CANADIAN ENCYCLOPEDIA OF SOCIAL WORK

CANADIAN ENCYCLOPEDIA
OF SOCIAL WORK

Francis J. Turner, editor

Wilfrid Laurier University Press

We acknowledge the financial support of the Government of Canada through the Book Publishing Industry Development Program for our publishing activities.

Library and Archives Canada Cataloguing in Publication

Encyclopedia of Canadian social work / Francis J. Turner, editor.

Includes bibliographical references.

ISBN 0-88920-436-5

1. Social service—Canada—Encyclopedias. I. Turner, Francis J. (Francis Joseph), 1929–

| HV12.E53 2005 | 361'.003 | C2005-903942-6 |

© 2005 Wilfrid Laurier University Press
Waterloo, Ontario, Canada N2L 3C5
www.wlupress.wlu.ca

Cover and interior design by P.J. Woodland.

Every reasonable effort has been made to acquire permission for copyright material used in this text, and to acknowledge all such indebtedness accurately. Any errors and omissions called to the publisher's attention will be corrected in future printings.

∞
Printed in Canada

For Jamie, Madeline, Luke, and Teya
—our grandchildren—
who have brought much joy
and fulfilment to Joanne and me.

List of Contributors

WARREN BROOKE, executive director, Family Services, London, ON

KEITH BROWNLEE, associate professor, School of Social Work, Lakehead University, Thunder Bay, ON

MAURICE D. BRUEBACHER, executive director, Family and Children Service of Wellington and Guelph County, Guelph, ON

GORD BRUYERE, First Nations assistant professor, School of Social Work, University of Victoria, Victoria, BC

C

SUSAN CADELL, professor, Faculty of Social Work, Wilfrid Laurier University, Waterloo, ON

CAROLYN CAMPBELL, assistant professor, Maritimes School of Social Work, Dalhousie University, Halifax, NS

WENDY CARMICHAEL, director, Residential Services, Fraser Health Authority, Abbotsford, BC

DAVID CHAMPAGNE, practitioner, Kitchener, ON

CAROLE PIGLER CHRISTENSEN, professor, School of Social Work, University of British Columbia, Vancouver, BC

PETER CHRISTIAN, consultant, Waterloo, ON

SHIRLEY CLEMENT, consultant, Office of the Worker Advisor, London, ON

ROSEMARY A. CLEWS, associate professor, St. Thomas University, Fredericton, NB

NICK COADY, associate professor, Faculty of Social Work, Wilfrid Laurier University, Waterloo, ON

KEN COLLIER, professor of Community Services, Athabasca University, Edmonton, AB

JOHN COSSAM, professor, School of Social Work, University of Victoria, Victoria, BC

LISA CROCKWELL, executive director, Newfoundland and Labrador Association of Social Workers, St. John's, NL

RICK CSIERNIK, associate professor, School of Social Work, King's College, University of Western Ontario, London, ON

DIANNE CULLEN, administrative co-ordinator, Manitoba Institute of Registered Social Workers, Winnipeg, MB

DEBBIE I. CURTIS, practitioner, St. John's, NL

D

ANDREA DALEY, practitioner, Community Mental Health, Toronto, ON

GARY D. DAVIES, practitioner, Head Injury Association of London and District, London, ON

ROGER DELANEY, director and professor, School of Social Work, Lakehead University, Thunder Bay, ON

JANE DEMPSTER, professor, School of Social Work, Memorial University, St. John's, NL

JANET DEVREUX, practitioner, St. Joseph's Health Centre, London, ON

PETER J. DOHERTY, practitioner, Catholic Family Services, Calgary, AB

SHARON DRACHE, writer, Ottawa, ON

HUGH DROUIN, executive director, Family Services Ontario, Toronto, ON

SUZANNE DUDZIAK, professor, Department of Social Work, St. Thomas University, Fredericton, NB

BLAIR DUNBAR, consultant, Canmore AB (formerly, Yellowknife, NT)

PETER A. DUNN, associate professor, Faculty of Social Work, Wilfrid Laurier University, Waterloo, ON

E

ADELE EAMER, professor, Department of Social Work, St. Thomas University, Fredericton, NB

JOHN ENGLISH, professor, Department of History, University of Waterloo, Waterloo, ON

RAYMOND O. ENSMINGER, practitioner, Edmonton, AB

REBECCA ERICKSON, practitioner, Therapy Partners Inc., Guelph, ON

PATRICIA ERVING, executive director and registrar, Newfoundland and Labrador Association of Social Workers, St. John's, NL

DAVID ESTE, associate professor, Faculty of Social Work, University of Calgary, Calgary, AB

DONALD G. EVANS, president, Canadian Training Institute, Toronto, ON

F

SHEILA FAUCHER, consultant, Toronto, ON

JANELLE FELDSTEIN, practitioner, Orleans ,ON

MARK FELDSTEIN, practitioner, Orleans, ON

MARGARET FIETZ, director, Family Service Canada/ Services à la Famille, Ottawa, ON

MARSHALL FINE, associate professor, Faculty of Social Work, Wilfrid Laurier University, Waterloo, ON

CAROL FRASER, executive director, Ontario Association of Credit Counselling Services, Toronto, ON

DONALD M. FUCHS, dean and professor, Faculty of Social Work, University of Manitoba, Winnipeg, MB

LUKE FUSCO, dean, Faculty of Social Work, Wilfrid Laurier University, Waterloo, ON

G

WILFRED A. GALLANT, associate professor, School of Social Work, University of Windsor, Windsor, ON

GERRY GAUGHAN, consultant, Almonte, ON

TINA GANDHI, child and family clinician, Intense Child and Family Services, Cambridge, ON

JOAN GILROY, professor, Maritime School of Social Work, Dalhousie University, Halifax, NS

ROBERT GLASSOP, executive director, Vanier Institute of the Family, Nepean, ON

MATTHEW GOODMAN, consultant, Goodman and associates, Hamilton, ON

KENNETH H. GORDON, director, School of Social Work, King's College, University of Western Ontario, London, ON

EUNICE GORMAN, doctoral student, Faculty of Social Work, University of Toronto, Toronto, ON

JOHN R. GRAHAM, Murray Fraser Professor of Community Economic Development, Faculty of Social Work, University of Calgary, Calgary, AB

ERIN GRAY, assistant professor, Faculty of Social Work, University of Calgary, Calgary, AB

JAMES GRIPTON, professor emeritus, Faculty of Social Work, University of Calgary, Calgary, AB

KLAUS GRUBER, executive director, Family Services, Saskatoon, SK

DORIS E. GUYATT, senior practitioner, Toronto, ON

H

JEAN HAASE, practitioner, London Health Sciences Centre, University Hospital, London, ON

BUDD L. HALL, dean of Education, University of Victoria, Victoria, BC

SUSAN HANNA, practitioner, Homewood Health Centre, Guelph, ON

SHERI HARDCASTLE, practitioner, Kitchener, ON

SHEILA HARDY, assistant professor, School of Social Work, Laurentian University, Sudbury, ON

HEATHER HARMONY, practitioner, Stratford, ON

DELMA HEMMING, consultant, Board of Registration for Social Workers of BC, Vancouver, BC

H. PHILIP HEPWORTH, practitioner, Ottawa, ON

DOROTHY CHAVE HERBERG, professor emerita, School of Social Work, York University, Toronto, ON

EDWARD N. HERBERG, consultant, Mississauga, ON

MARILYN HERIE, researcher, Centre for Addictions and Mental Health of Ontario, Toronto, ON

MARY A. HILL, practitioner, Vancouver, BC

SUSAN HILLOCK, professor, Social Work, Okanagan University College, Kelowna, BC

MICHIEL HORN, professor of history, Glendon College, York University, Toronto, ON

GARSON HUNTER, assistant professor, Faculty of Social Work, University of Regina. Regina, SK

I

ALLAN IRVING, professor, School of Social Work, King's College, University of Western Ontario, London, ON

J

EDWARD T. JACKSON, director and professor, Centre for the Study of Training, Investment and Economic Restructuring, Carleton University, Ottawa, ON

ROSE MARIE JACO, professor emerita, School of Social Work, King's College, University of Western Ontario, London, ON

CORNELIUS J. JAENEN, professor, Faculty of History, University of Ottawa, Ottawa, ON

LINDSAY H. JOHN, assistant professor, School of Social Work, McGill University, Montreal, QC

ELSIE JOHNSON, professor, Faculty of Social Work, University of Calgary, Calgary, AB

KATHY L. JONES, director, Community Services, Southern King's Child and Community Services, PE

K

GREGORY S. KEALEY, professor of History, Memorial University, St. John's, NL

JOAN KEEFLER, doctoral student, School of Social Work, McGill University, Montreal, QC

MARGARET KENNEDY, director, Child and Family Addictions and Mental Health, Services, Summerside, PE

M. DENNIS KIMBERLEY, professor, School of Social Work, Memorial University, St. John's, NL

ROSS A. KLEIN, professor, School of Social Work, Memorial University, St. John's, NL

AL KOOP, practitioner, Family and Children's Services Guelph, ON

L

JAN LACKSTOM, assistant professor, Faculty of Medicine, Department of Psychiatry, University of Toronto, Toronto, ON

DANIEL W.L. LAI, professor, Faculty of Social Work, University of Calgary, Calgary, AB

GRANT D. LARSON, professor, School of Social Work, University College of the Cariboo, Kamloops, BC

JEAN LAFRANCE, assistant professor and division head, Faculty of Social Work (Edmonton Division), University of Calgary, Edmonton, AB

BILL LEE, professor, School of Social Work, McMaster University, Hamilton, ON

IARA LESSA, assistant professor, School of Social Work, Ryerson University, Toronto, ON

DEBBIE LEVINE, practitioner, Toronto, ON

CHRISTINE H. LEWIS, professor, School of Social Work, Okanagan University College, Kelowna, BC

M

PIERRE MAHEU, professeur, École de Travail Sociale, l'Université du Québec à Montréal, Montreal, QC

KATHERINE MARCOCCIO, directrice, École de travail social, Université de Moncton, Moncton, NB

LORNA MARSDEN, president, York University, Toronto, ON

ANNE-MARIE MAWHINEY, professor, École de Service Social, Laurentian University, Sudbury, ON

GILLIAN MCCLOSKEY, associate director, Ontario Association of Social Workers, Toronto, ON

W.H. MCCONNELL, professor of law, University of Saskatchewan, Saskatchewan, SK

ERNIE MACDONALD, consultant, Charlottetown, PEI

FRANK MACDONALD, retired, Catholic Family Services, Windsor, ON

J. GRANT MACDONALD, professor, School of Social Work, York University, Toronto, ON

JUDY MACDONALD, assistant professor, Maritime School of Social Work, Dalhousie University, Halifax, NS

LYNN MCDONALD, professor, Faculty of Social Work, University of Toronto, Toronto, ON

ROBERT J. MACFADDEN, professor, Faculty of Social Work, University of Toronto, Toronto, ON

FRANK MCGILLY, professor (retired), School of Social Work, McGill University, Montreal, QC

ANNE MACGREGOR, student, Department of Social Work, St. Thomas University, Fredericton, NB

SHARON MCKAY, professor, Faculty of Social Work, University of Regina, Regina, SK

SUZANNE MCKENNA, executive director, New Brunswick Association of Social Workers, Fredericton, NB

BRAD MCKENZIE, professor, Faculty of Social Work, University of Manitoba, Winnipeg, MB

JOAN MACKENZIE-DAVIES, executive director, Ontario Association of Social Workers, Toronto, ON

SUE MCKENZIE-MOHR, clinician, Counselling Services, University of New Brunswick, Fredericton, NB

FRED MACKINNON, retired author and civil servant, Halifax, NS

DOROTHY MCKNIGHT, consultant, Waterloo, ON

KAREN MCNAUGHTON, associate, Pace Home Care, Kitchener, ON

IAN MACPHERSON, professor, Department of History, University of Victoria, Victoria, BC

ELLEN SUE MESBUR, director and professor, Department of Social Work, Renison College, University of Waterloo, Waterloo, ON

SUSAN TAYLOR MEAN, social historian, Open Learning Agency, Vancouver, BC

JEAN-MARC MEUNIER, directeur, Module de travail social, Université du Québec en Outaouais, Gatineau, QC

ROBERT H. MILLS, general secretary, Canadian Council of Churches, Toronto, ON

FAYE MISHRA, assistant professor, Faculty of Social Work, University of Toronto, Toronto, ON

EUGENIA REPETUR MORENO, executive director, Canadian Association of Social Workers, Ottawa, ON

MARY MOSS, practitioner, Montreal, QC

JOHN MOULD, president, Canadian Association of Social Workers, Ottawa, ON

NICK MULÉ, assistant professor, School of Social Work, York University, Toronto, ON

ALEX MUNROE, consultant, Waterloo, ON

ANNE MUNROE, practitioner, Waterloo, ON

N

HERB NABIGON, professor, School of Social Work, Laurentian University, Sudbury, ON

PAUL NEWMAN, professor (retired), School of Social Work, University of Manitoba, Winnipeg, MB

SHEILA M. NEYSMITH, professor, Faculty of Social Work, University of Toronto, Toronto, ON

O

ELLEN OLIVER, professor, School of Social Work, Memorial University, St. John's, NL

RITA ORTIZ DE WASCHMANN, chartered practitioner, Catholic Family Services, Calgary, AB

M. LOUISE OSMOND, practitioner, Advance Therapy and Consulting Services, St. John's, NL

BRIAN OUELLETTE, professor, Department of Social Work, St. Thomas University, Fredericton, NB

P

JEFF PACKER, practitioner, Community Support Team, Oshawa and District Family Court Clinic, Oshawa, ON

RENÉ PAGÉ, registrar and executive director, Ordre professionnel des travailleurs sociaux du Québec, Montreal, QC

MARILYN PARSONS, clinical social worker, Child and Adolescence Centre, London Health Science Centre, London, ON

DIANA PEDERSEN, assistant professor of history, Concordia University, Montreal, QC

DAVID PEDLAR, director of research, Veteran's Affairs Canada, Charlottetown, PEI

CARLOS J. PEREIRA, research assistant, Canadian Encyclopedia of Social Work, Toronto, ON

ALEX POLGAR, practitioner, Hamilton, ON

SUSAN PRESTON, assistant professor, School of Social Work, McMaster University, Hamilton, ON

NORMA JEAN PROFITT, associate professor, Department of Social Work, St. Thomas University, Fredericton, NB

R

SHELDON L. RAHN, professor emeritus, Faculty of Social Work, Wilfrid Laurier University, Waterloo, ON

STEVEN A. RAIKEN, consultant, Cap Jemini Ernst and Young Canada Inc., Toronto, ON

BRIAN RASMUSSEN, professor, Department of Social Work, Okanagan University College, Kelowna, BC

CHERYL REGEHR, professor, Faculty of Social Work, University of Toronto, Toronto, ON

LOUIS J. RICHARD, directeur adjoint, École de travail social, Université de Moncton, Moncton, NB

GRAHAM RICHES, director, School of Social Work and Family Studies, University of British Columbia, Vancouver, BC

ELIZABETH RIDGELY, director, George Hull Centre, Toronto, ON

DAVID RIVARD, executive director, Children's Aid Society of the District of Sudbury and Manitoulin, Sudbury, ON

ROBERTA ROBERTS, professor, Faculty of Social Work, University of Toronto, Toronto, ON

GAYLA ROGERS, dean, Faculty of Social Work, University of Calgary, Calgary, AB

GILLES RONDEAU, professeur titulaire et ancien directeur, l'École de service sociale, l'Université de Montréal, Montréal, QC

MICHAEL ROTHERY, professor, Faculty of Social Work, University of Calgary, Calgary, AB

WILLIAM ROWE, dean, University of South Florida, Tampa, FL (former director, School of Social Work, McGill University, Montreal, QC)

S

DANIEL SALHANI, associate professor, Faculty of Social Work, University of Regina, Regina, SK

BENJAMIN SCHLESINGER, professor, Faculty of Social Work, University of Toronto, Toronto, ON

WENDY SEAGER, administrative co-ordinator, School of Social Work, University of Victoria, Victoria, BC

MARGARET SELLICK, associate professor, School of Social Work, Lakehead University, Thunder Bay, ON

BEN ZION SHAPIRO, professor, Faculty of Social Work, University of Toronto, Toronto, ON

NANCY M. SHEEHAN, dean of Education, University of British Columbia, Vancouver, BC

WES SHERA, professor, Faculty of Social Work, University of Toronto, Toronto, ON

MARILYN SHINYEI, practitioner, Edmonton, AB

SUSAN SILVER, associate professor, School of Social Work, Ryerson University, Toronto, ON

LINDA SNYDER, assistant professor, Department of Social Work, Renison College, University of Waterloo, Waterloo, ON

JACK SPENCE, consultant, Family Services Ontario, Toronto, ON

PATRICIA SPINDEL, professor, Social Services Program, Humber College, Toronto, ON

RICHARD SPLANE, professor emeritus, School of Social Work, University of British Columbia, Vancouver, BC

CAROL A. STALKER, associate professor, Faculty of Social Work, Wilfrid Laurier University, Waterloo, ON

MALCOLM STEWART, Faculty of Social Work, University of Toronto, Toronto, ON

SILVIA M. STRAKA, McGill Centre for Studies in Aging, McGill University, Montreal, QC

G. ELAINE STOLAR, professor, School of Social Work, University of British Columbia, Vancouver, BC

NANCY E. SULLIVAN, professor, School of Social Work, Ryerson University, Toronto, ON

TRACY SWAN, professor, School of Social Work, McMaster University, Hamilton, ON

T

KWONG-LEUNG TANG, professor and chair, Social Work Program, Faculty of Health and Human Sciences, University of Northern British Columbia, Prince George, BC

LAURA TAYLOR, assistant professor, School of Social work, University of Windsor, Windsor, ON

SHARON TAYLOR, professor, School of Social Work, Lakehead University, Thunder Bay, ON

GARY TEEPLE, professor, Department of Sociology and Anthropology, Simon Fraser University, Burnaby, BC

BARBARA THOMLISON, professor, Florida International University, Miami, FL

RAY J. THOMLISON, director, Florida International University, Miami, FL

ANNE TOTH, practitioner, St. Clair Corporate Centre, Sarnia, ON

ANGELA TOWNEND, program supervisor, Catholic Family Service of Durham, Oshawa, ON

ANNA TRAVERS, practitioner, Sherbourne Health Centre, Toronto, ON

MING-SUM TSUI, senior lecturer, Department of Applied Social Sciences, Hong Kong Polytechnical University, Hong Kong

DAVID TURNER, professor, School of Social Work, University of Victoria, Victoria, BC

FRANCIS J. TURNER, professor emeritus, Faculty of Social Work, Wilfrid Laurier University, Waterloo, ON

JOANNE C. TURNER, professor emerita, Department School of Social Work, Renison College, University of Waterloo, Waterloo, ON

LINDA M. TURNER, assistant professor, Department of Social Work, St. Thomas University, Fredericton, NB

LESLIE M. TUTTY, professor, Faculty of Social Work, University of Calgary, Calgary, AB

ROBERT TWIGG, professor, Faculty of Social Work, University of Regina, Regina, SK

V

MARY VALENTICH, professor, Faculty of Social Work, University of Calgary, Calgary, AB

BENOIT VAN CALOEN, directeur, Département de service social, Faculté des lettres et sciences humaines, Université de Sherbrooke, Sherbrooke, QC

WILL C. VAN DEN HOONAARD, professor, Department of Sociology, University of New Brunswick, Fredericton, NB

W

SUSAN WATT, professor, School of Social Work, McMaster University, Hamilton, ON

LISA J. WELLS, graduate student, Department of History, Memorial University, St. John's, NL

ANNE WESTHUES, professor, Faculty of Social Work, Wilfrid Laurier University, Waterloo, ON

BRIAN WHARF, professor emeritus, School of Social Work, University of Victoria, Victoria, BC

GAIL WIDEMAN, practitioner, Portugal Cove, NL

MARTHA WIEBE, acting director, School of Social Work, Carleton University, Ottawa, ON

ANNE WILSON, practitioner, Waterloo, ON

MICHELLE WOLFE, practitioner, Family Services of Haliburton County, ON

GLORIA KRUPNICK WOLFSON, program head, Social Services, Social Work, and Substance Abuse Counselling, University College of the Fraser Valley. Abbotsford, BC

MICHAEL R. WOODFORD, doctoral student, Faculty of Social Work, University of Toronto, Toronto, ON

MARGARET M. WRIGHT, professor, School of Social Work, University of British Columbia, Vancouver, BC

ROBIN WRIGHT, professor, School of Social Work, McGill University, Montreal, QC

Y

MIU CHUNG YAN, assistant professor, School of Social Work and Family Studies, University of British Columbia, Vancouver, BC

Z

JOANNE ZAMPARO, professor, School of Social Work, Memorial University, St. John's, NL

MICHAEL KIM ZAPF, head, Department of Social Work Access Program, Faculty of Social Work, University of Calgary, Calgary, AB

Credits

Included by kind permission of McClelland and Stewart Ltd., The Canadian Publishers, from *The Canadian Encyclopedia* (2000): Antigonish Movement (Ian MacPherson); Canadian Bill of Rights, 1966 (W.H. McConnell); Canadian Congress of Labour (Irving Abella); Canadian Council of Churches (Donald H. Anderson, revised by Robert Mills, current general secretary); Canadian International Development Agency (Susan Taylor Mean); Canadian Labour Congress, Abraham Feinberg (Sharon Drache); Ginger Group, Imperial Order Daughter's of the Empire (Nancy M. Sheehan); League for Social Construction (Michiel Horn); Paul Joseph James Martin (John English), Trades and Labour Congress of Canada (Gregory S. Kealey); United Farmers of Ontario (Ian MacPherson); Young Men's Christian Association (Dianne Pedersen); and Young Women's Christian Association (Dianne Pedersen).

Acknowledgments

As we finally go to press with this project, I want to express in the most enthusiastic and heartfelt manner possible my gratitude and appreciation to the more than three hundred colleagues who contributed their wise counsel and or sensitive writing to this task. In particular, I want to thank three individuals who made particular significant contributions from an operational perspective. First, I want to mention Rob Jones and Carlos Pereira, who contributed greatly to the setting up, managing, and editing of the computer data bases and hard copy; Carlos Pereira also assisted with research and verifying numerous facts and details in the months leading to publication. Second, Michael Woodford from St. John's, Newfoundland, a doctoral student at the University of Toronto Faculty of Social Work, who proved to be an excellent sleuth in tracking down material and a writer of entries. I personally have gained much through the process of interacting with this cadre of our profession.

I am also most grateful to Wilfrid Laurier University Press throughout this process, in particular the support of the director, Dr. Brian Henderson, the assistance of managing editor Carroll Klein, and contractual copy editor Susan Quirk. Their knowledge and perception greatly helped to bring the original manuscript into a much more polished format, with a much higher level of consistency in style.

As always, I have greatly appreciated, of course, the support of Joanne Turner throughout this process of mail, fax, couriers, phone calls, parcels at the door, and hand-delivered material that became part of our daily lives for several years. I am truly grateful. As well, I learned much about our profession. In particular, the idea that first began this endeavour was confirmed: there is indeed a distinct profile of social work, which in its unity also reflects that diversity of values, history, life styles, beliefs, regionality, geography, climate, ethnicity, and cultures that comes together in that exciting entity known as Canada. *A mari usque ad mare.*

Francis J. Turner

Introduction

THE IDEA FOR THIS ENDEAVOUR emerged from a visit to the book display at the annual Learned Societies meeting at Brock University in 1996. Among the many works on display was a Canadian encyclopedia of music and as I glanced over its table of contents, I thought, Why not social work? Although I believe that that was the first time a definite concept of an encyclopedia of Canadian social work came to mind in a concrete way, I know that the project had been germinating for some time without my being fully aware of it. I now think that this preconscious cognitive process had actually begun with the publication of the nineteenth edition of *The Social Work Encyclopedia* edited by Dr. Dick Edwards and published by the NASW Press in 1995. I continue to be as impressed with this work as I have been over the years when I have frequently turned to it for information. Comprehensive and useful as this excellent work is, it clearly reflects an American view of our profession and, in so doing, omits the rich and distinctly different profile of social work as it has developed and exists in Canada. This omission ought not to be construed as a criticism of the prestigious US encyclopedia but, rather, an observation of an appropriate limitation inherent in the effort to focus a clear spotlight on the profession in one part of the world. In earlier editions of the NASW Press project, two or three entries usually spoke to Canadian issues; as the profession has expanded in scope and complexity— as manifested by the growth of this work from the single volume fifteenth edition to the current three-volume format—even these few have been eliminated. Thus, in the nineteenth edition, Canada appears only once: a brief description of social work education in our country located in the index.

Determining the Content

The process that produced the volume you are now reading reflects a developmental purview of growth, in that it has matured through several sequential stages. In its early conception, this work was envisaged as a supplement to the American encyclopedia. I presumed that producing a similar or parallel volume might involve considerable redundancy, given the many similarities in the profession as it exists in these two countries. Even from the first draft of a possible table of contents, I recognized that the concept of a supplemental volume was not feasible. In the project's formative stages, I consulted several senior colleagues, too numerous to mention individually. Very early in our deliberations the question of a supplement versus a stand-alone volume emerged. Its resolution represented an important step toward a unique work rather different from what had first been envisaged. As this issue was considered, the possible redundancy dwindled as my colleagues and I realized how much could be said about the social work profession from a Canadian perspective. I am grateful to Julie Foley, then president of the Canadian Association of Social Workers, who brought this issue more clearly into focus and led to the decision to work toward a stand-alone work. The entity called "Canadian social work" that is truly distinct from the profession in other countries does exist. Thus, while the initial draft table of contents drew heavily on that of the American volume, subsequent versions quickly began took on a life of their own—including the final one, which emerged after some twenty-three prior drafts, each of which emerged from suggestions by my colleagues; the final draft seemed to capture the spectrum for which we had collectively been searching.

As my colleagues and I examined other discipline-oriented encyclopedia, we became aware that an important function of this endeavour would be that it serve as a repository of information about certain personages who have played a significant role in the development of the profession in Canada. Glittering stars light our firmament but no single guide to share information about them has been produced. One of the fascinating facets of the project's development was watching the list of these personages emerge, as colleagues throughout the country made suggestions about whom to include. In true Canadian fashion, we tend to hide rather than celebrate our accomplishments. The work of Dr. Don Bellamy, Dr. Howard Irving, and Dr. Joanne Turner in *Canadian Social Welfare* is an exception to this; from their writing, I came to realize how many are our heroes and how quickly we seem to forget them. In particular, I became aware that, because of the size of the country, persons of note in one region may be unknown elsewhere. Contacts with colleagues everywhere helped to ensure that many of these lesser-known persons are identified. The list that finally emerged is impressive, even though it is clear some have been missed; perhaps they can be included in subsequent editions. This volume holds to the convention of excluding entries for living persons. A small regret is that, in an encyclopedia like this one, only succinct biographical summaries are appropriate. It is hoped that they might inspire compilation of a database from which a who's who of Canadian social work pioneers, theorists, educators, activists, and practitioners can be produced.

Financing

A second major challenge to make this encyclopedia a reality related to financing. In embarking on this project, I had a clear idea both of the considerable expense to be incurred in its production and of the perception by commercial publishers that it might not be their idea of a profit-generating product. Nevertheless, discussions were held with some commercial publishers and some university presses. Two factors became evident from these discussions. The first was that positive interest in the project came more from curiosity about a distinctly Canadian view of the profession than from perceptions that this encyclopedia might be a high priority. The commercial presses confirmed our assumption that they would support the project but would not view it as appropriate for their markets. Two university presses showed strong interest but would only consider it if a significant sum of money could accompany the final manuscript to assist with substantial production costs. With this understanding, the search was underway for funding support. Some was possible within the network of Canadian funders of academic projects; however, in view of the extant climate of drastic reductions, the probability for obtaining sufficient support was slim. During this search, some book preparation and general research funds became available to assist with the very large amount of multimedia software support needed to start and maintain the process of gathering and organizing entries. I am particularly grateful to the research offices of Wilfrid Laurier University and York University for their assistance in this aspect of the project. Finally, the decision was made to secure private funding for publication; this was secured and a contract with the Wilfrid Laurier University Press was concluded.

Scholarship

The third challenge to get this encyclopedia to the press was the structure and development of the project so that scholarly integrity was maintained. In keeping with academic and social work traditions, a network of authoritative and representative authors would have to be compiled, contacted, and consulted with regard to material to be produced. The size and diversity of the profession in this country dictated the need for an elaborate committee and sub-committee structure to handle this process. Several designs were conceived using such variables as proximity, regional representation, fields of service, language, professional associations, and faculties and schools of social work; after a long struggle with the feasibility and cost of such an endeavour—and strongly impressed with an effective but unconventional strategy for project development as described in a very non-social work, *Ship of Gold*—I decided to pursue a single-perspective approach that avoided the use of a formal organization or committee structure. This strategy carries with it the need for one person to take primary responsibility for the contents: what is included and what has been omitted, either by design or oversight. I gladly accept this responsibility and will be delighted to accept corrections, constructive criticism, and recommendations for omissions toward editorial revisions and, perhaps, new editions. This strategy required a considerable amount of ongoing discussion and consultation with many colleagues, to whom I am grateful in the extreme.

Once this decision was made, the challenge of who would be invited to write the entries and how such a coterie would be located had to be faced. After considering several possibilities, I decided that one of the ways to neutralize the possible biases of a single scholarly editor was to have each of the more than 440 entries written by a different colleague and those selected ought to represent as great a geographic breadth and professional diversity as possible. I began with a list of thirty colleagues throughout the country, to whom letters were sent asking them to write on topics within their expertise and requesting them to identify other colleagues whom they would recommend for particular topics. As well, all faculties and schools of social work and all provincial/territorial professional associations were contacted and asked to provide entries on their organization, as well as to recommend authoritative authors and topics. Overall this process worked well. I am greatly impressed and most grateful for the cooperation and enthusiastic participation from throughout our profession to contribute directly and indirectly to produce the entries for this encyclopedia. In only a few instances do we have more than one entry composed by one author, aside from the entries I chose to write myself. In terms of representivity, however, our francophone colleagues are undoubtedly under-represented. One of my original aspirations for this volume—and for other social work publications—was that it appear in a bilingual format. The omission of materials in translation has been a source of ongoing frustration for Canadian scholarship in most disciplines. In this respect, the very title of the work is remiss: some might suggest that a more accurate title should be "The Canadian Encyclopedia of English-Speaking Social Work in Canada."

Scholarly Editing

A fourth challenge that emerged as the encyclopedia entries were being organized as they arrived was the issue of just how they should be shaped. Several encyclopedia were examined to compare and contrast their approach to presentation of information. Each work had a profile of its own with some similarities. There emerged a perception that the purpose of a professionally focused encyclopedia like this one should provide a reader with a snapshot of each topic as it exists at the time of publication—here, the beginning of a new millennium. Further thought devoted to the desired form and content of a social work encyclopedia resulted in a determination that the main goal is to give an instant reference to the ordinary reader and to students, rather than to persons who are already expert in our field. Thus, the encyclopedia strives to give readers sufficient facts and information about each topic to advance their knowledge without attempting to be exhaustive. Implicit is the provision of a resource to check facts about which the reader is cognizant but seeks confirmation. In particular, we impressed on contributors that an encyclopedia is not a purveyor of opinion; rather, as described in the Columbia Encyclopedia, it ought aim at presenting generally accepted judgments. Thus, this encyclopedia is not an instrument for the presentation and defence of theories; it does report on the role of theories as has been done in this work. This encyclopedia is not a place to argue viewpoints or present solutions to issues; rather it gives readers in a succinct form a description of a particular person, event, or aspect of social work as it currently exists in Canada. Where appropriate, some historical perspective or a presentation of critical issues is offered. These are not argumentative nor ideological in perspective but strive to describe and inform what is, rather than what should be. This of course does not rule out the identification of trends or speculation. To assist readers who wish to pursue more detail or trends beyond our publication date, relevant entries close with a reference to a Web site and a list of works cited in entry references. Entries on persons begin with a synopsis of vital biographical data. Each entry begins with a succinct definition or description of the topic, and is followed by the author's identity and a list of cross-references to related entries in this volume. In several of the specialized encyclopedic works consulted, the entries were often unsigned; typically, the explanation given was that it avoided an undue influence on the reader carried by the reputation of a particular writer. While this rationale is understandable, my colleagues and I did not feel compelled to follow it; rather, we realized that, as this publication was a first for our profession, it was important that the authors be identified by name and professional locus of practice. Our reasons were twofold: to ensure that their contribution was acknowledged and to reflect the scope of representivity.

In examining other encyclopedia, the one that appeared closest to what was envisioned for this work was the second edition of *The Canadian Encyclopedia* (2000). I am most appreciative to the staff of McClelland and Stewart for their co-operation in permitting us to draw on some entries for this volume. Having their co-operation and permission to use a number of entries directly from their volume gives this work an additional Canadian flavour. As this was envisaged as a first step in the development of a Canadian work about our profession, by design, few restrictions were imposed on the entry authors. Hence the variety of formats is broad. One of the strengths of this diversity is that it truly portrays a mosaic of professional perceptions as diverse as the reality of our country. Another is the resulting amalgam of styles, content, viewpoints, and perceptions to present an integrated picture of social work in Canada in the year 2004.

One of the realities of a book such as this is that, once in print, it is fixed in time. Discussions with colleagues throughout the preparation process frequently raised the proposition that we use available technology such as CD-ROM to expand access to the work and to facilitate revisions and updates. Dr. Rob McFadden of the University of Toronto was particularly helpful in this regard. Should the resources become available, this stands as a high priority for this work. Overall, I have learned much throughout the stages of this work's maturation in an effort to present Canadian social work to Canadians—and, I trust to interested readers elsewhere. Although I write this introduction at the end of a long and complex process, I anticipate that it may be the beginning of a further process that will ensure subsequent editions.

Users of This Encyclopedia

The *Canadian Encyclopedia of Social Work* in its present format will be of assistance to those many persons and systems in society directly and indirectly related to that complex societal network called social welfare. Virtually every member of Canadian society at some time comes into contact with the social welfare system. Therefore, in addition to the vast quantity of professional social work literature that abounds, we are offering this much more accessible resource that surveys the total spectrum of the field. Individuals and groups involved in this system—or who want to understand aspects of it more thoroughly—can find information readily available in this single knowledge source. Beyond Canada, there is considerable interest in the Canadian welfare system, social work education, and social work profession. Practitioners, educators, and policy makers elsewhere in the world often look to the Canadian experience when they are developing or refining their own approaches to social work services. This encyclopedia stands as a useful first level of information for persons and groups seeking to become better informed about Canadian social work.

A

Aboriginal issues

Understanding current issues facing Aboriginal peoples requires an understanding of history, as Aboriginal peoples have had to struggle to maintain their languages, cultures, traditions, and land rights throughout the periods of contact with Europeans and Canadians. For more than a century, the peoples indigenous to the lands that became Canada have been subjected to oppression and colonization by dominating societies, as has occurred and is occurring in many other countries. Oppressing and colonizing practices have been initiated by church, government, education, economic, and justice institutions, as well as health and social systems, including services provided by social workers. Repeated attempts to impose values, beliefs, knowledge, and ways of doing by such institutions within the dominant societies have been devastating to Aboriginal societies and their ancestral lands. Residential schooling provides an example of such practices, when Aboriginal children were removed from their families and communities and sent to schools intent on stripping them of their language and culture; tragically, about half the children taken to these schools lost their lives there, mostly from infectious diseases. The history of social work with Aboriginal peoples has often not been supportive of the peoples' rights to self-government and self-determination. In the 1960s, for example, child welfare workers participated in a widespread "scoop" that removed Aboriginal children from their families and placed them into the care of provincial social service systems. To move from these negative experiences from the past, Aboriginal peoples have articulated the need for models of social practice that are congruent with and complimentary to the peoples' diverse ways of life, belief, knowledge, and values.

Aboriginal social work practice, an emerging profession, has grown out of the need to develop culturally based solutions to the existing issues in Aboriginal communities. Issues that Aboriginal peoples face include: high rate of poverty and social dependency (Williams 1997; WUNSKA 1997; Canada 1996b), substandard housing and lack of adequate water systems (Barsh 1994), lower levels of and lack of access to education, high rates of unemployment (Canada 1996a; AFN 1988; Canada 1991a), poorer health (CICH 1994; CMA 1994; Canada 1991b; Canada 1991c), and such social issues as high rates of suicide (Canada 1991c), and drug and alcohol abuse (Canada 1996a). Aboriginal solutions to such issues need to come from within Aboriginal communities with support from Canadian society. What needs to be understood clearly is that Aboriginal societies know best what has happened to them, what the effects have been, and what they need to do. Central to guiding the practice of Aboriginal social work is the development of processes and structures that support the pursuit of Aboriginal governance and self-determination. The inherent right of Aboriginal self-government, which is recognized by the government of Canada, includes for Aboriginal peoples the provision of community caring through delivery of Aboriginal social, health, and justice programs. The report of the 1993 Royal Commission on Aboriginal Peoples outlines four specific elements for social change: "healing of individuals, families, communities and nations; improving economic opportunity and living conditions in urban and rural Aboriginal communities; developing human resources; and developing Aboriginal institutions and adapting institutions" (Canada 1996b). Groups such as WUNSKA, a national association of Aboriginal social workers and educators in Canada, promote the practice of social work with Aboriginal peoples that is built on the diverse values, beliefs, ways of doing, knowledge, and being of Aboriginal cultures. This practice recognizes that the methods and resultant ways that practice is expressed and carried out may differ substantially from non-Aboriginal practice. The work of building a more appropriate practice for social work in Aboriginal communities—which requires, requires human and financial resources, as well as a revised knowledge base—is well underway.

[*Sheila Hardy*]

RELATED ENTRIES

Aboriginal Services, Assembly of First Nations, Canadian Charter of Rights and Freedoms, Culture, Diversity, Education in Social Work, Ethnic-Sensitive Practice, Ethnocultural Communities Services, Healing Theory (Cree), Indian & Northern Affairs Canada,

Marital & Family Problems, Poverty, Practice Methods, Racism-Sensitive Social Work, Remote Practice, Remote & Rural Practice Methods, Sensitizing Concepts, Services for Women, Social Welfare Context, Social Welfare History, Theory & Practice, Wellness

REFERENCES

AFN. 1988. *Tradition and Education: Towards a Vision of Our Future*. Ottawa: Assembly of First Nations.

Barsh, R.L. 1994. Canada's Aboriginal Peoples: Social Integration or Disintegration? *The Canadian Journal of Native Studies* XIV, 1, 1–46.

Canada. 1991a. Aboriginal Peoples Survey: Language, Tradition, Health, Lifestyle and Social Issues. Ottawa: Statistics Canada

———. 1991b. Aboriginal Peoples Survey: Schooling, Work and Related Activities, Income Expenses and Mobility. Ottawa: Statistics Canada.

———. 1991c. Health Status of Canadian Indians and Inuit. Report by Department of National Health and Welfare. Ottawa, ON.

———. 1996a. *Gathering Strength*. Vol. 3. Report of the Royal Commission on Aboriginal Peoples. Ottawa: The Commission. (Chairs: G. Erasmus and R. Dussault).

———. 1996b. *Renewal. A Twenty-Year Commitment.* A Report of the Royal Commission on Aboriginal Peoples. Ottawa: The Commission. (Chairs: G. Erasmus and R. Dussault).

CICH. 1994. Aboriginal Children. In *The Health of Canada's Children: A CICH Profile*. 2nd ed. Ottawa: Canadian Institute of Child Health.

CMA. 1994. Bridging the Gap: Promoting Health and Healing Aboriginal Peoples in Canada. Submission to the Royal Commission on Aboriginal Peoples. Ottawa: Canadian Medical Association.

Williams, A. 1997. Canadian Urban Aboriginals: A Focus on Aboriginal Women in Toronto. *The Canadian Journal of Native Studies* 1, 75–101.

WUNSKA Research Group. 1996. First Nations youth inquiry into tobacco use. SK: First Nations Social Research Institute.

———. 1997. First Nations community-based social welfare inquiry: A national inquiry into experiences and insights. Regina, SK: First Nations Social Research Institute.

Aboriginal services

For almost as long as human beings have inhabited North America, Aboriginal peoples have looked after themselves. "Almost" is an important qualifier, reflecting how recent the time has been during which Aboriginal peoples and their lands have been colonized, when they have not been in control of the resources necessary to care for themselves. Pre-colonial Aboriginal societies developed and implemented diverse systems of governance and distribution of resources and wealth. Aboriginal peoples' systems to care for one another were inspired and guided by relationships with the land and its natural wealth, and those relationships were formalized and regulated through spiritual ceremonial practices. For example, such west coast nations as the kwak̲wak̲a'-wak̲w and Wet'suwet'en used a hereditary system of leadership with delineated custodial responsibilities for resources and elaborate means to record and effect the distribution of those resources. East coast nations such as the Mik'maq and Rotinohshonni organized formal confederacies as a means of mutual support and protection. The primary mechanism by which Aboriginal societies throughout the continent served and supported one another was the family and clan, a system that differs considerably from non-Aboriginal social welfare systems. Aboriginal communities were largely left out of the development of the Canadian welfare state that emerged in the first half of the twentieth century for two reasons: as a responsibility of the federal government under the Indian Act, Indians—but not other Aboriginal peoples—were controlled in an all-encompassing fashion through the Department of Indian Affairs with little contact from other government agencies. Second, the interest promoting the development of Aboriginal lands was not the well-being of Aboriginal residents but colonial settlement and natural resource exploitation. In the 1950s, the federal government began to wind down the churches' operation of residential schools for Aboriginal children and to increase delegation of its constitutional responsibility for Aboriginal peoples and lands to the provinces (and, later, territories). Mainly as a means to cut costs, such services as education, health care, social assistance, and child welfare were transferred to the provinces and given legitimacy under section 88 of the Indian Act. Later delegation from the provinces to Band and Tribal councils on reserve has created a jurisdictional quagmire that Aboriginal peoples have been left to overcome; this delegation has also resulted in Aboriginal peoples delivering to their own people social and other services that are inappropriate, irrelevant, and inadequate.

As early as the 1950s in Toronto, Vancouver, and Winnipeg, friendship centres emerged to serve Aboriginal peoples and address their particular social conditions. But it was not until the early 1970s that these organizations coalesced into federally funded regional and national networks throughout Canada. Now underfunded—even though the need for them increases annually—these centres precariously continue to provide adult basic education, employment services, addictions counselling, family support, youth programs, and other services in a culturally relevant manner. In the often hostile urban environment, where indifference to the unique histories and cultures of Aboriginal peoples remains high, friendship centres strive to keep addressing overwhelming needs with insufficient human and financial resources as urban Aboriginal populations rise. Their efforts are representative of the struggles faced by social programs and services initiated by Aboriginal peoples throughout Canada. Their endurance, because they continue to attract and help Aboriginal people, reflects the increase and effectiveness, snowball fashion, of such agencies in these early years of the twenty-first century. That Aboriginal services have been developed and implemented in and beyond Aboriginal communities reflects, in part, self-government arrangements negotiated within Canada. Most Aboriginal organizations have an incremental kind of governance through authority delegated by federal, provincial, or territorial legislation and policy, or through tripartite funding agreements for specific service provision. Reconciling these dictates from dominant societies with the desire and need of Aboriginal peoples to provide services that draw on Aboriginal cultural practices and beliefs is a undertaking both difficult and contentious, yet rewarding. Acculturative dynamics—consisting in part of racism, neo-colonialism, ignorance, and apathy—characterize relations between Aboriginal and non-Aboriginal peoples. Despite these dynamics—indeed, because of them—Aboriginal service providers recognize the effectiveness of offering services that are based on traditional beliefs and practices, and can draw on useful aspects of non-Aboriginal social work practice.

[Gord Bruyere]

RELATED ENTRIES
Aboriginal Issues, Assembly of First Nations, Culture, Diversity, Ethnic-Sensitive Practice, Ethnocultural Communities' Services, Healing Theory (Cree), Racism-Sensitive Social Work, Remote Practice, Remote & Rural Practice Methods, Sensitizing Concepts, Theory & Practice

abortion

Pregnancy termination at the request of a woman has been legal since Parliament struck down the prior prohibition in 1969. While many legal, medical, social, and political restrictions remain, a 1988 ruling by the Supreme Court of Canada left the choice to a woman and her physician. The profession of social work, however, has been more ambiguous than the judiciary. In 1966 the Canadian Association of Social Workers developed its first "Policy Statement on Planned Parenthood," which recommended the right of individuals and couples to control their fertility by the use of contraception, and in March 1974 the association issued a "Policy Statement on Family Planning," which included a section on abortion. While the policy stated that the association did not "endorse abortion as a family planning method," it asserted that "the woman's free choice be respected." The policy statement was reissued in November 1986 in a somewhat shorter format, accepting the definition of family planning by the World Health Organization's Expert Committee and eliminating the statement regarding non-endorsement of abortion. No further revisions have been forthcoming. The association's 1986 statement on abortion reads:

CASW believes that social workers, by virtue of their training and experience, can offer a specialized contribution to the knowledge of their clients about contraceptive methods. In addition they can provide guidance and personal assistance designed to give an unwanted child an accepting environment. Social workers can furnish post-intervention services, which the woman and/or her family might need. They should also point out alternatives available to women seeking an abortion. However, in cases where the client's individual choice is that of abortion, even when [she has] been made aware of alternatives, we will ensure that the woman's free choice be respected, that she receives professional assistance, and that she not be forced to resort to clandestine methods.

We recommend that research be encouraged in all areas, and that the concept of family planning be given full support so that the future incidents of unplanned pregnancies may be significantly reduced.

No explanation in the statement is offered for the reference to the association's 1983 Code of Ethics in support of a client's rights to exercise self-determination and the social worker's "obligation to respect and promote the right to choose [and] inform the client of their biases" in relation to contraception but not when a client's choice is abortion.

[*Mona Acker*]

RELATED ENTRIES

Bioethical Issues, Canadian Association of Social Workers, Codes of Ethics, Ethics, Family Planning, Parenting, Pregnancy, Sensitizing Concepts, Services for Women, Single Parents, Wellness

abuse

Abuse is a generic term that describes a broad spectrum of maltreatment—such as child, elder, or spousal abuse—of individuals and groups of people, many of whom are counselled or treated by social workers. For instance, child welfare workers have clearly defined legal responsibilities to report and to take action on alleged or actual child abuse. Abuse that occurs within marginalized communities is frequently unseen, unrecognized, or ignored, even by those whose role is to prevent such occurrences. In a general sense, one of the functions of social work is to bring patterns and instances of particular and systemic abuse to the public view, as well as to develop strategies to eliminate them. As abuse is highly newsworthy, the media have assisted in bringing public attention, if not education, to patterns and situations of abuse; such public disclosure may facilitate change, even legislation. In the 1990s and 2000s, numerous reports have emerged documenting widespread abuse in earlier decades in institutions serving elderly people and children, especially orphans and juveniles in industrial schools and Aboriginal children in residential schools. Outcomes of some of these disclosures have included prosecution of offenders, payment of compensation, and provision for counselling of victims of abuse. Essentially, abuse is a misuse of power. Social work has played three major roles in

minimizing this societal evil: much work has been done with individual persons who have survived abuse; the profession has brought to light situations of abuse and identified the psychosocial trauma suffered by its victim of abuse; and social work has actively and successfully lobbied for needed societal change to remedy or reduce abuse, nominally through well-designed research with accurate data and sound analysis.

[*Francis J. Turner*]

RELATED ENTRIES

An Act for the Prevention of Cruelty to and Better Protection of Children, Child Abuse, Bereavement, Clinical Social Work, Elder Abuse, Sensitizing Concepts, Sexual Abuse of Children, Substance Addiction, Suicide, Therapy, Torture & Trauma Victims, Treatment, Vicarious Traumatization, Wellness, Women Abuse

accountability

Accountability in Canadian social work practice refers to that commitment of all components of the profession to assume responsibility for the quality and effectiveness of all its services. The profession has always accepted that not only must services be provided in an ethical and effective manner but these qualities must be demonstrably evident. For much of its history, as with many other professions, there was a presumption that the stated ethical commitment of all professionals was sufficient to guarantee quality services; in recent decades, the demand for demonstrated quality has acquired more objective dimensions more closely connected to outcome measures and, at times, fiscal performance. Accountability has three distinct but interrelated facets:

- First, accountability is required for quality and ethical practice to be provided by individual social work practitioners. Formal codes of ethics and standards of practice are enforced through disciplinary bodies of the profession (i.e., through the Canadian Association of Social Workers). As well, informal monitoring for such accountability is maintained by the media, as the actions and activities of social workers and social agencies are often newsworthy—especially perceptions or allegations of unprofessional, unethical, or incompetent behaviour.

- Second, accountability is demanded by the funders of social services and programs, who rightly expect that resources provided achieve their goals. As it is important to ascertain whether less expensive or more effective ways can achieve similar goals with no diminution of quality, funders now commonly require a formal evaluation of programs and services, perhaps carried out by an arm's-length party.

- Third, accountability relates to assessing how well social service or program objectives are being achieved. Many Canadian agencies engage in ongoing program evaluation, often monitoring components of service delivery with formal research methods. Three issues relating to program evaluation are of particular note:
  - First, partly from a lack of resources, many agencies have turned to universities and colleges for assistance, forging positive research links.
  - Second, to enhance their ability to assess and demonstrate accountability, many agencies have changed and upgraded data collecting, recording, and record keeping processes to ensure data standardization.
  - Third, articles and publications about positive and effective aspects of practices have been produced, aiding in the dissemination and advancement of knowledge for the profession.

Overall, increased public demand, commitment by the profession, and technological resources and methodologies to assess practice have encouraged social workers to take responsibility for demonstrable accountability. The Canadian Association of Social Workers has moved from having a statement of intent to developing a highly complex network of evaluations to ensure that accountability is a concrete, demonstrable, and observable component of the profession's activities.

[FJT]

RELATED ENTRIES

Administrative Theory & Practice, Agency-Based Research, Canadian Association of Social Workers, Codes of Ethics, Ethics, Legal Issues, Organizational Theory, Professional Issues, Professional Liability, Program Evaluation, Provincial/Territorial Associations, Recording, Theory & Practice

addiction

"Addiction" was in use in everyday and legal English long before it came to be associated with substance abuse. Kalant (1995) points out that, in the sixteenth century, addiction denoted someone who was legally bound or given over, as in a servant/master relationship, or given over to a practice or habit. The notion of loss of liberty relates to a more contemporary definition of addiction as a repeated failure to refrain from use of drugs and other substances, despite prior resolutions to do so. It is important to acknowledge, however, that many perspectives on addiction go beyond a focus on psychoactive substances; indeed, addiction can generally be understood as denoting excessive appetitive behaviours. In this view, addiction is an interplay of incentives and restraints: pleasure in the behaviour, accompanied by increasing negative consequences and ambivalence over its continuation. Thus, individuals can develop addictions to substances but also to such behaviours as gambling, sex, or eating. Here, the focus is on the more well-researched phenomena of addictions to such substances as alcohol and other drugs. Recent conceptualizations of alcohol and other drug use have focused on three stages of drug-taking behaviour (IM 1996): drug use (i.e., drug-taking), drug abuse (i.e., any excessive or harmful use), and drug dependence (substance dependence as defined by standard diagnostic criteria). Sources for standard diagnostic criteria include the *Diagnostic and Statistical Manual of Mental Disorders* and the World Health Organization's 1992 *International Classification of Diseases and Related Health Problems*. Bohn & Meyer (1999) provide an excellent review and discussion of the historical and contemporary typologies of addiction screening and diagnosis.

Despite considerable research in the area of addictive behaviour, there is no international consensus on the definition of substance abuse, dependence, and addiction. As West (2001) points out, the main challenges in understanding addiction are in explaining both the individual and the social factors associated with it, along with the ways in which addiction can be prevented or ameliorated individually and socially. West summarizes the diverse and often overlapping theories of addiction that attempt to come to grips with this phenomenon, including:

- behavioural or social theories that conceptualize addiction as some combination of biological, psychological, or social processes;
- theories that emphasize the effects of addictive stimuli (i.e., why some properties of a drug are more addictive than others);
- theories that attempt to explain why some individuals are more likely to become addicted than others;
- a theoretical focus on environmental and social conditions associated with addiction; and
- theories that stress the processes of relapse and recovery.

Part of the challenge in developing and testing theories about addictive behaviour is that addiction is understood within a social and cultural context. Therefore, definitions about what constitute the causes and consequences of addiction change over time as socio-cultural norms and beliefs shift and change. For example, the American prohibition of alcohol in the late nineteenth and early twentieth centuries was inextricably linked with social forces. This period also saw competing theories of alcohol addiction, between the conceptualization of alcoholism as a moral failing (by proponents of prohibition), and as a disease (by the medical community). It is also important to note that responses to addiction are determined by the way in which it is understood. If addiction is regarded as a disease over which the individual has no control, then lifelong abstinence makes sense in that context; on the other hand, quite different treatment implications emanate from such biological factors as genetic predisposition, or from such psychological explanations as conditioning and reinforcement, character traits, low self-esteem, or a need for excitement. Such environmental factors as role models, social norms, and the media likely also play a part in addictive behaviour, as do cultural and religious beliefs, life stage, and socio-economic factors. An integrative approach to understanding addictions that combines biological, psychological, social (including cultural and spiritual) factors has been proposed as a way of accounting for the myriad potential causes and consequences of addiction; this biopsychosocial approach holds that addiction is the result of a number of causes

and influences, and can best be understood in this broader context; thus, addiction is a multidimensional, complex phenomenon that cannot be explained by any single set of factors (Ogborne 1997).

Social workers continue to play a vital role in all areas of addiction research, policy, and treatment (Meeks & Herie 1999). Given the stigmatization of individuals who misuse or abuse alcohol and other drugs, advocacy and policy formation are critical in issues relating to social justice and access to essential programs and services. Frontline treatments tailored to individual needs and circumstances of diverse client populations are also key, and can be delivered through a range of specialist and non-specialist service settings. For the foreseeable future, the addictions field will continue to be a centre for lively debate and discussion, as the understanding of this complex and multi-dimensional phenomenon evolves and develops.

[*Marilyn Herie*]

RELATED ENTRIES

Abuse, Clinical Social Work, Counselling, Medication, Pharmacological Therapy, Practice Methods, Psychotropic Medication, Research, Sensitizing Concepts, Substance Addiction, Suicide, Theory & Practice, Therapy, Treatment, Wellness, Women's Christian Temperance Union

REFERENCES

Bohn, M.J., and R.E. Meyer. 1999. Typologies of Addiction. In M. Galanter and H.D. Kleber (Eds.) *Textbook of Substance Abuse Treatment*. 2nd ed. 97–108. Washington, DC: American Psychiatric Press.

IM [Institute of Medicine]. 1996. *Pathways of Addiction*. Washington, DC: National Academy Press.

Kalant, H. 1995. Addiction: Concepts and Definitions. In J.H. Jaffe (Ed.) *Encyclopedia of Drugs and Alcohol*. vol. 18–23. New York: Simon and Schuster / MacMillan.

Meeks, D.E., and M.A. Herie. 1999. Alcohol Dependence. In F.J. Turner (Ed.), *Adult Psychopathology: A Social Work Perspective*. 2nd ed. 572–610. New York: Free Press.

Ogborne, A. 1997. Theories of "Addiction" and Implications for Counselling. In S. Harrison and V. Carver (Eds.) *Alcohol and Drug Problems: A Practical Guide for Counsellors*. 2nd ed. 3–18. Toronto: Centre for Addiction and Mental Health.

West, R. 2001. Theories of addiction. *Addiction* 96, 1, 3–13.

administrative theory & practice

Administrative theory and practice for social and mental health services in Canada have evolved from a body of experience and literature common to both Europe and North America (Mouzelis 1969). In Canada social and mental health services are administered by a mix of incorporated non-profit agencies, government departments or Crown corporations, and for-profit organizations. In social systems theory, every post-feudal organization is composed structurally of four subsystems: a policy board, management and supervisory personnel, "staff" units serving the organization's needs (i.e., budget and finance, research and information systems, public relations, employment arrangements, salary/cheque distribution, fringe benefits), and "line" units devoted to serving the clients or patients. Research has confirmed that the greatest hazard to productive and creative internal personnel relationships is role ambiguity and role conflict among board members, management personnel, and employees in the staff and line units. The prevention of role-related stress is understood to depend chiefly on the clarity of written terms of reference for the board and each board committee (standing or ad hoc), on the clarity and quality of written job descriptions for each employee, and on a thorough readable manual of organizational regulations and procedures. A computerized manual eases employee access and convenience for ongoing revision. Also of importance is distinguishing carefully between decision control and decision participation, in such areas as approval of budget (by board), selection and employment of personnel (by manager), and decision making around diagnosis, choice of treatment plan, and conduct of treatment interview (by line-unit professionals); on the other hand, decision participation can be widely distributed within and among the four subsystems.

In settings where social work is the host profession (i.e., children's aid societies, family service agencies, children's mental health centres), line units are likely to be referred to as programs or teams, with the participation of other professions often on a separate contract basis. In settings where social work is a secondary rather than a host profession (i.e., hospitals, secondary schools, business and industrial corporations), line units are generally by departmentation based on human problem (e.g., mental illness, emotional and behaviour problems, family dysfunction, or specific disease or physical disability) rather than by profession. Departments are more likely to be referred to as programs, which are now often composed of interprofessional, rather than single-profession, teams. Whether in host or secondary settings, line-unit social workers within program/team structures have experienced such qualitative changes as less centralized administrative supervision, more collegial consultation, increased practice autonomy, local unit accountability, heightened knowledge and awareness of other professions, and in some settings mandatory membership in a provincially certified college of social workers and social service workers. Staff unit departmentation, particularly in hospitals, has remained largely unaltered except for qualitative changes in the way directors relate to their line colleagues. Medical social work departments, for example, continue to carry such functions as personnel recruitment, hospital orientation, in-service training, continuing education arrangements, and social work interns field practice assignments. Program evaluation and information systems store and retrieve data primarily from fact sheets in client/patient charts or files, and worker time and activity forms are routed every day or so to an agency information clerk or are entered directly at a computer manual. Client/patient chart information includes demographic data, notes on presenting problems, and, in recent years, client level-of-functioning data based on subjective worked ratings, client self-ratings, or short-form standardized test scores as to level-of-functioning at intake, once or twice during treatment, and at case closing.

For budgeting and funding, there has been a shift from earlier global line-item budgeting to program budgeting for programs defined either by presenting problems, by functions, by geographic service areas, or some combination of the three. Increasingly, funders have requested unit/cost data (e.g., cost per interview hour, per foster-home placement, per assessment, per home visit) as comparative efficiency indicators among competing service providers.

Many front-line workers in some settings feel that worker time and activity report forms, required by funders for unit/cost data, are burdensome. It is not unusual for line personnel to have to report daily on time spent, not only with client or patient—which is essential—but also time spent in committee meetings, travel time, telephone calls, case consultation meetings, case recording, referrals, missed appointments, and more. Program evaluation has evolved from a focus on volume of service, to a focus on unit costs (i.e., for efficiency), to a focus on cost-outcome reports (i.e., for effectiveness) for cases in progress and at case closing (Burch 1999). A recent operating agency demonstration of cost-outcome reporting found that, while certain other worker time and activity items are also needed on an ongoing basis or from a two-week annual time study, a cost-outcome report can be generated with just one information item from line personnel: time spent each day with client or patient (McCready et al. 1996). Data for cost per closed case, when linked to case-outcome ratings from patient charts or client files, are seen as providing valuable insights for professional self-development, as well as for management planning, board members, and funders.

[*Sheldon L. Rahn*]

RELATED ENTRIES

Accountability, Boards, Goal Setting, Organization Theory, Personnel, Supervision, Theory & Practice

REFERENCES

Burch, H.A. 1999. *Social Welfare Policies and Choices*. New York: Haworth Press, 360–61.

McCready, D.J., S. Pierce, S.L. Rahn, and K. Were. 1996. Third Generation Information Systems: Integrating Costs and Outcomes (Tools for Professional Development and Program Evaluation). *Administration in Social Work* 20, 1, 1–15.

Mouzelis, P. 1969. *Organization and Bureaucracy*. Chicago: Aldine.

Rahn, S.L., and D.J. McCready. 1985. Notes on Social Service Provision in Canada. *Canadian Public Policy* XI, 3, 625–28.

adoption

Adoption is the legal process of transferring the custody and guardianship of a child from one parent or parents to another parent or parents, who then have all rights and responsibilities of raising the child. The primary function of adoption is to provide for the care of children within a permanent family. Some form of adoption, with significant variations, is practised in all cultures. In Canada child welfare services, including adoption, fall within provincial/territorial authority and, therefore, adoption laws and practices differ from jurisdiction to jurisdiction. While such professions as law, medicine, and psychology may be involved, social work continues to be the predominant profession in adoption. Several distinct types of adoption are recognized: relative, public, private, and international. Adoption by a relative (i.e., intra-family, step-parent) is often treated as a private matter with no social work involvement. Public adoption (i.e., government, ward) is the placement of infants and older special needs children who, usually, have been apprehended from their birth family for reasons of neglect. Private adoption includes direct placement by the birth family, unlicensed intermediary placement, and placement by a licensed agency or individual. International adoption is the placement of foreign-born children into Canadian homes (The Hague Conference 1993; Bascolm & McKelvey 1997). One central issue in these adoption practices is the need to establish and maintain standards that ensure the well-being of children and families.

For many years, agencies believed that, for non-relative adoption, the adoptive family ought to be completely separated from the birth family. Until recent decades, that belief, along with the environment/heredity child-rearing debate, influenced adoption laws, policy, and practice; while parents were advised to tell a child of his/her adopted status, few post-placement services were available to assist families (Reitz & Watson 1992). Now adoption is viewed as a life-long process, with an emphasis on preparation and education of prospective adoptive parents, and provision of post-adoption services as vital for sustaining placements. Governments, agencies, national organizations (e.g., the Adoption Council of Canada, Parent Finders), and provincial adoptive parent support groups play a role in developing and delivering post-adoption services. One of the pioneers of reform was Canadian sociologist and adoptive parent, H. David Kirk; in 1964, he introduced to the adoption community the concepts of acknowledgment and rejection of difference in *Shared Fate: A Theory of Adoption and Mental Health*. His basic premises were that forming a family by adoption differs from forming a family by birth, and that, while tensions are inherent in the acknowledgment of this fact, adoptive families who do so fare better. Such developments as adoption self-help groups (both adoptive parent, and search-and-reunion) in the early 1970s and open adoption in the early 1980s challenged the practice of secrecy and the complete separation of birth and adoptive families. Open adoption recognizes that adopted persons have two sets of parents, both of which are important in the healthy growth and development of adopted children. Open adoption involves the birth parents selecting the adoptive family, exchanging identifying information, and making an agreement for ongoing contact. Such arrangements give birth parents peace of mind regarding their decision, adoptive parents a sense of entitlement, adopted children access to information about themselves (Gritter 1997). In the past birth fathers were ignored in the adoption process, but current adoption practice now addresses their rights and needs (Mason 1995) in accordance with legislation that requires notification and/or consent of birth fathers.

By the mid-1970s fewer infants were available for adoption: birth control and abortion were more available, more single mothers were raising their children, and Aboriginal communities were challenging agency practice of placing their children in non-Aboriginal families (Fournier & Crey 1997). The decrease in the number of children available prompted couples and single people wanting to adopt children to consider other options including private, international, older and special needs adoption, as well as new reproductive technologies. Government child welfare services turned their attention to finding adoptive homes for the many older and special needs children in care (Fahlberg 1991). This shift in focus resulted in such practices as encouraging foster families to adopt children in their care; recruiting families to foster with the intention of adopting (called "fost-adopt") if, and when, the child is legally free for adoption; starting permanency planning on the day the child is first taken into care; and considering kinship adoption as an option (Webber 1998). Birth parents (Petrie 1998) and adopted persons (Sorosky, Baran, & Pannor 1978) have had to live with secrecy for most of the twentieth century; now many actively seek to be reunited (McColm 1993). All provinces have legislation to facilitate reunions, the most common being mutual consent registries maintained by government departments. Most provinces have provisions for active searches for the other party when only one registers; British Columbia grants access, with veto provisions, to original birth records for adult adopted persons, or to amended birth records for birth parents. The debate continues over one party's right to know versus the other party's right to privacy. Ongoing research examines process, practice, and adoption outcomes, especially how adopted persons fare in adoption. Further research might study services needed by birth families so that children do not have to come into care, how children in care can be moved into permanency in a timely fashion, and the kinds of supports that adoptive families need as they raise their children, many of whom have significant special needs. Adoption in some form has always been, and will continue to be, part of the fabric of families. Societies must have alternatives for children who cannot be reared in their birth families. Adoption is an institution that will continue to evolve to better meet the needs of all participants. Information from the Adoption Council of Canada can be found online at <www.adoption.ca>.

[*Raymond O. Ensminger* and
Marilyn Shinyei]

RELATED ENTRIES

Aboriginal Issues, Child Advocacy, Child Custody & Access, Child Welfare, Children's Aid Society of Toronto, Family Planning, Family Research, Family Therapy, Sister Mary Henry, Marital & Family Problems, Parenting, Pregnancy, Private Adoption, Royal Commission on New Reproductive Technologies, Services for Children, Services for Families, Services for Married People, Services for Women, Single Parents, Toronto Infants Home

REFERENCES

Bascolm, B.B., and C.A. McKelvey. 1997. *The Complete Guide to Foreign Adoption: What to Expect and How to Prepare for Your New Child.* New York: Pocket Books.

Fahlberg, V.I. 1991. *A Child's Journey through Placement.* Indianapolis, IN: Perspectives Press.

Fournier, S., and E. Crey. 1997. *Stolen from Our Embrace: The Abduction of First Nations Children and the Restoration of Aboriginal Communities.* Toronto: Douglas and McIntyre.

Gritter, J.L. 1997. *The Spirit of Open Adoption*. Washington, DC: CWLA Press.

Mason, M.M. 1995. *Out of the Shadows: Birthfathers' Stories*. Edina, MN: O.J. Hoyrard.

McColm, M. 1993. *Adoption Reunions*. Toronto: Second Story Press.

Petrie, A. 1998. *Gone to an Aunt's*. Toronto: McClelland and Stewart.

Reitz, M., and K.W. Watson. 1992. *Adoption and the Family System*. New York: Guilford Press.

Sorosky, A.D., A. Baran, and R. Pannor. 1978. *The Adoption Triangle*. Garden City, NY: Anchor Press.

The Hague Conference. 1993. The Hague Convention on Protection of Children and Co-operation in Respect of Intercountry Adoption.

Webber, M. 1998. *As If Kids Mattered: What's Wrong in the World of Child Protection and Adoption*. Toronto: Key Porter.

advocacy

Advocacy refers to that century-old commitment of social workers whereby practitioners respond to specific psychosocial needs of individuals, dyads, families, and small groups, and use skills and knowledge to bring about systemic changes deemed to be necessary to the psychosocial growth of individuals or segments or all of society. Advocacy is a critically important concept in Canadian social work practice, representing one component of the social work dichotomy, of which direct service provision is the other. Within the socio-political climate of the intra-professional ethos, this dichotomy has unfortunately been presented as an either/or situation. Heated debates that ensued over which holds the greater importance has resulted in criticism of practitioners who under- or over-support either commitment. This dichotomy was reinforced in part in the education of social workers, where some curricula led students to elect one component of practice over the other. In recent years, considerable progress in disagreements as to the perceived prominence of either direct work or advocacy is diminishing, and all social workers are viewed as having a responsibility in advocacy; hence, even though both areas of practice require a broad spectra of knowledge and skills, specialized expertise in advocacy is required, along with an underlying need for mutual respect and understanding among specialists. The broad range of social work activities

involved in advocacy encompasses an individual social worker acting on behalf of an individual client, to the entire profession's efforts to effect changes of relevance to the entire population. This practice method is complex, requiring detailed knowledge of systems and subsystems as well as expertise and strategies to work effectively within larger systems, including the body politic; advocacy requires the ability to gather and analyze accurately available data as well as political lobbying to make use of such data. In Canada most agencies are involved in advocacy, while some— such as the Canadian Council on Social Development and Family Services Canada—exist entirely as advocacy bodies. In addition to the activities of direct service agencies, individual practitioners, special advocacy bodies, and organizations, various professional associations throughout the country advocate on client needs as well as on the welfare and development of the profession. Numerous letters, projects, briefs, petitions, delegations, research projects, policy papers, and data analysis have been produced by the profession on social issues, mostly by provincial/territorial associations, as much of the responsibility for the provision of welfare services rests with the provinces and territories. The national body, the Canadian Association of Social Workers, co-ordinates and shares information, as well as taking a direct advocacy role on matters of national and international concern.

[*FJT*]

RELATED ENTRIES

Anti-oppressive Social Work, Canadian Association of Social Workers, Canadian Council on Social Development, Child Advocacy, Education of Social Workers, Practice Methods, Provincial/Territorial Associations, Social Justice, Social Welfare History, Social Work Profession, Theory & Practice, Toronto Infants Home

agency-based research

Agency-based research—frequently called practice research—is a concept of increasing importance in Canadian social work practice for several reasons. For a long time the profession and much of the public assumed that social work interventions were effective in assisting clients; it was also assumed that even more effective practice was prevented only by either a shortage of trained personnel or a lack of sufficient resources. These assumptions, however, have rapidly changed. Clients, practitioners, administrators, researchers, funders, insurers, and the public are increasingly asking for evidence of effectiveness to justify the large amounts of public and private funding that maintain the ever-expanding social networks in Canada. Issues relate not only to how efficient a particular service is but to how practitioners can improve it. This interest in and demand for evidence of effectiveness come from beyond and within the profession; in agency delivering services, a strong climate exists for assessing differential outcomes of diverse services modalities, techniques, theories, and interventions. Practitioners are aware from experience that social work interventions at micro and macro levels are highly influential, but also understand that not every client is helped, or is helped sufficiently. New theories and formats of intervention move the profession toward finding more effective and efficient ways to bring about the individual and societal effects to which the profession is committed. This commitment to increase the knowledge base of the profession has been greatly enhanced by research capabilities and the concurrent extraordinary expansion of technique and strategies to measure and assess practice methods. Graduates of schools of social work have acquired strong research skills in their professional training, as research is increasingly regarded not only as a function of the university-based scientist but as a requirement of all practitioners. From this expansion has emerged a dramatic development of evaluative activities within even the smallest agencies, resulting in the production of clear and precise treatment plans and case objectives with measurable indicators of change, and strategies for evaluation at relevant intervals. Agencies are keeping much more accurate and consistent records, usually computerized; data can be more rapidly and accurately evaluated. Trends in practice are being fed back to practitioners in ways that assist them to alter interventions on either a case-by-case or an agency-wide basis. Agency-based research can identify more readily which segments of the population are not served, what kinds of problems are least helped, and what kinds of interventions have no, or even negative, impacts. One of the most positive outcomes of intensified agency-based research into front-line prac-

tice is the evidence demonstrating that social work is indeed effective and that the majority of people are helped by agencies. It appears that this awareness has greatly encouraged front-line workers to continue assessments and to value agency-based research as a means to enhance their practice. An interesting spin-off of this value shift in the profession has been the growing comfort derived from much closer relationships between agencies and schools of social work in the development of practice research.

[*FJT*]

RELATED ENTRIES

Accountability, Education in Social Work, Information & Communication Technologies, Organizational Theory, Practice Methods, Program Evaluation, Research, Services for Children, Services for Elderly People, Services for Families, Services for Married People, Services for Offenders, Services for People with Disabilities, Services for Refugees, Services for Women, Services for Youth, Social Services

Alberta College of Social Workers

The Alberta College of Social Workers serves as the regulatory body for the profession of social work in Alberta. Its early history predates 1950, when colleagues formed the Northern Alberta Branch and, later, a Southern Alberta Branch of the Canadian Association of Social Workers. Throughout the 1950s these small groups struggled for professional recognition, culminating in the legal incorporation of the Alberta Association of Social Workers in 1961. The initial Social Workers Act (1969) provided regulation for those with a master's degree in social work or its equivalent, and controlled the title "registered social worker"; registration, however, was voluntary. A few years later, when the bachelor's program in social work was introduced at the University of Calgary, the legislation was revised to include registration of individuals with this degree and two years' experience in practice. In 1984 another legislative revision enabled a graduate to become a registered social worker immediately on graduation. Currently, the Alberta association operates under the Social Work Profession Act (1991, and proclaimed in 1995). This legislation established an approved two-year social services diploma as the minimum educational requirement for registration. Several regulatory committees were established, and the organization's name became the Alberta Association of Registered Social Workers. In 1999 the Act was amended several times:

- to introduce mandatory registration for professionally trained and practising social workers, with some transitional exemptions;
- to provide a one-year transitional opportunity for those individuals working within scope and who identify with the profession but who did not have social work education; and
- to change the organization's name to the Alberta College of Social Workers.

As a result, membership in the association increased dramatically to more than 4,600 in 2002. The legislative amendments were necessary steps to prepare Alberta social workers for inclusion in the Health Professions Act, which was proclaimed for social work on April 1, 2003. The Act provides control of title, a broadly defined scope of practice, regulations in regard to continuing competency activities, and the practice of restricted activities and a specialty register for clinical social workers. Registration is mandatory with no exceptions. The Act applies to thirty professions and comes into force in stages, as the schedules and regulations for each respective profession are approved. Under the Act, mandated objectives of the Alberta College of Social Workers are:

- to serve and protect the public interest;
- to provide direction and to regulate the profession;
- to establish, maintain, and enforce standards for registration, continuing competence, and standards of practice;
- to establish, maintain, and enforce a code of ethics; and
- to approve educational programs for registration purposes.

The registration process requires applicants to provide an original transcript of educational standing, two letters of reference indicating good character and reputation, a criminal records check, and payment of an administrative fee with the first year's dues. Current membership categories are registered, invalid/retired, student, and honorary. The governing council of the Alberta college is comprised of voting members that include ten elected members and four public members appointed by the government, as well as non-voting members that include the past president and the chairs of the regulatory committees (i.e., Registration, Professional Social Work Education, Clinical, and Competence). The Aboriginal Social Work Advisory Committee advises the council on Aboriginal issues. The Executive Committee deals with issues management and advocacy activities. Membership interests are served by committees related to Children's Issues, Annual Conference, Gerontology, Private Practice, Retired, Health and Computers. The college maintains an office in Edmonton, Alberta. Current information can be found online at <www.acsw.ab.ca>.

[*Rod Adachi*]

RELATED ENTRIES

Accountability, Advocacy, Canadian Association of Social Workers, Education in Social Work, J.G. Hutton, International Federation of Social Workers, National Association of Social Workers (US), Provincial/Territorial Associations

An Act for the Prevention of Cruelty to and Better Protection of Children

Introduced into the Ontario Legislature in February 1893, An Act for the Prevention of Cruelty to and Better Protection of Children passed into law in May of that year (Jones & Rutman 1981) and became widely known as the Children's Protection Act or the Children's Charter. Reformers across Ontario had been pressing for such legislation, but it was not until the formation of the Toronto Children's Aid Society in 1891 that "Sir Oliver Mowat's Liberal government [was stimulated] to implement [these] proposed reforms" and to appoint a Superintendent who would guide and oversee the provisions of the Act throughout Ontario. John Joseph Kelso, the first president of the Toronto Children's Aid Society, was appointed as the province's first Superintendent of Neglected and Dependent Children, in July 1893. Mowat's provincial secretary, J.M. Gibson, spent a year preparing the bill and, with assistance from Kelso, the Reverend J.E. Starr of Toronto, Lady Aberdeen of Ottawa, and A.S. Allan of Guelph, it was ready for submission in the spring session of Parliament of 1893. The Act granted local children's aid societies wide powers:

- to apprehend and assume guardianship of neglected, ill-treated, and abandoned children;
- to supervise and manage local shelters for the temporary care of these children;
- to select, supervise, and manage foster homes for the ongoing care of these children;
- to establish visiting committees to visit foster children at least every three months, with powers to remove children from one foster home to another should this prove necessary; and
- to assume the role of friend to juvenile offenders.

Under the provisions of the Act, an apparently neglected child under the age of fourteen could be apprehended without a warrant and brought before a magistrate to be placed under the care and guardianship of an accredited children's aid society. A child was considered neglected if found: begging; receiving alms; thieving; wandering at late hours; not having any home or proper guardianship; associating or dwelling with a thief, drunkard, or vagrant; growing up without salutary paternal control and education; being destitute; being an orphan; and undergoing imprisonment for crime. In its emphasis on the protection of children, the Act specified that parents or others found guilty of neglecting or exploiting children could face fines of up to $100 and imprisonment of up to three months. Municipalities were responsible for the cost of caring for these children but were empowered to recover the costs from parents.

The Children's Protection Act (1888) had set the stage for these sweeping changes. The earlier Act had given courts the authority to place neglected children into authorized children's homes and established public responsibility for the care of neglected and abandoned children by requiring that municipalities cover costs of up to two dollars per week for each child placed into one of these homes. Children remained in these newly established homes until they reached the age of sixteen. This Act also reaffirmed that neglected children could still be committed to one of the province's industrial schools established by public school boards under the Industrial Schools Act (1874). Prior to this Act, dependent children were placed in orphanages or sent to adult shelters and houses of refuge until they could be apprenticed or fostered out as labourers to a local employer or farm family. In his first several years as superintendent, Kelso travelled throughout the province advocating for the formation of local children's aid societies. A detailed account of his address on November 17, 1893, to concerned citizens was reported the next day in the *Guelph Mercury*:

> Mr. J.J. Kelso upon being introduced spoke of the claims of neglected, abandoned and orphaned children, showing that the work of the Humane Society and the work that he was immediately interested in should go hand in hand. We had come now practically to the age of enfranchisement of children and had to protect them. The society for the prevention of cruelty to animals was sixty years in advance of that for the protection of children. The old laws of England were so that a man could be put in jail for cruelty to his child but the child could not be taken from him. Now there were laws in every civilized part of the world where the children could be taken away from the parents if not properly cared for and trained. The endeavour was to secure the enforcement of these laws relating to neglect and dependent or juvenile offenders, and take them away from the homes of vice, keep them from running on the streets and save them from crime. The parents of these children were generally so low and degraded that they had no regard for their welfare and left them in the state of physical as well as moral destitution. By the Children's Protection Act the child was made a citizen from the time of its birth.

By 1899 thirty-five voluntary societies had been formed in Ontario and most children, who resided in adult houses of refuge had been placed into children's shelters and foster homes under the supervision of a local inspector and an appointed visiting committee. Ontario's legislation to deal with neglected, abandoned, and dependent children was a first in Canada; its Children's Protection Act became a model for other jurisdictions.

[*Al Koop*]

RELATED ENTRIES

Abuse, Child Abuse, Children's Aid Society, J.J. Kelso, Sexual Abuse of Children, Services for Children, Toronto Infants Home, Wellness

REFERENCES

Jones, A., and L. Rutman. 1981. *In the Children's Aid: J.J. Kelso and Child Welfare in Ontario.* Toronto: University of Toronto Press.

Antigonish Movement*

Antigonish Movement, a social and economic movement sponsored by the Extension Department of St. Francis Xavier University, Antigonish, Nova Scotia. During the 1920s, following several decades of adversity in fishing, mining and agriculture in eastern Nova Scotia, St. Francis Xavier became involved in a series of social and economic programs, and in 1928 it established the Extension Department. The department was under the direction of Father Moses Coady, but it relied heavily on the inspiration of Father J.J. "Jimmy" Tompkins and on the organizing zeal of Coady's assistant, A.B. Macdonald. The "Antigonish Movement" was unusual—a liberal Catholic movement at a time when conservatism was dominant in the Roman Catholic Church....It focused on Adult Education as a means towards social improvement and economic organization. Typically, one of the movement's organizers would enter a community, use whatever contacts could be found and call a public meeting to assess the community's strengths and difficulties. A study club would be created and a program for a series of meetings developed. Usually, at the end of these meetings, one or more co-operatives would be established to help overcome the difficulties that had been discussed. The Credit Union was most common, but the movement also organized co-operatives for selling fish, retailing consumer goods, building homes and marketing agricultural produce.

During the 1930s the Antigonish Movement spread to, or was imitated in, many areas of Atlantic Provinces. It also became well known in other parts of Canada and in the USA, publicized by its own leaders, the churches and the credit union movement. During the 1940s a series of articles and books made the movement known in Europe, Latin America and Asia. In the 1950s adult educators and social activists began coming to study the movement in Antigonish, and in 1959 the Coady International Institute was established. The institute, a training centre for adult education and social action, soon attracted students for courses on the Antigonish method. Thousands of community organizers have studied in Antigonish. Upon returning to Asia, Latin America and Africa they have attempted, with differing degrees of success, to duplicate the movement's early accomplishments in Nova Scotia. In recent years the movement has played an important role in Canada's Foreign Aid programs. Locally the Antigonish Movement has found its study club approach difficult to sustain since the 1950s. The arrival of television, road improvements and a gradually increasing standard of living made it difficult to assemble groups for sustained study and community activism. The movement has been forced to embrace new communication and information technology and to face current issues, most of which are not resolved through co-operatives, in order to maintain its momentum. The success of these efforts is not as easily demonstrable as were the very concrete accomplishments of the 1930s and 1940s.

[*Ian MacPherson*]

* Used unedited by permission from *The Canadian Encyclopedia*. 2000. Toronto: McClelland and Stewart.

RELATED ENTRIES

Church-Based Services, Citizen Participation, M.M. Coady, Community Development, Co-operative Movement, Non-governmental Organizations, Social Welfare History

anti-oppressive social work

The history of social work has been characterized by a dynamic tension among those who understand its mission to be one of cure and control, and those who see it as one of transformation and resistance. Anti-oppressive theory and practice, an umbrella term for a variety of approaches that promote the latter mission, is presented as a means of promoting emancipatory struggles toward social justice. Social workers involved in the settlement house movement, the progressive era, the rank and file movement, the new deal, the social gospel movement, and the League for Social Reconstruction, among others, were all dedicated to social reform. Since 1970, however, social workers have witnessed the unprecedented development of anti-oppressive approaches—with roots in the radical and Marxist social work—as alternatives to the traditional social work model of personal rehabilitation and individual self-fulfilment. Subsequently, concerned that radical social work focused on class analysis at the expense of other factors, Canadian scholars developed what has become known as the structural approach to practice. Feminist social workers critiqued this structural approach, noting that the theoretical analysis and resultant practices had not adequately integrated issues of gender. Similarly, structural and feminist theory was criticized for lack of attention to racism, and anti-racism social workers challenged the Eurocentric bias of much social work, placing race at the centre of their analyses. At the start of the twenty-first century, while still contesting the terrain, these approaches have drawn together under the banner of anti-oppressive theory and practice.

Practitioners who subscribe to an anti-oppressive approach share the values of equity, inclusion, empowerment, interdependence and community, and have a vision of an egalitarian future. Understanding that a person's state of consciousness is related to the nature of society, such practitioners link the personal thoughts, feelings, and behaviour of individuals to socio-political issues and conditions. A recognition that power and resources are unequally distributed leads to personal and institutional marginalization, and relationships of oppression and domination. A capacity to encourage, support, and centre the knowledge and perspective of those who have been marginalized is essential for such practitioners, as well as recognizing and challenging privilege. Anti-oppressive practitioners seek to work collaboratively with individuals, groups, and communities to explore the transformative potential of social work through the elimination of oppression and domination. This collaborative work includes individual counselling and support in which the definition of problems is grounded in a critical analysis of the material and social realities of clients' lives. For example, a person who is having difficulty managing on monthly social assistance payments is not seen as having personal deficits that can be addressed through budgeting or life-skills programs; rather, inequities in income distribution and the inadequacy of the support payments are defined as problematic. Similarly, when working with a person with physical challenges, anti-oppressive workers strive to identify inhibiting and limiting structures facing the person. Such problem definition does not deny individual agency or influence but does affect the nature of the work done with clients. In doing this collaborative work, anti-oppressive

practitioners apply many of the same skills and methods used by other practitioners: counselling, supporting, assessing, referring, and advocating; they work to enhance the strengths of individuals and their environments, assist people in gaining more control of their lives, connect clients with others in similar situations, and defend client access to services and resources. Anti-oppressive workers may work in traditional or alternative social services. They may participate directly in social action and social change, and work with unions and other social justice groups.

[*Carolyn Campbell*]

RELATED ENTRIES

Aboriginal Issues, Antigonish Movement, Assembly of First Nations, Barnardo Homes, B'Nai Brith, Canadian Council on Child Welfare, Canadian Council on Social Development, Community Development, Dalhousie University Maritime School of Social Work, Diversity, Empowerment Theory, Fabian Society, Feminist Theory, Fred Victor Centre, Interprofessional Issues, League for Social Reconstruction, Progressive Social Work, Race & Racism, Racism-Sensitive Social Work, Radical Social Work, Sensitizing Concepts, Settlement House Movement, Social Gospel Movement, Social Justice, Social Planning, Social Policy, Social Welfare History, Social Work Profession, Theory & Practice

Assembly of First Nations

Before Canada emerged as a nation state, Aboriginal peoples organized and governed themselves according to their traditions. Within the Canadian state, Aboriginal peoples have been subjected to policies and practices that corroded traditional cultures, distribution of resources, and governance. Systematically marginalized, the peoples indigenous to this land have seen the resources on which they relied for survival redistributed to benefit non-Aboriginal citizens. Realizing the pressing need to form a national lobby to fight for their rights, the First Nations of Canada first attempted to do so soon after the First World War with the League of Indians in Canada. After the Second World War, Aboriginal peoples established the North American Indian Brotherhood. In 1961 the National Indian Council was formed to represent three of the four major groups of Aboriginal people in Canada: Treaty or Status Indians (now referred to as First Nations), Non-status Indians, and the Métis; the Inuit were excluded (McFarlane 1993). From that time, Aboriginal Peoples have always had a national lobby group to represent them in Ottawa. Yet these organizations failed because of internal factionalism and government actions intent on suppressing them. Subsequently, Inuit, Métis, and Aboriginal women established their own national organizations, while the Status and Treaty Indians in 1967 formed the National Indian Brotherhood (later renamed the Assembly of First Nations). This organization has became an increasingly articulate advocate for Aboriginal rights in Canada under the leadership of such individuals as George Manuel, Walter Dieter, Noel Starblanket, Delbert Riley, Dr. David Ahenakew, Georges Erasmus, Ovide Mercredi, Matthew Coon Come, and Phil Fontaine.

Soon after the National Indian Brotherhood came into existence, the federal government revealed its infamous 1969 White Paper, in which then Indian Affairs Minister Jean Chrétien introduced plans to eliminate the distinct status and rights of Treaty peoples. Responses from Aboriginal leaders and communities were quickly organized, with the national organization acting as the focal point for successful lobbying of the Canadian public and Parliament to have the White Paper withdrawn. This was the first collective effort by Aboriginal peoples throughout the country to publicly criticize government policy. In 1972 the national organization's policy paper, "Indian Control of Indian Education," was a breakthrough in gaining support from the Indian Affairs department to implement First Nation philosophy on self-governance and to promote the philosophy of Aboriginal control by Aboriginal communities. Between 1983 and 1987, the Assembly of First Nations and three other national Aboriginal organizations attended First Ministers Conferences to identify, define, and discuss Aboriginal and Treaty rights by then included in the Canadian Charter of Rights and Freedoms. These conferences marked the first time that Aboriginal peoples were represented in constitutional talks that directly affected them. The participation by national Aboriginal organizations helped to protect the undefined Aboriginal and Treaty rights recognized in Aboriginal societies and international law, against tremendous pressure from sev-

eral provinces and the federal government, which sought to define and control them within the Canadian legal system.

Despite numerous successes, bringing the diverse First Nations throughout Canada into a cohesive voice to lobby government for change was a formidable challenge for the National Indian Brotherhood. An important structural transition was the shift in 1982 to community representation and accountability to members; at that time, the National Indian Brotherhood, which had brought together regions, became the Assembly of First Nations, an organization of Chiefs representing more than 630 First Nations (AFN 1999). Thereafter, community leaders directly formulated and administered the policies of the newly restructured organization. The Assembly of First Nations Secretariat represents the views of those communities in such areas as Aboriginal and Treaty Rights, Economic Development, Education, Languages and Literacy, Health, Housing, Social Development, Justice, Taxation, Land Claims, Environment, and specific common issues that arise from time to time. The Chiefs meet annually to set national policy and direction through resolutions and to elect the National Chief at three-year intervals. The Chiefs also meet quarterly or as needed in a forum called the "Confederacy of Nations" to set ongoing direction; the membership of the confederacy consists of Chiefs and other regional leaders chosen according to a formula based on the population of each region. Current information on the Assembly of First Nations can be found online at < www.afn.ca >.

[*Gord Bruyere*]

RELATED ENTRIES

Aboriginal Issues, Aboriginal Services, Anti-oppressive Social Work, Canadian Charter of Rights and Freedoms, Culture, Diversity, Healing Theory (Cree), Human Rights, Indian Affairs & Northern Development, Non-governmental Organizations, Racism-Sensitive Social Work

REFERENCES

AFN. 1999. *History of the Assembly of First Nations.* Online at time of writing at < www.afn.ca / afnstorv .htm >.

McFarlane, P. 1993. *Brotherhood to Nationhood: George Manuel and the Making of the Modern Indian Movement.* Toronto: Between the Lines.

assessment

Assessment in Canadian social work practice refers to the process of ensuring that professional decisions about a client situation are based on a search for full understanding of all significant facets of a client and the inter-influences that impinge, or appear to impinge, on the presenting situation. Although often presented as a unitary act, assessment is a process that continues throughout a case, as situations change or are more clearly understood and as new information emerges. It is the process whereby the social worker is continually making a broad sweep of the client's reality to ensure that the diagnosis reached is accurately focused. In much contemporary practice and literature, assessment is viewed as coterminous with diagnosis. For those who view diagnosis as a narrow search for pathology, assessment is a preferable term, apparently because it is held to be a less problem-focused and broadly systematically based process.

In the assessment process, the social worker is attempting to understand a client's personal, resource, and systemic history, and present reality, as well as to identify orders or levels of significance to ensure proper, economical, ethical, and strategic foci of attention throughout a case. In the past assessment was seen as the formulation of a detailed history from which a diagnosis would emerge, leading to the formulation and implementation of a treatment plan. As practice methods have matured, it has become evident that an open-ended gathering of historical material was frequently a misuse of the time of a social worker who, as a result, often failed to connect with the client and identify the client's reality at contact. Therefore, for assessment that is an ongoing evaluation, it is critical for a social worker to determine what he/she knows, what he/she does not know, and what he/she wishes to know in order to arrive at a diagnosis—a conclusion about what he/she should do—at intervals throughout a case. Formulating a diagnosis is a process separate from assessment, in that the decisions made serve as the basis for intervention. Assessment is a much richer concept than the mere gathering of information that is implied by the phrase "client history." One of the challenges facing contemporary practice, with its diverse theoretical base, is the awareness of the complexity of client situations with which social workers are confronted. The myriad ways a client's life is influenced to shape personality as well as the set of life skills that derive from personal identity and history create a vast array of highly individualized psychosocial responses to life's challenges and to the range of influences that effect change. In an assessment process, therefore, a social worker must sort out from a potential mass of data what is needed and what can be left untouched. The skill that the social worker brings to practice is determining the importance and relevance to information about a client's psychosocial life. In the past psychodynamic thinking lent the assessment process a strong retrospective quality that began in a client's early life and led up to the present; contemporary practice is much more oriented to the present and a client's past is viewed from an assessment perspective only when deemed necessary rather than as a matter of course. Responsible practice demands that a social worker needs to report periodically on what aspects of the assessment process are deemed essential in forming the diagnostic judgments on which intervention is based.

[*FJT*]

RELATED ENTRIES

Accountability, Agency-Based Research, Diagnosis, Intervention Research, Interviewing, Practice Methods, Program Evaluation, Quality Assurance, Recording, Research, Theory & Practice, Therapy, Treatment, Wellness

Associated Charities of Toronto

The Associated Charities of Toronto (est. 1888) sought as its goal the bringing of cohesive order and planning to the many programs, services, and institutions with numerous sponsors dealing with various aspects of charity and welfare. Organizations such as this had emerged in other large cities and were the forerunners of social planning councils and the United Way. The first president of the Toronto organization was Goldwin Smith, who was very concerned about the highly disorganized nature of services at that time. While his intentions and those of the organization were good, the sought-for co-ordination of services did not take place.

[*FJT*]

RELATED ENTRIES
Church-Based Services, Non-governmental Organizations, Sectarian Social Services, G. Smith, Social Welfare History

Association of Social Workers in Northern Canada

The Association of Social Workers in Northern Canada (est. 1974) represents professionals in Canada's three northern territories: Northwest Territories, Yukon, and Nunavut. Before 1974 social workers from the Yukon and Northwest Territories were members of and represented as individuals by the Canadian Association of Social Workers; the association for northern social workers was established when the national association no longer accepted individual memberships. Although the association has existed in name since then, it has had extended periods of inactivity. The creation of Nunavut in 1999 provided the impetus to consider resurrecting the association, which had been dormant since the late 1980s. A report identified the barriers to maintaining a professional association of northern social workers, including:

- constraints of distance and geography;
- the lack of sufficient financial support;
- a small membership base;
- a consistently high turnover of social workers in northern communities;
- a high turnover of original association board members;
- an inability to agree on association membership requirements;
- vast differences in the educational and experiential backgrounds of northern social work practitioners;
- the division of the Northwest Territories to create Nunavut;
- the perception of social workers as paraprofessionals rather than as professionals;
- lack of a strong social work presence within territorial ministries of health and social services;
- dilemma in handling complaints regarding ethical conduct;
- a dilution of the role of social work education; and
- a backlash due to past social work decisions with northern and Aboriginal populations.

A meeting of territorial social workers was held in Inuvik in 1998. Supported by the national association, a decision was made to proceed with establishing a new northern association and an executive was chosen, along with three directors, one from each territory, to work with the executive. As the cost of holding face-to-face meetings is prohibitive, the board of directors meets monthly via teleconference. An annual conference has been held each year, combining an educational component with the annual general meeting. Membership in the association, which is voluntary, is open to graduates of university and community college social work programs and to others employed in social work. The association endeavours to promote the profession of social work in the territories and advocates for improved social conditions, provides advice to government bodies, attempts to raise awareness of social issues, and provides a communication link for northern social workers. To date, there has been no legislative regulation of territorial social work practice. As the Government of the Northwest Territories is considering introducing a health professions Act in 2003, it is possible that social workers there will have to be licensed and have their practice regulated under this Act. The association has full membership in the Canadian Association of Social Workers. Information about the Association of Social Workers in Northern Canada can be found online at < www.socialworknorth.com >.

[*Blair Dunbar*]

RELATED ENTRIES
Canadian Association of Social Workers, Education in Social Work, International Federation of Social Workers, National Association of Social Workers (US), Provincial/Territorial Associations, Remote & Rural Practice

Attention Deficit Hyperactivity Disorder

The inattentive, impulsive, and hyperactive behaviour of children more troublesome to others than to themselves was addressed prior to the twentieth century by punitive measures essentially aimed at suppressing bad conduct: beating the "devil" out of such children reflects the manner in which misconduct was perceived and "treated." The predictably less than optimal re-

sults obtained and changes in societal conceptualizations of childhood eventually gave rise to two
diverse views and concomitant interventions, one
being grounded in a medical model, the other
from a psychosocial systems perspective.

The first effect of the medical model was the
diagnostic label Attention Deficit Disorder, later
broadened to Attention Deficit Hyperactivity Disorder (ADHD). Problems with concentration,
impulsivity, and hyperactivity were transformed
by the act of labelling into numerous criteria, six of
which must be satisfied according to the prescripts
of the American Psychiatric Association's *Diagnostic and Statistical Manual of Mental Disorders*
in order for the label to be applied. The medical
model is based on an elaboration of the reality
that all children are born with certain natural
propensities. Troublesome children in particular
are believed to be born with inherited factors that
are manifested in abnormal brain morphology
associated with an underlying neurological dys-
regulation and underarousal of the frontal lobes.
While the purported physiological innate factors
do not readily translate into biochemical factors,
the medical intervention for children with ADHD
is essentially pharmacological, along with the
introduction of behavioural strategies in the
child's academic and, sometimes, home environment. The most commonly used drug is methyl-
phenidate (Ritalin™), which is available in both
short-acting and long-acting forms. This and similar drugs are reported to increase attention span
and make it easier for a child to focus on a task.
Teachers and parents report academic and behavioural improvements. Often the drugs are not
prescribed for weekends or during the summer
break from school. The prevalence of the medical
response to ADHD is attributable to two broad reasons. The first pertains to the environmental etiology of the troublesome behaviours and the effect
these have on the adults in the child's life: the
fussy, demanding, and difficult temperament of a
newborn combined with inadequate parenting
rapidly escalates into progressively more troublesome behaviours, culminating in either a cry for
help and/or an external identification of a problem. The second reason pertains to the almost
immediate relief produced by pharmacological
intervention. Side effects of the drugs vary and
include reduced appetite and difficulty going to

sleep. While the side effects are claimed to be controlled or to subside in time, there are nevertheless
short and prolonged consequences. Appetite loss
and sleep deprivation can create their own performance problems. Attention Deficit Hyperactivity Disorder often occurs with other problems
such as depressive or anxiety disorders. Especially
with depressed or anxious children, stimulant-
like drugs most often fail to produce the intended
results. In such cases, the stimulant like drugs can
make the behaviour of children worse. The pharmacological treatment of choice in these cases is
antidepressants and/ or major tranquillizers,
drugs that have their own type of side effects.
Moreover, it has been argued that major tranquillizers and antidepressants used with children produce no better results than the administering of a
placebo. The course of ADHD primarily addressed
with the use of pharmacological intervention is
worrisome. In one study 66 percent of children
with ADHD continued to have symptoms of the
"disorder" in adulthood and 23 percent were
found to have developed an antisocial personality
disorder (Weiss et al. 1985). Many adults with ADHD
are reported to continue to find taking stimulants
such as Ritalin™ helpful.

The non-medical behaviour of troublesome
children is defined within the psychosocial systems perspective, which reflects the dynamic
nature of interactions between the child and
his/her environment, with particular importance
given to developmental processes (Sroufe 1997).
Specifically, poor attachment relationships and
subsequent negative experiences are identified as
culminating in the manifestation of progressively
debilitating troublesome behaviours, as well as
cognitive, perceptual, and attributional dysfunc-
tionalities. This perspective contextualizes troublesome behaviour without negating the reality
of natural innate propensities. Furthermore, the
emphasis on environmental factors is reinforced
by research concerning brain development. There
is physiological evidence that sustained traumatic
experiences (i.e., childhood abuse), neglect, or
failure to form secure attachment in the early
years of life can create a chronic state of hyper-
arousal in a child and neuroendocrine activities in
the brain that can cause devastating consequences, including ADHD (Perry 1994). Emphasis,
therefore, is on environmental factors, specifically

parent/child interactions. Instead of addressing symptoms, the focus here is on the root causes of the problem. The justification of this approach is also based on the empirically established reality that environmental factors can enhance or diminish negative innate propensities. Essentially determined by the quality of parenting, a child born with a difficult temperament can grow up to be an adult no different in any way from a child born with a calmer temperament (Maziade et al. 1990). Mitigating the effects of a difficult temperament is acknowledged by the psychosocial systems perspective to be a difficult and challenging task that requires extraordinarily intuitive parents capable of recognizing and accepting in a timely manner the unusual needs of the child, and of drawing on specialized strategies and community resources. From a psychosocial systems perspective, attempts to change behaviour by means of intervention focused only on the child, without simultaneously changing the family environment by means of family therapy and other systemic interventions are considered to be futile. Early environmental intervention that is systemically focused and psychosocially grounded markedly diminishes the progressive actualization of negative innate propensities and the later life manifestation of anti-social behaviours. The determining factor is the extent to which parents can be guided to modify the nature of their interaction patterns with the troublesome child. As such, it is the response of the environment to the child's difficulties that determines the final outcome. Notwithstanding the conceptual and intervention differences between the medical and psychosocial systems models, both have markedly similar implications for the introduction of environmental measures with which to prevent the actualization of a child's innate negative propensities.

[*Alex Polgar*]

RELATED ENTRIES

Behaviour Theory, Clinical Social Work, Medication, Parenting, Person-in-Environment Perspective, Pharmacological Therapy, Practice Methods, Psychotropic Medication, Therapy, Treatment, Services for Children, Services for Youth, Wellness

REFERENCES

Maziade, M., C. Caron, R. Cote, C. Merette, H. Bernier, B. Laplante, P. Boutin, and J. Thivierge. 1990. Psychiatric Status of Adolescents Who Had Extreme Temperaments at Age Seven. *American Journal of Psychiatry* 147, 11, 1531–36.

Perry, B.D. 1994. Neurobiological Sequelae of Childhood Trauma. In M. Murbery (Ed.) *Catecholamine Function in Post-traumatic Stress Disorder.* Washington, DC: American Psychiatric Press.

Sroufe, L.A. 1997. Psychopathology as an Outcome of Development. *Development and Psychopathology* 9, 251–68.

Weiss, G., L. Hechtman, T. Milroy, and T. Perlman. 1985. Psychiatric Status of Hyperactives as Adults: A Controlled Perspective 15-Year Follow-up of 63 Hyperactive Children. *Journal of the American Academy of Child Psychiatry* 24, 211–20.

Reuben Baetz (1923–96)

Baetz, Reuben Conrad, social worker, Ontario MPP, *Cabinet minister; b. May 09, 1923, Chelsey, Bruce County, ON (of parents Harry William Baetz, Alice F. Henrich); m. Julie Annette Anderson, Aug. 05, 1950; children: Mark Conrad, Annette Alice, Carla Patricia; d. Oct. 1996*

Reuben Conrad Baetz spent a large portion of his life serving others, leaving no doubt that his heart lay in social work. Following the Second World War, when he served in the Canadian Active Service Force, he earned a bachelor's degree (*cum laude*) in political science in 1947 from the University of Western Ontario, and a master's degree in political science and history in 1948 at Columbia University. From 1949–56, he worked with the Lutheran World Federation Service to Refugees, becoming assistant director in 1952 and director in 1953. In 1957 Baetz received a bachelor of social work from the University of Toronto. Later, he was awarded honorary doctorates by both Wilfrid Laurier University and the University of Windsor. From 1957 to 1963, he was the assistant national commissioner of the Canadian Red Cross, and became a field director for the International Red Cross. In 1963 Baetz became executive director of the Canadian Welfare Council, where he led the organization through its transformation into the Canadian Council on Social Development. He remained the director until 1977, when he entered politics, and retains the distinction of being among the council's longest-serving executive directors (CCSD 1996). From 1972–76, while still directing the council, Baetz also served as president of the International Council on Social Welfare. Baetz began his political career in June 1977 as the MPP for Ottawa West. He quickly moved into the higher political ranks, becoming minister of Energy briefly in 1978, then minister of Culture and Recreation (1978–82), minister of Tourism and Recreation (1982–85), and minister of Intergovernmental Affairs (1985). Baetz was also a member of such organizations as Ontario Economic Council, Canadian Manpower and Immigration Council, Canadian Association of Social Workers, the board of governors of the Waterloo Lutheran University (now, Wilfrid Laurier University), and was a trustee of the Canadian Institute for Research on Public Policy. He died following a prolonged illness in 1996.

[*Michelle Wolfe*]

RELATED ENTRIES

Canadian Council on Social Development, Canadian Welfare Council, Social Planning, Social Policy, Social Welfare History

REFERENCES

CCSD [Canadian Council on Social Development]. 1996. *Perception*. 20, 3. Online at time of writing at <www.ccsd.ca>.

Barnardo homes

Barnardo homes were founded by Dr. Thomas John Barnardo (1845–1905), a pioneer in social work who established thirty-five homes and eighty centres for various kinds of child care. A convert to evangelical Christianity, he began a mission in 1866 in the east end of London, England, and four years later opened his first home for boys whom he had found sleeping on the streets or in lodging houses (Wymer 1962). The boys were fed and clothed in uniforms in the spartan atmosphere of this home, where they were given basic education and training in trades. Dr. Barnardo had a large sign erected on the boys' building, which read "No Destitute Child Is Ever Refused Admittance." In 1876 Barnardo opened the Village Home for Girls, a homey setting where girls attended school and were taught domestic skills. While more children were cared for through the continual expansion of Barnardo's efforts despite the constant struggle to find funds to support them, other children

had to be placed elsewhere. In 1882 Barnardo started to organize emigration of children to Canada. As a developing country, Canada was in need of labourers and it was expected that immigrant children, when grown, would have more opportunities in life than if they remained in England. In 1883 he set up permanent immigration headquarters in Ontario, one for boys (in Toronto) and one for girls (in Peterborough). After arriving by ship, children were taken to these headquarters for a brief stay. When a family applied for a child, the boy or girl would leave alone, most often by train to work on a farm; for children from cities in England, farm life was initially unfamiliar. Dr. Barnardo tried to build in safeguards for the subsequent welfare of children sent to Canadian families by having those who applied for a child supply a letter of reference from their church minister; he also expected twice-yearly follow-up visits. The children were also to attend school when they were not needed for work. The children's experiences varied widely. Some were raised as a member of the family they went to live with, were loved, were educated, and found good jobs. Many attended school sporadically and did not go beyond grade eight. Some were fed and clothed poorly, were physically abused, worked long hours, were isolated from the family, and rarely or never attended school. Barnardo's efforts to provide follow-up supervision sometimes fell short and some children were left feeling alone and unsupported; some felt like slaves. Many of the children faced the prejudices of those who felt resentful that the children, from the dregs of English society in their view, were taking jobs from local people; opinions circulated—supported by some influential Canadians and newspaper articles—that the children were of low character and intelligence with criminal tendencies. In 1887 Barnardo established an industrial farm near Russell, Manitoba, which housed up to ninety adolescent boys to be trained for farm labour; they generally led lives of hard work and monotony. Every summer and fall, new boys came and the former incumbents were hired by farmers; they fared no better in public opinion than had the children in Ontario: "As a result of the prejudice … no matter how honest their character or exemplary their work once they were hired, they were rumoured all over the West to be villainous and criminal" (Bagnell 1980: 168). In 1908 the industrial farm was sold by the trustees, much of it to men who had been boys there, and the money from the sale was used to fund other Barnardo programs.

In 1924 the Bondfield Commission went to Canada to study the thousands of children being sent by as many as fifty organizations in England; it recommended that only children of fourteen—at that time, school-leaving age—should go to Canada as farm labourers. Child immigration ended in the 1930s; by then, Barnardo homes accounted for 30,000 of the 80,000 children sent to Canada. As adults, these children married, raised families, and became members of Canadian society. Some who had lost contact with their families in England have sought information from the after-care department of the Barnardo organization (online at <www.barnardos.org>).

[*Brenda Brett*]

RELATED ENTRIES

Adoption, An Act for the Prevention of Cruelty to and Better Protection of Children, Child Welfare, Immigrants & Immigration, Services for Children, Social Welfare, Social Welfare History

REFERENCES

Bagnell, K. 1980. *The Little Immigrants*. Toronto: Macmillan.
Wymer, N. 1962. *Dr. Barnardo*. London: Longman.

behaviour theory

Behaviour theory is based on the premise that all behaviour can be understood by using a stimulus/response model in which an event (stimulus) happens and is followed by another event (response). The story of a colleague suggests that this basic behavioural model was known long before the behaviourists "discovered" it: his grandfather, an Aboriginal rancher, banged on a pail (stimulus) to get his horses to return to the barn (response). The Russian psychologist, Pavlov, explained how this might work when he experimented with a dog. Pavlov gave a dog food and noticed that the dog salivated in anticipation of eating; he then began to ring a bell while the dog was feeding and, finally, rang the bell and did not offer the dog food. He discovered that the dog salivated at the sound of the bell. Pavlov called the salivating behaviour to the sight of food an unconditioned response, and the salivating behaviour

to the sound of the bell a conditioned response. By consistently pairing the unconditioned response with the conditioned response, the salivation (unconditioned stimulus) became paired with the sound of the bell; to complete the model Pavlov also showed that a new (conditioned) response could be paired with an unconditioned stimulus by using the same technique.

The behavioural model had a significant impact on North American psychology and Canadian social work in the 1950s and 1960s. Behaviourism was seen as a competitor of Freudian psychology, which had had a significant impact during and immediately following the Second World War. The main developer of North American behaviourism, B.F. Skinner and his followers, took Pavlov's model and applied it to all forms of human and animal behaviour, to the extent that, in his later years, Skinner advocated raising children in a modified version of his famous "Skinner box." As understood by these psychologists, behaviour was created, and could be changed in two ways. The first was based on the classic conditioning model developed by Pavlov, where changing the stimulus changed the behavioural response. The second model, operant conditioning, posited that changing the response to the behaviour (reinforcement) could change behaviour. Under this model, behaviour would be continued if it received positive reinforcement (praise or treats) and stopped if it received negative reinforcement (no response, criticism, or punishment); behaviour reinforced occasionally (intermittent reinforcement) will continue over time as if it had been positively reinforced. The more likely the behaviour is to be rewarded positively, the longer it will last; the less frequent the reinforcement, the quicker it will cease. Behaviour could also be shaped by positively rewarding behaviours that were similar to the desired behaviour, selectively rewarding behaviour that came closest to the desired behaviour. Behaviour shaping by successive approximation is still used in many forms of skill development. Other behaviourists, arguing that an explanation for human behaviour needed more than the stimulus/response model, developed cognitive behaviourism, a model in which an individual chooses the response to the stimulus. In this model, in all but unconditioned responses, which are natural or biological, the individual makes a choice, not always a conscious one, as to how he/she responds. This chosen response is based on both the meaning the individual ascribes to the stimulus event and to the response repertoire the individual has developed. Using this cognitive model, behaviour change is made by helping the individual attach a different meaning to the stimulus event (reframing), or by teaching a new and more adaptive set of responses. The basic cognitive model was modified and developed into several different schools of cognitive behaviourism, including reality therapy, rational emotive therapy (Albert Ellis), cognitive therapy (Aaron Beck), and cognitive behavioural therapy (Donald Meichenbaum). Each of these cognitive behavioural theory is a distinct school that shares the same basic principles.

[Robert Twigg]

RELATED ENTRIES

Organizational Theory, Theory & Practice

Ken Belanger (1949–98)

Belanger, Ken, social worker, social justice activist; b. 1949; d. Aug. 14, 1998

Ken Belanger immigrated to Nova Scotia from Pennsylvania in the early 1970s, later becoming a Canadian citizen. He graduated in 1976 from the Maritime School of Social Work in Halifax, Nova Scotia, with a master of social work, and worked in social work positions in Halifax hospitals, mental health centres, and the Association for Family Life. In 1984 Belanger established a successful private practice, which he maintained until his death. In his practice, he offered counselling, group work, consultation, child custody assessments, and home study reports; he worked primarily with victims and perpetrators of abuse, persons with HIV/AIDS, and gay, lesbian, and bisexual youth and adults, their partners, and relatives. As a skilled facilitator and teacher, Belanger conducted many workshops with community organizations and agencies, sharing his expertise in violence and gender issues.

Ken Belanger practised social work with a high level of caring, responsibility, and ethical standards: his moral integrity was clearly evident in the congruence of his words and actions. He found the courage to carry what Sandra Butler calls "the burden of witness," to recognize the pain of his own and others' oppression in the dominant culture's refusal to recognize social inequalities and the suffering they bring. Belanger was a pioneer in the maritime social work community when, in 1985, he established Project New Start, a program for men who abuse their female partners. He facilitated men's groups for several years and collaborated closely with Bryony House, the Halifax transition house for abused women. Belanger successfully developed and maintained Project New Start, forming and implementing programs, supervising staff, educating the community, and training mental health, police, and other professionals. Belanger was also revolutionary in the social work community as one of the first social workers to be publicly and proudly a gay man. He tirelessly educated social workers about the many forms of systemic and personal heterosexism, and the realities and needs of gay, lesbian, bisexual, and transgendered persons. His willingness to risk and his unfailing commitment to advocate against oppression and injustice, for his own well-being and that of others, were exemplary. Belanger was part of the movement of people—primarily gay, lesbian, bisexual, and trangendered persons and their allies—who fought to have sexual orientation included in the Nova Scotia Human Rights Act as a prohibited ground of discrimination, as achieved in 1991.

Ken Belanger served the profession of social work as a faculty field instructor for the Maritime School of Social Work. Students knew him as a social worker who held high expectations of them in their field placements. Belanger was also active on the social action committee of the Nova Scotia Association of Social Workers and a registered private practitioner with the association. Generous in sharing his time and skills with community groups and organizations, he was a member of the men's action group, Men for Change, the advisory board of the Nova Scotia Persons with AIDS Coalition, and a counsellor on the gay and lesbian youth help line. After a long and courageous struggle with depression, Belanger died in 1998. He is remembered for his moral courage and fierce commitment to social justice. The Ken Belanger Commemoration Award, instituted by the Nova Scotia Association of Social Workers in 1999, honours him and recognizes social workers who demonstrate an explicit and unfailing commitment to pursue social justice and challenge oppression.

[*Norma Jean Profitt*]

RELATED ENTRIES
Anti-oppressive Social Work, Gay-Sensitive Services, Gender Issues, Human Rights, Lesbian Services, Nova Scotia Association of Social Workers, Sexual Orientation

R.B. Bennett: "New Red"

Richard Bedford Bennett, prime minister (1930–35); b. July 03, 1870, Hopewell, NB; Viscount Bennett of Mickleham, Calgary, and Hopewell; d. June 26, 1947, Mickleham, UK

Richard Bedford (R.B.) Bennett became the eleventh prime minister of Canada ten months after the stock market crash and the onset of the great depression of 1930s, when Canada was plunged into unprecedented economic and social impoverishment. Bennett's background as a very rich corporate lawyer, initially committed to unfettered capitalism, would seem an unlikely foundation for a social reformer; he was often caricatured as a plutocrat in a top hat. During the first four years of his term of office, his responses to the desperate pleas of voluntary agencies, provinces, and municipalities alike were primarily twofold: grossly inadequate annual grants, and the establishment of harsh work camps for unemployed men. R.B. Bennett's redemptive record began with his belated recognition, expressed early in 1935, that "The old order is gone. It will not return.... I am for reform! And in my mind reform means government intervention. It means government control and regulation. It means the end of laissez-faire." He sought to act on his new conviction through a broad legislative program he put before Parliament aimed at a more progressive taxation system, a minimum wage, closer regulation of working conditions, unemployment insurance, health and accident insurance, a revised old age pension, and agricultural support programs (including marketing boards). Bennett had left reform too late in his tenure: he was soundly defeated in 1935 by Mackenzie King. Most of Bennett's programs were later found to be unconstitutional; his legacy, however, is notable: he challenged uncontrolled capitalism and placed before Parliament, for the first time, the range of social and economic programs

needed to create what is now known as the welfare state—a process that would require nearly forty years to accomplish.

[*Richard Splane*]

RELATED ENTRIES
Great Depression (1930s), Social Planning, Social Policy, Social Welfare History, Unemployment Insurance, Welfare State

bereavement

Bereavement—grieving and mourning in response to a loss—is an acknowledged reality in all societies that have developed customs, beliefs, traditions, and practices to help individuals, families, and communities respond to their losses and to reintegrate into society in a new or renewed role. Only since the Second World War, however, has this social reality been incorporated into a recognized function of such helping professions as social work. This seems to have emerged within the developments of crisis theory and its many spin-offs of understanding high-stress situations and how best to respond to them therapeutically when needed. Not all bereavement requires professional help: some people recognize that various types of loss are a natural part of life and find in themselves or in their family and/or acquaintances satisfactory ways of readjusting. Persons who do not respond to loss in a healthy or growth-enhancing way may benefit from professional help. From this perceived professional need, a broad range of theories relate to the nature of loss and therapy for bereaved persons to readjust to their loss. This area of practice has become important for social workers as understanding of biopsychosocial reactions to loss expands. In particular, an awareness is growing that many life experiences may produce a sense of overwhelming loss from which a person may seek help to recover. Thus, loss of a pet, a slight change in one's health, moving to a new home, or separating from a friend—while not as serious as losses associated with war, assault, or major health conditions—may nevertheless be experienced as a form of bereavement. More than the actual loss, the meaning of the loss to the person and to their significant others affects the pattern and duration of their bereavement. Consequently, one event, such as loss of employment from a business closure, may be experienced by one employee as a challenge to be faced, and by another as so incapacitating that he/she seeks intervention. In response to this growing understanding of diverse kinds of loss, a broad range of techniques and services have emerged in social work, including crisis clinics, critical-incident stress debriefing, trauma response services, post-traumatic stress services, and grief counselling for the loss of a loved one. A dramatic change in practice relates to the timing of intervention, the need for which is often unpredictable in many high-stress situations; many services are now available outside standard operating times—twenty-four-hour crisis lines and clinics, for example—and the development within traditional agencies of critical response incident services offered at need. Most agencies and practitioners are also aware that different cultures have differing patterns of healthy responses to bereavement, a familiarity with which can assist social workers and other helping professionals to assist individuals, families, or communities that require or request intervention.

[*FJT*]

RELATED ENTRIES

Abuse, Disasters, Hospices, Immigrants & Immigration, Long-Term Care, Palliative Care, Sensitizing Concepts, Suicide, Torture & Trauma Victims

William Beveridge (1879–1963)

Beveridge, William Henry, social reformer, politician (UK); b. Mar. 05, 1879, Rangpur, India; knighted, 1919; made Baron Beveridge of Tuggal, 1946; d. Mar. 16, 1963

Baron Sir William Beveridge, a founder of the British welfare state, was born into a household that boasted twenty-six servants in the heyday of the British Empire. His life spanned two world wars, the depression between them, the 1950s when Britain was reported never to have had it so good, and the outset of the hippie era, when he felt himself a "slightly bewildered spectator of a pattern of social change that he himself had helped to create" (Harris 1977: 3). Beveridge's career ranged from social work (sub-warden in a famous settlement house at Toynbee Hall in London's impoverished east end), through journalism and academic appointments (a fellowship in law at Oxford University, and directorship of the London School of Economics) to politics as a civil ser-

vant, Liberal member of parliament, and Liberal peer. He thought deeply and wrote prolifically about social and economic issues in twentieth-century Britain. His complex philosophy included beliefs in self-help, individual initiative, and voluntary action attractive to those on the political right, while also advocating state provision of universal health and welfare appealing to those on the left. Beveridge's ideas were welcomed by the depression- and war-weary British public.

Beveridge is most renowned for his 1942 report, *Social Insurance and Allied Services*, in which he described his ambitious idea to eliminate want in Britain by an insurance-based universal system of social security that would provide cradle-to-grave coverage (Halsall 1999). The Beveridge Report, one of a number commissioned by the British government to guide post-war social reconstruction, offered a blueprint for universal health and welfare in Britain, Canada, and elsewhere. Beveridge and his committee identified want, disease, squalor, ignorance and idleness as the major peace-time obstacles to social well-being and suggested a strategy for establishing full employment policies, universal health-care, family allowances, and a system of social insurance and assistance. Government was to provide to those in need an income sufficient for subsistence but low enough to encourage voluntary action and individual responsibility. A social insurance system based on six principles was the mechanism for assuring income security. A flat-rate benefit (irrespective of other income that the insured person might have) was to be provided for those who were unemployed, disabled, or retired, and a flat-rate insurance contribution was to be made by each insured person or employer, irrespective of means. Unification of administrative responsibility was to be achieved by a single social insurance fund for all contributions and benefits, and by one-stop offices in each locality to handle all benefit claims. While it was anticipated that voluntary effort and personal resources would supplement income, it was also presumed that, for many people, this would not always occur; for such people, an adequate benefit for subsistence without a means test would be provided as long as their need existed. Beveridge's Report recommended that a comprehensive insurance system should cover most needs that could be predicted, and that a means-tested social assistance program should be a financial safety-net for the occasional non-insured risk. A system of classification would result in different contribution and benefit rules based on different reasons for income cessation. Beveridge's suggestions were well received throughout Britain, and legislation based on the report seemed inevitable. In 1944 a government White Paper recommended that many of the proposals should be adopted, and the 1946 National Insurance Act established a unified ministry of national insurance.

Some of Beveridge's recommendations—such as transition-period benefits to allow the insurance fund time to accumulate—were not adopted. Benefit levels set were lower than those proposed by Beveridge and were inadequate for subsistence; further, the purchasing power of benefits declined because annual increases in benefits did not keep pace with inflation. Thus, the reliance on the "national assistance" safety net was far greater than Beveridge had anticipated. The principle of comprehensiveness was eroded further when benefits were removed from the insurance scheme. Beveridge's ideas for social reconstruction also found favour in Canada; medicare and income security services that were established, however, were not as comprehensive as Beveridge had recommended. In Canada as in Britain, both unmet need and means-tested targeting are now frequent features of health and welfare provision. Beveridge's work went well beyond this report: eighteen books, numerous pamphlets, and forty-two unpublished collections of his work on unemployment, education, party politics, the economy, social security, family life, and gender (Harris 1977: 477–79). The London School of Economics has five hundred boxes of his academic work and personal papers. Never satisfied with his achievements, the final words Beveridge uttered on March 16, 1963, were: "I have a thousand things to do."

[*Rosemary A. Clews*]

RELATED ENTRIES

Canada Assistance Plan, Income Security, L. Marsh, Marsh Report, Social Planning, Social Policy, Social Welfare History, Unemployment Insurance, Welfare State

REFERENCES

Halsall, P. 1999. *Modern History Sourcebook: Sir William Beveridge: Social Insurance and Allied Services*. The Beveridge Report, 1942. Online at time of writing at <www.fordham.edu/halsall/mod/1942 beveridge.html>.

Harris, J. 1977. *William Beveridge: A Biography*. Oxford, London UK: Clarendon Press. London School of Economics. 1999.

Morgan, K.O. 1988. The Twentieth Century. In K.O. Morgan (Ed.) *The Mini Oxford History of Britain*. Vol. 5 *The Modern Age*. Oxford: Oxford University Press.

bioethical issues

Bioethics is a branch of philosophy that studies the rightness and wrongness (ethical behaviour) in a range of moral decisions emerging from a broad sense of health care. Health care professionals have always faced ethical issues; in recent decades, however, advances in technology related to human health—and specifically in biotechnology—have added complex dimensions. The consensus of health care professions, including social work, is that practitioners should aspire to do what is ethical and avoid what is unethical, in accordance with standards outlined in each profession's codes of ethics. In practice, however, differences of opinion as to the meaning and application of various ethical code standards may render the application of this principle unclear. Uncertainty in many situations can result in conflict for individual practitioners, colleagues in different professions, and clients and their significant others. The issue of abortion, for example, is an area where strongly divergent views can produce confusion and lack of support for a client in need. Other bioethical issues that arouse professional debate or a lack of clarity for appropriate intervention with clients include suicide, assisted suicide, euthanasia, needle exchanges, organ transplants, decisions relating to assessments for organ transplants, surrogate motherhood, new reproductive technologies, and alternate medicine. As well, bioethics may arise in issues relating to the allotment of health resources, research methods, and consent for participation in such processes as experimental drug treatments or medical treatments, and some types of research. Often, the ethical dilemma arises when the practitioner's personal convictions conflict with a client's request for a particular intervention or approach to care.

Clients and patients are demanding to be, and are involved, in many complex and critical decisions over their own or their loved one's life and death. Access to some information about health issues and technologies may prompt even more anxiety, uncertainty, and guilt than are conventionally evoked at such times. Social workers accustomed to handling such situations can bring calm reassurance and help clients and their families work through available knowledge, but must also expect to be understanding about the moral dilemma involved—even when the practitioner holds moral convictions that differ from those of the client and/or family members. Few social workers, nor indeed practitioners from any discipline, will view themselves or be viewed as experts in bioethics. Practitioners need sufficient self-awareness to determine their personal ability to work with clients in particular circumstances and, should they prefer not to continue, to be willing to refer such clients to another practitioner or agency. Responsible practitioners are prepared for issues that have such ethical parameters with information about appropriate resources that clients can contact to explore their options with someone who can understand and respect the moral convictions of the client. Many current bioethical issues create enough debate within a profession that their representative professional associations move to revise their codes of ethical conduct in response. Members along the continuum of morality on each issue have the opportunity to contribute to the development of such code of ethics revisions. In these ways, clients continue to be provided with a broad range of available services and resources, and members of the profession can find parameters for conduct that do not alienate their personal convictions.

[FJT]

RELATED ENTRIES

Abortion, Accountability, Codes of Ethics, Ethics, Knowledge Base, Legal Issues, Professional Liability, Professional Issues, Malpractice, Royal Commission on New Reproductive Technologies

biopsychosocial theory

Biopsychosocial theory, coterminous with psychosocial theory, is an important concept in contemporary thinking that represents a new stage in the development of psychosocial theory, that of

including an interest in, and concern about, the physical condition of a social work client and how it influences psychosocial functioning. It is in fact a return to an older purview of practice, which included the client's physical condition as a matter of course. Why general practice moved away from this important area of a client's life may relate to the profession's wish to establish a distinct identity separate from that of other professions, in this instance, medicine. As well, distinct fields of practice were emerging within the profession, such as medical social work, which might have been perceived as a specialty with a specific interest in a client's physical condition. Never an either/or situation, all practitioners were aware in general terms of the impact of a client's physical condition or functioning. Two factors refocused the profession's interest in the biological condition of clients. One is the movement in all human service professions toward a holistic view of clients, including all significant systems and subsystems of potential impact on an individual or family's function. The second is a parallel interest in systems theory, which emphasizes the need to take a broad sweep of a client's life and the interconnection of systems. To what extent the need to understand more of the biological realities of clients has affected contemporary Canadian curricula in social work is not clear. A return to the former model of curriculum that included a course on medical topics is unlikely; rather, relevant material is more likely to be incorporated into the teaching of human development. This new interest demonstrates that social work has much to teach other professions as social workers become more sensitive to the complex interactions of persons, and how these relationships influence and are influenced by their physical realities.

[FJT]

RELATED ENTRIES

Person-in-Environment Perspective, Psychosocial Theory, Theory & Practice

Ernest Blois (1878–1948)

Blois, Ernest H., social justice activist, social welfare pioneer; b. June 18, 1878, Gore, Hants Cty, NS; m. Jennie MacMillan; Companion of the Imperial Service Order, 1946; d. Mar. 29, 1948, Halifax, NS

Educated in Halifax County Academy and Dalhousie University, Ernest Blois taught for a time in a public school at Tangier, Nova Scotia, before joining the teaching staff of the Halifax Industrial School in 1901. Five years later, Blois became the superintendent of the school, which provided institutional care for delinquent boys: the beginning of a life of public service devoted to social justice. In this task, Blois received the support and encouragement of other Halifax citizens who were shaping social policies affecting children, such as Bessie Egan, Judge R.H. Murray, Judge W.B. Wallace, A.K. MacLean, and Mary Fletcher. Mrs. Egan, for example, worked with the Society for the Prevention of Cruelty to Animals, which also played a very significant role in helping abused and neglected children. Nova Scotia had laws to protect animals long before it passed specific legislation for the protection of children, and the society became the focal point of pressure for child-welfare legislation and for the creation of a separate organization to help families and children.

In 1905, Blois was a member of a committee set up by the provincial government to make recommendations on protective laws for minors. As a result of its work, a children's aid society was organized in Halifax and the Children's Protection Act became law in 1906. The groundwork was laid for the appointment in 1912 of a superintendent of neglected and dependent children and chief probation officer, a position held by E.H. Blois. As such, he became responsible for the development of children's aid societies, providing leadership in the development of services for the protection of neglected children; under his direction, children's aid societies were organized in most urban areas, while three new children's homes were opened. At Blois's urging, a Royal Commission was appointed—with Blois himself as a member—in 1919 to study the possibility of paying mothers a government allowance. Passage of mother's allowance legislation occurred in 1930, and Blois became the director of the Mother's Allowances Commission. Three years later, when Nova Scotia joined in the federal old age pensions program, Blois assumed the role of provincial director, in addition to his responsibilities for child welfare and mother's allowance.

Based on his experience at the Halifax Industrial School, Blois became greatly concerned about the dearth of facilities for training children with intellectual challenges. In 1927 a commission chaired by Mr. Justice W.L. Hall recommended the establishment of a training school for what were then called "feeble-minded" youths. Despite great financial stringency in the province, the Nova Scotia Training School opened at Brookside near Truro in 1929, with Blois as secretary of the first board of management. The training school remained one of his major interests until his retirement. Juvenile courts were also a special concern of his. The six juvenile courts in existence by 1929 placed emphasis on treatment aspects of juvenile offences. E.H. Blois saw to it that these courts were placed under the minister responsible for Social Welfare rather than under the attorney general's ministry, as was the case in other provinces. During the Second World War, many British children were evacuated to Canada, and Blois took an energetic part in the selection of foster homes and the placement of refugee children coming to Nova Scotia; he visited many foster homes and wrote personal letters to parents of many such children. In 1941 Blois became the first chairman of the board of the newly formed Maritime School of Social Work, which is now part of Dalhousie University. A few years later in 1944 Blois became the first deputy minister of Public Welfare and in 1946 he became president of the Canadian Conference on Social Work, presiding over its annual meeting. E.H. Blois retired in 1947. Co-workers spoke of him with affection and respect not untempered by awe. E.H. Blois—like J.J. Kelso and other pioneers of his generation—is one of the visionaries who were truly the founders of the social welfare movement in Canada.

[*Fred MacKinnon*]

RELATED ENTRIES

Children's Aid Societies, Child Welfare, Family & Youth Courts, Mother's Allowance, Services for Youth, Social Justice, Social Planning, Social Policy, Social Welfare History, Youth Criminal Justice Act

B'Nai Brith

In October 1843 twelve German-Jewish immigrants in New York City's Lower East Side formed a group named B'Nai Brith (trans. "Children of the Covenant"). The organization was to become a self-help group providing assistance to others in the community, and to engage in advocacy for the Jewish community. Its interest was in local, national, and international issues. In 1870 with violence against Jews sweeping Romania, B'Nai Brith took an advocacy role; a former B'Nai Brith president was appointed as honorary US consul to Romania, where he served for five years, setting the stage for decades of advocacy by B'Nai Brith for Jews around the world. The organization first became active in Canada in 1875 and, at present, it has chapters in fifty-eight countries. B'Nai Brith now has a long history of service, philanthropy, and advocacy with programs falling into five key areas: public policy, Jewish identity, community action, youth, and senior services.

In its early development, the organization took on a number of significant projects in the United States; it was among the first to promote secular Jewish learning. In 1851 its members built Covenant Hall, North America's first Jewish community centre, which housed the first Jewish public library. In 1868 when floods threatened Baltimore, the organization was among the first to launch a disaster relief campaign. During the Civil War in the United States, B'Nai Brith opposed attempts Ito expel Jews from several states under military rule; it succeeded in having the expulsion order revoked. After the Civil War, B'Nai Brith opened the Cleveland Jewish Orphan's Home. And in 1899 when a Denver tuberculosis hospital stood empty owing to lack of funds, B'Nai Brith purchased it and opened what would become the National Jewish Medical and Research Centre, which has become a global leader in lung, allergy, and immune system diseases.

On August 18, 1897, a small group of women gathered in San Francisco to promote sociability for B'Nai Brith members and their families; twelve years later, this auxiliary formally became B'Nai Brith Women. During the Second World War, B'Nai Brith Women sold war bonds, outfitted recreation rooms in hospitals, and raised money for Jewish refugees. In 1943 the organization founded its Children's Home in Israel to care for a group of young Holocaust survivors who had been severely traumatized and were in need of specialized care. Today the organization is independent and operates under the name Jewish Women International.

Over the years, B'Nai Brith has established a number of service organizations that it funds directly. One, the Anti-Defamation League, launched a counterpart in Canada in 1913 as The League for Human Rights devoted to fighting anti-Semitism, extremism, and bigotry. The League has taken up the issue of discrimination and racism as it relates to other groups, although its main focus is anti-Semitism. The mission of the organization is, in its own words, "to expose and combat the purveyors of hatred in our midst, responding to whatever new challenges may arise." B'Nai Brith Youth Organization (est. 1923) is an organization for teenagers. It is divided into three components: AZA (for the Hebrew letters Aleph, Zadik, Aleph for males in grades nine to twelve), B'Nai Brith Girls (for females in grades nine to twelve), and B'Nai Brith Teen Connection (for males and females in grades seven and eight). The B'Nai Brith Youth Organization is a youth-led, worldwide organization, which provides opportunities for Jewish youth to develop their leadership potential, a positive Jewish identity, and commitment to their personal development; youth can participate in democratically functioning small groups under the guidance of adult advisors and professional staff. B'Nai Brith Hillel is a foundation for Jewish campus life, also founded in 1923. With centres on more than five hundred university and college campuses, Hillel provides religious and social activities as well as support services for Jewish students; the organization, which does not require membership for participation, is committed to a pluralistic vision of Judaism that embraces all movements. Hillel is found on campuses in the United States and sixteen other countries. In addition to these organizations, B'Nai Brith maintains a full-time presence at the United Nations and at the European Union, and non-governmental status at the Organization of American States and MERCUSO (South America's economic development bloc). Information about B'Nai Brith in Canada can be found online at <www.bnai brith.ca>.

[*Ross Klein*]

RELATED ENTRIES

Church-Based Services, Foundations, Human Rights, Jewish Social Services, Non-governmental Organizations, Religion, Sectarian Social Services, Services for Youth

Board of Registration for Social Workers of British Columbia

The Board of Registration for Social Workers is the professional regulatory body for the practice of social work pursuant to the Social Workers Act in British Columbia. It carries out its mandate to set standards and protect the public by establishing requirements for registration and standards of practice, approving social workers for independent practice, and maintaining a complaints review process. Registration is not mandatory, except for those in independent practice. After many years of effort by the BC Association of Social Workers, the initial Social Workers Act was proclaimed in 1969. The Act created a five- to seven-member board appointed by Cabinet, providing for voluntary registration of social workers. In the first year under this Act, anyone working in a social work position could gain registration through transitional provisions, after which entry criteria was by either a social work degree or an upgrading program administered by the board. Hundreds of social workers without professional degrees took advantage of the upgrading program during the 1970s, the goal being to ensure that those working in social work positions were brought up to certain standards of knowledge and skill. In 1982 the upgrading program was phased out, as it was not considered an appropriate long-term method for setting standards, and social work degrees were becoming more accessible. Currently, entry criteria are either a bachelor's degree in social work, or its equivalent.

In 1984 the board adopted the code of ethics of the BC Association of Social Workers. In 1989 a significant amendment to the Social Workers Act was made to provide for control of title in the independent practice of social work. The board was expanded to twelve members, including two lay members, and administrative fairness was brought to the complaints review process through separation of the investigative and adjudicative functions of the board. Since 1989, the board, which focuses on an educative approach to ensuring appropriate standards of practice, has processed an average of ten complaints a year. The board has also received a number of complaints regarding non-registered social workers over whom it has no jurisdiction. Through its independent practice committee, the board developed standards of practice for independent practitioners, and approves about thirty-five new applications annually for independent practice. Currently the board has over 1,300 registrants, of whom 340

are approved for independent practice. During the 1980s and 1990s many submissions were made to government regarding the need for mandatory registration for all social workers through a self-regulating scheme. The board, in co-operation with the BC Association of Social Workers, continues to pursue this goal. Information about the board can be found online at <www.brsw.bc.ca/>.

[*Delma Hemming*]

RELATED ENTRIES
British Columbia Association of Social Workers, Canadian Association of Social Workers, International Federation of Social Workers, National Association of Social Workers (US), Provincial/Territorial Associations

boards

Organized social services in Canada, as in most countries, have always had boards of directors—citizens who oversee the operation of a particular agency or service. The function of a board is to set objectives for a service and to ensure that they are carried out. The general purpose of boards is to provide a form of public accountability for the agency functions and for the use of available resources. Board directors keep themselves separate from the day-to-day operation of the service and are apprised of operations through the agency director who is directly responsible to the board. In complex settings this accountability is ensured through committees and sub-delegation of the directors' responsibility. Board directors of agencies, who are generally not paid, serve in a voluntary role, except for some legislatively based services where board members may receive an honorarium or per diem for service. The duties and functions of boards in general are controlled by legislation applying to the specific nature and function of the service through the development of policies and procedures. Recently, board composition has shifted from the convention of inviting prominent community persons to be directors, to appointing persons with expertise or experience that reflects the nature of the service and the populations served by it, including clients and other potential consumers of the service. This latter trend has resulted in a dramatic diversification of boards, as opposed to earlier efforts to court board directors who could draw on their political, social, and business networks to attract sponsorships and funding. Membership on contemporary boards is now viewed not as just an honorary position but one requiring a considerable degree of commitment and expenditure of time and effort. Most boards now have well-designed orientations for new board members, written terms of reference, time-bound periods of service, and high expectations of regular attendance at meetings and of carrying responsibility for some aspects of the board's work. As the role of boards becomes much more accountable, much effort has gone into clarifying and explicating board responsibilities and duties, and their relationship to the functioning of the agency. In the past these areas were often unclear and unevenly implemented. An essential function of boards of social services is to oversee the financial operation of the service, as well as the nature of services being offered. As in the past, one role that continues to fall to boards of social services is fund-raising; given recent curtailing of funding for social welfare, this role may pose challenges for boards that no longer have as directors many high-profile people with access to political and voluntary dollars. Many boards now also take a firm role in public relations, public education, and enhancing the image of the service.

[*FJT*]

RELATED ENTRIES

Accountability, Administrative Theory & Practice, Canadian Association of Social Workers, Foundations, Organizational Theory, Voluntarism

Marguerite Bourgeoys (1620–1700)*

Bourgeoys, Marguerite, founder of the Congrégation de Notre-Dame de Montréal; b. Apr. 17, 1620 Troyes, FR; canonized Oct. 31, 1982; d. Jan. 12, 1700, Montréal, QC.

In 1640 Marguerite Bourgeoys joined a noncloistered congregation of teachers attached to a Troyes convent directed by the sister of Governor Maisonneuve of Ville-Marie (Montreal). She sailed for Canada in 1653 and in 1658 opened a girls' school in a stable on Montreal Island. Besides chaperoning girls sent from France as brides for settlers (*Filles du Roi*), she recruited French and Canadian girls as teachers, organized a boarding school for girls in Montreal, a school for native girls on the Sulpician reserve of La Montagne, and a

domestic arts school. Her "sisters" began teaching in rural parishes. She justified their refusal to become cloistered by observing that the Virgin Mary had remained "secular." Bishop Laval refused to permit them to take vows, but his successor Bishop Saint-Vallier invited them to open a school on the Île d'Orléans. Soon they had a domestic arts school and a primary school in the town of Quebec. On July 1, 1698 the secular sisters took simple vows and became a recognized noncloistered religious community. In the same year, Marguerite Bourgeoys began writing her memoirs, in which she deplored some departures from the initial austerity observed in her congregation. She spent her last two years in meditation and prayer, already revered as a saint by the colonists when she died. The Sisters of the Congregation of Notre Dame now number several thousand and have expanded their work to the United States and Japan.

[*Cornelius J. Jaenen*]

* Used unedited by permission from *The Canadian Encyclopedia*. 2000. Toronto: McClelland and Stewart.

RELATED ENTRIES

Congrégation de Notre-Dame, Church-Based Services, Religion, Sectarian Social Services, Social Welfare History

Ignace Bourget (1799–1885)

Bourget, Ignace, bishop; b. Oct. 30, 1799 at Pont Lévis; d. June 8, 1885 at Sault-au-Recollet

Ignace Bourget, the second Catholic Bishop of Montréal in the mid-nineteenth century, was educated at Point Lévis School, followed by the Seminary of Quebec and Nicollet College. His rapid progression within the Catholic Church saw his appointment on March 10, 1837 as coadjutor to Bishop Lartigue of Montréal and, on July 25 of the same year, as Bishop of Telemessa in Lycia; Bourget became Bishop of Montréal on April 23, 1840. From 1866–67 he began restructuring the parish of Montréal by emphasizing that its division into smaller parishes would benefit the people. This decision resulted in more than forty new parishes in the diocese of Montréal. Among his many charitable works, he founded L'institut de la Providence, the mission of which was the care of aged and infirm women, a movement that spread throughout Canada and the United States. He also

founded Les Soeurs de Misericorde, an order of
nuns engaged in a range of charitable and social
service programs. Bourget opened institutions in
Montréal for the care of children, people with
physical challenges, and the mentally ill. In his
work he was particularly committed to the provision of services to immigrants. In 1876 he tendered
his resignation as Bishop of Montréal, consequently being named titular Archbishop of Martia-
nopolis, where he withdrew to Sault-au-Recollet,
living at the St. Janvier residence until his death.

[*FJT*]

RELATED ENTRIES

Church-Based Services, Religion, Sectarian Social
Services, Social Welfare History

Frank Swithun Barrington Bowers
(1908–1992)

*Bowers, Frank Swithun Barrington, Oblate, educa-
tor, founder, St. Patrick's School of Social Welfare;
b. June 27, 1908. Place, UK; m. Margaret Moores,
1968; d. July 13, 1992, Calgary, AB*

Frank Bowers completed elementary and secondary school in England, before emigrating to
Canada as a youth of twenty. He entered an Oblate
order in the mid-1930s, taking the name Swithun;
following his ordination in 1942, he was an assistant at St. Joseph's Church, Ottawa, until 1946. He
completed an undergraduate degree in the mid-
1940s after the Oblates had chosen him to develop
a new school of social work at St. Patrick's College,
University of Ottawa. He was a lecturer in religion
(1945–47) and a professor of sociology (1946–47) at
St. Patrick's College. In December 1948 Father
Swithun Bowers received a Master of Social Work
from entered the New York School of Social Work
at Columbia University and in January 1949 he left
New York to begin the preparatory work that culminated in his greatest achievement: the establishment of what quickly became known in
Canada as the school for social casework. The
doors of St. Patrick's School of Social Welfare
opened in June 1949 to its first class of seventeen
students. Bowers' associate director was Frank
Hennessy, newly graduated with a Master of Social
Work from Fordham University in New York City.
Together, they shared the teaching load, while
Swithun Bowers was simultaneously completing
advanced courses in psychology at the Institute

of Psychology, University of Ottawa (1949–50). As
a speaker with dramatic flair, he was sought by
schools of social work and social work associations for presentations on current professional
issues and future directions. Students found his
lectures thought-provoking, inspiring, and uniquely "Swithunesque"—serious commentary laced
with dry humour, delivered in eloquent language
with moments of tension as audiences waited for
lengthy cigarette ash to drop. His vibrant voice
and sense of timing were impeccable. Father Bowers demonstrated political and financial savvy
early in his career when he persuaded Prime Minister Louis St. Laurent to include St. Patrick's in a
federal grant originally designated only for the
existing seven Canadian schools of social work in
1951 the school's program was granted accreditation by the American Association of Schools of
Social Work. In 1967 the school became affiliated
with Carleton University, where it was located in
1972.

During the 1950s and 1960s Father Bowers became a major influence in social work education in
Canada. He and Dr. Chick Hendry, director of the
University of Toronto School of Social Work, were
central in decisions and actions of the National
Committee of Canadian Schools of Social Work,
the forerunner of the Canadian Association of
Schools of Social Work. Through his capacity to
articulate the nature of social work, he became
known internationally, often engaging in work of
the Council of Social Work Education. By 1964 he
had published over thirty articles, his best-known
work being a tripartite definitive article in 1949 on
"The Nature and Definition of Social Casework"
that for years was the touchstone for scholars and
practitioners. Bowers received an honorary
doctorate from the University of Buffalo in 1961.
Bowers also effected some surprising personal
changes to his life. For several years he had been
quietly withdrawing from his priestly role; in 1968
he married Margaret Moores, a welfare worker
from Newfoundland who had graduated in 1965
from St. Patrick's School and then practised in
Ottawa. Bowers remained director of the school
until he retired in 1971 to Algarve, Portugal. In 1983
he returned to Ottawa for an alumni event, delight-
ing the audience with reminiscences on the development of St. Patrick's and giving thanks to the
faculty and students who had contributed to an

era in Canadian social work. In July 1992 Bowers suffered a stroke after visiting the King family in Three Hills, Alberta, where he had worked as a ranch hand from 1932 to 1934. His voice was silenced, but two days prior to his stroke he had typed his first words on a computer:

> I am about to embark on an adventure into modern technology I find myself very nervous, almost as though I am on the threshold of a strange new world. Perhaps the Portuguese Discoverers must have had this feeling of expectant awe as they set foot on some wild shore hitherto unknown to Western man. But my own feeling of awe gives way to the uncomfortable realization that I am not really equipped for the twenty-first Century.

[James Gripton and *Mary Valentich]*

RELATED ENTRIES

Canadian Association of Schools of Social Work, Carleton University School of Social Work, Church-Based Services, Education in Social Work, C.E. Hendry

brief treatment

While there is no formal definition as to what time frame is envisioned by "brief," this type of treatment is generally held to be an intervention with a client that encompasses fewer than six contacts. In the past treatment of this brevity was viewed as second best, a form of band-aid intervention, which could not be sufficiently intense to deal with a client's deep-seated sources of difficulty. So, even though many contacts with social workers were short term, such intervention was not given a great deal of attention. Interest in this modality grew, however, as the theoretical base of the profession has expanded and research has demonstrated that many clients do find that much of what they were seeking from contact with a social worker did take place in a very short time. Clients can, in fact, be very satisfied with a contact comprising three or four interviews. From these observations and practice experience, such approaches as planned short-term treatment, task-centred therapy, problem-solving theory, and much of the theoretical base of crisis intervention emerged.

An important concept underlying this perception of intervention in a time-bound manner is the growing understanding of the importance to clients of task- and problem-solving to life's challenges rather than personality analysis and change. This understanding legitimized briefer intervention, but initially failed to understand that the issue related to what the client needed and wanted; thus, the length of time of intervention became a variable in treatment rather than a value. Two further factors that have reinforced support for brief intervention stems from the stringent financial cutbacks in the public funding of social work services, and the increase in the amount of social work treatment financed by industry and insurance programs. These factors strongly favour short-term intervention and question the validity of longer-term treatment. From these administrative and economic realities, brief solution-based treatment emerged. In spite of these systemic realities, current thinking in the profession stresses the importance of viewing time as a variable in treatment rather than part of a short-term/long-term dichotomy: ideally, treatment should be as long as a client needs, ranging from highly therapeutic single contacts and cases that remain open for years.

[FJT]

RELATED ENTRIES

Assessment, Diagnosis, Direct Practice, Family Therapy, Individual Therapy, Interprofessional Issues, Personal Social Services, Problem-Solving Theory, Task-Centred Theory, Theory & Practice, Therapy, Treatment, Wellness

British Columbia Association of Social Workers

The British Columbia Association of Social Workers was incorporated as a non-profit professional society under BC law in 1956. The founding members were individual members of the BC chapter of the Canadian Association of Social Workers. Now, the association is one of the member organizations of the national association, which is itself now a federation of provincial and territorial professional associations. In addition to providing services to members, BC association's objectives include uniting and strengthening the social work profession. Pursuit of this objective led to the BC Social Workers Act of 1969, which created the Board of Registration for Social Workers in BC as a regulatory body separate from the association to control the title "registered social worker." Between 1969 and 1996, the BC professional association and board have collaborated on several initiatives to persuade government to amend the Social Workers Act to increase the board's control over the private practice of social work; however, the goals of establishing control of the title "social worker," having a scope-of-practice statement in law, and transforming the board into a professional college have proven elusive.

The BC association provides a number of services to members, including publication of the magazine *Perspectives* and an annual newsletter. An annual conference is usually held in conjunction with the annual general meeting and the election of the board of directors. The association's internal structure includes a number of geographically determined branches, each of which appoints a board member, and standing and ad hoc committees dealing with a range of professional interests, areas of practice, or matters of public policy, internal policy, and service design. Most of the association's members are registered social workers and hold degrees in social work or similar professional qualifications obtained in other countries. They agree to abide by the code of ethics, which includes the commitment to work with respect for and in the interests of clients, as individuals, families, groups, and communities. Thus, social workers' professional concerns extend from the details of particular client's situations to broad issues of social development, public policy, and social justice, as set out in an objective in the association's constitution. The association has a long record of advocacy with and for individuals and social groups, addressing the federal and provincial governments, Royal Commissions, task forces, and committees on a wide range of public policy issues and their implications for people, the provision of health and social services, and social workers. Briefs and submissions have addressed such topics as child protection and child welfare, poverty and the economy, health care, the care of senior citizens, reproductive technologies, death and dying, anti-racism, multiculturalism, legal aid. A commitment to maintain a critique of public policy and programs, and the activities associated with promoting the social work profession sometimes appear to be contradictory: the former implies a willingness to speak out against provincial government policies and actions, whereas the pursuit of improved professional regulation requires the development of a collaborative relationship with government. The association has been accused at times of neglecting the interests of clients and being too cosy with government; at other times, the association is described as overly concerned with policy and advocacy at the expense of advancing the profession's interests. The association attempts to negotiate issues toward realizing both objectives. Current information about the British Columbia Association of Social Workers can be found online at <www.bcasw.org>.

[*Stuart Alcock*]

RELATED ENTRIES

Canadian Association of Social Workers, International Federation of Social Workers, National Association of Social Workers (US), Provincial/Territorial Associations

bullying

Bullying among Canadian schoolchildren—peer bullying—is common. A 1998 report for Human Resources Development Canada concluded that the percentages of bullying and victimization in school-aged children in Canada are comparable to those reported in other countries: 14 percent are bullies and 5 percent are victims (Craig, Peters, & Konarski 1998). Peer bullying is a form of childhood aggression, seen to be an element of school life for many years (Charach, Pepler, & Ziegler 1995), occurring when a person is "exposed repeatedly and over time, to negative actions on the part of one or more persons" (Olweus 1978), and characterized as involving an imbalance of power (Smith & Brain 2000). Bullies appear to cause intentional distress to their victims; and victims, as less powerful than the bully, are unable to protect themselves: "Bullying can be direct physical or verbal aggression, or indirect, such as threats and intimidation, exclusion or gossip" (Charach, Pepler, & Ziegler 1995). Boys are more typically seen to engage in direct bullying methods, while girls are more likely to use indirect strategies (Smith & Sharp 1994). Research has demonstrated that children who are involved in bullying and victimization are at risk for developing problems later in life, including anxiety, depression, school drop out, criminal activity, and unemployment. Peer bullying has raised the attention of educators in particular, as most bullying occurs on school grounds rather than on the way home from school (Charach, Pepler, & Ziegler 1995). Peer bullying and the hidden violence in schools has serious implications for the well-being of children, academically, socially, and emotionally.

It is apparent that bullying requires a comprehensive scope, beyond but including social workers in schools and supporting fields. School social workers are likely, therefore, to intervene and deal with peer bullying in the school setting. Social workers in, for example, children's mental health, young offender programs, and private practice also provide education and support to the families of children and adolescents who are being bullied or are bullying others. School social workers offer a broad range of services, including advocacy, classroom interventions, group work, individual counselling, outreach to parents, parenting strategies, prevention of problems, and staff development. Social skills training, cognitive behavioural programs, and parent training programs are some of the interventions that have been tried to address aggressive behaviour in children at the individual and family level, with partial success (Charach, Pepler, & Ziegler 1995). Social workers have also played a role in working with the families of bullies and victims, as parental attitudes and/or parenting practices may be serving to perpetuate the problem of bullying and victimizing behaviours in their children (Craig, Peters, & Konarski 1998). These particular services allow social workers to direct their interventions to the development of anti-bullying initiatives and strategies with individual bullies and victims, school staff, the entire student population, and parents. Social workers have long been aware of the need to address peer bullying within Canadian society, as well as within the family, school, and community. They have encouraged sensitivity to the potential of peer bullying by highlighting the need to examine societal discrimination on the basis of race, ethnicity, class, and sexual orientation. Children who experience such discrimination, who are seen as different, are more likely to be victimized. The fact that many victims are fearful of reporting bullying incidents requires collaborative intervention and prevention programs which reach beyond treating the

individual student. Given the cutbacks in social spending over the past decade in Canada, social workers are more limited in their resources and ability to satisfactorily address the needs of children.

[*Ramona Alaggia*]

RELATED ENTRIES

Child Welfare, Conflict Resolution, Cults, Gangs, Mediation, Parenting, School Social Workers, Services for Children, Services for Youth, Treatment, Wellness, Youth Criminal Justice Act

REFERENCES

Charach, A., D. Pepler, and S. Ziegler. 1995. Bullying at School—A Canadian Perspective: A Survey of Problems and Suggestions for Interventions. *Education Canada* 35, 1, 12–18.

Craig, W., R. Peters, and R. Konarski. 1998. *Bullying and Victimization among Canadian School Children.* Internet ed. Ottawa: Human Resources Development Canada, Applied Research Branch. Online at time of writing at <http://www11.hrsdc.gc.ca/en/cs/sp/hrsdc/arb/publications/research/1998-000130/page04.shtml>.

Olweus, D. 1978. *Aggression in the Schools: Bullies and Whipping Boys.* Washington, DC: Hemisphere.

Smith, P.K., and P. Brain. 2000. Bullying in Schools: Lessons from Two Decades of Research. *Aggressive Behavior* 26, 1–9.

Smith, P.K., and S. Sharp. 1994. *School Bullying: Insights and Perspectives.* London: Routledge.

C

Caledon Institute of Social Policy

The Caledon Institute of Social Policy (est. 1992) is Canada's leading social policy think-tank. The institute does rigorous, high-quality research and analysis. It seeks to inform and influence public opinion and to foster public discussion on poverty and social policy; the institute also develops and promotes concrete practicable proposals for the reform of social programs at all levels of government, and of social benefits provided by employers and the voluntary sector. A private non-profit organization with charitable status located in Ottawa, the Caledon Institute is primarily supported by the Toronto-based Maytree Foundation. As it is not dependent on government funding and is not affiliated with any political party, the institute can be an independent and critical voice. While the institute occasionally undertakes contracts for governments and projects funded by other foundations that fit the institute's research agenda, such work does not define it. The Caledon Institute's work on poverty and other social and economic inequalities covers a broad range of social policy areas including income security (e.g., pensions, welfare, child benefits, unemployment insurance, benefits for Canadians with physical challenges), taxation, social spending, employment development services, social services, and health. While the Caledon Institute focuses on Canadian issues, it draws on international experience and innovations in social policy, and informs social policy experts and policy makers in other countries on developments in Canadian social policy.

Underlying work by the Caledon Institute is a quest for sustainable social policy, for strong cost-effective solutions to challenges posed by Canada's ageing population, insecure labour market, and rapid pace of social change. The institute believes passionately in the enduring need for strong social policy to fight poverty, ensure social and economic security, and achieve social justice; equally, it believes that fundamental changes in the economy and society demand fundamental reforms to social programs. The Caledon Institute emphasizes the vital links between social and economic policy, and its proposals are based on what can be achieved. The institute has had an extraordinary influence on public policy, as well as on the process and substance of social program reform; Caledon has had an unprecedented role in recent major social policy initiatives: the national child benefit, re-indexation of the taxation system, the proposed seniors benefit, reform of incomes and supports for Canadians with physical challenges, and a federal social security review. In this role the Caledon Institute takes leadership to get these issues on the political agenda through its expertise in policy analysis and development and its reputation for rigorous, tough-minded, and clearly written work that is not blinkered by ideology. The organization, which appears prominently and regularly in the media, is building a solid, rich, and authoritative body of knowledge on poverty, social issues, and social policy. Its staff of five complements its own publications by producing many

other commentators, including some of the country's leading thinkers. Its work is widely read and used by politicians, government officials, social and economic researchers and policy organizations, social advocacy groups, academics, editorial writers, journalists, and others interested in poverty and social policy. Current information on the Caledon Institute of Social Policy can be found online at <www.caledoninst.org>.

[*Ken Battle*]

RELATED ENTRIES

Non-governmental Organizations, Research, Social Policy

Canada Assistance Plan (1966–98)

The Canada Assistance Plan (CAP) was a federal/provincial program through which the federal government bore half the cost of social assistance and welfare services provided by the provinces, and their approved social agencies. Seen during its thirty-two years as Canada's basic social safety net, the program extended to some two million persons annually; by the late 1980s yearly budgetary costs to the federal government exceeded five billion dollars. Under CAP, provincial governments were responsible for the administration of the social assistance programs, including their design, comprehensiveness, eligibility requirements, and method of delivery. Sharing extended not only to social assistance and child maintenance but also to welfare services provided to those in need and likely to be in need. Welfare services were broadly defined to include rehabilitation services, casework, counselling and assessment services, and homemaker, daycare, and similar services. The provinces were required to provide assistance to all applicants through a needs test, including those coming from other provinces. They were also required to establish procedures for applicants/recipients to appeal administrative decisions, and were prevented from requiring recipients to work as a condition for the receipt of aid.

The Canada Assistance Plan emerged during the 1960s as part of a nation-wide comprehensive social security scheme conceived during the Second World War and developed incrementally through the 1940s, 1950s, and 1960s. More specifically, CAP was the product of federal/provincial discussions on replacing existing shared-cost measures—unemployment assistance, old age assistance, blind person and disabled person allowances—with a comprehensive measure that would also include welfare services, and be free of unnecessary restrictions. CAP was designed to "encourage the further development and extension of assistance and welfare services programs throughout Canada" and, accordingly, resulted in dramatic improvements in those programs in the years following its enactment in 1966. CAP was widely regarded as the foremost example of co-operative federalism, and as an integral and defining component of the Canadian welfare state. From the outset, it was highly regarded in public opinion polls as well as by the social welfare community, and was frequently proclaimed as the most telling evidence of Canada's provision for its neediest citizens. In the 1980s and 1990s, however, CAP became a target of anti-welfare ideologies. It was weakened by the Mulroney (Conservative) government in 1986 and eliminated by the Chrétien (Liberal) government in 1998. With the removal of the Canada Assistance Plan's standards and financial support, social assistance levels fell in most provinces and work requirements were imposed. Canada no longer had a nationwide social safety net.

[*Richard Splane*]

RELATED ENTRIES

Social Assistance, Social Policy, Welfare State

Canada Health Act

The Canada Health Act, 1985, is Canada's current federal health insurance legislation. The Act establishes criteria and conditions related to insured health care services—the national standards—that the provinces and territories must meet in order to receive full federal government transfer payments under the Canada Health and Social Transfer (Charles & Badgley 1987; Health Canada 2001). The provinces and territories are responsible for the administration and delivery of health care services. The social policy goal of the national health insurance program is to ensure that all residents of Canada have reasonable access to medically necessary insured services without direct charges. The Canada Health Act superseded the federal Hospital Insurance Diagnostic Services Act, 1957, and the Medical Care Act, 1968, which had resulted in the national health insurance program that cov-

ered medically necessary hospital and physician services for all residents. In 1984 Parliament passed the Canada Health Act, which retained and entrenched the criteria or basic principles underlying the national health insurance program from the earlier legislation:

- *Public administration*: The health care insurance plan must be administered on a non-profit basis by a public authority responsible to the provincial government and subject to financial audits. The public authority may appoint an agency to receive or carry out payments under the health care plan.
- *Comprehensiveness*: All insured health services provided by hospitals, medical practitioners, dentists and, where provincial law permits, analogous services of health care practitioners must be insured by the health care plan of each province.
- *Universality*: Every insured provincial resident is entitled to receive uniform terms and conditions of the health services covered under the plan.
- *Portability*: The province may not impose a minimum waiting period or minimum period of residence in excess of three months to be eligible for insured health services. Further, if an insured resident is temporarily out of the province but still in Canada, payment must be made for health services received at the rate approved by the health care insurance plan unless special arrangements are made between the provinces. For services received outside of Canada, payment must be made in the amount to which the resident would have been entitled in the home province for similar health and hospital services. If a resident relocates to another province and must fulfil a minimum period of residence or waiting period, health services must be covered as if the resident had not ceased to reside in the province.
- *Accessibility*: Under the Canada Health Act, provinces must provide reasonable access to health services that are neither impeded nor precluded by charges or other means made to insured persons. In addition a provincial health care insurance plan must provide reasonable compensation for insured health services by medical practitioners, dentists, and hospitals (Charles & Badgley 1987; Health Canada 2001).

Health care services covered by the Canada Health Act include insured health care services (i.e., medically necessary hospital services, physician services, and surgical-dental services) and extended health care services are certain aspects of long-term residential care (i.e., nursing home intermediate care, the health aspects of home care, and ambulatory care services). The Canada Health Act also contains the conditions required for provinces and territories to receive full transfer payments. First, each provincial/territorial government is expected to provide information to the Minister of Health in relation to health care and extended health care services. Second, these governments are obligated to recognize appropriately the federal government's contributions toward the services covered under the Act (Health Canada 2001). The major difference between the earlier acts and the Canada Health Act was the addition of provisions aimed at eliminating direct charges to patients in the form of extra billing and user charges within insured health care services. Extra billing and user charges are discouraged under the Act by being subject to mandatory dollar-for-dollar deductions from the federal transfer payments to the provinces and territories.

[*David Este*]

RELATED ENTRIES

Social Planning, Social Policy, Social Welfare Context, Therapy, Treatment, Wellness

REFERENCES

Canada. 2001. *Canada Health Act Annual Report 1999.* Ottawa: Health Canada.

Charles, C., and R.F. Badgley 1987. Health and Inequality: Unresolved Policy Issues. In Shankar Yelaja (Ed.) *Canadian Social Policy.* 47–64. Waterloo, ON: Wilfrid Laurier University Press.

Canada Health and Social Transfer

The Canada Health and Social Transfer was first proposed in a February 1995 budget speech as a new block funding arrangement to help the provinces carry out their constitutional responsibilities for delivering health, education, and social assistance. This new transfer payment from the federal government was to bring together and redefine two prior agreements that had been created in 1977. Before 1996 transfers for welfare and social assistance services had been made under the Canada Assistance Plan, and transfers for health and post-secondary education had been made under federal/provincial fiscal arrangements and the federal Post-Secondary Education and Health Contributions Act, more commonly referred to as the established program financing. Following the announcement of the Canada Health and Social Transfer in the 1995 budget speech, two separate parliamentary actions were required for the new arrangement to be implemented: the Budget Implementation Act, 1995, created the new transfer, specifying the amount of the transfer, the provincial/territorial allocations, and the terms and conditions under which the transfer would be paid in the 1996 fiscal year; the Budget Implementation Act, 1996, established the terms and conditions for the period 1997 through 2003. In the first year, total transfers paid under the Canada Health and Social Transfer were set at $26.9 billion and, for each fiscal year from 1997 through 2000, they were reduced to $25.1 billion. From 1997 onward, the transfer calculation had been based on the average Gross Domestic Product (GDP) less a predetermined coefficient; for example, if the GDP growth in the three years prior to 2000 were to average 3 percent and if the coefficient for that year were 2 percent, the amount of health and social transfer paid would be equal to the preceding year's amount plus 1 percent. Starting in 1998 the population of the province or territory was also figured into the calculation for the Canada Health and Social Transfer (Madore and Blanchette 1996: 6).

In effect, the Canada Health and Social Transfer expanded the previous federal block-funding arrangements—under established program financing for medicare and post-secondary education—to include welfare and social assistance services. The funding structure of the newer transfer payment was similar to that under prior arrangements: transfers were in the form of cash and "tax points." When the initial program financing arrangement was created in 1977, the federal government had reduced its personal and corporate income tax rates and the provinces and territories had raised their rates proportionately—that is, a shift in taxing powers transferred tax points from the federal to the provincial and territorial governments. On an annual basis, Ottawa had calculated the established program financing transfer by subtracting the tax revenues from program financing entitlements and paying the remainder in cash. The Canada Health and Social Transfer operated in a similar fashion but, under it, the provinces and territories received cash from Ottawa in the form of consolidated revenues that were not specifically earmarked for medicare, post-secondary education, welfare, or social assistance services (NCW 1995: 10).

The Canada Health and Social Transfer was designed so that the provinces and territories could have greater flexibility in the financing of social programs. As part of this flexibility, some of the national standards that had existed under the Canada Assistance Plan were relaxed under the newer transfer. When the Canada Assistance Plan was introduced in 1966, it had an open-ended federal/provincial cost-sharing arrangement with the federal government contributing half of the costs, under which a single social assistance program was created for all individuals and families in need. The federal standards for the Canada Assistance Plan required the provinces to provide adequate levels of assistance, to develop welfare services, to abolish provincial residency requirements and waiting periods, and to establish an appeals procedure. Of these national standards, only prohibition of a minimum residency period continued to apply under the Canada Health and Social Transfer (Scott 1998: 8). With respect to health care, national standards remained unchanged under the more recent transfer. For the delivery of all insured health services, provinces and territories still had to adhere to the terms and conditions of the Canada Health Act: universality, accessibility, comprehensiveness, portability, and public administration, as well as prohibiting user fees and extra billing; non-compliance with the national standards under the transfer could result in the cash contributions being reduced or withheld (Madore and Blanchette 1996: 8). The Canada Health and Social Transfer enabled the federal government to set limits on spending at a time when political pressure demanded paying down of the national debt and deficit. It also provided the provinces and territories more latitude in planning and delivering services while maintaining some national standards.

[*Thomas E. Brenner*]

RELATED ENTRIES

Canada Assistance Plan, Canada Health Act, Health Canada, Social Planning, Social Policy, Social Security

REFERENCES

Madore, O., and C. Blanchette. 1996. *The Canadian Health and Social Transfer: Operation and Possible Repercussions on the Health Care Sector*. Ottawa: Research Branch, Library of Parliament

NCW. 1995. *The 1995 Budget and Block Funding*. Ottawa: National Council of Welfare.

Scott, K. 1998. *Women and the CHST: A Profile of Women Receiving Social Assistance in 1994*. Ottawa: Status of Women Canada.

Canadian Association of Schools of Social Work / Association canadienne des écoles de services social

The Canadian Association of Schools of Social Work/Association canadienne des écoles de services social replaced its predecessor, the Canadian Association for Education in the Social Services (est. 1962). The context for the birth of the initial organization was the development of a number of social work programs in English-language universities (in 1914) and later in French-language universities (in 1942). The wish was to promote a national professional and academic identity for social work as well as for education for the profession. Up to the early 1960s, with a small number of schools, some Canadian social work programs had relied on the US Council on Social Work Education for accreditation. Social work leaders decided that there was a sufficient critical mass to promote Canadian educational policies and standards for the profession, in part because Canadian programs reflected a mix of influences and traditions: American, British, English-Canadian, and French-Canadian. The federal government, in part led by civil servants who were social workers, also supported the professionalization of social work and the establishment of national standards for professional education. With Canada taking the lead in North America in 1966 to embrace the bachelor of social work as a credible first professional degree (CAESS 1969), and to develop and apply nationally and locally relevant accreditation standards for master's and bachelor's degree programs, the Canadian Association for Education in the Social Services evolved in 1967 into the Canadian Association of Schools of Social Work (CAESS 1969). The association took over the accreditation function in 1970 and the first Canadian educational policy and accreditation standards were applied in 1972.

As an active participant on the international stage with the International Association of Schools of Social Work, the International Federation of Social Workers, and the International Council on Social Welfare, as well as within Canada, the national association has pursued the goals of promoting the profession of social work through educational policies and educational program standards that enable quality control, equalization, public protection, and the application of regionally and culturally relevant norms. The notion of equalization was interpreted in terms of promoting comparable standards for knowledge, skill, and competence throughout Canada. The concern over public protection was addressed through liaison with the Canadian Association of Social Workers (est. 1926) and through the promotion of practice skills and competency-based education, as evident in 1978 and 2002 standards for accreditation and related educational policies. As the organization has developed, its main themes have expanded to include more commitment to knowledge about minorities, psychosocial diversity, marginalized persons, and those most oppressed in society and the global village. The notion of relevance has been expanded to include more cultural sensitivity as well as more transparent and effective attention to such issues HIV/AIDS. As well, the association's concern with regional relevance has expanded to promote attention to social work, social work education, and social issues on a global scale. Attention to the goal of public protection includes ensuring relevance and effectiveness of social work education in terms of current community and societal needs and problems.

The association's commitments to promoting discussion, debate, and research related to social work, social work education, and social problems have been implemented in a number of ways. The association publishes a journal, originally *The Canadian Journal of Social Work Education* and subsequently renamed *The Canadian Social Work Review*. With a history of sponsoring and co-sponsoring studies and projects, the associa-

tion's reach has focused on education for the profession regionally, nationally, and internationally. Throughout Canada, the organization has promoted the active participation of its individual and institutional members in academic and professional discussion and debate at The Learned Societies (renamed the Humanities and Social Sciences Federation of Canada/Federation canadienne des sciences humaines et sociales). As well, sometimes in partnership with other national and international organizations, the association has co-sponsored international gatherings of social workers and academics. At the time of writing, membership in the national organization includes schools and faculties representing more than thirty baccalaureate degree and more than twenty-six master's degree programs. While the association does not accredit doctoral programs in social work, it does promote such studies. The association administrators and executive actively represent the interests of social work students and faculty regionally, nationally, and internationally. Current information about the Canadian Association of Schools of Social Work can be found online at < www.cassw-acess.ca >.

[*M. Dennis Kimberley*]

RELATED ENTRIES

F.S.B. Bowers, Doctorate in Social Work, Education in Social Work, Faculties of Social Work, Gender Issues, Human Rights, International Practice, Racism-Sensitive Social Work

REFERENCE

CAESS. 1969. *The First University Degree in Social Work.* Ottawa: Canadian Association for Education in the Social Services.

Canadian Association of Social Workers

Founded to monitor employment conditions and to establish standards of practice within the profession, the Canadian Association of Social Workers (est. 1926) is a federation of ten provincial and one territorial social work organizations, which has evolved into a national voice on behalf of some 17,000 social workers. By joining the appropriate provincial/territorial associations, social workers automatically become affiliated with the national association. Its mission is to provide a national leadership role in strengthening and advancing the social work profession in Canada, and the association's main purposes are to provide services to members of member organizations, to influence national social and public policy, to address national professional practice issues, and to advance the interest of the profession internationally. Recent initiatives include:

- A multi-year study of the human services sector in Canada, funded by Human Resources Development Canada and project partners (Canadian Association of Schools of Social Work, Regroupement des unités de formation universitaires en travail social du Quebec, and Canadian Committee of Deans and Directors of Schools of Social Work, as well as the Canadian Association of Social Workers).
- The planning of the joint conference of the International Federation of Social Workers and the International Association of Schools of Social Work, attended by two thousand delegates representing more than eighty countries.
- Promotion of the Profession National Project, aimed at social workers, students, academics, allied professions, governments, employers, the public, and the media. As part of its promotional strategy, the national association commissioned the development of a social work pin.
- The child welfare project, Creating Conditions for Good Practice.
- The social work forum, an initiative to foster a better understanding of and respect for the educational, regulatory, and practice perspectives of the social work profession in Canada and how they intersect, in an effort to ensure that the public is well served.

The national association participates in such national coalitions as Campaign 2000, Children's Alliance, Health Action Lobby, Quality-of-Life Care Coalition, Canadian Coalition on Enhancing Preventive Practices of Health Professionals, National Coalition on Housing and the Homeless, Canadian Mental Health Service Network, Canadian Coalition of Organizations Responding to AIDS, Canadian HIV/AIDS Legal Network, and Canadian Council on Health Services Accreditation. The *Canadian Social Work Journal* and the *CASW Bulletin*, both of which are published in English and French and sent to each member of affiliated organizations, are regular publications of the asso-

ciation: the journal addresses current issues of interest to the Canadian social work community, and the bulletin provides information on initiatives by the national association and activities of its member associations. The association has developed a code of ethics, national policy and position papers, research projects, reports, and books. It also acts as a clearinghouse for its member organizations, providing information related to social work policy and practice. The board of directors, which determines and oversees general and financial policies, includes one member from each provincial/territorial organization to assure a unified voice for the Canadian profession. The board works from a national, as well as an international perspective, to benefit the social work profession. Provincial/territorial contributions are also brought to annual general meetings between the national association's board and provincial/territorial presidents. A biennial conference provides the opportunity for individual members to gather and share information. Current information about the Canadian Association of Social Workers can be found online at < www.casw-acts .ca >.

[*Eugenia Repetur Moreno*]

RELATED ENTRIES

Accountability, Codes of Ethics, Ethics, Legal Issues, International Federation of Social Workers, I. Munroe-Smith, National Association of Social Workers (US), Professional Issues, Professional Liability, Provincial/Territorial Associations, A. Rose, Social Planning, Social Policy

Canadian Bill of Rights*

Prime Minister John Diefenbaker's path-breaking 1960 human rights charter, the Canadian Bill of Rights, applied only to federal law because the requisite provincial consent was not obtained. It recognizes the rights of individuals to life, liberty, personal security and enjoyment (not "possession," which is provincial) of property. Deprivation of these is forbidden "except by due process of law." It protects rights to equality before the law and ensures protection of the law; protects the freedoms of religion, speech, assembly and association, and the press; and legal rights such as the rights to counsel and "fair hearing." Laws are to be construed and applied so as not to detract from these rights and freedoms. One of the bill's weaknesses was that many judges regarded it as a mere interpretative aid. Section 2 provides that Parliament can override the mentioned rights by inserting a "notwithstanding" clause in the applicable statute; this has been done only once, during the 1970 October Crisis. To the extent that it is not superseded by the 1982 Canadian Charter of Rights and Freedoms, the bill remains in effect.

[*W.H. McConnell*]

* Used unedited by permission from *The Canadian Encyclopedia.* 2000. Toronto: McClelland and Stewart.

RELATED ENTRIES
Canadian Charter of Rights and Freedoms, Human Rights, Visible Minorities, Sexual Orientation

Canadian Charter of Rights and Freedoms

The Canadian Charter of Rights and Freedoms became part of the Canadian constitution on April 17, 1982, with the exception of section 15 (enacted in 1985). The Charter outlines rights and freedoms that Parliament believed were necessary in a free and democratic society, including:

- freedom of expression;
- the right to a democratic government;
- the right to live and to seek employment anywhere in Canada;
- the legal rights of persons accused of crimes;
- the rights of Aboriginal peoples;
- the right to equality, including the equality of men and women;
- the right to use either of Canada's official languages;
- the right of French and English linguistic minorities to an education in their language; and
- the protection of Canada's multicultural heritage.

The passing of the Charter meant that human rights became a legally recognized intrinsic and irrevocable part of Canadian identity. The Charter aims to protect individual rights by preventing laws that unfairly discriminate or that take away human rights. It acknowledges that everyone regardless of colour, religion, race, or belief possesses certain fundamental rights that no government can remove without cause. Prior to the enactment of the Charter, other laws, such as the Canadian Bill of Rights, 1960, protected many of the rights since included in the Charter. Laws that

limit Charter rights may be judged invalid by the courts, because the Charter is part of the constitution, as it is the supreme law of Canada, and other laws must be consistent with it. Under section 1 of the Charter, governments are allowed to place limits on Charter rights as long as they are reasonable and justified. Governments can pass laws that take away some rights under the Charter, as the notwithstanding clause in section 33—rarely invoked—empowers Parliament or a legislature to make a particular law exempt from the fundamental freedoms in section 2, the legal rights in sections 7 to 14, and the equality rights in section 15; however, a law that limits Charter rights under the notwithstanding clause expires after five years.

[*Michael R. Woodford*]

RELATED ENTRIES
Aboriginal Issues, Assembly of First Nations, Canadian Bill of Rights, 1960, Developmental Challenges, Human Rights, Physical Challenges, Visible Minorities, Sexual Orientation, Social Welfare Context

Canadian Congress of Labour*

Canadian Congress of Labour (CCL), was founded in the fall of 1940 as a merger of the All-Canadian Congress of Labour and the Canadian section of the Congress of Industrial Organizations. For sixteen years the CCL was in the forefront of Canadian union activity and organization. From an initial membership of some 77,000, it had enrolled some 360,000 workers by 1956, when it joined with the Trades and Labor Congress (TLC) to form the Canadian Labour Congress. Its affiliates included the international Industrial Unions in Canada: packinghouse workers, steelworkers, woodworkers, autoworkers, clothing workers, miners, electrical workers, and the mine, mill and smelter workers, as well as several large national unions led by the Canadian Brotherhood of Railway Employees. The president of this latter union, Aaron Mosher, also headed the CCL though the real power lay with secretary treasurer Pat Conroy, a strong nationalist who resigned in 1951 in a dispute with some of the international union leaders.

The CCL was more aggressive than its Craft Union counterpart, the TLC, and organized thousands of unskilled workers whom most labour experts thought were unorganizable. In 1945 the CCL officially allied itself with the Co-operative

Commonwealth Federation and many of its leaders ran in provincial or federal elections. As well, following World War I, the congress took the lead in expelling influential communist-dominated unions from its ranks. As the voice of Canadian industrial unionism, the CCL played an important role in national political and economic affairs.

[*Irving Abella*]

* Used unedited by permission from *The Canadian Encyclopedia*. 2000. Toronto: McClelland and Stewart.

RELATED ENTRIES

Canadian Labour Congress, Co-operative Commonwealth Federation, Employee Assistance Programs, Employment, Industrial Social Work, Non-governmental Organizations, Trades and Labour Congress

Canadian Council of Churches*

Canadian Council of Churches (CCC), founded 1944, is the national ecumenical fellowship of Canadian churches: Anglican, Armenian Orthodox, Baptist, British Methodist Episcopal, Canadian Conference of Catholic Bishops, Christian Church (Disciples of Christ), Christian Reformed Churches in Canada, Coptic Orthodox, Ethiopian Orthodox, Evangelical Lutheran Church in Canada, Greek Orthodox, Orthodox Church in America, Polish National Catholic Church, Presbyterian, Reformed Church of America—Classis of Ontario, Religious Society of Friends, Salvation Army, Ukrainian Orthodox Church, and United Church. The word "ecumenical" comes from the Greek *oikoumene*, meaning "the whole inhabited earth."

The purpose of any ecumenical organization is to seek unity for a divided church and to remind Christians that they share Christ's mission for reconciliation, peace, dignity and justice for the whole community. Within individual member churches, local needs and specifically denominational concerns have, at times, taken precedence over ecumenical efforts, but all CCC members nevertheless maintain a theological commitment to ecumenism. The council works closely with non-member Christian churches, as well as with communities of other faiths. It participates in Canadian inter-church coalitions for social justice, the Canadian Churches' Forum for Global Ministries and local councils of churches.

The Canadian Council, which provides an agency for consultation, planning and common action, was founded to co-ordinate the growing number of Canadian co-operative ventures in social service, religious education, evangelization and overseas mission, and to participate in the international ecumenical movement leading to the 1948 formation of the World Council of Churches (WCC), in which Canadians were prominently involved. The council communicates and co-operates with other national councils. It works closely with the WCC, though it neither contributes funds to nor receives financial support from the World Council. The CCC, with headquarters in Toronto, is governed and supported by its members through a semi-annual Governing Board and Triennial Assembly. Two commissions co-ordinate its work: Justice and Peace and Faith and Witness.

[*Donald W. Anderson* and *Robert H. Mills*]

* Used unedited by permission from *The Canadian Encyclopedia*. 2000. Toronto: McClelland and Stewart.

RELATED ENTRIES

F.S.B. Bowers, Church-Based Services, Non-governmental Organizations, Religion, Sectarian Social Services, Social Welfare History

Canadian Council on Child Welfare

The Canadian Council on Child Welfare (est. 1920) came into existence amid growing concerns about social issues throughout Canada and the realization that unified national responses were required (Splane 1996). Moreover, economic growth of the early 1900s meant the country had the resources to deal with related social and health issues. One response was the establishment of the federal Department of Health in 1919. When a large proportion of the country's adult male population died in the First World War, much attention turned to children. In response to public pressure to create a federal body primarily concerned with child well-being, the Department of Health held a conference, one result of which was the formation of the Canadian Council on Child Welfare. To advance its concerns, the council acted as a clearinghouse for information, began publishing its journal, *Canadian Child Welfare News* (in 1924) and participated in Canadian conferences about child welfare. In 1926 Charlotte Whitton became the council's executive secretary; despite her conservative views, Whitton fostered dramatic growth and development within the council and worked to establish the organization as an important entity in social policy issues. The council strongly influenced federal and provincial welfare programs, for example, assisting the drafting of the federal Old Age Pension Act, 1927, the first federal/provincial cost-shared program, and promoting with other agencies revisions to the Juvenile Delinquents Act, 1908, which came into effect in 1929. In light of its changing operational context, the council broadened its mandate in 1930 to include families, and was renamed the Canadian Council on Child and Family Welfare. In 1935 it became the Canadian Welfare Council and, in 1971, it was transformed into the present Canadian Council on Social Development.

[*Michael R. Woodford*]

RELATED ENTRIES

Canadian Council on Social Development, Canadian Welfare Council, Child Welfare, Children's Aid Society, *Dawn of Ampler Life*, Non-governmental Organizations, Research, Services for Children, Services for Families, Social Planning, Social Policy, Social Welfare History

REFERENCES

Rooke, P.T., and R.L. Schnell. 1987. *No Bleeding Heart: Charlotte Whitton, A Feminist on the Right.* Vancouver: UBC Press.

Splane, R.C. 1996. *Seventy-five Years of Community Service to Canada: The Canadian Council on Social Development 1920–1995.* Ottawa: Canadian Council on Social Development.

Canadian Council on Social Development

The social agency known since 1971 as the Canadian Council on Social Development has an undisputed claim as the country's foremost agency for the promotion of the social well-being of Canadians, reaching back to 1920. Its lineage is traceable through three predecessors: the Canadian Welfare Council (1935–68), the Canadian Council on Child and Family Welfare (1930–35), and the Canadian Council on Child Welfare (est. 1920). As these names indicate, the purposes of the organization changed over time, from a focus on children to the well-being of families, then more broadly to social welfare, and finally to the expressive and open-ended term by which the council is now identified, social development. Differences in

the objectives, roles, and functions of the organization have not broken the thread of common purpose as a human service association. The community service of the council in its former manifestations continuing into the twenty-first century, spanning well over half of Canada's life as a nation. As social welfare needs of Canadians emerged, humanitarian responses have been elicited from individual citizens, groups, and organizations under different auspices with diverse concerns and plans of action. The genius of the council has been to provide leadership for such responses and to act as a medium for concerted thinking, policy formulation, and advocacy on the social needs and aspirations of Canadians. This process is reflected by the support of citizen membership in the council from all regions of Canada, as well as in the community leaders who have served on its boards and committees. The thirty-two presidents of the council since 1920 have been drawn from throughout Canada and from many sectors of Canadian society, including the corporate world and the social welfare community. Highly competent professional and administrative staff and a succession of gifted and committed professionals as executive directors have served the council. The first of the thirteen full-time or acting executive heads of the council serving from 1920 to the early years of the twenty-first century was Charlotte Whitton (1920–44), credited with its early development and strong national performance. Whitton's contributions during the 1920s, the great depression of the 1930s and the early years of the Second World War mark her as one of the outstanding leaders in Canadian society, a standing confirmed in her later career as the first woman to become the mayor of a Canadian city (Ottawa). Her three successors—George Davidson, R.E.G. Davis, and Reuben Baetz—moved the council into the post-war era of social insurance, demogrants, and the full range of the government provisions in the welfare state. Throughout the 1950s and much of the 1960s, the council kept its character as a central agency within whose sphere virtually all components of Canadian social welfare were accommodated and nurtured. The predictable outward movement of distinctive aspects of what had been the council's composite program became autonomous organizations able to concentrate their attention and resources on a particular social problem or organizational approach. Since the late 1970s, the council has promoted policy positions that counter neo-conservative measures that sought to eliminate or weaken the social welfare measures that had been developed since the 1940s. The council was again guided through a demanding period by a succession of able executive directors: Agnes Benidickson (a former president, serving on an interim basis), Terrance Hunsley, Valerie Sims, Patrick Johnston, and David Ross. Through highly regarded research, consultation, public education, and well-focused advocacy, the council has promoted policies to reduce poverty—especially child poverty—unemployment, homelessness, and many other social and economic inequities. The council continues to be an authority in Canadian social and economic issues because of the quality of its analysis. It promise to continue as the foremost voice for social development in the twenty-first century. Current information about the Canadian Council on Social Development can be found online at < www.ccsd .ca >.

[*Richard Splane*]

RELATED ENTRIES

R.C. Baetz, Canadian Council on Child Welfare, L. Holland, L. Marsh, Non-governmental Organizations, Social Planning, Social Policy, Social Welfare History, Wellness

Canadian International Development Agency*

Canadian International Development Agency (CIDA) is the federal government agency responsible for administering most of Canada's official co-operation programs with developing countries and countries in transition. Formed in 1968, CIDA now has a presence in over one hundred countries and manages a budget of approximately $2.1 billion a year. CIDA's mandate is to support sustainable development in developing countries in order to reduce poverty, and to contribute to a more secure, equitable and prosperous world.

To achieve this purpose, CIDA concentrates its efforts on the following priorities: basic human needs, full participation of women, infrastructure for the poor, human rights/democratic development and governance, private-sector development and the environment. Approximately twenty-five percent of CIDA's resources are devoted to basic human needs.

CIDA works with a variety of partners to deliver assistance program. Bilateral projects are based on government-to-government agreements with developing countries. CIDA also enters into contribution agreements with Canadian partners, such as volunteer organizations, universities, co-operatives, professional organizations, churches and so on, to implement projects overseas. CIDA also supports mutually beneficial, development oriented commercial partnerships between Canadian and developing country private sector firms. Finally, CIDA also contributes to the assistance programs of multilateral development banks such as the World Bank and the African Development Bank, UN agencies like UNICEF and a variety of international organizations.

Canadians play a key role in their development co-operation program. CIDA's mandate and priorities are arrived at after cross-country public consultations, and most of the co-operation programs are implemented by Canadian suppliers of goods and services. Over the years, Canadians have made important contributions in a wide range of development projects and programs. For example, Canada is a world leader in supporting the full integration of women as equal partners in the development of their societies. Canadian engineers have helped build dams, communication systems airports and railroads. Canadian professionals have also shared their skills in immunization programs, educational, community development and environmental protection. In addition because of Canada's lack of colonial past and its reputation as middle power and an "honest broker," Canada has been able to play constructive roles in sensitive areas such as human rights, governance and postwar reconstruction programs. [Current information about the Canadian International Development Agency can be found online at < www.acdi -cida.gc.ca >.

[*Susan Taylor Mean*]

* Used unedited by permission from *The Canadian Encyclopedia*. 2000. Toronto: McClelland and Stewart.

Canadian Labour Congress*

Canadian Labour Congress (CLC) is a national Union Central founded on April 23, 1956 from the merger of the Canadian Congress of Labour and the Trades and Labor Congress of Canada. The One Big Union was absorbed into the CLC, but Quebec's Catholic unions chose to remain apart. In 1961 the CLC and the Co-operative Commonwealth Federation leaders joined to form the New Democratic Party, a link that has been maintained ever since. In 1997 there were 2.5 million trade unionists affiliated with the CLC through fifty-one international and national unions. Economic and legislative questions of national importance constitute a major focus of the CLC. Provincial and territorial federations of labour and municipal labour councils co-ordinate comparable programs of CLC affiliates. Every third year some 3000 delegates from affiliated unions convene to set policy for the central body. Between conventions, policy decisions are made by the forty-seven member executive council. The CLC headquarters are in Ottawa. [Current information about the Canadian Labour Congress can be found online at <www.clc -ctc.ca>.]

* Used unedited by permission from *The Canadian Encyclopedia*. 2000. Toronto: McClelland and Stewart.

RELATED ENTRIES
Canadian Congress of Labour, Co-operative Commonwealth Federation, Employee Assistance Programs, Employment, Industrial Social Work, Nongovernmental Organizations, Trades and Labour Congress

Canadian Mental Health Association

The Canadian Mental Health Association was originally the Canadian National Committee of Mental Hygiene (est. 1918). It operated initially on College Street in Toronto with Dr. Clarence Hincks, Dr. C.K. Clarke, secretaries Ann Abbot and Doris Secord, and a graduate nurse, Marjorie Keyes, who subsequently took classes in psychiatric social work studies at Smith College. In its first years, the organization succeeded in establishing 150 special classes for children at the time identified as "retarded," established mental hygiene clinics throughout Ontario, worked with soldiers suffering from shell shock in co-operation with the director general of military medical services, and raised awareness of mental health issues among new immigration. The organization also succeeded in improving professional education and

public awareness about mental health and illness. Dr. Clarke, by then dean of medicine and professor of psychiatry at the University of Toronto, became the organization's first director, guiding it to national prominence; he is remembered in the institute that carries his name, the Clarke Institute of Psychiatry. On Clarke's death in 1924, Dr. Hincks became director of the Canadian National Committee of Mental Hygiene until his retirement in 1952. The organization was renamed the Canadian Mental Health Association in 1952. The association continued to dedicate itself to improving the training of physicians, promoting public education around mental health and illness, and providing psychiatric screening for school children and immigrants. The national organization now has provincial branches and many local affiliates. Information about the Canadian Mental Health Association can be found online at <www.cmha.ca>.

[*Laura Taylor*]

RELATED ENTRIES
Developmental Challenges, Developmental Challenges & Families, *Diagnostic and Statistical Manual of Mental Disorders*, C.M. Hincks, Industrial Social Work, Wellness

Canadian Multiculturalism Act

Described in full as "An Act for the preservation and enhancement of multiculturalism in Canada," the Canadian Multiculturalism Act, 1985, was proclaimed in 1988, making this the first country in the world to adopt multiculturalism as a national law. The Act acknowledges multiculturalism as a fundamental characteristic of Canada and provides equal protection for every individual under the law and equal status to all Canadians. It includes policy objectives for the full and equitable participation of individuals and communities of all origins in the social, political, and economic spheres. The Act focuses on the elimination of racism and discriminatory barriers based on national or ethnic origin, colour, and religion; increased cross-cultural awareness; and the preservation and enhancement of language and cultural heritage. Further, it promotes programs and services that are accessible and better suited to all Canadians (Fleras & Elliott 1996: 12). To ensure accountability, the government is required to provide an annual report to Parliament on progress achieved. The Act recognizes that initiatives are needed to strengthen communities, encourage dialogue, and help people overcome barriers to their participation in society; specifically, it calls for efforts to connect Canadians and their communities to "promote the understanding and creativity that arises from the interaction between individuals and communities of different origins." It takes the position that societal change is the responsibility of the entire society, including major institutions and the government itself (Gauld 1992: 12).

Support for specific multiculturalism promotion began in 1971 when Canada's first official policy was announced by then Prime Minister Pierre Trudeau to address concerns by ethnic communities on the appointment of the Royal Commission on Bilingualism and Biculturalism in 1963. Although the policy advocated full involvement and equal participation of minorities in mainstream institutions without denying them the right to identify with select elements of their cultural past, it initially focused on European immigrants and their descendents and was geared to the preservation and sharing of their cultural activities, language, and heritage education (Fleras & Elliott 1992). The purpose of the multiculturalism policy was to encourage every Canadian to maintain and share their language and cultural heritage with others and thereby promote tolerance of diversity and positive attitudes (Berry & Laponce 1994). The policy was largely put into practice through support for cultural programs and activities, and language and heritage education. As immigration trends altered the composition of the Canadian population, criticism arose in the 1980s from people of non-European heritage who felt their cultures and contributions to Canadian society would be devalued by comparison to those of British and French ancestry (Reitz & Breton 1994); they also expressed concern that their role in Canada was relegated to secondary status. Parallel factors—including the weakening of British cultural presence in Canada with the decline of the British Empire after the Second World War, and an increasing American presence—led to fears of loss of identity. The 1967 Immigration Act revised the immigration system to be less discriminatory against immigrants from non-European cultures, making the development of an official policy on multicultur-

alism an inevitable next step. With the increasingly multicultural character of Canadian society, systemic discrimination in employment, housing, and education emerged, leading to the implementation of race relations policies and programs to eradicate racial discrimination at the personal and institutional levels, such as through the establishment of the Canadian Race Relations Foundation in 1991. Pressures resulted in a shift from biculturalism to multiculturalism; thus, while the Official Languages Act, 1969, legally recognized the role of British and French cultures in Canadian society, the 1971 multiculturalism policy was put in place to recognize the contributions of other cultures (Bibby 1990). Multiculturalism was to establish Canada as a unique nation, unlike any other, to differentiate Canadians from Americans (Bibby 1990). Multiculturalism was designed as a national symbol for Canadians, fulfilling the need for a distinctive identity and source of pride. Less than ten years after the announcement of the 1971 policy on multiculturalism, the multicultural character of Canada gained constitutional recognition, where section 27 of the 1982 Canadian Charter of Rights and Freedoms specified that the courts were to interpret the Charter "in a manner consistent with the preservation and enhancement of the multicultural heritage of Canada" (Fleras & Elliott 1992). The Act can be found online at <www.canada.justice.gc.ca>.

[*David Este*]

RELATED ENTRIES

Aboriginal Issues, Canadian Charter of Rights and Freedoms, Chinese Immigration Act, Citizenship & Immigration, Diversity, Human Rights, Immigrants & Immigration, Race & Racism, Racism-Sensitive Social Work

REFERENCES

Berry, J.W., and J.A. Laponce. 1994. Evaluating Research on Canada's Multiethnic and Multicultural Society: An Introduction. In J.W. Berry and J.A. Laponce (Eds.) *Ethnicity and Culture in Canada: The Research Landscape.* 3–16. Toronto: University of Toronto Press.

Bibby, R. 1990. *Mosaic Madness: The Poverty and Potential of Life in Canada.* Toronto: Stoddart.

Fleras, A., and J.L. Elliot. 1992. *Multiculturalism in Canada: The Challenge of Diversity.* Scarborough, ON: Nelson Canada.

———. 1996. *Unequal Relations: An Introduction to*

Race, Ethnic and Aboriginal Dynamics in Canada.
2nd ed. Scarborough, ON: Prentice-Hall.

Gauld, G. 1992. Multiculturalism: The Real Thing. In
Stella Hryniuk (Ed.) *Twenty Years of Multicultural-
ism: Success and Failures.* 9–16. Winnipeg, MB:
St. John's Press.

Reitz, J., and R. Breton. 1994. *The Illusion of Differences.* Toronto: C.D. Howe Institute.

Canadian Research Institute for Social Policy

The Canadian Research Institute for Social Policy (est. 2000) is a "multi-disciplinary research
organization dedicated to improving the effectiveness of social policy in Canada, to help Canadian
communities provide better education and care
for their children, and to contribute to capacity-
building efforts in developing countries" (UNB
2002). Based at the University of New Brunswick,
the centre is the successor of the Atlantic Centre
for Policy Research. The institute researches factors that promote or restrict polices and practices
with an emphasis on positive outcomes. In recent
years in collaboration with the New Brunswick
Department of Education, the institute has studied those factors in schools and teaching that facilitate learning. In addition to the publication of its
original research, the institute produces a quarterly publication, *Policy Brief.* Current information about the Canadian Research Institute for
Social Policy can be found online at <www.unb.ca
/crisp>.

[*FJT*]

RELATED ENTRIES

Education in Social Work, Non-governmental Organizations, Research

REFERENCE

UNB. 2002. Canadian Research Institute for Social
Policy. University of New Brunswick. Online at time
of writing at <www.unb.ca/crisp>.

Canadian Social Work Foundation

The Canadian Social Work Foundation (est.
1983) is a charitable organization that was formed
to extend the scope and improve the effectiveness
of social work within the field of social welfare.
The foundation aims to increase public understanding of the field and, in particular, the contribution of social work to human well-being. The

foundation's activities include the Dransfield-
Dewhurst Fund recently used to support several
conferences by the International Federation of
Social Workers and International Association of
Schools of Social Work, as well as scholarships to
social workers from eastern Europe, South and
Central America, Africa, and Asia. Through this
fund as well, the Canadian Association of Social
Workers and AON scholarship is awarded annually to assist a member of a member organization
of the national association to attend a national or
international social work event.

[*Eugenia Repetur Moreno*]

RELATED ENTRIES

Canadian Association of Social Work, Education in
Social Work, Foundations, Non-governmental Organizations

Canadian Welfare Council

Throughout its history, the Canadian Council
on Social Development has operated under four
different names; its three previous names were
Canadian Council on Child Welfare (1920–30),
Canadian Council on Child and Family Welfare
(1930–35), and Canadian Welfare Council (1935–
71). As the Canadian Welfare Council, the organization expanded its mandate to include the broad
social welfare issues affecting all Canadians, rather
than only children and families. This change in
focus was a direct result of the tremendous increases in social needs and related macro policy
issues that had arisen during the great depression
of the 1930s. Given the likelihood of a second world
war, the council played an active role in mobilization efforts to deal with mounting social problems.
The council's contributions included holding a
conference on voluntary services for the armed
forces, helping to establish official welfare services (e.g., Dependants Allowance Board, Dependants Board of Trustees), assisting with plans to
provide services for 7,000 guest children from
Britain, and working to establish day nurseries for
children whose mothers were involved in the war
effort. With the onset of war in 1941 and the federal
government turning its attention to the creation of
post-war economic and social policies, the council also offered its assistance. Under the leadership of George Davidson, the council advocated
the development of a comprehensive national

social security program. Davidson's position was distinct from that of his predecessor, Charlotte Whitton, who had not supported earlier proposals for comprehensive social security. In the early 1940s the council also advanced the provision of national allowances for children. The council developed greatly, with growing resources, under R.E.G. Davis, who became the executive director in 1946 (Splane 1966). During the period 1946–63, educating the public, providing information toward social policy, and entering international issues became important council activities; moreover, the council started to work with the corporate sector and, to a lesser degree, labour groups, to obtain their support for social policy development. The council also maintained its role in national social policy advocacy, proposing such programs as unemployment assistance, national medicare, and tax reform: "Tangible progress in unemployment assistance, old age security and other income support programs, hospital insurance and other health and social service measures attested to the Council's influence" (Splane 1996: 33–34). In 1963 some of the council's program divisions were pressuring for a split from the organization; as a result, the council established a commission to review its operations and carried out its recommendations for reorganization in the following years. In 1971 the Canadian Welfare Council became the Canadian Council on Social Development, a name it still holds today. Current information about the Canadian Council on Social Development can be found online at <www.ccsd .ca>.

[*Michael R. Woodford*]

RELATED ENTRIES
Canadian Council on Social Development

REFERENCE
Splane, R.C. 1996. *Seventy-five Years of Community Service to Canada: The Canadian Council on Social Development, 1920–1995*. Ottawa: Canadian Council on Social Development.

Canadians In and Out of Work

Leonard Marsh wrote *Canadians In and Out of Work: A Survey of Economic Classes and Their Relation to the Labour Market* in 1940. Its detailed analysis of the country's socio-economic conditions was said to be the most comprehensive study of the Canadian social structure and employment

of its time. Marsh's analyses led to proposals for a national welfare policy structure on which Canada's post-war social network was based.

[*FJT*]

RELATED ENTRIES
Employment, L. Marsh, Marsh Report, Poverty, Social Welfare History

capacity assessment

Capacity assessment is a planning tool that a community can use to determine its existing resources that can be useful for people to develop their community. This assessment tool, such as the one devised by John Kretzmann and John McKnight in 1993, is based on a belief that community development should be defined by the aspirations of people living within that community (i.e., "inside out") rather than defined by policy makers or planners living outside the community (i.e., "outside-in"). Capacity assessment is also based on a belief that a focus on capacities or strengths of community members will empower and encourage them to become active in addressing local concerns (Kretzmann & McKnight 1993; 1997). While these are not new values for community workers, what has attracted interest in Kretzmann and McKnight's work is their provision of well-developed manuals or guides that permit a community worker to carry out an asset—or capacity—inventory, as well as extensive advice on how to do this work in a way that community members animate and empower themselves to create the place they want to live. For their approach to capacity assessment, which was created to revitalize low-income urban neighbourhoods, Kretzmann and McKnight (1993) describe five steps. First is a thorough mapping of the capacities and assets of individuals, citizen's associations, and local institutions within an identified neighbourhood. Capacity inventories are surveys carried out by people within the community and to identify skills, abilities and talents, experiences, and interests. Skills people have that they can use in support of community building include care giving, office and retail skills, maintenance and repair skills, or construction; abilities and talents that might be of use include crafts, storytelling, gardening, or teaching. Experiences that residents might share include travel, having successfully advocated for themselves, or having a family member within a social or health services organization. Finally, people are asked which of their skills they would be interested in sharing with others in the community, or areas of interest for learning. Developing this capacity inventory is followed by building relationships among people and organizations identified as being assets for mutually beneficial problem solving within the community, for example, by linking an individual in need of respite care for a disabled child with somebody who has experience caring for children with special needs. People who want to improve public transportation or establish a seniors centre could get together. Such linking may be done informally or through creation of a local information exchange (Kretzmann & McKnight 1998), for example, finding ways to involve homebound seniors or disabled people in the management of a food bank. The third step is mobilizing for economic development and/or information sharing—for example, increasing availability of such critical resources as child care or identifying retirees in the community who can assist local groups with professional expertise; enhanced civic involvement is another possible use of this information, perhaps through volunteering to help with youth activities or sports teams or by providing support to young families. The fourth step is a community visioning process with a broadly representative group and development of a plan for implementing this vision. Once representative community members have defined what they want to accomplish, the last phase is leveraging resources to support this local development plan, often from government or the profit sector. Byproducts of these tangible actions are a building of trust and an increase in social capital within the community, as people get to know one another and become aware of resources they can draw on within the community. Kretzmann and McKnight emphasize the importance of carrying out capacity assessment in a way that supports the development of this sense of trust as well as enhanced social capital.

Once inventoried, these capacities can be mobilized for many different community-building projects. This process can be used in a broad way, or for a focused specific purpose. Its primary purpose may be to support local economic development, for instance, or to reduce isolation of elders

and mothers with young children. Having a clearly defined purpose can shape the approach and questions to be asked. Residents must also decide how best to gather capacity information: through face-to-face interviews, a self-administered questionnaire, or focus groups, for instance. Distributing or presenting gathered data could include innovative ideas such as showing the location of the assets on an enlarged map of a neighbourhood (Dewar 1997; Turner, McKnight, & Kretzmann 1999). Critics of capacity assessment argue that it is not a new idea and may rely overmuch on certain resources, possibly reinforcing a neo-conservative stance within the community (McGrath et al. 1999). This critique can be made of all community-building efforts that foster self-determination and citizen empowerment. The key to using Kretzmann and McKnight's tool without falling into the trap of neo-conservatism appears to be in the final step—leveraging outside resources, public and private, to support the locally defined development plan.

[*Anne Westhues*]

RELATED ENTRIES

Assessment, Community Development, Community Organization, Empowerment Theory, Participatory Research, Research

REFERENCES

Dewar, T. 199. *A Guide to Evaluating Asset-Based Community Development: Lessons, Challenges and Opportunities.* Chicago: ACTA Publishers.

Kretzmann, J.P., and J.L. McKnight. 1993. *Building Communities from the Inside Out.* Chicago, IL: ACTA Publishers.

———. 1997. *A Guide to Capacity Inventories: Mobilizing the Community Skills of Local Residents.* Chicago: ACTA Publishers.

———. 1998. *A Guide to Creating a Neighbourhood Information Exchange.* Chicago, IL: ACTA Publishers.

McGrath, S.K., Moffatt, U. George, and B. Lee. 1999. Community Capacity: The Emperor's New Clothes. *Canadian Review of Social Policy.* 44, 9–23.

Turner, N., J.L. McKnight, and J.P. Kretzmann. 1999. *A Guide to Mapping and Mobilizing the Associations in Local Neighbourhoods.* Chicago, IL: ACTA Publishers.

caregiving

Social work is frequently referred to as one of

the caring professions. Caregiving emerged as a public issue in Britain, Canada, and the United States in the early 1980s. Two catalytic pieces were *A Labour of Love: Women, Work and Caring* (Finch & Groves 1983)—which documented the economic and social costs borne by adult daughters caring for elderly parents, and the research of social psychologist Carol Gilligan (1982) on the differential development of boys and girls in the debate over justice versus care, based on principles of ethical thinking. The justice/care debate continues, and many writers have tried to blend the two (Clement 1996; Koehn 1998). During this same period, research on ageing was marked by an emphasis on the burden of care and the costs to the health care system of an ageing population. Now, a considerable literature in ethics and health economics, as well as social policy, examines various aspects of caregiving. The debate, however, has taken a particular form in social work. Substantively, caregiving is central in services to people in need of some kind of assistance with daily living (i.e., children, people with physical challenges, and elderly persons). Since the 1970s policy has shifted to providing health and social services in people's homes rather than in institutional settings. This shift resulted from a combination of concerns about the projected rising costs of health care and increasing evidence that people enjoy a better quality of life if they remain in their home and community. While the shift to home-based services is widely supported, many questions persist about who provides the care and under what conditions—part of a larger debate around the nature of the partnership among government, families, and for-profit and not-for-profit sectors. Traditionally, the family—in particular women—provided most of the hands-on care; however, the assumptions underpinning this model degrade as family structures and the welfare state change.

At this time caregiving has become one of several arenas in which the implications of economic and social restructuring of the welfare state are felt. In Canada the state (i.e., federal and provincial/territorial governments) provides most of the funding but services are contracted out and delivered by a mixture of public, voluntary, and for-profit agencies—a model often referred to as the mixed economy of care. The amount and nature of this mix differs from jurisdiction to jurisdiction because health and social services are a provincial/territorial responsibility. Canada, unlike such countries as Australia, does not have a national home and community care program alongside the Canada Health Act, and has only experimented with state allowances for carers and other forms of consumer-directed care. It is estimated that families do about 80 percent of caregiving. Reliable longitudinal data have not been compiled, but the combined effects of early discharge from hospitals, an ageing population, and a policy direction that emphasizes home-based care suggest that the work expected to be done by families will increase in the years ahead. Several equity issues in policies that affect caregiving are surfacing. State provisions have decreased: in the 1990s, the amount of federal funding transferred to the provinces and territories plummeted, and the amounts spent on home care are still less than 5 percent of provincial/territorial health care budgets. Combined with the economy of care, this decrease has resulted in an expanding market for social care. People with sufficient resources can purchase additional help but are calling on a service market comprised of paraprofessionals where salaries are low, turnover is high, and quality control is difficult to regulate. Consumers usually are not in a position to exercise much choice. More than two decades of research has documented the effects of caregiving responsibilities on the mostly female kin who do it on a daily basis; the economic, as well as social, effects on women are long term (i.e., their ability to secure employment-related benefits for their own old age is reduced). Another issue under debated is the way in which unpaid work is valued in Canadian society: if caregiving is valued, how is this to be translated into rights and benefits? Under present policies, those who provide unpaid caregiving are being excluded from entitlements that those who are employed can claim. Thus, the relationship between caring and social justice is played out in social policy. Research on caregiving suggests that, under current policy approaches, the work of caregiving will continue to be undervalued and continue to be the responsibility of unpaid women. An alternative and potentially more equitable approach might be to assume that all citizens are caregivers at different points in their lives, and that this needs to be reflected in employment and tax policies in ways that do not disadvantage those who offer caregiving services.

[*Sheila M. Neysmith*]

RELATED ENTRIES

Case Management, Clinical Social Work, Deinstitutionalization Movement, Hospices, Long-Term Care, Managed Care, Palliative Care, Practice Methods, Sensitizing Concepts, Social Services Workers, Theory & Practice, Therapy, Treatment, Volunteering, Welfare State, Wellness

REFERENCES

Clement, G. 1996. *Care, Autonomy, and Justice: Feminism and the Ethics of Care.* Boulder, CO: Westview Press.

Finch, J., and D. Groves, Eds. 1983. *A Labour of Love: Women, Work and Caring.* London: Routledge and Kegan Paul.

Gilligan, C. 1982. *In a Different Voice.* Cambridge, MA: Harvard University Press.

Koehn, D. 1998. *Rethinking Feminist Ethics: Care, Trust and Empathy.* London and New York: Routledge.

Neysmith, S., Ed. (2000). *Restructuring Caring Labour: Discourse, State Practice and Everyday Life.* Toronto: Oxford University Press.

Carleton University School of Social Work

The Carleton University School of Social Work had its fiftieth anniversary in 1999 with a large number of alumni celebrating social work education. The school was first established by Father Swithun Bowers at St. Patrick's School of Social Welfare; it joined Carleton University in 1967 but was not moved from its downtown location until 1973 to become part of the Carleton campus. When the school first opened in 1949 it offered both a bachelor's and master's degree in social work, but the bachelor's program was soon dropped; in 1991, a new four-year program toward a baccalaureate was offered in recognition of the changing nature of the field. The Ontario Association of Professional Social Workers Eastern Branch and a number of local employers, who had long encouraged the development of an undergraduate degree program, welcomed this initiative. The bachelor's program is structured to meet the needs of students ranging from those with little human service experience and no prior post-secondary education, to those with considerable experience and training.

The master's program is for students holding a bachelor's degree in social work, or an honours degree in another program. Applicants with a bachelor's degree enter a one-year master's program, while those coming from a different discipline enter a two-year program. The practicum, an important aspect of both bachelor's and master's programs, provides students with the opportunity to apply, test, develop, and integrate knowledge, theory, and skills. Students can work under supervision in a wide range of community and organizational settings, such as hospitals, children's services, community health centres, correctional services, women's health and crisis centres, and non-governmental organizations. Being located in the nation's political capital also affords Carleton students the opportunity to work in federal government departments. The school is also dedicated to ensuring accessibility to mature students, recognizing that they may have commitments to partners, children, family, friends, and employers as well as studies. Both the bachelor's and master's programs offer part-time and full-time studies.

Carleton School of Social Work has played a central role in the development of what has come to be called structural social work, the impetus for which originated in the social and political turmoil of the 1960s and 1970s. Many community and political activists were among those who contributed to the development of structural approaches to social work. They developed a critical analysis of social work education, practice, and research wherein it was argued that a social work focus on individual pathology and on individual change did not adequately address people's hardships. Instead, structural social workers advocated for broad-based social, political, and economic change, as the root cause of people's problems were seen as stemming from social, political, and economic inequities. Structural social work is directed at bringing about social change and creating a more fair and just society, and is committed to working with individuals and supporting them in their time of immediate need. In this regard being committed to the provision of immediate relief is as important as being committed to social change. Over the past two decades, structural social work has moved beyond class/gender analyses to incorporate an analysis of sexual orientation, physical and intellectual disability, and race. The School of Social Work has been active in implementing the principles of education equity. The school's mission statement on education equity recognizes people who have faced historical exclusion and marginalization: Aboriginal peoples, people of colour, people with physical and intellectual challenges, people disadvantaged by their economic situation, and lesbian, gay, bisexual, and transgendered persons; in response to structural impediments such persons may have faced, the school affirms the principle that all people should have the opportunity to learn and to contribute in a supportive environment that validates and develops their knowledge, insights, and perspectives within that environment. Education equity is seen as a structural issue requiring a rigorous review of established norms. As such, the school affirms that educational equity is consistent with the principles of quality education as it recognizes and develops academic excellence and practice competence. In the past ten years the school has been involved in delivering the bachelor's degree programs in a number of First Nation communities in Ontario and Quebec, where the programs have been developed through discussions initiated by the communities. The school is currently in the process of developing a doctoral program in social work in response to a growing need in Canada for doctoral graduates in social work: it is expected that the first cohort of students will be admitted for 2004. Current information about the Carleton University School of Social Work can be found online at < www.carleton .ca/ssw >.

[*Martha Wiebe*]

RELATED ENTRIES

F.S.B. Bowers, Diversity, Doctorate in Social Work, Education in Social Work, Faculties of Social Work, Practicum Instruction, Ontario Association of Social Workers

case management

Case management is a style of practice, which emerged in the late 1970s and early 1980s, that attempts to organize and co-ordinate a cluster of community services to meet the complex needs of clients in a manner that an individual service may not. It Canada its development was linked in part to the deinstitutionalization movement and to the accompanying integration of community-based services. The complex changes in the financing and provision of services in interaction with the network of services in a community were a result of attempts to meet a broad spectrum of client needs. The goal of case management is to foster a high degree of co-operation between and among agencies to avoid duplication of services and to ensure that the optimum profile of available resources is constructed and monitored in the best interests of the client. The motivations for case management include a strong wish to maximize the differential impact of various interventions and services, reduce duplication, respond to gaps in the service network, and enhance efficiency. Underlying support for this style of practice is a perception that case management reduces costs and increases effectiveness.

This practice revolves around the person of a case manager, whose task it is to identify the profile of the service needed for a case, to assemble and build the required team, to ensure an accurate assessment and diagnosis of a situation, to plan and establish the perceived needs of a client, to oversee the plan, to monitor change in the identified target situation, to do the same in the planned implementation strategy, and to ensure that a process of ongoing evaluation is introduced and maintained. Depending on where a case manager—frequently, a social worker—is located in the service structure, he/she can draw on a variety of approaches to case management practice. The form it takes depends on the case manager's commitment to sharing, co-ordinating, and co-operating on the part of the involved service givers and the accompanying history, politics, rivalries, and resource availability. As with all delivery systems, case management dynamics can be subject to interpersonal conflict or power struggles which could be detrimental to a client's welfare. The concept is a sound one, however, offering greater flexibility and ready access to resources in a much less structured way than in the former mode of service delivery. Successful case management requires a high degree of group and administrative skills on the part of the case manager as well as a firm commitment by the network of professionals, persons, resources, and systems involved. A creative process, case management can and does bring the strength of a diverse, organized, and flexible service profile to clients.

[*FJT*]

RELATED ENTRIES
Caregiving, Networks, Program Evaluation, Social Networks, Social Policy & Practice, Theory & Practice

Marie-Thérèse Casgrain (1896–1981)

Casgrain, Marie-Thérèse (née Forget), social activist, suffragist, senator; b. July 10, 1896, Montréal, QC; m. Pierre Casgrain, 1916; first woman to lead provincial party (NDP, 1996); Officer of the Order of Canada (1967); d. Nov. 02, 1981, Montréal, QC

Marie-Thérèse Casgrain, the daughter of a banker and conservative member of Parliament, Sir Rodolph Forget, received her first education at the Convent of Sacred Heart in Montréal. She became a dedicated and passionate social activist for civil liberties and human rights in Canada and around the world, through organizations she founded and through her own political career. Her husband, Pierre Casgrain, became a Liberal member of Parliament in 1921. Casgrain worked relentlessly to improve living conditions for poor women in Quebec and for the protection of and better educational opportunities for neglected children. In 1926 she founded Ligue de la Jeunesse Feminine, a volunteer organization for social work, promoting and fighting to improve the legal status and rights of Quebec women throughout the subsequent fifteen years. In 1928 Casgrain became president of the Provincial Franchise Committee—later renamed La Ligue des Droits de la Femme / League for Women's Rights; she led this organization's campaign for women's rights, despite a marked lack of support from the provincial government, the church, and rural women. She was able to overcome this resistance by reaching out to women through her influential radio program, *Femina*, broadcast in both French and English. Her leadership in the campaign for women's suffrage in Quebec eventually helped most women there to achieve the right to vote in 1941. During the Second World War, Casgrain was one of two presidents of the Women's Surveillance Committee for the Wartime Prices Trade Board. Following the war, she continued to press for child protection laws, prison reform, government appointments for women, and amendments to Quebec's Civil Code.

In her political career, Marie-Thérèse Casgrain was elected nine times to both federal and pro-vincial legislatures from 1942 to 1962. She resigned as vice-president of the National Federation of Liberal Women in 1946, also leaving the Liberal Party, which she had supported for years to join the Co-operative Commonwealth Federation (CCF); from 1951 to 1957, she led the provincial wing of the CCF in Quebec. When the New Democratic Party succeeded the CCF in 1961, Casgrain continued her support in the position of national vice-chairperson. During this period, she helped to found the Fédération des femmes du Quebec (est. 1966). In 1967 she was named an Officer of the Order of Canada and, in 1970, Prime Minister Pierre Elliott Trudeau appointed Casgrain, by then seventy-four years of age, to the Senate. Marie-Thérèse Casgrain was a great humanist who steadfastly fought for the rights of Canadian women, men, and children.

[*Carlos J. Pereira*]

RELATED ENTRIES
Co-operative Commonwealth Federation, Feminist Theory, Human Rights, Social Justice

REFERENCES
Benson, J. 2003. Thérèse Casgrain. Profiles of Women. Online at time of writing at <www.canoe.com/MoneyWomenProfiles/casgrain_woman.html>.
Dumont, M., M. Jean, M. Lavigne, and J. Stoddart. 1987. *Quebec Women, A History*. (Trans.) Roger Gannon and Rosalind Gill. Toronto: The Women's Press.
The Heroic Heart—Thérèse Casgrain. 2003. Online at time of writing at <www.pch.gc.ca/special/poh-sdh_2000/english/routeone/r1-hero1.html>.

Harry Cassidy (1900–51)

Cassidy, Harry Morris, social scientist, social welfare reformer, social work educator; b. Jan. 18, 1910, Vancouver, BC (of Herbert Francis Cassidy & Maria Rendall Morris); m. Beatrice Pierce; children: Norah, Jane, Michael; d. Nov. 04, 1951, Toronto, ON

Harry Cassidy was a tireless crusader for public social welfare services in Canada and the United States in the 1930s and 1940s. His 1926 doctoral dissertation in economics from the Robert Brookings Graduate School of Economics and Government laid the groundwork for his lifelong interest in problems of poverty, living standards, industrial relations, and social legislation. While teaching at the University of Toronto (1929–34), Cassidy conducted research studies on unemployment, housing conditions in Toronto, and labour conditions in the clothing trades, which were among the first detailed empirical studies of Canadian social conditions by a social scientist. His two books of the 1940s, *Social Security and Reconstruction in Canada* (1943) and *Public Health and Welfare Reorganization* (1945) were the first to describe and analyze in detail Canadian social welfare programs at both the federal and provincial levels. Cassidy was a prominent member of the League for Social Reconstruction (est. 1931–32) a blend of the UK Fabian Society and the US New Deal liberalism. A strong advocate for social reform and a vision of a democratic socialist Canada, the league very soon became the brain trust for the newly formed Co-operative Commonwealth Federation (est. 1933). League members assisted in writing the Regina Manifesto, the party's founding document, and the party's 1935 book *Social Planning for Canada*, of which Cassidy wrote several chapters. Cassidy's thinking was in tune with the league's reformist program of research on social problems and on education to inform and enlighten citizens on the need for social change. As director of social welfare for British Columbia (1934–39), Cassidy developed that province's social services and drew up extensive plans for universal public health insurance; had Cassidy's scheme not been derailed by the medical profession, it would have been the first such program in Canada. Cassidy was among the first generation of Canadian social scientists who were technical experts; as he saw his work from the perspective of social engineering, he moved to refashion the province's social services in line with modern methods of management that favoured practical, efficient solutions to social problems. Cassidy had little interest in social theory and was of the view that empirical data spoke for themselves. Social progress for Cassidy depended on technology and bureaucracy. As a social work educator, Cassidy developed a school of social work at the University of California, Berkeley (1939–45), and one at the University of Toronto (1945–51); his plans for both schools were close to impossibly ambitious. The base of university education for social workers needed to be broadened, he argued, by placing much greater emphasis on the social sciences, social research, and the legal and administrative features of social welfare. It was his hope that graduates of these strengthened programs would be able to assume

leadership roles in the more efficient and humane administration of public social welfare. Cassidy had enormous drive and determination and he became very well known in the 1930s and 1940s as an economist, a public welfare administrator, a social scientist, a university administrator, a prolific author, and an expert on social security. His colleague and friend, R.E.G. Davis commented in 1979, long after Cassidy's death, that Harry Cassidy "was the closest we ever came to having a leader in social welfare in Canada" (Irving 1981). It is a legacy unlikely ever to be surpassed.

[*Allan Irving*]

RELATED ENTRIES

W.H. Beveridge, Co-operative Commonwealth Federation, Education in Social Work, Fabian Society (UK), L. Holland, League for Social Reconstruction, Marsh Report, Regina Manifesto, Research, Social Planning, Social Policy, Social Welfare History, University of Toronto Faculty of Social Work

REFERENCE

Irving, A. 1981. Canadian Fabians: The Work and Thought of Harry Cassidy and Leonard Marsh, 1930–1945. *Canadian Journal of Social Work Education* 7, 1, 7–28.

Catholic charities

The social work profession thinks of Catholic charities in three different ways. In their most general context, Catholic charities are the visible discharge of the fundamental commitment of Catholicity, to the corporal works of mercy. As with all Christian denominations, the Catholic Church and all its members have an obligation to care for and minister to the needs of those in want. Over the centuries in all parts of the world, the church has conducted a range of formal and informal activities, the goal of which was to minister to the needs of persons and groups out a spirit of charity. From its very earliest days in this continent, the Catholic Church established and developed charitable institutions and missions (i.e., orphanages, hostels, hospitals, schools, and residences), many established by dioceses for the sole purpose of serving the needy; much of this work was carried out by the personnel of religious orders. As the nature of needs changed, and as service provision became increasingly professional and publicly financed, many of these service facilities from the past diminished. Some ceased to exist and others, as with all social services, took on a more contemporary format. Many retained their names and identities connecting them to the Catholic church, becoming autonomous entities with little or no formal administrative contact with one another other except through the diocese in which they were located. In modern Canada, then, Catholic charities are those organized services, institutions, and programs sponsored by a parish or diocese to provide care to specific groups in society. A further use of the term relates to those situations where, rather than functioning as autonomous entities, each agency or service in a diocese is linked as part of a formal network of services; thus, Catholic charities refers to the overall administrative structure within a diocese, under a director and board of directors. The function of these entities is to ensure a co-ordination of services, an ongoing assessment of need, and, when necessary, the establishment of new services, the establishment of standards of service and an ongoing process of evaluation, and, in some instances, accreditation on a regular basis. To partake of services from these large networks of diocesan agencies, clients need not be members of the church; rather, the services exist for all who seek or are identified as needing assistance from a service that is based on particular values and commitments.

[*FJT*]

RELATED ENTRIES

Associated Charities of Toronto, Church-Based Services, Foundations, Non-governmental Organizations, Religion, Sectarian Social Services, Social Welfare, Voluntarism, Wellness

child abuse

Child abuse is physical, sexual, or emotional harm inflicted on a child by a parent or caregiver. Physical abuse includes excessive physical punishment or discipline, deliberate violence, torture, cruelty, deprivation of basic physical needs, and confinement; it can include serious isolated incidents, and/or a pattern of repeated but less severe incidents. The abuse may result in bruises, broken bones or fractures, cigarette burns, brain damage caused to an infant through shaking, malnutrition, failure to thrive, or even death. For many abuse victims, there are no physical symptoms, but, for all victims, the long-term emotional im-

pact of abuse can be just as damaging as any physical scars. Sexual abuse ranges from sexual harassment to full sexual intercourse; it includes touching, fondling, molestation, exhibitionism, and/or sexual exploitation of a child by the parent or caregiver. Sexual abuse may be perpetrated on a child by an adult caregiver, or by another older child where there is a significant difference in age, development, or size. The essence of sexual abuse is the violation of a child's trust and the caregiver having taken advantage of the child's dependency. Sexual abuse is usually progressive, moving from suggestive comments, to touching, to sexual intercourse. In serious cases, the child may experience physical harm, such as bleeding or bruising in the genital or anal area. The emotional impact of sexual abuse can result in depression, anxiety, the inability to trust others and share in intimate relationships, sexual dysfunction, low self-esteem, suicidal behaviour, and prostitution. Emotional abuse is the most difficult kind of child abuse to identify. The emotionally abusive caregiver may humiliate or degrade a child, reject a child, or fail to respond to a child's needs for affection and love. Repeated emotional abuse can have devastating effects on the ability to function long into adulthood. The concept of child abuse may also include child neglect, or harm resulting from a caregiver's failure to provide for a child's physical, medical, or safety needs. Differences in community standards, the realities of poverty, and cultural expectations can make identifying child neglect difficult. The concept of child abuse is relatively recent. In the past child welfare agencies focused on providing care for orphaned, abandoned, and neglected children, and the police handled assaults against children. In the early 1960s child abuse was identified as a special child protection issue. One of the sources of this concept was Dr. C. Henry Kempe; with his colleagues, Kempe identified "battered child syndrome" (Kempe, Helfer, & Helfer 1968). By the early 1970s, child welfare legislation in Canada had incorporated the concept of child abuse. Sexual abuse came to the forefront in the early 1980s in a US study by David Finklehor that uncovered the widespread sexual victimization of children; similar facts were documented in Canada through the 1984 Badgley Report, commissioned by Health and Welfare Canada, on sexual offences against children and youth.

The reasons why parents or caregivers abuse their children are complex and not fully understood; the underlying causes of physical abuse, sexual abuse, and neglect are often quite different. Child abuse is not usually caused by any single factor, but by the combination of several interacting issues. Parents or caregivers who were abused themselves as children or who have severe stress, mental illness, substance abuse, or physical or intellectual challenges are more likely to abuse their children. Family crises and unhealthy family dynamics also increase the risk of abuse: parents are more likely to abuse within a family where, for example, adult relationships are characterized by violence and where power and control issues are prevalent. A parent with unrealistic and age-inappropriate expectations of a child, or a parent who is socially isolated may become abusive under stress. All of these issues are exacerbated by economic circumstances. Living in poverty is a critical factor that contributes to both abuse and neglect. In fact, poverty is the one factor most likely to determine which children will be removed from families (Lindsey 1994: 144); for this reason, it is important for protection workers not to discriminate against poor children. Child abuse and neglect have another causal dimension for Aboriginal children who may have been reared within caring extended families. The economic, political, social and cultural realities of Aboriginal life have been severely disrupted and, over several generations, very many Aboriginal children were taken from their families and raised in non-Aboriginal foster homes or in church- and government-operated residential schools. As a result, they lost family and cultural ties, parenting and life skills, and even their lives, as about half the Aboriginal children sent to residential schools died, most from infectious diseases; many were neglected and/or seriously abused. The ensuing cycles of abuse have had a devastating impact on succeeding generations.

Since child abuse has been defined as a special child protection issue, the incidence of reporting has increased dramatically. Child protection legislation throughout Canada now includes a formal requirement that professionals and the general public report any suspicion of child abuse. Government policy and agency practice also encourage the early identification and reporting of high-risk situations, in order to help families before abuse occurs. Professional training and community education programs discuss the physical indicators of abuse (i.e., unexplained bruises, fractures, bumps, and genital/rectal bleeding), as well as behavioural and emotional indicators (i.e., an abused or neglected child may be withdrawn, fearful, and depressed, or may be angry and display aggressive outbursts). A sexually abused child may exhibit sexually inappropriate or acting-out behaviour. Since child abuse can take so many different forms and children can react in so many ways, an untrained person may have difficulty identifying signs of abuse accurately. Therefore, it is critical for any suspicion to be reported. Child welfare authorities are responsible for investigating all allegations of abuse and reports of suspected abuse. Legal and professional obligations limit the amount of information that can subsequently be shared with the reporting person, without the full consent of all family members; however, the reporting person may be in a good position to provide ongoing support to the child during and following the investigation. The immediate task for the investigating social worker is to assess immediate safety needs and ensure the child's safety. The protection investigation will determine the extent and severity of the abuse, and a full abuse investigation will be conducted jointly with police under a joint protocol. Many provinces and territories have formal risk assessment models that help to ascertain future harm; such models address the factors that are associated with risk of abuse and neglect, and can assist in development of an appropriate service plan with the family and other professionals. In serious situations, the abuser and the victim need to be separated until the risk of future abuse is minimized. It is preferable that the perpetrator—rather than the child—leave the family. If the child cannot be protected within the family, extended family or friends might be available to provide care. As a last resort, the child may be placed in foster care. Cases of verified abuse will be sent to a family court.

Sexual abuse treatment programs include individual and group therapy for the child victim, for the offending adult, and for other care-taking adults who did not protect the child from abuse. Treatment programs assist child victims to disclose the full extent of abuse, to understand they were not responsible for it, to gain self-esteem, and to learn ways to protect themselves from further abuse. Treatment for non-offending adults helps them to acknowledge the abuse, to believe the victim, and to provide consistent parental support to the victim. Treatment for the offender focuses on issues of power and control, relationships, and sexuality, and requires the offender to take full responsibility for the abuse. In less serious situations, risk can be minimized through support programs. Counselling can address parental issues of past abuse, substance abuse, marital conflict, and family violence. Mental health and developmental services can help parents and children with emotional, psychological, or developmental challenges. Community support programs, lay home visitors, and mutual aid programs can reduce social isolation and provide concrete assistance to parents struggling with daily life. Many Aboriginal communities and agencies offer community programs and healing circles that draw on cultural traditions. Family preservation programs include intensive, in-home interventions to help families resolve crises and learn new ways of interaction. All intervention programs have been shown to be most effective when provided in an integrated way, in close collaboration with the child protection social worker involved (Cameron & Vanderwoerd 1977). Primary prevention programs serve high-risk children and families. Some jurisdictions provide universal screening for high-risk conditions at birth and home visiting for all new parents of high-risk infants, because the first years of life are critical to healthy development. Other prevention programs are geared to high-risk groups. The Ontario Better Beginnings, Better Futures program responds to the fact that children are most at risk within economically disadvantaged neighbourhoods. Other programs may provide special supports for parents with psychiatric or developmental challenges. Many jurisdictions also have community education programs that raise awareness about child abuse—for example, school curricula that include personal safety programs for young children, and positive parenting courses for older youth.

[*Maurice D. Bruebacher*]

RELATED ENTRIES

Abuse, An Act for the Prevention of Cruelty to and Better Protection of Children, Barnardo Homes, Child Advocacy, Child Custody & Access, Child Welfare, Children's Aid Society, Clinical Social Work, Crisis Intervention, Counselling, Elder Abuse, Family Research, Family Services Canada, Family Therapy, Marital & Family Problems, Parenting, Peer Counselling, Play Therapy, School Social Workers, Sensitizing Concepts, Services for Children, Sexual Abuse of Children, Single Parents, Therapy, Treatment, Torture & Trauma Victims, Vicarious Traumatization, Women Abuse

REFERENCES

Cameron, G., and J. Vanderwoerd. 1977. *Protecting Children and Supporting Families: Promising Programs and Organizational Realities.* Toronto: Aldine de Gruyter Press.

Kempe, C., H. Helfer, and R.E. Helfer. 1968. *The Battered Child Syndrome.* Chicago: University of Chicago Press.

Lindsey, D. 1994. *The Welfare of Children.* New York: Oxford University Press.

child advocacy

The Ontario Office of the Children's Lawyer (est. 1827) has a mission to investigate, protect, and represent the personal and property rights and obligations of children, and advocate for children in proceedings before the courts of Ontario. This children's lawyer represents the interests of children before the court in custody and access matters, child welfare proceedings, and civil litigation and estate matters. The children's lawyer is an independent officer of the Crown appointed by the lieutenant governor-in-council on the recommendation of the attorney general, to represent children within the administration of justice. The office was formally established in Toronto in 1881 to protect the property and financial interests of children under eighteen years of age. Originally the official guardian, the name of this office was changed in April 1995 to the children's lawyer. Office staff working with the children's lawyer include lawyers and social workers. Social workers have been retained by the office since the early 1950s, when concern about the rising post-war divorce rate caused the government to require all divorces with minor children to be served on the official guardian. An investigation and report to the court by the official guardian was required before a divorce could be granted. In the late 1970s the focus of legal representation moved to include more personal rights of children, including issues related to their custody and access by parents in divorce and separation, and within the context of child welfare proceedings before the court. The Ontario attorney general established the child representation program to be administered by the office of the then official guardian after a judicial enquiry into the death in 1982 of Kim Anne Popen (Allen 1982). After the enquiry, several concerns were expressed about why and how the system had failed this child. Of the eighty-seven suggestions made, Mr. Justice Allen recommended that it be incumbent on the court in all proceedings under the Child Welfare Act (now, the Child and Family Services Act) to determine if separate representation is necessary or desirable to protect the interests of the child. At present, the involvement of the children's lawyer is mandatory in all child protection cases when ordered by the court (under s.38 of the Child and Family Services Act) and is discretionary in custody and access matters (under s.112 and subs.89(3.1) of the Courts of Justice Act). When the children's lawyer consents to become involved in custody and access cases, the form of intervention may be legal representation, a social work report, an issue-focused legal representation or social work report, or a team approach involving reports by both a lawyer and a social worker. In custody and access matters, the focus of the lawyer is to represent a child's interests independently on a solicitor/client basis before the court and to assist the adult parties in resolving their dispute in the interests of the child. The role of the child's lawyer is to act as the child's legal representative. This includes acting as advocate for the child client to have his/her voice and interests heard and communicated to the parties and to the court. The child's lawyer may not represent the "best" interests of the child, as they are to be determined by the court. The child's lawyer or social worker does not take instructions from the child but places their interests within the context of the court proceeding. Lawyers and social workers explore each child's views and preferences where they can be ascertained and provides a context for those views in certain circumstances. Both lawyers and social workers ensure that all relevant evidence (psychosocial, emotional, and legal) is presented to the court, so that each child's wishes

can be placed in context to assist the judge in his/her decision making.

[*Rachel Birnbaum*]

RELATED ENTRIES

Advocacy, Child Custody & Access, Child Welfare, Children's Aid Society, Criminal Justice, Family Therapy, Family & Youth Courts, Marital & Family Problems, Parenting, Practice Methods, School Social Workers, Services for Children, Services for Youth, Toronto Infants Home

REFERENCE

Allen, Mr. Justice H. Ward. 1982. *Report of the Judicial Inquiry into the Care of Kim Anne Popen.* By the Children's Aid Society of the City of Sarnia and the County of Lambton. Vol. 1-4. Toronto: A.P. Gordon, Queen's Printer for Ontario.

child custody and access

Child custody refers to the agreement under which parents who are separated or divorced settle the parenting arrangement for dependent children. Sole or joint custody are the most common arrangements. If sole custody is granted, then the non-custodial parent may be granted access to the children according to a specified pattern. In joint custody, both parents must consult and agree on major decisions affecting the welfare of the child. The child custody arrangements may be settled between the parents, often with the help of a mediator or, in disputes, by the provincial/territorial courts. The courts tend toward joint custody on separation unless there is animosity between the parents, or should one of the parents not want custody. Canada and many other jurisdictions have engaged in a process of reassessment of family law related to the determination of child custody and access on marital breakdown (Canada 1998). This process affects federal and provincial/territorial jurisdictions: the federal government is responsible for changes to the Divorce Act, while provincial/territorial governments are responsible for access enforcement. In 1997 through a review by the Special Joint Committee on Child Custody and Access, Parliament sought the concerns and recommendations of families and professionals for improving the family law system. Following this consultation, the federal government, in its reform of family law, replaced such existing concepts as "custody" and "access" with clearly defined language that can promote a focus on the best interests of child and help to maintain meaningful relationships for the child after divorce. Four principles guide the reform (Canada 1999). First, to assist in minimizing the negative impacts of divorce on children, a child's perspective will be promoted. This paramount strategy is based on individual needs, best interests and well-being of the children. Second, the federal government recognizes the need to work together with other levels of government to co-ordinate efforts in the area of family law. Third, educational and social services need to be improved to provide a more holistic and effective supports for children and families facing divorce. Finally, no one model of parenting and support is suitable for all children and families after the parents separate. Issues driving the need to reform family law regarding child custody and access are aimed at improving outcomes for children:

• a growing concern for children's rights;
• a desire to reduce conflict at the time of marriage breakdown in an attempt to minimize the negative impacts on children;
• a movement towards shared parenting and parenting plans;
• when possible, adopting a non-adversarial dispute resolution mechanisms such as mediation or facilitating the court process through unified family courts that tend to all family law matters; and
• a focus on widening the circle of persons involved with children of divorce, such as grandparents, other extended family members, and mental health professionals (Canada 1998).

The broad effective measures needed to support families going through separation and divorce require collaboration between governments as well as with such disciplines and professional groups as legal, child protection, and mental health. Professionals recognize that divorce and separation are difficult for all parents and children. Some families seem to get stuck during the transition phase, where one or both parents are intent on maintaining a high degree of conflict and tension, making it impossible to resolve parenting decisions without a great deal of intervention. The incidence of such divorces is estimated at between 10 and 20 percent of the divorcing population (Canada 1999).

Social workers or other professionals may encounter these high-conflict families in several ways; for example, courts may appoint a professional, usually a social worker or psychologist, to provide a family assessment. Social workers may become involved in the custody process through the child welfare system, as it is not uncommon for allegations of abuse and neglect to be raised during divorce proceedings. Social workers who work with women and children victimized by domestic violence often assist these women and advocate for them on custody and access issues. Those involved with the rights and concerns of persons belonging to minorities (e.g., sexual orientation, religious, and ethnocultural) are also making their voices heard around the issue of custody and access.

[*Cathryn Bradshaw*]

RELATED ENTRIES

Abuse, Child Abuse, Child Advocacy, Child Welfare, Children's Aid Society, Family Demographics, Family: Non-traditional, Family Research, Family Services Canada, Family Therapy, Marital & Family Problems, Parenting, Separation & Divorce, Services for Children, Services for Youth, Sexual Minorities, Single Parents, Women Abuse

REFERENCES

Canada. December 1998. *For the Sake of the Children*. A report to Parliament of the Special Joint Committee on Child Custody and Access. Online at time of writing at <www.parl.gc.ca>.
———. May 1999. Government of Canada's response to the report of the Special Joint Committee on Child Custody and Access: Strategy for Reform. Online at time of writing at <www.canada.jus tice.gc.ca>.

child welfare

Child welfare is the field of social service whereby the state undertakes the roles and functions generally assumed by parents or caregivers. In Canada child welfare services are provided by provincial/territorial governments either directly through a government ministry, or in partnership with a private organization, usually a children's aid society. The first children's aid society in Canada was created in Toronto in 1891, and the first child welfare legislation, An Act for the Prevention of Cruelty to and Better Protection of Children, was proclaimed in 1893. As with all child welfare legislation, the 1893 Act stipulated the circumstances under which the state could intervene in the life of a family to protect and monitor the well-being of children. Current child welfare legislation generally addresses abuse, sexual abuse, neglect, and, in some jurisdictions, emotional abuse. Families often become involved with the child welfare system on a voluntary basis, whereby children are supervised in their own homes. Court proceedings resolve family disagreements about the involvement of child welfare authorities, with all parties represented legally. Typically, authorities must have reasonable grounds to apprehend a child and place him/her in care; legal definitions of a child in need of protection, which are used to determine whether a province/territory can intervene, are very similar throughout Canada.

To augment protective services, child welfare organizations generally provide a spectrum of support services to families. In the 1980s a focus on family autonomy and preservation resulted in changes to child welfare legislation that emphasized the least intrusive form of intervention, the most noteworthy changes having occurred in Ontario and Alberta. The emphasis on family preservation was accompanied by the development of a variety of support services such as group work, parenting education, family preservation, and family support services, all of which were generally geared to reflect the needs of the local community. Child protection also involves the collaboration of other professionals, such as police, medical and mental health practitioners, teachers, and day care providers. While such collaboration has always been viewed as important, the necessity gained significance in the 1980s when the pervasive extent of child sexual abuse was realized with the release of the Badgley Report (Canada 1984). Accordingly, major changes in child welfare and criminal laws were undertaken; in many jurisdictions, protocols were developed to provide for co-ordinated investigation by police and child welfare authorities. Severe funding cuts in the 1990s to child welfare services throughout Canada eroded much of the support developed in the previous decade, contributing further to the need for collaboration with other community services. At the same time, questions were being raised about the viability of family preservation initiatives, and about policies that were perceived to be leaving children in or returning them to inadequate parental care. Restricted funding forced many child welfare organizations to assume a more residual approach to service. The tragic death of several children finally brought an end to funding cuts: the public outcry over these deaths led to comprehensive investigations and equally comprehensive changes to child welfare legislation that placed greater emphasis on the protection and well-being of children and less emphasis on family preservation. Accompanying changes in the legislation in New Brunswick, Quebec, Ontario, and British Columbia were efforts to standardize the investigation of child abuse and neglect through safety and risk assessment tools.

Child welfare legislation generally specifies the period of time a child may remain a temporary ward before either being made a permanent ward of the Crown or being returned to her/his family. Should a child be taken into care, he/she may be placed in one of several settings, the most common of which is foster care where the child remains in a family environment for the period stipulated by a wardship order. If the plan is to reunite the child with his/her family, then efforts are made to address the circumstances that contributed to the child's apprehension; frequent contact and visiting between the child and family is encouraged. Should a child become a permanent ward of the Crown, then the placement options most frequently chosen are adoption or long-term foster care or other out-of-home resources, including group homes (most frequently used for adolescents), treatment foster homes, and placement resources that provide care for children with special needs (i.e., intellectual, emotional, physical, and/or developmental challenges). These resources are generally funded and licensed by the same ministry that addresses child welfare matters, and tend to be staffed by paid employees who work shifts. While the education and training of these workers may vary, they are generally poorly paid and tend not to stay in their positions long. Potential foster caregivers are approved and employed by the child welfare system for which they provide care. Initial screening processes usually involve criminal police checks, inquiry into their motivation, marital status, child care/parenting experience, community supports, and mental and emotional health. While most provinces and territories provide an orientation and ongoing training for caregivers, participation in training is not mandatory. Local, provincial/territorial, and national foster parent associations also offer training and advocacy for foster caregivers, who also tend to be poorly compensated for the service they provide. Unfortunately, the experience of children in care has often been characterized by considerable instability as a result of placement breakdown, multiple moves, limited long-term permanency planning, and staff turnover. The emphasis in the 1980s on family preservation also contributed to children entering care at a later age, often with more complex needs; these trends put considerable strain on out-of-home resources. The financial cuts of the 1990s also affected the availability of placements; foster care, for example, has for many years had a critical shortage of recruitment and retention. As a consequence, decisions as to where and with whom a child will be placed are most frequently dictated by placement availability, rather than by the best resource for the child.

Most current child welfare legislation now reflects the importance of maintaining a child's cultural heritage, even though efforts to recruit foster homes in diverse cultural communities are not always successful. Many children of African and Caribbean ancestry, for example, are still placed in families with European backgrounds. This issue has been particularly controversial in Canada with regard to the placement of Aboriginal children, where attempts to assimilate them through fostering and residential schooling date from the early nineteenth century. Child welfare agencies have played a role in the colonization of Aboriginal peoples. A prominent example occurred under the 1965 Indian Welfare Agreement, by which child welfare services were to be extended to Aboriginal peoples identified as Status Indians; the result is referred to as the "sixties scoop" when Aboriginal children were placed, most often in the homes of non-Aboriginal families, at a rate four times that for the rest of Canada (Armitage 1993). While Aboriginal children are still overrepresented in the in-care population, increased community interest in improvements has led to the development of Aboriginal child and family services in most provinces and territories.

Recent legislative changes also indicate that Aboriginal children removed from parental care are to be placed in Aboriginal homes whenever possible, and that Aboriginal services are to be informed and consulted.

Historically, the child welfare field has been criticized for ignoring social conditions that contribute most to child abuse and neglect. Poverty, gender oppression, and racism are rarely addressed in the provision of child welfare services. Gay, lesbian, bisexual, and transgendered youth constitute another highly vulnerable in-care population of children that remains largely neglected by child welfare authorities; some initiatives in one children's aid society, however, suggest that the unique needs of these young people are beginning to be recognized. Critics have identified child welfare as an arm of the state that perpetuates the oppression of the most vulnerable in society by maintaining structural inequity. By focusing on the inner workings of the family, rather than the conditions that contribute to abuse and neglect, the child welfare system is further victimizing some clients—in particular, poor women. Social workers who recognize this situation are faced with an ideological conundrum between caring and control (Wharf 2000).

At the beginning of this millennium, those involved in child welfare services are faced with many challenges, some a legacy from changes made in the 1990s. Changes to provincial/territorial standards that lowered the eligibility threshold for a child in need of protection have resulted in increased reporting of abuse and caseloads. Some view efforts to standardize practice through risk assessment and record keeping mechanisms as a quick fix that consumes considerable worker time and has the potential to undermine professional judgment. These changes are seen as contributing to sufficiently high rates of rapid worker turnover, particularly at the entry level, and burnout of more seasoned workers that child welfare in Canada is described as being in crisis. One consequence—the necessity to hire staff without social work training—may signal that social work is on the precipice of losing its time-honoured niche in child welfare. Responses to these challenges are coming from the child welfare community, with some hopeful signs. Ongoing discussion involving provincial/territorial ministries, child welfare representatives, and schools/faculties of social work may address the identified need for well-trained professional social workers in child welfare. Despite the residual approach that has evolved in recent years, the importance of advocacy and creating partnership with clients is being recognized: the resurgence of community work and an increased emphasis on family group conferencing, for example, offer some promise in this regard (Lee 1999). Reconceptualizing "clients" as "citizens" could open the door for more active partnership in child welfare (Wharf 2000; Savoury & Kufeldt 1997). These aspects of child welfare work may not be mutually exclusive—as they are commonly conceptualized; rather offering temporary care as a support to families may result in a more positive perception of those who require intervention, perhaps bridging the divide between care and control.

[*Tracy Swan*]

RELATED ENTRIES

Aboriginal Issues, Adoption, An Act for the Prevention of Cruelty to and Better Protection of Children, Barnardo Homes, Child Advocacy, Child Abuse, Child Custody & Access, Children's Aid Society, Crisis Intervention, Family Allowance Act, Family Demographics, Family: Non-traditional, Family Research, Family Services Canada, Family Therapy, Sister M. Henry, C. Hincks, E.D.O. Hill, L. Holland, Marital & Family Problems, Parenting, Play Therapy, Practice Methods, Private Adoption, School Social Workers, Sensitizing Concepts, Services for Children, Services for Families, Services for Women, for Youth, Separation & Divorce, Sexual Orientation, Single Parents, Social Welfare, Theory & Practice, Toronto Infants Home, Visible Minorities

REFERENCES

Armitage, A. 1993. Family and Child Welfare in First Nation Communities. In B. Wharf (ed.), *Rethinking Child Welfare in Canada*, 131–71. Toronto: McClelland and Stewart.

Canada. 1984. *Sexual Offences against Children*. Vol. 1–2: Report of the Committee on Sexual Offences against Children and Youths. Ottawa: Ministry of Supply and Services. (Chair: R. Badgley).

Lee, W. 1999. A Community Approach to Urban Child Welfare. In L. Dominelli (Ed.) *Community Approaches to Child Welfare: International Perspectives*. 64–94. Aldershot, UK: Ashgate.

Savoury, G.R., and K. Kufeldt. 1997. Protecting Children Versus Supporting Families. *The Social Worker* 65, 3, 146–54.

Wharf, B. 2000. Cases or Citizens? Viewing Child Welfare through a Different Lens. *Canadian Social Work* 2, 1, 132–39.

Children's Aid Society (Toronto)

The Children's Aid Society of Toronto (est. 1891) is the largest board-operated child welfare organization in Canada, offering a wide range of programs to serve Canada's largest and most complex urban environment: integrated family and children's services; protective services, family support; high-risk infant program; pregnancy and after-care; day treatment; community work; research; community education; branch children's services; long-term care; foster care; health services; adoption and Crown ward disclosure; volunteer involvement. The society began with the work of journalist J.J. Kelso, who in 1887 wrote about the conditions of children and animals and the need for an organization that would prevent cruelty to both. Encouraged by a positive community response, he founded the Toronto Humane Society. The need for a separate organization for children soon became clear, however, and he was asked to establish a children's aid society with objectives to provide adequate schools for the poor, separate treatment for juvenile offenders, more playgrounds and youth clubs, and a shelter for neglected children. (A separate society was established for Catholic children.) In 1893, the agency received a charter from the Ontario government to protect Toronto's non-Catholic children in their own homes and to place neglected, abandoned, or orphaned children in suitable institutions or with volunteer foster families.

The first shelter was opened, with a reciprocal agreement with the Infants' Home (est. 1875), by a remarkable public health nurse, Vera Moberly, to provide institutional and foster care for vulnerable young children. The agencies were combined in 1951. For its first thirty years, the Toronto children's aid society was a volunteer organization with few staff members: by 1911, four social workers were responsible for all cases as well as out-of-town foster homes. An executive director was not hired until 1923. The society initially ran a shelter and juvenile detention home, which was taken over by the city in 1920 and the number of admissions to the shelter dropped significantly; the introduction of an Adoption Act in 1921 and the decision to pay foster parents also decreased admissions, so that the shelter was closed in 1928. Like other agencies during the great depression of the 1930s and the Second World War, the society faced more serious challenges (Macintyre 1993) and was reorganized to focus on the protection of children from abuse and neglect, and the care of children orphaned or unable to live at home. Municipal and private funding increased, as did staffing with preference being given to university trained social workers; amalgamation with the Infants Home brought the agency 195 new staff. In 1957 the agency assumed responsibility for child welfare in the entire metropolitan area of Toronto, then encompassing the recent amalgamations into the city.

Amendments to child welfare legislation in 1965 gave children's aid societies in Ontario a mandate to develop preventive services. With a historic interest in family well-being, the Toronto society embraced preventive work, taking strong stands on such issues as housing, adult only buildings, child poverty, universal and comprehensive child care, and workfare. In 1968 the society deployed child protection workers into so-called high-risk communities; this approach has evolved a developmental orientation that engages community capacities, provides public education on social issues affecting children, and encourages mobilization (Lee & Richards 2002; Lee 1999). The society is the only child welfare organization to maintain community work as a significant aspect of its work for children. In 1999 legislative changes presented child welfare agencies across Ontario with increased responsibilities. As governments become less interested in protecting vulnerable citizens (Rice & Prince 2000), the children's aid society is operating in a more challenging environment; for example, 73 percent of the children served now live in families at or below the poverty line. Further, with 47 percent of families served identifying themselves as members of a minority culture, the Toronto society has broadened its programs and approaches to try to meet the needs of all segments of the city's increasingly diverse population.

[*Bill Lee*]

RELATED ENTRIES

Adoption, An Act for the Prevention of Cruelty to and Better Protection of Children, Barnardo Homes,

E.H. Blois, Child Abuse, Child Advocacy, Child Custody & Access, Child Welfare, Crisis Intervention, Ethnic-Sensitive Practice, Family: Non-traditional, Family Research, Family Services Canada, Family Therapy, J.J. Kelso, Non-governmental Organizations, Marital & Family Problems, Parenting, Private Adoption, Social Welfare History, Services for Children, Sexual Abuse of Children, Single Parents, Toronto Infants Home, Wellness

REFERENCES

Lee, B. 1999. A Community Approach to Child Welfare in Urban Canada. In L. Dominelli (Ed.) *Community Approaches to Child Welfare, International Perspectives.* 65–94. Aldershot, UK: Ashgate.

Lee, B., and S. Richards. 2002. Child Protection through Strengthening Communities. In B. Wharf (Ed.) *Community Work Approaches to Child Welfare.* Peterborough, ON: Broadview Press.

Macintyre, E. 1993. The Historical Context of Child Welfare in Canada. In B. Wharf (Ed.) *Rethinking Child Welfare in Canada.* Toronto: McClelland and Stewart.

Rice, J., and A. Prince. 2000. *Changing Politics in Canadian Social Policy.* Toronto: University of Toronto Press.

Chinese Canadian National Council

The Chinese Canadian National Council (est. 1980) was founded with the mandate to promote the recognition and protection of the rights of all individuals, in particular, those of Chinese ancestry, and to encourage their full and equal participation in Canadian society. The council promotes understanding and co-operation between Chinese Canadians and all other cultures in Canada. The council works closely with other communities and government to identify needs and priorities, and to lobby for adequate funding for services specific to its members. Similarly, the council has been conducting ongoing consultation with government health, education, and service institutions regarding culturally sensitive services and better access to these services. Current information about the Chinese Canadian National Council can be found online at < www.ccnc.ca >.

[*Carlos J. Pereira*]

RELATED ENTRIES

Canadian Multiculturalism Act, Chinese Immigration Act, Diversity, Ethnic-Sensitive Practice, Non-governmental Organizations

Chinese Immigration Act

The Chinese Immigration Act is one part of a series of legislative measures used by the federal government to regulate Chinese emigration to and immigrants in Canada in the late nineteenth and early twentieth centuries. These measures are often cited as examples of the racist and discriminatory nature of the Canadian immigration policy in the past. Canadians of Chinese ancestry have long constituted the largest visible minority in Canada. Social workers wishing to practise with cultural sensitivity can benefit from an understanding of the settlement experience of Chinese immigrants to Canada, which has not been smooth. It is believed that some Buddhist monks came from China to the lands that became Canada as early as 458; in formal records, Chinese immigration began in 1885 when workers from China arrived from California during the Fraser River gold rush. Their presence in British Columbia was not welcomed initially, but Chinese labour soon became indispensable to economic development at the time, particularly in the building of the transcontinental railway. Chinese labourers became adept at detonating dynamite, a vital contribution to the construction, which proved fatal to many who made it. When British Columbia experienced economic hardship, however, anti-Chinese sentiment grew. Public opinion shifted from perceptions of Chinese workers as patient, hard-working, and making significant contributions to western development, to culturally inferior, racially unfit, undesirable immigrants unlikely to become assimilated into Canadian society. From a sense that Chinese labour represented an economic threat, in an atmosphere in which discrimination flourished openly in social and political milieu, the federal government of Sir John A. Macdonald in 1885 passed An Act to Restrict and Regulate Chinese Immigration Into Canada, to impose a head tax of $50 on all persons of Chinese origin entering Canada. This mimicked passage of the US Chinese Exclusion Act of 1882. The government of Wilfrid Laurier increased the head tax in 1900 to $100, and in 1903 to $500—both exorbitant amounts intended to deter further emigration from China. Between 1885 and 1923, Canada collected approximately $23 million in head taxes. Evidently feeling justified by persistent public anti-Chinese sentiment, governments openly restricted the rights of Chinese residents to vote, own land or businesses, be employed, or become citizens. A Royal Commission on Chinese and Japanese Immigration was struck in 1902, but nothing changed. Between 1911 and 1923, the number of immigrants from China declined from a total of 21,564 (from 1911 to 1915), to 7,261 (from 1916 to 1920), and to 4,353 (from 1920 to 1923). In 1923 the Mackenzie King government brought in the Chinese Immigration Act to prevent anyone from China other than diplomats and students entering Canada. No limits were placed on immigration from Europe. The Act also imposed further controls on residents of Chinese origin or ancestry who were by then living throughout Canada; they were required to obtain a government certificate and provide written details on routes and destinations for foreign travel (Li 1998). This racially based immigration Act virtually halted immigration from China: between 1924 and 1944, only 15 immigrants entered Canada from China.

The Chinese Immigration Act remained in effect during the Second World War, even though China was among the allies to which Canada was also allied. Contributions to the war effort by Chinese Canadians helped to increase societal support for the community so that, with much lobbying, Mackenzie King was persuaded in 1947, the final year of his tenure, to repeal the Chinese Immigration Act. Yet, by comparison to the experience of immigrants from Europe and the United States, Chinese immigrants continued to experience discrimination until 1967, when Canada introduced a universal point system to be applied to all immigrants regardless of origin. The immigration measures applied by the federal government solely on the basis of race, and the discriminatory restrictions imposed on residents of Chinese origin or ancestry resulted in considerable financial and emotional burdens on Chinese families, many members of which were separated for years. Since the mid-1980s, descendents of people who paid the head taxes developed a campaign to educate Canadians about these measures and to lobby government for redress; they are demanding an official apology and financial compensation. So far, Canada has refused to offer either, but petitioning and political action continue.

[*Daniel W.L. Lai*]

RELATED ENTRIES
Canadian Multiculturalism Act, Chinese-Canadian National Council, Diversity, Race & Racism, Visible Minorities

Brock Chisholm (1896–1971)

Chisholm, Brock, physician; first director-general, World Health Organization; 1948: b. May 18, 1896, Oakville, ON; d. Feb. 02, 1971, Victoria, BC

Brock Chisholm trained in medicine and psychiatry, and rose to international prominence when he became the first director-general of the World Health Organization in 1948. It was observed at the time that he assumed responsibility for the largest practice any physician had ever had: more than 3 billion people (Irving 1998). A few years earlier, when Dr. Chisholm was Deputy Minister for Health in the federal Department of National Health and Welfare, Canadians had been shocked by his declaration at a home and school meeting in Ottawa that children should not be taught thought-crippling myths. "Any child who believes in Santa Claus has had his ability to think permanently destroyed," Chisholm had told astonished parents. The Santa Claus incident of 1945 and many similar statements are indicative of Chisholm's iconoclastic personality, earning him a reputation for kicking up dust every time he spoke in public; his audiences were seldom disappointed. In the two decades following the Second World War, Chisholm was one of Canada's most controversial figures, at times reviled as a dangerous individual, at others praised as an enlightened modern humanist. Throughout his work, though, a central theme predominated: the absolute necessity for people to free themselves from standard clichés and prejudices of one's time and upbringing, to be free-thinking independent individuals; the very worst thing for younger generations, he repeatedly emphasized, is the prospect that they "might turn out like us." Underlying Chisholm's provocative statements was the rock-solid conviction that the human race had to achieve emotional health and learn to live in harmony—or perish.

For much of his life—from small-town physician in Oakville, Ontario, until long after his retirement at the southern tip of Vancouver Island—Chisholm displayed a knack for pinpointing problems before they became the concern of soci-

ety or political leaders. He took up such causes as world peace, sex education, birth control and the population explosion, racial tolerance, and the admission of China to the United Nations. He warned of world food shortages, the depletion of the world's irreplaceable natural resources, and the dangers of nuclear and biological warfare. He was a tireless advocate for the idea of world citizenship. Chisholm's greatest contribution was the work he accomplished from 1946 to 1948 in helping to lay the groundwork for the World Health Organization (est. 1948). where he served as the first director-general (1948–53). Chisholm himself proposed the name World Health Organization to reflect the facts that disease knows no political boundaries, that health—like security and peace—is indivisible, and that no one can be considered safe while prevention and treatment of disease are denied anywhere in the world. Chisholm was responsible for many of the key phrases in the global organization's constitution insisting, for example, that the clause on child health and welfare reflect global concerns: "the ability to live harmoniously in a changing total environment is essential to the healthy development of the child." Chisholm also can be credited with the organization's expansive definition of health: "a state of complete physical, mental and social well-being and not merely the absence of disease or infirmity." By 1948 Chisholm was the undisputed captain of the movement for world health. What Chisholm accomplished in the years 1946 to 1953 was nothing short of heroic: as long as there is a world, he will always be remembered for what he achieved in those crucial years.

[Allan Irving]

RELATED ENTRIES
Wellness

REFERENCE
Irving, A. 1998. *Brock Chisholm: Doctor to the World.* Markham, ON: Fitzhenry and Whiteside.

church-based services

Canadian churches and synagogues have played a critical role in the provision of social welfare and social work services, carrying on a millennia-old worldwide tradition of providing care to the needy. In earlier centuries, the majority of such institutions as hostels, hospitals, orphanages, and homes for the aged and the indigent in Canada were sponsored by organized religions. The motivating factor for such sponsorship emerged from the range of theological views underlying the churches' views of their responsibility to help those deemed to be less fortunate. More recently, many such services were duplicated by community bodies or government agencies, which officially at least did not advance a particular religious position. A complex network of public and sectarian, or church-sponsored agencies, emerged as social services became more professional, and governments increasingly understood the necessity of ensuring service availability to all, the cost of providing these services increased, and as the range and number of philanthropic organizations, often for specific projects or clients, expanded. Within this network, there were and continue to be apparent service duplication. For some observers, this situation is undesirable, while for others it is seen as giving clients and potential clients a broader range of choices—especially clients seeking a particular service where particular beliefs, values, and/or traditions will be respected. Most services with a religious affiliation are funded by the sponsoring religion, whereby the services may not be identified or recognized as being needed by the public or public funders; however, especially in recent years, many church sponsored services receive all or part of their funding from foundations, the United Way, or through many tax-based sources. Public funding of religious-sponsored services can create tensions when, for instance, the funding source wishes to direct the nature of the services offered; perhaps the most prominent example involves the moral and ethical appropriateness of offering or not offering abortion services and counselling. The underlying rationale for the continuation of religious-based commitment services beyond the theological commitment to service and social justice is twofold: the first being to meet the needs of clients whose biopsychosocial difficulties touch on matters of religious morals and ethics, so that services are available where such matters are understood and respected. Second, the very long history of religious-based social services offers a strong accumulation of knowledge and wisdom from which social workers can draw; as such, the profile and quality of these services continue to

advance a standard of excellence. An interesting development in recent years is an increase in clientele actively seeking church-based services not on the basis of the client's belief system but rather out of a sense of perceived comfort with receiving services, which are based on a particular viewpoint. Few such agencies now—and perhaps only rarely in the past—require adherence by the client to a specific theological commitment. Church-based services continue to comprise a high profile in the mosaic that is the Canadian social welfare network, with strong indicators that their role is increasing rather than diminishing.

[*FJT*]

RELATED ENTRIES

Antigonish Movement, B'Nai Brith, M. Bourgeoys, I. Bourget, Catholic Charities, Citizen Participation, Congrégation de Notre Dame, Fred Victor Centre, Jewish Social Services, R. Leger, Non-governmental Organizations, Religion, Salvation Army, Sectarian Social Services, Sister Mary Henry, Social Gospel Movement, Social Welfare History, Voluntarism, Women's Christian Temperance Union, Women's Missionary Society, Young Men's Christian Association (YMCA), Young Women's Christian Association (YWCA)

citizen participation

Definitions of citizen participation vary, but many agree that it is a means of making government administrations more responsive to citizens' preferences. According to Wireman (1977), citizen participation has been defined as a process by which individuals take part in decision making in the institutions, programs, and environments that affect them. Thus, participation in social service organizations can provide citizens with an opportunity to influence policy development, the allocation of resources, and the design of new programs. Much of the literature in public administration, political science, and social work favours the involvement of communities and citizens in the development and delivery of human services programs. Frequently called for in response to perceived bureaucratic insularity and insensitivity, citizen participation is perceived as a way to introduce alternative views, reduce impersonality, and bring about increased familiarity with the problems and needs of client populations and communities. Many forces may impel citizens into participative roles with human service organizations, but their effectiveness is uneven, as large public bureaucracies generally have a poor response performance, often excluding citizens from participation. In part, this lack of responsiveness may have resulted from the changes in human services more than thirty years ago produced by an increase in formal organizational structures with the accompanying paraphernalia of professionalism and regulations. The 1960s and 1970s saw a proliferation of new kinds of citizen participation, stimulated in part by efforts by the federal governments in Canada and the United States, because of the perception that their agencies created to serve the poor were not sufficiently responsive, and by the belief that better mechanisms and approaches were needed to assist the poor and minorities. The objectives of the Canada Assistance Plan, paralleling the early "War on Poverty" declarations in America, led to the creation of demonstration projects throughout the nation that were designed to give poor people a voice in local agency policy development and decision making (Armitage 1975). These efforts by government to encourage social or grassroots action were soon accompanied by citizen activism of a political nature, often about local concerns. According to Armitage (1975), pressures to curb the perceived militancy of local citizen groups led to the demise of government-sponsored citizen participation in the 1980s. Social workers have involved citizens in many other ways, such as in the settlement house movement, where local citizens were invited to be advisors on boards or committees, and policy makers on neighbourhood councils and local community organizations. Social workers have collaborated with mutual aid and self-help groups, informal helpers, in various experiments with social animation and with citizens at the neighbourhood level (Pincus 1984; Katz 1970). During the 1970s and early 1980s, social workers increasingly found employment in agencies with large bureaucracies and minimal interest in citizen participation in policy and operational plans. By the 1990s, many government jurisdictions had moved toward regional structures that involve citizens as board members and advisors, and in public consultation of their views on important or controversial issues. As social workers increasingly find

employment in community service delivery organizations and local government administrations (Schmidt et al. 2001), they may be able to make stronger connections with citizens in future.

[*Jean Lafrance*]

RELATED ENTRIES

Advocacy, Antigonish Movement, Capacity Assessment, Church-Based Services, Community Development, Community Organization, Community Service, Co-operative Commonwealth Federation, Co-operative Movement, "Democracy Needs Socialism," Empowerment Theory, Mutual-Aid Societies, Natural Helping Networks, Non-governmental Organizations, Participatory Research, Peer Counselling, Progressive Social Work, Radical Social Work, Sectarian Social Services, Self Help & Mutual Aid, Self-Help Groups, Settlement House Movement, Social Justice, Social Networks, Social Planning, Social Policy & Practice, Social Welfare History, Theory & Practice, Voluntarism

REFERENCES

Armitage, A. 1975. *Social Welfare in Canada: Ideals and Realities.* Toronto: McClelland and Stewart.

Katz, A.H. 1970. Self-Help Organizations and Volunteer Participation in Social Welfare. *Social Work* 15, 1, 51–60.

Pincus, C., and E. Herman-Keeling. 1984. Self-Help Systems and the Professional as Volunteer: Threat or Solution. In F.S. Schwartz (Ed.) *Voluntarism and Social Work Practice: A Growing Collaboration.* New York: Landham.

Schmidt, G., A. Westhues, J. Lafrance, and A. Knowles. 2001. Social Work in Canada: Results from the National Sector Study. *Canadian Social Work* 3,2, 83–92.

Wireman, P. 1977. Citizen Participation. In J.B. Turner (Ed.) *Encyclopedia of Social Work.* 17th ed. Washington, DC: NASW Press.

Citizenship and Immigration Canada

Citizenship and Immigration Canada is a department of the federal government, responsible for two aspects of social history that have played a central role in the development of Canada as a nation. Under the British North American Act, 1867 (now, Constitution Act, 1867), the federal government is responsible for all matters concerning immigration and citizenship, as implemented through the Citizenship Act, 1985, and the Immigration and Refugee Protection Act, 2001 (which replaced the former Immigration Act) (Armitage 1988). The federal department grants Canadian citizenship to eligible individuals. Current law automatically grants citizenship to any baby born in Canada, independent of the parent's immigration status. Immigrants can apply for citizenship after they have lived in this country for three years. Current federal policy allows three classes of immigrants to enter Canada: family class (i.e., close family members sponsored by a Canadian citizen or resident); independent class (i.e., individuals selected because of their potential to contribute economically to Canada, such as skilled workers and business immigrants); and refugee class. Refugees are persons identified under the Geneva Convention relating to the Status of Refugees, other displaced persons resettled from abroad with government assistance or private sponsorship, and persons who have successfully claimed Convention refugee status in Canada. The Immigration and Refugee Board, an independent administrative tribunal, adjudicates in-land refugee claims; the board also conducts inquires and detention reviews, and hears appeals concerning denial of admission, removal orders, and refusals of family class sponsorship applications.

Many provincial/territorial governments have specific intergovernmental agreements on immigration, of which the Canada–Quebec Accord is the most comprehensive. Under the accord, Quebec is empowered with selection powers and control over its own settlement services. British Columbia has a similar agreement that is not as comprehensive as Quebec's. To meet local labour market needs, other provinces have agreements enabling them to select immigrants with specific competencies. Canada retains responsibility for defining immigrant categories, setting immigration levels, and carrying out enforcement activities. Citizenship and Immigration Canada also issues documents, such as passports and visa, that verify Canadian citizenship. The federal department administers three programs that foster immigrant settlement and integration. Community agencies are funded through the Immigrant Settlement and Adaptation Program to provide basic assistance with orientation, housing, and referral to social services. The Host Program involves volunteers assisting newcomers to become familiar with their new community. And a third program funds community agencies and private institutions to deliver basic language instruction to adult newcomers in English and French. Current information about Citizenship and Immigration Canada can be found online at <www.cic.gc.ca>.

[*Michael R. Woodford*]

RELATED ENTRIES

Barnardo Homes, Chinese Immigration Act, Diversity, Immigrants & Immigration, Services for Refugees, Social Welfare Context, Torture & Trauma Victims

REFERENCE

Armitage, A. 1988. *Social Welfare in Canada: Ideals and Realities.* 2nd ed. Toronto: McClelland and Stewart.

clinical social work

Clinical social work practice encompasses individual, couple, family, and group counselling that is focused on helping people overcome intrapsychic, interpersonal, and environmental problems and enhance their social functioning. Other terms that describe clinical practice are micro practice, direct practice, and social casework. While the dominant role of clinical practitioners is that of counsellor or therapist, other common roles include broker of services, case manager, educator, mediator, and advocate. Clinical practitioners practise in a wide variety of settings that includes child welfare agencies, family service agencies, child and adult mental health centres, hospitals, schools, correctional facilities and services, and private practice. Given the range of settings within which clinical social work practice takes place, clinical social workers encounter and deal with a wide range of presenting problems, such as depression, anxiety, couple and parent/child relationship difficulties, child abuse and neglect, and environmental and social stressors (e.g., poverty, lack of social support, various forms of oppression). In many work settings, clinical social workers typically work closely with other helping professionals such as psychologists and psychiatrists. Some of the roles of other helping professionals are distinct from those of clinical social workers— for example, psychologists do psychological testing and psychiatrists diagnose mental disorders and prescribe medication—yet much overlapping occurs among helping professionals with regard to the role of counsellor or therapist. Despite such overlap, clinical social work practice has traditionally been distinguished from that of other helping professions by its greater emphasis on:

- a person-in-environment perspective that pays attention to the role of environmental and social factors in human problems;
- the normalcy of human problems;
- clients, strengths, and resources; and
- a collaborative and egalitarian working relationship that focuses on supporting and empowering the client.

Clinical social workers draw on diverse knowledge, theory, and skills. One foundational meta-theory on which they rely is ecological systems theory (Rothery 2001), used to operationalize a person-in-environment perspective. To guide the helping process, clinical practitioners also apply the generic principles and skills of the problem-solving model, those principles and skills related to engagement, data collection and assessment, planning and contracting, intervention, evaluation, and termination (Coady & Lehmann 2001). Classified as psychodynamic, cognitive-behavioural, humanistic, feminist, and post-modern approaches (Lehmann & Coady 2001), clinical theories are used by social workers, as well as other helping professionals, in individual, couple, family, and group counselling. Practitioners also need substantive and up-to-date knowledge about problems that clients frequently present (e.g., depression, anxiety, child abuse). In addition the 1994 code of ethics developed by the Canadian Association of Social Workers provides essential guidelines for all social work practice.

[*Nick Coady*]

RELATED ENTRIES

Abuse, Addiction, Assessment, Canadian Association of Social Work, Codes of Ethics, Direct Practice, Ecological Theory, Ethics, Feminist Theory, Home Care, Hospices, Medication, Micro Practice, Natural Health & Complementary Wellness, Person-in-Environment Perspective, Practice Methods, Program Evaluation, Psychotropic Therapy, Psychotropic Medication, Suicide, Theory & Practice, Therapy, Treatment, Wellness

REFERENCES

Coady, N., and P. Lehmann. 2001. The Problem-solving Model: An Integrative Framework for the De-
ductive, Eclectic Use of Theory and Artistic, In-tuitive-Inductive Practice. In P. Lehmann and N. Coady (Eds.) *Theoretical Perspectives for Direct Social Work Practice: A Generalist-Eclectic Approach*. 46–61. New York: Springer.

Lehmann, P., and N. Coady. 2001. *Theoretical Perspectives for Direct Social Work Practice: A Generalist-Eclectic Approach*. New York: Springer.

Rothery, M. 2001. Ecological Systems Theory. In P. Lehmann and N. Coady (Eds.) *Theoretical Perspectives for Direct Social Work Practice: A Generalist-Eclectic Approach*. 65–82. New York: Springer.

Moses Michael Coady (1881–1959)

Coady, Moses Michael, adult educator, co-operative and community development promoter; b. Jan. 03, 1881, Northeast Margaree, NS; founder of Antigonish Movement; d. July 28, 1959, Antigonish, NS

Born into a farming family in Cape Breton, Moses Michael Coady first trained as a school teacher and subsequently graduated in 1905 from St. Francis Xavier University in Antigonish. Father Coady was ordained a priest in Rome in 1910, simultaneously earning doctorates in theology and philosophy at the Urban College in Rome and, in the same year, returned to St. Francis as a faculty member. Five years later, he had obtained a master of education degree at the Catholic University of America and returned to Antigonish as principal of St. Francis Xavier High School and lecturer at the university. The role he played in the revitalization of the Nova Scotia Teachers' Union in 1920 and his service as its secretary-treasurer for many years presaged his career as a leader in collective action. In Antigonish, Coady worked closely with his mentor, Father Jimmy Tompkins; while vice-principal of St. Francis Xavier, Dr. Tompkins had become imbued with the mission of adult education through contacts in Britain and observation of the extension work of the University of Wisconsin. Convinced that existing institutions, especially universities, were failing to address deficiencies in the education of the majority of adults, Coady devoted much of his considerable energy to adult education. He believed that the capacities of adults were best stimulated by focusing on practical issues meaningful to them. As such, he began to guide groups of miners, farmers, and fishers in rural Nova Scotia to study reasons for their depressed economic circumstances, which were embedded in the workings of the prevailing capitalist system; he encouraged them to organize themselves to change their circumstances through the creation of consumer and producer co-operatives and credit unions. These initial efforts formed the basis for what has come to be known as the Antigonish movement.

Coady's credibility was greatly enhanced by his presentation to the 1928 federal Royal Commission on the Maritime Fisheries, the creation of which was inspired in large measure by Father Tompkins. Following a recommendation of the commission, Coady was engaged by the provincial agriculture ministry to organize fishers; from these efforts, the Maritime Fishermen's Union was established. Also in 1928, Coady became the first director of the St. Francis Xavier Extension Department, carrying out its dual mandate: adult education through co-operation. He always insisted that the Antigonish Movement was primarily concerned with adult education in the fullest sense: "We want our men ... to be men, whole men, eager to explore all the avenues of life and to attain perfection in all their faculties." The organization of co-ops and credit unions was secondary, a means to an end. Accordingly, the department's organizing process always began with the formation of study clubs, whose members were called on to think through their problems collectively before developing strategies to overcome them; the co-ops organized through the leadership of the department regularly dedicated a substantial part of their resources to continuing education. Despite the singularly difficult economic environment of the 1930s, thousands of participants organized hundreds of producer and consumer co-operatives and credit unions, with their associated study clubs in the Maritime provinces. The great majority enjoyed substantial financial success.

Coady achieved wide recognition for his work. His 1939 book, *Masters of Their Own Destiny: The Story of the Antigonish Movement of Adult Education through Economic Co-operation*, has been translated into at least seven languages. In 1949 he was elected president of the Canadian Association for Adult Education and was invited to address the plenary session of the Economic and Social Council of the United Nations. All historians and observers of the Antigonish movement attribute much of its success to Coady's charisma and

personal abilities, not least the inspirational power of his oratory: one writer describes him as "a saintly though forceful figure whose physical presence and searching intellect dominated most meetings he attended." His oft-repeated message was that the prevailing economic system exploited primary producers and workers unjustly—and, for good measure, narrowed the lives of the exploiters as well; at the same time, the people must accept some responsibility for their plight and could indeed become "masters of their own destiny" by their own efforts. To critics who said that a focus on "the prices of lobsters and lambs" was unbecomingly materialistic for a priest, Coady retorted that religious people should want to change a system "that sins against nearly every ethical principle." Coady's themes—which comprised concrete solutions for felt problems, acceptance of responsibility, and the explosive possibilities of democratic group action—resonate sympathetically with community organization and community development as practised by social workers; Coady, however, did not directly involve himself with social work. Coady retired as director of the extension department in 1952 and died of leukaemia in 1959. The work to which he had devoted his life is now carried on by the Coady International Institute. With assistance from the United Nations, St. Francis Xavier attracts considerable numbers of international students who come to learn the principles and practices of co-operation and of adult education.

[*Frank McGilly*]

RELATED ENTRIES

Antigonish Movement, Community Development, Community organization, Co-operative Movement, Social Justice

REFERENCES

Coady, M.M. 1971. (Ed.) Alexander F. Laidlaw. *The Man from Margaree: Writings and Speeches of M.M. Coady, Educator/Reformer/Priest*. Toronto: McClelland and Stewart.

codes of ethics

Codes of ethics exist in Canadian social work as in all professions to ensure protection of the public against the risks of inappropriate, incompetent, and unethical practice of social workers. This protection is offered in a general way by providing a basis where concerns or complaints related to alleged unethical behaviour can be adjudicated and remedies applied. In a more positive way, the professional association carries out on behalf of practitioners an ongoing review of the complex ethical issues that emerge in contemporary practice; this review gives direction and assistance to individual practitioners on appropriate standards of practice, as well as a forum where such issues can be discussed and reviewed. The formalizing of codes of ethics for social workers has long been the responsibility of the Canadian Association of Social Workers, the national professional association to which individual social workers belong voluntarily. In joining the national association, members committed themselves to its code of ethics. As practice has become more complex, such issues as record keeping, private practice, and the potential for abuse in the helping relationship have prompted several revisions of this national code. In the 1970s as the provinces and all the territories moved to establish their own associations, most provincial/territorial associations initially adopted the national code of ethics; inevitably, however, changes were made to individual provincial/territorial codes to respond to particular situations related to each province and accordance with the national code of ethics became less certain. Since membership in a provincial/territorial association and the national association is voluntary and since, essentially, there were few differences among the codes, adherence to more than one code created little difficulty for most practitioners. In recent years two factors have made this situation more complex. First, the public profile of social work has greatly expanded and, as the types of services being requested and expected of social workers became more complex, the potential for allegations of unethical behaviour to be levelled at practitioners greatly increased. For the first time such allegations acquired a quasi-legal nature as social work clients turned to lawyers to help them address behaviour by their social workers that they perceived as unethical. and as social workers sought to defend themselves from such allegations. Many of these cases were argued on the basis of the practitioner's adherence to or deviation from components of the respective code of ethics by which the social worker was bound. This argument, in turn, raised questions about which code of ethics should be the basis for a complaint.

Second, within provinces, such as Ontario and Alberta, with a college or board as well as a professional association both representing social workers, more than one code of ethics might bind members in addition to that of the national association. Since for the most part these associations are voluntary, the decisions of a complaints body within them reviewing issues of professional misconduct—even when argued on the basis of adherence to a code of ethics—had no legal standing. A matter of unethical behaviour taken to a provincial tribunal with legislative jurisdiction, however, would have legal standing and legal consequences.

The national association, while without a legislative basis, did help to shape provincial codes through its initial development of national standards; close co-operation between and among provincial/territorial associations has further refined individual codes so that consistency is maintained as much as possible. As legislation for social workers was developed in the provinces, codes of ethics became embedded in the statutory framework, thereby expanding the significance and sanctions of compliance for practitioners, which ceased to be voluntary. Social workers in each province with a legislated code were then bound to comply with its concept of ethical practice. One of the important roles of professional codes of ethics and legislated statutes intended to protect the public is ongoing clarification of professional social work issues for the profession as a whole, as well as for individual instances. Publications have also emerged over the years from professional associations to raise ethical implications of aspects of practice in relation to the code(s) of ethics. Thus, practitioners throughout the country have evolved clearer understandings of various kinds of ethical practice; they have been included in amendments to professional codes of ethics, which in turn greatly strengthen the ability of the profession to protect the public.

From the emergence of social work as a senior human service profession in Canada, practitioners have recognized that the practice of individual members of the profession need be governed by a common set of professional commitments and a resulting set of practice responsibilities and expectations flowing from them, as incorporated within codes of ethics. The essential nature of such codes and their ongoing reformulations have established that the primary responsibility of the social worker is to seek the good of the client; inherent in this responsibility are commitments to confidentiality and the development and maintenance of appropriate standards of competence. Having different codes of ethics nationally and in most provinces could have produced different standards of practice; in reality, the profession has challenged itself to work toward commonalties and consistency of standards throughout the country. Similar questions about differing standards in different jurisdictions arise around the issue of portability of social work competence and ethics among nations. To date, most Canadian social work issues related to codes of ethics have emanated from national and provincial practice; as practice becomes more international in scope, international ethical issues are likely to increase in importance, perhaps necessitating their addition to Canadian codes of ethics.

[*FJT*]

RELATED ENTRIES

Accountability, Canadian Association of Social Workers, Diversity, Ethics, Human Rights, International Practice, Legal Issues, Malpractice, Professional Issues, Professional Liability, Provincial/ Territorial Associations, Recording, Sensitizing Concepts

cognitive theory

The principal tenet of cognitive theory is that the major determining factor in a person's behaviour and emotions is thinking. Generally an optimistic approach to the human condition, cognitive theory encompasses a strong belief that people are able to shape and alter their significant environments, including their own inner life, to be accomplished by learning to recognize and reshape irrational aspects of their lives and their responses to others and situations. People are creative and able to find solutions to the challenges of life (Goldstein 1984). Alfred Adler is considered to be the founder of this theory; an early student of Freud, Adler's disagreements with Freud led to his development of a therapeutic approach in which a person's social drives predominate. In recent decades, several significant social work contributions have augmented this theory, for example, Harold Werner's pioneer work in 1965, *A Rational*

Approach to Social Casework (Werner 1982). Adler and Werner viewed human nature as highly flexible; for them, change comes about when people in a therapeutic milieu are able to reflect on, and alter, misconceptions in their thinking processes which create problems in their lives. In the process of treatment the client is led to focus on distortions of their own internal communications, which in turn lead to misperceiving themselves, others, and situations. To facilitate this process of rethinking, an approach to practice that draws on cognitive theory has developed a range of specific techniques, including homework in which the client maintains a written record of their responses and perceptions of various events. While this theory focuses on individual treatment in much of the initial literature, its usefulness for families and groups has been indicated in research. It has been demonstrated to be effective in the treatment of depression, when the source of the depression stems from irrational thoughts internalized by the client. Since this theory is built on a highly positive perception of the human potential, it fits well with current social work practice with its stress on strengths and a holistic perception of persons.

[*FJT*]

RELATED ENTRIES

Theory & Practice

REFERENCES

Goldstein H. 1984. *Creative Change: A Cognitive-Humanistic Approach to Social Work Practice.* New York: Methuen.

Werner, H. 1982. *Cognitive Therapy: A Humanistic Approach.* New York: Free Press.

Albert Comanor (1909–85)

Comanor, Albert, social service administrator, social activist, educator; b. Oct. 27, 1909, New York, US, d. Feb. 1985

"It was ultimately his humanity that impacted those who knew him best," reminisced Frank Clark about his colleague, Albert Comanor, at the Faculty of Social Work in the early 1970s at the University of Calgary. This sentiment was echoed by anyone who relates anecdotes about this complex, brilliant, and ethically driven man. Albert Comanor grew up in a culturally Jewish household with two brothers and a sister "imbued with a love of words" by their parents, according to his younger brother, Milton Comanor: "Even I, the baby of the family, couldn't sit down to breakfast without bringing something to read." Early success in the theatre brought an angry response from his usually reasonable father ("Don't even think of it") precipitating—so Milton recalls—a lengthy clash of wills. The resulting "non-compromise" with his father's wish for him to enter law was Comanor's earning of a bachelor's degree in economics from the University of Pennsylvania, Wharton School, in 1930, followed by a master's degree sociology, economics, and political science in 1931 and a social work certificate from the Pennsylvania School of Social Work in 1935. Milton remembers his brother as "the brightest and most articulate person I have ever known." Albert Comanor plunged with zest into a career starting as a caseworker, then supervisor with the Jewish Family and Children's Service in Pittsburgh, Pennsylvania. He continued with this work in the US Army, from which he was granted a special discharge to work in China with the United Nations Relief and Rehabilitation Administration (1945–47). From there, he became the assistant director of community relations and, later, assistant executive director for the United Service to New Americans, an international migration and resettlement agency, before returning to the Jewish Family and Children's Services as executive director in Dade County, Florida (1950–60). No account of Albert Comanor's life is complete without mention of the loves of his life, a miniature Schnauzer, Twinkle, and his wife of his last seventeen years, Pearl, also a social work educator. Equal to him in intellect and capacity, Pearl was his soul mate; he loved her more than any person on the planet and she, him. While Comanor appeared to some as overbearing, brash, cocky, and even intimidating, those children and adults lucky enough to know him well found him to be among the most warm-hearted, loving, and generous persons they had the fortune and pleasure to know.

Albert Comanor was drawn into academe by an offer of an assistant professorship from the Graduate School of Social Work at Rutgers University, New Brunswick, New Jersey, where he was promoted to professor in 1964. He then went to San Francisco State College in 1967, where his plans to develop a new social work program encountered difficulty: according to records in the University of Calgary archives, "Labour unrest and other difficulties at the College conspired against him." In January 1969 the University of Calgary lured him to Canada as a full professor. Tim Tyler, dean of the faculty at the time, had invited him for a consultation but was so impressed by his explosive enthusiasm that he found a way to hire him. Comanor remained there as a senior faculty member until his retirement in June 1975, when he was awarded recognition as professor emeritus. Not content to retire to a well-earned rest, he assumed the directorship (pro tem) of the School of Social Work at Memorial University of Newfoundland at St. John's (1976–77); he was a visiting professor with the Faculty of Social Work at the University of Regina, Saskatchewan, to assess the feasibility of a gerontology program (1977–78); and he was a part time consultant to the Faculty of Social Welfare, University of Calgary (1978–79). He finally retired to a house on the beach in Tofino on Vancouver Island, where he immersed himself in local social action and continued to be sought after as a consultant, speaker, and writer on social work and social issues until his death at the age of seventy-five. Even on his deathbed, as he moved in and out of a coma, his zeal for the truth was evidenced, according to Frank Clark, by his insistence on knowing why he was dying. "I want that diagnosis and I want it written in stone," he demanded. Albert Comanor's frequent involvement in conferences, symposia, workshops, and other training venues is reflected in the large number of papers he presented, which are now held in the University of Calgary archives along with his personal correspondence and some academic articles. His 1937 article in the journal *Social Work Today*, in which he argued for professional collaboration among social work entities and organized labour, showed his devotion to progressive causes and willingness to speak in print. His continued insistence on professionalism and involvement in professional social work issues resulted in the formation of the National Association of Social Workers. From advocating for the profession to calling for services for refugees (1940s and 1950s) and for the aged (1950s and 1960s), to political action (1960s), to social action on environmental issues (1970s and 1980s), he lived his life according to his principles.

[*Mona Acker*]

communication theory

The importance of communication theory is evident in the reliance of much social work practice on effective communication between the social worker, clients, and others. This theory focuses on communication patterns and rules of clients, which govern their interactions with others in problem-producing or -maintaining. The goal of this focus is to aid persons in developing more effective and satisfactory ways of feeling, thinking, and behaving (Greene 1996). The theory establishes basic axioms that underlie all human communications; in examining the processes and patterns by which humans communicate, the theory has developed a unique vocabulary. One important term in this lexicon is "double bind," a concept that studies patterns of communication that contain paradoxes, which in turn create confusions and a sense of being put down, which in turn creates anxiety. Communication theory emerged in the 1950s from the work of Bateson, Haley, and Jackson as well as other work carried out in The Mental Research Institute. Although not a major theory in social work practice, communication theory has been formally addressed in social work literature as well as significant writing on communications in general (Nelsen 1980). Treatment from this perspective focuses on client-defined problems and an examination of communication patterns that maintain them. In seeking to alter problematic communications, a series of techniques has been developed to include such things as reframing and behavioural prescriptions. In addition to work with individual clients, the techniques of communication theory have been used successfully by social workers working with organizational structures and communities. In working with individuals, this theory has proven effective on a broad spectrum of problems and client types, including work with depression and chronic pain, and with a special interest in couples and family problems. Communication theory underscores the importance of training and super-vision, and numerous training centres using its techniques have been developed in North America and Europe. To date the empirical base of this theory is still emerging, much of it relying on individual cases. One of the reasons this theory has not been widely accepted in the general professional ethos relates to a discomfort felt by some social workers that the interventive techniques have a manipulative quality that seems contradictory to their concept of social work values. Nevertheless, trained practitioners have achieved powerful effects using the techniques of communication theory.

[FJT]

REFERENCES
Greene, G.G. 1996. Communications Theory and Social Work Treatment. In F.J. Turner (Ed.) *Social Work Treatment.* 115–45. 4th ed. New York: Free Press.
Nelsen J. 1980. *Communications Theory and Social Work Practice.* Chicago: University of Chicago Press.

community colleges

Community colleges have a very broad mandate, which can vary significantly by province, region, and college. In general their main functions are to address the training and educational needs of business, industry, and the public service sectors, while also meeting the needs of secondary school graduates seeking a vocation. Colleges have generally offered two-year diploma and certificates; this may now be changing as some jurisdictions, particularly Ontario, move toward the granting of applied degrees. Colleges are also entering into transfer agreements (often called articulation agreements) with universities whereby students can gain credit toward university degrees for courses taken at a community college. Ontario's Humber College has gone a step further and is blending some of its programs with the University of Guelph, so that students can earn both a diploma in social services work, and a degree in family and child studies in four years. Social services diploma and certificate programs vary considerably across the country in content and length. The broadest array of social services diploma programs are in Ontario, where most colleges offer them; in other provinces, only two or three colleges may offer such programs. Social services programs in community college generally offer smaller class sizes than universities and more direct contact with faculty. This is important in social work as a field that requires individual growth and the development of critical thinking. Colleges that have signed extensive articulation agreements with university programs in social work, or which are now entering into blended programs with universities, offer both conceptual and concrete learning opportunities through a blend of theory and practice in social work. Since colleges have within their mandates the requirement that they address the economic and social needs of the communities in which they are located, many colleges with social services programs place students in local agencies. They may also become involved in what is called, in the United States, "service learning," when students contribute in some way to their community while learning about social issues and conditions and meeting people who require their help. Social services programs in community colleges also maintain close ties to employers of their graduates; employers often serve on advisory committees to many of these programs, and faculty maintain contact with their students as field supervisors. Many colleges also offer professional development and opportunities for skills upgrading to front-line workers in human services agencies.

Colleges serve a student population that is highly diverse in ages and cultures. Students from all over the world, as well as immigrants, have found in colleges a welcoming learning environment and an opportunity for upward mobility. More students with university degrees are seeking the unique hands-on training opportunities and practical experience offered in community colleges to enhance their career prospects, as most community colleges boast high job-placement rates. Mature students attending community colleges to earn academic credentials in their fields of interest find high levels of adjunct support available to them; they find colleges to be an excellent transition from work life back to academia.

The national and international voice of Canada's colleges and institutes is the Association of Canadian Community Colleges. Member colleges represent student populations of more than 900,000 full-time and 1.5 million part-time learners. More than 30,000 faculty are employed in more than 900 campuses. Annual college budgets range from $9 million to $120 million per year, and 45 to 80 percent of college funding comes from provincial or territorial governments, with the rest coming from student fees, and private, or industry contracts. The association acts as a national marketing and advocacy organization, and provides a means by which colleges can share information and experiences, and create partnerships among institutions and other agencies and sectors. The Association of Canadian Community Colleges can be found online at < www.accc.ca >.

[*Patricia Spindel*]

RELATED ENTRIES
Education in Social Work, Para-professionals, Social Services

community development

Community development, like social work, incorporates two complex concepts into a set of social practices. The concept "community" derives from the Latin *communis* (common). Cultural sociologist Raymond Williams has suggested that, by the eighteenth century in England, community was used as a term that "distinguished the body of direct relationships from the organized establishment of realm or state" (1976:75). Williams later argued that modern usage of the concept development relates to a society's planned use of resources; he noted, however, that the same word holds very different meanings if it refers to the use of resources by internal local interests or to external exploitation of the resources by others (Williams 1976: 103–104). Community development for community social workers has evolved to mean a set of practices that can be help local people to engage in relations that can improve the conditions of their lives. Whether the body of direct relationships is supported by exploiting local resources or resources in the broader society depends on the level of autonomy that the state is prepared to extend to a particular community— and has a profound impact on the way in which the social worker engages with local people. An early example of development practices in rural communities can be seen in the transformation of the imperial British Agricultural Board in the colonies during the 1790s. The board, charged with promoting good crops, dispensed knowledge necessary for proper record keeping and other fundamentals of organization for purposes of trade in the colonial outposts, imported British assumptions about local needs and predetermined agenda for local change and improvement (Talman 1933). By the 1820s, scientific ploughing techniques, 4-H clubs, and women's institutes were operating independently in thirteen district agricultural societies throughout Upper Canada.

A significant twentieth-century departure from this approach is provided by the Antigonish movement in eastern Canada. Father Moses Coady, a Catholic priest in Nova Scotia, during the great depression of the 1930s worked with extension staff at St. Francis Xavier University to establish study clubs throughout the Antigonish area. Farmers and small business people gathered in local halls to share skills and hear ideas about how local conditions could be improved; then they acted on their ideas, forming credit unions and farm co-operatives that saw them though the hard times. This mixture of grassroots and top-down community development, which took care of social as well as economic needs, persists as one model currently applied by social workers (Turner 1997: 224–36). Coady's approach was an improvement on the approach two centuries earlier of the British Agricultural Board, in that extension staff worked with the local people to determine what their local priorities were and taught local people about possible solutions. In the mid-1960s in Quebec social worker Michel Blondin promoted a new community development movement called *animation sociale*, which synthesized the confrontational approach of Saul Alinsky (1946) and the consensual approach of Murray Ross (1967). It was employed to mobilize local people to participate in a process of advocacy and pressure tactics in promotion of specific desired community changes. This approach has gained currency under the rubric of community economic development, a form of which has surfaced again recently in Ontario as the "Healthy Communities Coalition." Firmly grounded in the top-down approach, where ideas for action and strategies come from outside a community, *animation sociale* encouraged community groups to seek out consensus with authori-

ties—but "as they met with resistance at city halls and other institutions ... many turned to political action for solutions" (Jacob 1997: 91–92). In the 1970s an approach called conscientization, developed by Brazilian literacy activist Paulo Freire, was imported by Catholic missionaries returning from assignments in Brazil and has continued since. Conscientization became popular in Quebec and elsewhere in Canada. Quebecois academic social practitioners working with oppressed people through training sessions based on conscientization that are sensitive to the learning needs of disadvantaged people. Their goal was to build the confidence of the oppressed in their local strengths and solutions, rather than looking to external authority for guidance (Dore 1997: 93–94).

At the outset of the twenty-first century, a new way of looking at community social work is emerging from a deeper understanding of the concepts of community and development. Banks and Mangan (1999) conducted original research on local perceptions of neighbours about the social networks that are strengths in their lives, that is, those networks that give them autonomy, a sense of some control over the conditions of their lives. In conducting this action-research, the authors have themselves become actors in the development of the community in which they conducted their research. This is not a solitary perspective. For years, American community development commentator John McKnight has talked about capacity-based social work where residents are not clients but "citizen actors." Recently other social workers in key positions have been developing research tools, such as capacity assessment, that will help local people to identify community assets. Community development is, then, a set of practices that facilitates people in their "body of direct relationships" to identify their assets and to act on change.

[*Ken Banks*]

RELATED ENTRIES

Advocacy, Antigonish Movement, Anti-oppressive Social Work, Capacity Assessment, Church-Based Services, Citizen Participation, M.M. Coady, Community Organization, Community Service, Co-operative Movement, "Democracy Needs Socialism," Empowerment Theory, Mutual-Aid Societies, Natural Helping Networks, Non-governmental Organizations, Participatory Research, Progressive Social

Work, Radical Social Work, Sectarian Social Services, Settlement House Movement, Social Development, Social Networks, Social Planning, Social Policy & Practice, Social Justice, Social Welfare History, Theory & Practice, Voluntarism

REFERENCES

Alinsky, S. 1946. *Reveille for Radicals*. Chicago: University of Chicago Press.

Banks, K., and M. Mangan. 1999. *The Company of Neighbours: Revitalizing Community through Action Research*. Toronto: University of Toronto Press.

Dore, G. 1997. Conscientization as a Specific Form of Community Practice and Training In Quebec. In H. Campfens (Ed.) *Community Development around the World*. Toronto: University of Toronto Press.

Jacob, A. 1997. CD Issues and Trends. In H. Campfens (Ed.) *Community Development around the World*. Toronto: University of Toronto Press.

Ross, M.G. 1967. *Community Organization Theory, Principles, and Practice*. New York: Harper and Row.

Turner, F.J. (Ed.) 1999. *Social Work Practice: A Canadian Perspective*. Toronto: Prentice Hall / Allyn and Bacon.

Williams, R. 1976. *Keywords*. London: Fontana.

community organization

Community organization is a long-standing set of practices that predate community development, grounding a tradition for social workers that predates even the settlement house movement. Lappin and Ross of the University of Toronto School of Social Work, reported from a comprehensive study that community organization, as "originally perceived by the leaders of the Charity Organization Society movement, called essentially for the involvement of the affluent, leaving the friendly visitor to deal with the pauper" (Ross 1967: 3–4). Charity organization societies were assemblies of business and church leaders in the progressive era (c.1880–1920) that responded to the social devastation produced by industrialization with the belief that a systematic, even scientific, approach could be taken to resolve poverty and community disruption. Their prescriptions depended on the expertise of human services professionals and the moral suasion of dedicated men and women of the upper classes. Their influence is seen well into the twentieth century in the United Way, social

planning councils, and neighbourhood organizations formed by local business and church leaders with experts from outside a community who, for years, were mostly community social workers.

For the social worker, whose task is to identify local social needs and to plan services to address those needs, the process of community organization begins with a focus on a task or problem. Typically, this task or problem may come to the attention of, for instance, a United Way affiliate with responsibility for that particular geographic area or community, which may dispatch a social worker to assess the situation and commence action. Initially, the worker will identify existing local resources—most likely knowledgeable individuals who may or may not be connected to community agencies—that may help to address the problem. The worker might conduct interviews with local school principals, priests and ministers, members of municipal council, and key volunteers of service organizations (e.g., university women's club, Canadian Legion). An important tactic is to ask each informant for other community contacts who can also be interviewed. After a dozen or so such visits, he/she will have gathered enough information on the task or problem to begin to develop a strategy for action. The next step is to determine where community people have consensus on aspects of the task or problem. Given this agenda, the worker can then call together whichever of the informants are prepared to follow up, and form a working group to develop strategies to lead to action and community change on the task or problem.

A modified version of this approach is the visioning technique, such as the one in the World Health Organization's Healthy Communities Program; local public health departments have taken on responsibility for these programs, so the workers are often trained nurses rather than social workers. Indeed, few schools of social work still teach these approaches. In a visioning process, the worker may be invited into a community that is seen to be in transition. Initial steps are similar to the earlier process: gathering and analyzing information from key informants to guide a series of open meetings with the community. Several meetings draw out the visions of local people for enhancing community strengths, examine model projects, and focus on several doable improvements. Participants are recruited to form an association with access to municipal resources that can organize and take part in dialogue with authorities for collaborative planning and action to implement the vision. Recently, social workers have gravitated to the more grassroots approaches of community development, which is more consistent with the client-driven practices of the profession than the top-down approaches of community organization.

[*Ken Banks*]

RELATED ENTRIES

Advocacy, Antigonish Movement, Capacity Assessment, Church-Based Services, Citizen Participation, M.M. Coady, Community Development, Community Service, Co-operative Commonwealth Federation, Co-operative Movement, "Democracy Needs Socialism," E.D.O. Hill, Mutual-Aid Societies, Natural Helping Networks, Non-governmental Organizations, Organizational Theory, Participatory Research, Peer Counselling, Progressive Social Work, Radical Social Work, Self Help & Mutual Aid, Self-Help Groups, Settlement House Movement, Social Development, Social Justice, Social Networks, Social Planning, Social Policy, Social Policy & Practice, Social Welfare History, Theory & Practice, United Way, Voluntarism

community service

Social work's participation in community service was influenced historically by the themes of social reform, clinical understanding, community development, and self-help. Social reform predominated in the United Kingdom and the United States in the 1880s, when well-intended wealthy people would fund, among other facilities, neighbourhood houses for the purpose of providing leadership to local residents and addressing issues through collective action. This pattern was repeated in those countries, as well as in Canada in the 1920s and 1930s. In the United States, public health outreach proliferated in the first two decades of the twentieth century, while the role of social work remained one of social reform. By 1920 health and social services began to retreat into hospital clinics and the profession's focus moved to individual maladjustment and away from communities. In Canada this shift occurred around the end of the First World War. Community Chests and United Way organizations began to emerge to consider issues of social planning and

the collective funding of needed services. In Canada service provision seemed to split along gender lines, with many women preferring clinical services and many men favouring community involvement. In the 1960s through the 1980s the profession in Canada saw huge developments in clinical knowledge and practice, while community social service primarily featured outreach clinics to deliver developed services. Pockets of poverty and the ghettoization of people of African and Latin American ancestry in the United States began to focus the profession there on serving whole families and whole communities through self-help, prevention, and early intervention strategies. Trends in Canada followed the US experience, as real attention to community service with community development and self-help strategies was not prevalent until the mid-1980s in Canada except in some rural areas. Social workers also found that traditional practices tended not to work well for clients within the large concentrations of immigrants from non-European cultures, creating the impetus for the profession to revisit community service models with new energy and commitment. Current community service trends favour strength-based empowerment and community development strategies. Agencies in large cities often hire staff from diverse cultures to ensure sensitivity of service to language, culture, and local needs.

[*Warren Brooke*]

RELATED ENTRIES

Church-Based Services, Citizen Participation, Community Development, Community Organization, Deinstitutionalization Movement, Non-governmental Organizations, Sectarian Social Services, Social Planning, Social Policy, Social Services, United Way, Wellness

conflict resolution

Conflict resolution refers to the ways in which individuals, families, communities, corporate entities, or other social units deal with differences between/among them. Differences may be based on divergent beliefs, values, identities, or interests, whether real or perceived. The primary ways in which people deal with differences include avoidance, accommodation, competition, compromise, and collaboration, depending on whether they focus on satisfying their own interests or those of others. Professionals trained in conflict resolution techniques tend to favour collaborative processes, where they assist parties to resolve differences through voluntary amicable agreement. This contrasts with the conflict model of social work, in which social workers challenge oppressive structures in society through such unilateral action as strikes, protests, or civil disobedience. One of the tensions among conflict resolution professionals is how to balance the values of peaceful resolution with social justice, particularly significant power imbalances exist between parties. Social workers draw from a variety of theoretical bases, including systems, communication, political science, game, and ethnocultural theories, to support conflict resolution. Approaches to conflict resolution can be classified as task-oriented, power-based, rights-based, interest-based, transformative, therapeutic, and feminist. Under the task-oriented approach, parties work though a rational, sequenced problem solving designed to resolve the presenting issues in dispute. Using a power-based approach, the parties try to influence one another through competitive means. Sources of power that can be used in conflict resolution can include physical might, informational advantages, communicative skills, financial resources, and sanctioning power. Rights-based conflict resolution refers to processes in which parties debate competing legal rights or entitlements (i.e., as in a court of law). The interest-based approach encourages parties to look at underlying interests rather than positions, rights, or power to resolve their disputes. Interest-based conflict resolution focuses parties on satisfying their joint and individual interests and needs, collaborating to produce win/win solutions. The transformative approach fosters mutual understanding and empowerment between the parties, where the process is more important than outcome; this approach downplays the task of resolving a particular dispute, instead encouraging parties to listen to one another and promoting self-determination, choice, and autonomy. A therapeutic approach to conflict resolution uses methods derived from individual and family therapies to help conflicting parties deal with relational and emotional issues. Feminist approaches to conflict resolution incorporate principles of feminism into the conflict resolution practice, working to remedy power differences between the sexes, empowering the parties to develop their own decisions, and relating private issues with political ones; in their practice, social workers may play such diverse roles as negotiator, advocate, facilitator, healer, expert/consultant, and mediator. Social workers negotiate, for example, with clients on behalf of their agencies (e.g., contracting with involuntary clients to ensure that children are not abused or that offenders do not engage in criminal activities). As advocates, social workers assist clients in advancing their needs and interests, speaking on behalf of clients, empowering clients to represent themselves more effectively, or ensuring that others hear a client's voice. As facilitators, social workers help people speak and listen to one another, removing barriers to communication and creating a safe environment for people to communicate. Social workers use a variety of therapeutic processes to help people heal from the scars of past conflict. As experts or consultants, social workers can provide recommendations for how people can resolve disputes (e.g., by providing a custody evaluation for separating parents). Other conflict resolution roles—such as arbitrator, administrator, buffer, and penalizer—are less common for social workers. Common contexts in which social workers act as conflict resolution practitioners are divorce/separation cases, parent/youth conflict, victim/offender reconciliation, disputes between clients and other helping professionals, cross-cultural conflicts, and public policy development.

[*Allan Barsky*]

RELATED ENTRIES

Bullying, Communication Theory, Feminist Theory, Mediation, Organizational Theory, Peer Counselling, Practice Methods, School Social Workers, Sensitizing Concepts, Systems Theory, Theory & Practice, Treatment

REFERENCES

Chetkow-Yanoov, B. 1997. *Social Work Approaches to Conflict Resolution: Making Fighting Obsolete.* Binghampton, NY: Haworth.

Mayer, B. 2000. *The Dynamics of Conflict Resolution: A Practitioner's Guide.* San Francisco, CA: Jossey-Bass.

Congrégation de Notre-Dame de Montréal

The Congrégation de Notre-Dame de Montréal (est. 1659) was the first community of non-cloistered sisters in the land that became Canada. It was founded by Marguerite Bourgeoys, whose reason for coming from France was to establish the first school for colonists' children; recognized as Canada's first social worker, Marguerite Bourgeoys was widely known for her compassion and her refusal to accept any privilege that would set her apart from ordinary people (Martel 1982; Simpson 1997). She looked after the *filles de roi*, the women brought from France to marry settlers, affirming the importance of these women's roles in family and society, and supporting them in many different ways; her education of the women was based on the profound conviction that the future of the new country lay in their hands. Bourgeoys and her Congrégation sisters also nursed the sick, helped families with problems, and fought against poverty and family violence. The educational work of the Congrégation over the past two centuries has continued to focus on children in low-income areas with assistance to families through their role in the schools. More recently, however, the nature of their work has shifted, owing to the fact that school education is now universally provided; the Congrégation has returned to their social work roots The present mission of the Congrégation sisters is to follow Jesus in his emphasis for helping those who are poor, excluded, and marginalized, preferably by living in solidarity with them. They exercise this option for living among the poor through "liberating education," and committing themselves to participate actively in the transformation of society for a more just world. Today, the Congrégation is found in nine countries on four continents: about 1,400 sisters—1,000 of whom are francophone—in seven provinces in Canada, and another 360 sisters in other countries. The current work of the Congrégation is situated within a Christian critical social analysis, with which they seek to understand the roots of oppression in order to take action to help transform society. Their notion of "liberating education" aims to empower oppressed people to act in solidarity with one another, on their own behalves and for the transformation of their communities. Non-violence and peace are important social goals, in society and in the family. Congrégation sisters have a particular interest in the liberation of women, as well as families in difficulty, and youth. In Canada the Congrégation continue to teach in schools, but less than before. Some sisters currently work in pastoral work in parishes, prisons, and the health care system, while others focus on spiritual growth and faith education. A few work in cultural education, such as in museums devoted to Marguerite Bourgeoys. Other Congrégation initiatives are more directly linked to social work. At the macro level, Congrégation sisters are active in social action work (e.g., Groupe solidarité justice, Comité justice et foi). The Congrégation is also engaged in community practice, through the sisters' work with refugees, women, students, seniors, and small children; the Juan Moreno House in Montréal, for example, provides short-term housing for women and children refugees, and Le Baluchon, also in Montréal, is an after-school program for children living in poverty. At the micro level, the Congrégation sisters work directly with individuals and families in difficulty, providing counselling services; they are also active in literacy, employment, job training, and substance abuse rehabilitation (i.e., the Congrégation's Shalom Centre in Sydney Mines and Exodus House, both in Nova Scotia, work with women recovering from alcohol addictions). All the work of the Congrégation is interconnected with the belief that social change begins with education—education that liberates and empowers those who are marginalized and excluded.

[*Silvia M. Straka*]

RELATED ENTRIES

M. Bourgeoys, Church-Based Services, Religion, Sectarian Social Services, Social Welfare History

REFERENCES

Martel, S. 1982. *Au temps de Marguerite Bourgeoys.* Montréal, QC: Éditions Méridien.

Simpson, P. 1997. *Marguerite Bourgeoys and Montreal, 1640–1665.* Montreal and Kingston: McGill-Queen's University Press.

constructivism

Constructivism refers to the view that reality (i.e., what people perceive to be the world around them and their experience of it) is a product of human mental processes, and that people actively construct reality as opposed to mechanically react to an external objective reality; from this point of view, reality cannot be regarded as an external value-free foundation for knowledge. Constructivism is a theory relatively new to social work (Carpenter 1996), but it does have a long history within other disciplines "with roots in philosophy, psychology and cybernetics" (Von Glasersfeld 1987: 162). With only two texts within the literature devoted specifically to this theory (Fisher 1991; Rodwell 1998), social work continues to be hesitant about embracing constructivism; still, constructivist ideas do form the basis for other major social work theorizing, such as social constructionism and narrative theory. Historically, the status of reality has formed a point of disagreement between constructivist theorists. Two theoretical camps can be distinguished: the radical constructivists—such as von Foerster, von Glasersfeld, Maturano, Varela, and Watzlawick—who argue that reality does not exist beyond personal experience, and critical constructivists—such as Guidano, Hayek, Kelly, Mahoney, Piaget, and Weimer—who do not deny the existence of a real world but suggest that people co-create personal reality. What these thinkers agree about that, if reality is a construction, then as many realities exist as there are perceivers of reality. The position that experience is constructed poses questions about how such constructions are organized, and the answers reveal a divergence within constructivist thinking. Neo-Piagetian is constructivist theory, allied with the ideas of Piaget, that is mostly concerned with individual personal or psychological processes in the organization of knowing; Piagetian constructivists sought to develop theoretical models based on developmental stages that were seen as invariant and applicable to all persons and cultures. The stages determine how information was organized and whether new information would lead to the creation of new meaning and knowledge or whether it would be selectively perceived and be incorporated within old, existing structures. This approach—usually referred to as constructivist theory, sometimes personal constructivism—is the branch of theorizing that has tended to become more affiliated with education and has found greatest expression by educational theorist. On the other hand, theorists who have drawn

inspiration from Vygotsky's ideas that wider social considerations influence the organization of knowing (1978) have come to be known as social constructivists; these theorists, less allied with individualist traditions, are concerned with how social relationships influence the understanding of reality. These ideas are extended by social constructionists who are concerned with the political implications of knowledge and knowledge development, and who choose to explore the ways in which reality is constructed within society through social discourse. Social constructionists are less concerned about trying to articulate universal principles and are more interested in directing attention to society's particular habits in constructing the world. The aim of social constructionism is to demonstrate the problems that arise from these constructions or conventions, and to invite alternative conceptions of the world or what is considered to be good.

[*Keith Brownlee*]

RELATED ENTRIES

Narrative Theory, Theory & Practice

REFERENCES

Carpenter, D. 1996. Constructivism and Social Work Treatment. In F.J. Turner (Ed.) *Social Work Treatment: Interlocking Theoretical Approaches.* 4th ed. New York: Free Press.

Fisher, D.D.V. 1991. *An Introduction to Constructivism for Social Workers.* New York: Praeger.

Rodwell, M.K. (Ed.) 1998. *Social Work Constructivist Research.* New York: Garland.

Vygotsky, L. 1978. *Mind in Society: The Development of Higher Psychological Processes.* Cambridge, MA: Harvard University Press.

Co-operative Commonwealth Federation

The Co-operative Commonwealth Federation (CCF) (est. 1933) was brewed in the twin crucibles of the Great Depression and the Second World War. One following the other threatened people's sense of security and well-being, eliciting political responses to improve social welfare. In many countries, socialism and communism emerged in post-war politics; in Canada, too, the politics shifted to the left. The two main political parties had to adjust their policies, as the Canadian electorate responded to articulations from a newly formed party known as the Co-operative Commonwealth Federation or, more popularly, the CCF. Under the leadership of J.S. Woodsworth, representatives from labour and farm groups met in Saskatchewan with academics, some from the League for Social Reconstruction, to found the party. Its guiding principles were expressed in the Regina Manifesto, written by members of the league; the manifesto stated an intent to "replace the present capitalistic system, with its inherent injustice and inhumanity, by a social order from which the domination and exploitation of one class by another will be eliminated, in which economic planning will supersede unregulated private enterprise and competition, and in which genuine democratic self-government based upon economic equality will be possible" (cited in Van Loon & Whittington 1976). Initially rather militant, the new party moderated its ideological position, particularly after its federal electoral support peaked in 1944–45 without having produced a political victory. The party declared that it would no longer strive to eliminate all forms of capitalism, but would continue as a strong voice for more egalitarian national policies. CCF policies had resonance throughout Canada, prompting Conservatives to become progressive and Liberals to become more socially conscious. Prime Minister Mackenzie King, for example, asked Leonard Marsh to produce a policy report on social security that reflected ideas expressed in the UK Beveridge Report. Finkel notes that "both the Liberals and the Conservatives, wishing to stem the growth in support for socialism, began to advocate extensive programs of social insurance, labour rights, and job creation" (1997: 7). In an effort to attract more than 16 percent of the popular vote and to have greater national appeal, the CCF dissolved in 1961 to launch the New Democratic Party. Some saw this transformation as a "socialist sell-out" (Gonick 1975), while others described it as "agrarian pragmatism" (Bennett & Krueger 1971). Winn and McMenemy noted that: "Moderation of the socialist ideology was an international phenomenon. Socialist parties in Germany, the United Kingdom, and elsewhere underwent similar changes" (1976: 40). While the electorate never fully embraced the CCF, the party did have regional appeal. In a provincial election in 1933, for instance, the CCF won enough seats to become the official opposition in British Columbia. In 1934 the party formed the opposition in Saskatchewan, and in 1944 it was elected to govern that province and continued to do so for almost twenty years. In post-war Ontario, where Conservatives dominated governance for decades, the CCF in 1943 came within five seats of victory. Its successor, the New Democratic Party, was elected to govern in Saskatchewan in the late 1960s, in Manitoba and British Columbia in the 1970s, and Ontario in the 1990s.

[*Thomas E. Brenner*]

RELATED ENTRIES

H. Cassidy, Citizen Participation, Community Development, Co-operative Movement, T.C. Douglas, League for Social Reconstruction, A. Macphail, Regina Manifesto, F.R. Scott, Social Justice, Social Planning, Social Policy, Social Welfare History, J.S. Woodsworth

REFERENCES

Bennett, J., and C. Krueger. 1971. Agrarian Pragmatism and Radical Politics. In S.M. Liset (Ed.) *Agrarian Socialism: The Co-operative Commonwealth Federation in Saskatchewan*. London, UK: University of California Press.

Finkel, A. 1977. Origins of the Welfare State in Canada. In Leo Panitch (Ed.), *The Canadian State: Political Economy and Political Power.* Toronto: University of Toronto Press.

Gonick, C. 1975. A Long Look at the CCF/NDP. *Canadian Dimensions* 21–34.

Van Loon, R., and M. Whittington. 1976. *The Canadian Political Systems: Environment, Structure and Process.* 2nd ed. Toronto: McGraw-Hill Ryerson.

Winn, C., and J. McMenemy. 1976. *Political Parties in Canada.* Toronto: McGraw-Hill Ryerson.

co-operative movement

The co-operative movement refers to means through which communities can gain economic empowerment through collective ownership. (Craig 1993). Roots of the movement in Canada can be traced in large part to a group of weavers who called themselves the Rochdale Society of Equitable Pioneers, which began selling staples in a co-operative store in 1844; co-operatives spread throughout Britain in response to the traumatizing effects of industrialization, urbanization, technological advances, and large-scale farming in the mid-nineteenth century. A form of social devel-

opment, co-operatives have "always been intended by their founders as solutions to social
questions.... [T]hey address themselves to perceived inadequacies in the prevailing system of
organizing the economy: if the prevailing system
worked perfectly, no one would be impelled to
form a co-operative" Fairbairn (1990: 136). Some of
the earliest co-operatives in Canada include
mutual insurance companies, creameries, credit
unions, and grain growers' associations. An often-
cited example is the Antigonish movement,
headed by Father Moses Coady and Father Jimmy
Tompkins, which combined adult education with
economic aims that radically transformed the lives
of farmers, fishermen, and miners. Today co-operatives are found throughout Canada in forms as
diverse as daycare centres, funeral homes, and
consumer co-op stores. Co-operatives reflect community development in several ways, including
the emphasis on local control over decision making, respect for community above self-interest, the
potential role of the co-operative as a site of social
activity, and the ongoing potential for generating
additional economic activity (Kettilson 1992). The
Evangeline region of western Prince Edward Island
represents a successful tribute to the notion that a
network of co-operatives can provide a viable and
productive community development approach
(Wilkinson & Quarter 1996). Seven principles associated with the co-operative movement include
voluntary and open membership, democratic control, member economic participation, member
education and training, co-operation among co-
operatives, and concern for community, autonomy and independence (Craig 1993).

[*Linda M. Turner*]

RELATED ENTRIES

Antigonish Movement, Capacity Assessment, Citizen
Participation, M.M. Coady, Community Development, Community Organization, Co-operative Commonwealth Federation, Non-governmental Organizations, Participatory Research, Settlement House
Movement, Social Welfare History, Voluntarism

REFERENCES

Craig, J. 1993. *The Nature of Co-operation*. Montréal:
Black Rose.
Fairbairn, B. 1990. Co-operation as Politics: Mem-
bership, Citizenship and Democracy. In M.E. Fulton
(Ed.), *Co-operative Organizations and Canadian
Society*. 129–40. Toronto: University of Toronto Press.

Wilkinson, P., and J. Quarter. 1996. *Building a Com-
munity-controlled Economy: The Evangeline Co-
operative Experience*. Toronto: University of Toronto
Press.

correctional services

A correctional service encompasses a wide
range of services including correctional institutions, probation, and parole. Responsibility for
correctional services in Canada is divided between
the federal and provincial/territorial governments.
Correctional Service Canada has federal responsibility, under the solicitor general's department,
and administers the sentences of offenders sentenced under federal laws to imprisonment for
two years or more. The Corrections and Conditional Release Act, 1992, provides the legislative
mandate for the correctional service that manages federal penitentiaries for men sentenced for
federal offences, five regional centres for women
sentenced for federal offences, community correctional centres for conditional released offenders, and parole offices for the supervision of conditionally released offenders in the community.
The correctional service is responsible for the care
and custody of inmates; the provision of programs
that contribute to the rehabilitation of offenders
and to their successful reintegration into the community; the preparation of inmates for release;
parole and statutory release supervision; and
maintaining a programs of public education about
the operations of the federal service. The National
Parole Board is also responsible to the federal
solicitor general under the Corrections and Conditional Release Act, 1992; it makes independent
decisions about conditional releases, pardons, and
recommendations for clemency. The purpose of
parole is to contribute to the maintenance of a
just, peaceful, and safe society by means of decisions related to the timing and conditions of an
offender's release. British Columbia, Ontario, and
Quebec have provincial boards, with jurisdiction
for parole of offenders serving sentences in provincial correctional facilities in that province; in
provinces and territories without a provincial
parole board, the National Parole Board has jurisdiction. Provinces and territories are responsible
for offenders sentenced for provincial/territorial
offences of less than two years. Provincial/terri-
torial governments are also responsible for pro-

viding institutions for accused persons who have been remanded in custody pending trial and sentence; providing various services to the courts (i.e., pre-sentence reports); and probation services. In the provinces and territories, the ministry responsible for adult corrections varies considerably throughout the county.

Probation, which involves the conditional release of an offender into the community, is the most common form of criminal sanctioning in Canada. Consequently, the largest group of offenders who are placed under correctional supervision are those on probation. While probation is a judicial function, provincial/territorial correctional authorities are responsible for administering probation. For a variety of programs, governments may contract for services from community agencies—both non-profit and for-profit—which have become an integral part of correctional services. Throughout the history of correctional services, non-governmental agencies have worked to improve conditions in prisons and to assist offenders on their release from prison. Churches and such voluntary organizations as the Salvation Army, the John Howard Society, St. Leonard's Society, the Elizabeth Fry Society, and the Mennonite Central Committee have made significant contributions to the improvement of correctional services in Canada. Treatment interventions for offenders rely on studies by Canadian researchers, which are grounded in cognitive-behavioural approaches. Ongoing research is conducted into programs likely to increase the likelihood of an offender's successful reintegration into society and, today, the emphasis in governmental and non-governmental programs is toward more effective services based on this research. This evidence-based practice is led by Correctional Service Canada and is gaining ground in provincial and community settings. This reaffirmation that rehabilitation is the key function for correctional service provides for the possibility of a successful re-entry of offenders into communities.

[*Donald G. Evans*]

RELATED ENTRIES

E.H. Blois, Criminal Justice, Forensic Practice, Family & Youth Courts, J.J. Kelso, Kingston Penitentiary, Legal Issues, Practice Methods, Probation, Services for Offenders, Services for Youth, Wellness, Young Offenders Act, Youth Criminal Justice Act

Council on Social Work Education (US)

The Council on Social Work Education (est. 1952) is an organization committed to the preparation of competent social workers in the United States. In 2002 the council, celebrating its fiftieth anniversary, represents more than 3,000 individual members, and 146 master's and 433 bachelor's programs of professional social work education. Launched in January 1952, in New York City, the present council is recognized by the Council for Higher Education Accreditation as the sole accrediting agency for social work education in the United States. Membership includes individuals from the field of social work including graduate and undergraduate educational programs, public agencies, voluntary agencies, social work educators, field instructors, and interested persons. The twenty-nine elected board directors provide governance for the organization and establish commissions, committees, and task forces to examine relevant issues. They are able to draw on the knowledge, skills, and expertise of social workers from educational and agency fields. Board directors, who come from throughout the country and represent educational programs, faculty, practitioners, and diverse cultures, volunteer their knowledge and time. Since 1952 the council has had eighteen presidents and ten executive directors. The formation of the council emerged from the competition between and ultimate co-operation of the American Association of Schools of Social Work and the National Association of Schools of Social Administration to assert accreditation of social work degrees. A primary source of the early conflict was the proper role of undergraduate education in training students for social work practice and, in particular, training for public social services. The debate continues today regarding the relationship of undergraduate and graduate training, and the particular continuum of preparation; the original basic areas of knowledge identified were social services, human behaviour, and social work practice (casework and group work) with the later addition of community organization as an accepted concentration method. The first fifty years of the council were devoted to the quantity and quality of practitioners working in social welfare. A goal was to ensure the recruitment of professional social workers nationwide, with quality education and a foundation of skills and knowledge defined as professional social work.

Major functions of the council include faculty development, knowledge dissemination through publications and conferences, research into the goals and function of social work education, public policy (e.g., national legislation, administrative policies), and collaboration with national and international organizations in social work and related fields. Although the council has expanded its mandate throughout its history, it has held the primary role of periodic and systematic review of its member educational programs. This process of accreditation requires each school to review its programs in relation to a detailed set of educational standards set by the council; these reviews usually recur at five- to seven-year intervals. The process requires a self-evaluation of the program to be reported by the faculty. This report is reviewed by the commission on accreditation, which subsequently appoints a review team of social work educators. This team visits the university to meet with faculty, students, administration and various other constituencies. This team then provides the commission with a report on adherence to council standards. Subsequent review of this report by the commission results in a determination as to whether a program will be accredited or reaccredited, or will be required to meet certain conditions before achieving accreditation. The council limits its accreditation function to programs that prepare students for professional social work practice (i.e., bachelor's and master's degree programs); in general, associate degree programs (i.e., at community colleges) are not eligible for accreditation. In addition the council does not set standards nor accredit doctoral programs in social work; however, more than sixty such programs exist in the United States. Historically, prior to the development and acceptance of the accreditation role of the Canadian Association of Schools of Social Work, some Canadian social work programs applied for and received accreditation by the US council; at one time, programs at British Columbia, Calgary, Carleton, Dalhousie, Laval, Manitoba, McGill, Montreal, Ottawa, Toronto, and Wilfrid Laurier universities were accredited by the US Council on Social Work Education. No Canadian schools are accredited by the US council today, nor do the Canadian and US organizations have formal agreements for reciprocal recognition of one another's accreditation. Talks initiated by the Canadian national association have taken place in the past, but achieving this goal has not attracted sufficient interest; the standards in both countries do not differ dramatically. For the most part, the absence of a reciprocal accreditation agreement has not disadvantaged graduates from Canadian and US programs in employment in either country; generally, accreditation by either organization is accepted. Many Canadian social work faculty maintain individual membership in the US organization, apparently to remain abreast of US academic research, attend the council's annual program meeting, and to maintain for professional networks. Current information on the Council on Social Work Education can be found online at <www.cswe.org>.

[Ray J. Thomlison]

RELATED ENTRIES

Education in Social Work, Faculties of Social Work, National Association of Social Workers (US), Nongovernmental Organizations

counselling

Counselling refers to a social work process involving a professional relationship with a client that seeks to enhance psychosocial growth, usually through the amelioration of some problem or issue in the client's life related to him/herself or his/her interaction with others, or systemic issues. The counselling process is viewed as a professional responsibility that requires knowledge of human development and behaviour, socio-cultural issues, and systemic factors as well as skills in the ability to relate therapeutically to a broad diversity of human persons and situations. Initially, counselling emerged from Carl Roger's client-centred school as term to replace the concept of therapy or psychotherapy, on the basis that these terms had an underlying concept of pathology requiring treatment. (The client-centred theory is now referred to as personal-centred theory.) While counselling was originally seen as a term of equal status with treatment, a shift in usage implied that therapy was a more rigorous and demanding process that required a more intensive level of training, knowledge, and skill. This distinction then became caught up in the sociology of the professions, so that therapy and psychotherapy were viewed as restricted to the domain of specific professions, while counselling was viewed as a more general practice within a broader range of professions. This imprecision remains within social work, in that some practitioners understand and designate their work as a form of treatment that can be identified as therapy, psychotherapy, or psychosocial therapy, while others refer to the same activities as counselling. In Canadian social work practice counselling is provided from a broad spectrum of theories, each of which presents a specific perception of persons and situations. Whichever theoretical base underlies counselling, the social work code requires that a client's situation be assessed or diagnosed as the rationale for intervention. In this process, the wants and values of the client are to be respected, and accurate records and an ongoing evaluation are to be kept. As well as describing a social work practice, the term "counselling" also refers to the activities of any professional who engages in a process in which a client seeks the expertise of the professional in relation to some aspect of the client's biopsychosocial reality.

[*FJT*]

RELATED ENTRIES

Biopsychosocial Theory, Bioethical Issues, Bullying, Credit Counselling Canada, Peer Counselling, Personal-Centred Theory, Practice Methods, School Social Workers, Social Welfare Context, Theory & Practice, Therapy, Treatment, Wellness

creativity

Creativity has long been recognized as a significant and central component of social work practice (Gelfand 1988; Siporin 1988). Creative social work practitioners have been characterized as having a willingness to risk, from mistakes, and change; holding the ability to seek tools from a variety of methods; exhibiting a high tolerance for ambiguity, and displaying flexibility, originality, ease of expression, and the ability to redefine situations. Creativity is vital according to Gelfand: "The introduction of imaginative techniques into the daily practice of social workers in a structured and systematic manner can greatly enhance the performance of practice" (1988: 499). Another author claims that creative practitioners have "the

ability to come up with novel deviations and changes which add a distinctive touch to the schemas, or ultimately result in new schema—doing something better, or doing something quite different" (Weissman 1990: 62). An overview of the literature on creativity and social work produced a framework of five categories (Turner 1999): creative expression, creative presentation of self by the social worker, creative conceptualization at the direct practice level, creative conceptualization at the community practice level, and the "creative cosmology" paradigm. Creativity will continue to be required and called on as social work practice evolves. The point is emphasized by Ife, who claims that, if social workers are "to provide appropriate help to clients, and if they are to continue to work towards social justice, they will need to develop and display a degree of creativity and imagination generally not hitherto found in the profession" (1988: 21).

[*Linda M. Turner*]

RELATED ENTRIES

Practice Methods, Progressive Social Work, Theory & Practice

REFERENCES

Gelfand, B. 1988. *The Creative Practitioner*. New York: Haworth.

Ife, J. 1988. Social Work Education for an Uncertain Future. In E. Chamberlain (Ed.) *Change and Continuity in Australian Social Work*. Melbourne, AU: Longman-Cheshire.

Siporin, M. 1988. Clinical Social Work as an Art Form. *Social Casework* 69, 3, 177–83.

Turner, L. 1999. Forms of Creativity in Social Work: A Framework for Practitioners. *Social Work Canadian* 1, 1 (Fall), 91–97.

Weissman, H. (Ed.) 1990. *Serious Play: Creativity and Innovation in Social Work*. Silver Spring, MD: NASW.

Credit Counselling Canada

Credit Counselling Canada (est. 2000) is a national network of not-for-profit agencies and provincially/territorially legislated programs for the orderly payment of debt. It was formed to enhance the quality and availability of not-for-profit credit counselling for all Canadians. Prior to its establishment, separate services existed throughout the country and belonged to provincial/territorial bodies; the Ontario organization (est. 1918), for example, currently has 726 accredited agency members. Credit counselling agencies have helped hundreds of thousands of individuals and families resolve their debt problems and learn to use money and credit wisely. Credit counsellors review with clients their financial position to obtain a clear picture of each client's unique situation and explore solutions to resolve their problems and concerns. Many clients require only budgeting or credit guidance to manage their situation, while others benefit from assistance with arranging appropriate solutions with creditors, for instance through debt-repayment plans whereby clients pay the agency based on their ability to pay and creditors receive equitable payments. All clients receive referrals to other appropriate community services when necessary. Agencies may also provide workshops or seminars on personal budgeting and using credit wisely to businesses, community groups, schools, and the general public. Agencies can offer their services and programs at little or no cost to consumers, as funding of their programs comes largely from generous support by creditors, United Way, government grants, and voluntary contributions. Information on Credit Counselling Canada can be found online at <www.creditcounsellingcanada .ca>.

[*Carol Fraser*]

RELATED ENTRIES
Counselling, Non-governmental Organizations, Practice Methods, Theory & Practice, Treatment, United Way, Wellness

criminal justice

Criminal justice in Canada refers to the implementation and administration of the Criminal Code. The main government parties in criminal justice in Canada are the police, forensic laboratories, Crown prosecutors, the judiciary, courts, correctional institutions, probation officers, and parole boards. Numerous agencies and organizations, acting on behalf of offenders and of victims, play a role in criminal justice, as do a plethora of lawyers, para-legals, investigators, and other independent professionals. Social workers play a variety of roles as counsellors, classification specialists, or probation/parole officers. Some observers refer collectively to these components as a system, but others suggest that the complexity of Canada's criminal justice does not operate in the orderly,

well-integrated sense that the term "system" implies (Griffiths and Verdun-Jones 1994). At the heart of criminal justice in Canada is the federal Criminal Code, changes to which can be made only by Parliament. Administration of the Code, however, is a provincial/territorial responsibility, whereby courtrooms and Crown prosecutors conduct day-to-day business. Canadian criminal justice regards a violation of the Code as an offence against the state rather than against an individual. For this reason, the crime is prosecuted by an attorney who represents the Crown rather than one who represents the victim. Under subsection 722(1) of the Code, victims of crime can make a statement at sentencing about the impact of the crime on them. Other than this statement, victims have no other formal role in the prosecution of an accused other than as a witness. (The recently implemented Youth Criminal Justice Act, 2002, has its own procedures for youth who become involved in criminal justice.) for Public opinion plays an important role in the criminal justice process. In spite of a consistent downtrend in the crime rate in Canada, the public, when polled, appears to believe that there are problems with crime control. Some researchers attribute this belief to the way in which crime is used by politicians and portrayed in the media (Sprott 1999; Sprott & Doob 1997).

Criminal justice starts with the police who can be municipal employees (e.g., Vancouver Police Department), provincial employees (e.g., Sûreté de Quebec), or federal employees (the Royal Canadian Mounted Police); the RCMP provide police services in provinces or territories that do not have a separate force. Either acting on a complaint from a member of the public or on their own observation that a crime may have been committed, a police officer issues a warrant to arrest an individual. Many complaints and observations of possibly criminal behaviour do not result in an arrest but may be handled informally by the police officer involved (Cunningham and Griffiths 1997: 5–6). Information about the arrest is assessed by a Crown prosecutor who decides whether to proceed to court with the charge. The prosecutor may elect to drop the charge if he/she thinks that a trial is unlikely to result in a conviction. He/she may offer the accused person the opportunity for an alternative to the court process; for example, a person charged with shoplifting or soliciting a prostitute may attend educational or therapeutic workshops or groups as an alternative to going to trial. The prosecutor may also negotiate with the attorney for the accused for a guilty plea in return for the processing of the offence under a less serious section of the Code. If the charges proceed to a trial, the accused can plead not guilty or guilty. If the accused pleads guilty or is convicted, the judge determines what type of sentence the convicted person will receive. Options available to a judge include non-custodial and custodial sentences. Non-custodial sentencing options include:

- absolute discharge (i.e., no penalty and no official criminal record);
- conditional discharge (i.e., conditions set by the judge while under a period of supervision that, if offender meets them, result in no criminal record);
- a fine (i.e., payment of an amount of money set by the judge);
- a suspended sentence (i.e., suspension of a period of incarceration while offender is on probation and, if probation is completed successfully, offender does not serve custodial sentence); or
- a conditional sentence (i.e., incarceration served in the community, an option only available where no minimum term of imprisonment is imposed for the offence and a provincial/territorial sentence of incarceration would normally be imposed).

Custodial sentences require either federal or provincial/territorial incarceration. A federal sentence is any sentence to a period in custody of two years or more. A provincial/territorial sentence is two years less a day or less. Federal sentences generally are served in federal operated institutions but there are agreements in place that allow some federally sentenced prisoners to serve their periods of incarceration in provincial/territorial institutions. Probation is a period of community supervision that could be the sole disposition of the court, part of a suspended sentence, or an additional sentence tacked onto provincial incarceration. Any offender convicted of an offence where there is not a prescribed minimum period of imprisonment is eligible to receive a probation disposition. Probation may or may not involve reporting regularly to a probation officer. The probation order will outline expectations of the offender (i.e., to keep the peace, to be of good behaviour) as well as such conditions as attendance at rehabilitation programs or reporting to a probation officer. Parole is a period of supervision in the community that occurs after a sentence of incarceration has been partially served—a concept that dates from August 11, 1899, when Parliament enacted An Act to Provide for the Conditional Liberation of Convicts, informally known as the Ticket of Leave Act. Offenders serving time in federal institutions apply to the federal board of parole, while offenders in provincial/territorial institutions apply to the appropriate provincial/territorial board of parole. Boards of parole are arm's-length administrative tribunals that determine whether offenders who are eligible (e.g., generally after serving one third of their sentence) can be released on parole. The BC Board of Parole, for example, bases its decisions on whether an offender will not, by reoffending, present an undue risk to society, and whether the release of the offender will contribute to the protection of society by facilitating the reintegration of the offender into society as a law-abiding citizen.

[*Margaret M. Wright*]

RELATED ENTRIES

Aboriginal Issues, E.H. Blois, Correctional Services, Criminal Justice, Cults, Ethics, Forensic Practice, Family & Youth Courts, J. Gandy, J.J. Kelso, Kingston Penitentiary, Legal Issues, Practice Methods, Probation, Services for Offenders, Services for Youth, Wellness Young Offenders Act, Youth Criminal Justice Act

REFERENCES

Cunningham, A.H., and C.T. Griffiths. 1997. *Canadian Criminal Justice: A Primer.* Toronto: Harcourt Brace.
Griffiths, C.T., and S.N. Verdun-Jones. 1994. *Canadian Criminal Justice.* 2nd ed. Toronto: Harcourt Brace; Ottawa: Justice Canada.
Sprott, J.B. 1999. Are Members of the Public Tough on Crime?: The Dimensions of Public Punitiveness. *Journal of Criminal Justice* 27, 5, 467–74.
Sprott, J.B., and A.N. Doob. 1997. Fear, Victimization, and Attitudes to Sentencing, the Courts, and the Police. *Canadian Journal of Criminology* 39, 3, 275–91.

crisis intervention

Crisis intervention focuses on the immediate relief of symptoms. The term "crisis" is defined in diverse ways, as a "subjective reaction to a stressful life experience" (Bard & Ellison in Roberts 1990: 8), a "temporary state of upset and disorganization" (Slaikeu 1990: 15), an "upset in a steady state" (Parad 1965: 24), and an "acute emotional upset" (Hoff 1995: 4). Perhaps the explanations most helpful to social work are Greek and Chinese: the Greek word *krinein*, from which "crisis" is derived, meaning decision making or, more broadly, turning point, while the Chinese symbol for crisis (*wei ji*) is composed of two characters, which mean danger and opportunity (Slaikeu 1940: 15). These two meanings capture the dual reality of crisis work—where there is danger (things can get worse), but also opportunity for informed decision making and for turning the crisis into a positive turning point. The roots of crisis intervention lie principally in psychiatry, and the original focus was on the mental health crises of psychiatric patients. Now, the practice of this brief mode of intervention encompasses a wide range of presenting problems; it has developed clearly delineated intervention goals for restoration of a client to a precrisis level of functioning, and for helping a client to develop new adaptive coping methods, rather than insight or growth. In crisis intervention, the social worker may assume a direct, active, and goal-oriented role, and may mobilize community resources to assist the client through the crisis; moreover, the social work values of self-determination and focus on client strengths are still emphasized in crisis intervention (Golan 1978).

Models of crisis intervention have been developed by such social work theorists as Rappaport's three-stage model (Rappaport 1967) and Golan's three-phase model (Golan 1978). More recently, Roberts (1991) proposed a seven-stage model, which includes assessing lethality and safety needs, establishing rapport and communication, identifying the major problem, dealing with feelings and provide support, exploring possible alternatives, assisting in formulation of an action plan, and following up. Another comprehensive model of crisis intervention identifies two levels of crisis intervention: psychological first aid (first-order intervention), and crisis therapy (second-order intervention) (Slaikeu 1990); this model identifies two possible levels of intensity in intervening in a crisis and provides for possible roles for para-professionals, family members, and front-line caregivers. While much crisis intervention literature has a strong direct practice focus, crisis models can be applied to families, groups, or communities. Further, from its earliest beginnings, crisis intervention has had a preventive focus (Slaikeu 1990: 10), which has led to the creation of suicide prevention programs, crisis lines, drop-in centres, and eventually to crisis programs and agencies that respond to such diverse situations as sexual assault, family violence, psychiatric emergencies, medical conditions, school trauma, and community disasters. Crisis intervention has long been an integral fact of social work practice, and will continue to be a primary mode of intervention, particularly in response to economic restraint, increased caseloads, and calls for greater effectiveness and efficiency (Golan 1978: xii). Despite critiques that crisis theory has tended to disregard the impact of social, structural, and systemic dimension of crisis, or that it is merely band-aid intervention (Hoff 1995: 6), research in Canada indicates that social workers in direct practice with HIV/AIDS work see crisis intervention as one of their primary intervention modalities (CASW 1995: 7). Studies on the effectiveness of crisis intervention are sparse and research that evaluates the outcomes of specific intervention techniques is nascent (Roberts 1990: xvi). Social work has made significant contributors to this multidisciplinary and multi-faceted field (Golan 1978; Parad 1965 and Roberts 1991) and is seen as having to offer in modern, effective, crisis intervention services.

[*Brian Ouellette*]

RELATED ENTRIES

Abuse, Counselling, Direct Practice, Disaster Practice, HIV/AIDS, Marital & Family Problems, Practice Methods, School Social Workers, Sensitizing Concepts, Suicide, Theory & Practice, Therapy, Torture & Trauma Victims, Treatment, Vicarious Traumatization, Wellness, Women Abuse

REFERENCES

CASW. 1995. *Social Work Practice and Practice Wisdom in the Field of HIV/AIDS Research Report*. Ottawa: Canadian Association of Social Workers.

Golan, N. 1978. *Treatment in Crisis Situations*. New York: Free Press.

Hoff, L.A. 1995. *People in Crisis: Understanding and Helping.* San Francisco, CA: Jossey-Bass.

Parad, H.J., and L.G. Parad. 1965. *Crisis Intervention: Selected Readings.* New York: Family Service Association of America.

Roberts, A. 1991. *Contemporary Perspectives on Crisis Intervention and Prevention.* Englewood Cliffs, NJ: Prentice Hall.

Slaikeu, K. 1990. *Crisis Intervention: A Handbook for Practice and Research.* Boston: Allyn and Bacon.

cults

A cult is one of a wide variety of groups broadly characterized by collective behaviour that is unorthodox and possibly anti-social, and may be expressed through ritual or religious devotion. A cult may have begun as a splinter group in a state of tension with a predominant religious group; another may be a new religious movement on its way to becoming a religious denomination. Examples of prominent cults are the Hare Krishna and the Unification Church (or Moonies). Cults are often portrayed in the media as threatening or dangerous, as for instance when the Aum Shinriko cult released the nerve gas Sarin into the Tokyo subway, killing six people. In most cases, however, cults may be most destructive to the members themselves. Cults are associated with the use of deceptive practices and/or mind-control techniques to retain members, who are typically encouraged to sever ties with their family and friends. Members of some cults have been required to surrender property and years of their lives by working for the leader, who is usually charismatic and holds the devotion of cult members who believe in the leader's abilities, character, and knowledge. In extreme cases, membership in a cult leads to the death of all or some of its members, such as the 913 followers of Jim Jones in Guyana in 1978, the 39 Heavens Gate members who committed suicide in 1997, and the 6 deaths by shooting and 80 by fire as a result of the 1994 siege and assaults by US officers on the Branch Davidians in Waco, Texas. In March 1997, 5 members of the Order of the Solar Temple committed suicide in a house in St-Casimir, Quebec. Apparently believing that they would travel to the star Sirius after death, these people set fire to the house, bringing to 74 the number of lives claimed by this cult since 1994. Many of the victims were well educated and successful, including the former mayor of Richelieu.

Among theories about the process of becoming a member of a cult, Sirkin (1990) identified five stages in the process of cult affiliation: hooking, joining, intensification and social disengagement, and realignment. Several family dynamics are related to cult affiliation by their children. A child with parents who set standards unlikely to be attained, for example, may feel driven to seek acceptance and reinforcement from a cult (Wynne 1958). Families with a high rate of involvement of their children in cults express less emotion and more criticism (Sirkin 1990). Wright and Piper (1986) noted that alienation from family relationships precedes cult membership. Zimbardo and Harley (1985) reported that 50 percent of high school students included in their survey had been approached about joining a cult. While cults have high conversion rates, they also have high rates of defection (Bromley 1991). Stoner and Parke (1977) divided cult disaffiliation into the stages of re-evaluation of life in the cult, readjustment to life outside the cult, and reacceptance of life outside the cult. According to Goldberg (1982), cult members who undergo deprogramming move through three stages: initial post-deprogramming, when individuals still exhibit many symptoms of their cult behaviour and personality; re-emergence of precult personality; and integration of cult experiences into their lives. Ash (1985) listed depression, guilt, shame, fear, and anger as part of the former cultist's affective demeanour, with the provision that, where conflicts were part of the member's precult personality, they will re-emerge during cult disaffiliation. Cult affiliation affects the cult member and his/her family members (Robinson & Frye 1997). Social workers should refer former members for a complete medical examination, as they are likely to have had a poor diet and a generally unhealthy lifestyle. The second need requiring a social worker's intervention is the ex-members' psychological need to cope with the cognitive and emotional aspects of the cult experience, especially such separation problems as adjusting to the outside world, confronting lingering doubts about leaving, and coping with a sense of personal failure (Bromley 1991). Families may need help in resolving issues and problems that occurred before cult membership, as well as issues that surfaced and accelerated during cult involvement. Members of a cultist's family may need therapy to deal with issues arising from the cultist's decision to remain in a cult rather than return to the family. Families that have attempt to remove family members in a cult in an attempt to deprogram them have met with mixed success. Likely, much-publicized cult tragedies are only a small percentage of cults operating in Canada. Secrecy surrounding particular cult practices and beliefs make it difficult for researchers and mental health professionals to estimate of the number of people affected by cults, or to determine appropriate actions. Evidence that the Solar Temple cult tried to expand into Manitoba in 1993 could not be verified, for instance, as information abut the cult operation has not been available since the 1997 fire. Determining when a group is becoming destructive cult is also complex. Educating the public about the nature of destructive cults and providing training for therapists who deal with families are two ways to deal with the effects of cults in Canadian society.

[*Peter J. Doherty*]

RELATED ENTRIES

Counselling, Organizational Theory, Peer Counselling, School Social Workers, Services for Children, Services for Youth, Theory & Practice, Wellness

REFERENCES

Ash, S.M. 1985. Cult-induced Psychopathology, Part 1: Clinical Picture. *Cultic Studies* 2, 31–90.
Bromley, D.G. 1991. Unravelling Religious Disaffiliation: The Meaning and Significance of Falling from Faith in Contemporary Society. *Counseling and Values* 12, 67–78.
Goldberg, L. 1982. Group Work with Former Cultists. *Social Work* 27, 165–70.
Robinson, B., and E.M. Frye. 1997. Cult Affiliation and Disaffiliation: Implications for Counselling. *Counseling and Values* 41, 2, 166–88.
Sirkin, M.I. 1990. Cult Involvement: A Systems Approach to Assessment and Treatment. *Psychotherapy* 27, 1, 116–23.
Stoner, C., and J.A. Parke. 1977. *All Gods Children: Salvation or Slavery?* Radnor, PA: Chilton.
Wright, S.A., and E. Piper. 1986. Families and Cults: Familial Factors Related to Youth Leaving or Remaining in Deviant Religious Groups. *Journal of Marriage and Family* 48, 15–25.
Wynne, L.C. 1958. Pseudomutuality in the Family Relations of Schizophrenics. *Psychiatry* 21, 205–20.
Zimbardo, P.G., and C. Hartley. 1985. Cults Go to High School: A Theoretical and Empirical Analysis of the Initial Steps in the Recruitment Process. *Cultic Studies Journal* 2, 91–147.

culture

Culture, as it is used in social work practice, is difficult to define, as the term is used inconsistently. In particular, it is often viewed as co-terminous with "ethnicity"; this usage is especially prevalent in US literature, which is frequently used in Canadian faculties and schools of social work. For some people, cultural and ethnic identity might be identical. In Canadian usage, the term "culture" refers to the patterns of customs, values, behaviours, and traditions found in an identifiable group of persons that are formed or shaped by their identification with a particular geographic location. Reference is often made to "Canadian culture" as meaning those sets of values, interests, customs, and attitudes that are commonly found in someone who identifies themselves as being Canadian. A broader use of the term refers to North American culture as those commonalties of personality that would mostly but not universally be found in persons from North America that might differentiate them from someone from, for example, India. "Ethnicity" is generally to be understood in a more focused way as referring to a person's identity with his/her historical origins or background. It sometimes spoken of as a singular term (i.e., Irish or Pakistani or Vietnamese); increasingly in Canada's multicultural diversity, ethnicity is spoken of as double or multiple (i.e., Polish-Scots, Finnish-Canadian, or German-French-Brazilian).

From a social work perspective, it is interesting that many aspects of a client's personality may come from their cultural or ethnic identity as much as from being Canadian. It is important for practitioners not to overlook differences between the two concepts. For example, a person who is a Canadian with Polish and Irish roots might be different from his brother living in the United States who might also identify himself closely with the same roots but might also be influence by his identity with American culture. In Canada and the United States, a broad diversity of ethnic identities exist, which might influence to some extent the worldview of persons attached to them. But there also exists a Canadian culture, which in its formation over the years has developed some commonalties despite ethnic differences. As social work continues to focus on the importance of understanding diversity, it is important not to let this term become oversimplified. Rather, diversity needs be viewed as a many-faceted phenomenon that creates subtle but powerful similarities as well as differences between/among people. A segment of this diversity is a person's cultural identify, stemming from his/her identify or lack thereof with a large component of the world's population.

[*FJT*]

RELATED ENTRIES

Aboriginal Issues, Aboriginal Services, Diversity, Ethnic-Sensitive Practice, Ethnocultural Communities' Services, Healing Theory (Cree), Peer Counselling, Minorities, Racism-Sensitive Social Work, Sensitizing Concepts, Visible Minorities

Dalhousie University Maritime School of Social Work

The Maritime School of Social Work of Dalhousie University (est. 1941) was founded to meet the need for professional education in social work in the Atlantic region. It is the fourth oldest school of social work in Canada after Toronto, McGill, and British Columbia. Beginning as an independent school operated by a board of trustees, it affiliated during the 1950s with five maritime universities: Acadia, Mount Allison, Saint Francis Xavier, Saint Mary's, and the University of King's College. Membership in the board of trustees included the presidents of the affiliated universities, deputy ministers of provincial departments of social welfare in the Atlantic provinces, and individuals from business, social work, and community organizations throughout the region. Faculty of affiliated universities also served on admissions and curriculum committees together with faculty from the school. These five universities granted master's degrees in social work to students who had undergraduate degrees and who had fulfilled academic and field requirements for the two-year program. In addition provision was made for

admission of a limited number of employed social service practitioners who did not have undergraduate degrees; they were awarded a diploma on successful completion of the program (Hancock). This arrangement lasted until 1969 when the school joined Dalhousie University, where it is currently located in the Faculty of Health Professions along with professional schools for nursing, occupational therapy, physiotherapy, health services administration, human communication disorders, health and human performance, pharmacy, and allied health professions. The school also relates to the Faculty of Graduate Studies with respect to the master's program. In 1980 following a national trend, the school established a bachelor of social work program, which was offered on campus and decentralized to several sites in the maritime provinces. Decentralized programs were successful in making a first professional degree in social work accessible to persons employed in social welfare and related human services who could not relocate to Halifax because of employment, family, and community responsibilities. Staff in social services, the majority of whom were women, were afforded an opportunity to upgrade their qualifications for the positions they held and enhance their career potential.

The school's affirmative action and educational equity initiatives—implemented in the master's program in the 1970s for members of indigenous Aboriginal, Black, and Acadian communities—were extended to the bachelor program on campus and in decentralized sites. As much of the student body was comprised of experienced, mature persons often carrying full time work, parenting, and community responsibilities, adult education philosophies and methods were selected as the most appropriate models in both decentralized and on-campus programs. A strong feature of the decentralized bachelor program was a model of community involvement in planning and delivery, incorporating two central themes. One consisted of advisory committees in every site, composed of representative students, employers, labour, and culturally and ethnically diverse communities. The second theme was an extensive degree of co-operation with other maritime universities—University College of Cape Breton, University of Prince Edward Island, University of New Brunswick at Saint John, and University

Ste. Anne—and with major employers, community groups, and professional associations in the maritime provinces. The model developed for decentralized bachelor programs in the 1980s harmonized with the themes of co-operation among universities, governments, employers, and other interested parties, as well as with the affirmative action initiatives that were part of the founding vision and a forerunner of the current emphasis on co-operation in order both to maintain quality programs and conserve limited resources. In addition to decentralized programs, the school and Mi'kmaq communities in Nova Scotia initiated a bachelor of social work program for employees of Mi'kmaq social agencies. This five-year externally funded project operated with the assistance of advisory and curriculum committees, a full-time co-ordinator and academic skills instructor. It was designed to connect social work theory and practice with Mi'kmaq culture, ways of knowing, and community life in order to assist Mi'kmaq communities to take over such social programs as family and child welfare, addictions and family violence, and to shape these programs to meet more adequately the social and health needs of Mi'kmaq communities. Certificate courses were also offered in community health and alcohol/drug treatment for staff of First Nation programs.

Today the Maritime school is one of four schools of social work in the Atlantic provinces and one of more than thirty in Canada. The undergraduate and graduate degree programs are offered on a full- and part-time basis on campus, and part-time through distance education to students from throughout Canada. The current student body numbers well over three hundred students: just under two hundred in the bachelor program and more than one hundred and twenty in the master's program. Of this number, more than seventy students are enrolled in the undergraduate and just under forty in the graduate distance education programs. Distance education programs rely primarily on Internet-based instruction, field work done onsite under the supervision of local practitioners and with administrative personnel to co-ordinate programs and technical support. By far the majority of students entering the bachelor program have an undergraduate degree and many have work experience in human services. In addition to core courses in

social policy, history and ethics, practice theory, community development, and research, field practice is required. Admission to the master's degree, a five university-credit program, depends on having a bachelor of social work degree and work experience. The field program operates in close co-operation with human service agencies and community-based programs locally, regionally, and nationally. Both programs are fully accredited by the Canadian Association of Schools of Social Work. Faculty members have a range of research, scholarly, professional, and community interests which are reflected in the core and elective curriculum. The undergraduate and graduate levels incorporate analyses of systemic inequity based on such social factors as gender, sexual orientation, ethnicity, culture, poverty, and physical challenges. School faculty over the years have developed theory and practice in feminist, structural, anti-racist approaches in social work (currently combined under the umbrella of anti-oppressive practice). Reflecting contemporary global interconnections among human needs, social problems, and eco-political issues, the school has participated in international projects, the most recent being in child welfare. Funded under the Canada/European Union program for co-operation in higher education, the school partnered with other Canadian and European schools to develop child welfare curricula in an international context. This project involved student exchange, international conferences, publications, and an Internet-based course in child welfare. Since 1987, the school has also had a strong and vibrant continuing education program, which offers a wide range of professional development courses and workshops to social workers and related human service professionals in various locations in the maritime provinces. This program employs a full-time co-ordinator and support staff and is operated with an advisory committee made up of representatives from major fields such as health, community services, and community volunteers.

The Maritime School of Social Work has been a pioneer and leader in post-secondary education in the fields of feminism, diversity, and affirmative action in both its recruitment of students and its curriculum. The maritime regional consciousness that the school has consistently incorporated into its program is now expanding to include national and international themes. The school remains committed to ensuring that its academic programs are accessible to members of the diverse communities, notably African Nova Scotian and Mi'kmaq and other First Nations, persons with physical challenges, and mature persons who are working in the field of human services. Its affirmative action policies begun in the early 1970s have produced an enviable record of admitting and graduating students from diverse communities who go on to hold responsible positions in social work and, as such, have contributed to advancement of anti-oppressive practice as individuals and through such organizations as ABSW (Association of Black Social Workers), MFCS (Micmac Family & Children's Services), Persons with Disability Commission. Current information about the Maritime School of Social Work can be found online at < www.dal.ca/socialwork>.

[Joan Gilroy]

RELATED ENTRIES

Anti-oppressive Social Work, Diversity, Education in Social Work, Faculties of Social Work, Nova Scotia Association of Social Workers, Racism-Sensitive Social Work

REFERENCE

Hancock, L.T. *The History of the Maritime School of Social Work, 1941–1969.*

Dawn of Ampler Life

Dawn of Ampler Life (1943) was a report written by Charlotte Whitton at the request of John Bracken, then leader of the Conservative party. The report consisted of Whitton's analysis and comparisons of various contemporary designs for social welfare as might be developed and implemented after the Second World War. Unlike many observers at the time, Whitton criticized Leonard Marsh's report recommending social welfare strategies, which had been based on the philosophy of William Beveridge's report in Britain. Two of her major criticisms of Marsh's report were that it did not respond to the needs of Canadian citizens and it overemphasized income security.

[FJT]

RELATED ENTRIES

W.H. Beveridge, H. Cassidy, Canadian Council on Child Welfare, L. Marsh, Marsh Report, Social Welfare History

deafness

Social work service to people who live with deafness has many challenges. People who identify themselves as deaf need to be perceived in similar ways to other clients seeking to solve problems; if the sole focus rests on a client's deafness, the opportunity to see significant linguistic and cultural differences may be lost. Within audiological, linguistic, and cultural literature on deafness, observers sometimes spell the word "deaf" differently to differentiate audiological limitations indicative of severe-to-profound hearing loss ("deaf") and members of a linguistic and cultural community ("Deaf") (Toth 1999, Hill 1993); people who identify themselves as Deaf may or may not meet audiological deficit requirements, although they use sign language and are accepted as members of the culturally Deaf community (Woodward 1972). Deafness has been defined in relation to onset as well as by degree of hearing loss. The Canadian Hearing Society describes most hearing loss as congenital, conductive, or sensorineural. Congenital hearing loss is associated with a biological condition that occurs before or at birth. Conductive hearing loss is a loss of hearing sensitivity resulting in the inability of sound to pass from the outer ear through the middle ear, frequently associated with problems of the bones in the middle ear, a closing off of the canal by atresia, or a narrowing of the canal by stenosis. Sensori-neural hearing loss is permanent and reflects damage to the hair cells in the inner ear or along nerve pathways to the brain as a result of complications in pregnancy, birth, disease, the toxic effect of drugs, or trauma to the skull. The society uses a fourth category, "mixed," to describe a combination of sensori-neural and conductive damage. As well, hearing loss can be inherited. Audiological assessments provide information about the degree and impact of hearing loss, to be analyzed and explained by audiologists and speech-language pathologists. Figure 1 offers a general understanding about what an audiogram can indicate about the degree of hearing loss and its implications for receiving and producing verbal language (CHS 1999).

Deafness ranging from mild-to-profound hearing loss may be experienced within the population as a whole, and many people may use assistive devices or have surgery to augment or repair

FIGURE 1: Degree of Hearing Loss

Degree of hearing loss	Audiogram Decibel Level (dB)	Manifestation
Normal hearing	Very soft levels between –10 to –5 dB can be heard.	All speech sounds heard, even when whispered.
Mild	Without amplification and/or changes to the listening environment, people who score 16 to 50 dB will not hear all speech sounds.	Most vowel sounds can be heard, but some consonant sounds such as "th," "f," "s," "h" may be difficult to hear or missed altogether.
Moderate	Cannot hear normal conversation without the use of hearing aids or other devices when audiogram shows 51 to 70 dB.	Conversation will sound very faint and may consist of vowels only.
Severe	Cannot hear normal speech sounds when audiogram shows a hearing loss between 71 and 90 dB.	Speech may or may not be detected even when spoken loudly or close to the ear.
Profound	Little or no measurable hearing if audiogram shows a hearing loss greater than 90 dB.	Even with hearing aids, most speech sounds will not be detected and atonal voice quality will be present.

audiological damage (CHS 1999). Deafness for children requires different considerations depending on when hearing loss occurs. While pharmacological or surgical treatment can result in the improvement or restoration of hearing, greater difficulty may be experienced in the ability to understand or produce language by a child who loses his/her hearing before he/she has learned to speak (pre-lingual) than for the child whose hearing loss occurs after speech and spoken language have been acquired (post-lingual) (CHS 1999). Language may, however, be acquired in a visual, gestural form of signed language and may be used to provide a child with a viable means of communication even as auditory and verbal therapy continue to be pursued (Drasgow 1998; Wilcox & Wilcox 1991). A child may be educated in a mainstream school with the assistance of interpreters and devices, or may be admitted to a special school where he/she could expect to be taught through a signed language (i.e., the American Sign Language), a written language, and exposure to teachers and students who also have hearing loss. Children who have a hearing loss of at least 70 decibels are considered to be "deaf" and may be eligible for assistance in special education (i.e., as under an Ontario program [1997]), as described by admission criteria of schools for the deaf (Robarts 1996). Because degree of hearing loss may not be immediately identified and parents may initially prefer to pursue speech therapy and the use of augmentative communication methods and devices, children may consider themselves as being hearing impaired or deaf long before they learn sign language or become involved in activities of Deaf cultural communities.

Deafness presents psychosocial considerations for social workers. While social and educational difficulties presented by hearing loss are significant, people who are deaf have to face even greater communication challenges. Most deaf children are born to hearing families and only 10 percent of the population can be expected to be deaf (Sacks 1990); the resulting isolation of deaf people has made communication an important factor in the way in which professionals work with them. Attempts to address deafness-as-disability and deafness-as-difference have uncovered stresses to accommodate limitations imposed by deafness in the family, school, community, and workplace; these issues have been the focus of a variety of therapeutic interventions (Toth 2000). Many people, having taken stock of their deafness, have decided to join the hearing population by whatever means available (i.e., hearing aid, cochlear implant, oral method). Others have actively cultivated relationships with those who use signed language and identify themselves as members of the culturally Deaf community; such people may not want or need to overcome their deafness and become hearing in order to be considered "normal," in fact, identifying themselves as Deaf and not disabled for socialization, marriage, creation of artefacts, and exchanges of information about everyday living. Social workers can best serve clients who are deaf by considering the whole person within his/her situation, as well as how deafness is perceived by the client. Trained to empathize with clients' circumstances, social workers have a unique ability to honour difference and use those it to help clients help themselves.

[*Anne Toth*]

RELATED ENTRIES

Developmental Challenges, Developmental Challenges & Families, Personal-Centred Theory, Physical Challenges, Minorities, Practice Methods, Sensitizing Concepts, Visual Impairment, Wellness

REFERENCES

Bienvenu, M.J. 1991. Can Deaf People Survive Deafness? *Perspectives in Deafness* 41, 21–25.
Calderon, R., and M. Greenberg. 1993. Considerations in the Adaptation of Families with School-aged Deaf Children. In M. Marschark and M. Clark (Eds.), *Psychological Perspectives on Deafness*. 27–47. Hillsdale, NJ: Lawrence Erlbaum.
CHS. 1999. *Starting Point: A Resource for Parents of Deaf or Hard of Hearing Children*. Toronto: Canadian Hearing Society.
Drasgow, E. 1998. American Sign Language as a Pathway to Linguistic Competence. *Exceptional Children*. 64, 3, 329–42.
Gannon, J. 1981. *Deaf Heritage: A Narrative History of Deaf America*. Silver Spring, MD: National Association of the Deaf.
Hill, P. 1993. The Need for Deaf Adult Role Models in Early Intervention Programs for Deaf Children. *Journal of Canadian Educators of the Hearing Impaired* 19, 6, 12.
Padden, C., and T. Humphries. 1988. *Deaf in America: Voices from a Culture*. Boston, MA: Harvard University Press.
Lucas, C. (Ed.) 1989. *The Sociolinguistics of the Deaf Community*. San Diego, CA: Academic.
Mendelsohn, M., and F. Rozek. 1983. Denying Disability: The Case of Deafness. *Family Systems Medicine* 1, 2, 37–47.
Sacks, O. 1990. *Seeing Voices: A Journey into the World of the Deaf*. New York: HarperCollins.
Toth, A. 1999. Improving the Delivery of the Sign Language Instruction Program for Parents of Children Who are Deaf and Receiving Services from a School for the Deaf. [Unpub. practicum report.] Fort Lauderdale, FL: Nova Southeastern University.
Toth, A. 2000. Reducing the Risk of Psychosocial Problems for Children Who Are Deaf at a School for the Deaf. [Unpub. practicum report.] Fort Lauderdale, FL: Nova Southeastern University.
Wilcox, S., and P. Wilcox. 1991. *Learning to See: American Sign-language*. Englewood Cliffs, NJ: Regents/Prentice Hall.
Woodward, J. 1982. *How You Gonna Get to Heaven if You Can't Talk with Jesus: The Educational Establishment vs. the Deaf Community*. Silver Spring, MD: T.J. Publishers.

deinstitutionalization movement

The movement for deinstitutionalization emerged in the early 1950s. It sought to move large numbers of elderly people, as well as persons with, for example, intellectual, developmental, and physical challenges, from big publicly financed institutions into a variety of much smaller, more community-based and specialized settings. This movement had strong public support, some on humanitarian grounds as increasing publicity was given to real and alleged negative aspects of populous institutions; other support was motivated by the saving of public dollars in the belief that less expensive methods of caring for such citizens could be found in community care. Lobbying by groups of institutional residents for less restrictive care and a more normal lifestyle was given support by many helping professions. Advances in pharmacology and community-based psychosocial services assisted many persons to demonstrate that they did not need the restrictive life of the big institutions but could function and enhance personal growth in community facilities. As a result, the emptying and closing of institutions became popular among professionals and politicians, with firm public support. There is much less agreement, however, as to whether moving the former residents of large institutions into communities has been beneficial to them. Clearly, the movement has resulted in a broad expansion and community acceptance of a range of targeted services and specialized group-living arrangements. Many persons in these living arrangements have more satisfying lives with more opportunities than before for personal growth and for living closer to relatives and friends, in a community familiar to them. Accompanying trends are a reluctance to consider institutionalization as a first response to persons in need, and much briefer stays when institutionalization is deemed necessary. On the other hand, the available community services have proven to be very expensive and, frequently, public funds are insufficient to support needed resources. Some community residents may not be fully supportive of some types of services, such as neighbourhood group homes. Finally, as not everyone can function in a community-based arrangement, the need for institutions continues. At the outset of this millennium, a slight shift in the negative perceptions of larger institutions is producing calls for the identification of the proper and most beneficial roles of such institutions to foster the optimum development of each person's potential without the earlier negative effects of institutional living.

[*FJT*]

RELATED ENTRIES

Caregiving, Case Management, Community Service, Developmental Challenges, Social Planning, Social Policy, Social Services, Theory & Practice, Treatment, Wellness

democracy needs socialism

A catchphrase in Canadian social welfare, "democracy needs socialism" arose from the title of a 1938 book written by the research committee of the League for Social Reconstruction. Framers of many pieces of social legislation, the league's researchers used ideas from this book, arguing that the values and the participatory and democratic goals underlying the ideas should be reflected in programs to help Canadian citizens. Socialism, active at the time, was a system that emphasized positive and active citizenship, social cohesion, and concern for the quality of community life balanced with healthy and fulfilling individual life. The phrase "democracy needs socialism" is founded in beliefs developed and extended since the publication of the book, and is used to reflect the ideas that citizens should be encouraged, through open and accessible formal and informal avenues—including societal organizations and institutions—to intervene in political, economic, cultural, gender-based, national, ethnic and other issues without unreasonable fetters. Popular notions of democracy in nations such as Canada focus on such formal political dimensions as election campaigns, political parties, legislative bodies, and media circulation of democratic activity. By contrast, proponents of the view that "democracy needs socialism" hold a broader concept of democracy; they cite low voter turnout and participation in political parties as indicators that citizens have little involvement. Instead, they note that citizens ought to participate more actively, to intervene against societal forces—notably capitalism—that affect citizens and impinge on them unevenly and unfairly. One current aim is to counter what is characterized as "democracy equals capitalism," a position in which the market defines access to money or other essential resources, and limits the ways in which people may engage them. "Democracy needs socialism" has come to represent a conviction that people take part in activities to counter issues that affect them negatively in whatever ways their circumstances, personalities, and motivations allow. Social workers with the conviction that "democracy needs socialism" draw on it as a basis for work with their clients to help individuals, groups, families, organizations, and communities engage into more broadly based activities of citizenship.

[*Ken Collier*]

RELATED ENTRIES

Citizen Participation, Community Development, Community Organization, League for Social Reconstruction, Social Welfare History

demography

Demography is the statistical study of whole populations and specific segments of a population (i.e., size, distribution, density, age, migration, and rates of birth, fertility, life expectancy, and death) to analyze patterns of change and predict future trends. Understanding and utilizing demographics is useful for such social work activities as direct clinical practice, the development of social policy, and program design and management, in particular, to help analyze the environment in which these interventions take place. Three key current demographic issues in Canadian are ageing, migration, and family composition. Canada's ageing population has resulted from several factors, one of the most prominent being the change in fertility rates since 1945. A baby boom from the mid-1940s until the mid-1960s produced a rise in the fertility rate to more than three children per woman; since then, the fertility rate has fallen rapidly, remaining below the rate for natural replacement in the population. The baby boom will influence Canadian society for many years to come. An increasing number of people are also living longer today: in 1999, the life expectancy from birth for a female was 81.7 years and 76.3 years for a male; these numbers represent gains in life expectancy of 0.4 years and 0.5 years, respectively (Canada 2002a). Scientific and technological advancements and improvements in living standards continue to contribute to increased life expectancy. Mortality rates also reflect the trend that Canadians are living longer: in 1981, 1 in 5 males (20%) and 2 in 5 females (41%) could expect to reach the age eight-five; but in 1999, 1 in 3 males (33%) and almost 1 in 2 females (49%) could expect to live to that age (Canada 2002a: 34). As baby boomers age and life expectancy increases, social workers and policy makers will be challenged in their responses to such issues related to an ageing population as chronic health conditions and housing. Immigration and migration within a population, reflecting movement from one community to another, are both affecting current population patterns. With the number of births falling in 1999 for the ninth consecutive year, net migration within Canada currently accounts for 61 percent of overall population growth, making it the main component of growth in the country (Canada 2002a: 9). In 2000 Canada received 227,300 immigrants, more than 54 percent of whom were admitted within the independent class (i.e., business and skilled workers) of the immigration policy; as well, 30,058 refugees were

admitted in this year (Canada 2002a: 39). Social workers will continue to be needed to work with immigrants and refugees, and particularly those interested in responding to their cultural, linguistic, and other specific needs. The composition of families in Canada continues to shift. The number of traditional families—that is, one consisting of a mother, a father, and children under the age of twenty-four and living at home—has decreased from 55 percent in 1981 to 44 percent in 2001; over the same time period, couples without children have increased from 34 to 41 percent (Canada 2002b). More Canadians are also choosing to live in common-law relationships, which increased from 5.6 percent in 1981 to 14 percent in 2000, with the proportion of married-couple families falling from 83 percent in 1981 to 70 percent in 2000 (Canada 2002b). Family composition is changing in others ways, too. Seniors are increasingly residing with their adult children and the number of same-sex common-law partnerships currently represents 0.5 percent of all Canadian couples (Canada 2002b). Issues relating to ageing, migration, and family composition are only some of demographic trends that will impact on social work practice in Canada. Demography can provide tools to reveal the shape of the work social workers may be asked to undertake. It can help frame the context of social work practice and provide important information to those who design the health and social services that social workers typically deliver. Demography is an important aspect of social work to identify, analyze, and understand population trends as they emerge and affect practice.

[*Matthew Goodman*]

RELATED ENTRIES

Family Demographics, Family: Non-traditional, Family Statistical Patterns, Immigrants & Immigration, Research, Services to Elderly People, Single Parents, Social Planning, Social Policy, Theory & Practice

REFERENCES

Canada. 2002a. *Report on the Demographic Situation in Canada 2001: Current Demographic Analysis.* Ottawa: Statistics Canada.

———. 2002b. 2001 Census: Families and Household Profile: Canada. Ottawa: Statistics Canada. Online at time of writing at <www.statscan.ca/>.

developmental challenges

Developmental challenges is the current terminology used to describe delayed intellectual maturation. Many other terms have been used, such as mental retardation, mental deficiency, mental handicap, mental impairment, intellectual deficiency, intellectual challenge, intellectual disability, developmental handicap, and developmental disability; some of these terms are still in widespread use. A basic definition is a "below-average general intellectual functioning with associated deficits in adaptive behavior that occur before age eighteen" (Anglin & Braaten 1978). Developmental challenges, which have consistently affected 1 to 3 percent of the population, constitute a failure or delay in normal maturation in intellectual, emotional, social, and often physical and physiological areas as defined by societal norms. The degree of disability ranges from borderline to profound impairment. A score below seventy on a standard intelligence quotient test is considered a sign of developmental disability. A diagnosis of a developmental challenges is generally formulated when the individual is unable to exhibit age-appropriate adaptive behaviours in such areas as language, motor skills, learning, judgment, and speech. Among the many causes of developmental challenges, the most generally accepted are: pre- and post-natal trauma; infections such as rubella, meningitis, encephalitis, and HIV; chromosomal abnormalities such as Down syndrome, Fragile X syndrome, and Prader-Willi syndrome; genetic abnormalities; inherited metabolic disorders such as Tay-Sachs disease, Rett's disorder, and phenylketonuria; toxicity such as exposure to lead poisoning, alcohol, and various opiates; nutritional deficiencies such as malnutrition; and environmental factors associated with poverty. There is no cure for developmental challenges. Where causes are attributed to chromosomal or to genetic and inherited metabolic disorders, genetic counselling and pre-natal screening, can decrease the incidence of developmental challenges, especially for families at risk.

Over the centuries, treatment has varied markedly depending on the public's perception of individuals with developmental challenges. The earliest forms of formal treatment in Canada—when developmental disabilities and mental illness were considered one category—involved custodial care in large institutions. The objects of custodial care was the protection of the public, and some training of children and adults with developmental challenges. The rationale for protecting the public was the belief that those with developmental challenges were dangerous and very promiscuous, potentially populating the community with "defective" children—attitudes that began to change very slowly. Parents were urged to place their children with developmental challenges as early as possible in institutions, as they were perceived as incurable and having only minimal abilities. Residents in institutions were there for life. Initially, they were housed in jails or in psychiatric facilities known as lunatic asylums. Some visionaries, notably J.W. Langmuir, inspector of asylums and prisons in 1871, perceived that "That class of defective (those under twelve years of age) can be successfully treated in an independent institution possessing all the means and scientific appliance of a modem training school for children, the establishment of which is required both in the interests of humanity and public economy" (Anglin & Braaten 1978). This recommendation resulted in the establishment in Orillia in 1867 of an Asylum for Idiots and Feebleminded. Several other such specialized institutions were also built, with the title later changing from asylum to training school. These large institutions were self-sufficient, with residents growing their own food, making some of their own clothing, and generally assisting in the maintenance of the institution: this self-sufficiency was viewed as training for, where feasible, future employment as farm hands or domestic help. Programs in community institutions such as schools and recreational facilities were similar to those for the general population; instead of adapting the programs, program managers expected people with developmental disabilities to adapt to the programs. Their inability to do so was further evidence that isolation in large institutions was the appropriate societal solution.

While institutional care was considered the norm, some authorities were convinced that people with developmental challenges could be trained and could live in communities with their families. Pioneers such as Dr. Helen MacMurchy, Inspector for the Feebleminded for Ontario, strongly believed that early education for children with developmental challenges could help them to become productive adults. This perception encouraged the Toronto Board of Education to open classes in twenty-one schools for more than eight hundred children with intelligence quotient results over fifty (Anglin & Braaten 1978). As similar classes followed, the Ontario government enacted the Special Classes Act in 1911 to permit boards of education to establish classes "for all children who are backward and abnormally slow in learning." Parallel to the formation of special classes in local schools was a movement of parents wanting to keep their children at home. In 1948 an organized group of parents first met in Toronto; three years later, the Parents' Council for Retarded Children was incorporated, with a membership consisting of 200 representing 140 children. The council has changed its name over the years to Association for the Retarded Children, to Association of Retarded Children and Adults, and is now known as the Association for Community Living. Today, the council is one of 420 local associations within the Canadian Association for Community Living, one of Canada's largest charitable organizations. The association has a national office and twelve provincial/territorial organizations representing 40,000 members throughout Canada. Over the years, local associations have established special schools from their own moneys, which later became part of boards of education. Where, in the past, children with various disabilities were educated in segregated classes, more recently, they have become integrated and maybe assisted by educational assistants trained in special needs.

Parents' groups also developed residential homes in communities for children and adults who could not live at home. Sheltered work was established to provide employment and training for jobs in the community. By 1973 the belief was growing that individuals with developmental disabilities could live in their own communities as long as supports were put in place, thereby making institutional care unnecessary. Another notable shift in practice occurring at the time was that developmental disability, which had been considered a health issue—with institutions employing physicians, nurses, and other health care professionals—changed to become a social issue. In 1970 in Ontario for example, the admin-

istration and funding of institutions and community services were transferred from the Ministry of Health to the Ministry of Community and Social Services. This shift was part of the broader movement throughout the 1970s to 1990s to deinstitutionalization, when community-based organizations were encouraged to provide services funded by government, such as recreation, family support, training, employment, and residences. While residents with developmental challenges in institutions were placed in community residences, public funding was inadequate to include those residing in their homes but requiring specialized residences. In other words, parents who kept their children at home and who eventually required placement were left out. While placement in institutions was not an option, programs such as Special Services at Home (in Ontario) and respite care in and out of the home were developed to ease the burden of care for families. Social work has been an important partner in the provision of services to persons with developmental challenges and their families. Parents with children with any disability face emotional stress, and practical problems, such as access to even commonplace services like schools, recreation, housing, babysitting, or transportation. As well, parents need time and support to accept the disability of their child; in fact, many parents mourn the loss of a normally healthy child at each phase of maturation and may require ongoing or renewed support. Social workers are also involved in policy making and administration of programs and services to people with developmental challenges and their families. In addition to services provided for children and adults and their families, research with the focus on prevention and treatment has been ongoing. Genetic research into many health problems has contributed much to further knowledge about developmental disabilities.

[*Rose Blackmore*]

RELATED ENTRIES
Canadian Charter of Rights and Freedoms, Canadian Mental Health Association, Deinstitutionalization Movement, *Diagnostic and Statistical Manual of Mental Disorders*, Developmental Challenges & Families, C. Hincks, Minorities, Peer Counselling, Personal-Centred Theory, Physical Challenges, School Social Workers, Sensitizing Concepts, Services for People with Disabilities, Treatment, Wellness

REFERENCES

Anglin, B., and J. Braaten. 1978. *Twenty-five Years of Growing Together: A History of the Ontario Association for the Mentally Retarded.* Toronto: Ontario Association for the Mentally Retarded. Online at time of writing at <www.healthanswers.com>.

developmental challenges and families

The arrival of a developmentally challenged child can have different effects on the structure, function, and development of a family than does the arrival of a normally functioning child. Children with special needs take up a lot of time, energy, resources, and emotions; parents caring for such a child experience a great amount of stress, even on the spousal relationship. The stress of seeing medical specialists, dealing with differences in opinion on decisions, and addressing the needs of work and/or other children contribute to physical exhaustion and ongoing tension in the home. The father and the mother, who used to be a close couple, each may find him/herself feeling isolated and depressed, not least from chronic sorrow over the loss of a normal child. A developmentally challenged child may be seen as a burden or responsibility with which their family has to deal, rather than a beloved addition. Parents have to reorganize their attitudes, goals, and lifestyle rapidly; and siblings may discover that they will have family responsibilities that their friends may not. Siblings of a child with special needs may have more responsibilities at home, changes in routine, and role distribution that may produce feelings of neglect, resentment, or hostility toward their brother or sister. Often, the developmentally challenged child becomes the youngest child regardless of his/her actual chronology and, consequently, the actual youngest sibling may be required to grow up faster and perform tasks not expected of him/her while the parents' attention is transferred to the developmentally challenged child's greater needs. In the literature, this pattern is called "role tension" (Farber & Rychman 1965, cited in McHale & Simeonsson 1981). These unplanned disruptions to family life may create tension and conflict in the family, sometimes referred to as a "tragic crisis" or arrest in the life cycle (Farber 1960, cited in McHale &

Simeonsson 1981: 161; Rodger 1985). Under what observers call "family mythology" (San Martino & Newman 1974), each family member adapts in ways that best meet his/her own needs in the context of the family's needs, thereby determining his/her version of the mythology for him/herself at each stage of their development.

How a family responds to a developmentally challenged child is likely to be determined by the parents' attitudes. If parents are accepting toward their developmentally challenged child, siblings will react similarly. The ability and willingness of parents and extended family adults to be positive and communicate openly about the special needs of their child greatly influence family adjustment. Lack of communication within a family teaches children that some topics are taboo and maintains false ideas about their reality. Parents need to ensure that other children feel confident about approaching them to discuss their feelings or concerns that their problems are being subsumed by the special needs of their brother/sister. Otherwise, siblings may be at risk for emotional problems that do not come to their parents' attention (Vandasy et al. 1984). Brothers and sisters of a child with developmental challenges may feel emotions ranging from anger and resentment, guilt, curiosity, concern, sorrow, and anxiety, through excitement and joy, to pressure, fear, loneliness, protectiveness, frustration, longing, jealousy, fear, confusion, embarrassment, and/ or unhappiness. These feelings may vary in intensity and may emerge in response to specific events (Powell & Ogle 1985); if such feelings remain unresolved, they may cause major problems for the siblings and interfere with the development of positive relationships. Issues of identity, of being similar and different to the developmentally challenged child may be of concern to siblings as they wonder what other characteristics they share with their brother/sister and whether they are defective in some way. They may avoid identifying with their developmentally challenged sibling because they are fearful of being developmentally challenged. Siblings may feel denial and, as a result, reject their brother/sister or feel guilty about their negative feelings. Some siblings may try to compensate for the limitations of their brother/sister with special needs overachieving. Other siblings may be confused about their role as both sibling and "surrogate parent." The situation may also move siblings generally into developmental stages earlier than their friends, perhaps robbing them of important relationships and experiences (Seligman 1983). Older siblings may be concerned about the future for their developmentally challenged brother/sister, perhaps wondering who will care for him/her, as well as genetic implications for themselves. Adolescents fearful of rejection may feel isolated from their peers and try to keep dating partners from learning about their developmentally challenged brother/sister. Parents must ensure that all their children feel loved, even as their attention seems to be focused on the developmentally challenged child, and that other children understand that they matter, that their sole importance in the family is not to help meet their brother/sister's special needs. Some parents may need help to balance their own well being and needs with those of their developmentally challenged child and those of other children.

Social workers can help families find community resources to help raise their developmentally challenged child, as well as clarify and resolve negative feelings or tensions a constructive way. Through family counselling, practitioners can guide family members to handle their feelings openly and honestly, or face having make adjustments later. Social workers can provide information about the nature of their child's disabilities, and resulting strengths and limitations. Special support may be recommended for siblings to help them understand their feelings and work through ways of personal integration (Featherstone 1980, cited in Milunsky 1981). Group counselling for siblings of developmentally challenged children may be an effective forum for some to gain information and share experiences, as siblings learn that they are not the only ones in their situation. In group counselling, social workers can provide a safe environment for siblings to ask questions, express feelings, and solve problems (i.e., how to deal with teasing from peers at school, telling friends about their developmentally challenged sibling, handling parental expectations, and effects on future relationships). In general counselling helps these children to gain a better understanding of their situation, which in turn enhances their own psychosocial development.

[*Tina Gandhi*]

RELATED ENTRIES

Canadian Charter of Rights and Freedoms, Canadian Mental Health Association, Developmental Challenges, Family Therapy, C. Hincks, Parenting, Peer Counselling, Physical Challenges, School Social Workers, Sensitizing Concepts, Services for Families, Services for People with Disabilities, Treatment, Wellness

REFERENCES

McHale, S.M., and R.J. Simeonsson. 1981. Research on Handicapped Children: Sibling Relationships. *Child: Care, Health and Development* 7, 153–71.

Milunsky, A. (Ed.) 1981. *Coping with Crisis and Handicap.* New York: Plenum.

Powell, T.H., and P.A. Ogle. 1985. *Brothers and Sisters: A Special Part of Exceptional Families.* Baltimore, MD: Paul H. Brookes.

Rodger, S. 1985. Siblings of Handicapped Children: A Population at Risk? *Exceptional Child* 32, 1, 47–56.

San Martino, M., and M.B. Newman. 1974. Siblings of Retarded Children: A Population at Risk. *Child Psychiatry and Human Development* 4, 3, 168–77.

Seligman, M. 1983. Sources of Psychological Disturbance among Siblings of Handicapped Children. *Personnel and Guidance Journal* 61, 9, 529–31.

Vandasy, P.F., R.R. Fewell, D.J. Meyer, and G. Schell. 1984. Siblings of Handicapped Children: A Developmental Perspective on Family Interactions. *Family Relations* 33, 155–67.

diagnosis

Diagnosis, as a term and concept in Canadian social work, has sparked considerable conflict. For some, it is the process and formally stated series of judgments that serve as the basis of each action taken or not taken throughout a case, for which a social worker is prepared to accept responsibility; practitioners who perceive diagnosis in this way think of it as the essence of responsible practice. Ethical practice demands that everything done by the social worker in each particular situation in a case must be based on a conscious decision relevant to social work knowledge and theory. As a facet of intervention, diagnosis is now viewed both as a process and a fact, in contradistinction to earlier perceptions when diagnosis was seen as a separate and one-time act carried out after the gathering and analysis of a client's social history. As a process, diagnosis is viewed as ongoing from the initial contact with a client and proceeding throughout the life of the case; each diagnosis is also the concrete stated fact of decisions made, for which a practitioner is to be held ethically accountable.

Others, however, view diagnosis as a term that has been borrowed from medicine and used by social work in an inappropriate way, as it is said to be a concept that imbues social work practice with an overly pathological orientation. This negative view of diagnosis—more often reflected in text books than in practice literature—seems to have emerged from the desire to distance social work from a basis that may be perceived as too close to mental health practice; instead, such commentators have encouraged a wider holistic psychosocial basis for social work, now known as a biopsychosocial. Since the term diagnosis has been long associated with a psychopathological tradition, the term is viewed by many who are attempting to broaden the focus of social work practice as too narrow, too unitary, too overly dependent on a single theory, too exclusive of clients, and too closely identified with the *Diagnostic and Statistical Manual of Mental Disorders*. The unwillingness of some social workers to use the term "diagnosis" could have negative effects on their clients in depriving them access to resources where a specific diagnosis is required.

The broad spectrum of needs to be addressed by social work client systems and subsystems require highly competent judgments for practitioners to determine what is to be done. The lack of a profession-wide consensus about a diagnostic paradigm or system is a major challenges for social workers, further complicated by the spectrum of intervention theories, each with its own lexicon. The discussion within the profession about the interface of diagnosis and outcome often enters the realm of polemics, as, aside from agency records, very few examples of social work diagnoses are available for comparison. Thus, it is difficult to distinguish relationships among diagnosis, intervention, and outcome, as evaluation of practice and outcomes become a more integrated component of practice records of data are now available to link the processes of diagnosis, intervention, and outcomes.

[*FJT*]

RELATED ENTRIES

Accountability, Agency-Based Research, Assessment,

Codes of Ethics, *Diagnostic and Statistical Manual of Mental Disorders*, Ethics, Intervention Research, Interviewing, Practice Methods, Program Evaluation, Recording, Research, Theory & Practice, Therapy, Treatment, Wellness

Diagnostic and Statistical Manual of Mental Disorders

The *Diagnostic and Statistical Manual of Mental Disorders* developed by the American Psychiatric Association is a broadly accepted system for identifying types of mental disorders; the most recent edition, the fourth published in 1994 and revised in 2000, is widely known as DSM-IV. The most recent publication of the International Classification of Mental and Behavioural Disorders, issued by the World Health Organization, is also used by practitioners, primarily outside North America. The manual provides operational criteria for various mental disorders and a definition of abnormality. Before the manual, virtually every medical teaching centre and university used a different classification system for mental disorders, and mental health professionals often made diagnoses by clinical "feel" or intuition; meaningless communications and arguments between professionals occurred as a result (Reid & Wise 1995). The American Psychiatric Association published the first diagnostic manual in 1952, the second edition in 1968, the third in 1980 with a further revision in 1987. DSM-III offered a significant improvement over previous editions, as field trials were used in an effort to improve reliability and entries became atheoretical, as the focus moved away from endorsing any one theory of abnormal psychology. Previous editions had been highly influenced by psychoanalytic theory. DSM-IV is a collaborated effort of professionals in all fields in mental health, including social workers representatives from all over the world—including twenty-seven Canadian psychiatrists and psychologists. To make DSM-IV more sensitive, rigorous field trials in seventy sites were set up, where six thousand patients were evaluated. One of the goals was to have the DSM-IV to be more consistent with the World Health Organization's classifications. There was also a desire to promote communication of ideas and understanding of the various disorders. The multi-axial approach to diagnosis begun in 1980 with DSM-III continues in DSM-IV, with minor modification. The use of the five axes provides additional patient information to the diagnosis:

- Axes 1 and 2 are used to describe a patient's current condition; multiple diagnoses can be made on axes 1 and 2, as necessary. Axis 1 lists disorders usually first diagnosed in infancy and adolescence (i.e., substance abuse, eating disorders, mood disorders and sexual and gender identity disorders). Axis 2 lists personality disorders (i.e., paranoid, anti-social, histrionic, and obsessive-compulsive).
- Axis 3 lists general medical conditions that may affect psychological functioning of a patient or the management of a case; endocrine and nutritional conditions are also coded on this axis.
- Axis 4 lists psychosocial and environmental problems that affect a patient's functioning.
- Axis 5 estimates an individual's level of functioning at the time of the evaluation, or at other specified times, using the global assessment of functioning by which a client is assigned a number from zero to one hundred based on behaviours to indicate how well he/she is handling stress.

DSM-IV is not without criticisms. Many professionals argue that the diagnostic endeavour is flawed because of its adherence to the medical model. Others argue that psychiatric labels unfairly stigmatize an individual or lead to self-fulfilling prophecies. This can be particularly serious when children are concerned (Rapoport & Ismond 1996). A frequent criticism of the manual is that it takes a categorical approach to classification. Rather than recognize a continuum from normal to abnormal, an individual is considered either to have a disorder or not. Problems with reliability seem to remain, where clinicians cannot agree on the diagnosis of a particular patient. Some critics note that the manual tends to pathologize non-medical behaviour related to reproduction. Another criticism is that the manual makes the assumption that psychological problems are largely attributable to the individual, rather than taking life circumstances into account. Others complain of gender and cultural biases. While attempts were made to include cultural differences, the manual is largely determined by a consensus of English-speaking scientists trained primarily in the United States. The diversity of Canadian society requires sensitivity to cultural and attitudinal factors in assessment. Despite these criticisms, DSM-IV can be useful to social workers and other mental health workers, for example, as a guide to intervene with appropriate strategies in the treatment plan. DSM-IV can provide additional information about a client's prognosis for recovery or response to an intervention. DSM-IV conceptualizes its Axis 4 as a means to measure psychosocial stress or problems that may affect the diagnosis, treatment, and prognosis of mental disorders (Smart & Smart 1997). The global assessment of functioning in Axis 5 can provide a baseline from which to determine if the client is improving from an intervention. Familiarity with this diagnostic manual can assist social workers to communicate with other mental health professionals about a treatment plan. The development of a diagnostic classification system is an ongoing process requiring continual refinement and study. With further research and field trials, the reliability of the diagnostic manual will continue to improve and its usefulness grow.

[*Peter J. Doherty*]

RELATED ENTRIES

Assessment, Clinical Social Work, Diagnosis, Theory & Practice, Treatment, Wellness

REFERENCES

Rapoport, J.L., and D.R. Ismond. 1996. *DSM-IV Training Guide for Diagnosis of Childhood Disorders*. New York: Brunner/Mazel.

Reid, W.H., and M.G. Wise. 1995. *DSM-IV Training Guide*. New York: Brunner/Mazel.

Smart, D.W., and I.F. Smart. 1997. DSM-IV and Culturally Sensitive Diagnosis: Some Observations for Counselors. *Journal of Counseling and Development* 75, 392–97.

direct practice

Direct practice is a term frequently used in Canadian social work parlance to describe practice that is carried out with an individual, dyad, group, or family, as opposed to activities carried out on behalf of clients, such as work with some significant aspect of the client's life. The term may be used somewhat imprecisely, as it is also used to distinguish work done on behalf of a client involving someone in the client's life (i.e., a life partner) who, while not the direct client, is nevertheless an important part of the situation that brought the client into contact with the social worker. As well, the term tends to be used to distinguish micro from mezzo and macro practice, where the focus is to bring about social change to an issue that is generally problematic for large numbers of persons not identified as clients. The difficulty with restricting the term to face-to-face work with clients is that, in much current social work, the interaction of the worker with an individual or small group is in a position to bring about some desired change and, in this regard, does require skills in interviewing and relationship. A further difficulty with the term is that direct work may be viewed as more important and requiring a more intensive level of skill than other areas of social work practice; thus, the term takes on intraprofessional value significance, perhaps contributing to intraprofessional tensions. Nevertheless, a considerable amount of social work practice does consist only of direct interaction with clients, either as individuals or with others in similar situations. In this facet of practice, the social worker draws on knowledge stemming from an understanding of human growth and development, of the impact of significant societal systems, on knowledge and skill in professional relationships, and of familiarity and expertise with the network of helping/hindering resources in a client's life. For many clients, a brief face-to-face contact with a skilled practitioner can suffice to bring about the sought-for change in direction; for other clients, the relationship with a social workers may take weeks to develop and the process of helping might continue for many months or even years. While the current political perception is that social work treatment should by definition be short term, experience has shown that this is too simplistic; clients who have been severely damaged by life experiences may need time to trust helpers and may require the most intense level of therapeutic knowledge and skill. The skill of the social worker is in the ability to diagnose accurately who the client is, what he/she wishes, and what resources the persons can draw on to achieve a sought-for level of psychosocial growth and development.

[*FJT*]

RELATED ENTRIES
Assessment, Brief Treatment, Diagnosis, Indirect Practice, Macro Practice, Micro Practice, Mezzo Practice, Personal Social Services, Practice Methods, Theory & Practice

disaster practice

Tornadoes rip through a rural area, destroying homes and buildings; in its wake, teams of Mennonites join residents to rebuild barns and houses. A bus tumbling down a mountainside kills forty-three passengers from the same community, where people mourn and offer mutual support. For months after a jet plane crashes into coastal waters, rescue workers and military officials recover body parts and debris, and local people comfort relatives of victims. Each of these tragic events is a disaster. They resulted in loss of life and dreams, and elicited heroism and community efforts to help friends and strangers. They are unique opportunities for social workers to apply a range of skills and abilities from front-line crisis intervention through community organization and advocacy, to program and policy planning. The people most directly affected people by such events are survivors and victims' families, who experience a range of emotional, cognitive, and behavioural symptoms, as described in a large body of literature (APA 1994; Herman 1992; van der Kolk, McFarlane, & Weisaeth 1996). More recently, it has been recognized that rescue workers exposed to mutilated bodies, mass destruction, and life-threatening situations may also become hidden victims (McFarlane 1988; Regehr, Hill, & Glancy 2000). As well, communities as a whole are affected by disasters that occur in their midst. Social workers can play a role with each of these affected groups.

Responses of family members and survivors in the wake of a disaster occur in three broadly defined phases: the awareness phase, when people first hear of a disaster; the waiting phase, during which people wait to learn fate of loved ones and the extent of their loss; and the confirmation phase, when people begin to mourn their loss and make plans for the future. Disaster intervention with survivors and families focuses on three primary needs: information, empathy, and instrumental assistance. These needs are differentially addressed during each of these phases. In the awareness phase, reactions can span panic to anger or shock; at this point, social workers must remain calm and in control, provide as much information as possible, and begin the process of setting up an emergency centre for those directly affected. An emergency centre must have shelter, communication facilities, food, access to medical resources, and must insulate people from intrusive media. It is often in this environment that families will pass the waiting phase, which may last several hours or days, weeks, or months. During this phase, social workers can assist people by helping to mobilize natural support systems, advocate for survivor and family needs, and bear witness to their pain. The need for detailed information—sometimes beyond that which might be appropriate—cannot be overemphasized. Social workers can ensure that this need is met. The confirmation phase, while signalling that the disaster may be over, is by no means end of the trauma for survivors and families. Social workers can play a vital role in grief counselling and in assisting individuals to make plans for honouring the dead and for their own future (Figley, Bride, & Mazza 1997).

Critical incident stress is a term that identifies a set of traumatic reactions in individuals who respond to disasters. recent programs target the needs of emergency responders in order to lessen the impact of disasters on their lives and subsequent work. These programs, often headed by social workers, offer three levels of service. The first level is on-scene assistance in prolonged events, during which a critical incident stress team is responsible for setting up a rest centre for rescue workers and ensuring that their needs are met. Following a disaster, crisis debriefing is offered to groups of emergency responders aimed at helping them to share experiences, normalize responses, provide strategies for self-care, and develop a climate of mutual aid among members. While crisis debriefings perform an important role for increasing support among emergency responders, they do not lessen the effects of trauma on severely affected individuals; social workers can offer such individuals one-on-one trauma counselling (Regehr & Hill 2000). Finally, social workers also play an important role in program and policy

development regarding services for workers in these high-stress professions.

Another level of intervention for social workers in disasters is with communities as a whole. There is a need to create a means of remembering the dead, to put plans in place to avoid a recurrence of the disaster wherever possible, and to develop more effective means for dealing with future disasters. In this respect, the community organization and policy development skills of social workers are invaluable. Disaster mobilizes social workers to go beyond normal coping abilities and to use the full extent of their skills. Trauma spreads and secondary traumatic reactions are common to all mental health professionals who provide assistance. It is therefore vital that anyone providing assistance also pays attention to the significant impact that sharing the profound grief of others has on them.

[*Cheryl Regehr*]

RELATED ENTRIES

Bereavement, Crisis Intervention, Family Therapy, Non-governmental Organizations, Sensitizing Concepts, Theory & Practice, Torture & Trauma Victims, Wellness

REFERENCES

Figley, C. 1995. *Compassion Fatigue: Coping with Secondary Traumatic Stress Disorder in Those Who Treat the Traumatized.* New York: Brunner/Mazel.

Figley, C., B. Bride, and N. Mazza. 1997. Death and Trauma: The Traumatology of Grieving. Washington, DC: Francis and Taylor.

Herman, J.L. 1992. *Trauma and Recovery.* New York: Basic Books.

McFarlane, A. 1988. The Phenomenology of Post-traumatic Stress Disorders Following a Natural Disaster. *Journal of Nervous and Mental Disease* 176, 1, 22–29.

Regehr, C., and J. Hill. 2000. Evaluating the Efficacy of Crisis Debriefings for Emergency Responders. *Social Work with Groups* 23, 2.

Regehr, C., J. Hill, and G. Glancy. 2000. Individual Predictors of Traumatic Reactions in Firefighters. *Journal of Nervous and Mental Disease* 188, 6, 333–39.

van der Kolk, A. McFarlane, and L. Weisaeth. 1996. *Traumatic Stress: The Effects of Overwhelming Experience on Mind, Body and Society.* New York: Guilford Press.

diversity

Diversity in Canadian society refers to its multicultural composition, sometimes described as an essential aspect of Canadian identity. Canadian multicultural policies, which promote a "cultural mosaic" to enable people from different cultures and/or ethnic ancestries to coexist, are said to contrast with the American "melting pot" that is criticized for attempting to remove such social differences to produce homogeneity (MacKey 1999). Some critics claim that the advancement of Canadian diversity has become a moral imperative and that failure to promote it is labelled "unCanadian" (Winterdyk & King 1999). Social workers have an ethical duty to pursue the best interest of clients and the responsibility to promote social change. The code of ethics of the Canadian Association of Social Workers requires social workers to attend to the needs and wishes of diverse populations. Comfort with diversity has been identified as a distinguishing feature of Canadian social work (Turner 2002: 2). Diversity appears often in social science and social work literature but is frequently not defined; sometimes "diversity" and "difference" are used interchangeably. Hardy and Mawhiney define diversity as "the ways that people are different from one another and how these differences shape various ways of living and thinking, different assumptions, values and beliefs" (2002: 58). Another analysis suggests that diversity has four dimensions: heterogeneity, social stratification, social inequality, and minority group status (Winterdyk & King 1999: 3–10); drawing on the work of Blau (1977), these authors suggest that heterogeneity is a horizontal differentiation of people in terms of nominal parameters (or prescribed and recognized characteristics). Social stratification refers to the vertical differentiation in a hierarchy of status differences. Social inequality exists "when social status is reinforced through the exercise of social power" (Winterdyk & King 1999: 8), and minority group status results when dominant societies exercise power to the disadvantage of another segment or other segments of the population. These four dimensions of diversity tend to be implicit rather than explicit in social work discourses. Other forms of population diversity have been explored by other observers, with the greatest attention focused on diversity based on class, gender, ethnicity, race, and culture; still others have identified diversity in family patterns, age, sexual orientation, physical and mental ability, and spirituality.

Ideas about how social workers should approach work with diverse populations compete and conflict. Some theorists and practitioners concentrate on social work with particular populations (i.e., women, or people with a distinct ethnicity). Claims have been made that differences within, as well as between, gender, ethnicity, and social class—identified as the most fundamental forms of diversity—are not always acknowledged by social workers. Thus, women from visible minorities or from non-European cultures have commented that much social work theory, even feminist theory, has a Eurocentric bias that denies their experiences. Some suggest that, instead of exploring a particular form of social difference, social workers should consider experiences such as oppression that are common to many communities. Advocates of competent practice recommend that social workers gain knowledge and skills to respond to the needs and wishes of distinct communities within mainstream society, while anti-oppressive practice challenges the domination of people who are identified as marginalized. Thus, much women-centred practice within a competence tradition calls on social workers to focus on issues faced by women, while much feminist practice urges social workers to identify and challenge oppressive patriarchal cultures, structures, and social systems. The competing voices are a strength rather than a weakness of social work, as diversity of approach is needed if particular client populations are to receive services that respond to their distinct conditions, rights, wants, and needs.

[*Rosemary A. Clews*]

RELATED ENTRIES

Aboriginal Issues, Anti-oppressive Social Work, Assembly of First Nations, Canadian Charter of Rights and Freedoms, Canadian Multiculturalism Act, Chinese Immigration Act, Culture, Ethnic-Sensitive Practice, Ethnocultural Communities' Services, Feminist Theory, W. Head, D.G. Hill, Immigrants & Immigration, League for the Advancement of Coloured People, Minorities, Minority-Sensitive Practice, Race & Racism, Racism-Sensitive Social Work, Sensitizing Concepts, Services for Refugees, Social Welfare Context, Visible Minorities

REFERENCES

Blau, P. 1977. *Inequality and Heterogeneity: A Primitive Theory of Social Structure.* New York: Free Press.

Hardy, S., and A.M. Mawhiney. 2002. Diversity in Canadian Social Work Practice. In F.J. Turner (Ed.) *Social work Practice: A Canadian Perspective.* 2nd ed. 57–68. Toronto: Pearson Education.

MacKey, E. 1999. *The House of Difference: Cultural Politics and National Identity in Canada.* London: Routledge.

Winterdyk, J.A., and D.E. King (Eds.) 1999. *Diversity and Justice in Canada.* Toronto: Canadian Scholars Press.

doctorate in social work

The doctoral degree in social work began to emerge as an important facet of Canadian social work education in the late 1950s. Before that time, only a few faculty members and senior policy makers and researchers with doctorates identified themselves as social workers. In English-speaking Canada the first social work doctorate was established at the University of Toronto. Two factors appeared to have contributed to this development. Canadian universities were moving toward the establishment of social work programs, increasingly at the graduate level, with strong recommendations for the need for faculty members with doctoral training. At the same time, the profession itself was promoting the enhanced quality of master's degree programs in social work, and encouraging further studies and advanced research. While no new doctoral programs were established in Canada in the 1960s, many US and UK universities had developed doctoral programs in social work and in fields closely allied to the profession. Even though the motivation for undertaking doctoral studies was not necessary to pursue an academic career, the majority of doctoral graduates of the 1960s and 1970s did eventually move into academia. As the doctorate gained appeal, the issue of preferred designation of the degree as a DSW or PhD emerged. At this time, the majority of social work doctoral programs originally conferring a DSW are now designated as a PhD. At the start of this millennium, the social work doctorate has attained a higher profile in Canada. Even though many continue to view the degree as preparatory for academia, the number of social workers with doctorates in non-academic

positions, including front-line practitioners, is also increasing. A significant number of social workers have completed doctorates in such allied disciplines as economics, sociology, education, and political science, thereby contributing their specialized knowledge to social work practice. The development of programs has been rapid: nine universities in Canada now offer a doctoral program in social work, including some joint programs with other disciplines, and others are planned. The place of the doctorate has yet to be clarified within the social work profession. The doctorate is not mentioned by many regulatory bodies for social workers throughout this country, which still perceive the master's degree as the significant senior qualification. Interest in the doctoral level of academic training in social work is rapidly expanding, however, and could soon become the generally recognized senior standard for the profession.

[FJT]

RELATED ENTRIES

Council for Education in Social Work (US), Education in Social Work

Thomas C. Douglas (1904–86)

Douglas, Thomas Clement, sociologist, premier of Saskatchewan, leader, New Democratic Party; b. Oct. 02, 1904, Falkirk, Scotland; d. Feb. 24, 1986, Ottawa, ON

Tommy Douglas was a champion boxer, sociologist, printer, and preacher, as well as Canada's "best-loved political leader" (Whelan & Whelan 1990). His work contributed greatly to social worker, but he himself was not a practitioner. As a sociology graduate in the early 1930s, Douglas decided that private charity and individual initiatives were inadequate responses to social deprivation and injustice. Throughout his fifty years of public service, he sought to discover root causes of these phenomena and bring about changes that would benefit Canadians. The humanitarian and egalitarian ideals of social work were reflected in the "Humanity First" slogan of Douglas's socialist government in Saskatchewan and were powerfully expressed in his courageous political initiatives. Douglas was the first to introduce medicare to a Canadian province. Free medical treatment by a Winnipeg surgeon saved one of Douglas's legs from amputation in early childhood; as an adult, he initiated a policy for all citizens to have access to free health services. In 1959 Douglas brought to Saskatchewan an insurance-based medicare scheme that was characterized by universal coverage, high-quality service, and administration by a public body responsible to the legislature. The scheme was resisted by the province's medical establishment—to the extent of a physicians' strike, but medicare in Saskatchewan survived and became the model for similar schemes adopted throughout Canada. After his political defeat following the introduction of medicare, Douglas called on his party workers to "fight on… I will lay me down and bleed awhile and then I'll rise and fight again." He did so. Douglas endeavoured to eliminate social distance between himself and his constituents, making himself accessible through invitations to "come and talk to the government of Saskatchewan." His demeanour was described as "cheerful and relaxed, as if there was only one man in the world, the one he was talking to" (Whelan & Whelan 1990: 25). On one occasion he left a Cabinet meeting to offer condolences to a recently bereaved constituent and on another he stopped a New Democratic Party procession to greet a wheelchair-bound friend (Whelan & Whelan 1990: 24, 124). Douglas displayed great courage in his pursuit of social justice. When Prime Minister Trudeau introduced the War Measures Act in 1970, Douglas, as leader of the federal New Democratic Party, declared it to be an infringement of personal liberty and spoke out strongly against it. Douglas's stance led to an extreme public reaction against the party and Douglas himself, yet he persisted in his resistance. This preacher-politician personifies the humanitarian and egalitarian ideals of social work.

[*Rosemary A. Clews*]

RELATED ENTRIES

Co-operative Commonwealth Federation, Regina Manifesto, Social Planning, Social Policy, Social Welfare History

REFERENCE

Whelan, E., and P. Whelan. 1990. *Touched by Tommy*. Regina, SK: Whelan Publications.

eating disorders

The eating disorders anorexia nervosa and bulimia nervosa have received comprehensive attention only in the past thirty-five years, although they have been reported for many years. Anorexia nervosa is marked by self-imposed dietary restraint in an effort to satisfy an intense and extraordinary drive for thinness. The anorexic—usually female—has a distorted view of her body, seeing herself as fat when in fact she is extremely thin and experiencing medical and psychosocial complications from starvation; the anorexic person does not respond to reassurance that she is not fat. Bulimia is marked by the consumption of a large amount of food in a discrete period of time accompanied by a feeling of being out of control (binge eating) and some sort of compensatory behaviour (e.g., vomiting, laxative use, exercise, post-binge dieting) designed to undo the calories consumed during the binge; the bulimic experiences the same drive for thinness that anorexics report. Bulimia nervosa may also co-occur with anorexia nervosa. These two eating disorders compromise the health and well-being of a significant proportion of Canadian society: prevalence rates of 0.5 to 1 percent for anorexia nervosa and 1 to 3 percent for bulimia nervosa do not capture an even larger group of people who are below the threshold for diagnostic criteria but who also suffer health, social, and psychological impairment. Most of the people with eating disorders (90%) are women. Eating disorders typically begin in adolescence; it is not uncommon, however, for children to come into care for them, nor for young adult women in their twenties to experience an initial episode. Eating disorders can take many years to recover from and for a small group will be chronic in nature. Mortality rates of 10 percent are reported in the *Diagnostic and Statistical Manual of Mental Disorders*. The etiology of eating disorders is thought to be multi-dimensional, with a primary focus on cultural, individual, and family factors. Cultural norms equating thinness with beauty and success emphasize individual appearance as a measure of esteem and competence. Individual factors (i.e., difficulties with identity, autonomy, depression, perfectionism, and chronic illness) combine with family factors (i.e., problematic parent-child relationships, history of eating disorders, substance abuse, depression, and a magnification of cultural issues). A vulnerable person may begin to diet as a result of an incident that challenges or lowers his/her self-esteem in an effort to become thinner and, thereby, improve his/her sense of self-worth and effectiveness; successive diets and persistent lack of self-confidence, however, trap him/her in the eating disorder. Initially illnesses based in affluent societies, eating disorders are spreading as values about appearance in affluent societies become accepted elsewhere. An appreciation of cultural differences is essential to proper identification and treatment. Treatment of anorexia and bulimia nervosa is multi-modal and interdisciplinary, with physicians and dieticians as key members of the treatment team augmented by social workers, occupational therapists, and psychologists. The first step toward recovery is helping a client to normalize their eating to the extent that they are medically stable and able to engage in psychological work. People who are unable to do this in the community will typically be referred to an intensive in-patient or day program in a hospital; many initial programs are followed by some sort of relapse-prevention program. Less intensive treatments focus on psycho-education, individual, group, and family therapy where many different models maybe advanced to change eating and purging behaviours, address body-image disturbance, and resolve psychological and interpersonal issues. For people who remain chronically ill, a health promotion approach is recommended.

[*Jan Lackstom*]

RELATED ENTRIES

Assessment, Bioethical Issues, Counselling, Diagnosis, Peer Counselling, Personal-Centred Theory, School Social Workers, Services for Youth, Theory & Practice, Therapy, Treatment, Wellness

ecological theory

Ecological theory is an approach to social work practice that focuses on the transactions between a client and his/her significant social systems. It emerged as a framework for social work in the 1970s, and has since been widely considered the best available conceptual map to help practition-

ers understand clients and their needs. It is a general, abstract theory, variously referred to as a perspective, or a "life model" or even a "metaphor" as a way of thinking about situations. While ecological theory directs attention to what is fundamental in social work, it allows considerable leeway regarding the focus for assessment and intervention: a practitioner can and should find room within the perspective for a range of less abstract approaches for understanding different clients' problems and considering options for helping to solve them. A well-known aspect of social work's history is the ongoing struggle to reconcile the two priorities of helping individuals and families function more effectively versus improving the social conditions that are often the source of their difficulties. Although these goals can be complementary, they remain a source of tension. Practitioners focusing on personal change are accused of ignoring the social conditions that cause distress; those who emphasize social change are accused of downplaying individual needs and potentials. This tension has driven the search for a self-definition declaring a professional commitment to both personal and societal change. In 1949 Father Swithun Bowers, founder of St. Patrick's School of Social Welfare, collected every definition of social casework he could find and distilled them into one. "Social casework," he concluded, "is an art in which knowledge of the science of human relations and skill in relationship are used to mobilize capacities in the individual and resources in the community appropriate for better adjustment between the client and all or any part of his total environment" (Bowers 1949: 417). What distinguished the profession was the dual focus on people and their environments, and the recognition of the need for a match of individuals' needs with community resources. The basic premises identified by Bowers have proven very durable. Theoretical development in the half-century since has added depth to Bowers' themes without challenging them in any basic sense; his definition is remarkably congruent with the ecological or ecosystems theory perspective that guides current practice. Steps on the path from Bowers to the present include the influential psychosocial model, which reinforced the commitment to simultaneously address personal and environmental aspects of clients' lives (Turner 1978).

Another important development was general systems theory, often credited to Ludwig von Bertalanffy (1968). Working at the universities of Ottawa and Alberta, von Bertalanffy initially sought ways of understanding biological phenomena, but soon realized that his ideas could illuminate human issues as well. Coeval with von Bertalanffy's early work, Gordon Hearn devoted his time as Cassidy Research Visiting Professor at the University of Toronto's School of Social Work to an exploration of general systems theory and its potential importance to social work theory. With the publication of *Theory Building in Social Work* in 1958, Hearn established social work as the first and most prominent helping profession to embrace systems theory with the following central concepts:

- Systems are groups of people (e.g., families) that are organized, in as much as there is pattern and predictability in how members relate to one another.
- The reasons things happen in systems are more often circular than linear (i.e., people or events have a reciprocal back-and-forth influence on each other).
- Although they are organized, systems are not entirely predictable, so the effects of efforts to influence them—the outcomes that interventions produce—cannot be confidently known in advance.

Social work theorists in the 1970s joined systems theory to ecology, a perspective borrowed from the life sciences to produce the ecological or ecosystems perspective. Several pointed out that, as systems, clients and their families are constantly involved in transactions with other systems (Meyer 1988, Germain & Gitterman 1996); these transactions define an ecological niche or social space within which a person lives. The transactions make demands of the person (i.e., stresses and problems) and support the person in adapting to those demands; if demands outweigh resources, a person tends to suffer; if resources are adequate, a person can adapt effectively. This balance of demands and supports, mediated by individual differences in perception and capability, is a powerful determinant of health and happiness, referred to as "goodness of fit," a critical aspect of the ecological niche each person occupies (Rothery 2001). Taken together, systems and

ecological concepts have significantly advanced the understanding of how people and their environments shape one another. One concern about ecosystems theory, however, notes that its potential use as a rationale for expecting clients to adapt to oppressive circumstances would be inappropriate; as ecology theory lacks a systematic statement of values for what a just social environment comprises, this concern is valid. Still, the theory has beneficial applications of its encouragement of a broad, holistic understanding of clients' needs, and its promise as a general theory that integrates a range of methods and techniques. With its emphasis on the mediated balance of demands and resources as determinants of social well-being, ecology theory rests on basic assumptions for which there is very strong empirical support.

[*Michael Rothery*]

RELATED ENTRIES

F.S.B. Bowers, H. Cassidy, Environmental Issues, Organizational Theory, Person-in-Environment Perspective, Systems Theory, Theory & Practice

REFERENCES

Bowers, F.S.B. 1949. The Nature and Definition of Social Casework: Part III. *Social Casework* 30, 10, 412–17.

Germain, C., and A. Gitterman. 1996. *The Life Model of Social Work Practice: Advances in Theory and Practice*. 2nd ed. New York: Columbia University Press.

Hearn, G. 1958. *Theory Building in Social Work*. University of Toronto Press.

Meyer, C. 1988. "The Eco-systems Perspective." In R. Dorfman (Ed.) *Paradigms of Clinical Social Work*. 275–95. New York: Brunner/Mazel.

Rothery, M. 2001. "Ecological systems theory." In P. Lehmann and N. Coady (Eds.), *Theoretical Perspectives for Direct Social Work Practice*. 65–82. New York: Springer.

Turner, F.J. 1978. *Psychosocial Treatment in Social Work*. New York: Free Press.

von Bertalanffy, L. 1968. *General Systems Theory: Foundations, Development, Applications*. New York: Braziller.

education in social work

Formal education for social workers has existed in Canada since the University of Toronto opened its school (later, faculty) of social work (est. 1914).

Before then, the majority of students seeking professional preparation at a university sought it in one of the US programs, and a few to such UK programs as the ones at London School of Economics and Oxford. Unlike the format followed by most other professions, university education for social workers began at the graduate level, with master's degree programs. However, because university regulations in some early programs required that students held an undergraduate degree in the subject in which they were seeking a graduate degree, the first year of the master's of social work program at Ottawa and Toronto was designated as a bachelor of social work year, for which the students were awarded a formal degree. In a few instances, students with this bachelor's degree moved directly into practice; nevertheless, the master's degree remained the baseline for membership in the profession. In the 1970s, two advances in social work education were seen in Canada: community college programs, and the offering of baccalaureate programs at universities. The rapid development of diploma programs in community colleges emphasized social welfare curricula. Initially, there was little formal interface between community college programs and university-based programs; however, as college programs continued to flourish and their graduates found positions in a broad range of social welfare positions, this separation began to change. Many community college graduates, after some experience in the field, found themselves interested in formal social work recognition and sought admission to university social work programs; frequently, such students reported that some of their first-year university course material was a repetition of material taught in college. Another perspective on the closer relationship between colleges and universities offering these programs is that many faculty in university programs were also teaching in college programs; they also reported a high degree of commonality of course material and student abilities. Social workers teaching in community college programs reported that, overall, the quality of the curricula was strengthening. Recently, formal dialogue among various colleges and universities began, on a discipline-to-discipline basis; to date, this dialogue is uneven but ongoing. Some universities schools and faculties now recognize material learned in colleges

courses, particularly if the college courses were taught by university staff.

The increased interest in a formal bachelor of social work program led to its development in the 1970s to become the baseline degree for the social work profession. Most of the then-existing Canadian schools of social work offered a bachelor's program, and new departments, schools, and faculties of social work were opened in other Canadian universities. Alongside this accelerated movement to the baccalaureate program, an interest in Canadian accreditation emerged. Until this time, the US Council on Social Work Education was accrediting only master's degrees in social work throughout North America; thus, the many new Canadian schools offering the bachelor program would be excluded from having their graduates accredited. By the time the US council moved to the accrediting of bachelor's degrees, the Canadian accrediting body, the Canadian Association of Schools of Social Work (est. 1967), had long been functioning. The Canadian accreditation system, now accepted as authoritative, establishes and maintains the quality of university-based programs. A reflection of its influence is seen in the fact that several provincial statutes set graduation from an accredited school of social work as the basis for the recognition of formal education credentials leading to qualification as a registered social worker. One of the thrusts of the Canadian accreditation process is to maintain the sensitive balance between respecting the autonomy of a university to set and shape its own curricula, while ensuring that each program meets the content and standards of the profession.

Demand for entry into university programs of social work has continuously increased, permitting schools and faculties to set and maintain high admission standards. Students in turn have expectations of an excellent educational experience, putting continual pressure on social work programs to enhance the quality of their curricula. The need for competent, well-trained, and knowledgeable graduates to begin practice also continues to grow, ensuring employment for graduating students. In recent decades, further expansion of education for social work relates to the interest in advanced research conducted in doctoral degrees, which also provide training for new faculty in social work programs to meet increasing needs. In a very short time, the profession has moved from having a single Canadian doctoral program to nine, with others in planning stages.

[*FJT*]

ego psychology

Ego psychology, an outgrowth of Freudian psychoanalytic theory, is the study of the ego that was favoured by a majority of clinical social workers from the 1940s to the 1970s. While Freud himself laid out a grand plan for understanding the human psyche, his own thinking and writing focused primarily on the id, drives, and the unconscious; consequently, his work is now often referred to as "id psychology." Ego psychology moved the emphasis of psychoanalysis from the id to the ego, the rational executive function of the psyche, similar to the adult in transactional analysis. The founders of the ego psychology school were Heinz Hartman, Ernst Kris, and Rudolph Lowenstein, joined by Anna Freud, Sigmund Freud's daughter. Hartman was the "founding father" of ego psychology and his goal was to develop this new approach to psychoanalysis in a way that built on, but did not contradict, Freudian theory. At a time when other members of Freud's Vienna circle were developing their own theories, Lowenstein and his colleagues desired to stay within the Freudian fold. The major emphasis of ego psychology is the functioning of the ego. It is understood that the ego needs to develop a certain amount of autonomy from the id and superego so that it can make the decisions it needs to keep the individual mentally healthy: Freud's definition of mental health was the ability to love and work. The ego is required to negotiate and find a balance between the demands of the id, the censure of the superego, and the reality of the environment. In doing so, the ego is often required to settle for what are called compromise formations, the bases of neuroses. The basic understanding of the functioning of the ego is that it consists of areas of primary and secondary autonomy. The areas of primary autonomy are those functions that should develop to their full potential from birth in a conflict-free state, independent of any interference caused by psychological conflicts. It is understood that, if these areas of functioning are hampered by psychological issues, the person has a very serious psychological problem. The areas of secondary autonomy are the psychological aspects of the personality. These areas of ego functioning are born and develop in conflict between the id, superego, and environment; they create neuroses and, in extreme cases, psychoses. The significance of ego psychology to social work practice can be understood by putting its introduction to North America into a time frame. Psychoanalysis had come to North America in the 1930s and 1940s and was firmly entrenched in the medical profession—something that Freud had not wanted to happen—by the outbreak of the Second World War. During this same period, as social work was struggling for professional recognition, social workers were finding their way into hospital settings and adopting the dominant language of the medical field, namely psychoanalysis; they were accused by their non-clinical peers of violating the basic tenants of the budding profession. After the war, when Freudian psychoanalysis was no longer thought to be the perfect answer to all human issues, clinical social workers began to question their use of it. Ego psychology found its way across the waters and, with its emphasis on adaptation and the relationship between the ego and the environment, breathed new life into the devotion of clinical social workers to psychoanalytically based therapy. Ego psychology was the dominate form of clinical social work practice from the end of the Second World War until the 1970s, when the rapid growth of new theories of individuals, families, and groups, presented clinicians with many new and appealing options.

[*Robert Twigg*]

elder abuse

Elder abuse is harmful behaviour directed toward older people by family members or professional caregivers whom an older person loves or trusts or on whom he/she depends for assistance. Abuse that occurs where an older person lives, whether alone or with a caregiver, is referred to as domestic elder abuse, while abuse that occurs in hospitals, nursing homes, and long-term care facilities is referred to as institutional abuse. The abuse could include physical, psychological, and material harm to an older person. Physical abuse refers to the use of bodily injury, physical pain, or impairment inflicted by physical force (i.e., striking, hitting beating, pushing, or burning). Medical maltreatment, such as the overuse of physical restraints, and sexual assault are sometimes included within physical elder abuse. Psychological abuse, also referred to as verbal or emotional abuse, involves the intentional inflicting of mental anguish on an older person (i.e., name-calling, humiliation, intimidation, threats of abandonment). Material abuse, often referred to as financial abuse, involves the intentional, illegal, or improper exploitation of an older person's material property or financial resources (i.e., fraud, theft, or use of money or property without the person's consent). Some, but not all, forms of elder abuse may be prosecutable crimes (i.e., fraud, theft, physical assault, sexual assault). Neglect, also considered to be a form of elder abuse, refers to the intentional or unintentional failure to fulfil a caretaking responsibility to an older person. Sometimes self-neglect—an older person's own behaviour that threatens his/her health and safety—is included as a form of elder abuse. Recently, violation of civil rights has been included as institutional elder abuse, and abandonment has been considered within domestic elder abuse. The only national study of the prevalence of domestic elder abuse (i.e., number of occurrences in a lifetime) found that 4 percent of Canadians reported some type of abuse: 2.5 percent material abuse, 1.4 percent chronic verbal aggression, 0.5 percent physical abuse, and about 0.4 percent neglect (Podnieks et al. 1989). There is no Canadian study about the incidence of domestic elder abuse (i.e., number of new occurrences in a specific time) and no national prevalence or incidence studies of institutional elder abuse. No causes of elder abuse have been confirmed, but explanations abound (e.g., hypotheses for caregiver stress or that abuse is learned in the family). No combination of risk factors has been identified to assist detection, and the efficacy of most intervention methods has not been established; at best, research suggests that victims of psychological and physical abuse have good health but psychological problems, while their abusers typically have a history of psychiatric illnesses and/or substance abuse, live with the victim, and depend on them for financial assistance. Physical abuse is more likely to be inflicted on disruptive older people with dementia who live with family caregivers. While financial abuse does not have a typical victim, it may be more serious when the abused person is dependent on the abuser. Victims of neglect tend to be very old with cognitive and physical frailties.

Four major programs have developed in response to elder abuse: statutory adult protection, domestic violence model, advocacy, and integrated approaches. Adult protection legislation characterized by legal powers of investigation and intervention has been enacted in various forms in Nova Scotia, Prince Edward Island, New Brunswick, and British Columbia; Nova Scotia also has mandatory reporting. Domestic violence programs include crisis intervention services, emergency sheltering, support groups, and education for victims and the public. Advocates for the abused ensure that the needs of victims are met and their rights are known and respected; this is possible only when the advocate is independent from the formal delivery system. The integrated model includes delivery of a broad array of health and social services. Prevention of elder abuse has been approached through education of the victim, the public, and professionals. Social work has played an extremely important part in the brief history of recognition and response to elder abuse in Canada beyond involvement in the design and delivery of intervention. Many of the first studies to identify the problem were carried out by social workers (Pittaway & Westhues 1993), and the first four books ever written in Canada about elder abuse were by social workers: Schlesinger and Schlesinger's 1988, *Abuse of the Elderly: Issues and Annotated Bibliography*; McDonald et al.'s 1991 *Elder Abuse and Neglect in Canada*; MacLean's

1995 *Abuse and Neglect of Older Canadians: Strategies for Change*; and Reis and Nahmiash's 1995 *When Seniors Are Abused: A Guide to Intervention.*

[*Lynn McDonald*]

RELATED ENTRIES

Abuse, Assessment, Caregiving, Child Abuse, Crisis Intervention, Peer Counselling, Personal-Centred Theory, Sensitizing Concepts, Services to Elderly People, Therapy, Treatment, Torture & Trauma Victims, Vicarious Traumatization, Women Abuse, Wellness

REFERENCES

Pittaway, E.D., and A. Westhues. 1993. The Prevalence of Elder Abuse and Neglect of Older Adults Who Access Health and Social Services in London, Ontario, Canada. *Journal of Elder Abuse and Neglect* 5, 4, 77–93.

Podnieks, E., K. Pillemer, J.P. Nicholson, T. Shillington, and A.F. Frizzell. 1990. *National Survey on Abuse of the Elderly in Canada.* Toronto: Ryerson University.

employee assistance programs

Employee assistance programs provide management and labour with the opportunity to improve job performance as well as enhance worker health, safety, and well-being by providing assistance to employees and their families with such problems as alcoholism, substance abuse, and related behaviours. While inaugural programs had mandatory participation components, current programs typically rely on supervisory, union, peer, or medical referral with an ever-increasing emphasis on voluntary use. These programs attempt to resolve employee concerns by directing workers to appropriate treatment or self-help groups. Successful plans are most often administered by a joint labour/management committee that develops a formal written policy and administers the program (Dickman et al. 1988; EAPA 1990). Critics of employee assistance program claim that workplace intervention is merely a mechanism of social control, that provide employers with a sanctioned systematic method for handling employees judged to be deviant or unfit for the workplace. This criticism has led to reproaches against clinical practice models that ignore poor working conditions, stressful work environments, and lack of worker participation as determinants of employee

problems. Practitioners interested in prevention as well as treatment draw attention to the need for these programs to also create positive organizational change and to empower employees through ongoing involvement in program development, promotion, administration, and workplace change (Corneil 1984; Karasek & Theorell 1990). Clinical services to individuals with personal problems have been delivered in some fashion in the workplace since the mid-1800s. Welfare capitalism, which was the forerunner of employee assistance programs, was primarily a paternalistic effort to obtain worker loyalty by meeting some basic employee needs. The demise of welfare capitalism occurred in the late 1930s, just as Alcoholics Anonymous was emerging as a social force. In the 1940s Alcoholics Anonymous went to industrial leaders with its method to help alcoholic employees. With employees being drawn into the Second World War, employers needed every available employee and many accepted the Alcoholics Anonymous model, which became the base on which occupational alcoholism programming was created. While social work in its infancy had been a foundation for earlier workplace interventions, the profession expressed little interest in doing so in this period. Workplace intervention became the role of managers and supervisors, much to the chagrin of many members of the labour movement who charged that occupational alcoholism programs were witch hunts to find and discharge union members (Csiernik 1992; Popple 1981). By the 1970s psychoactive drugs had entered the North American consciousness and a broader orientation to workplace problems led to the formal emergence of employee assistance programs. Greater use of counselling emerged as more behavioural problems were being identified as the source of employee issues. The rush to embrace the US medical treatment model led to the proliferation of third-party counsellors covered by private insurance to deal with the range of problems identified through the workplace (Wrich 1980). This trend came to Canada in the late 1980s with an explosion of private practitioners in the field. Interest in employee assistance programs has now increased, owing to the recognition of the interrelationship between job-based difficulties and personal problems. Acknowledgment of the fact that problems from home manifest themselves in the workplace and that problems from work go home with employees has led some organizations, particularly in western Canada, to change the name of their employee assistance plans to employee and family assistance programs. Over time three distinct models of delivering assistance have emerged in Canada:

- *internal volunteers*: recovered individuals (through AA), union counsellors, peer counsellors, and referral agents; and formal self-help groups in the workplace;
- *internal professionals*: social workers and associated counselling professionals, medical staff (occupational health nurses and occupational physicians), human resources staff; and
- *external professionals*: private practice social workers and associated professionals, large multidisciplinary agencies, and consortia.

Currently, clinical services provided by these programs focus on crisis intervention, brief solution-focused counselling, critical-incident stress debriefing, and case management. Many organizations have also added a health promotion and wellness orientation. As well, the legacy of Alcoholics Anonymous persists in strong self-help and peer-assistance orientations among employee assistance plans, particularly within unionized workplaces. Despite periods of limited activity, occupational social workers have made vital contributions to the field. Social workers bring an ecological orientation to employee assistance programs; increasingly progressive programs are also examining the impact of the workplace on existing problems as well as how the nature of work creates employee problems (Csiernik 1996, 1998).

[*Rick Csiernik*]

RELATED ENTRIES

Clinical Social Work, Ecological Theory, Employment, Health & Unemployment, Industrial Social Work, Medication, Peer Counselling, Psychotropic Medication, Substance Addiction

REFERENCES

Corneil, W. 1984. History, Philosophy and Objectives of an Employee Recovery Program. In W. Albert, B. Boyle, and C. Ponee (Eds.) *EAP Orientation*. 54–72. Toronto: Addiction Research Foundation.

Csiernik, R. 1992. The Evolution of Employee Assistance Programming in North America. *Canadian Social Work Review* 9, 2, 214–28.

———. 1996. Occupational Social Work: From Social Control to Social Assistance? *The Social Worker* 64. 3, 67–74.

———. 1998. An Integrated Model of Occupational Assistance. *The Social Worker* 66, 3, 37–47.

Dickman, F., B. Challenger, W. Emener, and W. Hutchison. 1988. *Employee Assistance Programs: A Basic Text*. Springfield, MA: Charles C. Thomas.

EAPA. 1990. Introduction to the Employee Assistance Professionals Association. Arlington, PA: Employee Assistance Professionals Association.

Karasek, R., and T. Theorell. 1990. *Healthy Work: Stress, Productivity and Reconstruction of Working Life*. New York: Basic Books.

Popple, P. 1981. Social Work Practice in Business and Industry, 1875–1930. *Social Service Review* 55, 257–69.

Wrich, J. 1980. *The Employee Assistance Program*. Centre City, MN: Hazelden.

employment

Employment is not only a major source of income and psychosocial recognition for individuals; in modern capitalist society, where labour is seen as a commodity, it is also a property to be regulated by the labour market. Idealized conditions for a perfect labour market, which might be expected to satisfy allocative efficiency and full employment, are unachievable (Casson 1979); therefore, government measures are expected to protect individuals as well as broader societal interests against insecurity caused by labour market failures. In most welfare states based on Keynesian economic theory, including Canada, full employment was seen as a major component of the overall welfare system. The Marsh report on social security in 1943 and the 1945 white paper on employment and income had both recommended a full-employment policy; however, federal governments since then have frequently been criticized for their lack of commitment to maintaining this policy (Guest 1990). More recently, a "natural" rate of unemployment based on the concept of the non-accelerating inflation rate of unemployment, has replaced the Keynesian ideal of full employment (McQuaig 1999). In the 1990s Canada's average official unemployment rate frequently exceeded 9.5 percent, based on the monthly Labour Force Survey of about 50,000 Canadian households. Moreover, since the survey counts only people who are actively seeking employment during the survey week, the official rate of unemployment tends to underestimate the actual situation; such forms of unemployment as involuntary part-time work, loss of overtime or shortened work hours, and discouraged workers who give up looking for work remains undetected. Major causes of unemployment include personal preference (i.e., searching for a better job, inducing income for other purposes), the nature of the job market (i.e., money-wage rigidity, wage differentials in different occupations, information problems), and structural factors (i.e., changes in technology and economic demands, seasonal fluctuation of demands, and discrimination) (Casson 1979). In Canada personal preference as a cause of current unemployment rates is insignificant; on the other hand, economic globalization, as a structural factor that emphasizes free trade and competition, has been indicated as a major cause of high unemployment. Unemployment has traditionally been perceived as a problem of male adults (Giddens 1994). Youth, immigrant, and female workers are ignored within employment trends when they work in low-wage and part-time jobs with low job and income security. Youths have also experienced employment difficulties; throughout the 1990s unemployment rates among youth in Canada were consistently above 14 percent. Despite a confirmed correlation between years of education and level of earning, there is a trend toward teens aged fifteen to nineteen years old being neither employed nor studying full-time; in the same age group, there is a trend for males dropping out of school to work (Canada 2000). Many of the 200,000 immigrants who come to Canada each year face unique barriers to employment, including language problem, unrecognized credentials and foreign experience, and lack of Canadian work experience; as a result, immigrants are being segregated and marginalized from the dominant job market. Following spectacular increases in the 1980s, the labour force participation rate of women levelled off in the 1990s. Meanwhile, women are spending more time working in unpaid positions and in work that is not covered by employment insurance (Canada 1997). The documented history of social workers' involvement with the unemployed dates from at least 1929 (Irving & Daenzer 1990). Social work has a mandate to serve the unemployed (Riches & Ternowetsky 1990), yet most contemporary employment services are provided by employment and career counsellors. Recently, many community colleges have offered formal training programs in employment counselling, largely based on the assessment component of employment counselling model.

The Unemployment Insurance Act, 1940, was to provide income protection to workers who became unemployed; renamed as employment insurance in 1996, the program tightened eligibility and decreased the amount of benefits. Since then a statistic called the beneficiary/unemployed ratio is calculated for a given week by dividing the number of regular employment insurance beneficiaries by the total number of unemployed people; records of this statistic show a substantial decline in the number of people receiving unemployment benefits, from 80 percent in the 1980s to 40 percent in the 1990s (Roller 1999). In 1996 the federal government presented a labour market development proposal that outlined retraining and job creation programs, including employment counselling, job search preparation, retraining courses, job placement, support services for self-employment, and grants for businesses. To respond to regional variation in unemployment conditions, this proposal permitted each province and territory to develop its own labour market program to reflect its priorities and needs. Some wonder if national standards for protecting the unemployed risk further weakening as a result; nonetheless, most of these programs are based on the eligibility of employment insurance. In turn, employment became a prerequisite for labour entitlement, which determines who has a right to share the social wealth through an insurance system founded on a male adult labour market.

[*Miu Chung Yan*]

RELATED ENTRIES

Employee Assistance Programs, Employment Insurance, Employment Insurance Act, Great Depression (1930s), Globalization, Health & Unemployment, Income Security, Industrial Social Work, Marsh Report, Private Practice, Private-Sector Employment, Privatization, Social Welfare Context, Trades & Labour Congress of Canada, Unemployment Assistance Program, Unemployment Insurance Act, Vocational Rehabilitation, Workers Compensation

REFERENCES

Canada. 1997. *Economic Gender Equality Indicators.* SW21-17/1997E. Ottawa: Status of Women Canada.

——. 2000. *Profile of Canadian Youth in the Labour Market.* RH61-1/2000E. Ottawa: Publication Office, Applied Research Branch, Strategic Policy, Human Resource Development Canada.

Casson, M. 1979. *Youth Unemployment.* London: Macmillan.

Giddens, A. 1994. *Beyond Left and Right: The Future of Radical Politics.* Cambridge, UK: Polity.

Guest, D. 1990. Government and Market: Response to Unemployment. In G. Riches and G. Ternowetsky (Eds.) *Employment and Welfare.* Toronto: Garamond.

Irving, A., and P. Daenzer. 1990. Unemployment and Social Work Practice: An Historical Overview—1929–1987. In G. Riches and G. Ternowetsky (Eds.) *Employment and Welfare.* Toronto: Garamond.

McQuaig, L. 1999. *The Cult of Impotence: Selling the Myth of Powerlessness in the Global Economy.* Toronto: Penguin.

Riches, G., and G. Ternowetsky (Eds.) 1990. *Unemployment and Welfare: Social Policy and the Work of Social Work.* Toronto: Garamond Press.

Roller, S. 1999. *Report on the Main Results of the Employment Insurance Coverage Survey, 1998.* 73F0008-XPE. Ottawa: Statistics Canada, Income Statistics Division.

employment insurance

Employment insurance is a federal government program the main objective which, since its inception, has been to insure against the risk of temporary and involuntary unemployment for those who are active in the labour market. The original program was introduced through the Unemployment Insurance Act, 1940; under the Employment Insurance Act, 1996, the name of the program changed to employment insurance. A significant part of the income security system, the program has been revised several times over the last sixty years. Important reforms in the 1970s broadened the goals of the program to include special benefits for individuals unemployed as a result of the birth or adoption of a child, illness, and temporary disability. The program has always been financed through employer/employee premiums, where employers pay 1.4 times the employee contribution, based on a percentage of employee weekly earnings up to an annual maximum salary (currently, $39,000). Employment insurance is administrated by a federal agency now known as the Canada Employment Insurance Commission, which is part of the Human Resources Development Canada ministry; the commission sets program policy and regulations, including the premium rate. Almost all employed persons, including self-employed persons who fish are covered by employment insurance. A person who becomes unemployed must have demonstrated their attachment to the labour force by having paid into the employment insurance program, and must have worked a minimum number of hours throughout the previous year as minimum eligibility to receive benefits while unemployed. Coverage is denied to people who cannot show just cause in cases of voluntary withdrawal or dismissal from employment. Eligibility is based on the hours of work accumulated during the previous year. The minimum required hours vary according to regional unemployment levels: in regions where the unemployment rate is low (i.e., less than 6%), a minimum of 700 hours is required, while claimants residing in regions where the unemployment rate is high (i.e., greater than 13%) must acquire a minimum of 420 hours. Notable exceptions include people entering the workforce for the first time and, in most cases, people re-entering the workforce after an absence of two or more years, who must work a minimum of 910 hours to be eligible. People who apply for maternity, parental, or sickness benefits must have acquired 600 hours of work to qualify for benefits. No benefits are paid for a waiting period of two weeks. While unemployed people are receiving benefits, they must demonstrate their willingness and ability to work in order to remain eligible. Depending on the regional unemployment rate and the number of hours the person has worked over the preceding year, the duration of benefits range from fourteen to forty-five weeks. When the number of hours is held constant, the duration of benefits is typically longer in regions with higher rates than in regions with lower unemployment rates. The basic benefit is 55 percent of a claimant's average weekly insured earnings. Although a claimant can receive benefits by meeting the minimum regional requirement, he/she must have worked at least two weeks longer in order to receive the basic benefit rate. Low-income families receiving the child tax benefit may qualify for the family income supplement; in such instances, the benefit rate may exceed 55 percent. Average weekly insured earnings are calculated by dividing the total earnings accumulated over the previous twenty-six continuous weeks by the greater of either the number of weeks worked in this time period or by a set divisor adjusted to the regional unemployment rate. This amount is multiplied by the applicable benefit rate to determine the weekly income benefit. In all cases, benefits do not exceed $413 per week. Once a recipient's benefits have been exhausted, he/she must once again acquire the required minimum hours of employment and contribute to the system in order to qualify again. As with other programs created to respond to social need, there is much debate about the purpose of employment insurance and its program effects. Criticisms stem from the opinion that employment insurance creates disincentives to work and, thereby, exacerbates unemployment. Other concerns point to how restraints to employment insurance contribute to the loss of income security for many Canadians.

[*Erin Gray*]

RELATED ENTRIES

Employment, Health & Unemployment, Income Security, Social Welfare Context

Employment Insurance Act

The Employment Insurance Act, 1996, provides the legislative authority for the federal government program the main objective for which, since its inception, has been to insure against the risk of temporary and involuntary unemployment for those who are actively involved in the labour market. The original Unemployment Insurance Act, 1940, underwent major revision in 1955 and 1971, and in 1996, when the name of the program was changed. Each Act has been amended a number of times during its tenure. Prior to 1940, responsibility for issues concerning unemployment fell under provincial authority as prescribed by the British North America Act, 1867 (now Constitution Act, 1867). However, the hardships experienced during the great depression of the 1930s overwhelmed the capacity of provinces and municipalities to provide relief to millions of jobless Canadians who

could not control the economic downturns that had led to unemployment. The challenges posed by soaring unemployment pointed to the need for a national social insurance program. The Employment and Social Insurance Act, 1935, was defeated by Parliament on constitutional grounds, as it was alleged the federal government had attempted to intrude in an area of provincial jurisdiction. Nevertheless, the constitution was eventually amended to give the federal government the authority needed to pass the Unemployment Insurance Act in 1940. Initially, unemployment insurance covered about 42 percent of the labour force. Coverage was restricted to those employed in work considered to be at moderate risk for unemployment only, whereas those employed in either secure or highly unstable work including seasonal employment, were excluded. The costs of the program were shared among employees, employers and the federal government. The 1955 Act broadened benefits and extended coverage to about 75 percent of the labour force. Eligibility requirements were relaxed, benefit rates were increased, and benefit periods were lengthened. Allowable earnings regulations were eased and seasonal benefits—introduced as supplementary benefits in 1950—were increased to match the rate of regular benefits. With economic growth accompanied by heightened public expectations, unemployment insurance served as a federal policy instrument to carry out macroeconomic objectives. The 1971 Act vastly liberalized unemployment insurance as access into the program was eased further and a more comprehensive range of benefits was offered. Coverage became almost universal (nearly 93%). Benefit rates were increased and eligibility was extended to those who experienced an interruption in employment as a result of pregnancy or sickness. While cost sharing among employees, employers, and government continued, the federal government assumed fiscal responsibility for benefits related to higher rates of unemployment (4%+). High unemployment rates persisted in the period following the 1971 Act, and the growing demand on federal resources led to a concerns about government spending. Amendments later that decade tightened eligibility criteria, reduced benefit rates, and shortened benefit periods. Provisions were made so that regional differences in the unemployment rate affected the terms of eligibility and the duration of the benefit period. Divergent opinions emerged about whether unemployment insurance should be based fundamentally on insurance principles, or whether it should address issues of income redistribution; a series of studies on the purpose of unemployment insurance in the 1980s revealed that opposing and competing positions were widespread throughout Canadian society. Reform, as it has unfolded since the late 1980s, contrasts sharply to the liberalization of the previous decade. Unemployment insurance costs were skyrocketing, becoming a target for governments facing demands for spending cuts and financial restraint; as a result, funding responsibility for the unemployment insurance program shifted to the employer and employee alone in 1990, when federal financial support was withdrawn. Citing pressures stemming from structural economic change, the government instead expanded active employment strategies for unemployment insurance. The Employment Insurance Act, 1996, invoked more far-reaching restraint than before, including much tighter eligibility rules, reduced benefit amounts, and shorter benefit periods. An offer made to the provinces and territories for transfer of responsibility related to active re-employment benefits (i.e., wage subsidies and support for self-employment) would see the federal government withdraw from the purchase of labour market training. The evolution of the legislature on unemployment insurance reflects historical efforts by governments to rationalize social security during times marked by changing social and economic circumstances and shifting political imperatives.

[*Erin Gray*]

RELATED ENTRIES

Employment, Health & Unemployment, Income Security, Social Welfare Context, Unemployment Insurance Act

empowerment theory

Empowerment theory in social work seeks ways for people to participate actively to overcome divisions between personal troubles and public issues, and effect changes in themselves and their milieu. This theory has attained a high degree of importance in social work practice in the last decade. This theory draws on the potential of other theories as well as its own concepts to link the personal and political potential for supporting oppressed groups to bring about positive change in their lives. Empowerment theory seeks connections between personal suffering and social justice. Empowerment theory sees its historical roots in the work of Jane Adams, Bertha Reynolds, and the African American Woman's Clubs (Lee 1996). Current influences include liberation theology, the work of Germain and Gitterman (1996) and their stress on the interconnection of all aspects of reality, and systems theory. A social worker cannot give empowerment to clients but can help clients to seize it for themselves through a positive sense of self-knowledge of their reality and the development of strategies to attain freedom from oppression. Educative processes can assist people to articulate and better understand the reality that must be changed, and to achieve comfort in seeking power as a goal. This approach draws heavily on reflective thinking, support, resource generation, encouragement, self-awareness, and consciousness raising. Practitioners must work hard at understanding the client's story and history of oppression. As in practice that draws on feminist theory, persons often have to learn to deal with their own personal problems before they can feel confident enough to move to broader systemic issues. Practice using this theory may be with individuals or with communities, where a heavy reliance on group work can be useful (Schwartz 1974). Social workers have a responsibility to include all persons, especially those who are oppressed and frequently overlooked by more traditional theories, many of which are seen to create systemic barriers to them. Working through this theory requires knowledge and skill in working with individuals, small groups, and large systems, including political bodies. Empowerment theory has widespread support as a basis for work with oppressed people and communities within national and international contexts.

[*FJT*]

RELATED ENTRIES

Anti-oppressive Social Work, Citizen Participation, Community Development, Natural Helping Networks, Peer Counselling, Personal-Centred Theory, Practice Methods, Race & Racism, Racism-Sensitive Social Work, Theory & Practice

REFERENCES

Germain, C., and A. Gitterman. 1996. *The Life Model of Social Work Practice: Advances in Theory and Practice.* 2nd ed. New York: Columbia University Press.

Lee, J.A.B. 1996. The Empowerment Approach to Social Work Practice. In F.J. Turner (Ed.) *Social Work Treatment.* 4th ed. 218–49. New York: Free Press.

Schwartz, W. 1974. Private Troubles and Public Issues: One Social Work Job or Two? In R.W. Klenk and R.W. Ryan (Eds.) *The Practice of Social Work.* 2nd ed. 62–81. Belmont, CA: Wadsworth.

environmental issues

Always fundamental to social welfare and the practice of social work, environmental issues currently focus on two major perspectives: professional practice (i.e., person-in-environment) and environmental change (i.e., global social policy):

Person-environment practice is an emergent model of direct practice that makes strategic use of time to accomplish three things:

- improving a client's sense of mastery in dealing with stressful life situations, meeting environmental challenges, and making use of environmental resources;
- achieving this end through active assessment, engagement, and intervention in the environment, considered multidimensionally, with particular emphasis on the mobilization of personal social network; and
- linking individual concerns in ways that promote social empowerment through collective action. (Kemp, Whitakker, & Tracy 1997: xi)

The person-environment practice model comprises positive building blocks for partnership, mutuality, reciprocity, social assets, resilience, optimization of improvement, natural helping, social integration (coping skills), coherence (sense of meaning), and hope. Kemp, Whitakker, and Tracy further note that: "Despite the centrality of 'person-environment' as a key construct... the core focus of direct practice, assessment and change strategies has centred more on 'person' than 'environment'" (1997). The assessment of human needs from a person-in-environment perspective is essential to social work theory and practice. Factors in the environment (i.e., transportation, housing, socialization opportunities, accessibility of health services and social supports)

have been a major focus of intervention and policy development. Ironically, while new technology and research have led to better health and social services, environmental barriers often prevent access to these resources; expensive new services, for example, are usually located centrally and may be out of reach or unknown to people living a distance from them. Similarly, barriers exist due to gender, age, social class, and ethnic issues. With the advancement of high-speed communication, transportation, and world markets, these barriers have become both more obvious and less acceptable.

Throughout the 1970s, 1980, and 1990s, environmental issues have acquired a global meaning equally as critical as those directly related to practice. That is, weather change, depletion of natural resources, pollution and environmental ecosystem conflicts have challenged the quality of life for people all over the world. Direct social work intervention and research on these issues have been limited, except for addressing the increased human suffering that results from them. Current social work policy statements on the environment, such as that articulated by the National Association of Social Workers, indicates clearly that environmental exploitation violates the principle of social justice and is a direct violation of the association's code of ethics (1999). The same concerns exist in Canada. More than 90 percent of Canada's land area is primarily uninhabited, as urban centres constitute only 0.3 percent of the land area. (Keating 1997: 81). Because Canada has more environmental land area per person than most affluent nations, environmental issues have a unique importance to its population and policies. Much of the economy is dependent on exploitation of natural resources. Depletion of the uninhabited resource areas, and increasing pollution of virtually all areas have had an enormous economic social welfare impact on Canadians' quality of life. Pollution has produced harm to health as well as the economy. These impacts are creating additional needs for financial, clinical, and community development intervention. Canada's Aboriginal peoples are particularly hard hit (Gordon & Suzuki 1990; Knudtson 1992). From a positive perspective, the Canadian standard of living has repeatedly been rated in the top ten in the world according to the United Nations Development

Program's Human Development Index, using life expectancy, education, and national income indicators (Keating et al. 1997: 54). Canada has not experienced the widespread severe poverty that affects much of the world; however, depletion of such natural resources as forests, marine life, and fresh water is beginning to harm some Canadians. Environmental depletion and change are closely associated with conflict as well as poverty. Reduction of supplies such as forest and fish stocks have created harm as well as policy disputes. Increased environmental disasters such as floods and severe weather, owing in part to global warming, have created trauma as well as financial losses. In short, environmental problems, and conflict between economic systems and ecosystems have escalated (Keating et al. 1997: 65–75), adding to the need for social welfare policies, programs, and resources. While Canada ranks high in the world in quality of life, global environments are interdependent: "Ecological interactions do not respect the boundaries of individual ownership and political jurisdiction" (WCED 1887: 46–47). Canada's environmental and social welfare advantages are diminishing, as global dimensions of economic and ecologic issues affect them.

[*Peter E. Bohm*]

RELATED ENTRIES

Assessment, Diagnosis, Ecological Theory, Personal-Centred Theory, Person-in-Environment Perspective, Theory & Practice

REFERENCES

Gordon, A., and D. Suzuki. 1990. *It Is a Matter of Survival*. Toronto: Start.

Keating, M., and Canadian Global Change Program. 1997. *Canada and the State of the Planet: The Social, Economic, and Environmental Trends Are Shaping Our Lives*. Toronto: Oxford University Press.

Kemp, S.P., J.K. Whittaker, and E.M. Tracy. 1997. *Person-Environment Practice*. New York: Aldine deGruyter.

Knudtson, P. 1992. *Wisdom of the Elders*. Toronto: Stoddart.

National Association of Social Workers. October 1999. Policies: Five Added, 17 Revised. *NASW News*. Washington, DC: National Association of Social Workers Press.

WCED. 1987. *Our Common Future*. New York: World Commission on Environment and Development, Oxford University Press.

Gerald Erickson (1935–89)

Erickson, Gerald Dale, social work educator, administrator: b. 1935, Ashland, WI; d. 1989

Gerald Erickson became a scholar, social work educator, administrator, and leader in mental health practice. Following his service in the US army, he graduated from Northland College, in his home town and, in 1963, received a master's degree in social work from the University of Michigan. Erickson was employed by the Wisconsin Department of Health and Social Services for two years before becoming the chief psychiatric social worker at the Marshfield Clinic in Marshfield, Wisconsin (1965–69). He moved to Canada in 1969, where his skills as an educator and administrator were soon evident in positions as associate professor of social work at the University of Manitoba (1969–78), director of the Psychological Services Centre, University of Manitoba (1976–78), chairman and associate professor of the Department of Social Work at York University in Toronto (1978–82), and director and professor of the school of social work at the University of Windsor (1982–89). He was a decisive, democratic, and innovative administrator who strongly believed that a university served the needs of the community. Erickson was, for example, the founding graduate program director of a unique part-time master's program in social work, based on a tutorial model at York University. At the University of Windsor, he advocated for a part-time master's program as well as evening and weekend classes, and upgraded the quality of field placements. During a two-year sabbatical from the University of Manitoba, he moved to York, England, to pursue his doctorate. In the thirteen years between achieving his doctoral degree in 1976 and his death in 1989, Dr. Erickson achieved a remarkable body of scholarly research, teaching, writing, and developing social work education. He served on the editorial boards of *Canada's Mental Health, the International Journal of Family Therapy, and the Canadian Journal of Community Mental Health.* He presented papers at many national and international conferences, and was a consultant to numerous human service organizations. Erickson was the author of articles published in many prominent journals in his field. In 1975 he published the seminal article, "The Concept of Social

Network in Clinical Practice" which, in combination with subsequent articles in the same area, substantially increased his reputation in the field of social network theory. His July 1988 article, "Against the Grain: Decentering Family Therapy" elicited more responses, according to the editor, than any previous article in the history of the *Journal of Marital and Family Therapy*. Despite his comparatively late start in entering the world of academia, Dr. Gerald Erickson made an enduring contribution to social work education and to the literature on family therapy, social networks and social support.

[*Rebecca Erickson*]

RELATED ENTRIES

Clinical Social Work, Education in Social Work, Family Therapy, Marital and Family Problems, Social Planning, Social Policy, University of Windsor (School of Social Work)

ethical issues

Ethics in social work practice serve to articulate the principles that distinguish this profession from others. Concepts such as social justice, equitable distribution of resources, and focusing on the best interests of the client provide a framework under which social workers practice. Practitioners are continually faced with deciding among interventions or courses of action for which they must weigh ethical values—their own, the client's, the profession's, and others'—as well as legal implications. An ethical dilemma is rarely simple and is usually multi-dimensional. For this reason, social workers operate within a framework where ethical dimensions of decisions can be weighed. The literature articulates a variety of means to make such decisions, with the following critical areas in common:

• What is the ethical dilemma?
• What are the conflicting ethical principles and standards?
• What are the different possible courses of action, including risks or consequences?
• What other issues may have an impact on the decision (e.g., legal considerations)?
• What action do you choose?
• What are the outcomes of this chosen action?

Professional standards for social workers are outlined by the Canadian Association of Social Work-

ers code of ethics, most recently set in 1994 but, at the time of writing, undergoing review. The code is subject to periodic review to keep pace with the ever-evolving state of social work regulation. Most provinces and territories use this code in whole or part to hold their members accountable. In general codes of ethics serve four key purposes:

• to provide a statement of moral principle that helps the individual professional to resolve ethical dilemmas;
• to help establish the group as a profession;
• to act as a support and guide to individual professionals;
• to help meet the responsibilities of being a profession. (Sinclair et al. 1991)

The social work code of ethics also most often intersects with the legal obligations of practitioners. From a legal point of view, the practitioner's first point of reference is the law under which he/she practices (e.g., child protection); few practitioners perceive an ethical conflict on limitations of confidentiality where the law requires mandatory reporting of child abuse. Similarly, social workers inevitably comply with the legal "duty to warn" in situations of imminent harm, such as when he/she knows that death threats have been made against an identifiable person, despite owing confidentiality to a client. In weighing situations where ethical responsibilities appear to be in conflict, social worker can rely on the law and their professional code of ethics as their frames of reference. While the national association's code of ethics provides the lead for Canadian practitioners, more and more organizations that employ social workers are developing their own workplace codes or statements of ethical principles, under which social workers must also practice. In addition specific practice areas, for example, mediation and family therapy have a further code for their members. For the most part, the ethical values or principles in these separate codes or statements will coincide with those in the professional code for social workers. When this is not the case, the professional code must take precedence. Social workers can practise through ethical standards that differ from those in written codes, depending on personal preference, perhaps from spiritual beliefs, cultural traditions, or commitments to particular approaches to practice. When personal ethics conflict with the professional code, the professional code must take priority.

In this era of rapid complexity and increasing client workloads, two areas of ethical decision making can provide further reassurance for social workers. One is the process of evaluating potential outcomes, and the other is consultation. Often, the selection of an outcome for a difficult decision is when things goes wrong. To aid future decision making, an experienced social worker will take the necessary time to review ethical situations and share his/her assessment, so that opportunities for learning can also be lost. The role that consultation plays in resolving ethical issues cannot be underestimated. Practitioners should not hesitate to consult colleagues, supervisors, administrators, or even a social work regulatory body about a decision to be made, and document this consultation in detail. While the pace of practice has escalated dramatically in recent years, it is nevertheless critical that consultation—particularly in weighing ethical dilemma—continue to be fundamental to social work. It is especially vital when decisions must be made that override a client's rights, that is, when the law takes precedence so that client confidentiality may be set aside. Many agencies now have legal specialists available for such consultations. Consultation can serve to lessen the natural discomfort that practitioners feel when ethical issues arise.

[*Kathy L. Jones*]

RELATED ENTRIES

Accountability, Bioethical Issues, Canadian Association of Social Workers, Codes of Ethics, Diversity, Human Rights, International Practice, Knowledge Base, Legal Issues, Malpractice, Professional Liability, Provincial/Territorial Associations, Research, Recording, Sensitizing Concepts

REFERENCES

Jones, K. 2002. Ethical Issues. In F. Turner (Ed.) *Social Work Practice: A Canadian Perspective*. 417–29. Toronto, ON. Prentice Hall.

Sinclair, C., S. Poizner, K. Gilmour-Barrett, and D. Randall. 1992. *The Development of a Code of Ethics for Canadian Psychologists*. 1–11. [Companion manual to the Canadian Code of Ethics for Psychologists, 1991.] Canadian Psychological Association.

ethnic-sensitive practice

Canadian social workers are uniquely positioned to show global leadership in practice that is sensitive to clients' ethnicity. Europeans from several countries began the mixing of cultures by emigrating to the lands inhabited by diverse Aboriginal peoples that eventually became Canada. Since contact, ongoing immigration has contributed to an increasingly diverse social mosaic. Strong influences in social work from the United States and the United Kingdom, however, have meant that until recently the Canadian social work orientation has been limited to models of practice that tended to be ethnocentric to dominant cultures in those countries. Such approaches in social work have constrained the profession's ability to be effective in helping people whose ethnicity, culture, and languages differ from those of the dominant cultures. Recently, an understanding of these ethnocentric biases and their effect on practice has helped social workers to develop alternative practice models and approaches that demonstrate sensitivity to ethnicity and cultural differences. Many social workers have yet to ensure that their practice methods are sensitive to ethnic and cultural differences. The profession has taken some preliminary steps to set policy to advance practice sensitivity; for example, the Canadian Association of Schools of Social Work now requires as part of its accreditation standards that schools incorporate Aboriginal and multicultural content into their curricula, taking into account the specific ethnic and cultural composition of their catchment area. Social work programs in northern Ontario, for instance, are offered in French, in English, and for First Nations, as a reflection of the high numbers residents with francophone, bilingual (English/French), anglophone, and several First Nation ancestries. In larger urban centres, where recent immigration features increases in people from Asia, the Caribbean, and war-torn regions, curricula are to reflect each of these realities. The complex needs of ethnic-sensitive social work practice, however, will require considerations beyond establishing professional curriculum standards. The profession could act to advance ethnic-sensitive practice by, first, determining a common understanding of what ethnic-sensitive practice is and how social workers can know when they have achieved it. Teachers of social work can be encouraged to test their own assumptions and biases and, in turn, guide students to work through any internalized oppression they may have. The process of helping social workers achieve ethnic-sensitive practice is still experimental and practitioners in the field as well as students can benefit from ongoing educative guidance to work effectively with people from a different ethnicity or culture from their own. Social workers and teachers also need to take into account that diversity exists within ethnic and cultural identifications. Finally, the profession can promote greater recruitment from among ethnicities and cultures beyond those of the dominant societies, so that they can provide leadership in the development of ethnic-sensitive practice. The profession needs to be more reflective of the Canadian mosaic than at present. Social workers educated in ethnocentric models of social work can benefit from educative efforts that can enhance their awareness and help them to operate from an ethno-sensitive perspective. Leadership for this rests among those in the profession from cultures beyond the dominant societies with the experience and expertise gained from their own ethnic-sensitive perspective. Being open to learning from social workers who come from within this perspective—rather than appropriating knowledge from it—can help social workers from outside it to accept their colleagues from different cultures as the leaders of ethno-sensitive social work practice. Respect for difference and diversity has always been part of social work's professional ethos, but only in the last few years this commitment been addressed in ways that are meaningful for practice. Social workers face challenges and opportunities for supporting and guiding one another toward practice that truly reflects sensitivity to colleagues and clients for enhanced working relationships and a more balanced society.

[*Anne-Marie Mawhiney*]

RELATED ENTRIES

Aboriginal Issues, Anti-oppressive Social Work, Culture, Diversity, Ethnocutlural Communities' Services, Healing Theory (Cree), Minorities, Practice Methods, Race & Racism, Racism-Sensitive Social Work, School Social Workers, Sensitizing Concepts, Theory & Practice, Visible Minorities

ethnocultural communities' services

An ethnocultural community demonstrates the multiple facets of ethnicity, where ethnicity refers to any or collectively all aspects of the phenomena related to an ethnic community, and particularly to people possessing a common national or geographic origin, culture, or religion (Isajiw 1999: 17). Members of the dominant societies in Canada still tend to have the decisive voice in major institutions that provide social services, and people from within minority ethnocultural communities have been—and still are—characterized as possessing less social, political, and economic power in Canada, as a result of either legislation that mandates this or of entrenched social practices that continue social inequality (E.N. Herberg 1989: 17–21; 1990: 207–209), despite official policies of multiculturalism and anti-discrimination. Persistent social inequalities are particularly problematic for members of minority ethnocultural communities because the social foundation of relations between the dominant societies and minority communities has been a tension between maintaining their sense of common identity and heritage on the one hand and the need to participate in mainstream institutions outside their ethnocultural community on the other (E.N. Herberg 1989: 10). To provide appropriate ethnocultural social services, social workers need to understand elemental factors internal to each ethnocultural community that influence the pattern of its own community services, or/and that of mainstream services:

1 *The total number of members in an ethno-racial community in a particular locale*: Obviously, the pattern of ethnocultural services must be different for communities that possess hundreds of thousands of members than for those that have many fewer members, in comparison.

2 *The percent that the group membership number comprises of the total population in the region*: Groups that constitute a tiny fraction of the area population invariably receive less assiduous attention by mainstream agencies in planning, developing and providing ethnic community or mainstream services than for ethnoracial communities that makes up a majority or large minority of the total local population.

TABLE 1: Values in High- and Low-Context Cultures

High-Context Values (in Ethnocultural Communities)	Low-Context Values (in Mainstream Society)
The family is central.	The individual is central.
Members are hierarchically ordered.	Members are egalitarian.
Men and women are segregated.	Men and women are integrated.
All are highly interdependent.	Independence is paramount.
The society is religious.	Secularism is dominant.
Traditions are unquestioned.	Everything is questioned.
Time is polychronic.	Time is monochronic.
Approach is holistic.	Approach is fragmentary and analytical.
Communication is oral.	Communication is written.
Place of origin is important.	Mobility is essential.

Source: D.C. Herberg [1993] 35–51

3 *The percentage of each ethnoracial community and the entire region that are immigrants to Canada*: Immigrants have very different service needs than those in the second or later (Canadian-born) generations. And, recent immigrants need quite different kinds of services than immigrants who are long-time residents in Canada.

4 *Ethnic language—retention and use*: The diversity and nature of services need be different for ethnoracial communities possessing higher degrees of retaining and using their heritage language than in communities that have become largely linguistically assimilated.

5 *Residential concentration of the community's members*: Very different patterns of service content and locations are needed for ethno-racial communities that have a great majority of members living in proximity to other group members than for communities in which the group's members are thoroughly dispersed across the entire region.

6 *Degree of religious monopoly*: The extent that affiliation with only one religion exists in the ethnoracial community: A community whose members almost entirely belong to the same religion will have or need a different set of services than one in which religious participation is spread over many different faiths, with no one dominating.

7 *Degree of institutional completeness*: The extent of diversity in and number of ethnic social institutions existing within an ethnoracial community, parallel to the institutions of the mainstream society: The communities with a very great degree of institutional completeness will be largely self-sufficient in serving its members, compared to the great reliance on mainstream service agencies by minority communities with few or no internal community agencies. Prominent amongst ethnoracial community institutions are their own health and social agencies, educational services, community governance, and media (E.N. Herberg 1989: 93–95, 226–39).

Each of these phenomena affects different ethnocultural communities differently. Some members of ethnocultural communities have maintained a social, even geographic, separation from others so as to retain their culture (i.e., some Jewish, Muslim, Mennonite, Hutterite, Mediterranean, Asian, and Aboriginal communities), while other individuals have abandoned much or most of their heritage, culture, and community boundaries. In turn, the pattern each minority ethnocultural community develops in its members' adaptation to Canadian society has strongly influenced the nature and depth of its own internal social services as well as the form and content of services in mainstream institutions delivered to each ethnocultural community. As in the past, ethnocultural communities continue to develop social services to meet objectives shared by many community members, or to meet their universal needs in ways traditional to their culture. The first such services to emerge are usually mutual-benefit organizations, often were established under the aegis of clergy or/and congregants of a religion prominent within the community (Harney 1978). Faced with few people to serve and few resources, recent immigrants, for instance, organize themselves to provide the kinds of assistance that in their home country was provided by the extended family, village, or national government (Canada 1970: 107–108; Harney 1979); soon a formal immigrant-aid agency is organized to help subsequent members of this community who emigrate, especially with orientation, getting around the city, finding employment, obtaining health care and schooling for their children. As each immigrant community develops—and especially as their Canadian-born children form their own families—a variety of other organizations emerge to guide adaptation to their adopted homeland or development of ways to continue to practise their traditional culture. Thus, distinct social services formed within ethnocultural communities are distinguishable from mainstream services. Usually, services are provided by people from the same background who speak the communities' language(s). Official language provision in mainstream social services tends to be in English and French in most of Canada; Quebec and the territories provide services in the official languages under their jurisdictions. These policies, however, can be a challenge for members of ethnocultural communities who may have little proficiency in these official languages. Further, some people may have poor literacy skills in official languages and be unable to read vital information or complete forms to get services from mainstream social services.

Social workers from many mainstream social services may also use such terms as "relationship," "personality," "aptitude," "motivation," "early childhood," or "empowerment" assuming that all clients understand them and their underlying presumptions. A treatment centre may expect parents of a disturbed child, for example, to report on or keep written notes about their child's early developmental experiences in the expectation that the parents are able to read, write, and complete forms, and/or have some knowledge of psychology fundamentals. People may feel reluctant to give personal information about an individual's problems social workers who are perceived to be ethnocultural strangers. Furthermore, services are provided strictly at prearranged appointment times, because clock-time is important to most caregivers and many clients in institutions focused on efficiency. By contrast, minority ethnocultural community services may operate under different assumptions and values, drawing on cultural expectations of the ethnocultural community they serve, with the flexibility to use oral and written reporting in appropriate languages and behaviours. Non-linear high-context modes of thought are still likely to be held by recent immigrants and elderly people; even among the second and third generations, linear thought patterns common in mainstream society are often not deeply ingrained. Caregivers, accordingly, are expected to act as extended family members or, at least, people of their own ethnocultural community who can be entrusted with personal information. If a person cannot be helped by family members, then he/she may believe that service from an agency within their ethnocultural community is their sole acceptable resource. The values in Table 1 based on the theories of Hall (1984) sketch several dimensions of how ideas and beliefs of the traditional societies (from which many of the immigrants to Canada have come since the introduction of the colour-blind Immigration Act, 1968 (repealed in 2001) vary from the low-context expectations and values of post-industrial Canadian society. High-context values are generally found in ethnocultural community service agencies—and only in rare instances in mainstream social services.

To complicate the situation, each ethnocultural community is to some extent divided by religious and political ideologies. In addition while immigrants come here with the similar objectives of achieving a better life for themselves and their children, the disparate means by which they achieve them create other differences within the community. Some people try to adapt to Canadian ways by making significant personal changes, while others expect and try to achieve their objectives with very little change to their values or cultural practices. Minority community ethnocultural services experience a range of cultural adherence among clients, as some people's more traditional ways and others' become transitional. Conflict over cultural adherence and identity invariably affect families and community ethnocultural organizations. Those who follow traditions strongly may view with disapproval those who change as disloyal to their cultural heritage and practices, and consciously erect barriers of social distance to them. Clearly, ethnocultural service workers need to become aware of the variety of dimensions in which they work. Social workers also need to be taught to recognize and understand that many factors, such as rifts within minority ethnocultural communities, may interfere with effective service delivery. A major issue of this multifaceted area of service delivery is where ethnocultural services should be located: in an ethnic community or a mainstream agency. Ethnocultural community agencies quickly learn what funders appreciate most in service provision (i.e., efficiency, fiscal restraint), and have responded by amalgamating or partnering with other ethnocultural agencies or even with a mainstream agency. Various models of co-operation among ethnocultural community and mainstream agencies have merged, in which a primary concern is to assure that social workers in ethnocultural agencies educate their colleagues in mainstream agencies. Thus, mainstream agency staff learn to provide social services that complement, not contradict, minority communities' cultural values and practices (Herberg & Herberg 2001).

[*Dorothy Chave Herberg* and
Edward W. Herberg]

RELATED ENTRIES

Aboriginal Issues, Aboriginal Services, Anti-oppressive Social Work, Citizenship & Immigration Canada, Codes of Ethics, Culture, Diversity, Ethics, Ethnic-Sensitive Practice, Immigrants & Immigration, Minorities, Peer Counselling, Race & Racism, Racism-Sensitive Social Work, Sensitizing Concepts, Services for Refugees, Visible Minorities

REFERENCES

Canada. 1970. *The Cultural Contributions of the Other Ethnic Groups.* Report of the Royal Commission on Bilingualism and Biculturalism. Book 4. Ottawa: Information Canada.

Hall, E.T. 1984. *The Dance of Life: The Other Dimension of Time.* Garden City, NY: Anchor Press Doubleday.

Harney, R.F. 1978. Religion and Ethnocultural Communities. *Polyphony: Journal of Ontario Multicultural History Society* 1, 2, 3–10.

———. 1979. Introduction, and Records of the Mutual Benefit Society. *Polyphony: Journal of Ontario Multicultural History Society* 2, 1, 1–3, 5–18.

Herberg, D.C. 1993. *Frameworks for Cultural and Racial Diversity: Teaching and Learning for Practitioners.* Toronto: Canadian Scholars Press.

Herberg, E.N. 1989. *Ethnic Groups in Canada: Adaptations and Transitions.* Toronto: Nelson Books Canada.

———. 1990. The Ethno-Racial Socioeconomic Hierarchy in Canada: Theory and Analysis of the New Vertical Mosaic. *International Journal of Comparative Sociology* 31, 206–21.

Herberg, D.C., and E.N. Herberg. 2001. Canada's Ethno-Racial Diversity: Policies and Programs in Canadian Social Welfare. In J.C. Turner and F.J. Turner (eds.) *Canadian Social Welfare.* 4th ed. Toronto: Pearson Education, and Allyn and Bacon Canada.

Isajiw, W.W. 1999. *Understanding Diversity: Ethnicity and Race in the Canadian Context.* Toronto: Thompson Educational.

experimental research designs

Experimental designs are used by social work researchers who desire to isolate direct relationships of cause and effect. Typically, these research designs are viewed as limited to laboratory experiments, where researchers measure the effect of a particular stimulus (e.g., when an educational film about the harmful effects of smoking on a person's health is used to change a subject's patterns of smoking). Experimental designs are also commonly used in social work practice to evaluate the effect or effectiveness of intervention. An experimental design is attractive because it allows the research practitioner to control such threats to internal validity as

• *extraneous events* that coincide with the period of intervention and which may mediate the influence of the intervention on its targeted attitude or behaviour;

• *maturation of the subject over time*, as when a bereaved client improves with time independent of a counsellor's intervention;

- *the effect of the testing experience*, and of the instrument used, on the effect being measured;
- biases that are inherent in the selection of subjects/clients for participation in treatment; and
- *ambiguity about the direction of a causal relationship*, as when it is unclear whether behaviour change was the result of completion of intervention or that completion of intervention was the result of behaviour change (i.e., did the intervention make the client better, or did the client's getting better allow for them to complete the program of intervention).

Experimental designs control for threats to internal validity through the use of an experimental group, members of which receive the intervention being tested or evaluated, and a control group, members of which do not receive the intervention, but administer the measurement instruments that are used to gauge the effect of the intervention on the experimental group. An experimental design is distinct from pre-experimental and quasi-experimental designs, which use a comparison group rather than a control group to measure against the experimental group. The key difference is that a control group is equivalent in important characteristics to an experimental group. Equivalence is not a strict concern when using a comparison group. Equivalence of the experimental group and control group is achieved in an experimental design through random assignment and matching: research participants are randomly assigned to the experimental group and the control group, and are matched according to relevant demographic or other characteristics. For example, in a study looking at the effect of cognitive therapy in teaching anger management skills to a prison population, the experimental and control groups will be comprised of the same proportions of population characteristics (i.e., ethnicity, age, and gender) as well as characteristics specific to the study (i.e., violent offenders, non-violent offenders). Through random assignment and matching, the researcher practitioner is able to control for the mediating influence of demographic and other relevant differences on the effect of the intervention.

A research study may be designed in accordance with one of three main types: classic (also called pre-test/post-test control-group design),

post-test/only control-group design, and the Solomon four-group design. In classic experimental design includes an experimental group, which receives pre-testing, an intervention, and post-testing, and a control group, which is given pre-testing and post-testing but no intervention. By comparing the difference in pre-test and post-test scores for the two groups, the researcher practitioner is able to separate the effect of the intervention on the post-test score from the effect of taking the pre-test and its effect on the post-test. As well, because both groups take the pre-test and the post-test at the same time, extraneous historical events that may influence post-test scores can be controlled. The post-test–only control-group design is used when it is not practical to administer a pre-test before intervention. A researcher practitioner who wants to determine the psychological effect of sexual victimization on a child, for example, is not able to measure a particular child's psychological traits before victimization; however, it is possible to construct a control group that is equivalent on all relevant demographic and other characteristics to a group of children who have been sexually victimized, and then compare the two groups on characteristics that would be affected by victimization. The design assumes that the process of random assignment and matching removes any significant differences between the experimental and control groups. Consequently, the researcher practitioner can identify specific psychological and emotional effects of victimization. The most elaborate experimental design is the Solomon four-group design, which has two experimental groups and two control groups. As with other designs, participants are randomly assigned to the four groups and are matched for equivalence. One experimental group receives the pre-test, intervention, and post-test; the other experimental group is not given a pre-test, but is provided intervention followed by the post-test. One control group receives the pre-test and post-test; the other control group is given only the post-test. Through this design, the researcher practitioner is able to isolate the effect on the post-test scores of the pre-test, extraneous historical events, and the interactive effect of the pre-test with the intervention. In other words, through comparison of the four groups, it is possible to distinguish independent effects of the pre-test and intervention, as well as the interactive effect of the pre-test with the intervention. Although this design is the most sensitive to measuring the effect of intervention, it is not commonly used in social work studies, as forming four distinct groups is difficult, as is coordinating the pre-tests and post-tests to occur at the same time for four groups.

[*Ross A. Klein*]

RELATED ENTRIES

Capacity Assessment, Demography, Research

F

Fabian Society (UK)

The British Fabian Society (est. 1884) was founded to promote evolutionary socialism in accordance with the highest moral responsibilities (de Schweinitz 1972). It has been referred to as the best-known and most successful agent of social reform in English history (Cole 1969). Implementation of major parts of the Beveridge report in 1942 to usher in the welfare state in 1948 have been referred to as the "Fabian dream come true" (Cole 1969). The Fabian Society attracted to itself the most enthusiastic and original body of women and men, some of whom represent English intellectual legend: dramatist Bernard Shaw, sexologist Havelock Ellis, futuristic novelist H.G. Wells, economist Sidney Webb and his wife, sociologist Beatrice Webb, two future prime ministers Ramsay Macdonald and Clement Atlee, suffragette Emily Pankhurst, labour theorist Harold Laski, philosopher Bertrand Russell, and social reformer Annie Besant. One unique characteristic for its time was the presence of four women among the founding members. The name "Fabian"—from Fabius, the commander of the Roman army that defeated the mightier army of Hannibal of Carthage by a cautious strategy of delay and avoidance of direct encounter—reflects the society's axiomatic approach to social reform. The Fabians' strategic approach was to bring about socialism incrementally by means of electoral and parliamentary advances, and redirection of the existing state institutions, for instance, by public ownership of industry, social services, and re-distributive taxation (Tivey & Wright 1989). The gradualist notion of social action was a rejection of Marxist theory of class struggle; Karl Marx's *Das Kapital* had been translated into English in 1880 and circulated widely in academic circles. Instead, the Fabians hoped to promote equality for all through collective ownership and democratic control of the nation's resources. They concerned themselves with a long succession of practical reforms, such as suffrage for women, the eight-hour work day, municipal water supply, housing, public education, and a standard minimum wage (de Schweinitz 1972). To contextualize the Fabians' contribution to the profession of social work, their ideology can be compared to that of another philanthropic organization of the time, the Charity Organization Society. Both the Fabians and the Charity Organization reacted to the 183 harsh amendments to the English Poor Laws, but the latter society preferred to remedy instances of injustice that resulted from the reformed Poor Laws rather than change or repeal the laws themselves. The Fabians, on the other hand, looked beyond individual injustices to the underlying class and social structure. For the Fabians, poverty was not a problem of individual character but a problem of economic and industrial organization (Titmuss 1963). Nonetheless, in 1912, the two societies formally merged and together established the London School of Economics, which made a commitment to social investigations and the need for social policy to be grounded in a firm empirical base. The school's emphasis on research gave rise to some germinal research projects that were used to inform and subsequently change existing policies (Bulmer, Lewis, & Piachaud 1989). Another major accomplishment of the Fabians was the leading role they played in the creation of the British Labour Party. No group of people has come together in the quest for social justice comparable to the Fabian Society as successful agents for social change.

[*Lindsay H. John*]

RELATED ENTRIES

W.H. Beveridge, Poor Laws (UK), Social Planning, Social Policy, Social Welfare History, Welfare State

REFERENCES

Bulmer, M., J. Lewis, and D. Piachaud. 1989. Social Policy: Subject or Object? In M. Bulmer, J. Lewis, and D. Piachaud (Eds.) *The Goals of Social Policy.* London: Unwin Hyman.

Cole, M. 1969. *The Story of Fabian Socialism.* Stanford, CA: Stanford University Press.

de Schweinitz, K. 1972. *England Road to Social Security*. New York: A.S. Barnes.

Titmuss, R.M. 1963. *Essays on the Welfare State*. London: Unwin University Books.

Tivey, L., and A. Wright. 1989. *Party Ideology in Britain*. London: Routledge.

faculties of social work

Social work curricula throughout Canadian universities, brought about by the process of accreditation, have much in common. One area of difference, however, is the location of social work programs within universities: the three major administrative structures in English-language universities are departments, schools, and faculties. In the United States the distinction between a school and a faculty is blurred with many schools of social work having a dean as their principal administrative officer. In Canadian universities, there is a much clearer distinction in that deans of faculties report to a university vice-presidents, and directors of schools report to deans. At this time in Canada there are five social work programs in English-language universities with the designation of faculty (Calgary, Manitoba, Regina, Toronto, and Wilfrid Laurier). Within the profession and the accreditation process, no distinction is made between a faculty and a school, as long as it has a distinct social work identity. Within a university, however, a program headed by a dean has much more influence over university policies in general as well as in its ability to attract resources. Also, within the university, graduates of a faculty have a clearer identity in the university's overall profile. Whether the faculties of social work are likely to increase in number is not clear, as it is not a topic of current concern to the profession. From a longer perspective in the sociology and politics of academe, the development of more programs in faculties could strengthen the position and profile of social work in universities generally and, thereby, further enhance the profession as a whole. A factor in this development may be the increasing importance of the doctoral degree in the profession.

[*FJT*]

RELATED ENTRIES

Canadian Association of Schools of Social Work, Carleton University, Doctorate, Education in Social Work, Knowledge Base, Practicum Instruction, Professional Continuing Education, Universities of Manitoba, Regina, Toronto, Wilfrid Laurier; also Schools/Departments of Social Work or Social Services at: Carleton University, Dalhousie University, Lakehead University, McGill University, Memorial University, Okanagan University College (Kelowna), Ryerson University, St. Thomas University, Université de Moncton, Université de Montréal, Université de Sherbrooke, Université du Québec à Montréal, University College of the Cariboo, University College of the Fraser Valley, and Universities of: British Columbia, Calgary, Manitoba, Northern British Columbia, Regina, Toronto Victoria, Waterloo (Renison College), Western Ontario, Windsor

Families and Schools Together Canada

Families and Schools Together Canada (est. 1999) is based on the program originally developed by Dr. L. McDonald and her family service colleagues in Madison, Wisconsin. There, an innovative two-year collaborative prevention and early intervention program with parental involvement is aimed at assisting children between six and nine years old identified by their school as having academic and behaviour difficulties. Over the years, the US program has been highly effective in prevention and amelioration of the problems. Originally brought to Canada, where it is known as F@ST by Catholic Charities of Calgary, the program has now spread to a broad range of Canadian family service agencies, principally in Ontario through the work of Family Service Ontario. Later, in 2001, it was taken over by Family Service Canada/Services à la famille—Canada in Ottawa.

[*FJT*]

RELATED ENTRIES

Family Services Canada/Services à la famille—Canada, Services for Families

Family Allowance Act

The Family Allowance Act, 1944, enabled the federal Department of Health and Welfare to start administering family allowances (also known as children's allowances) in 1945. At the time, the Act was considered one of the most comprehensive initiatives in the world, in that it provided for universal cash allowances for all children under sixteen. One contemporary commentator noted that the Family Allowance Act was the "first piece of legislation in Canada, which extends to all citizens on an equal basis, a helping hand in the task of rearing their children. In effect it says to all children that they have an equal right to share in the revenues of their country, that they all are entitled to freedom from the pressures of poverty" (Gould 1945: 31). Although the idea of a national family allowance program did not become reality until 1945, it was debated on several earlier occasions: "The subject received careful considerations in 1929 by a Parliamentary Committee of the Liberal Government, and in 1932 by the Quebec Social Insurance Commission" (Stepler 1944: 2). It was again discussed in 1942 at the national convention of the Co-operative Commonwealth Federation, where support was given for a national family allowance program. It was not until 1943 when Leonard Marsh's report on social security was released that the necessary work for adoption of family allowance legislation began. This report recommended family allowance as an integral component of a national social security system (Stepler 1944). Marsh had argued that "children's allowances have a basic claim in any really clear-sighted system of social security, for both normal and dependency situations" (cited in Stepler 1944: 6). Why family allowance at that time? In the context of post-war Canada, emphasis in social planning was given to freedom from want and, given the conditions of the day, meeting children's needs was financially challenging for most families; poverty was widespread (Stepler 1944; Gould 1945). Family allowance, as an income security program for families with dependent children, recognized this reality (Armitage 1988). Family allowance, however, also had the goal of improving Canada's post-war economy (Armitage, 1988; Battle & Torjman 1992).

The introduction of family allowance into Canadian social welfare encountered much resistance. While strong advocates, such as Margaret Gould (1945) and Dorothy Stepler (1944), offered viewpoints in favour of the system, some well-respected social policy advocates, such as Charlotte Whitton (1945) and Claris Edwin Silcox (1945), argued against the proposed family allowances. Two criticisms emerged. First, as inadequate levels of payment were administered, child poverty was not being addressed by the program. Second, universality did not differentiate family incomes, so that the same benefits were paid to high- and low-income families (Armitage 1988). Changes were later made to income tax legislation in response to the latter criticism, along with other changes throughout its tenure (see Battle & Torjman for a summary); however, it always remained an initiative for lower-income families. In 1993 the Children's Special Allowance Act virtually ended the federal government's role in universal social welfare programs. Instead, the Family Allowance Act was replaced by a graded system of tax relief to people at various income levels, including a child tax benefit. As a result, the poorest families in the country not only lost their family allowance income but, as well, received no benefit from the new tax benefits.

[*Michael R. Woodford*]

RELATED ENTRIES

Co-operative Commonwealth Federation, Dawn of Ampler Life, Family Research, Family Services Canada, Income Security, Marsh Report, Poverty, Social Planning, Social Welfare History, B. Touzel

REFERENCES

Armitage, A. 1988. *Social Welfare in Canada: Ideals, Realities, and Future Paths*. 2nd ed. Toronto: McClelland and Stewart.

Battle, K., and S. Torjman. 1992. *Child Benefit Primer: A Response to the Government Proposal*. Ottawa: The Caledon Institute of Social Policy.

Gould, M. 1945. *Family Allowances in Canada: Facts Versus Fiction*. Toronto: Ryerson.

Silcox, C.E. 1945. *The Revenge of the Cradles: Population and Family Allowance*. Toronto: Ryerson.

Stepler, D. 1944. *Family Allowances for Canada*. Rev. ed. Toronto: Canadian Institute of International Affairs and Canadian Association for Adult Education.

Whitton, C. 1945. *Baby Bonuses: Dollars or Sense?* Toronto: Ryerson Press.

family and youth courts

Family and youth (formerly, juvenile) courts are generic terms for courts responsible for determining legal issues related to family relationships and people under the age of majority (generally, eighteen years old). The legal or formal names of these courts may vary within a and from province to province or territory. Before the 1970s, courts were very fragmented, with different courts having limited responsibility for different types of decisions (Gall 1995). Family divisions of provincial/territorial courts, for instance, could make decisions about child custody, access, and support but could not grant divorce decrees—while family divisions of superior courts could make decisions about all these matters. Consequent problems that arose included different standards being applied in different courts for similar issues, judge shopping by lawyers, and the inability of judges to deal with related issues in a single forum. Since the 1970s, unification of courts has given judges the power to make decisions across different types of legal issues. As these reforms were implemented, some jurisdictions decided to link more social services to the court, thereby making family and youth courts more than venues for people to litigate disputes (Vayda & Satterfield 1997). Today, courts popularly known as family courts have jurisdiction over issues related to separation and divorce, including parenting responsibilities, primary residence of the child, child and spousal support, possession of the matrimonial home, and division of property; child welfare, including abuse, neglect, adoption, and foster care; and some issues related to abuse by intimate partners, including restraining orders—though similar orders for protection may be sought through criminal court. Courts popularly known as youth or juvenile courts deal with minors who have been charged with criminal offences; only under very specific circumstances can minors be brought into adult criminal court for such serious crimes as murder. Social workers can play the following roles in these courts:

- *as court counsellors*: providing supportive or therapeutic interventions for families under stress, as an adjunct to court services;
- *as educators*: providing legal information to help clients negotiate their way through the legal system, particularly for non-contested issues or matters that do not require legal advice (note that social workers can provide legal information, but not advice, which would be considered unlawful practice of law);
- *as mediators*: facilitating collaborative conflict resolution as an alternative to litigation (e.g., custody and access mediation, child protection mediation, or victim-offender reconciliation programs) (Barsky 2000; Kruk 1997);

- *as diversion counsellors*: offering minors charged or convicted with a crime alternative measures for making amends to the victim of the crime or society in general (e.g., community service rather than incarceration);
- *as probation officers*: ensuring that minors convicted of a crime follow through on the terms of their probation orders and offering psychosocial interventions (including referrals to community-based help);
- *as witnesses*: providing testimony in a court proceeding, which may include fact evidence (information they have observed directly) or opinion evidence (if they have been qualified by the court as an expert witness) (Barsky 1997).

Courts provide opportunities for interprofessional collaboration among social workers, lawyers, judges, and other court and custodial officials. Working in courts can also pose ethical and role conflicts for social workers, including client self-determination versus public safety, family autonomy versus child safety, and confidentiality versus the court's need for full information to make just decisions.

[*Allan Barsky*]

RELATED ENTRIES

Aboriginal Issues, Abuse, E.H. Blois, Bullying, Criminal Justice, Counselling, Cults, Ethics, Family Therapy, Interprofessional Issues, J.J. Kelso, Legal Issues, Mediation Services, Peer Counselling, Practice Methods, Probation, Services for Families, Services for Offenders, Services for Youth, Social Welfare Context, Young Offenders Act, Youth Criminal Justice Act

REFERENCES

Barsky, A.E. 1997. *Counsellors as Witnesses*. Aurora, ON: Canada Law Book.
———. 2000. *Conflict Resolution for the Helping Professions*. Belmont, CA: Brooks/Cole.
Gall, G. 1995. *The Canadian Legal System*. 4th ed. Toronto: Carswell.
Kruk, E. 1997. *Mediation and Conflict Resolution for Social Work and the Helping Professions*. Belmont, CA: Brooks/Cole.
Vayda, E., and M. Satterfield. 1997. *Law for Social Workers: A Canadian Guide*. Toronto: Carswell.

family demographics

To identify and understand the needs of individuals, families, groups, and communities as well as the social issues they confront, social workers often turn to the interdisciplinary study of demography, which provides a picture of the population(s) they serve. By observing, anticipating, and explaining changes in birth, mortality, and migration rates that together determine the size and composition of human populations, demographers demonstrate how changes in the age structure and living circumstances of a population have a direct bearing on the social, economic, and cultural environments within which they exist. Family demographics as a social work profession is "concerned with helping individuals, families, groups and communities.... Social work is concerned with individual and personal problems but also with broader social issues" (CASW 2001).

Several current demographic trends are likely to have an impact on families. The growing cohort of older persons which, by virtue of differences in the life expectancy of men and women, consists of larger numbers of elderly women than men is "projected to place severe strains on health and social services because of their numbers and their expected longevity" (Schmidt 2000). The anticipated growth in the numbers of children and youth living in low-income families including disproportionate numbers of poor lone-parent families and poor Aboriginal families will, it is suggested, also increase demand on social service programs. (In most Aboriginal communities, one quarter of the population comprises people under the age of twenty-five.) Canada has an increasing reliance on immigration to sustain the size of the overall population and/or modest levels of population growth; with this reliance comes the challenge of meeting, in an appropriate and sensitive way, the differing needs of an ethnically, culturally, and linguistically diverse population. The central demographic trend that accounts for the general trend of ageing in Canadian society is the continuing trend toward fewer births and smaller families, as reflected in a total fertility rate of 1.54 births per woman as recorded in 1998, the lowest rate every recorded (Belanger, Carriere, & Gilbert 2001: 29). (Again, the trend in Aboriginal communities is a contrast, as birth rates, particularly for Inuit women, are among the highest in the world.) Since the early 1970s, most Canadian women have chosen to bear fewer children than would be necessary to replace themselves, resulting in a proportionate decrease in the number of children and a corresponding increase in the proportion of older Canadians. Among the factors accounting for the decrease in the average number of children born to women during their childbearing years are delayed age at union formation, postponement of childbearing till later in life occasioned often by prolonged periods of education; a generalized preference for smaller families, the prevalence and broad acceptance of sexual relations outside of marriage, the increased instability of conjugal relationships (both marriages and common-law unions), and the increased labour-force participation of women reflecting fundamental changes in the culturally defined roles and responsibilities of men and women.

Other significant trends of family formation and functioning that shape the issues confronted by social workers include increases in the numbers and proportions of stepfamilies following divorce or separation. In the context of an economy in which most households rely on the earnings of two wage-earners, families that have, by virtue of choice or circumstance, only one earner are disproportionately represented among the ranks of low-income families. The rates of child poverty recorded in Canada toward the end of the twentieth century remained persistently high, with roughly one in every five children living in a low-income family (Vanier Institute 2000: 118–19). Evidence suggests that other families with more financial security often experience high levels of stress in balancing the often competing demands and obligations of their jobs and their families; it is most often women who experience the highest levels of work and family stress as they assume a disproportionate level of responsibility for domestic labour, child care, and elder care. When Canadians decide to marry or live together, to raise a family of whatever size, to separate or divorce, to move from one area of the country to another, they do so as individuals; yet these individual decisions reflect discernible patterns throughout the population, patterns that define the demographic contours of Canada as a society and nation. The choices, needs, and circumstances of family members change as they adapt to the social, economic, and cultural circumstances in which they find themselves. This process of adaptation has laid the foundation for a society that is older and more culturally diverse than the Canada of a hundred years ago. Present-day Canada will call on renewed commitments to and/or entirely new public policies designed to satisfy the income security, health, educational, and social needs of its population. Individuals and communities will be needed to respond to challenges and needs for social support and human services unique to this new era.

[*Robert Glassop*]

RELATED ENTRIES

Demography, Family Planning, Family Research, Family Statistical Patterns, Knowledge Base, Marital & Family Problems, Research, Separation & Divorce, Single Parents, Social Planning, Social Policy, Vanier Institute for the Family

REFERENCES

Belanger, A., Y. Carriere, and S. Gilbert. 2001. *Report on the-Demographic Situation in Canada: Current Demographic Analysis.* 91-209XPE. Ottawa: Statistics Canada.
CASW. 2001. *CASW Presents the Social Work Profession.* Ottawa: Canadian Association of Social Workers. Online at time of writing at <www.casw-acts.ca/>.
Schmidt, Glen. 2000. *The Canadian Social Work Sector: Implications for Education and Professional Development.* Colloquium presentation to the Joint Conference of the International Federation of Social Workers and the International Association of Schools of Social Work. Montreal, July 29–August 02, 2000. Online at time of writing at <www.arcaf .net.social_work proceedings/>.
Vanier Institute. 2000. *Profiling Canada's Families II.* Ottawa: Vanier Institute of the Family.

family: non-traditional

Family construction, traditionally based on blood or marital relationships, has been changing. As a result of changing social norms—especially those concerning women—and the prevalence of divorce, remarriage, individuals choosing not to marry, adoption, multiracial families, and openly gay and lesbian relationships, the conventional conceptualization of the nuclear family no longer reflects current family realities. Forms of family that exist today include the traditional nuclear family (i.e., mother, father, and their children) and such alternate models as extended, single-parent, childless, blended, and same-sex-headed families, as well as families of choice. While some of these non-traditional family struc-tures may appear to be relatively new, some have been commonplace for decades, particularly in cultures where extended family members are part of the immediate family system, such as among the Inuit. In today's society, diverse non-traditional family forms may be more typical than the conventional nuclear family. Nevertheless, the nuclear family model seems to retain its privileged status as the benchmark against which other family forms are evaluated (Okun 1996): "What we take to be 'the family' mid 'family life' is influenced by the ideologies and discourses inherent in the society in which we live at a particular historical point" (Dallos & Draper 2000: 7). Moreover, social work training in family intervention and therapy has been founded on the assumption of "the family as a stable two-parent [heterosexual] social system that remained together over time" (Gorell Bames 1998: 8). Research that informs practice and theory has focused primarily on nuclear families that are primarily white, middle class, city dwellers (Okun 1996). These benchmarks and assumptions are no longer sufficient in today's sociocultural context, especially given social work's commitment to client self-determination, diversity, empowerment, and social justice. Effective preparation for practice considers the diversity of family forms and meaning-making processes within such systems. Constructivist and other postmodern approaches can assist social workers to intervene effectively with alternate family forms (Gorell Barnes 1998). All types of families experience problems and practitioners must critically assess current assumptions about what constitutes a normal healthy family; such concepts are social constructions that are neither phenomenological nor objective. Social workers and other helping professionals need to understand the different ways families are "created, constructed and maintained, and the potential effects on subsequent relational dilemmas" (Gorell Barnes 1998: 9). It is also necessary to maintain flexible conceptual maps of how families translate their lived experience: "Diverse structures for conceptualizing these processes of mutual influence and for exploring the dissonance that can occur between them will help therapists to explore variations in family forms and the relationship of these to the way different families handle troubling events" (Gorell Barnes 1998: 9). From there, developing insight into the psychosocial or conventional issues facing the family, not necessarily related to their structure or composition, is necessary. Considering these in light of family strengths and resources, environmental interactions, and the historical and sociocultural context is fundamental to effective practice. In terms of social welfare, the persistence of the bias toward the traditional nuclear family in many Canadian social policies, as in those of other affluent nations, has oppressed and excluded alternate family models from the public policy environment and made them ineligible for some benefits extended to traditional families. While efforts have been made to reform social policies and programs to be inclusive of non-traditional families, a concerted effort for further change is required: "Unfortunately, at the very times when diverse types of families are ever more prevalent, governmental policies, the radical right, the culture in general, and even the literature on the family field consistently operate to marginalize and pathologize alternative families" (Okun 1996: vii). Calls to return to "family values" have become associated with decreased tolerance for difference and diversity (Okun 1996). Social workers can advocate for policy change that is inclusive of all family forms, thus enabling all models of family to be visible and celebrated parts of Canadian communities.

[*Michael A. Woodford*]

RELATED ENTRIES

Family Demographics, Family Research, Family Statistical Patterns, Gender Issues, Marital & Family Problems, Parenting, Separation & Divorce, Services for Families, Vanier Institute for the Family

REFERENCES

Okun, B.F. 1996. Foreword to C. Anderson, *Understanding Diverse Families: What Practitioners Need to Know*. New York: Guilford.
Dallos, R., and R. Draper. 2000. *An Introduction to Family Therapy: Systemic Theory and Practice*. Buckingham, UK: Open University Press.
Gorell Barnes, G. 1998. *Family Therapy in Changing Times*. Houndmills, UK: Macmillan.

family planning

Family planning programs assist clients with achieving or avoiding a pregnancy through medical intervention, education, counselling and provision of birth control. Family planning can potentially improve the quality of life by creating social, emotional, physical, and economic benefits to both individuals and society (FHI 1998b). With the advent of more sophisticated forms of reproductive technology, the risk of HIV/AIDS and sexually transmitted diseases, as well the exceptional needs of pregnant teens, social workers today play an increasingly significant role in the area of family planning. Their interdisciplinary responsibilities in medical and family-oriented settings provide them with the opportunity to broaden the focus of treatment beyond the medical domain by applying a psychosocial model of assessment and treatment, emphasizing both psychological and social influences. Canadian policies on reproductive health have long recognized the social costs of unplanned pregnancies and the need to assist families with attaining a balance between the desire for children and available resources. In 1969 the federal government's legalization of contraceptives paralleled the establishment of family planning clinics, operating mostly in hospitals and regional health departments. As federal government policies on family planning began to take greater form, the first National Conference on Family Planning took place in Ottawa on March 2, 1972. One proposal at that time identified the need to ensure that information, including training programs, were accessible in a variety of settings. Health Canada continues to emphasize the importance of accessible family planning programs and, in addition, stipulates that these programs be comprehensible, effective, culturally sensitive, and respectful of individual choices (Canada 1999). At present, about 76 percent of Canadians use some form of contraception, while approximately 10 to 20 percent of couples are deciding not to have children at all (CCT 1995). Historically, social workers as a profession have played a limited role in directly providing family planning services; more recently however, the increase in elective single motherhood, the prevailing economics associated with raising children, as well as the increasing number of women in the labour force, have led to an increase in the need for social workers to address problems and concerns related to family planning. The cost effectiveness of family planning programs is also very attractive in comparison to the long-term expenses associated with unplanned pregnancies. In 1994 the province of Ontario alone spent $18 million on family planning programs, many of them aimed at prevention (CCT 1996); for teenagers in particular, family planning is assumed to refer to prevention or "planning to not conceive." Despite efforts to educate teens and make birth control more accessible, however, in 1997 for the first time, the percentage of teen pregnancies ending in abortion (50.3%) occurred at a higher rate than those ending in live births (46.8%) (Canada 2001). The controversy over birth-control counselling for teens persists but, for social workers, acknowledging the importance of family planning, including abstinence, is a critical task to educate and thereby protect this vulnerable population.

The overriding need for medical intervention with regards to family planning has typically resulted in the administration of services by medically trained personnel such as family physicians or public health nurses. While social workers have traditionally played a secondary role in this area (Schlesinger 1977), the increasing complexity of family issues has generated ongoing referrals by physicians and nurses, particularly in public health, thereby provoking greater involvement by the profession. Essentially, social workers deliver three forms of service to clients with regards to family planning: education, referral, and advocacy and counselling (Bradshaw et al. 1977). The responsibility to educate and to recognize the importance of raising family planning issues in therapy is essential to the profession's commitment to excellence and to serving the best interests of the client. Acknowledging such consequences of unintended pregnancies as post-natal complications, poverty, child abuse, academic failure, or post-abortion trauma provides education with the potential to nurture both insight and protective behaviours on the part of a client. While Canada spent $30 million on abortion services in 1993, it is estimated that each dollar spent on family planning services results in $10 being saved in social welfare costs (CCT 1996). Referrals to family planning services are made by social workers from a variety of settings who encounter individual and couples needing to more fully address the medical aspect of this issue in their lives. Historically, referrals were given to women alone; today, males are also encouraged to explore the many benefits of

family planning and to recognize their responsibilities in this area. It is presumed that, when males are educated about family planning and included in the process, they are more likely to use birth control and consequently improve the rates of effectiveness (FHI 1998a). Today many family planning services have designed more inclusive marketing strategies, appealing not only to men but to differing ages, sexual orientations, and marital status. Social workers are trained to respond sensitively to diverse client backgrounds, honouring how decisions regarding family planning vary according to age, gender, socio-economic status, and culture. Family planning issues are often revealed indirectly during the assessment process: the client who initially presents with marital conflict around intimacy may in fact fear another pregnancy because he/she cannot find an acceptable form of birth control; or the partner who believes another child will restore a failing marriage in spite of the fact that they are ill-equipped in many ways to raise another child. Regardless of the model of therapy used, social work intervention in the form of traditional casework establishes and more clearly defines the link between family planning and specific presenting concerns. For example, the basis of a particular client's alcohol abuse as well as anxiety related to yet another unplanned pregnancy compels the social worker to identify treatment goals to address both the fundamental concern of effective birth control as well as the dynamics underlying the problematic nature of other issues such as stress management or a sexually abusive relationship. Family planning services are an investment in the overall health of society. Policies and programs that enable individuals, couples, and families to access reliable and cost-effective means to safeguard their fertility and their family planning goals, benefit the entire community. Social workers play an important role in supporting the family planning efforts of their clients through both direct intervention and referral. Their contribution to this aspect of reproductive health is both preventive and treatment-based; ensuring access to services and information is a primary responsibility they undertake, particularly with those clients most at risk for unplanned pregnancies. The social work value of self-determination is critical when working with clients on the very personal matter of family planning. Future directions for social workers therefore include broadening their knowledge base of family planning resources, continuing to support those needing assistance to utilize these services, recognizing and promoting the significant role of males in family planning, and taking a stand on the development of federal policies and programs related to advanced reproductive technologies.

[*Angela Townend*]

RELATED ENTRIES

Abortion, Family Demographics, Family Research, Family Services Canada, Family Therapy, HIV/AIDS, Marital & Family Problems, Parenting, Pregnancy, Royal Commission on New Reproductive Technologies, Services for Families, Services for Women, Single Parents

REFERENCES

Bradshaw, B., W. McIlhaney Wolfe Jr., MD, T. Wood, and L. Stansbury Tyler, MD, 1977. *Counseling on Family Planning and Human Sexuality.* New York: Family Service Association of America.

CCT. 1996. *The Economics of Contraception, Abortion and Unintended Pregnancy.* Toronto: Childbirth by Choice Trust.

Family Health International. 1998a. Male Participation in Reproductive Health. *Network* 18, 3.

———. 1998b. Contraception Influences Quality of Life. *Network* 18, 4.

Canada. 1999. *Report from Consultations on a Framework for Sexual and Reproductive Health.* Ottawa: Health Canada.

———. 2001. *Sexual and Reproductive Health.* Fact Sheet. Ottawa: Health Canada.

Schlesinger, Ben. 1977. *Family Planning in Canada. A Source Book.* Toronto: University of Toronto Press.

family research

Social workers have faced profound changes in working with Canadian families over the past fifty years and, in the course of responding effectively, have used family research to guide practice. Significant demographic changes revealed by research have prompted social workers to advocate for those whose needs to care for and provide a nurturing environment for family is compromised by inadequate socio-political conditions. With a constant rise in divorce rates since amendments to the Divorce Act, 1985 (Canada 2001), the very essence of family structure has changed; as a result, social workers often counsel separating and divorcing, single-parent, and blended families. Demographic changes in traditional gender roles, employment patterns, and relationship trends have resulted in couples delaying child bearing and raising children at older ages. As people are living longer, family care responsibilities have been compounded, so that intensive elder-care and child-care needs occur concurrently. At the same time, affordable and accessible day care for children and care for ageing parents are pressing social demands that continue to be under-funded. Family research has also demonstrated an increasing trend in violence against women (Canada 2001). Social work programs responding to the significant rise in reported woman abuse, have evolved to counsel women and children in the aftermath of family violence, as well as to provide treatment for battering partners. Initiatives to address the problem of family violence at all levels of government have been in large part driven by social workers who are creating ground-breaking interventions at family, community, and policy levels. Front-line child welfare workers are also identifying and intervening with families to reduce the occurrence of child maltreatment and promoting parenting practices that support optimal development of children and youth. The unfortunate reality remains that, since the late 1970s, incidences of child abuse and neglect persist at alarming rates (Trocmé et al. 2001). Other demographic factors that have expanded the scope of family social work services include rising rates of immigration and the resulting diversity of culturally varied families (Al-Krenawi & Graham 2002). Studies of immigrant families find that immigration can significantly disrupt parent/ child relations, exacerbate high-risk adolescent behaviour, intensify intergenerational conflict, and contribute to separation of families; the process of acclimatization to a new country is emotionally and physically taxing, as family members reorganize psychologically and socially (Alaggia & Marziali 2002; Ward 1996). Immigration, child poverty, and recent legislation that recognizes gay and lesbian unions have propelled social workers to develop policies and offer interventions to communities at the margins of Canadian society. Important investigations in family research are testing the effectiveness of such intervention models as structural, strategic, multigenerational, and behavioural approaches and developing new approaches. Contemporary models—e.g., brief solution-focused and narrative therapies—have emerged most recently and incorporate important social justice concerns. Certain family systems approaches for specific problems—such as behavioural interventions for families dealing with youth with conduct disorders, family therapy for prevention of drug and alcohol abuse relapse, or family treatment for anxiety orders in children—appear to be more effective than individual interventions alone (Kazdin 2000). From demographic analyses to treatment outcome studies, advances in family research are invaluable in providing social workers with important guidelines for effective practice.

[*Ramona Alaggia*]

RELATED ENTRIES

Family Demographics, Family Statistical Patterns, Knowledge Base, Marital & Family Problems, Research, Social Planning, Social Policy, Vanier Institute for the Family

REFERENCES

Al-Krenawi, A., and J. Graham (Eds.) 2002. *Multicultural Social Work in Canada.* Toronto: Oxford University Press.

Canada. 2001. Census: Violence Against Women Survey. Ottawa: Statistics Canada.

Kazdin, A.E. 2000. Treatments for aggressive and antisocial children. *Child and Adolescent Psychiatric Clinic of North America* 9, 4, 841–58.

Trocmé, N., B. MacLaurin, B. Fallon, J. Daciuk, B. Billingsley, M. Tourigny, M. Mayer, J. Wright, K. Barter, G. Burford, J. Hornick, R. Sullivan, and B. McKenzie. 2001. *Canadian Incidence Study of Reported Child Abuse and Neglect.* Final Report. Ottawa: Health Canada.

Ward, C. 1996. Acculturation. In D. Landis and R.S. Bhagat (Eds.) *Handbook of Intercultural Training.* 124–47. 2nd ed. Thousand Oaks, CA: Sage.

Family Services Canada /
Services à la famille—Canada

The formation of Family Services Canada/Services à la famille—Canada (est. 1977) resulted from a task force set up early in the 1970s by a group of family service agency social workers to develop a national organization for the well-being of families and children. In its five years Family Services Canada operated through a steering committee with regional representatives from throughout Canada; led by its executive secretary, Henry Stubbins, the structure and mission for this new organization was developed. Thanks to grants from the federal government, the organization hired an executive director, Trevor Williams, opened a one-room office in the Canadian Council on Social Development's building in Ottawa. At the inaugural general meeting and conference held in June 1982 in Montreal, Dr. Frank Turner was the keynote speaker. The original signatories in April 1983 to the letters patent of Family Services Canada were: Jacques Alary, Reverend V.R. Boutilier, Frederick A. Day, Nancy Dickson, James Gallagher, Gerard V. Gaughan, Martin Johns, Michelle Lachance, Gilles Lacroix, Jacques Larin, Jacques Lizee, Evelyn McCorkell, Reverend Paul McCraken, Ernest MacDonald, Tom Mills, Jill Oliver, and Trevor Williams. These dedicated family service professionals had the foresight to develop a national organization, on the model of an association that respects the direction of its members, to provide leadership and service to its member agencies and advocacy for families in Canada. Family Services Canada is a national voluntary organization and a registered charity, with a membership of more than a hundred family service agencies throughout Canada. Its vision of "Strong Families in a Caring Society" is supported by its mission of "promoting families as the primary source of nurture and development of individuals, promoting quality services which strengthen families and communities and advocating policies and legislation, which advance family well-being in Canada." Family Services Canada provides leadership in policy, advocacy, and quality services to children and families through its membership and nationally sponsored programs. Social workers have been the primary professional staff of family service agencies throughout Canada. Member agencies have been instrumental in advancing social work theory and practice through practica for students at schools of social work, participation in research studies with local universities, and fostering working environments that encourage innovation and continuous improvement. Social workers employed in Family Services Canada agencies have been active members in their professional associations and tenacious advocates for child and family well-being. Family Services Canada's national committees, programs, and conferences provide networking opportunities for staff, boards, and volunteers to share and develop their knowledge and expertise. Over its twenty years of operation, Family Services Canada has engaged in many exciting endeavours from the development of its national Employee assistance program in 1982; a four-year program of international development in Bogotá, Colombia; a national family week public awareness program in 1985; annual executive director training program of in 1986; the Canadian certified family educator program in 1990; special projects on literacy, HIV/AIDS, ethnocultural diversity service delivery, anti-violence and parenting public service announcements on television and radio, early intervention projects, and strengths-based practice program; leadership awards; an evaluation program for quality assurance through outcomes; research on planned short-term treatment and on family strengths and assets; annual conferences in cities throughout Canada; social action and advocacy on behalf of families on its own and in partnership with national coalitions; and to its national sponsorship beginning in 1998 of Families and Schools Together Canada. The governance board structure of Family Services Canada now consists of twelve members: two from each of Ontario and Quebec, one from each of seven other provinces, and one from the three territories. In 1984 after twelve years of service, Trevor Williams resigned after twelve years of service to be followed by Margaret Fietz. Family Services Canada's mission and operating values and principles promote working in partnership with its members and other like-minded organizations, respecting and honouring all family types, and advocating for those disadvantaged and disengaged to promote full participation in society. Family Services Canada has been and is a strong national organization maintained by the collegiality, co-operation, and commitment of its members, be they family service agencies, volunteer board members, or interested individuals. All can be proud of the contributions made over the years that have prepared the organization for the present and the future, working together to build strong families in a caring society. Current information about Family Services Canada / Services à la famille—Canada

can be found online at <www.familyservicecanada.org>.

[*Margaret Fietz*]

RELATED ENTRIES

Family Demographics, Family Planning, Family Research, Family Statistical Patterns, Family Therapy, Families and Schools Together Canada, Marital & Family Problems, Non-governmental Organizations, Parenting, Services for Families, Social Planning, Social Policy, Theory & Practice

family statistical patterns

Tremendous changes in relation to family life have occurred in Canada since the end of the Second World War—particularly since the 1990s. By July 1, 2000, the total population had reached 30,750,087, with 78 percent of Canadians living in urban areas, and 22 percent in rural areas. During the past five years, 43 percent of Canadians moved at least once. At present, family size is statistically small at an average of 3 persons, in part owing to the steady decline in the birth rate over the past decade; in 1998, of the total 338,963 births, 96,631 were to single women and one third were to mothers aged thirty years of age and older.

Legal marriages have also been declining and Canadians are generally older at first marriage. In 1999, 153,900 couples married; for brides, the current average age at marriage was twenty-seven and, for grooms, twenty-nine years of age. The fastest growing form of couplehood was cohabitation, with 14 percent of all Canadian couples has been common-law couples, more than 40 percent of whom live in Quebec. The number of divorces appears to be levelling off, with 69,088 divorces in 1998. Of couples who were married, 36 percent had dissolved their marriage before their thirtieth anniversary. In divorce proceedings, courts placed 60 percent of the children with their mother, 10 percent with their father, and 30 percent in joint custody. In 1996 at least one partner in 25 percent of all marriages had married for the second time. One in five persons who had remarried had previously been divorced.

The 1996 census found 1.1 million lone parents; single-parent families constituted 13 percent of all families, resulting in one in five Canadian families with children being headed by a lone parent. Female single-parents headed 85 percent of all such families, while 15 percent were headed by men. That census also indicated that 20 percent of children in Canada had experienced the break up of their parents by their tenth birthday.

It is estimated that about half a million gay and lesbian parents are raising children in Canada. In 1999 in Alberta two lesbian couples adopted the sons of their same-sex partners, as Alberta now allows adoptions by same-sex couples. British Columbia, Ontario, Nova Scotia, and Quebec have similar legislation. As a result of court cases, gays and lesbians in some provinces could marry in 2003; same-sex couples were attempting to legalize their relationships throughout Canada.

In 1999, more than half (50.4%) of all Canadians were women. In 1996 close to one in five women living in Canada was an immigrant, 11 percent of the female population identified themselves as members of a visible minority, and 12 percent had a university degree. Of the total female population over the age of fifteen, 13 percent were living alone. A girl born in Canada in 1997 could expect to live for more than eighty-one years. In the late 1990s, the majority of employed women worked in occupations such as teaching; nursing and related health occupations; and clerical, sales, and service occupations.

The population of seniors constituted 12.5 percent of all Canadians in the year 2000 and it is estimated that, by the year 2041, this segment of the population will almost double to 23 percent of the total population. Of all seniors, 26 percent were born outside of Canada. Senior women represent 58 percent of all seniors; however, of seniors aged eighty-five years and over, women represent 70 percent. About one in five seniors is considered to have a low income. Almost all Canadian seniors describe themselves as very happy or happy with their lives. In 1996 two million Canadians provided informal care to seniors with long-term health care problems; more than two-thirds of the caregivers were between the ages of thirty and fifty-nine, and more than two-thirds work for pay and are married. One in four takes care at the same time of children under the age of fifteen. Women who look after senior relatives and children at home constitute the so-called sandwich generation. Three-generation households in 1996 represented 3 percent of all households and nearly half were headed by immigrants.

In Canada it cost nearly $160,0000 to raise a child from newborn to age nineteen. This cost does not take into account the income that a parent forgoes if he/she leaves the labour force to stay at home with the children. Child-care costs take 32.5 percent of the total costs, shelter 23 percent, food 20 percent, and clothing 10 percent. The rest is spent on health and personal care, recreation, and transportation. In 1996, 84 percent of all women aged fifteen years of age and over were living with either their immediate or extended family, and 23 percent of all women between the ages of twenty and thirty-four still lived at home with their families. Of all the men between twenty and thirty-four, one-third were still living at home.

In 1997, 57 percent of all families with children under the age of sixteen were dual-earner families. Women accounted for 45 percent of all paid workers, spent 38 hours per week on unpaid work, and were the sole earners in 25 percent of families. In 1998 the average after-tax family annual income was $49,626, and family taxes averaged $12,500. It cost $113.00 a week on average to feed a family. Almost 26 percent of all households spent 30 percent or more of their income on shelter.

In 2000, one in five children in Canada lived in poverty. The average poor family earned $9,4890 below the poverty line. The amount required to lift the 1,338,000 children out of poverty was calculated as $12.7 billion. Most poor children live in a two-parent family, led by an adult who is in his/her late thirties, who has graduated from high school, and lives in rental accommodations in a large community. At the end of 1998, 100,000 households were waiting for social housing in fourteen large urban centres.

Canada had only enough regulated child-care spaces to serve one out of every ten children under twelve years of age. Less than one in three of the children using regulated child care has a fee subsidy. It is estimated that 40 percent of food bank users are children. The majority of food bank users receive social assistance.

An estimated 135,573 child maltreatment investigations were carried out in Canada in 1998, of which 45 percent were substantiated, 22 percent remained as suspected, and one-third were unsubstantiated. According to Statistics Canada, three in ten women who were married or had been previously married have experienced at least one incident of physical or sexual violence at the hands of her partner. Approximately 4 percent of older adults (i.e., sixty-five years or older) living in private homes reported experiencing abuse or neglect. The most prevalent was material abuse involving widowed older adults living alone and perpetrated by a distant relative or non-relative. Chronic verbal aggression ranked as the second most prevalent form of abuse.

[Benjamin Schlesinger]

RELATED ENTRIES

Demography, Family Demographics, Family Research, Research, Single Parents

family theories

Family theories were developed primarily within the social sciences in order to understand functioning among family members and between families and society. Families differ from other social groups in that they tend to last over very long periods of time and they are intergenerational; they usually contain both biological and affinal relationships between and among members, and the biological and affinal aspects link families to a larger kinship network (Klein and White 1996). Of late, the definition of family has been undergoing revision for two major challenges. The first came from feminist critiques over recent decades—particularly with regard to the family's grounding in patriarchy (Cheat 1991). The second challenge has been to the notion of the traditional North American nuclear family— that is, a heterosexual married couple and their own children—from the increasing diversity within society that has resulted in, for example, single-parent families, remarried families, ethnic family configurations, and gay/lesbian families (Baker 1984). Prominent family theories that have been used by North American social scientists and social workers include symbolic interaction, exchange theory, structural functionalism, feminist family theory, conflict theory, family systems theory, and family development (or family life cycle or life span) theory. Symbolic interactionism addresses ways in which people interpret reality symbolically and how these interpretations are influenced by the external social environment

(Baker 1984); it focuses on how family members arrive at a shared sense of the world given their varied interpretations (LaRossa and Reitzes 1993). Behaviour is seen, through this theory, as the outcome of the fit between the family and/or oneself and valued external groups. Exchange theory, in simplistic terms, posits that people make choices based on a cost/benefit ratio that typically involves a process of negotiation and bargaining (Sabatelli and Shehan 1993); for example, in deciding to marry or cohabit, one might consider whether the personal benefits of being with a particular person outweigh the costs. Structural functionalism views the family as a central player in a functional and stable society. The family's structure is largely determined by the roles that family members play among themselves and in society, and the basic functions of families have been viewed through this theory as reproduction, maintenance, social placement, socialization of the young, and personality stabilization of adults (Cheat 1991). Feminist family theorists have been critical of the static and gender-biased roles assigned to men and women—that is, instrumental and affective leaders, respectively—that have served to isolate and disadvantage women (Cheat 1991). Conflict theory views conflict as a core element of social life, in which individuals and/or groups are typically motivated by their own interests, values, and goals (Farrington and Chertok 1993). Conflict can arise when interests differ (e.g., when a parent wants to rest and the children want to play) or when interests are similar but resources are scarce (e.g. when each partner wishes to buy his/her own choice among several options but they do not have enough money for both). Power, which plays an important role in this view of the family, has been seen by many conflict theorists as a resource that has been inequitably distributed to men and the more privileged in society (Klein and White 1996). Family systems theory, which highlights the interconnectedness of human beings and human systems, has had a large impact within family social work practice (Baker 1984). The family, as a system, is composed of interrelated subsystems and a change in one will likely have an impact on others; for example, the loss of a job for a parent will likely affect the lifestyle of all members of his/her family and the nature of the family's interactions with outside systems, such as friends and social institutions. Systems theory suggests that behaviour can best be understood within the context in which the behaviour takes place; therefore, the individual can best be understood in light of the family, society, and culture in which he/she is embedded (Whitchurch and Constantine 1993). Given the importance of the family for the sustenance and socialization of members within society, it is interesting to note that only one theory has been developed specifically with family in mind: family development/life cycle theory (Klein and White 1996; Rogers and White 1993). All other family theories have been adapted from pre-existing theories that were constructed to comprehend other aspects of life, for example, individual, biological, mechanical, or sociopolitical functioning. Instead, family development/life cycle theory focuses on the developmental stages of families and family members over their life span (Baker, 1984). Transitions—such as single to couple, couple incorporating children, launching, retiring—are seen as key factors in understanding the functions of, and changes within, families. Indeed, family social workers using this perspective note that difficulty making transitions from one stage to another can be one reason families experience problems (Carter and McGoldrick 1999). Being out of "phase" can create stress; for example, some immigrant families may feel conflict and isolation if their traditional family ways are at odds with transitional expectations within Canadian society.

[*Marshall Fine*]

RELATED ENTRIES

Conflict Resolution, Family: Non-traditional, Family Research, Feminist Theory, Functional Theory, Knowledge Base, Social Work Theory, Systems Theory, Theory & Practice

REFERENCES

Baker, M. 1984. *The Family: Changing Trends in Canada.* Toronto: McGraw-Hill Ryerson.

Carter, B., and M. McGoldrick. 1999. Overview: The Expanded Family Life Cycle: Individual, Family, and Social Perspectives. In B. Carter and M. McGoldrick (Eds.) *The Expanded Family Life Cycle: Individual, Family, and Social Perspective.* 3rd ed. 1–26. Needham Heights, MA: Allyn and Bacon.

Cheat, D. 1991. *Family and the State of Theory.* Toronto: University of Toronto Press.

Farrington, K., and E. Chertok. 1993. Social Control Theories of the Family. In P.G. Boss, W.J. Doherty, R. LaRossa, W.R. Schumm, and S.K. Steinmetz (Eds.) *Sourcebook of Family Theories and Methods: A Contextual Approach.* 357–81. New York: Plenum.

Klein, D.M., and J.M. White. 1996. *Family Theories: An Introduction.* Thousand Oaks, CA: Sage.

LaRossa, R., and D.C. Reitzes. 1993. Symbolic Interactionism and Family Studies. In P.G. Boss, W.J. Doherty, R. LaRossa, W.R. Schumm, and S.K. Steinmetz (eds.) *Sourcebook of Family Theories and Methods: A Contextual Approach.* 135–66. New York: Plenum.

Rogers, R.H., and J.M. White. 1993. Family Development Theory. In P.G. Boss, W.J. Doherty, R. LaRossa, W.R. Schumm, and S.K. Steinmetz (eds.) *Sourcebook of Family Theories and Methods: A Contextual Approach.* 225–54. New York: Plenum.

Sabatelli, R.M., and C.L. Shehan. 1993. Exchange and Resource Theories. In P.G. Boss, W.J. Doherty, R. LaRossa, W.R. Schumm, and S.K. Steinmetz (eds.) *Sourcebook of Family Theories and Methods: A Contextual Approach.* 385–411. New York: Plenum.

Whitchurch, G.G., and L.L. Constantine. 1993. Systems Theory. In P.G. Boss, W.J. Doherty, R. LaRossa, W.R. Schumm, and S.K. Steinmetz (eds.) *Sourcebook of Family Theories and Methods: A Contextual Approach.* 325–52. New York: Plenum.

family therapy

Family therapy applies many theories of behaviour to help understand the person, the family system, and the larger context of the family system. An integrative framework incorporates systemic, developmental, feminist-informed, and intergenerational theories considered within patterns of culture and gender. Working with families requires the treatment of the context of the problem alongside of the actual problem, through a series of purposeful conversations with different combinations of people listened to by other combinations of people. The use of systems theory for understanding the context of and the interactive components of the problematic behaviour of an individual is central to family treatment. The idea that the whole is larger than the sum of the parts and that the behaviour of others have a circular influence on one's own behaviour led to a new direction for treatment of children, resulting in a shift from the child-guidance model in which the a child was seen by a physician and the parents or caregivers by a social worker. The presenting problem of a child is seen as a warning that indicates a need for change in the system, while at the same time preventing change. The symptom of school avoidance, for example, indicates the need for change as a youth demands greater autonomy; this symptom also prevents change as the parents or caregivers become more vigilant. The complementarity of the interaction between youth and parents or caregivers moves simultaneously, as the less the youth goes to school, the more the parents or caregivers scrutinize—and the more the parents scrutinize, the less the youth goes to school. The premise is that the problem lies in the structure of the family, within the organization of the parts of the system that prevents the system from finding new solutions required at new developmental stages. Understanding the interactional patterns in a family system reaches beyond the nuclear family and into the family of origin and larger kinship system. Just as spatial relationships are useful for thinking about the nuclear family, so interactional patterns are necessary for thinking about the nuclear family in relation to the extended family, by looking at forces that keep the family isolated, vulnerable, and disengaged: an orphan. The alternative is the nuclear family that does not distinguish itself from the extended family, at the expense of individuation, differentiation, or connection through cherishing of differences: an appendage.

While family therapy considers the whole, family members—the part—is the vehicle for change. As a youth increasingly attends school, parents or caregivers become less vigilant. Developmental theory of the individual is part of all family treatment thinking; it considers the age and stage of the individuals who make up the family. Crises commonly occur at points of transition between eras, whereby one way of being must yield to a new way of being. The work to meet new developmental tasks is supported or confounded by intrapsychic, interpersonal, historical, and cultural factors. The equilibrium of the whole is in constant flux as it grapples with the growth and development of the parts. The task of the family is to have adequate flexibility to respond to the changing needs of its members while maintaining a core of stability to facilitate a sense of identification and belonging. At the same time, the parts of the whole

are not equal. Children are not equal to parents or caregivers, and feminist-informed theory would indicate that women are not equal to men in families, as men still frequently carry more power. Family treatment explores the distribution of power within the family and the symptoms, which come from inequality. Family treatment takes into account the larger systems within which the family functions. Culture, citizenship, and economics are the major contexts for families. Culture shapes identity, tradition, rituals, worship, and language as well as provides a larger context that guides the family's values and the ways in which those values are implemented. Citizenship within the global economy has been changing, bringing periods of dislocation, necessary re-education, and lengthy processes of acclimatization for families. Some cultural traditions can help with the process of acclimatization, while others may hinder settlement and create family conflict, as rigid adherence to former practices, behaviours, and activities may not fit well in the immigrant family's new country. Work with all families includes conversations relating past to present, and maintaining connection to the past without denying the present. The economic life of the family determines different opportunities, from menus to housing to neighbourhoods. This aspect of the family needs to be understood and discussed as part of treatment, as it indicates areas of inclusion and exclusion. Family therapy ends with a semi-colon, never a period, to reflect its ongoing nature. Families need to feel welcome to return to treatment at different stages of the family cycle. In this spirit, this entry ends with a semi-colon;

[*Elizabeth Ridgely*]

RELATED ENTRIES

Caregiving, Clinical Social Work, Family Planning, Family Research, Family Services Canada, Family Theories, Marital & Family Problems, Parenting, Peer Counselling, Play Therapy, School Social Workers, Separation & Divorce, Services for Families, Systems Theory, Theory & Practice, Therapy, Treatment, Vanier Institute for the Family, Wellness

Abraham Feinberg (1899–1986)*

Feinberg (ne Nisselevicz), Abraham, rabbi, singer, peace activist; b. Sept. 14, 1899, Bellaire, OH; d. Oct. 5, 1986, Reno, NV

Raised and educated in the United States, Abraham Feinberg held rabbinical pulpits there in the 1920s. He left the rabbinate in 1930, and after changing his name to Anthony Frome embarked on a new career as a singer. With his own radio show in New York from 1932–35, he became known as the "Poet Prince of the Air Waves." Alarmed by the rise of Hitler and Nazi Germany, Feinberg became a rabbi again. In 1943 he came to Toronto as rabbi of Holy Blossom Temple, Canada's largest Reform Jewish congregation. During his tenure at Holy Blossom from 1943–61, he earned a worldwide reputation for his championship of the downtrodden, his embrace of radical causes, and his efforts to remove the barriers between Jews and non-Jews. Dedicated to world peace and social justice, he protested against the Vietnam War. Perhaps his greatest moment as a peace activist was his 1967 visit to Vietnam when he met with Ho Chi Minh. In the 1970s Feinberg moved back to the United States of America, where he became rabbi-in-residence at the Glide Memorial Church in San Francisco. He was the author of three books, *Storm the Gates of Jericho* (1964), *Hanoi Diary* (1968) and *Sex and the Pulpit* (1981), and wrote for *Saturday Night*, *Maclean's*, the *Globe and Mail*, and *The Toronto Star*.

[*Sharon Drache*]

*Used unedited by permission from *The Canadian Encyclopedia*. 2000. Toronto: McClelland and Stewart.

RELATED ENTRIES

Jewish Social Services, Religion, Sectarian Social Services, Social Justice, Social Welfare History

feminist theory

The second wave of feminism in North America during the 1960s and 1970s prompted the development of feminist theory and feminist social work practice. Women social workers and other helping professionals, typically calling themselves feminist counsellors and therapists, began to incorporate concepts, themes, and perspectives deriving from feminism and the Women's Liberation Movement into their practice with women. Writers such as Betty Friedan, Germaine Greer, Kate Millet, Shulamith Firestone, Robin Morgan, and Andrea Dworkin as well as musicians, poets, and artists provided the wellspring for feminist practice and education. The feminist rallying cry "per-

sonal is the political" was not solely a reflection of their efforts seeking to end patriarchal arrangements within society and advocate for equality of women and men; it was a lens for seeing women's individual problems within the context of oppressive social conditions that kept women subordinate to the dominant group, namely, men. Through consciousness-raising groups and individual and group counselling, feminists enabled women to tell their stories of child sexual abuse, rape, and battering by their male partners. A women's health movement emerged to enable women to make their own decisions about medication, surgery, and practices related to birth control, pregnancy, childbirth, and abortion. Social workers focused on helping women find their own voices, free from self-blame and a sense of pathology. Mental health services came under attack for their perceived subordination of women to men and their dismissal of women's concerns as primarily intrapsychic and treatable through medication, electroshock, and compliance with traditional gender roles (Chesler 1972; Penfold & Walker 1983). The development in the 1970s of rape crisis centres—later known as sexual assault centres—and battered women's shelters demonstrated that feminist ideas were gaining societal currency. During the 1970s and 1980s, feminist theory and feminist practice gained prominence. Most social work education faculties included at least one or two feminist women educators who promoted courses that addressed women's or gender issues in social work as well as feminist practice. James Gripton's 1974 national survey of Canadian social workers identified the inequitable distribution of social workers by gender within their organizations, and defined sexism within organizations as pertaining to inequities in the allocation of preferred statuses and rewards. Through Helen Levine's leadership, Carleton University's School of Social Work became known for its feminist focus. Mary Russell's *Skills in Counselling Women* affirmed that feminist theory begins with woman at centre stage and conceptualized the emerging practice with women as:

a collaborative process between counsellor and client in which both identify, analyze, and attempt to remediate the social, cultural, and psychological barriers to women's optimal functioning, setting as the immediate goal the alleviation of the client's personal distress and as the long-term goal the effecting of social change. (1984: 15)

A Women's Caucus of the Canadian Association of Schools of Social Work met first in 1975 to examine educational issues. In the mid-1980s the association accreditation processes called for examination of a program's curriculum with respect to women's issues. "Feminism and social work practice" was published in the third edition of *Social Work Treatment: Interlocking Theoretical Approaches*.

Initially feminist practitioners drew on traditional theories to understand and to help women, despite their criticism of theories that were perceived to subordinate women to men. Key theoretical advancements included the separation of sex and gender; the idea that rape is a crime of violence rather than sexual expression; that sexual harassment is a form of discrimination; and that women's choices are constrained by socialization and limited opportunities. Feminists viewed their practice with women through such ideological perspectives as ending patriarchy, empowerment, emphasis on process, and validation of the non-rational (Bricker-Jenkins & Hooyman 1986). Other ideological frameworks with theories of women's societal place and implications for practice included conservative perspectives focusing on sex, liberal perspectives focusing on gender, and radical perspectives focusing on sex, gender, and sexuality (Valentich & Gripton 1984). Gaining favour were new theories on women's voice (Gilligan 1982); self-in-relation focusing on women's connectedness (Miller 1986; Surrey 1985); and women's ways of knowing (Belenky et al. 1986). These theories were developed by women studying women, often using qualitative methods. Overall, however, there has been only a moderate development of social work research related to feminist theory and practice. By the 1990s feminist theory had permeated mainstream social work practice; most programs, however, usually offered only one or two elective courses on women's or gender issues. In order to integrate feminist and masculinist practice approaches (McKecknie & Valentich 1989) and to overcome feminist theory's lack of attention to men, Valentich (1992) proposed gender-sensitive practice. Social workers sought empowerment of women in diverse realms of practice (Bricker-Jenkins, Hooyman, & Gottlieb 1991;

T. Laidlaw et al. 1990; Valentich 1996) and in work with individuals, couples, families, groups, communities, policy development, and administration. Where possible, feminist social workers transformed existing sociological and psychological theories (Worell & Remer 1992) to make them more compatible with goals of helping women take charge of their lives. New paradigms such as postmodernism were vigorously examined for their implications for practice (Chambon & Irving 1994; Van Den Bergh 1995), often with controversy, as the relativistic nature of all perspectives suggested that action might not ensue. However, standpoint theory (Van Den Bergh 1995) affirmed that women's realities were grounded in gender, but emphasized the multiplicity and diversity of women's experiences.

In recognition of global issues relating to women and ethnicity and oppression, the ideological frameworks (Jagger & Rothenberg 1993) now include multicultural feminism and global feminism, in addition to conservatism, liberalism, classical Marxism (focusing on class), radical feminism, and socialist feminism (focusing on gender and class). Saulnier (1996) identifies liberal, radical, socialist, lesbian, womanism, and global feminism, as well as cultural and ecofeminist theories, and postmodernism as major branches of feminist theory with implications for practice. While the earlier period of theory-building was characterized primarily by a liberal perspective with white women taking the lead, the latter period reflects a more inclusive feminism. Despite a degree of societal backlash to feminism and a trend to societal conservatism, feminist theory and feminist social work practice stands at a threshold. While securely established within social work, the further development of feminist theory and feminist social work practice remains in the hands of increasingly overburdened and politically constrained social workers and social work educators.

[*Mary Valentich*]

RELATED ENTRIES

M.-T. Casgrain, Gender Issues, Knowledge Base, N. McClung, A. Macphail, E. Murphy, I. Parlby, Royal Commission on New Reproductive Technologies, Royal Commission on the Status of Women, Services for Women, Theory & Practice

REFERENCES

Belenky, M.F., B.M. Clinchy, N.R. Goldberger, and J.M. Tarule. 1986. *Women's Ways of Knowing: The Development of Self, Voice, and Mind.* New York: Basic Books.

Bricker-Jenkins, M., and N.R. Hooyman (Eds.) 1986. *Not for Women Only: Social Work Practice for a Feminist Future.* Silver Spring, MD: National Association of Social Workers.

Bricker-Jenkins, M., N.R. Hooyman, and N. Gottlieb (Eds.) 1991. *Feminist Social Work Practice in Clinical Settings.* Newbury Park, CA: Sage.

Chambon, A.S., and A. Irving (Eds.) 1994. *Essays on Postmodernism and Social Work.* Toronto: Canadian Scholars Press.

Chesler, P. 1972. *Women and Madness.* New York: Avon.

Gilligan, C. 1982. *In a Different Voice.* Cambridge, MA: Harvard University Press.

Gripton, J. 1974. Sexism in Social Work: Male Takeover of a Female Profession. *The Social Worker* 42, 78–89.

Jagger, A.M., and P.S. Rothenberg (Eds.) 1993. *Feminist Frameworks.* New York: McGraw-Hill.

Laidlaw, T., C. Malmo, and Associates. 1990. *Healing Voices: Feminist Approaches to Therapy with Women.* San Francisco, CA: Jossey-Bass.

McKechnie, R., and M. Valentich. 1989. Male-focused Clinical Social Work Practice. *Arete* 14, 1, 10–21.

Miller, J.B. 1986. *Toward a New Psychology of Women.* 2nd ed. Boston, MA: Beacon.

Penfold, S., and G.A. Walker. 1983. *Women and the Psychiatric Paradox.* Montreal, QC: Eden.

Russell, M.N. 1984. *Skills in Counseling Women— The Feminist Approach.* Springfield, IL: Charles C. Thomas.

Saulnier, C.F. 1996. *Feminist Theories and Social Work: Approaches and Applications.* Binghamton, NY: Haworth.

Surrey, J.L. 1985. *Self-in-Relation: A Theory of Women's Development* (Work-in-Progress Series, No. 13). Wellesley College, Stone Centre for Developmental Services and Studies.

Valentich, M. 1992. Toward Gender-Sensitive Social Work Practice. *Arete* 17, 1, 1–12.

Valentich, M., and J. Gripton. 1984. Ideological Perspectives on the Sexual Assault of Women. *Social Service Review* 58, 3, 448–61.

Van Den Bergh, N. (Ed.) 1995. *Feminist Practice in the Twenty-first Century.* Washington, DC: National Association of Social Workers.

Worell, J., and P. Remer. 1992. *Feminist Perspectives in Therapy: An Empowerment Model for Women.* New York: John Wiley and Sons.

Alfred Fitzpatrick (1862–1936)

Fitzpatrick, Alfred, Presbyterian minister, educator, founder of Frontier College; b. Apr. 22, 1862, Millsville, NS; Order of British Empire, 1935; d. June 16, 1936, Toronto, ON

Educated at Queen's University, Alfred Fitzpatrick received his bachelor of arts degree in 1890. Ordained in the Presbyterian Church in 1892, Fitzpatrick championed education, particularly for adults. Fitzpatrick "believed education was the God-given right of every person, male or female, not the exclusive privilege of the favoured few" (Morrison 1999: 34). In 1899 he became a missionary at Nairn Centre, Ontario and established the Canadian Reading Camp Association that was renamed Frontier College in 1919. Labourer-teachers took the classroom to forest, mine, and rail camps to teach reading and numeracy. Reading camps spread throughout Canada and into the United States. Today, Frontier College remains a volunteer-based organization that promotes literacy throughout Canada. With his assistant, Edwin Bradwin, Fitzpatrick wrote *Handbook for New Canadians* in 1919. A second book, *University in Overalls: A Plea for Part-time Study*, was published in 1920. Between 1922 and 1934, degree-granting status was conferred on Frontier College by an Act of Parliament so that people taking courses through correspondence could receive a bachelor's and master's degrees. In recognition of his work in adult education he was awarded the Order of the British Empire in 1935.

[*Brenda Brett*]

RELATED ENTRIES

Education in Social Work, Employment

REFERENCE

Morrison, J.H. 1999. Black Flies, Hard Work, Low Pay: A Century of Frontier College. *The Beaver* October/November.

food banks

Food banks provide groceries to people in need, and are of relatively recent origin in Canada, the first having been established in Edmonton, Alberta, in 1981. They form part of a growing web of community-based feeding programs (e.g., school lunch programs, collective kitchens, soup kitchens.) Food banks vary in aims, size, and function, from large food collection and distribution centres to small-scale emergency food pantries. A typical food bank is a "centralized warehouse or clearing house registered as a non-profit organization for the purpose of collecting, storing and distributing surplus food (donated, shared), free of charge, to front line agencies which provide supplementary food and meals to hungry people" (Riches 1986). Food banks are mainly organized by community and/or faith-based organizations, although they may also be provided by co-operatives, unions, and educational institutions. Food banks differ in their approaches to hunger or food poverty. The majority provide a charitable and voluntary service of redistributing food, while others (e.g., Daily Bread Food Bank in Toronto and the Regina Food Bank) also engage in public education and advocacy. The Canadian Association of Food Banks/Association de banques alimentaires du Canada (est. 1988) is a national coalition that co-ordinates donations of food and transportation across the country to ensure food is distributed quickly and efficiently to member food banks; provides liaison between food banks, industry, and government; and acts as the voice of food banks (CAFB 2002). In more recent years it has played an active role in national anti-poverty advocacy and support for a food security movement in Canada. The association conducts an annual hunger count survey, which is the only reliable source of information about food banks in Canada. According to the hunger count, in 2001, 615 food banks and 2,213 affiliated agencies were providing emergency groceries to 726,902 people in the month of March. The survey also reports that, since 1989, food bank use has risen more than 92 percent; that Ontario and Quebec serve the largest number of people using food banks; Newfoundland has the highest rate of food bank users as a percentage of provincial population (5.9%); that 77 new food banks opened in Canada since 1995; that almost 40 percent of food bank recipients are under the age of eighteen; that most food bank recipients are receiving social assistance; and that most food banks provide a three- to four-day supply of groceries and restrict requests for assistance to once per month. It has been argued

that food banks have become an institutionalized second tier in Canada's social welfare system (Gandy & Greschner 1989).

The emergence of Canadian food banks was strongly influenced by the growth and development of food banks in the United States, originating with the first food bank in Phoenix, Arizona, in 1967. In Canada the economic recession of the early 1980s combined with the failure of the social safety net to ensure eligibility and adequate benefits for the rapidly escalating numbers of unemployed persons were critical factors in the rise of food banks. Welfare reform, the scrapping in 1966 of the Canada Assistance Plan, and social spending cutbacks have further reduced benefit entitlements and the adequacy of income support. Lack of affordable social housing, high costs of rental accommodation in many communities, and soaring utility costs have resulted in the depletion of household food budgets, with the result that food banks have been meeting a basic need. To the extent that unemployment rises, income inequality and social exclusion deepen, and governments fail to address the income and housing needs of vulnerable people, it is likely that the demand for food banks will continue to grow. A Statistics Canada study (Che & Chen 2001) based on the 1998–99 national population health survey reports that 8.4 percent (2.4 million) Canadians were living in household where food was inadequate. They had to compromise their nutritional intake owing to lack of money, being unable either to obtain the variety or quantity of food they wanted, or to purchase enough food to eat. The existence of food banks raises a number of important issues and debates for Canadian social work and social policy, including

- whether food banks are evidence of hunger being met, or indicators of significant food poverty;
- the merits of charitable food redistribution as an effective response to hunger compared to full employment, income redistribution, and publicly supported social programs; and
- the public accountability of federal and provincial governments to ensure domestic compliance with their obligation to guarantee the human right to food, clothing and shelter under the United Nations International Covenant on

Economic, Social and Cultural Rights, ratified by Canada in 1967.

Food banks are playing an important role along with other organizations in the health and nutrition, food policy, agriculture, environment, international aid, and social policy sectors to build a national food security movement in Canada. Their effectiveness as an adequate response to the structural causes of food poverty is in doubt.

[*Graham Riches*]

RELATED ENTRIES

Poverty, Social Welfare, Social Welfare Context, Welfare State

REFERENCES

CAFB. 2000. *Hunger Count 2000: A Surplus of Hunger*. Toronto: Canadian Association of Food Banks. Online at time of writing at <www.cafb-acba.ca/>.

Che, J., and J. Chen. 2001. Food Insecurity in Canadian Households, Health Reports. Ottawa: Statistics Canada 12, 4, 11–12.

Gandy, J., and S. Greschner. 1989. *Food Distribution Organizations in Metropolitan Toronto: A Secondary Welfare System?* Working Papers in Social Welfare in Canada. University of Toronto, Faculty of Social Work.

Riches, G. 1986. *Food Banks and the Welfare Crisis*. Ottawa: Canadian Council on Social Development.

forensic practice

Forensic social work is a unique and relatively unrecognized field of practice that can be distinguished from other disciplines that involve the application of social work knowledge and practice in the combined fields of mental health and criminology. The forensic social worker can be associated with, but distinguished from, other occupations, such as parole and probation officers, and positions in such community organizations as the John Howard Society and the Elizabeth Fry Society, which are mandated to help ex-offenders reintegrate into a community. Whereas these associates interact primarily with the court system and with other psycho-social agencies and services, forensic social workers belong to interdisciplinary teams based on the traditional medical model and operate in facilities that are a hybrid of correctional institutions and psychiatric hospitals serving a clientele of federal inmates (persons convicted of a crime and

sentenced to serve two years or more in a federal penitentiary). Through federal/provincial agreements, provincial and territorial inmates serving sentences of up to two years less a day and meeting certain criteria may be accepted for treatment in these facilities. The recognition of the need for the treatment of mentally ill offenders in Canadian penitentiaries predates confederation in 1867 (Green, Robin, & Naismith 1991: 290–95). In the modern era, a number of federal government commissions have recommended the establishment of special facilities to treat mentally ill offenders, including the 1938 Archambault Commission; the 1956 Falteau Commission; the 1958 Royal Commission on Sexual Psychopaths; and the 1969 Ouimet Commission (Shrubsole 2000). In 1971 the Chalke Report commissioned by the federal solicitor general presented a detailed plan for the development of psychiatric services in the federal corrections system; the report recommended that a uniform psychiatric service be established in each region of the country, each to be professionally staffed to ensure adequate care and treatment at standards set by each province. In 1972 the solicitor general accepted the report and instructed the Canadian Penitentiary Service to establish centres in the Atlantic region (the Regional Treatment Centre associated with the Dorchester Penitentiary in Dorchester, NB), in Ontario (the Regional Treatment Centre in Kingston), in the prairie region (the Regional Psychiatric Centre in Saskatoon, SK), and Pacific region (Pacific Regional Health Centre in Abbotsford, BC). The facilities were planned, developed, and opened, the last becoming operational in Saskatoon in 1978. In Quebec contractual arrangements for the treatment of mentally ill federal inmates have been established with provincial psychiatric facilities. By February 2000, the centres in Kingston, Saskatoon, and Abbotsford had been awarded accreditation from the Canadian Council on Health Services Accreditation. In 2002 the association was in the process of assessing the Regional Treatment Centre in Dorchester against Canadian standards for mental health care.

The unique challenge presented to managers of these facilities was to develop models of treatment that blended established modes of organization in penitentiaries with the medical model of treatment—a model had to be built from the ground up. There was no previous experience within the correctional service in the operation of forensic mental health facilities; conversely, mental health professionals were not familiar with corrections. The top-down hierarchical control typical of corrections operation was in conflict with the medical model, which gave some weight to participatory management. Under the hierarchical control model, inmate activities were highly regimented in accordance with commissioner's directives which were, in effect, highly detailed behavioural guidelines aimed at minimizing the risk to staff of being in harm's way of aggressive inmates, and protecting the perimeter against escape. Newly hired health professionals resisted these strongly bureaucratic modes of operation. These competing visions of the organization and day-to-day functioning of the treatment facilities created challenges for their managers. In addition the health professionals themselves were at odds over how best to adapt the medical model to a correctional setting. These stresses were reflected in the initial design and delivery of programs. Since few aspects of existing mental health programming incorporated correctional concerns, little could be gleaned from the existing medical model. Experimentation was necessary in practice if not as an overt approach to development. Initially, a "functional matrix management model" (Green, Robin, & Naismith 1991: 290–95) was established in which each department provided various services to patients. This approach created distinct areas of responsibility across the health professions, reduced some of the interprofessional conflict by limiting the insecurities of the mental health professions; however, it also avoided co-operative patient-centred treatment approaches that focused primarily on the needs of the patient. By the early 1990s, however, the treatment centres had migrated to the program-management model, which by then had been adopted by most hospitals in Canada and the United States. One of the key features of this program was that it allowed for the measurement of results whereby program objectives could be set and assessed. The program-management model integrates the correctional perspective by having it shift from the static security model to a dynamic model, which incorporates the use of technological security systems. Electronic surveillance systems are em-

ployed to reduce the requirement for guard towers and perimeter security patrols. Similarly, the need for manned interior security stations are reduced by video monitors and electronically controlled access between areas, allowing correctional officers to move among the inmate-patients and become active members of program teams.

The reporting structure of the Regional Psychiatric Centre in Saskatoon illustrates the program-management model, and social workers' roles and responsibilities in the system (RPC 1999–2000: 15). Rather than have a separate social work department, social workers are integrated into each of the four programs at the centre: the psychiatric treatment program; the intensive healing program; the sex offender program; and the aggressive behaviour control program. In each team, social workers collaborate with psychiatrists, psychologists, nurses, recreational therapists, and occupational therapists. To provide an avenue for professional development and to address concerns related to treatment modalities that incorporate unique social work knowledge and practice; in lieu of separate departments for each discipline, informal committees are encouraged for all social workers and for each of the other professional disciplines. Other positions are also incorporated, depending on the orientation of each program. These include library technicians, patient work co-ordinators, behavioural science technicians, and program delivery officers. Given the disproportionate representation of Aboriginal inmates in Canadian correctional institutions—especially in the prairie region, which also receive offenders from the territories—Aboriginal Elders and Aboriginal program officers are also part of each team. Parole officers provide such pre-release planning as preparation for inmates' applications and appearances before the National Parole Board and serve as a bridge to the community by helping to establish support services to released offenders and their families. Social workers are developing approaches that blend their training and intervention strategies within the unique setting of these correctional mental health treatment centres. Because of their small numbers in Canada, social workers in these settings have received little recognition for the distinct contribution they are making in their role in multidisciplinary teams in forensic settings. Their work is at an early stage of development and has received little attention in professional journals to date; however, as the development of knowledge increases and as performance measurement provides quantifiable indicators of the results of social work intervention modalities, forensic social work will begin to be recognized for its contribution to the unique knowledge base of the profession.

[*Mark Feldstein*]

RELATED ENTRIES

Correctional Services, Criminal Justice, Family & Youth Courts, Practice Methods, Probation, Services for Offenders, Theory & Practice

REFERENCES

Green, C.M., P.D. Robin, and L.J. Naismith. 1991. Psychiatry in the Canadian Correctional Service. In *History of the Regional Psychiatric Centre*. A presentation by William Shrubsole of the Regional Psychiatric Centre at Saskatoon, SK, March 2000. *Canadian Journal of Psychiatry* 36, 290–95.

RPC. 1999–2000. Annual Report, 15. Saskatoon, SK: Regional Psychiatric Centre.

Shrubsole, W. March 2000. *History of the Regional Psychiatric Centre*. A presentation at Saskatoon, SK.

foundations

Foundations are non-profit organizations established to provide some support to eligible organizations, research or other projects. The Canadian Centre for Philanthropy recognizes six types of foundations: family, corporate, community, special purpose, government, service club (Van Rotterdam 1999). Foundations may also be classified as either public and private; this designation depends on the nature of the relationship among the directors, founders, or trustees, and on the source of funds. Public foundations raise funds to carry out their own programs and activities or to contribute to qualified donees. Private foundations—usually family foundations—receive money from a single source and disburse funds to qualified donees. The best known and most numerous foundations in Canada are family foundations, usually established by a wealthy individual or family. The organizations to which such foundations grant funds are frequently those to which the funder's or family's interests are committed; however, many of the larger family foundations now look at broader needs within the community. The family foundation with the most assets in Canada is The J.W. McConnell Family Foundation. Corporate foundations, which are also private foundations, derive their funds from profit-making businesses from which they are legally independent; they may be structured so that, in profitable years, the business can donate money for investment to the corporate foundation. Donations are then made from investment profits.

Public foundations established to meet the needs of a particular community are called community foundations. The Winnipeg Foundation, established in 1921, is the oldest such institution in Canada and the Vancouver Foundation is the largest in Canada, ranking among the top foundations in North America in terms of grants. They function much like private foundations, but funds are derived from donor contributions, often through bequests, and donors may designate their funds to particular areas of interest. Granting is usually restricted to the community in which the foundation is located. Special-purpose foundations may be private or public, and fund eligible entities within their own province. Prominent among these are foundations that raise funds for a particular hospitals. An exception is The Hospital for Sick Children Foundation, which allocates funds to institutions in the field of child health throughout Canada. Special-purpose foundations with a legal origin and focus receive their funds through interest accruing on lawyers' trust accounts, for example, the Law Foundation of British Columbia and the Law Foundation of Ontario. Government foundations function very similarly to other foundations, but they do not conform to formal definitions of foundations, in that they are most often established through lottery funds—for example, the Ontario Trillium Foundation and the Wild Rose Foundation in Alberta. They operate with varying degrees of independence from government. Such service clubs as the Rotary Club, the Shriners, and the Lions Clubs are among the most well-known social organizations in Canada, always having played an important role in the Canadian charitable sector. Some service clubs have also established charitable foundations, a number of which exist as a result of member bequests and donations. In some cases, funds are raised from special events. In general grant moneys contributed by foundations are small by comparison to the collective donations by individuals to receiving organizations.

[Robin Wright]

RELATED ENTRIES

Associated Charities of Toronto, B'Nai Brith, Canadian Social Work Foundation, Catholic Charities, Fundraising, Non-governmental Organizations, Voluntarism

REFERENCE

Van Rotterdam, I. 1999. *Building Foundation Partnerships: The Basics of Foundation Fundraising and Proposal Writing. A Manual.* Toronto: Canadian Centre for Philanthropy.

Fred Victor Centre

The Fred Victor Centre (est. 1894) is one of the oldest missions in Canada. It emerged with the assistance of the Massey Family and the Methodist Church in Toronto, as one of the outcomes of the social gospel movement. Fred Victor, son of a prominent Methodist family related to the Masseys, had wanted to commit himself to helping victims of industrialization but died at a very young age. In his memory, his father established the Fred Victor Mission, which began with a commitment to serve women and men living in poverty in Toronto. Over the years in addition to its functions as an inner-city mission it has evolved into an integrated multiservice organization aimed at creating a "just and caring society, which values and includes all people, no matter what their background or situation." It is important in Canadian social welfare history not only for its longevity and continuance of services. It is also an example of a centre that provides the essential needs of food, shelter, and social connections, as well as ways and means for persons to work toward a better future by having opportunities to develop skills and capacities. Current information can be found on the mission's website < www.fredvictor.org/ >.

[FJT]

RELATED ENTRIES

Church-Based Services, Employment, Non-governmental Organizations, Poverty, Sectarian Social Services, Voluntarism, J.S. Woodsworth

functional theory

Functional theory is essentially a theory of therapy that seeks to substitute concepts of growth rather than treatment. Functional theory holds that growth takes place through the process of the therapeutic relationship, which in turn is shaped by the structure of the agency in which the service is provided. As a theory of personality, it stresses the will as the organizing force in the person, and present experiences as the basis on which a person can change in a desired direction; it does not ignore the influence of the past and the unconscious but does not consider them to be all-determining. Functional theory views people as inherently creative, choosing to change and mature, and human nature as inherently good, possessing an innate drive to psychosocial growth. As well, the theory presumes that people are responsible for their behaviour. Functional theory originated from the ideas of Otto Rank, an early student of Sigmund Freud, and came into social work principally through the writings and teachings of Jessie Taft and the School of Social Work at the University of Pennsylvania, Virginia Robinson, and Ruth Smalley in the 1920s and 1930s. Shankar Yelaja at Wilfrid Laurier University, who had completed his doctorate at the Pennsylvania school, kept functional thinking alive in Canadian social work literature. Functional theory as a system questions the concept of diagnosis as a process of data collection and analysis, instead perceiving it as a process of helping clients understand themselves in ways that leads to a modification in their behaviour. History is also important but only to the extent that it influences present behaviour. The essence of the helping process is the client/therapist relationship, which is unique for each client. Through relationships with others throughout their lives, people grow or limit their growth. The ending of important relationships is given considerable attention in the therapeutic process under this theory. While functional theory was essentially developed as a basis for casework, its concepts were applied successfully to a broad range of groups and some aspects of community work. Supervision is considered to be a critical aspect of training for functional practice, with the implication that social work training to at least at a master's level could adequately prepare someone to practice functional therapy.

Functional thinking has a firm commitment to the testing of knowledge and practice and, hence, a strong element of research permeates functional writing and practice. As functional thinking is now considered to be outdated, it is rarely addressed in a formal sense in Canadian faculties and schools of social work. It was, however, the source of the first major theoretical split in the profession of social work in the emergence of the functional and diagnostic schools; as such, the theory has been seminal in social work history and the development of theory and practice. While functional theory as a discrete entity is not currently taught in North American schools of social work, many of its tenets mark contemporary thinking about social work practice.

[*FJT*]

RELATED ENTRIES

Interprofessional Issues, Theory & Practice, S. Yelaja

fundraising

Fundraising is the financial development process by which non-profit organizations gather funds from individuals, corporations, foundations, and government for their operations, projects, and services. Six basic methods are used to raise such funds: annual funds, capital campaigns, special gifts, planned gifts, grantsmanships, and direct-mail campaigns (Rosso 1991). In an annual fund, a non-profit organization reaches out and invites its constituency to share in its mission; as such, it is an effective strategy to involve and bond the constituency to the organization. The main objective of an annual fund is to obtain a donation from as many constituents as possible, to repeat such gifts annually, and to get them upgraded; a secondary objective is to build a base of donors or prospects, and to establish habits and patterns of giving. Annual fund parameters include a major fundraising event, a letter inviting constituents to renewal and upgrade their donations, a special gift letter, and/or a personal letter soliciting a major gift. As well, organizations may use such activities as phone-a-thons, telemarketing, door-to-door solicitation, collection boxes on store counters, car washes, and bake sales. A large amount of the money to be raised through the annual fund will likely come from a small number of contributors: the rule of thumb in fundraising

suggests that 10 percent of the gifts received during an annual fund have the potential to produce 60 percent of the money required to meet the goal set for that year. In general, 3 to 5 percent of contributors enrolled in an organization's donor base to have the ability make major gifts. The success of an annual fund enhances an organization's ability to raise funds using the five other methods. A capital campaign is designed to raise a specific sum of money within a particular time to meet such asset-development needs of an organization as the construction of a new building, the renovation or enlargement of an existing building, purchase of furniture or technical equipment, and endowment funds; such a capital campaign usually occurs every five to seven years. A special gift is a variation of capital fundraising, where the focus is on an array of special-purpose needs that may require major gifts. This strategy is to identify potential large contributors (individuals, corporations, or foundations) for a significant gift or grant to meet a special need, or to seek endowment funds (Frantzreb 1991). Planned giving programs encourage contributors to include donations from their estate (i.e., bequests in wills, transfer of insurance), trusts, and contracts in the form of cash, stock certificates, or personal property. The benefit of a planned gift is not available to the organization until a future date when the gift matures (Brain 1991). Grantsmanship is a fundraising method for obtaining a gift from a corporation, foundation or government source with no strings attached to accomplish agreed-on objectives. The purpose of a direct-mail campaign is not to obtain funds but to find future prospects. Through direct mail—the sending to a widespread segment of the general public of information with a letter requesting donations—an organization may just break even financially. As people receiving direct mail-outs have not expressed specific interest in the organization, the response is generally lower than campaigns directed to people who have. A positive response rate of 1 to 2 percent is an excellent return on a direct marketing process (Carver 1991). Fundraisers in non-profit organizations who are responsible for devising and implementing financial development strategies have expertise in identifying and cultivating funding agencies, in writing and supporting proposals in conjunction with colleagues responsible for operations, and maintaining positive relationships with existing and potential funders as well as the many volunteers who give their time to fundraising campaigns.

[Robin Wright]

RELATED ENTRIES
Foundations, Non-governmental Organizations, Voluntarism

REFERENCES
Brain, P. 1991. Establishing a Planned Giving Program. In H. Rosso (Ed.) *Achieving Excellence in Fundraising: A Comprehensive Guide to Principles, Strategies and Methods.* San Francisco, CA: Jossey-Bass.
Carver, R. 1991. The Power of Mail to Acquire, Renew, and Upgrade the Gift. In H. Rosso (Ed.) *Achieving Excellence in Fundraising: A Comprehensive Guide to Principles, Strategies and Methods.* San Francisco, CA: Jossey-Bass.
Frantzreb, A. 1991. Seeking the Big Gift. In H. Rosso (Ed.) *Achieving Excellence in Fundraising: A Comprehensive Guide to Principles, Strategies and Methods.* San Francisco, CA: Jossey-Bass.
Rosso, H. (Ed.) 1991. *Achieving Excellence in Fundraising: A Comprehensive Guide to Principles, Strategies and Methods.* San Francisco. CA: Jossey-Bass.

G

John Gandy (1918–99)

Gandy, John, social planner, social justice activist, educator; b. 1918; m. Katherine; children: Sharon, Alan; d. 1999

John Gandy encountered racial prejudice and discrimination throughout his years in Petersburg, Virginia, where he was born to African-American teachers. This experience fired a lifelong commitment to social change. Issues of social justice rather naturally became his central professional concern. Gandy took his first degree at Virginia State Teacher's College where his father was president. His first graduate degree, in sociology at Ohio State, prepared him well for productive interprofessional relationships in his social work career. Gandy started in social work in a severely deprived community in Chicago at the Cook County Department of Welfare, an experience that sharpened his concern about social problems at the grassroots. In 1942 Gandy completed a master's degree at the University of Chicago School of Social Service Administration, from which he went to senior research positions at the welfare council of Chicago. Issues of youth and social justice were the focus of a noteworthy demonstration project he directed (The Hyde Park Youth Project), involving the co-ordination of neighbourhood preventive and treatment services. After this, in 1958, he left the United States to build a new life with his family in Toronto, where he joined the Social Planning Council. As director of research and planning, Gandy served at a time when attention to service delivery and co-ordination was crucial in a city experiencing post-war expansion of the inner city and its surrounding suburbs; further, the establishment of metropolitan government in 1943 required planners to anticipate accelerating social needs and the failure of resources to measure up. In this work, Gandy was able to build on his Chicago experience. After five years at the Toronto planning council, Gandy's career took another turn when he enrolled for a doctorate in social work at the University of Toronto. In 1966 he joined the teaching faculty, where he remained until his retirement in 1987. From 1973 John Gandy was the graduate secretary of the doctoral program in social work at the University of Toronto for nearly ten years; his gregarious nature led him to take a personal interest in the induction and progress of every student. He was widely acknowledged as a supportive teacher whose involvement with the students went beyond the classroom to helping them with financial aid, research, and employment opportunities. His influence on social work education and practice in social welfare through this work was manifold and immeasurable. Throughout his twenty-two years on the faculty and into retirement as a professor emeritus, John Gandy made important contributions in such fields as criminal justice and race relations. Giving unity to his teaching and research was a deep lifelong commitment to the values and ethics of social work, which never overlooked the social context.

Along with a wholehearted commitment to his academic role, Gandy continued as a community activist. Building on his earlier experience, he contributed to Canadian social welfare in Toronto and other urban centres. A notable accomplishment was his chairing (1977–80) of a major research and planning project committee known as Suburbs in Transition carried out by the Toronto Social Planning Council. A special contribution of the substantial report that followed was its convincing analysis that extensive human problems coupled with serious institutional weaknesses in human service delivery were rampant throughout suburbs everywhere in Canada. In his achievements, Gandy moved with the times, for example, in the investigation of computer applications in social welfare agencies (1983–85) funded by the Social Services and Humanities Council of Canada. And, in 1990, with Lorne Tepperman, publication of *False Alarm: The Computerization of Eight Social Service Organizations.* Issues concerning the privatization of human services were another focus of collaborative research in his retirement. He gave leadership at numerous workshops and conferences was an active member of numerous official and non-governmental bodies (i.e., Ontario Ministry of Correctional Services, Ontario Board of Parole, Toronto John Howard Society, University of the West Indies, and York County Legal Aid Plan). He shared his teaching and experience in social planning and research in his many scholarly journal articles, book chapters, research reports and monographs, often co-authoring with students or colleagues. In 1994 St. Thomas University awarded him an honorary doctor of laws in recognition of his large contribution to social work education and social planning. Gandy was also an inveterate traveller, not only to conferences and offshore sabbatical postings in Ghana, Scotland, and the Caribbean. He travelled for the sheer pleasure of seeing new places, as well as keeping in touch with and enlarging his international network of friends. John Gandy's enormously productive and generous life ended on an ocean cruise in 1999.

[*Donald F. Bellamy*]

RELATED ENTRIES

Criminal Justice, Diversity, Education in Social Work, Information & Communication Technologies, Program Evaluation, Race & Racism, Social Justice, Social Planning

gangs

Gangs vying for territory and economic profit form a deviant and often lethal subculture of society. The Criminal Intelligence Service of Canada estimates that upward of 150 criminal organizations carry out activities in Canada today.

The history and influence of gangs in Canada likely parallels that of the United States, which stretches from at least the early 1800s (Bordewich 2002). Poor and desperate émigrés forcibly removed from the British Isles during the Industrial Revolution and Irish famine were resettled in North America. Living conditions for the newcomers were deplorable and the situation made worse by substantial unemployment, deadly disease, and ethnic intolerance. Historians conjecture that some newcomers unable to overcome hardship through legitimate means joined associates who likewise found society unreceptive and unsympathetic to perpetrate illegal means to survive. Research on gang formation supports the notion that dislocation, destitution, and disenfranchisement can forge solidarity between certain individuals who experience oppression and, out of desperation to survive, are propelled as a group to engage in illegal activities. Indeed, later waves of migrants had their substantial impact on the growth and development of Canada paralleled by the often glamorized exploits of criminal gangs that developed in and spread from their enclaves. The Klondike gold rush, the "roaring" twenties, and the Great Depression and the "dirty" thirties are among key events in the history of Canada and the development of organized crime; however, the majority of contemporary gangs owe their roots to the era following the Second World War. Coming home in 1945, many who served in the armed forces found their fame as war heroes short-lived. Men who had served their country valiantly faced a post-war economy that offered little opportunity or satisfaction. Feeling excluded from the social mainstream, veterans began to band together in the hope of rekindling the excitement and comradeship of the services. A prominent example is the Hells Angels gang, which began when some Second World War US fighter pilots— whose squadron's nickname was the Hells Angels—began travelling together on motorcycles and were viewed as wild, reckless, crude, and vicious; such films as *The Wild One* and *Easy Rider* deepened the public's fascination with the mystique of motorcycle gangs. Indeed, the role of the media is cited in some of the literature as a key component in the popularizing of gangs and the romanticizing of their amoral and unlawful acts in Canada and elsewhere around the world

(Fasilio & Leckie 1993). During counterculture movement of the 1960s, motorcycle gangs took on a new role, supplying hippies with drugs and offering them protection against law enforcement. The financial reward from gang endeavours was immense and set the stage for a transformation of motorcycle gangs from crude loosely knit bands of anti-social lawbreakers into efficient profit-motivated criminal organizations bent on expansion and control of the underworld marketplace. Motorcycle gangs continue to overshadow the contemporary organized crime scene in Canada: the Hells Angels, Rock Machine, Los Brovos, Bandidos, Satan's Choice, and other biker gangs can be found exerting their influence in every province and territory. Bikers, however, were not the sole occupants of the post-war gang scene in Canada. Long-established organized crime gangs, such as the Mafia and Cosa Nostra, continued to operate in the country engaging in activities ranging from drug trafficking, prostitution, extortion, gambling, and smuggling to money laundering. More recently, gang activities have extended to include illegally selling and disposing of chemical toxins and industrial waste, manipulating the stock market, counterfeiting money and documents, and migrant trafficking. Interestingly, these traditional crime organizations have been collaborating with biker gangs to extend their range of influence, particularly in the illegal drug trade, at home and abroad. Demographically, gangs in Canada are no longer confined to large urban centres, but can be found in rural communities as well. Gang membership and impact on citizenry are no longer specific to age, race, ethnicity, gender, or socio-economic circumstances. Asian gangs—such as the Red Eagles, Lotus Family, and Viet Ching—are typically large, structurally complex, and violent (Dubro 1992); limited at one time to estranged Asian youth, gangs tied to tong, triad, and yakuza now include many recent immigrants from India and the Pacific Rim region. Likewise, Aboriginal gangs have increased noticeably in recent years and have modelled themselves on the Black gangster subculture. Using such monickers as the Warriors, Native Syndicate, Redd Alert, and Indian Posse, Aboriginal gangs also have developed close business ties with non-Aboriginal gangs, notably the Hells Angels. Most recently, organized crime groups from Eastern Europe have emerged throughout Canada and have launched commercial dealings with biker, Asian, and Aboriginal gangs (Canada 2002; Hamilton 2000; JHS 2001).

At the heart of gang formation and involvement is a range of biopsychosocial characteristics that can coalesce to increase individual, group, and community susceptibility. A framework for resilience, presented in terms of risk and protective factors, which can be used to understand how certain individuals might be persuaded to join or be recruited into a gang. On the one hand, the presence of risk factor stimuli or processes can increase the vulnerability of an individual to external threats and influences. Biological traits that raise an individual's risk potential include being male and suffering from a genetic, neurological, or other medical disorder. Such psychosocial factors as poverty, discrimination, injustice, and inadequate educational and employment opportunities can also affect individual risk probability. At the family level, factors that contribute to an increase risk include ineffective parenting, child neglect and abuse, parent/parent conflict, and mental illness especially when combined with substance abuse. Typically, an individual who is thought to be at risk presents as behaviourally withdrawn or disruptive, cruel, delinquent, lacking in self-esteem, in poor health, and less intelligent. Protective factors that counterbalance risk and stimulate a resilient response to adversity encompass a similarly wide range of biopsychosocial attributes. Being a female and healthy are important protective requisites. Social support from caring and available adults in the home, school, and community has been shown to help lessen or alleviate an individual's risk. Vital to support and caring is the nature and effectiveness of the parent/child relationship. In summary, a protected person can be portrayed as positive, even-tempered, possessing good self-esteem, intelligent, and healthy. Accepting that individuals are resourceful and want to cope and survive, it is understandable that gangs would feed on those most vulnerable by manipulating the aforesaid risk and protective factors. Using Maslow's hierarchy of human needs construct, Jackson and Knepper (2003) offer an interesting view on how gangs groom their prospective converts by playing on their weaknesses. The foundational physiological needs of food, shelter, and clothing are met by gang members through their illegal money-making endeavours. Safety needs are met within gangs through their organizational structure, which ensures that vulnerable group members safeguard one another. Belonging to a group meets the social needs of members and replicates family life. Respect for oneself is realized within the gang through its structure by encouraging members to comply with and excel within the group. Finally, self-actualization is pursued through activities that help gang members maximize their potential. Resilience is spawned by the search for and acquisition of protection in the face of exposure to considerable risk. Consequently, resilience has more to do with coping and survival than it does with whether the outcome is positive or negative. It is about beating the odds and overcoming hardship. Interceding to reduce the impact of gangs involves a multifaceted approach, which includes curbing their activities and stifling their potential for growth and expansion. To date, however, the combined efforts of criminal justice and social service professionals have met with only limited results. It would seem that, unless socio-economic incentives that lead to the creation and continuance of criminal organizations are removed, gangs will be part of society.

[*Brent Angell*]

RELATED ENTRIES

Biopsychosocial Theory, Bullying, Family Therapy, Parenting, Peer Counselling, Poverty, School Social Workers, Services for Youth

REFERENCES

Bordewich, F.M. 2002. Manhattan Mayhem. *Smithsonian*, 33, 9, 44–54.
Canada. 2002. *Youth Violence and Youth Gangs: Responding to Community Concerns*. Ottawa: Solicitor General for Canada. Online at time of writing at < www.sgc.gc.ca >.
Dubro, J. 1992. *Dragons of Crime: Inside the Asian Underworld*. Toronto: Octopus.
Fasilio, R. and S. Leckie. 1993. *Canadian Media Coverage of Gangs: A Content Analysis*. Research Report No. 1993-14. Ottawa: Solicitor General of Canada.
Hamilton, H. 2000. Targeting Vulnerable Groups: The Impact of Organized Crime. *Gazette: A Royal Canadian Mounted Police Publication*, 62, 3, 8–9.
Jackson, M.S., and P. Knepper. 2003. *Delinquency and Justice*. Boston, MA: Allyn and Bacon.
JHS. 2001. Gangs: Executive Summary. Calgary, AB: John Howard Society of Alberta.

gay-sensitive services

The burgeoning AIDS crisis of the early 1980s played a direct role in changes to health care and social services for gay men. Health care and social service professionals—including social workers—struggled to understand this life-threatening disease and the realities of gay men's lives. A compassionate and concerned lesbian and gay community began to organize their own education of professionals on sensitive intervention with their communities. As a result, much has developed since then in specialized services for sufferers from HIV/AIDS, their families, and the gay community. More recently, gay men have been made more aware of other kinds of sexually transmitted diseases (i.e., different strains of hepatitis) as well as prostate cancer. Social workers often play a direct role in assisting gay men afflicted by any of these illnesses and numerous other life experiences (Mulé 1999). Issues that affect gay men are numerous; perhaps the most pressing—one unique to sexual minority communities—is the process of coming out, the public acknowledgment of one's sexual orientation; variances and complexities in this process can include self-acceptance, age and marital status, finding oneself on the sexual orientation continuum, and responding to the reactions of others. Other issues then become coloured by the fact that these men accept and openly identify themselves as gay, issues related to self-esteem, absence of role models, exploring their sexuality, fear of sexually transmitted disease, experiencing many deaths of friends, illness, career, family relations, building friendships, intimate relationships, addictions, sexual abuse, domestic violence, desire for children, parenting, ageing, and others (CLGRO 1997; Mulé 1999; van Wormer et al. 2000). With regard to interaction with social workers, gay men with a history of stigmatization and discrimination need practitioners be value-free and non-judgmental (CLGRO 1997); social workers who can do so can provide accessible, sensitive, and equitable services (Mulé 1999). Sexual orientation is included as a prohibitive ground of discrimination in the Canadian Human Rights Act and in the human rights codes of all ten provinces and two territories. These laws and others that now recognize and extend benefits to sexual minorities include wording that speaks to "services," which includes health care and social services. Advocacy for including sexual orientation in these laws came from gay and lesbian activists throughout the country educating the public, while applying pressure to politicians and making use of the courts. Canadian public opinion, as a result, has steadily shifted toward growing acceptance of sexual minorities, believing evermore that equality should be applied to all Canadians. As these rights have been won, those affected, such as gay men, have become increasingly aware that conventional social and health care service structures were not designed to be inclusive. Gay men and lesbians have had to advocate for changes to apparent limitations in the fields of health care and social services and the social workers that work within them. Thus, the convergence of legislative recognition of human rights and social and health-care benefits, social acceptance, and awareness of service limitations has brought the social work profession to a crossroads with gay men.

Based on their systemic experiences with HIV/ AIDS and a number of grassroots studies of health care and social services for sexual minorities, gay men have begun to demand access to equitable and sensitive services alongside other tax-paying citizens. As well, several openly gay social workers are challenging the profession to address these issues. Currently, a major stumbling block to affective change is lack of funds. The combination of the seriousness of the AIDS crisis and the work of AIDS activists pressured governments into funding for HIV/AIDS—specific services throughout the country. Few health care and social services, however, are specific to broader health matters for gay men. For the most part, the public sector takes an integrative approach in service provision to gay men, offering them within established mainstream settings, perhaps with gay-specific programming or gay-sensitive social workers. The latter provisions are usually instigated by client needs and/or advocacy on the part of gay-positive social workers. Alternately, the private sector sometimes offers specialized services in specific geographic location through diverse gay or gay-sensitive social workers who offer counselling and therapy in private practice specific to gay men. While social work codes of ethics includes sexual orientation as a prohibitive grounds for discrimination, few social workers are currently trained in sensitivity toward

gay men, the issues affecting them, or ways to provide services to address them. Few schools of social work in Canada provide formal training on these issues in their curricula to students, and few social work associations provide ongoing training in this area to social workers currently in the field (CLGRO 1997; Mulé 1999; van Wormer et al. 2000). While the profession continuously strives to meet the demands with which it is faced, it has made little progress on openness and acknowledgment of gay men. Today, in response, gay male clients and openly gay social workers are working to move the profession toward greater sensitivity, accessibility, inclusion, and equity. This transition presents positive opportunities as the profession slowly embraces gay men as a client base, and as gay men in their journey of self-acceptance and full inclusion are coming into their own rights to adequate and effective social work intervention. Current information on gay issues and services can be found online at <www.gaycanada.com>.

[Nick Mulé]

RELATED ENTRIES

K. Belanger, Bereavement, Education in Social Work, Gender Issues, HIV/AIDS, Lesbian Services, Natural Helping Networks, Mutual-Aid Societies, Parenting, Peer Counselling, Self-Help Groups, Self Help & Mutual Aid, Sensitizing Concepts, Sexual Harassment, Sexual Minorities, Sexual Orientation, Sexual Problems & Services, Social Services, Social Work Profession, Theory & Practice

REFERENCES

CLGRO. 1997. *Systems Failure: A Report on the Experiences of Sexual Minorities in Ontario's Health-Care and Social-Services Systems.* Toronto: Coalition for Lesbian and Gay Rights in Ontario.

Mulé, N. 1999. Social Work and the Provision of Health Care and Social Services to Sexual Minority Populations. *Canadian Social Work* 1, 1, 39–55.

van Wormer, K., J. Wells, and M. Boes. 2000. *Social Work with Lesbians, Gays and Bisexuals: A Strengths Perspective.* 22–24. Boston, MA: Allyn and Bacon.

gender issues

Gender issues are multiform human phenomena, existing as focal points of significance and concern relating to socially constructed, learned and maintained, culturally contextualized expectations of people based on their biological sex. Gender roles are the attitudes, feelings, values, aspirations, norms, and behaviours prescribed for a member of a cultural community to correspond with his/her sex, and to differentiate between the sexes. These gender differences reveal the respective worth and status ascribed to individuals by their community or the broader society, which in turn greatly determine their opportunities and choices, and the nature of their living experiences. Gender identity evolves as an individual adopts his/her cultural expectations, given that there may be variation among individuals in the extent of conformity to the community's traditional or stereotypical ideals (e.g., "tomboy," "man's man"). The parameters of acceptable variation in conformity are set by the community. Flexibility or rigidity in setting and enforcing the community's parameters create an environment that defines normalcy for its members, with demands for rigid adherence to cultural gender norms having the potential for members to suffer conflict and stress when they do not meet gender role expectations or when they display traits of the "wrong" gender (e.g., in many cultures, an assertive woman or a submissive man). Typically built into a culture's understanding of gender differences is a power differential across genders. Patriarchy is a belief enacted in daily living that sees males as superior to females and entitled legitimately to perceived male privilege over them. A system of power inequity or imbalance with regard to gender can lead to an abuse of power over women, who are deemed to hold less status and authority, and who may be viewed as vulnerable, weak, and even deserving of poor treatment or limited opportunities. These social, political, economic, and ideological conditions, which oppress women on the basis of their gender, are collectively called sexism. Though existing in the invisible structural realm of society, sexism's beliefs, attitudes, assumptions, and values disadvantage women in the form of discrimination against them in their personal lives (Bishop 1994).

Gender issues are important concerns for social workers in three ways. First, they form a values-based body of knowledge for social workers in direct practice, research, education, and policy. Awareness of the effects of gender for all people requires that social workers understand the relationship between the public/political dimension of society where the invisible forces of sexism

operate, and the private/personal sphere of actual people's lives in which those sexist forces are manifested as obstructions to empowerment and equality. The realities of interacting oppressions also are significant; that is, that gender discrimination often exists for women in combination with such other oppressions as racism, classism, ablism, ageism, and heterosexism. The term "feminization of poverty" reflects the prevalence of poverty among women, many of whom are single and/or elderly women, and sole-support mothers. Gender issues demand attention from social workers in a second way as a consideration in skilful gender-attuned practice. To uphold the social justice mission of the profession means that social workers direct their efforts toward social justice in the structures of society, and toward the enhancement of people's individual lives to augment their sense of satisfaction and participation in decisions that affect them, and toward assisting them to feel part of society rather than a marginalized nonentity. A further practice concern is the need for social workers to be mindful of different people's views on gender, recognizing that not everyone, not even every woman, sees gender issues similarly. Ethical anti-oppression practice means self-awareness of the social worker's own social identity characteristics, and respect for differences between him/her and others, and not assuming common attitudes, values, and beliefs within or across groups and communities. Gender awareness in practice reveals particular gender-related issues for some women: physical and/or sexual violence; poverty; career development barriers; balancing a job outside the home with family and household maintenance; mental health and medication concerns; culture conflict for newcomers to Canada attempting to maintain their heritage concurrently with making a new life; relationship discord with male partners; and the burdens of domestic caring, often pinning women in the sandwich of responsibilities for children and ageing relatives, perhaps while managing a home and job, and balancing a marital relationship. Gender-attuned practice is a whole-person perspective, which focuses on strengths, and helps create opportunities for all people to attain a sense of worth and competence, able to make the choices they desire, and with knowledge of the structural context and impediments to their advancement. The third concern for social workers about gender issues lies as an aspect of the profession itself. Social work is most often characterized as a female profession with its roots and current practice still very much an expression of women's caring (Baines, Evans, & Neysmith 1998). This reality points to the inherent gender issues of discrepant valuing and remunerating of the many front-line positions staffed by women, the less available advancement opportunities for women, and the ranking of social work itself as a lower-status profession by contrast to such male-associated professions as medicine or law. Experiencing the effects of gender discrimination directly in the social work profession serves as a valuable basis for social workers to be better able to empathize with women disadvantaged by sexism. Much work still is needed toward achieving social justice for all persons, a task for which social work is well-equipped. Members of this profession are educated in humanistic values and ethics, steeped in knowledge about the multidimensional construction of society, and solidly trained in theory-based practice. Gender issues are complex, daunting, and fundamental as they pervade virtually all cultures in public and private ways, posing challenges that social work can and must address.

[*Nancy E. Sullivan*]

RELATED ENTRIES

Anti-oppressive Social Work, K. Belanger, Education in Social Work, Empowerment Theory, Feminist Theory, Gay-Sensitive Services, Knowledge Base, Lesbian Services, Practice Methods, Sensitizing Concepts, Sexual Harassment, Sexual Minorities, Sexual Orientation, Social Justice, Social Services, Theory & Practice, Women Abuse

REFERENCES

Baines, C.T., P.M. Evans, and S.M. Neysmith (Eds.) 1998. *Women's Caring: Feminist Perspectives on Social Welfare.* 2nd ed. Toronto: Oxford University Press.

Bishop, A. 1994. *Becoming an Ally: Breaking the Cycle of Oppression.* Halifax, NS: Fernwood.

generalist practice

Generalist thinking in social work attempts to support a position that all theories are of equal value and utility, and that one is to be favoured over another only in situations when the nature of the presenting situation or the values and world view of the client indicates the application of a particular theory. Pedagogically, this approach creates several challenges. Do social work educators try to teach a little of each theory and combine them into a model of practice? Or do they teach abstract general principles of practice from the spectrum of theories that can be brought together into a generalized theory of practice? Two major concepts that drive this form of approach to practice are found in the literature of generalist practice. The first is that generalist thinking is not a theory in itself but a cluster of theories combined into an approach to practice. The second is a clear preference for systems thinking and problem solving, favouring the premises that clients have problems that they bring to a social worker, and that the function of intervention is to help the client find acceptable solutions to the problems. A further underlying theme in generalist thinking is that intervention is for the most part short-term. In Canadian social work teaching and thinking in the last fifteen years, the term "generalist" has acquired a range of meanings and a great deal of significance. It has become identified as the sought-for basis of bachelor of social work programs by the accrediting arm of the Canadian Association of Schools of Social Work and is the term used by many practitioners to describe the conceptual base of their practice. Generalist theory and practice has emerged as a way to avoid the identification of any one particular theory as the primary basis of practice in an era when more than thirty social work practice theories are current. As a concept, generalist thinking has sought and indeed achieved some success in minimizing intraprofessional struggles evident in earlier years when advocates of one theory or another vied for conceptual supremacy. Generalist practice can allow practitioners to tap the richness of the existing range of theories so that the strengths of each are available to help clients. Thus, generalist practice can be viewed as a particular form of practice that makes much more use of some theories than others, with the potential to evolve into a new theory of practice for social work.

[*FJT*]

RELATED ENTRIES

Education in Social Work, Interprofessional Issues, Micro Practice, Practice Methods, Theory & Practice

gestalt theory

As a theory of social work practice that is also applied by other professions, gestalt theory stresses the wholeness of the human experience. With roots in existential thinking and theory, gestalt is a highly present-centred approach to intervention, one in which practitioners nevertheless understand the importance for individuals to examine their pasts to understand how these experiences have influenced the present. Gestalt theory emerged in the 1940s, principally developed by Fritz Perls as a challenge to traditional psychoanalytic thought, stressing instead a therapeutic relationship that strives to minimize barriers between person seeking to achieve I/ Thou qualities. The theory stresses the wholeness of each person and their value as an individual. The focus in therapy is not to bring about change but rather awareness, that can foster the ability of the client to change if he/she so desires. In seeking to prompt this awareness, the therapist aims to expand the range of behaviours of the client and to take responsibility for who they are and to stress experiential experiences rather than only a cognitive perspective (e.g., unfinished work from the past is to be completed and worked through). In gestalt therapy, the client decides how long treatment should last; in general, however, a short-term process is preferred. Originally developed for one-to-one treatment, much gestalt work has been carried out with dyads, groups, and families. And, while gestalt has not been used directly to date in community work, it is viewed as useful in understanding systems, in particular institutions with a therapeutic thrust. Gestalt theory offers a system with a strong commitment to research that has demonstrated strongly positive evidence of its effectiveness on a broad spectrum of presenting situations. As such, it is a theory very attuned to social work thinking with its emphasis on person-in-environment and on starting with the client and his/her perspective. Although serving as a base for practice for some social workers, gestalt theory to date has not received much written attention from a social work perspective. In fact, gestalt theory and practice is thought to require specialized training in gestalt institutes after graduation from a social work program. As a system gestalt is not as popular as it was two decades ago, appearing to have strong credentials only in intervention with specific client groups. It is not espoused by practitioners who address issues of severe mental illness or a lack of such basic needs as money or housing. In view of its commitment to brief intervention, however, it fits well with current interest in brief treatment as the modal type of social work practice.

[FJT]

RELATED ENTRIES

Education in Social Work, Interprofessional Issues, Micro Practice, Practice Methods, Theory & Practice

Ginger Group*

Ginger Group, an independent group of members of Parliament who in 1924 split from the Progressive Party because they did not support a party structure that inhibited an MP's ability to act solely as the representative of his constituents. The group, named after the Tory MPs who in 1917 opposed the Military Service Act, was initially composed of United Farmers of Alberta representatives G.C. Coote, Robert Gardiner, E.J. Garland, D.M. Kennedy and Henry Spencer, and United Farmers of Ontario representative Agnes Macphail.

Later, working with Labour MPs J.S. Woodsworth, William Irvine, A.A. Heaps and Angus MacInnis, it included Ontario MPs W.C. Good and Preston Elliott, Alberta Independent Joseph Shaw, Milton Campbell from Saskatchewan and W.J. Ward from Manitoba. The Ginger Group declined along with the Progressive Party; some members later helped found the Co-operative Commonwealth Federation.

* Used unedited by permission from *The Canadian Encyclopedia*. 2000. Toronto: McClelland and Stewart.

RELATED ENTRIES

Co-operative Commonwealth Federation, A. Macphail, Social Welfare History, United Farmers of Ontario, J.S. Woodsworth

globalization

Globalization often refers to the continuous expansion of capitalism throughout history, but this notion is not helpful for understanding successive stages in capitalist development nor current worldwide economic expansion. The present era, characterized by intracorporate rather than international trade, is dominated by a few hundred transnational corporations and overseen by a global quasi-state. As national markets are being more or less transformed into a single world market, the world of nation states with separate economies is in transition. Globalization has also been referred to as the arrival of self-generating capital at the global level. That is, capital as capital, capital in the form of the transnational corporation, free of national loyalties, controls, and interests. This is not the mere internationalization of capital, which assumes a world of national capitals and nation states, but the superseding of the nation state by capital. It is a process that renders the national economy—and its associated borders, policies, programs, and political processes—more or less meaningless but that at the same time gives coherency to a global system as such. This process began in the aftermath of the Second World War when the two main prerequisites of a global market first appeared. One was the vast change in technology spawned by the war effort, technology with far more productive capacity than could be consumed by mere national markets. The other was the beginning of a global enabling framework established with the formation of the World Bank, the International Monetary Fund, and the General Agreement on Trade and Tariffs, which expanded in 1995 into the World Trade Organization. A technological revolution in the early 1970s, with the development of the modem computer, rapidly advanced these prerequisites. Early in this decade, it became clear that there was little in the entire range of the production of goods and services that could not be computerized. No arena of human endeavour was left unaffected. Not only could knowledge and information now be completely objectified, stored outside human carriers, but they could be accessed and employed by machines. Unprecedented in its implications, this new computer-dependent mode of production made it possible for corporations to minimize or eliminate humans at the point of production, embodied a permanent revolution in technology and science, and transformed the nature of production from analytic to synthetic. Its productive power required a global market. The implications of this technological revolution forced the deconstruction of national structures of capital accumulation, the political and economic shells of capitalism from an earlier stage in the development of the means of production. In this transition, the chief function of the national state became the harmonization of the national with the developing global regime of accumulation. In as much as the system remains capitalist, globalization is a process that is inevitable. But this is not to say that it is accepted; everywhere it is resisted for what it does and what it means. As the arbitrary global assertion of corporate right, it subordinates or violates the rights of individuals and other collective entities, presents no avenues for democratic representation, and challenges the need for specific social network structures.

Globalization may be understood as the unfolding resolution of the contradiction between ever-expanding capital and its national, political, and social formations. Prior to the 1970s, capital expanded with particular territorial and historical roots and character; afterward, capital began to expand more simply as corporate ownership and control corresponded less and less with national geographies. If capitalism had to create a national state and a defined territory in order to come into its own, in the form of the transnational corporations it has had to remove or transform this "shell" to create institutions to facilitate accumulation at the global level. Globalization is the close of the national history of capitalism, and the beginning of the history of the expansion of capital *sans* nationality. Globalization may be characterized as the shift of the main venue or site of capital accumulation from the national to the supranational level. The shift is marked by the transnational corporations that dominate the world economy, by their pervasive transborder operations, the preponderance of foreign direct investment, and numerous transnational corporate mergers and takeovers, joint-ventures, share agreements, cartels, and oligopolies. This shift, captured in the phrase "the end of [political] geography," has required the establishment of administrative agencies at the global level and transformation or harmonization of national laws that have become barriers to the global accumulation of capital. Globalization can be grasped as the "triumph of capitalism," that is, as the ascendancy of economics over politics, of corporate demands over public policy, of the private over the public interest, of the transnational corporation over the national state. This triumph is embodied in the powers of the International Monetary Fund, the World Bank, and the World Trade Organization, which are structured in the interests of corporate private property, without democratic access and unrepresentative of other interests. It is the subordination of national and other interests to those of transnational corporations.

[Gary Teeple]

RELATED ENTRIES
Employment, Welfare State

goal setting

Goal setting in contemporary social work refers to the necessary and important process of establishing and working toward clear and precise objectives with a client as to the desired outcome of a therapeutic intervention. Goal setting for the therapeutic process has, from the earliest days of social work practice been an essential component of responsible practice. While from the earliest days of social work practice the idea of having a goal for intervention was considered to be important, such goals were, for the most part, set by the social worker with varying degrees of client involvement and were usually imprecise and diffuse. Therefore, a practitioner might state that his/her goal was for improved marital relationship. Current practice holds that effective treatment requires much more specific objectives, such as that a goal in working with a couple might be to spend five sessions with the husband to improve his ability to express positive feelings, and five sessions with the wife to encourage her to be more open about her feelings. The development of acceptance for the precision of current goal setting was a gradual transition, dependent on the mode of intervention and theoretical base preferred by the practitioner. Further, increased client participation is also valued in current practice. Client participation in goal setting depended on the modality under discussion and the theoretical orientation of the practitioner. For example, more attention is given to goal setting in the earlier group and family literature, and less is given in the one-to-one intervention material. In recent decades however, practice has moved to a much greater emphasis on client involvement in the setting of objectives in many theories, especially those emphasizing a much greater focus on prac-

titioner/client partnerships. As well, in the sociopolitics of the profession, greater attention is being given to the setting of goals within management by objective and evaluation of outcomes. Operationally, the enhanced interest on concrete goal setting within treatment has led to the concept of formal contracts with clients, at times set out in writing, to outline the therapeutic objectives and how they are to be achieved. Some theories on which practice is founded (e.g., task centred) are built around this mutual setting of clear goals and contracts, which are used as the basis for subsequent social worker/client contacts. The very process of setting goals in itself is often therapeutic and may even represent the total content of the therapist/client interaction. Important as the emphasis on goal setting has become, practitioners are aware that this process can be overstressed in some situations. Experience shows that frequently what a client identifies as a desired goal for service may actually be a testing ground and an entré to a therapeutic process that needs to be experienced before the client is prepared to risk investing and involving him/herself into more complex objectives. This latter point keeps practitioners alert to the risk of not over-focusing on the setting of objectives in a way that closes the opportunity for a client to invest further in the relationship and in therapeutic process with renewed goals when he/she is sufficiently comfortable to do so.

[FJT]

RELATED ENTRIES
Administrative Theory & Practice, Capacity Assessment, Quality Assurance, Practice Methods, Program Evaluation, Task-Centred Theory, Theory & Practice

Great Depression (1930s)

The Great Depression of the 1930s had a tremendous effect on the development of social work and a broad range of social services in Canada. The immensity and duration of the economic depression, as well as the rapidity with which large numbers of people had to fulfil basic needs for survival—at times, one in five employable citizens—contributed to the growing understanding of poverty and the need for a comprehensive social network that was not built on the concept of deserving versus undeserving. During the 1930s the emphasis was on meeting the daily needs of people, rather than seeking long-term solutions, such as the universal programs that emerged following the Second World War. Various ideological and economic theories, many of which contradicted one another, were promulgated during the depression years for ways to terminate the economic conditions and relieve the needs of the indigent. For the most part, the theories were ignored.

Many factors contributed to the depression that affected most economies of much of the world from 1929 throughout the 1930s, with Canada being one of the hardest hit. In Canada these factors included a building boom; fallen prices for wheat, great quantities of which were stockpiled; and the stock market too high, with many people buying on margin. Canada's economy relied heavily on exports to foreign markets, which amounted to one-quarter of the gross national product: "Almost half the public debt and four-fifths of the private debt were in foreign hands. The West was built on foreign money" (Berton 1990: 25). The main exports were food, lumber, newsprint, and minerals: "In Canada the virtual disappearance of markets for export staples triggered the economic decline" (Grayson 1971: viii). Erratic patterns in the stock market for a couple of months before the stock market crash on Black Tuesday (October 29, 1929) was dismissed by financial experts simply as a correction, thereby falsely allaying investor confidence. Initially, Prime Minister Mackenzie King (1921–26, 1926–30, 1935–48) viewed the aftermath as a recession that would be of short duration. But, as a result of people's fear of governments, industry, banks and individuals stopped spending, investing, lending, and expanding (Braithwaite 1977: 9).

The Great Depression affected Canadians unevenly. Many wealthy people barely noticed it. Other people lacked such basic necessities as food, housing, and clothing. People who continued to work experienced pay cuts. Those who suffered the most hardship were young people coming into the job market for the first time, fishermen, and farmers. More than a quarter of the people residing in the wheat belt left, as drought led to severe dust storms and the invasion of food-producing fields by grasshoppers and such plants as Russian thistle. Some married men who lost their job and were unable to find another either deserted

their families or left home for long periods of time to look for work. Thousands of young men rode the rails trying to find jobs. In 1933, the worst year of the depression, 26 to 33 percent of employed people, mostly men, were out of work; many did not appear in statistics as unemployed because they lived with their families. Many of these men were veterans of the horrors of the First World War. Greatly disillusioned and embittered by the response of government to their plight, citizens throughout the country perceived inadequacies in the helping network and, further, understood that systemic, rather than personal, causes underlay the massive needs for social assistance. Many were sufficiently drawn to proposed solutions and ideologies of a radical nature that the government feared increased support for the Communist Party. As a result, immigration was drastically cut, deportations were increased, and work camps were established in 1932 for unemployed men, who worked eight hours a day for $0.12 per day, as well as room and board. Still, protest marches that were organized were well attended. The most famous was a march in 1935 by unemployed men on Ottawa that was forcibly stopped by the police. Another in Regina resulted in a riot.

Effects on society were felt everywhere, as the average age of marriage rose and the birth rate dropped. While it was illegal to provide information about birth control, by 1936 a nationwide network of nurses and social workers had interviewed people in poor working-class neighbourhoods and offered to mail them free contraceptive kits. For doing this, Dorothea Palmer, a part-time social worker in Ottawa, was arrested; she was acquitted in 1936. There were only a few score trained social workers in Canada at the time, and each one in every type of agency had an immense caseload. Churches, charities, the Canadian Red Cross, and many newly founded self-help groups collected and distributed food and clothing. Standards in relief throughout the country varied, and relief payments were low, partly to discourage alleged dependency and laziness. All three levels of government funded relief, but the federal government earmarked four-fifths of its portion for work projects. The programs, administered by municipalities, were marked by graft, patronage, and inefficiency. To protect local taxpayers, municipalities enforced residency requirements of varying lengths of time; consequently, many people were denied relief. Furthermore, the strong work ethic among Canadians prevented many people from accepting relief. Beyond this reluctance, it could also be humiliating, as homes were searched for such perceived luxuries as radios and telephones, the presence of which indicated that those people did not need social assistance. Liquor and drivers' licences had to be surrendered. Credit vouchers were used for food, and municipalities excluded certain foods. While the various government relief programs reflected a strong ethos of attributing blame to individual persons and families in need, the hundreds of volunteers and formal and informal non-governmental organizations that emerged—perhaps not economically sophisticated—began to understand and promote the concept that the problems were systemic. People were not to be blamed and punished but to be helped.

Prime Minister R.B. Bennett (1930–35) believed in "conservative principles of balanced budgets, strict maintenance of law and order, sound financing and the right and duty of every man to perform useful work" (Braithwaite 1977: 8). These had far-reaching effects. In 1932 Charlotte Whitton, a social worker who was director of the Canadian Council of Child Welfare, proposed to the prime minister that she do a three-month study of unemployment relief in the prairies. She reported that relief spending was handled incompetently and that many people should be excluded from unemployment relief. She recommended the federal government take control of relief spending and save money by hiring federal social workers. Declining this advice, Bennett refused to deal directly with the problems of poverty. By 1938 Prime Minister Mackenzie King reluctantly moved toward Keynesian economics of cyclical budgeting. Rain finally fell in western Canada, ending the drought in the prairies. The Second World War brought an end to this era, but the lessons from the great depression strongly influenced the development of assistance programs as well as the field of social work following the war.

[*Brenda Brett*]

RELATED ENTRIES

R.B. Bennett, W.H. Beveridge, Church-Based Services, Employment, L. Marsh, Marsh Report, Poverty, Sectarian Services, Social Welfare History, B. Touzel, Welfare State

REFERENCES

Berton, P. 1990. *The Great Depression*. Toronto: McClelland and Stewart.

Braithwaite, M. 1977. *The Hungry Thirties*. Toronto: McClelland and Stewart.

Grayson, L.M., and M. Bliss (Eds.) 1971. *The Wretched of Canada*. Toronto: University of Toronto Press.

group practice

Social work's approach to group work in Canada arose out of the settlement movement in the United Kingdom and United States in the late nineteenth century, with a mission of community-based practice focused on meeting people's needs in relation to their life issues and environmental conditions. Empowerment and social action toward personal, community, and societal change are concepts inherent in the history of working with people in groups. A social work group itself may be conceptualized as a "social microcosm … in that prevailing structures and dilemmas in the area of social relations will be reflected" in a group, allowing for a reciprocal affect outwardly to those "social, political, ideological, and cultural processes" of society, as members interact in their lives beyond the group (Shapiro 1990: 5). "Social group work" and "mainstream model" are terms that signify this approach that is distinctive to social work. It is a practice modality interwoven with ideological and functional principles that characterize a society within which people's opportunities and life chances are maximized: social equality, mutual aid, interdependence, natural networks of caring and helping, and social action. In a mainstream model group, "the group interaction process ranges freely, naturally, and spontaneously both with respect to how people communicate, to what substantive content is addressed and how, and to the variety of means and routes the group may use to process its goals" (Lang 1979: 210–11). The group worker acknowledges and respects the strengths, abilities, and perspectives of group members, and participates with them in order to assist them in forming a group as a means of achieving their goals. A sense of momentum and ownership is a desirable objective for group members, as the power of the group process is regarded as the agent of service and task accomplishment. The group worker brings knowledge of social group work principles and techniques, and a willingness to work with the group in the development of its power. The worker's role focuses less on leading a group, and more on helping a group discover its own leadership holdings and competencies that may be uncovered or learned using the strength of peer support and interaction (Sullivan 1995: 30). Group work practised by social workers has evolved over time to a contemporary state wherein different models have become integrated with influences from psychology, education, medicine, recreation, and self-help fields (Breton 1990). As a result, therefore, it is practised within a framework of multiple but related principles rather than as clearly defined model. The framework emphasizes interaction of the members, the group as an entity, the worker role, and group activities toward the achieving of purposes.

The range of group work practice in social work is evident in a study by Mesbur (1996) and in a paper presented in Toronto in 2000 at the Twenty-Second Annual International Symposium of the Association for the Advancement of Social Work with Groups. Mesbur found that groups have been problem-focused and population-specific, and were the modality of preference by practitioners for positive outcomes with these issues. Groups were comprised, typically, of vulnerable and marginalized populations (i.e., abused children and women, older adults, and seriously ill people) elicited such themes as social support, mutual aid, competency building, education, and skill acquisition. A majority were time-limited and semi-structured in format. The 2000 symposium program reaffirms this profile of group work practice in Canada; that is, it still highlights problems and specific people: assaulted women, children of violent families, adolescents in care, immigrant mothers, siblings of children with disabilities, disadvantaged women, young offenders with learning disabilities, Aboriginal peoples, HIV/AIDS youth, gay and bisexual youth, poor parents, street kids, multicultural families with children with disabilities, Black youth at risk, adopted teens and their families, care-givers of chronically ill people, women with heart disease, children with cleft lip and/or palate, men who batter, teen mothers, people with renal dysfunction, people with bladder exstrophy, older adults, social work students in the classroom, and bereaved people. Creative

innovations are evident in many practices, for example, meal planning and cooking, improvisational acting, online group work, and storytelling. Many of these papers indicated that many current group practices hold a component of social justice. With the hybridization and eclecticism of group work in social work, the original mission and mandate of working with disadvantaged people can become sidelined as influences from other disciplines become incorporated. Specialization to population, issues, and setting can distance group work practice from social work's unique private/public perspective. It may compromise, if not discard, the understanding of the role of oppressive ideologies and institutions in creating problems for people, as well as the right and potential efficacy of people in groups to challenge and change those elements of society in the direction of full inclusion and social justice.

[*Nancy E. Sullivan* and
Ellen Sue Mesbur]

RELATED ENTRIES

Anti-oppressive Social Work, Community Organization, Empowerment Theory, Mutual Aid, Natural Networks, Peer Counselling, Practice Methods, School Social Workers, Settlement House Movement, Social Justice, Theory & Practice

REFERENCES

Breton, M. 1990. Learning from Social Group Work Traditions. *Social Work with Groups* 13, 3, 21–33.

Lang, N.C. 1979. A Comparative Examination of Therapeutic Uses of Groups in Social Work and in Adjacent Human Service Professions: Part II — The Literature from 1969–1978. *Social Work with Groups* 2, 3, 197–220.

Mesbur, E.S., with F. Marra and C. Webb. 1996. Survey of Social Group Work in Metropolitan Toronto. Unpublished raw data.

Shapiro, B.Z. 1990. The Social Work Group as a Social Microcosm: Frames of Reference Revisited. *Social Work with Groups* 13, 2, 21.

Sullivan, N. 1995. Who Owns the Group? The Role of Worker Control in the Development of a Group: A Qualitative Research Study of Practice. *Social Work with Groups* 18, 2/3, 15–32.

James Harris (1922–99)

Harris, James, social work administrator, educator; b. June 15, 1922, Philadelphia, PA; m. (Rev.) Judi Carse; children: Jeffery, Joy; d. Sept. 17, 1999, New Hamburg, ON

Jim Harris, the youngest child in a sibling group of seven, served in the Second World War as a sergeant major, and pursued his early interests in music and sports by playing professional football with the Philadelphia Giants and, in 1948, by earning a bachelor's degree in music. He became a music teacher and programmer for ghetto children in Philadelphia, and later worked in public assistance and a training school for boys. In 1961 on completing a master's degree in social work, Harris became director of the Lutheran Social Mission Society and group services co-ordinator for the Philadelphia Housing Authority; subsequently, he led psychology and research for the Elwyn School for the Retarded and worked with the Philadelphia Women's Christian Alliance Child Placement Agency. In 1967 Jim Harris moved to Canada, first as co-ordinator of services for the Children's Aid Society of the County of Waterloo and, in 1971, as co-ordinator of the social services program at Conestoga College of Applied Arts and Technology in Kitchener. In 1980 he became associate professor and director of Social Development Studies at Renison College, University of Waterloo until he retired in 1988. Harris published numerous articles regarding social work, religion, social issues, ageing and race relations, authored two books (*Inner Peace: An Essential for Social Work Practice* and *Yea, I Have a Goodly Heritage: My Faith, My Life and Racism*), and contributed to the textbook *Canadian Social Welfare*. Throughout Jim Harris's outstanding career in social work, he was known for his compassion, kindness, patience, sensitivity, humbleness, his love of group work, and his quiet gentle manner.

[*Dorothy McKnight*]

RELATED ENTRIES

Anti-oppressive Social Work, Community Organization, Empowerment Theory, Mutual Aid, Natural Networks, Peer Counselling, Practice Methods, School Social Workers, Settlement House Movement, Social Justice, Theory & Practice

Wilson Head (1914–93)

Head, Wilson Adonijah, social worker, administrator, educator, founder Urban Alliance on Race Relations; b. 1914, Georgia; Harry Jerome Award, 1988; d. 1993

Wilson Head was the son of a Georgia share-cropper, the oldest of five children. In his memoirs, *A Life on the Edge,* Head reflects on the forces that shaped his life, in particular the sometimes brutal conditions, injustices, and indignities to which Black people in the southern United States were regularly subjected, which he experienced during his early years. He attended segregated schools and colleges, later making his way to the University of Georgia, where he earned a master's degree in social work, and to Ohio State University, where he earned a doctoral degree in sociology and social psychology. Much of his post-secondary work was done on a part-time basis, which gave him an understanding of how graduate work could be achieved by a person who had to be employed to attend university. Experiences of racial segregation motivated Dr. Head's lifelong commitment to fight against all manifestations of segregation and, in particular, the submissive behaviour expected of Black people and against the absorption of those expectations by Black people. In his autobiography, he gives many examples of the punishment meted out to "uppity" Black people, that is, anyone who stepped beyond the expected boundaries of oppression. Although Dr. Head had left America before the civil rights marches in Alabama, he had taken part in many of the earlier testing situations where Black people tried to integrate restaurants and places of public accommodation. He worked at times with the Congress of Racial Equality and the National Association for the Advancement of Colored People. Dr. Head's social work practice was nearly always in community development as, for instance, when he was director of community development and community organization at Flanner House, in Indianapolis, which served poor and indigent Black people. Elsewhere his practice involved helping youths to overcome mental health problems. In his practice, he always challenged not only bigotry and assumptions about the inferiority of Black people but anyone in authority who expected him either to be subservient or to provide lesser services to clients who were Black.

Another aspect of life in the southern United States that affected Head was his dislike of the militaristic atmosphere in some of the segregated schools he attended. He fought consistently against ideas and undemocratic behaviour that were imposed on him. As his understanding about the importance of racial equity grew, he developed sufficiently strong ideas about the immorality of war that he became a conscientious objector. When the Second World War started, he determined that he would not take part in US military service; he had to remain steadfast to achieve status as a conscientious objector, not an easy task. He carried out alternative service in hospitals, in some cases volunteering as a subject of medical research. The Society of Friends (i.e., Quakers) remained an important source of support for him throughout.

In 1959, Wilson Head emigrated to Canada to take the post of executive director of the Windsor Group Therapy Project; he later became director of the Windsor Social Planning Council. In 1965 he went to work on the Toronto Social Planning Council, where he was often sought by the media, especially on issues relating to poverty, tenant's rights, or police involvement in any aspect of human equality and social justice in the news. In the late 1960s Dr. Head was asked to start a social work program at York University. This initiative, coming from within Atkinson College (the part-time college of the university), started in the division of professional studies as a program in social welfare administration. Through Dr. Head's efforts this entirely part-time professional program overcame objections from within the liberal arts college as well as full-time professional programs at other universities. Later, the program was converted to a bachelor's degree in social work, which was more acceptable to the social work profession. A great many practising but untrained social workers in Toronto and the surrounding areas earned their bachelor's degree in this program through evening courses while working by day. Largely because of Wilson's vision and knowledge, many students and employed social workers have had the opportunity to get their education on a part-time basis. The York program has flourished and is now a full-fledged school of social work that awards both bachelor's and master's degrees in social work.

One of Wilson Head's enduring accomplishments was his founding of the Urban Alliance on Race Relations (est. 1975), which has become a model for other race relations and anti-racism organizations throughout Canada. The alliance advocates not only for social justice for Black people in Canada but also for people in other visible minorities, owing to circumstances within the social milieu. Unlike his US experience, Dr. Head found that other issues in Canada complicated the development of an organization advocating against racism. One was that many immigrants had strong ties to their place of origin and that those ties were at least as strong as ties to others of the same or similar ethnicity or culture. In addition those Black people who had been in Canada for many generations often identified themselves more as a Canadian than as a Black person. Further, people from many backgrounds who experienced racism in their daily lives did not initially want to organize about racism, because it was an unfamiliar way of approaching this long-extant problem in Canada. Dr. Head's consuming challenging views about racial inequity, stretching back to his early years, enabled him to keep in view what was needed. He knew, as few other Canadians did, that change must come from a demand by the victims of racism and not from the largesse of racially and economically secure people. In short, Dr. Head understood what the consequences were for the discriminated-against, and developed strategies they could employ to achieve redress. Wilson Head will be remembered in Canada as its foremost promoter of anti-racism advocacy. In 1988 he was given the Harry Jerome Award in recognition of his work, and in 1992, York University announced a scholarship in race relations in Dr. Head's name.

[*Dorothy Chave Herberg*]

RELATED ENTRIES

Diversity, Education in Social Work, Race & Racism, Racism-Sensitive Social Work, Social Planning, Visible Minorities

Heagerty Report on Health Insurance

On February 5, 1942, Dr. John Joseph Heagerty, federal director of public health services, was selected to chair an interdepartmental advisory committee on health insurance. Under Order in

Council P.C. 836, the committee's mandate was to study all factual data relating to health insurance, to draft a bill for comprehensive national health insurance, and to advise and report to then-minister of pensions and national health, Ian A. Mackenzie. The committee members carried out an intensive study of public health and medical care based on contemporary health problems in Canada; they complemented their examination by soliciting general views on health insurance from several appointed committees comprised of national interest groups and studied health insurance plans from thirty-nine countries. The Heagerty committee recommended that Canada establish national public health to focus on prevention and treatment and a national system of health insurance. The latter was to be based on compulsory fees payable by all residents of Canada by agreement with the provinces as well as contributory insurance funds to be paid by insured persons, employers, and both federal and provincial governments. Although the Heagerty report's recommendations on health insurance were released on March 16, 1943, they were not implemented, owing to federal and provincial disputes over funding of the scheme.

[*Carlos J. Pereira*]

RELATED ENTRIES

Health Canada, Rowell-Sirois Commission, Wellness

healing theory (Cree)

The Plains Cree have long had guidance for the healing of individuals and families. Healing based on Cree traditions builds stronger individuals, families, and communities, so that social problems can be decreased (Nabigon & Mawhiney 1995; Nabigon & Waterfall 1995). Elders, our spiritual masters, teach that illness and other things from which we need healing come from the dark side of life, defined by five little rascals: inferiority, envy, resentment, not caring, and jealousy. Elders emphasize the importance of listening and paying attention to everything around us, especially the natural world, often symbolized by the colour green to represent healing. Listening can help people make the appropriate changes to heal themselves from the effects of these rascals and move toward goodness (i.e., caring, feelings, relationships, and respect). Learning how to use the healing traditions of the Cree is a life-long learning process that includes fasting (i.e., sleeping and living outdoors for four days and nights without food and water) and participating in sweatlodge ceremonies. Fasting and sweatlodges must be done under the guidance of an Elder, as they can be dangerous if attempted alone.

At the heart of Cree healing traditions is the medicine wheel, which is used to teach people to seek a balanced way of life. The medicine wheel reflects many significant aspects of life, such as the four cardinal points of the universe symbolized by four colours. (The medicine wheel is common to other Aboriginal societies, which may associate other colours with the four directions.) Medicine wheel teachings begin with certain basic principles:

- The *east* (red), where the sun rises to start each day, represents renewal of mind, body, spirit, and life in spring.
- The *south* (yellow), where the sun stands at midday, represents the time needed to restore and maintain balance and healthy relationships, as in summer.
- The *west* (black), for night time or fall, represents inner strength and self-reliance.
- The *north* (white), for light in the night skies and snow in winter, represents endurance and sharing.

Today, where many Aboriginal individuals and communities are experiencing social disruption, the teachings of the medicine wheel can focus on the renewal and rebuilding of inner strength needed to restore harmony and well-being. Elders teach people that healing begins when we can shed our inner darkness (i.e., anger or resentment) so that we can take responsibility for ourselves and start rebuilding self-reliance. Having a steady job can increase healing and contribute to a sustainable economy in our communities. Healthy people can produce wealth from our ancestral lands and resources for equitable distribution to community members. This renewal is possible when we draw on our strengths and share our traditional values. The four colours of the medicine wheel also represent the peoples of the earth. Permeating all five colours or aspects of life are the spiritual teachings of honesty and kindness. The Cree believe that, through our spiritual teachings and values, we can build a world based on mutual respect and trust. The transition from racism and fear to developing such a world will take time but can be realized through healing based on our traditions. Elders and community leaders actively promote healing based on traditional knowledge as a way for our communities to start taking over responsibility for ourselves, as well as justice, health, economics, social services, and other aspects of governance.

[*Herb Nabigon*]*

*The author acknowledges the teachings which have guided and shaped this entry, of Michael Thrasher, Rebecca Martel (Kakegee Sikaw Wapestak, "Keeper of the Dawn"), the late Abe Burnstick and Eddy Bellrose, and one senior Elder who prefers to remain anonymous.

RELATED ENTRIES

Aboriginal Issues, Culture, Diversity, Natural Health & Complementary Wellness, Remote Practice, Remote & Rural Practice Methods, Theory & Practice, Therapy, Treatment, Wellness

REFERENCES

Nabigon, H., and A.M. Mawhiney. 1995. Aboriginal Theory: A Cree Medicine Wheel Guide for Healing First Nations. In F.J. Turner (Ed.) *Social Work Treatment*. 4th ed. 18–38. New York: Free Press.

Nabigon, H., and B. Waterfall. 1995. An Assessment Tool for First Nations Individuals Families. In F.J. Turner (Ed.), *Social Work Treatment*. 32–33. 4th ed. New York: Free Press. [Used with the permission of Weech-it-te-win Family Services, Training Learning Centre, Fort Francis, ON.]

health and unemployment

Health and poor employment conditions are two variables that cause some people to prosper and others to suffer conditions that frequently bring the attention of social workers. People who enjoy good health and are free from disabling conditions, in general, have better opportunities to find and maintain meaningful employment than people who do not; the reverse is also generally true. Employment in unhealthy environments can result in workers developing chronic illnesses, become injured, or may be killed on the job (i.e., high incidence of disability and death in rail construction, especially in mountainous areas; lung disease developed by asbestos and coal miners, and cancer in non-smoking restaurant workers from second-hand smoke of patrons). The relationship between the independent variables of health and unemployment is well documented.

A 1994 study for the Ontario Premier's Council on health, well-being, and social justice, for example, noted that 43 percent of poor Ontarians enjoyed good or excellent health, compared to 69 percent of more affluent Ontarians, and that poor Ontarians were much more likely to experience multiple health problems than wealthier Ontarians. A 2002 federal government study, *Report on the Health of Canadians*, corroborated the Ontario study, reporting that affluent, employed, and well-educated people are healthier than those who are poor, unemployed, and poorly educated. The inability of some population groups to acquire enough income to provide proper nutrition leads in turn to poorer health and lower chances of maintaining sustained employment. Clearly, many factors are involved. Research on the employment status of Canadians who are physically challenged mirrors that of research on the effect of health conditions on the ability to work; for example, the Canadian Council on Social Development studied the participation of disabled women in the labour force, reporting that: "The best defence against poverty for persons with disabilities is employment, but women with disabilities also have one of the lowest rates of labour force participation in the province of Ontario" (Fawcett 2000). The report asserts that "employment is a key element in full citizenship." In 2000, the Royal Bank of Canada released a study by economists McCallum and Holt, *Cautious Optimism on a Mounting Twenty-First Century Social Challenge*, that pointed to Canada's poor track record in including Canadians with disabilities in the general trend of economic growth. After presenting the evidence, the report challenged companies as well as governments and families to incorporate people with physical and intellectual limitations into society in a meaningful way. Researchers have clearly documented the relationship among the variables of health, education, work, and wealth. Some of the social consequences of being unhealthy and out of work were reported by Health Canada in 1997: "people who have been unemployed for any significant amount of time tend to die earlier and have higher rates of suicide and heart disease. Spouses of unemployed workers experience increased emotional problems. Children, especially teens, whose parents are unemployed, are at higher risk of emotional and behavioural problems. Recovery of physical and mental health after unemployment is neither immediate nor complete." In addition to social costs are financial costs. In 1998 SMARTRISK (est. 1992), a nationwide non-profit injury-prevention program, calculated that unintentional injuries cost $8.7 billion, of which $2.7 was related to loss of productivity. Health Canada reported that, in 1998, the cost of illness in Canada was $159.4 billion, of which 47.3 percent was indirect (i.e., the value of lost production). Experts suggest a number of solutions to the problems caused directly and indirectly by poor health, disabling conditions, and unemployment. Health Canada's 2002 *Report on the Health of Canadians* includes this list: improvement in social support networks, life-long learning, healthier working conditions, equitable income distribution, poverty reduction, adequate income, and a thriving sustainable economy with meaningful work for all. This latter report also recommend—as does the Royal Bank study—a collaborative approach among many sectors if the multiple challenges caused by health and unemployment problems are to be met and overcome.

[*Gary D. Davies*]

RELATED ENTRIES

Employee Assistance Programs, Employment, Health Determinants, Industrial Social Work, Poverty, Vocational Rehabilitation, Wellness

REFERENCES

Fawcett, G. 2000. *Bringing Down the Barriers.* Ottawa: Canadian Council on Social Development.
Canada. 1997. *Canada Health Action.* Ottawa: Health Canada. Online at time of writing at <www.hc-sc.gc.ca/>.
———. 1998. *Economic Burden of Illness in Canada.* Ottawa: Health Canada. Online at time of writing at <www.hc-sc.gc.ca/>.
———. 2002. *Report on the Health of Canadians.* Ottawa: Health Canada. Online at time of writing at <www.hc-sc.gc.ca/>.
McCallum, J., and D. Holt. 2000. *Cautious Optimism on a Mounting Twenty-First Century Social Challenge.* Toronto: Royal Bank of Canada.
Ontario. 1994. *Wealth and Health, Health and Wealth.* A report of the Premier's Council on Health, Well-Being, and Social Justice. Toronto: Queen's Printer.
SMARTRISK. 1998. *The Economic Burden of Unintentional Injury in Canada.* Toronto: SMARTRISK.

Health Canada

Health Canada is the current federal government department, formerly called the Department of Health and Welfare, which came into existence in 1944, and which superseded the Department of Pensions and National Health. In 1993 the department was combined with part of the former consumer and corporate affairs ministry to become Health Canada. Mackenzie King, the prime minister in 1944, determined that a new department was needed to oversee planned nationwide social security and health initiatives, including family allowances, health insurance, and old-age pensions (Guest 1987). Medical doctors Brock Chisholm and George Davidson, two pre-eminent health and social welfare advocates, filled the deputy minister portfolios for health and welfare, respectively. National Health and Welfare played a critical role in advancing nationwide health and social welfare policy. In 1949 for example, the department initiated the National Health Program, which provided federal grants to the provinces to strengthen their health facilities and support service development. The country moved toward a national health insurance system with the Hospital Insurance and Diagnostic Services Act, 1957, followed by the Medical Care Act, 1968; these statutes brought national standards to health care, a matter of provincial responsibility. The Canada Health Act (1984) outlines five principles that provinces and territories, which remain responsible for the administration of health care, are to follow: public administration, comprehensive services, universal access for residents, portability (i.e., between jurisdictions), and accessibility to all residents. These principles have elicited persistent debate. With respect to the initiation of social welfare in 1944, National Health and Welfare was responsible for many major policies that supported the development of a national social security system, such as the enactment of the Unemployment Insurance Act, 1940. In 1956 the department implemented the National Assistance Program. Outside of employment-related programs, National Health and Welfare in 1945 administered the Family Allowance Act, resulting in the first universal government cash grant. The Blind Persons Act, Old Age Assistance Act, and Old Age Security Act were all proclaimed in 1951 to replace the Old Age Pension Act, 1927. The Old Age Security Act was seen to be the most momentous of these because it signalled federal administration of the nationwide program that offered assistance to persons aged seventy years or older (later changed to sixty-five years of age). These measures were significant in that constitutional amendments were required to change employment and welfare from provincial to federal responsibilities. Currently, responsibility for the majority of federally operated social security programs lies with Human Resources Development Canada.

Health Canada continues to work with provincial and territorial governments to advance the health of all Canadians. The department maintains a leadership role in policy development while enforcing various health regulations, promoting disease prevention, and enhancing healthy living. As described in the departmental publication, *About the Department*, Health Canada currently has four priorities: preserving and modernizing Canada's health care system, enhancing the health of Canadians, safeguarding the health of Canadians, and working with Aboriginal peoples to attain a level of health comparable to that of other Canadian living in similar locations (Canada 2002). Current information about Health Canada can be found online at < www.hc-sc.gc.ca >.

[Michael R. Woodford]

RELATED ENTRIES

Canada Health Act, Health Determinants, Health & Unemployment, P. Martin, Wellness

REFERENCES

Guest, D. 1987. *The Emergence of Social Security in Canada*. 2nd ed. Vancouver: UBC Press.
Canada. 1949. Annual Report, Department of National Health and Welfare [April 1948–March 1949.] Ottawa: King's Printer.
———. 2002. *About Health Canada and Canada Health Act Overview*. Ottawa: Health Canada. Online at time of writing at < www.hc-sc.gc.ca/ >.

health determinants

Health, as defined by the World Health Organization, is viewed as a complete state of physical, mental, social, and emotional well-being rather than as a narrower concept as the absence of disease. Health is a resource for living that enables people of all ages to realize their hopes and needs, and to change or cope with their environments. This definition implies a positive state of being, including a physical dimension to the health of individuals and populations, such psychological dimensions as attitudes or awareness, social practices, and social conditions. This concept of health is referred to as the population health approach. Health Canada, within its framework for population health, identifies twelve determinants of health, which are categorized as environmental or individual determinants:

- *Income, income distribution, and social status*: Together these factors represent the single, most important determinant of health. Population studies show that health status improves as income and status rise. Societies with the healthiest populations are reasonably prosperous and tend toward an equitable distribution of wealth compared to similarly prosperous societies where wealth is distributed less equitably, regardless of the amounts spent on health care.
- *Social environments*: Societal values and rules (i.e., social stability, safety, tolerance, positive interpersonal relationships and community cohesion) have a significant influence on the health status of a population.
- *Education and literacy*: Health status improves with level of education and literacy, which also improve occupational opportunities and provide people with a greater sense of control over their life circumstances.
- *Employment and working conditions*: Level of control over work, workplace safety, and job security are closely related to health status.
- *Social support networks*: Supportive families, friends and communities are important determinants of health. Research results suggest that health effects related to social relationships are at least as important to health status as those associated with such risk factors as smoking, obesity, high blood pressure, and inactive lifestyles.
- *Accessible health and social services*: Access to health and social services supports population health status in that as it assures all who require service or support to attain or maintain optimal personal and/or family health and functioning are able to do so. Health and social services also

contribute to population health through health promotion and disease prevention activities.

• *Healthy child development*: Factors have a strong influence on one's life opportunities and health status as an adult include prenatal care, birth weight, caregiver/child relationship, early nurturing for learning during sensitive periods of brain development, stimulation, and nutrition.

• *Personal health practices and coping skills*: Personal behaviour and consumption patterns such as smoking, use of alcohol, drug abuse, diet, and physical activity are directly related to health outcomes.

• *Physical environment*: The physical environment—both natural (air, water, soil) and constructed (housing, work sites, community and road design)—represents a significant determinant of health.

• *Biological and cultural endowments*: Heredity and genetic endowment, gender, and culture are important determinants of health that are more or less fixed at birth.

Viewing health as influenced by both environmental and individual determinants is congruent with the social work profession's focus on person-in-environment and the code of ethics of Canadian Association of Social Workers. Helping individuals, families, and communities improve their functioning and prevent social problems from affecting them negatively requires that the social worker maintain a focus on an individual's traits and behaviours, and how they interact with the relevant people and systems in their lives. The role of the social worker is to address both person and environment simultaneously, as well as the transactions between them.

[*Margaret Kennedy*]

RELATED ENTRIES

Assessment, Diagnosis, Health & Unemployment, Health Canada, Person-in-Environment, Wellness

Charles Hendry (1903–79)

Hendry, Charles Eric (Chick), social work administrator, educator; b. 1903; d. 1979

Chick Hendry grew up in the Glebe neighbourhood of Ottawa, the son of a devout Baptist mother and a Presbyterian father, who was a moderately successful retail clothing and camping goods merchant. Hendry fell into community development at a young age, as he and several young friends started a lending library out of his family home—at its apex comprising more than 700 books and a membership of approximately 135 boys. As a teenager he met Taylor Statten, an eminent leader of recreational and social activities for youth, especially for the Young Men Christian Association (YMCA), and for the rest of his life Hendry was a devoted advocate of the YMCA movement. In summers he was a leader in one of Statten's boy camps, and he boarded with Statten's mother-in-law while pursuing undergraduate studies in political economy at McMaster University. Statten secured Hendry his first job as provincial secretary of the Alberta Boys' Work Board. Moving to New York City in 1928, Hendry earned two masters degrees, one in religious education from Union Theological Seminary and the other in educational sociology from the teacher's college at Columbia University. In 1931 he enrolled in a doctoral program in sociology at the University of Chicago but did not complete the degree. Here began a two decade-long career in the United States. He was director of research and personnel at the Kenosha, Wisconsin, chapter of the YMCA (1928–29), moving into a junior position in the Department of Sociology at the Y's George Williams College in Chicago (1929–37)—of which Hedley Dimock was director, gradually replacing Statten as Hendry's mentor. Hendry became the co-founder and, later, national chairman of the American Association for the Study of Group Work (1936–40). In 1937 he returned to New York City, where he became director of programs and personnel training for the Boys' Clubs of America (1937–40). Other assignments followed in quick succession: national director of research and statistical services of the Boy Scouts of America (1940–44); director of research for the American Jewish Congress National Commission on Community Inter-Relations (1942–46); part-time lecturer at the New School for Social Research (1942–44) and at the teacher's college at Columbia University (1942–46); and research associate at the Massachusetts Institute of Technology's newly founded Centre for Group Dynamics (1944–46). An advocate of action research and collaborative relationships, he was

> never strongly anchored to any one approach or method; impatient with detail, free-wheeling and unsystematic in thinking; a romantic, poet, dreamer, and charismatic personality; always

more of a doer than a thinker, more a promoter than a scholar.

His principal skills were relational, not intellectual. What he might have lacked by way of single-minded, disciplined devotion to scholarly detail he compensated for in other ways, particularly as a leader and motivator. By the time he returned to Canada he had acquired superb abilities to network within and beyond academia, to recognize and to maintain connections with people whose careers were clearly on the rise, to initiate social advocacy work, to raise money, to convince others to help champion social causes, to work crowds, and to generate interest in projects to which he was committed. Possessing a happy disposition, an enormously persuasive personality, a far-reaching imagination, and that "can do" spirit of enterprise that he had learned from the YMCA, everything he did was with great and contagious enthusiasm.... A skilled delegator, a risk-taker, a gregarious, innovative, energetic, and intensely ambitious behind-the-scenes operator, Hendry was eager to place his work beyond the confines of academia. He had a considerable aptitude for travelling and a natural sensitivity to the global village, and was in demand as a consultant in social policy, social work curricula, and professional development in and outside Canada. (Graham 1994: 161–62)

In 1946, Hendry and his family relocated to Toronto to take up a full professorship under Harry Cassidy, director of the University of Toronto School of Social Work. Five years later, following Cassidy's death, Hendry was appointed as director, retaining the position until his retirement in 1969. During Cassidy's leadership, the school had grown fourfold. Hendry oversaw its continued post-war expansion and recruited some superb scholars, in part to replace those who departed during this period of continent-wide university expansion. Not a prolific author, he had co-written with Dimock a 1931 YMCA study, *Camping and Character*, and he authored alone a 1933 polemical embrace of technology and progress and a 1936 study on community development in Cleveland. One of his best-received works was a 1969 study, *Beyond Traplines*, for the Anglican Church on its relations with Aboriginal peoples. Hendry cannot be understood without reference to Canadian Protestantism, the YMCA, American individualism, liberalism, positivism, and social science, as well as a social structure that favoured the leadership advancement of men, even in a profession numerically dominated by women. He was known among Canada's corporate, political, and social elite, and functioned with exceptional ease and relative success in these contexts.

[*John R. Graham*]

RELATED ENTRIES

F.S.B. Bowers, Canadian Association of Schools of Social Work, H. Cassidy, Education in Social Work, University of Toronto (Faculty of Social Work), YMCA

REFERENCES

Graham, J.R. 1994. Charles Eric Hendry (1903–1979): The Pre-war Formational Origins of Leader of Post-World War I Canadian Social Work Education. *Canadian Social Work Review* 11, 2, 150–67.

Sister Mary Henry (1902–96)

Mulligan, Mary (Sister Mary Henry), educator, farm manager, social worker, humanitarian; b. 1902, Newton PE; Benemerenti Medal, 1964; Order of Canada, 1975; d. 1996

Sister Mary Henry exemplified all that is best in those who fight for social justice and serve the poor and downtrodden in God's name. Born Mary Mulligan in Prince Edward Island, she attended the local schools and obtained her teacher's licence at Prince of Wales College in Charlottetown. After joining the Sisters of St. Martha, Sister Mary Henry was assigned at twenty-three years of age to St. Vincent's Orphanage, where she managed a 32-hectare (80-acre) farm and taught five grades of children. After various assignments teaching school and managing other farms owned by the order, Sister Mary Henry completed her bachelor of arts degree at the University of Ottawa and, in 1954, she graduated from St. Patrick's School of Social Welfare in Ottawa with her master's degree. On her return to Prince Edward Island, she was appointed executive director of Catholic Family Services Bureau in Charlottetown. In this position, which she held for the next twenty-three years, Sister Mary Henry played a leadership role in the organizing and development of new social welfare structures that have contributed much to the betterment of island families. She initiated innumerable programs for addiction, family life education, health services, unmarried mothers, as well as a non-denominational camp for children. In the early days, her office became a weekly meeting place where the only three trained social workers in the island province; with Eugene MacDonald (director of child welfare) and J.E. Green (director of family allowance), Sister Mary Henry devised methods of helping poor and hurt families in the province. This unique approach brought together federal, provincial, and private services focused on poverty and discrimination for the whole island. At that time, a large number of infants surrendered by unmarried mothers had no possibility of adoption on the island. In New Jersey, another member of the Sisters of St. Martha who was also a trained social worker, Sister Kathleen Kilbride established a foundation through which she placed children in adoptive homes. Sister Mary Henry began to place children from Prince Edward Island into the eastern United States, where adoption homes were available in large numbers. For hundreds of children, it meant escaping institutional life, and gaining acceptance into families who potentially could lavish them with love, protection, and a good education. Of the many and significant contributions Sister Mary Henry made for the welfare of people this living legacy is perhaps her greatest memorial. Sister Mary Henry was a strong and compassionate woman who spent the greater part of her ninety-three years improving conditions for the health and welfare of poor people. She died in 1996. In recognition of her commitments in life, she had been awarded the Benemerenti Medal by Pope John XXIII in 1964, chosen Islander of the Year by Prince Edward Island in 1966, given an honorary doctor of laws from St. Dunstan's University in 1968, and awarded the Order of Canada in 1975.

[*Ernie MacDonald*]

RELATED ENTRIES

Adoption, Church-Based Services, Religion, Sectarian Social Services, Services for Children, Social Welfare History

Daniel Hill (1923–2003)

Hill, Daniel G., chair, Ontario Human Rights Commission, Ombudsman of Ontario, founder, Ontario Black History Society; b. Nov. 23, 1923, Independent, MI; m. Donna; children: Daniel Jr., Lawrence, Karla; Order of Canada (Officer), 2000; d. June 27, 2003

Daniel G. Hill, educator, author, consultant and community activist graduated from Howard Uni-

versity in 1948, received a master's degree from the University of Oslo in 1951, and a doctoral degree in sociology from the University of Toronto in 1960. He became the first director, and then chair, of the Ontario Human Rights Commission (1962–73). In 1984 the Ontario government made Dr. Hill Ombudsman of Ontario for a five-year term. Dr. Hill consulted on human rights across Canada and in Bermuda. He also served as consultant for the Ministry of Correctional Services (Ontario), the University of Toronto where he held the rank of Adjunct Professor, the Canadian Civil Liberties Association and the Commission of Inquiry on Equality in Employment. His scholarly work including articles and books in the area of Black history is widely recognized. Dr. Hill's 1981 *The Freedom Seekers, Blacks in Early Canada* has become an approved Ontario ministry of education history text; his 1977 *Human Rights in Canada: A Focus on Racism* has been used extensively; and his address to the Black History Conference in 1978 was subsequently published (1984). With his wife, Donna and five associates, Dr. Hill founded the Ontario Black History Society (est. 1978), a non-profit charitable organization dedicated to the study Black history in Ontario. He was president emeritus of the society and an honorary fellow of the Multicultural History Society of Ontario. In 1981 he launched a provincial exhibit on Black History in Early Ontario sponsored by the Ontario Black History Society and the City of Toronto Archives. Prior to that, he and members of the Toronto Negro Business and Professional Men's Association had produced the exhibit *The Negro in Ontario in the Nineteenth Century*, a groundbreaking first. Dr. Hill has been honoured by many educational institutions and was presented with the Order of Canada for the year 2000 by Adrienne Clarkson, Canada's governor general at his home on October 21, 1999, presented there because of ill health. In the bestowing of the Order of Canada, Canada stated that "his career represents a lifelong quest for fairness" and that Dr. Hill "through his writings on Black history, has contributed to our awareness of this important aspect of Canada's heritage" (Canada 2000).

[*Laura Taylor*]

RELATED ENTRIES

Diversity, Human Rights, Race & Racism

REFERENCES

Hill, D.G. 1984. Black History in Early Toronto. A Presentation to the Black History Conference held in Toronto, February 18, 1978. *Polyphony* [Multicultural History Society of Ontario] Summer: 28–30.

Ontario Black History Society. 2002. Dr. Daniel G. Hill. The Society. Unpublished document. Online at time of writing at <www.blackhistorysociety .ca/>.

Canada. 2000. Order of Canada Members. Ottawa: Governor General. Online at time of writing at <www.gg.ca/>.

Ernest Hill (1919–68)

Hill, Ernest David Orlo, educator, social work administrator, community organization advocate; b. 1919, Vancouver, BC (of Walter Hill and Jean Lewis); m. Mary; five children; d. Mar. 04, 1968, Vancouver, BC

Ernest David Orlo (Ernie) Hill attended St. Anne's Academy and the Christian Brothers Vancouver College, where he edited the school paper in his senior year. Perhaps the influence of his parents—his devout Catholic mother and his Protestant father who leaned toward the Co-operative Commonwealth Federation—engendered an ability to move within environments of conflict with steadiness and optimism. After training at the normal school in Vancouver, Hill headed north, as was expected of newly graduated teachers, to teach in a one-room school. Eighteen months later he joined the Royal Canadian Air Force, was seconded to the RAF, Elizabeth City, NC, to install radar in bombers flying the Atlantic. Ernie Hill was among many veterans to attend university after the war. He received a bachelor of arts 1947 and a bachelor of social work the following year from the University of British Columbia. He worked for the Catholic Children's Aid in Vancouver until returning to the University of British Columbia for his master's degree in 1950. He then spent three years as head of the medical social service department of St. Paul's Hospital. The academic and professional experiences of these years, which also included activity as a founding member of the BC Association of Social Workers, led to an invitation from the Vancouver Community Chest and Council to join its staff in 1954. Two years later, he was appointed head of its health and social planning division. From this time, Ernie Hill's career focused on community organization and community development. His strong commitment to social change and a deep concern for others, complemented by an ability to assist individuals and communities to work together, allowed him to become "the chief architect of the local area approach to community welfare services in the Vancouver area" (BCASW 1968). With this approach, notions of local involvement and neighbourhood government flourished, in the words of a tribute to him: "he was at the heart of the processes for establishing new directions and innovations—whether for research and programs for multiproblem families, for a new social planning board at the City of Vancouver, or for citizen capacity development in disadvantaged areas of the city" (Cunliffe, Tributes 1968: 1). In 1965 Hill and his wife Mary travelled to Ottawa, where they became founding members of the board for the Vanier Institute of the Family. Hill was also a special lecturer in community organization at the University of British Columbia School of Social Work (1966–68). There, he was described as a dedicated teacher, able to make valuable connections between theory and social work practice. One of his students wrote that "his own great sense of humanity and justice came through—he wanted "to impart his feelings for people and their needs to his students" (Azzara, Tributes 1968: 34). In British Columbia, following a provincial welfare conference, Hill helped to establish the Voluntary Association for Health and Welfare, which subsequently became the Social Planning and Research Council of British Columbia. Ernie Hill died suddenly of a heart attack at the age of forty-nine. A memorial trust in his name was established jointly by the United Community Services (formerly the Community Chest and Council), the University of British Columbia School of Social Work and The BC Association of social workers "in support of social work education, particularly in the field of Community Organization" (Naphtali 1968). A tribute for Ernie Hill noted that "[h]is approach was one of great depth and understanding of the complex dimensions of social work practice. His counsel and leadership was sought and recognized in national undertakings—including the impetus he gave through teaching and educational responsibilities for staff of planning councils and funds across Canada" (Nicholls, *Tributes* 1968: 4).

[*Mary A. Hill*]

RELATED ENTRIES

Community Organization, Education in Social Work, Vanier Institute for the Family

REFERENCES

BCASW. 1968. *In Memoriam*. BC Association of Social Workers Newsletter. Spring 3.

Naphtali, H. 1968. Personal communication. Executive Director, United Community Services of Greater Vancouver. June 14.

Tributes. 1968. *A Memorial Tribute to Mr. Ernest D. Hill.* Transcript of radio broadcast, March 10. 1–4. School of Social Work, University of British Columbia.

Clarence Hincks (1885–1964)

Hincks, Clarence Meredith, physician, social work occupations; b. Apr. 8, 1885, St. Marys, ON (of Rev. William Henry Hincks and Martha Greene); d. Dec. 17, 1964, Toronto, ON

Clarence Meredith Hincks was born on April 8 (*Canadian Who's Who* 1961–63) 1885, and raised with a Protestant upbringing that he maintained throughout his life. Hincks attended University of Toronto, from which he received his bachelor of arts (1905) and his medical degree (1908), following his internship at Toronto General Hospital. While at university, Hincks suffered his first bout of mental illness, as a result of which he gained a conviction of the possibility of recovery that would shape his career commitment to mental well-being. Dr. Hincks began a private practice in Campbellford, Ontario, but after refusing to provide an abortion to a prominent citizen, he returned to Toronto where he was medical inspector of public schools (1912–17). In this work, he became increasingly concerned about children labelled at the time as "unteachable"; Hincks is credited with introducing intelligence quotient (IQ) testing in the Toronto schools to aid in screening children, particularly those who today would be identified as having developmental challenges. In 1914 Dr. Hincks and Dr. C.K. Clarke opened a social services clinic at Toronto General Hospital to work with children, and hired two nurses to act as social workers, and in 1915 Hincks was also appointed psychiatrist for the Toronto Department of Health. In spite of the mutual concern Dr. Hincks and Dr. Clarke had for children—and Hincks's own belief in the normalization and

potential for recovery for children with mental illness—both physicians became leading proponents of the eugenics movement of the time. Hincks's major commitment, however, remained mental well-being, or hygiene, as it was then called. With his colleagues Dr. Clarke and Dr. Colin Russell of Montréal, Dr. Hincks founded the Canadian National Committee of Mental Hygiene in 1918, with the patronage of Lady Eaton; known as a masterful organizer and fundraiser, Hincks started a series of "drawing-room meetings" throughout Canada with socially prominent women to gain additional support for the committee. He invited Clifford Beers, founder of the US mental hygiene movement, to join him in addressing these afternoon teas, as Hincks wanted to follow Beers's model; in 1913 Hincks had been introduced to Beers's book, *A Mind that Found Itself*, which had led him to believe that Beers's experience with depression was similar to his own. He also approached business and professional leaders to sit on the committee's board and each to pledge $1,000 toward the organization. Dr. Hincks's commitment was soon widely recognized: he served on the US National Committee of Mental Hygiene (1919–30) and, in 1926, he was awarded a Rockefeller Foundation Scholarship for studies in London, Zurich, and Munich. From 1918–22, the Canadian National Committee of Mental Hygiene was approached by most of the provincial governments to undertake a series of surveys of mental institutions. The findings were reported to each respective provincial governments in confidence, a procedure that avoided public shaming of a government while building trust with the governments. These reports exposed many appalling circumstances of the treatment of mental illness—including patients locked in coffin-like boxes in New Brunswick and a woman kept naked in a dark cupboard for two years in Manitoba—but they also motivated a national interest in mental health conditions. Dr. Hincks, who was among the first advocates of occupational therapy in psychiatric institutions, convinced provincial governments to commit more than six million additional dollars to improve mental hospitals. In 1924 Hincks was asked to sit on a committee that resulted in the founding of the Canadian Association of Social Workers. He is also credited with introducing mental hygiene to the curriculum of schools of social work and nursing, and was instrumental in the development of the School of Psychology at the University of Toronto. During the Second World War, Dr. Hincks organized the Canadian Children's Service (est. 1942), a group of Canadian women who provided mental health services in Britain's bombed cities. Arguably, Clarence Hincks's greatest legacy lies in his guidance of the Canadian National Committee of Mental Hygiene in its formative years. Throughout his directorship, Hincks advocated for tertiary prevention—the provision of services and treatment to prevent relapses, a return to community living for those with mental illness, and the normalization of mental illness.

Hincks lectured extensively throughout North America on subjects related to mental well-being and was internationally renowned for his advocacy in the field. He did not publish extensively but his concepts of mental health can be found in his 1919 article in *Canadian Journal of Mental Hygiene*, "The scope and aims of the mental hygiene movement in Canada." In 1953, he became a member of the *Comité d'honneur* of the World Federation for Mental Health, and served as chairman of the organizing committee for the fifth International Congress on Mental Health. In 1963 he received honorary doctorates from the University of Toronto and the University of British Columbia. He was a member of the Canadian Medical Association; the Canadian Psychiatric Association, the Royal Medico-Psychological Association (UK); a member of the Board of the National Council of Parent Education (US); and a member of Delta Tau Delta. Hincks made history in 1962 when he discussed his own bouts of mental illness, which included alternating depression and euphoria on CBC radio. In battling his own mental illness throughout his life, Dr. Hincks was accustomed to retreat to his cottage in Muskoka where he sought restful therapy in golf and sailing. Dr. Jack Griffin said of Hincks that he "let people know that it was possible to be mentally ill, to recover and carry on" (1996). Hincks's ideals continue in the Canadian Mental Health Association, the organization he helped found, and in the organization that bears his name, the Hincks Dellcrest Institute, which was initially, the C.M. Hincks Institute.

[*Laura Taylor*]

RELATED ENTRIES

Canadian Mental Health Association, Developmental Challenges, Developmental Challenges & Families, *Diagnostic and Statistical Manual of Mental Disorders*, Wellness

REFERENCES

Griffin, J. 1996. *Ottawa Citizen* July 01.

Roland, C. 2002. Clarence M. Hincks, Mental Health Crusader, 1885–1964. Online at time of writing at <http://collections.ic.ca/heirloom_seriesvolumes 5/78-79.htm>.

HIV/AIDS

The virus HIV, which stands for Human Immunodeficiency Virus, is commonly associated with Acquired Immune Deficiency Syndrome, better known as AIDS. HIV serostatus is the general term used to indicate the presence or absence of HIV antibodies in a person's bloodstream. In a human, the virus weakens the immune system of an individual who has tested positive for the presence of HIV antibodies in the blood and is, therefore said to be HIV-positive; people who have been tested and whose blood contained no antibodies are referred to as HIV-negative. A person who is HIV-positive may be symptom-free or may be ill with related conditions. As such, a person who is HIV-positive is not necessarily ill and does not necessarily have AIDS. Testing is still not entirely reliable immediately after exposure to HIV; screening practices, however, have made blood and blood products much safer. AIDS can be used in a technical sense to classify individuals who have developed one or more of an evolving list of opportunistic infections. Because HIV weakens the immune system, individuals succumb to opportunistic infections to which they would not have, had their immune systems not become compromised. Death occurs as a result of AIDS-related complications rather than directly of AIDS. Since AIDS is a technical reference as well as the word used to denote the whole disease, many have begun to use the more accurate term HIV disease. Disease progress varies widely. In some cases, people live for long periods of time with their immune system suppressed and a diagnosis of AIDS; in others, people are diagnosed and die quite quickly.

In North America, recent advances in medicine mean that HIV disease is now managed and treated more as a chronic illness than a fatal one. As there is no known cure for HIV infection, prevention is of utmost importance. Education about condom use and healthy needle-use practices are among the programs that have been implemented. While the epidemic has had a strong impact on Canadians, the picture worldwide is disastrous. Infection rates in sub-Saharan Africa, for example, are many times higher than they are in Canada, with a third of some countries having died and thousands of children becoming orphaned. In North America the psychosocial impact has been immense, both for those who are HIV-positive as well as those who care about someone with HIV/AIDS. The transmission of HIV occurs through exchanges of bodily fluids, the most common ones occurring through sexual contact and intravenous drug use, both highly stigmatized social activities. As a result, the syndrome is widely associated with negative perceptions. As screening for HIV antibodies took a long time to develop, many hemophiliacs were infected through tainted blood products, but most media portrayed these infections as innocent victimization. People living with HIV are often doubly stigmatized when they are also dealing with such issues as sexuality, drug use/addiction, or prostitution. The population most affected by HIV/AIDS is gay men—the population initially infected—but increasing numbers of women and teens are becoming infected. Violence, sometimes related to intravenous drug use or to working in the sex trade, is a particular problem in the lives of women who are living with HIV/AIDS (Canada 1998). The effect of the epidemic on gay people and their families has been devastating, as it is not uncommon for them to have lost dozens of friends. Regardless of the means of infection or the accompanying issues, HIV disease entails loss, loss of dreams, of sexual spontaneity, of health. Those who are infected as well as those who care for infected individuals are subject to AIDS-related multiple loss (Nord 1997). Social workers have a role in prevention and education as well as intervention throughout society concerning the effects of HIV/AIDS. Ethical issues, especially those around mandatory testing and reporting, are often raised in relation to HIV (Taylor, Brownlee, & Mauro-Hopkins 1996). HIV disease challenges social workers to

expand the boundaries of service and to confront many taboos, such as fear of death and issues of sexuality, for themselves and for their clients at personal and societal levels.

[*Susan Cadell*]

RELATED ENTRIES

Caregiving, Clinical Social Work, Family Planning, Gay-Sensitive Services, Hospices, Lesbian Services, Long-Term Care, Personal-Centred Theory, Treatment, Sensitizing Concepts, Sexual Orientation, Wellness

REFERENCES

Canada. 1998. *HIV and Sexual Violence against Women: A Guide for Counsellors Working with Women Who Are Survivors of Sexual Violence.* Ottawa: Health Canada.

Nord, D. 1997. *Multiple AIDS-Related Loss: A Handbook for Understanding and Surviving a Perpetual Fall.* Washington, DC: Taylor and Francis.

Taylor, S., K. Brownlee, and K. Mauro-Hopkins. 1996. Confidentiality Versus the Duty to Protect: An Ethical Dilemma with HIV/AIDS Clients. *The Social Worker* 64, 4, 9–17.

Laura Holland (1883–1956)

Holland, Laura, social worker, nurse; b. 1883, Toronto, ON; CMB, 1934; d. 1956

Laura Holland provided outstanding leadership in both her professions as a social worker and nurse locally, provincially, and nationally. It was said of her that "her innovative approaches were vital to the well being of people of all ages from infancy to adulthood" (Paulson, Zilm, & Warbinek 2000: 36). Laura Holland graduated from the Montreal General Hospital School of Nursing in 1914, then went overseas with the Canadian Army Medical Corps (1915–19); she was awarded the Royal Red Cross medal, first class for dedicated service (UBC Archives 1950). In 1919 she qualified in the social work course at Simmons College in Boston, then returned to work in eastern Canada with distinction until 1927, when she relocated to the west coast. In the early history of child welfare in British Columbia, a study by the then-Canadian Welfare Council (now, Canadian Council on Social Development) had recommended changes in the care of children from institutions to foster homes, the establishment of a family agency, and the employment of professional social workers. In response to the last recommendation, the story is recounted of the three wise women from the east, reflecting the arrival of Laura Holland, Zella Collins, and Katherine Whitman from Ontario. They were followed shortly after by Mary McPhedran, who headed the family welfare agency. Laura Holland was prominent among the list of reformers recommended to help introduce the new era of social work on the west coast (Paulson, Zilm, & Warbinek 2000: 37). She revolutionized the Vancouver children's aid society and "brought agencies together, improved the health of children in care, initiated and found foster homes" (Angus 1951 cited in Paulson, Zilm, & Warbinek 2000). In 1934 she was named Commander of the British Empire by King George V for her outstanding work in Ontario and British Columbia. When the Catholic children's aid was in crisis, she helped in a similar way (Fulton 2001), travelling to that agency from Victoria where she then worked as advisor to the ministry of health and welfare (1938–45).

The University of British Columbia School of Social Work (est. 1928) at first offered all instruction by local professionals called honorary lecturers. For many years, Laura Holland appeared weekly at the campus as a favoured lecturer; a scholarship in her name is an enduring memorial of her contributions. Holland also taught in the university's School of Nursing. At her retirement, in 1945, then-deputy minister of Social Welfare Harry Cassidy wrote: "Her wise counsel, her fine ideals, and her far-sighted vision are enshrined in the legislation and the regulations which have built the present system of services for health and welfare in British Columbia, the system which is now, I think, the finest in Canada" (Cassidy 1945: 2–3 cited in Paulson, Zilm, & Warbinek 2000). At the convocation of the University of British Columbia, May 12, 1950, Holland received a doctor of laws (*honoris causa*), the citation for which stated in part that her "compassion for the unprotected, made effective by abundant common sense and great executive ability, has been responsible in large measure for our provincial child welfare program and has contributed greatly by thought and action to the increasing efficiency of our national welfare services. [Holland] exemplified the highest devotion to human welfare herself but has also the rare faculty of inspiring a like devotion in others" (UBC Archives 1950).

[*Mary A. Hill*]

RELATED ENTRIES

Canadian Council on Social Development, H. Cassidy, Child Welfare, University of British Columbia School of Social Work

REFERENCES

Fulton, P. 2001. Personal communication. Former executive director, Catholic Children's Aid. Vancouver, 1941–45.

Paulson, E., G. Zilm, and E. Warbinek. 2000. Pioneer Government Advisor: Laura Holland, RN, RCC, CBE, LLD (1883–1956). *CJNL* 13, 3 September/October 36–38.

home care

Home care provides services for eligible persons in need in their home or place of residence to augment support services provided by family, neighbours and friends, and community agencies. Home care in some provinces originated as a way for older people to remain independent in their own homes and to defer admission to long-term care facilities; in other provinces, it was initiated to expedite discharge from acute-care hospital beds. While organizational structures, services, and delivery modes vary throughout the country, home care programs are usually delivered regionally to clientele in all age groups. Eligibility criteria usually include residence in the province or territory for a specified time period, possession of provincial/territorial health insurance, and an inability to access community agencies. Some programs cover the cost of medical supplies and rental of equipment, or issue a drug card to cover the cost of medication; other programs consider those costs to be the responsibility of the client and utilize an assessment tool to calculate the client's ability to pay for some services. Referrals to a home care program are usually initiated from such sources as individuals requiring care, agencies, families, physicians, or hospitals. Some programs draw on assessments of the need for home care by a case manager—either a social worker or a nurse—in a hospital to assist discharge planning staff to arrange for services to begin as soon as possible after discharge. In the community, the case manager assesses client needs and arranges for professional nursing, therapy, and/or support services, as needed; conducts case conferences; and monitors the changing needs of the client. Services—such as nursing, physiotherapy, occupational therapy, social work, nutrition counselling, respiratory therapy, speech and language therapy, personal support, laboratory services, or transportation—may be provided by professionals employed by the program or by providers supplied by contracted agencies. In some provinces (e.g., Prince Edward Island) home care also provides adult protection services. As treatment methods and technology continue to develop, the range of complex treatments available to clients served at home continues to expand. In an attempt to provide care for high needs clientele, specialized teams have been created to include, for instance, palliative care, mental health, acquired brain injury care, and pediatrics.

The federal department of Veterans Affairs Canada also offers home care services to eligible veterans. The Veterans Independence Program is designed to allow veterans to remain in their own home for as long as possible and to obtain access to intermediate care in community-based services. District counsellors, supported by client service agents, assess a client's needs and authorize funds to cover the costs of services not provided by the provincial home care program or other community agencies. Some of the services funded include home maintenance, transportation, home adaptation, oxygen services, and special equipment.

The home care social worker functions as part of a multidisciplinary team, which may be large or small, according to client needs. The role is varied and challenging, because the persons they serve are of all ages, stages of life, and physical and emotional condition. Social workers assist clients and their families who experience stress, grief, loss, turmoil, financial problems, and isolation related to their illness, as well as, in some cases, coexisting medical or psychiatric problems. Practitioners can offer treatment for marital or family conflict, caregiver stress and burnout, adjustment to deteriorating health or a palliative illness. The social worker may need to work with hospital staff, community agencies and professionals, schools and day care centres, long-term care or other facilities. Social work intervention, which is generally short term, can also provide clients with assistance in accessing disability pensions, affordable accessible housing, and funding for equipment not covered by government programs or private insurance. Since the commencement of home care programs, demand for services has expanded and it is anticipated that, as the Canadian population ages and funding for heath care decreases, the need for home care will continue to increase.

[*Karen McNaughton*]

RELATED ENTRIES

Caregiving, Clinical Social Work, Long-Term Care, Managed Care, Palliative Care, Personal-Centred Theory, Practice Methods, Sensitizing Concepts, Services for Elderly People, Theory & Practice, Veterans Affairs Canada, Wellness

hospices

Hospices in Canada offer facilities or services for the dying. Palliative care, which is often used as a synonym for hospice, is a multidisciplinary approach to caring for the dying, which involves dealing with fear of pain and suffering in an effective way (i.e., pain and symptom management), las well as treating the whole person (i.e., the psychological, spiritual, physical, intellectual and social selves). Most hospices are community-based organizations, while palliative care is usually offered within a hospital or similar institutional setting. Family and friends are central to care provision, as hospice and palliative care recognize that they are part of the care team. The goal of treatment is to facilitate a peaceful death, as well as helping those served to live as free from pain and anxiety as possible until they die. As a free-standing facility, a hospice may provide residential care as a home away from home, where people who are dying can receive care and support. Hospice care also describes volunteer support services offered to people in their own homes, for instance, to care for children, give respite to caregivers, provide emotional support for family members and the dying person, and offer bereavement support after the person has died. Regardless of setting, community-based hospice and institutionally based palliative care both offer services to the terminally ill and have similar values and goals for their treatment.

The term "hospice" has been in use for two thousand years (Stoddard 1992) and is similar in derivation to hospital, host, hospitality, hostel and hotel, having in common generosity to strangers and comfort. In the mediæval period pilgrims and the dying were housed together in hospices attached to religious houses, as the dying were perceived as prophetic pilgrims and valued by the community as spiritual leaders. The unified concept of hospice and hospital became distinct entities after the monasteries and convents were closed (Buckingham 1983). Today, care is client centred, rather than being driven by available technology and curing illness, which is more likely to be the case with treatment in acute-care hospital wards. The focus of hospice and palliative intervention is on care and life, not on preventing death. Hospice and palliative care in some provinces are represented by a single association for both (i.e., the British Columbia Hospice Palliative Care Association) or for only one (i.e., Manitoba's Palliative Care Association), while in others there are two separate entities (i.e., the Hospice Association as well as the Palliative Care Association in Ontario). Hospice care is one of the fastest-growing programs in Canada, one in which social workers make an important contribution.

The availability and training of social workers who can work with terminally ill persons differs throughout the country. The role of professional social workers with hospice care includes linking terminally ill persons to hospice services, while they provide psycho-social counselling and emotional support to them and their families. Social workers may also serve as volunteer hospice visitors or as board members. Social workers are part of the palliative care team in acute-care hospital wards, and may also be available to terminally ill persons as part of a community-based team. Practitioners may refer dying persons and their families to such resources as hospices and physicians specializing in palliative care. Social workers in palliative care provide psycho-social counselling and support, assist with estate planning and financing, facilitate family meetings, and lead or co-lead support or bereavement groups. The values of hospice and palliative care are consistent with social work values of self determination, advocacy, dignity of the individual, and holistic health care. Further, social work practitioners are in a key position to contribute to the continuing growth of hospice services in their role as educators of care professionals, clients, and the public,

as well as promoting the continuing integration of institutional and community-based services in a manner consistent with the goals of provincial associations; to make hospice care available to all those who need it. More information can be obtained online at <www.living-lessons.org> and <www.hospice.on.ca>.

[*Anne Munroe*]

RELATED ENTRIES

Bereavement, Bioethical Issues, Caregiving, Clinical Social Work, Long-Term Care, Managed Care, Palliative Care, Personal-Centred Theory, Sensitizing Concepts, Services for Elderly People, Suicide, Veterans Affairs Canada, Wellness

REFERENCES

Buckingham, R.W. 1983. *The Complete Hospice Guide.* New York: Harper and Row.
Stoddard, S. 1992. *The Hospice Movement: A Better Way of Caring for the Dying.* Rev. ed. New York: Vintage.

human rights

Human rights concepts, which have evolved throughout history, form the foundation of societal values, which in turn underpin social work theory and practice in Canada. Social work is deeply influenced by ideals and principles embodied in Canadian and international laws to uphold human rights. Concepts of human rights have been articulated by Greco-Roman philosophy and by such philosophers and humanists as St. Thomas Aquinas, Baruch Spinoza, Gottfried Wilhelm Leibniz, Hugo Grotius, John Locke, and Jean-Jacques Rousseau. Modern concepts that emerged in the eighteenth century were influenced by the French and American revolutions. By then, the focus was on the idea of individual rights, now referred to as "negative rights," the exercise of which did not require state intervention, such as the rights to freedom of expression, religion, and assembly. Human rights continued to evolve with the worldwide anti-slavery movement and the Geneva Convention of 1864, which protected medical installations and personnel during war, and the Hague Convention of 1899, which established humanitarian rules for naval warfare. These developing international standards did little to stop the atrocities of the First World War, with the result that "[p]eople realized that more had to be done—that an international organization must be created to ensure peace and protect individual." In response to this need, the League of Nations was formed at the end of the First World War. Among the league's formative proceedings was the imposition on several European states of treaties containing obligations to protect racial, religious, and national minorities. In 1948 the successor to the League of Nations, the United Nations, proclaimed the Universal Declaration of Human Rights. The declaration affirmed that each person is entitled to fundamental human rights simply by being human. John P. Humphrey, a Canadian human rights expert and professor of international law, was appointed as the first director of the human rights division of the UN Secretariat and was the principal drafter of the Universal Declaration of Human Rights. The universal declaration lists dozens of human rights, including rights to "life, liberty and the security of the person"; specific rights against enslavement, torture, arbitrary arrest, and exile; rights to due process in prosecution (i.e., the presumption of innocence); liberty rights (i.e., to marry, have a family, and divorce, and to movement, freedom of thought, and religious practice); political rights to participate in "genuine" elections; cultural rights to develop one's personality; economic rights (i.e., to work and join trade unions, and to favourable pay and paid holidays); welfare rights (i.e., to social security, health care, special assistance for child care, and free education). Canada is a signatory to the declaration.

Canada and some provinces have passed legislation on a range of human rights. For example, in 1944 Ontario introduced the Racial Discrimination Act and in 1947 Saskatchewan passed its Bill of Rights. Fair accommodation and fair employment practices laws were enacted throughout Canada after 1951, followed by equal-pay legislation for women. In the 1960s the provinces consolidated fair-practices statutes into comprehensive human rights codes, administered and enforced by permanent human rights commissions. The Canadian Bill of Rights, 1960, was enacted as the first federal human rights charter, which applied only to federal jurisdiction because the requisite consent of the provinces was not obtained. In 1982 the Canadian Charter of Rights and Freedoms was enacted to offer constitutional protection against government interference with

human rights. The Charter guarantees fundamental freedoms, democratic rights (such as participation in elections), mobility rights (to and from within Canada), legal rights, equality rights (including equal rights for men and women and protection of the multicultural heritage of all Canadians), language rights (and minority language rights), as well as the ability to enforce these rights. In 1977 the federal government had created a national human rights commission to ensure equality of opportunity and freedom from discrimination in federal jurisdiction. The commission's mandate is to make the Canadian Human Rights Act, 1977, work for the benefit of all Canadians by providing means for resolving individual complaints; promote knowledge of human rights in Canada and to help reduce barriers to equality in employment and access to services. Every province has also promulgated human rights legislation to deal with discrimination that is not covered by the Charter, such as discrimination between individuals, or between employers and employees.

In 1966 the Universal Declaration of Human Rights was supplemented by two binding covenants: the International Covenant on Civil and Political Rights, and the International Covenant on Economic, Social, and Cultural Rights. Canada ratified both covenants in 1976 (with the unanimous consent of the provinces), so that they are now binding on Canada in international law. Canada also ratified the Optional Protocol to the Civil and Political Rights Covenant providing the right of every individual in Canada to complain to the federal human rights commission if the Canadian government is not meeting covenant requirements. Canada also accepted another optional obligation, accepting complaints from other states that have ratified the covenant and thereby accepted this state party-to-state party complaint procedure. Since the ratification of the International Covenants, Canada has signed several other important human rights treaties, including the Convention on the Elimination of all Forms of Discrimination Against Women (ratified, 1981), the Convention against Torture and Other Cruel, Inhuman or Degrading Treatment or Punishment (ratified, 1987), and the Convention on the Rights of the Child (ratified, 1991). These international covenants have had a significant impact on Canada's obligations to uphold human rights. A report released in December 2001 by the Standing Senate Committee on Human Rights stated:

> As Canadians, we enjoy extensive human rights protections through our domestic legal system and, in particular, as a result of federal and provincial human rights legislation and the constitutional guarantees enshrined in the Canadian Charter of Rights and Freedoms. Beyond these domestic achievements, Canada has been at the forefront of the international human rights movement…. It is perhaps not surprising that Canada would become a world leader in human rights. Canada has had to confront and reconcile different cultures, languages, and religions from its very inception as a nation. Tolerance and mutual respect were the only way forward for Canada.

Notwithstanding the progress Canada has made in the field of human rights, enabling legislation has yet to be passed to fulfil a number of Canada's commitments with regards to international human rights instruments. Clearly, the way forward requires further action. Information on the concept and history of human rights can be found online at < www.udhr.org/ >; on Canada's human rights obligations at < www.pch.gc.ca/ >; and on the Canadian Human Rights Commission at < www.chrc-ccdp.ca >.

[*Janelle Feldstein*]

RELATED ENTRIES
Aboriginal Issues, Assembly of First Nations, K. Belanger, Canadian Bill of Rights, Canadian Charter of Rights and Freedoms, M.-T. Casgrain, Chinese Immigration Act, Diversity, W. Head, D.G. Hill, Knowledge Base, S. Monet-Chartrand, N. McClung, Minorities, Physical Challenges, Racism-Sensitive Practice, Sensitizing Concepts, Sexual Orientation, Visible Minorities

John Hutton (1944–90)

Hutton, John, social work administrator, educator; b. Apr. 24, 1944, Brockville, ON; d. Dec. 24, 1990, Edmonton, AB

John Hutton began his post-secondary education studying for a Christian ministry but changed his mind before ordination; instead, he pursued an education in social work, graduating with a master's degree from the University of Calgary in 1976. Hutton worked for the city of Edmonton social services department until 1979, when he

joined the faculty of the social work program at Grant MacEwan Community College. Hutton also contributed significantly to his profession, as a member of the council of the Alberta Association of Social Workers for a number of years and as its president (1984–85). In 1985 he took a two-year leave of absence to pursue a doctorate in social work at Columbia University. John described his time at Columbia University as a period of sustained happiness. He was thrilled to study with leaders in the social work profession, to be challenged academically, and to receive encouragement to develop his passion for social justice. He completed his course work, then returned to Edmonton to his position at Grant MacEwan both to work on his dissertation and for change in his community. An active participant in Edmonton, Hutton served on the boards of several inner-city agencies and an AIDS organization. Sadly, he passed away before his work on his dissertation and in the community was complete.

A man of some apparent contradictions, John Hutton was at once a relaxed casual person, while also a passionate—often impassioned—defender of underdogs. Hutton was continually alert to societal inaction to address instances of gross unfairness perpetrated on people unable to defend themselves. A gentle warm individual who loved to laugh, he reacted with visible outrage to instances of discrimination. Loyal and supportive in his relationships, John Hutton was also hard on friends, colleagues, and himself, when their or his actions on social justice fell short of his expectations.

[*John Mould*]

RELATED ENTRIES
Alberta College of Social Workers, Education in Social Work

hypnosis

Hypnosis is a model of intervention used by social workers to augment their usual clinical methods when working with clients suffering from a wide range of somatic and psychosocial problems (Nugent 1996, 2002). Present hypnotherapy stems from work done by Franz Anton Mesmer, an Austrian physician, in the latter half of the eighteenth century. Mesmer's view was that people in poor health could be cured by affecting their "animal magnetism." Inherent in Mesmer's method was the use of verbal suggestion and touch to bring about change (Buranelli 1975). Since the time of Mesmer, numerous approaches have come under the umbrella of hypnosis, but the system developed by Erickson and Rossi (1979) has had the most impact on social workers (Lankton & Lankton 1983), in large part owing to their use of metaphor in the helping process. In particular, the influence of Erickson's work has been felt in many popular approaches to practice that use imagery and allegory in their method (Bandler & Grinder 1975; Lankton 2000; Andreas 1991). The use of metaphoric storytelling in hypnotherapy helps to reframe the meaning that clients attach to their experience and entices them to seek alternative solutions to their problems. The subtlety of hypnotic suggestion effectively reduces client resistance to change and instils in them a platform for future transformation that can be an embarkation point to address other issues. As Lankton (2002) indicates, the use of metaphor helps clients to recover, connect, and convey the emotional and cognitive content of their perceptions in a manner that is personally significant and inspirational.

Erickson and Rossi describe three phases to hypnotherapy. As with all practice methods, the success of hypnosis is founded on the ability of the social worker to form an effective therapeutic relationship with the client (Nugent 1996, 2002). During the initial phase, the therapist builds rapport by gathering, validating, and anchoring information from the client's account of the problem, as well as other aspects of his or her life. In so doing, the social worker creates a repertoire of internally constructed experience-based solutions (Erickson & Rossi 1979). Presented in the form of narratives about the potential for change, content from the client's arousal and emotional experience is paraphrased and used to instil expectancy that change is probable. The subsequent phase in the change process involves the use of therapeutic trance. In this phase, the social worker chooses either a formal trance—by having the client focus inward on a recalled, occurring, or constructed auditory passage, a visual sequence, or a kinaesthetic feeling—or an informal trance—by having the client listen to a sensory-rich narrative created by the therapist (Erickson & Rossi 1979). The purpose of each of these trance techniques is to fix

the client's attention inward and away from the demands of the external world through a gradual and deliberate process. In each instance, the social worker uses verbal and nonverbal messages or suggestions to disrupt existing patterns of cognition and behaviour in a bid to free the client to search for solutions and to reframe experience. the client can be aware of the trance-induced change that results, or he or she may experience change as a spontaneous effect or epiphany. The final phase in hypnosis involves confirming with the client that change has indeed taken place. To do so, the social worker must work carefully to help the client become aware of and to accept changes that occurred during the trance. Success in having clients recognize and incorporate change is critical in staving off the interference of or the return to prior deleterious patterns of thinking and behaving (Erickson & Rossi 1979; Nugent 1996, 2002). The continued fascination with metaphor-based hypnosis by social workers assures its future clinical application. Those interested in using hypnotherapy need to be aware that ethical and lawful standards of practice require social workers to seek specialist training, supervision, and certification or licensing.

[*Brent Angell*]

RELATED ENTRIES

Bioethical Issues, Clinical Social Work, Ethics, Narrative Theory, Practice Methods, Treatment, Wellness

REFERENCES

Andreas, A. 1991. *Virginia Satir: The Patterns of Her Magic*. Palo Alto, CA: Science and Behavior Books.

Bandler, R., and J. Grinder. 1975. *Patterns of the Hypnotic Techniques of Milton H. Erickson*, MD. Vol. 1. Cupertino, CA: Meta Publications.

Buranelli, V. 1975. *The Wizard from Vienna: Franz Anton Mesmer*. New York: Putnam.

Erickson, M., and E. Rossi. 1979. *Hypnotherapy: An Exploratory Casebook*. New York: Irvington.

Lankton, S. 2002. Using Metaphor with Clients. In A.R. Roberts and G.J. Greene (Eds.) *Social Workers' Desk Reference*. 385–91. New York: Oxford University Press.

———. 2000. Milton Erickson's Contribution to Therapy: Epistemology—Not Technology. Online at time of writing at <www.lankton.com/epist.htm>.

Lankton, S., and C. Lankton. 1983. *The Answer Within: A Clinical Framework of Ericksonian Hypnotherapy*. New York: Brunner/Mazel.

Nugent, W. 1996. The Use of Hypnosis in Social Work Practice. In F.J. Turner (Ed.) *Social Work Treatment: Interlocking Theoretical Approaches.* 362–88. 4th ed. New York: Free Press.

———. 2002. Using Evidence-based Hypnosis. In A.R. Roberts and G.J. Greene (Eds.) *Social Workers' Desk Reference.* 441–46. New York: Oxford University Press.

immigrants and immigration

Immigrants comprise a vital component of Canadian society now, as they have since first contact with Aboriginal peoples and throughout the country's history. At an astonishing pace, Canada is becoming a beacon of hope for people wanting to escape oppressive political regimes, social chaos, and economic disintegration in their own country. An immigrant to Canada is a person who seeks landing (lawful permission) to establish permanent residence, while a refugee seeks refuge from a fear of persecution for reasons of race, religion, nationality, or membership in a particular social group or holding a certain political opinion. To help immigrant and refugee newcomers, three basic ideas are essential: people have a right to shape their destinies through migration; immigrants arrive on new shores as people of need; and the immigrant is to be revered. Underlying these ideas is a humanitarianism that cuts deep into Canadian religious and cultural upbringing. Current and future refugees and immigrants are as likely to contribute to Canadian society as others have in the past. Through Citizenship and Immigration Canada, the federal government maintains fair and open processes to reunite families, provide a safe haven for refugees, and encourage immigration for economic growth. Issues and challenges related to large numbers of immigrants permeate social service agencies and organizations, even those that are marginal to mainstream settlement and integration activity. Although immigrants come to Canada for many different reasons, they have something very important in common: they come here because they want to. Immigration to Canada is not cheap, however, as the federal government charges every adult refugee and immigrant a $975 fee to land in Canada,

and a family consisting of two adults and children must pay $1950 in landing fees. These fees are the equivalent of several months' salary in some places. As immigrants must pay these and immigration application fees, as well as transportation and other costs of arrival, considerable financial hardship and sacrifices must be undertaken for them to consider this step. The fact is that Canada is encouraging more and more immigration under its "independent skilled" category of immigration. These newcomers will probably not be a financial burden on the state (i.e., in need of welfare and support services), at least on their arrival. Bluntly speaking, the terms "independent" and "skilled," as they refer only to probability, are not synonymous with financially well off or arriving with a job offer. Regrettably, this pattern fuels a public misconception about the needs of many immigrants, potentially doing future migrants a great disservice—particularly in relation to the allocation of funds for community services that support immigrants.

Despite the promise of a new and prosperous life, immigration to Canada presents several psychological and emotional challenges to newcomers, particularly to children:

- culture shock and adjusting to newness (e.g., new residence or home, new buildings and architecture, new foods, new style of clothing, new toys, street signs, new flags);
- cultural awkwardness (e.g., different play things including technological play things, different heroes and heroines, different story book tales, and different language, expressions, and mannerisms);
- social isolation and stigmatization (e.g., ridicule and/or rejection by host community peers, degradation through labelling such as "greenie" or "greener" and exclusion from peer group activities, scapegoating or mimicking);
- fear of authority figures and adults in uniforms (e.g., residual effects, particularly for those children who come from oppressive regimes, generalized beliefs that such authority figures as the police, punish and hurt children as well as their loved ones);
- rebirth/birth of cultural and religious identity, whereby prior to immigration, a family that may not have felt safe to live and celebrate publicly its ethnicity or religious affiliation, finds consider-

able liberalism and tolerance of different religious practices in Canada; for others, ethnicity and religion may have been so suppressed at home that an entirely new dimension to their identities is acquired as part of the migration process;

• secondary migration and constant uprootedness (i.e., a sense of homelessness may readily befall children who, despite their young age, have been uprooted and moved from one country to another or more, never really knowing where the "proverbial pea" would drop and permanently root in the wheel of migratory change); and

• paradoxical lament: "Smile and the world smiles with you; cry and you cry alone." By all rights, the immigrant youngster should exude perpetual enthusiasm toward life anew—if not life redeemed—but the paradox is that many, if not all, immigrant children require permission, even prompting, in order to grieve. The predominant grief reaction for immigrant children specifically relates to "loss of the familiar," despite how perilous or unappealing that sense of familiar, in reality, had been. Loss of the familiar entails physical surroundings such as a former apartment; play or activity areas, neighbourhood, streets, but necessarily encapsulates as well: sounds (e.g., trolleys, ox carts, fog horns, brooks), smells (e.g., livestock, auto fumes, cooking oils, wild flowers), and other sensorial imprints.

To help newcomers adjust to the communities where they choose to settle, suitably trained professionals and community volunteers offer government-funded programs (i.e., language instruction) and a spectrum of vital settlement and integration services. Some newcomers find a welcome from organizations founded by members of their own ethnocultural or religious community who immigrated in earlier decades. Social work practitioners may be involved in the provision of many of these services, including community orientation, matching host families, vocational counselling, support groups, child and youth programs, temporary housing and emergency responses. Social workers and other professionals can help to assure newcomers of consistent good quality intervention, and can advocate for the availability and distribution of funds to

support these services. By empowering newly arrived adults and youth to participate actively on planning committees, task groups, and agency boards, communities can guarantee that immigrant service delivery will be pertinent and timely. As such, the seeds can be planted for integration into mainstream life that is so vital for robust Canadian communities.

[*Michael Briks*]

RELATED ENTRIES

Barnardo Homes, Bereavement, Chinese Immigration Act, Church-Based Services, Citizenship & Immigration Canada, Diversity, Ethnocultural Communities' Services, Jewish Social Services, School Social Workers, Sectarian Social Services, Services for Refugees, Torture & Trauma Victims, Visible Minorities

Imperial Order Daughters of the Empire*

Imperial Order Daughters of the Empire (IODE) was founded in 1900 by Margaret Polson Murray of Montreal, who envisioned an organization of women devoted to encouraging imperialism. Beginning with an educational mandate promoting Britain and British institutions through the schools, it became actively involved in both world wars in supporting Canada's efforts on behalf of Britain and the allies. Other areas of interest included immigration, child welfare, community health and social services. In recent years the IODE has concentrated more on community affairs, supporting Canadian educational, cultural and social developments. Although its membership has declined, it remains an active women's organization, with 9400 members in 422 branches in 1995.

[*Nancy M. Sheehan*]

* Used unedited by permission from *The Canadian Encyclopedia*. 2000. Toronto: McClelland and Stewart.

RELATED ENTRIES

Non-governmental Organizations

income security

Income security refers to social programs that provide cash payments in a variety of circumstances to individuals or families. Some income security programs cover various social risks that preclude or limit employment (e.g., disability, poverty, sickness, or unemployment); others provide money to individuals in various stages of life (e.g., to the elderly, or to sole parents whose child rearing responsibilities preclude full employment). The two major forms of income security programs are selective and universal. Selective programs have their roots in the Elizabethan Poor Laws in England brought to Canada with European colonization as a way to address unemployment. Today general welfare assistance programs—also called social assistance or a social allowance—are examples of selective programs where money is transferred from a level of government to an individual. Eligibility criteria form the essence of selective programs and individuals are evaluated using a means test. Means tests are carried out by social workers to assess a person's financial resources (i.e., income, assets, debts and other obligations) and any other criteria (i.e., number of dependants or health of the applicant). Personalizing problems of poverty—rather than focusing attention on broader societal structures beyond an individual's control that may create the conditions for poverty—is one of several criticisms levied against selective programs. For example, economic changes that cause the closure of a pulp and paper mill in a one-industry town and lead to loss of jobs for applicants of a selective program is the result of factors beyond the applicants' control. Selective programs have also been criticized because they may stigmatize people who, through factors outside their immediate control, experience temporary or permanent loss of income. These programs devote considerable administrative resources to monitoring the lives of individual clients, rather than focusing on broader community and societal changes that might improve clients' opportunities; however, proponents believe that selective programs are the most efficient means of targeting money to those in need. Some commentators believe that means tests may motivate recipients to return to the workforce, while critics say that the tests coerce. Some social assistance programs have introduced workfare requirements that compel recipients to participate in training and/or other work-related activities in return for benefits. Some policy makers hope that workfare will increase motivation and provide skills for the unemployed to return to the workforce; others criticize workfare both for punishing social assistance recipients and for rarely providing skills or a living wage.

Universal programs, in contrast to selective programs, provide cash benefits to those individuals in a society who fall within a specified category. They are based on eligibility as a right of citizenship rather than through a means test. Whereas selective programs focus attention on an individual claimant's worthiness to receive benefits, universal programs operate under manifestly different assumptions, whereby the state has expressed responsibility to provide income security for all citizens within each identified category. Further, the state implicitly recognizes the presence of conditions that are beyond an individual's control and may impede economic well-being. Stigma has little place in a universal program, since all people, regardless of level of need, may have access to benefits as long as they fulfil eligibility conditions (e.g., having children, for the family allowance program).

Over the past twenty-five years, two trends in income assistance have been particularly noticeable. First, benefit rates, eligibility requirements, and terms of programs have become increasingly strict; for example, as the National Council of Welfare has shown consistently that social assistance benefit rates fall below Statistics Canada's low-income cut-off measurement of poverty (NCW 2000). A second identifiable trend is that universal programs, which came to the fore during the Second World War, have been systematically eroded as selective programs found new favour; for example, in 1992 the universal family allowance program, which had been in effect since 1948, was replaced with a child tax benefit, whereby the former family allowance and child tax credits were combined for a single refundable income-tested child tax credit (Graham, Swift, & Delaney 2003: 41, 58).

Many argue that the income tax system's role is to counterbalance payments to the rich—and not the social program itself. This works with a progressive income tax system where the proportion of paid taxes increases with earnings; however, in a regressive tax system, taxes are not collected on an ability-to-pay basis. Regressive and progressive are relative terms, and the most extreme instance of regressive tax—such as a sales tax—is levied equally, that is, the sales tax charged remains the same percentage whether a person paying a sales tax is below the poverty line or the president of a major bank. Canada's federal tax system is somewhat—although far from completely—progressive; therefore, higher-income earners pay a greater proportion of their money on income tax than do those in lower-income categories. The argument may be made that universal programs do *not* wrongfully direct moneys to the better-off, given the existence (or potential existence) of a progressive income tax system (Muszynski 1987). What is more, with everyone receiving benefits from a universal program, some argue that the middle and upper classes are politically co-opted into supporting the program, and benefits are less likely to be reduced in scope or eligibility than in a selective program geared only towards the less politically powerful poor (Titmuss 1958, 1987). Income security programs were designed to provide the basic level of income necessary for each individual and family. Current poverty levels in Canada are high: many Canadians are living with insufficient means of subsistence. After the Second World War, Canadian income security programs made substantial inroads against poverty; at the beginning of the twenty-first century, with poverty levels greater than they were in the mid-1970s (Battle 1999), Canada's social policy makers need to respond with change.

[*John R. Graham*]

RELATED ENTRIES

W.H. Beveridge, Employment Insurance, Family Allowance Act, Income Assistance, L. Marsh, Marsh Report, Mother's Allowance, Mother's Allowance Commission, Parenting, Poor Laws (UK), Poverty, Single Parents, Social Security, Social Welfare History, Unemployment Assistance Program, Welfare State, Workfare

REFERENCES

Battle, K. 1999. *Poverty Eases Slightly*. Ottawa: Caledon Institute of Social Policy.

Graham, J.R., K. Swift, and R. Delaney. 2003. *Canadian Social Policy: An Introduction*. 2nd ed. Toronto: Allyn and Bacon.

Muszynski, L. 1987. *Is It Fair? What Tax Reform Will Do to You*. Ottawa: Canadian Centre for Policy Alternatives.

NCW. 2000. *Welfare Incomes 1999*. Catalogue No. H6B-27/1999E. Ottawa: National Council of Welfare.

Titmuss, R.M. 1958. *Essays on the Welfare State*. London: George Allen and Unwin.

———. 1987. *Selected Writings of Richard M. Titmuss: The Philosophy of Welfare*. London: Allen and Unwin.

Indian and Northern Affairs Canada

Indian and Northern Affairs Canada (or INAC) is a department of the government of Canada, also known as the Department of Indian Affairs and Northern Development (or DIAND). At present, this department has responsibility under the Indian Act for people and lands identified through treaties negotiated with the British Crown and referred to collectively as "Indian," as well as responsibility for the northern territories. As such, the department does not set policy nor fund programs for non-Treaty Aboriginal peoples (i.e., Métis, non-status Indians, and the many Treaty people whom the department has stripped of their status). For some decades in the last century, the department included Inuit under the Indian Act until Inuit advocated for their removal; however, the department continues to administer programs for Inuit. The department carries out the government's fiduciary obligation to protect the interests of Treaty peoples and lands, which it has often administered in a paternalistic and tutelary manner that has frustrated Aboriginal leaders seeking to reduce government control over their communities.

The department's role has changed throughout its history. The first government department concerned with Aboriginal peoples dates from 1755 when the British colonial administration established an Indian Department. The colonial Indian Department aimed to foster positive relations with the Nations with which the British had built military alliances. At confederation, subsection 91(24) of the British North America Act, 1867 (now Constitution Act, 1867) assigned authority over "Indians and lands reserved for Indians" to the federal government; for a hundred years after confederation, departments such as the Interior and Citizenship and Immigration held this mandate. By the mid-1940s, several Aboriginal Nations had successfully lobbied, sometimes in the international arena, for changes to the harsh policies of the department aimed at assimilating Aboriginal peoples into Canadian society; this lobbying process gained increasing momentum, motivating the government to make incremental changes. In 1966 Parliament created the Department of Indian and Northern Development with a direct role in the provision of such community and social services as housing, road maintenance, water and sewer systems, and economic self-reliance. The department was compelled to make more dramatic changes to its approaches after nationwide Aboriginal opposition to the 1968 White Paper that proposed abolition of the department and subsection 91(24) of the constitution, after the 1982 constitutional changes recognized Aboriginal and Treaty rights, and after Parliament in 1984 recognized that the right to Aboriginal self-government was inherent in the Canadian legal system. Today, the department sees itself as a facilitator of Aboriginal self-government that acts in advisory, support, and funding capacities. Moreover, the territorial legislatures and administrations now operate separately from the department and have responsibility for education, health, and social programs delegated from other federal departments to meet the varied and intense needs in northern communities. The department continues to maintain federal programs and research on Crown lands in the territories. At present, the department lists its four main responsibilities as: supporting Aboriginal self-government, supporting northern governments (i.e., Northwest Territories, Yukon Territory, and Nunavut), improving living conditions in First Nation communities, and settling land claims. These functions are highly interconnected and require co-operation from affected communities, provincial, territorial, and other federal departments. Today, the department asserts a vision of working to make Canada a better place for First Nation and northern peoples. In doing so, the department is committed to supporting the efforts by First Nations, Inuit and Inuvialuit, and territorial residents to achieve self-government, and to attain their rightful place as full partners in Canada. Current information about the department can be found online at < www.ainc-inac .gc.ca/ >.

[*Michael R. Woodford*]

RELATED ENTRIES

Aboriginal Issues, Assembly of First Nations, Remote Practice, Remote & Rural Practice Methods, Social Welfare Context

indirect practice

Indirect practice is not as frequently referred to in Canadian social work practice as in the past. It was most commonly used by practitioners practising from a psychosocial theoretical base to distinguish two general types of activity: one—direct practice—comprising clinical practice with face-to-face interaction with the client; and the other—indirect practice—consisting of any aspects of practice involving contact with significant others or systems in a client's life to bring about some changes a client seeks. In spite of the efforts of Florence Hollis and other psychosocial authors to give these two facets of practice equal importance, diverse practitioners over the decades have attempted to impute a higher status to therapeutic activities. As a result, the tendency has emerged in the profession for viewing direct practice as more demanding and of greater significance than indirect practice. Yet some observers, such as Hollis and Woods, persist in describing indirect practice as equally if not more demanding and complex than direct practice.

The term "indirect practice" is also used to distinguish between social work carried out in the interest of individuals, dyads, families, and groups, and social work that focuses on communities or larger systems. This usage is not common throughout the professional, and has generally become subsumed by other terms, such as micro and macro practice. This dichotomy seems also to reflect differences within the profession related to the value of each kind of practice, as if indirect practice has some quality that renders it of secondary importance to direct work. Within the profession are strong advocates for the primacy of both aspects of practice, contributing to the expenditure of considerable dialectic energy. In recent years, direct / indirect debate seems to have diminished in favour of growing usage of the terms "micro," "mezzo," and "macro" practice. Underpinning this move lies a commitment in Canadian social practice to all forms of practice, with the recognition that each is important and of value. Professional decisions are thereby made on the basis of strategy and resource availability rather than on the ascribed worth of one facet of practice over another.

[*FJT*]

individual therapy

In individual therapy, only two people are physically present, the client and the therapist. Even in this dyadic relationship, however, larger groups are involved, represented in the client's inner mind and fantasy (Foulkes 1964). Individual therapy is also known as psychotherapy, which has been described as: "the treatment, by psychological means, of problems of an emotional nature in which a trained person deliberately establishes a professional relationship with the [client, with the goals] of removing, modifying or retarding existing symptoms, ... mediating disturbed patterns of behaviour ... and promoting positive personality growth and development" (Wolberg 1967: 3). Such therapy relies on adequate communication, verbal and non-verbal, between the client and the therapist, who applies his/her training and expertise to alleviate the symptoms with which the client presents. Either explicitly or implicitly, a contract is formed between the client and therapist, in which they both agree to collaborate to help the client deal with issues that are causing significant discomfort for him/her, or are disrupting his/her life: "patients and their therapists define one or more major problems around which the treatment will focus" (Cristoph & Barber 1991: 3), and the emphasis is on helping the client discover truths about him/herself, life, and feelings, with the goal of making changes that the person wishes to achieve in therapy. Historically, the development of individual therapy originated in the "nineteenth century with the advent of psychoanalysis [which] was a fairly circumscribed entity" (Herron & Rouslin 1982: 3), comprised of the procedures used, the therapists who were trained in them, and the problems to be treated. Over time the focus shifted from treating only ill individuals, to helping people who were healthy become healthier (Herron & Rouslin 1982), and goals centred on self-actualization processes, such as self-fulfilment, development of positive attitudes toward life, and the building of gratifying relationships with people (Wolberg 1967). With this came an increase in the number "of proce-

dures, kinds of problems, types of therapists, and theoretical conceptions" (Herron & Rouslin 1982: 4). According to Cristoph and Barber, the length of therapy has shifted "toward tile brief therapy model as the standard, [while] long-term therapy is becoming the exception (1991: 1). Initially, the therapist must assess the level of motivation of the client in making change, since this is a major factor in the therapeutic outcome (Cristoph & Barber 1991). Most commonly, sessions occur weekly for approximately six to twelve sessions, at which time the issues and progress achieved in therapy are reassessed. The stages involved in individual work coincide with those in family or group therapy, as "initial evaluation and creation of the therapeutic relationship or alliance, therapeutic work and working through, and termination" (Cristoph & Barber 1991: 332).

[*Susan Hanna*]

REFERENCES
Cristoph, P., and Barber, J.P. (Eds.) 1991. *Handbook of Short-Term Dynamic Psychotherapy.* New York: Basic Books.
Herron, W.G., and S. Rouslin. 1982. *Issues in Psychotherapy.* Bowie, MD: Robert J. Brady.
Wolberg, L.R. 1967. *The Technique of Psychotherapy.* 2nd ed. Part I. New York: Grune and Stratton.

industrial social work

Industrial, or occupational, social work. is professional practice within the context of the occupational welfare system. This describes those social and health benefits, beyond salaries or wages, which are provided to those who are in some way attached to the workplace and where they exist, unions or associations. This system is directly funded by work organizations, unions or employees, through mandated legislated requirement, collective agreement, or on a voluntary basis. While there is no specific mandate for social work practice within provision of direct or indirect services within the workplace, the profession's systemic perspective and skills have been readily adaptable to this type of practice most predominantly—but not exclusively—in the provision of direct clinical services. It provides a venue through which social work can intervene to help preserve employees in a significant life's role through points of crises in their lives without being labelled by what ever presenting concerns they have.

Provision of social services in the workplace may have had its origins in the medieval feudal system, wherein aristocratic landholdings were worked by serfs in return for certain protections. With the industrial revolution in both the United Kingdom and the United States in the nineteenth century—prior to the advent of the origins of professional practice as it is currently practised—social services began to evolve as a part of corporate welfarism. By the early 1800s welfare secretaries—who were in-house—and industrial secretaries—who were contracted from YMCAS—were providing instrumental services and paternalistic individual support with a moralistic underlay to employees in a number of factories. Corporate motivations varied, including providing services needed by the labour force to function in the absence of community services; socializing immigrant workforces; encouraging the loyalty in its employees to stabilize its workforce; and discouraging attempts by unions to organize workplaces. As social work education evolved in the early twentieth century, many graduates took positions as welfare secretaries (i.e., New York School of Social Work graduates were taking more positions in industry than in any other field of practice). In the second decade of the twentieth century these programs began to lose their popularity among many employers. With the evolution of scientific management and the consequent dehumanization of labour in the twenties, it was increasingly logical for employers to identify employees as units of labour. As community services increased, immigrant children were acculturated through the public school system. Employees resented the paternalistic nature of services pro-

vided by welfare secretaries, and efforts at unionization continued unabated. At about this time social work organizations began criticizing workers' employment conditions. Early legislation, such as workers compensation to deal with industrial injuries, was introduced. With a few exceptions, the American social worker in the workplace disappeared. In Europe and elsewhere, the trend of employing social workers and providing social services through the workplace continued. In North America philanthropy provided a separation between work and social services through community-based social welfare agencies co-ordinated by red feather organizations to structure this philanthropy.

For the next several decades in the United States and Canada, Alcoholics Anonymous was to have a most profound effect on workplace services. This movement evolved in Akron, Ohio, in the 1930s as a means for those suffering from alcoholism to maintain sobriety through a twelve-step program based in spiritual fellowship with other sufferers, at a time when no other successful treatment existed. The movement has become worldwide in scope. Within the context of industry suddenly providing services to maintain a workforce during the Second World War, the potential benefits of Alcoholics Anonymous was not lost on employers. They saw few other resources in dealing with addicted employees other than dismissing them due to progressively deteriorating work performance. Initially some industries encouraged members of Alcoholics Anonymous to conduct meetings on the company premises. From the early 1940s through the 1960s, workplaces in the United States and Canada developed programs that focused on dealing with employees experiencing alcoholism. Over time, these evolved into Occupational Alcoholism Programs in which supervisors were trained to confront suspected alcoholic staff and to direct them into coerced treatment; as a result, these programs tended to reach employees experiencing middle- or late-stage alcoholism. Widely distrusted by employees, these programs were limited in number. By the late 1960s, the federal and provincial governments in Canada had developed policies to deal with the treatment of alcoholism. In 1970 Senator Samuel Hughs, an Alcoholics Anonymous member, initiated US legislation that established addiction programs in all branches of the national government, required them in all businesses that had substantial contracts with the government, and provided staffing in each state to encourage the development of such programs. In 1977 the federal treasury board in Canada established the expectation, criteria, and funding for all federal departments to establish employee counselling programs for substance abuse; this was paralleled by most provincial governments.

To avoid the stigmatization of the Occupational Alcoholism Programs, these programs were often redefined as Employee Assistance Programs (*see entry on these programs*). They differed in a number of ways:

- referral was based on job performance rather than trying to diagnose the cause of the problem;
- confidential voluntary use for non-work affecting problems was introduced;
- the possibility for joint management/union program collaboration was encouraged;
- the position of paid program coordinator to manage these programs became popular; and
- services were provided for broad range of problems rather than specifically alcohol.

In the initial stages of this evolution the broadening of presenting problems was still based on the assumption that the underlying cause of all problems was alcoholism. The standard of program effectiveness was that a large percentage of case finding dealt directly with alcoholism. The initial programs used Alcoholics Anonymous members in the role of program facilitator to some extent; they were responsible for organizing Employee Assistance Program joint committees, which under their guidance, established the purpose (i.e., to retain troubled workers), the policies (i.e., employee anonymity in use), the program, the process for accessing the program (both voluntary and mandatory), supervisory training in use of constructive confrontation to force employees with diminished job performance into treatment, employee outreach, and reliable assessment and treatment resources appropriate to the rationale of the program. They also monitored employees' treatment progress, evaluated program effectiveness, and maintained Employee Assistance Program visibility. A few Canadian programs circumvented the troubled-worker

approach by adopting a personnel social work model utilized in some European countries, notably the Netherlands; it purportedly provided clinical and referral services based on normal life cycle personal and workplace concerns of employees; special attention to demographically vulnerable groups; and the recognition that the employee stress could be exacerbated by conditions in the workplace.

The quality of Employee Assistance Program services had been an issue mostly because, in its evolution, many of those offering the services had no professional credentials or bodies to which they were accountable. To ensure some standard of quality control by the 1980s, there were two American self-governing Employee Assistance Program bodies: the Employee Assistance Professional Association, which established a standard of individual competence based on certification, and the Employee Assistance Society Association of North America, which was based on program competence but also established criteria for individual practitioners. Both required Employee Assistance Program or professional practice experience. While many Canadian Employee Assistance Program clinical providers had professional credentials, a number also obtained certification from the former US association; some of the larger external Canadian organizations providing Employee Assistance Program had obtained program certification. In 2000 the Employee Assistance Society Association of North America passed its mandate for program certification standards to the Council on Accreditation, which certifies a broad range of fields of practice in North America. Criteria for measuring the effectiveness of these programs have included degree of program utilization; user satisfaction (e.g., anonymity in use, program accessibility, attitude toward program user, helpfulness, effectiveness in problem resolution); and various measures of impact on work performance (e.g., absenteeism and cost-effectiveness). Most evaluations, where they exist, are conducted internally and are related to the rationale for which the program has been established. Only a few programs have utilized rigorous external evaluations.

Occupational social work is much broader in scope than Employee Assistance Programs but is similarly without exclusive sanction. Less visible in

Canada, it has continued to exist wherever social work practitioners are using their skills and values in the world of work: in work preparation programs; job placement services; public staffing departments or labour departments mediating or conciliating management/labour contract disputes; workers' compensation offices providing vocational rehabilitation and advocacy services; unions (as staff representatives or co-ordinators for union counsellor programs); union-sponsored workplace health and safety clinics; contracting services for employees (e.g., work adjustment, pre-retirement programs); in work organizations as human rights or harassment officers; ombudsman offices; unemployed help centres advocating for claimants' employee insurance rights. Their involvement in these roles is based on a recognition of their skill sets, values, and training.

Documented evidence indicates that, in the field of industrial social work practice, there continues to be a significant presence of social workers as well as psychologists. The predominant educational level of practitioners is a masters degree, although in Canada there has been little educational support for work-related practice within the academic social work community. At a graduate level, no courses are offered and, at an undergraduate level, only one broad workplace-sensitive practice course is taught periodically and it is more in line with courses taught in some American social work faculties. One university provides a distance education multidiscipline certificate course in employee assistance programming.

Industrial or occupational social work is a field of practice that provides services to employees and families in one of their most significant life roles, that of work. It has drawn on social work practitioners at different levels of practice depending on the venue in which they are employed, but primarily seasoned post-graduate professionals. Its catchment population represents roughly 65 percent of the Canadian adult population and their families in an expanding field of practice; as such, this under-reported and under-recognized field of practice actually touches the lives of many Canadians. Critics outside and inside the field question whether its practitioners are co-opted by the business community and whether it hampers efforts at addressing primary prevention of working conditions that exacerbate employee stress. Defenders argue that the same criticism can be levelled at any field of practice most of which deal with tertiary and, at best, secondary prevention; they argue that having the access to the workplace provides an opportunity to influence business practices in the direction of enlightened self-interest. Supporters of industrial social work agree, however, that criticisms are important to keep them vigilant in terms of maintaining employees at the centre of their practice.

[*Paul Newman*]

RELATED ENTRIES

Canadian Labour Congress, Canadian Mental Health Association, Education in Social Work, Employee Assistance Programs, Employment, Health & Unemployment, Social Work Profession, Substance Addiction, Theory & Practice, Vocational Rehabilitation, YMCA

REFERENCES

Csiernik, R. 2000. Employee Assistance Program Education in Canada: The State of the Nation. *Employee Assistance Quarterly* 15, 3:15–22.

McGilly, F. 1985. American Historical Antecedents to Industrial Social Work. *Social Work Papers*, University of Southern California. 19,1:1–13.

Popple, P.R. 1981, Social Work Practice in Business and Industry, 1875–1930. *Social Service Review* 55: 257–69.

information and communication technologies

Information and communications technologies in social work practice and education involve the electronic collection, storage, communication (i.e., exchange and dissemination), manipulation, and analysis of small to enormous amounts of information. New uses are being developed beyond individuals working with information on one computer to uses that mimic sophisticated human activity, those that supplement human intelligence, and those that have an impact on the way people live and work. Although these technologies are considered tools for accomplishing tasks, they are not value-neutral. As more and more individuals obtain access through decreasing costs and size of components, people have been prone to view these technologies through rose-coloured glasses. The developing technologies that have many positive attributes over manual information collection and retrieval also raise numerous issues that must be considered in decision making. The appropriateness of using electronic technologies for documenting and storing highly personal client information is a persistent ethical matter debated by practitioners. Beyond confidentiality and security (i.e., who should have access to what information), other issues of concern include an expanding information gap or "techno-divide" between those who have and those who do not have access or familiarity, accountability in Internet use (e.g., regulation of, and liability for, virtual counselling causing problematic interventions), information overload (e.g., is all the client information collected necessary), replacement of people with computers, ownership of information (e.g. client records and on-line courses), and costs (i.e., staying up to date with software and hardware compatibility, and training). These technologies put pressures on human service organizations, which have been slow to adopt them. Increasingly, agencies are using computers to store client information and other records in databases to meet the increasing needs for accountability and speed. Electronic mail is replacing the internal memo as well as external mail. Few organizations lack their own website, as the Internet is being used by organizations to disseminate their own messages and to obtain professional information, often without assessing sources. The Internet is adding hundreds of pages each day to the information available on social work practice and research topics. Many social workers now carry to interviews a notebook computer or palm pilot to record information and send it directly to their office. Educational institutions are not immune either to pressures to use these technologies. Social work education programs are making increasing use of web-based course organization platforms for the partial or total delivery of courses and entire local and distance education programs for bachelor's and master's degrees. While web-based courses increase access to students in rural and northern areas for degree programs and continuing education, the question of equal or enhanced quality, as compared to traditional classroom-based instruction continues to be debated. It is critical that social workers address value issues in the use of information and communication technologies

and advocate for guidelines in the Canadian Association of Social Workers code of ethics. One online source for computer use in social work networks is < www.uta.edu >.

[*Mona Acker*]

RELATED ENTRIES
Communication Theory, Codes of Ethics, Ethics, J. Gandy, Interviewing, Knowledge Base, Neurolinguistic Programming, Program Evaluation, Recording, Theory & Practice, Technology

integration of services

Integration of services within Canada's social network has been a challenge for Canadian social work from its earliest days. Because of the complex historical development of the welfare state, many social agencies and services have emerged with diverse sponsorship, funding, missions, legislative bases, targets, values, and cultural bases. One long-standing reality of this expansive social network is considerable duplication and overlapping of services. For some observers, this duplication and overlapping is to be valued as a positive reflection of diversity within the Canadian mosaic; for others, it is an uneconomical flaw that is undesirable in times of serious resource limitations. To address the fiscal restraints while maintaining the perceptible benefits of cultural diversity, administrators within many social services have striven to co-operate in various forms of service integration. Within governments, ongoing restructuring of federal departments and provincial/territorial ministries seeks better efficiency in the social network; however, differing political views, value bases, priorities, and resource availability can sometimes hamper smooth transitions, as do political conflicts over responsibilities among different jurisdictions. In recent decades, the movement for deinstitutionalization and basing more services locally has brought communities into these interjurisdictional conflicts. In communities of all sizes, the service network is now vast and many services located in communities are actively seeking ways for effective integration. Social workers have always worked in communities informally and formally; as such, they have supported structured strategies for local integration, many of which later developed into such bodies as community welfare councils, social planning councils, and United Way affiliates. In addition to community-wide structures that contribute to community planning, local co-ordinating agencies—such as Catholic social services, Jewish social services, or federal veterans services—strengthen efforts to integrate local services. Within the process of integration, new agencies and services also arise, sometimes offering new approaches and sometimes posing more challenges. In recent years, for instance, services have emerged from or been targeted to particular cultural or ethnocultural communities, especially in cities that have experienced increases in population from these communities, which do not feel served by existing services. In time, many such services may become integrated into existing agencies in a manner that maintains service sensitivity, language, and responsiveness to the identified needs of clients served by the currently separate agencies. Thus, ongoing enrichment of service delivery can develop from emergent organizations that fill identified service gaps to meet social needs and conditions within the changing dynamic of society. The process of integrating social services is ongoing and very long-term in response to a multiplicity of variables, not necessarily related to efficiency and fiscal constraints, but also reflecting changing needs and priorities from within the diversity of clients to be served. This complex process can foster rapid integration of some aspects of the social network—where objectives, approaches, and values coincide—and much lengthier integration of more disparate aspects, while at all times being driven by the North American societal values of efficiency and economies of scale.

[FJT]

RELATED ENTRIES

Aboriginal Services, Case Management, Church-Based Services, Community Service, Correctional Services, Deinstitutionalization Movement, Ethnocultural Communities' Services, Gay-Sensitive Services, Interprofessional Education, Interprofessional Issues, Jewish Social Services, Lesbian Services, Personnel, Sectarian Social Services, Services for Children, Services for Elderly People, Services for Families, Services for Married People, Services for Offenders, Services for People with Disabilities, Services for Refugees, Services for Women, Services for Youth

International Federation of Social Workers

The International Federation of Social Workers (est. 1956) comprised national social worker organizations from more than seventy countries to advance notions of best practice and co-operation among social workers worldwide, for the promotion of social justice. The idea for this federation emerged from the former International Permanent Secretariat of social workers that dissolved in 1939. The current federation was founded during the International Conference on Social Welfare in Germany. Canada was a founding member of this new federation with eleven other countries and has hosted two of the federation's international conferences (1984 and 2000). Governance of the federation is facilitated through the annual general meeting, where each member organization has one vote. More routine matters are addressed through the executive committee comprised of a vice presidential representative from each of the five global regions and, between executive meetings, by a core working group comprised of the president, first vice-president, and treasurer. The federation has also has been granted special consultative status with the United Nation's Economic and Social Council and Children's Fund. The aims of the federation include the promotion of social work, with a particular focus on ethics, human rights, and such major policy issues as health, migration, older persons, women, and peace, and social justice. The federation has a permanent human rights commission and a permanent committee on ethical issues. In co-operation with the International Association of Schools of Social Work and the International Council on Social Welfare, the federation produces the journal *International Social Work*. Other publications of the federation include its biennial conference proceedings, a regular newsletter, and documents specific to the social work profession (e.g., the definition of social work, and the principles and standards for the ethics of social work). The federation is a partner of, among other international bodies, Amnesty International, the European Union, and the International Labour Organisation. To support the work of the federation, individuals and agencies can join the federation as a friend, of which there are currently more than a thousand. Current information about the International Federation of Social Workers can be found online at <www.ifsw.org>.

[*Susan Preston*]

RELATED ENTRIES

Canadian Association of Social Workers, International Practice, National Association of Social Workers (US), Provincial/Territorial Associations

international practice

International social work is an area of study and practice that is not ordinarily included in Canadian literature as a social work method but, in view of its very rapid development in recent years, it appears to have attained this stature. While some practitioners within the profession in Canada have been actively interested in international social welfare issues and have sought to develop relationships with colleagues in other countries, this work has not attained profession-wide significance. In recent years, awareness of the profession's development worldwide has been growing, especially in view of expanding and diverse immigration to Canada that is drawing profoundly on social work expertise. Humanitarian values of the profession are leading more Canadian social workers to become concerned about the drastic needs elsewhere in the world, and to appreciate the potential leadership role that Canadian practitioners might take. As a result, international social work has become an important area of study within the profession. It is now common for Canadian social workers to take significant roles in international social work bodies and serve in international posts. International journals are produced in Canada and international conferences held here; international exchanges take place regularly between social workers from Canada and other countries. International practice has a firm foundation in Canada, with increasing numbers of practitioners applying the accumulating body of knowledge on international issues, and expanding specific and generic roles in international social welfare. Rather than being viewed as a minority interest, the understanding is growing profession-wide that sensitivity to international social welfare can benefit Canadian practitioners as part of their overall training. Another area of professional importance is the reciprocal recognition of social work quali-

fications between countries. Among the many immigrants to Canada are trained social workers whose expertise and language skills can contribute to services here if their qualifications can be shown to be equivalent to Canadian standards for practice. Similar processes in other countries can make it easier for Canadian practitioners who wish to work abroad to have their qualifications recognized.

[*FJT*]

RELATED ENTRIES

Canadian Association of Social Workers, Codes of Ethics, Immigrants & Immigration, International Federation of Social Workers, Knowledge Base, R. Leger, G.H. Lévesque

interprofessional education

Interprofessional education has gained increasing favour in faculties of health science and social work since the mid-1970s, so that students in both fields can achieve competence necessary for interprofessional practice. Goals of such education are to improve health outcomes and team functioning, to provide for patients with complex needs, and to foster cognitive and behavioural change among students. Students gain an increased awareness of other disciplines' roles, responsibilities, values, and training. For social work students, this increased knowledge and information about other professions, combined with opportunities to interact with students and faculty of other fields, can lead to improved team functioning, increased collaborative work and better patient/client, family, and community care. Interprofessional education differs from the more common uni-professional and multiprofessional approaches to health education. Uni-professional training involves individuals from the same discipline convening to master specific models of conduct, theories, and knowledge. Multiprofessional learning involves participants from a number of specialties meeting to better understand a particular health care issue. Interprofessional education brings students together from a variety of professions to learn as a team through collaboration, integration, and interaction in an effort to comprehend the core principles and concepts from each participating discipline. With the increasing complexity of patient/client, family and community health needs, treatment, and management, interprofessional practice is likely to expand. Social work, with its exquisite awareness of the social determinants of health, of psychosocial issues in illness, and of power dynamics within teams and organizations, is uniquely positioned to take a leadership role in interprofessional education.

[*Fran Aiken*]

RELATED ENTRIES

Education in Social Work, Knowledge Base, Multi-skilling

interprofessional issues

Every social work domain, from child welfare to geriatric services, in organizations and in communities, requires the engagement of other human service professions. These encounters range from brief telephone contacts to intensive and protracted interprofessional interaction. Social workers have always collaborated with other professionals as an efficacious technique for the identification and resolution of practice issues. Now, more than ever before, organizational leaders, as well as all human service professions, have also fully embraced the benefits of interprofessional transactions and have made them the modal form of work in human services. This new level of interprofessional interaction, potentially leading to more effective, efficient, and ethical services for clients, also entails profound ethical, practice, and organizational issues for the human service professions generally and for social work in particular. The history of this interaction has been advantageous for social work. Unlike some other human service professionals, social workers learn about the knowledge and skills of related professions, and how these professions operate in practice settings. Social workers' core knowledge, for example, of group dynamics, interpersonal behaviour and communication, and ethnocultural and gender differences, as well as their skills in dealing effectively with such issues, has proven very useful for guaranteeing that interprofessional processes work well. Indeed, it is very often the case that the social worker on the interprofessional team is asked by colleagues to take the lead in such processes as solving team process issues, resolving interprofessional conflicts, and

ensuring that decisions and processes undertaken by the team are ethical. Social workers in such situations may even assist team members with personal or work-related issues. These activities may also place an extra and sometimes onerous burden on social workers, who are also expected to carry client-related responsibilities.

With the increasing emphasis on interprofessional approaches to problem identification and resolution, social workers and their colleagues are likely to encounter practical and ethical issues. To ensure that interprofessional services are appropriate, and of the highest quality, processes must be put in place that ensure that client concerns and needs are not overwhelmed by professional goals, objectives, and organizational processes, and that client voices are heard and accounted for in all circumstances. Experience and the professional literature suggest that, when professionals from different disciplines work together, they do not always understand, trust, and respect one another's expertise. Issues that have the potential to interfere with or undermine the provision of quality and ethically sound client services include interprofessional competition, differing conceptions of the role of the client, the exercise of power in interprofessional interaction, theoretical and practice differences, the form and content of professional communication, overlapping professional mandates and work roles, interpersonal conflict, diversity and gender conflicts or misunderstandings, and undemocratic approaches to decision making and group processes. Practice experience and research indicate that potential sources of conflict between professionals and managers—for example, supervision and autonomy issues, allocation of work roles and tasks, and individual and group rewards—must be isolated and addressed if interprofessional work is to be successfully implemented in human service organizations. The enduring existence of such dynamics in interprofessional work relations is well documented. The consensus is that, while the benefits of interprofessional co-operation are significant, the potential harm to clients, professionals, organizations, and communities could be serious. It is therefore critical that social workers continue to employ their leadership, knowledge, and skills, and work closely with clients and other human service professions, to ensure that interprofessional work processes are technically and ethically sound.

[*Daniel Salhani*]

RELATED ENTRIES

Case Management, Education in Social Work, Knowledge Base, Legal Issues, Multi-skilling, Professional Issues, Personnel, Practice Methods, Social Planning, Social Policy & Practice, Theory & Practice

intervention research

Intervention research, which is becoming more prevalent in Canadian social work practice, refers to the profile of research strategies that aim specifically at efforts to describe the impact of social work services on clients and, in particular, those of a clinical nature. The importance of this type of research has been expanding in recent decades for several reasons. From an economic perspective, ongoing assessment of the impact of alternate interventions that produce comparable results can help allocate funds to the most cost-effective intervention. In a similar way, service administrators can study different ways of allocating resources to evaluate the most effective and efficient from the perspective of interventions with clients being carried out by different practitioners and/or different agencies. Perhaps, most importantly, practitioners can apply intervention research to understand better what impacts various practice methods are having on clients, especially in this era of rapidly expanding theories, techniques, and treatment strategies. Implicit in the concept of interventive research is the goal of seeking to assess what happens to and for the client when a practitioner undertakes particular interventive strategies. Challenges that emerge in such research include when the assessment is made, and who is to make the assessment—the client, the practitioner, the administrator, or the funder? Presumably, each evaluation of the impact of one or more interventions would differ; for example a family receiving treatment in a family agency could be very pleased with the treatment received from a social worker, whose assessment is that the family ought to be further along in its adjustment, while the agency and funding source may be disappointed by the time involved on this case. The best research approach would be to collect assessments from different perspectives and analyze them all. Researchers reporting their

findings need to be meticulous in documenting their approach, and professionals reading research reports need to be alert to the approach taken by the researcher.

Interest in intervention research has resulted in an increased awareness of and use of formal contracts with clients, in which the goals of each intervention are clearly set out and thereby much more easily assessed at intervals and on termination of a case. Various strategies of evaluation—such as verbal reports from clients, before/after measurements, questionnaires completed by clients, assessment by third-party researchers, and reports by significant others in a client's life—are now available for this type of research. To date, most interventive research has focused on overall outcomes of a case: that is, whether established case objectives were achieved or a client helped as a result of intervention. Little has been done to isolate differential impact of the various facets of intervention within a case or a series of cases, but such examinations are likely in the future. Increased impetus in support of this type of research has come from the mostly positive findings that have emerged regarding the impact of social work treatment: in general, clients involved with a social worker are found to have profited by the intervention. The challenge for the profession is to begin to identify how best to bring about more improvements and how to enhance them, as well as to identify situations in which certain interventions are not helpful and how to arrive at positive outcomes in such circumstances.

[*FJT*]

RELATED ENTRIES

Research

interviewing

Interviewing is a basic tool that is unique in social work practice, in that the interview occurs in a social work setting and follows social work values. Once mutually agreed by practitioner and client for the purpose of gathering information, this technique can be used to determine eligibility for a program (i.e., an assessment or intake interview), to identify a problem (i.e., an intake or casework interview), to recreate a healing environment (i.e., casework or treatment interview), or to contribute to evaluations (i.e., assessment, research, or employment interview). The purpose of a specific interview is partially determined by the setting. For example, an intake/assessment interview at a social assistance office will differ from an initial interview by a social worker on an oncology ward at a hospital, and from the first interview in a hiring process for a youth worker. A research interview differs from a therapy interview; however, they may both be part of explorations for healing a client's trauma: the research interview might looks at what helps the healing in a general way that can assist other practitioners, and the treatment interview looks at what helps a particular individual heal. Assessment (or intake), research, and employment interviews tend to be more structured, may involve the use of check lists, a formal outline, or categories of required information. Such interviews are directed by a practitioner as interviewer, who exerts a great deal of control. In the casework or treatment interview, a client can participate in shaping the interview. Clients may also participate in guiding qualitative research interviews, for instance, in a snowball technique or a focus group. The interview can be said to have three parts: beginning, middle, and end. The beginning sets the outline, the purpose of the interview (for assessment, treatment, information gathering), the role of each participant (i.e., interviewer- or client-directed), and time or other boundaries (i.e., task completion, time elapsed, breaks, permissible interruptions). In the middle phase of an interview, information is gathered verbally and nonverbally: the more structured the interview, the more reliance is placed on verbal (including written) information; the more unstructured, open, and interactive the interview, the more nonverbal information is included. Therapy interviews rely much more on nonverbal information when establishing a climate of safety; in using nonverbal cues that the client is open to a new experience or a new interpretation, or in using the relationship of the interview to effect change (i.e., as opposed to using the content of the interview). For example, an interviewer who observes and supports client who sobs to release held-back pain is using interview content to effect change; the relationship reframes a belief system or world view that allows the client greater choice in reaching change. This middle phase of an interview can be, for instance, when

the couple in marital therapy practice and experience more effective ways of communicating emotions and goals, or when the researcher completes the interview questionnaire with the client, or when the employer gathers the information and gets the feel of the suitability of a prospective employee (Shulman 1998). The end phase of an interview involves reviewing what was accomplished and what steps, if any, need to be taken depending on the type of interview (e.g., an applicant is eligible for the program, a hiring decision will be made, a couple is to practice new communication skills before the next appointment, or an interviewee can see a research report in six months).

Social work knowledge and theory go into preparing for the interview; into developing the intake sheet and the research questionnaire; and into selecting the appropriate therapy model to use. As well, practitioners draw from a wide range of behaviour theories in preparing for and assessing the results of an interview. How an interview is to be structured and what information is relevant for preparing an interview depends on the interview circumstances and purpose. Interviewing a child, for instance, differs from interviewing a young adult in jail for the first time or interviewing an elderly person about medical procedures for a terminally ill spouse. The social work adage "begin where the client is" sums up the perspective of a practitioner before each interview. Pre-interview preparation includes being aware of common emotional themes that occur for clients (e.g., lack of self-esteem, shame in applying for social assistance, anxiety over seeing a therapist for depression). Theories of human behaviour, systems interaction, how communities function, and organizational needs all shape the amount and type of personal information a client may be asked to reveal. Skills and techniques for establishing trust, keeping focus, and recalling forgotten information go into decisions about setting the structure and determining the pacing of the interview. Post-interview tasks include writing up the purpose and accomplishments of the interview; reporting the progress made on the interview purpose can become part of the process of preparing for the next interview. Intake information is passed on to the social worker, nonverbal content is described (e.g., the client seemed less anxious), a candidate's suitability for a position is compared to other candidate's, and the decision for a subsequent interview is made. For the research interview, the information from this interview is compared with that gathered from other interviews. Social work interviews are by nature intrusive and can harm an interviewee. As power differential between practitioner and client is always an issue in interviewing, part of practitioner training is sensitizing to treat interviewees in a supportive and respectful way. Confidentiality is vital to social work, and is especially crucial to every aspect of interviewing. Practitioners need to ensure that they handle personal information volunteered by clients with circumspection, so that rough notes and completed reports are stored with an awareness of where this information is and how it might be used. Clarity on information storage and retrieval, as well as use, needs to be established before an interview takes place.

[*Alex Munroe*]

RELATED ENTRIES

Assessment, Diagnosis, Personal-Centred Theory, Practice Methods, Recording, Research, Theory & Practice

REFERENCE

Shulman, L. 1998. *Skills of Helping Individuals, Families, Groups and Community*. Itasca, IL: F.E. Peacock.

J

Jewish social services

The Jewish community in Canada, like other ethnic and religious communities, has a number of formal organizations that provide social services and support. Canadian Jewry is about 370,000 persons strong, or about 1.4 percent of the total Canadian population. The community has established national fraternal and quasi-political organizations, as well as local philanthropic organizations and agencies. The Canadian Jewish Congress (est. 1919), for instance, serves as the official voice of Canadian Jewry and represents nationwide Jewish issues and concerns to provincial and federal governments. Acting on matters affecting the status, rights, and welfare of Canadian Jews, the congress is affiliated with most Jewish welfare

federations, community councils, and other Jewish organizations. B'Nai Brith Canada as part of the international fraternal organization, which also sponsors the League for Human Rights, has remained independent of the congress. Other national Jewish organizations include the National Council of Jewish Women, Hadassah-wizo, Canada-Israel Committee, and Canadian Zionist Federation. The National Council of Jewish Women (est. 1890) is a volunteer organization that works to improve the quality of life for women, children, and families. In addition to several projects in Israel, the organization has national projects in Canada devoted to prevention of domestic violence and improvement of child care and day care services; it also engages in political advocacy on a range of women's and family issues. Hadassah-wizo (est. 1917), a women's international Zionist organization, has as its purpose the provision of support to Israel—including medical services through the Hadassah Medical Organization (est. 1912)—as well as the support of youth and adults who are considering or are interested in emigrating to Israel; it sponsors Young Judea, a Zionist youth movement, and engages in social and political advocacy on local and national issues of interest to women and the Jewish community. The Canada–Israel Committee (est. 1967) is the official representative of Canadian Jewry on Canadian–Israeli relations; its aim is to promote and advance this relationship and to sensitive the Canadian public to Israel's perspective on Arab–Israeli relations. The Canadian Zionist Federation pulls together various organizations that have as their goal support for Israel, support for Canadians to visit Israel, and support for those considering and or desiring to emigrate (*aliyah*) to Israel.

At the local level, Jewish communities in most cities are organized around a welfare federation or a community council that are responsible for collecting funds for the United Jewish Appeal (an organization that provides funding to national and international Jewish charities, including support for resettlement and welfare services in Israel), and for disbursing funds to a range of local welfare, social, cultural, and recreational agencies. The Jewish Federation of Greater Toronto, for example, provides support to Jewish schools and Jewish community centres, a family resource centre, the Jewish Immigrant Aid Services of

Canada, Jewish Information Services of Greater Toronto (which publishes the *Jewish Community Services Directory of Greater Toronto*), and a "welcome wagon" for new community members and new parents. One of the largest such organizations is the Jewish Family and Children Services (est. 1868) in Toronto provides services to children and youth (i.e., child protection, foster care, adoption, respite care and family support, big brothers/big sisters, and a day-treatment program for adolescents with emotional or behavioural problems), rehabilitation and family services (i.e., individual and group counselling, family violence services, and a residence for ex-psychiatric patients), and community services (i.e., a volunteer bureau, chaplaincy services to Jewish residents in health care facilities and penal institutions, an adolescent outreach project, family life workshops, and a second-hand clothing store). Federations and community councils found in Vancouver, Edmonton, Calgary, Winnipeg, Ottawa, Montreal, and Halifax as well as Toronto; they provide many of the same services proportionate to their population and needs. The fundraising efforts of welfare federations is largely separate from the activities of other national and Israel-related organizations, and from the fundraising undertaken by such other Jewish institutions as schools and synagogues. Participation by members of the Jewish community in social service organizations is committed. According to a 1990 survey, 41 percent of the Jewish community in Canada made a contribution of $100 or more to their local federation's appeal, and for those households that gave more than this amount, the average contribution was $1,700. The Montreal appeal—a community of about 100,000 persons— raised approximately $30 million a year in the early 1990s. All of the organizations discussed rely heavily on voluntary participation and lay leadership. Thus, in 1990, 47 percent of Canadian Jews identified membership in a Jewish organization, 31 percent indicating that they performed volunteer work in a Jewish organization, and 25 percent indicating that they sat on a board or a committee. Current information on the Canadian Jewish Congress and links to other organizations can be found online at <www.cjc.ca>.

[*Ross A. Klein*]

RELATED ENTRIES

B'Nai Brith, Church-Based Services, A. Comanor, A. Feindberg, Immigrants & Immigration, Religion, Sectarian Social Services, Social Welfare History, Wellness

Philip Johnston (1937–99)

Johnston, Philip, public health and social service administrator; b. June 23, 1937, Niagara Falls, ON; d. June 20, 1999, Kitchener, ON

Philip Johnston was commissioner of social services in Waterloo Region, Ontario, for the latter part of the 1900s, at the pinnacle of a long and respected career in public health and social services. He received his first professional training in public health at Ryerson Polytechnic Institute in Toronto, then worked as a public health inspector in his hometown of Niagara Falls. Moving to the city of Waterloo, he also worked in public health until he was given responsibility for social assistance administration. With the formation of regional government in 1973, he became coordinator of social services for Waterloo Region. In 1981 Johnston completed his master's degree in social work at Wilfrid Laurier University, which enhanced his ability to improve social service administration. During his thirty-eight year career in municipal service, Phil Johnston was a passionate champion of the poor, advocating for better benefits, more effective service, and ways to preserve the dignity of clients. As president of the Ontario Municipal Social Services Association, he was a member of the Social Assistance Review Committee, which authored the landmark *Transitions Report* on social assistance in Ontario. He also served on several provincial task forces. Many progressive changes in social services in Ontario emanated from Phil Johnston's reasoned and steadfast efforts.

[*Linda Snyder*]

RELATED ENTRIES

Interprofessional Issues, Wilfrid Laurier University (Faculty of Social Work)

Jungian theory

Jungian theory is an approach to psychotherapy that was developed by Swiss psychologist Carl Gustav Jung (1875–1961). Born into a family that had produced many physicians and clergy, Jung himself initially qualified as a physician; but his interests in the human psyche soon took him far beyond medicine into the realms of philosophy, archaeology, and spirituality. While Jung had considerable respect for Freud and collaborated with him, he moved beyond Freud in his development of a concept of individualized vital energy rather than emphasis of the predominance of sexual energy. Jung held a positive and holistic perception of humans with a commitment to the idea that people inherit uniform archetypes from the past. In pursuing these ideas, he devoted considerable time and interest to the study of Aboriginal cultures worldwide. While to date Jung has not had an impact on social work comparable to that of Freud or Erickson, it is clear that much contemporary social work thinking is in concert with Jung's ideas about the human psyche and therapy. His views of the human person and the sense of wholeness of persons with self and the environment are congruent with therapeutic concepts of existentialism. For Jung, the goal of therapy is to help persons achieve wholeness by finding harmony between their conscious and unconscious lives. The present-day marked interest in spirituality can be viewed as a critical component of human existence that needs to be taken into account and addressed as social work practitioners strive to understand client realities. While a rediscovery of spirituality by social work has not been directly influenced by Jung, there is much in Jung's analytical psychology that reflects his thinking about this topic, much of which is congruent with social work thinking. Jungian theory strongly supports the creativity of the human soul, likewise a theme reflected in the positive social work approaches to building on the strengths and potential of clients rather than focusing on problems and pathology.

[FJT]

RELATED ENTRIES

Psychoanalytical Theory, Theory & Practice

K

John Joseph Kelso (1864–1935)

Kelso, John Joseph, social reformer, founder of Toronto Children's Aid Society, first superintendent of children (ON); b. Mar. 31, 1864, Dundalk, Ireland (of George Kelso & Anna MacMurray); m. Irene Martin June 25, 1901; children: Martin, Irene; Silver Jubilee Medal, 1935; d. Sept. 30, 1935

J.J. Kelso is largely responsible for the creation of the Ontario child welfare system and for creating a great demand for social workers and for professional social work education. He was the youngest of nine children who enjoyed a middle-class lifestyle in Ireland until fire destroyed their family starch manufacturing business and the family emigrated to Toronto in hopes of re-establishing a good life. On finding only a poorly paying clerical job, his father coped with his frustration by an increasing dependence on alcohol and his mother, a deeply religious woman, became the driving force in the family, providing training that gave religion a central place in J.J.'s life. At a young age, Kelso taught Sunday school and was very active in the Presbyterian Church, where he encountered the ideals of the social gospel movement and the spirit of social reform. Kelso worked at many odd jobs, mostly in the publishing industry, from a young age and aspired to become a journalist. He gave up his plans for university when offered a permanent job as a reporter, first for the *World* and then for the *Toronto Globe*. Kelso was then the major provider for his family and, as his career expanded, he was able to provide his parents and sisters with their own home and a better lifestyle. Kelso's observations of homeless children, children selling newspapers, and his friends put in jail for petty theft with adult offenders (he was fourteen at the time) contributed to his becoming one of the most influential reformers of the social gospel movement in Ontario. In 1886 he became known as "Tagger Kelso" because he obtained an amendment in the Municipal Act to prohibit children less than eight years old working on the streets and, for enforcement, required all children engaged in street vending, including those selling newspapers, to be licensed, or tagged. Kelso's next reform activity was the establishment in 1887 of a society for the prevention of cruelty to children and animals; from these roots, Toronto's separate humane society and children's aid society emerged. In 1888 Kelso began the Fresh Air Fund, modelled on similar organizations in England and New York, to provide outings for needy children; the fund thrived so that nine thousand children benefitted in 1891. The Fresh Air

Fund, now managed by the *Toronto Star*, continues to raise funds to send needy children to camp. Kelso also established a Christmas Fund to provide presents for needy children. In 1888 Kelso advocated for passage of the Children's Protection Act, under which neglected children in Ontario could be sent to children's homes, and for a separate judicial system for young offenders, which became a forerunner of for the current youth criminal justice system. On July 18, 1891, Kelso and other concerned citizens established a children's aid society and an emergency shelter for children, which opened in 1892 on Centre Street. Kelso served for its first six months as president but resigned owing to work commitments at the *Toronto Globe*. Somewhat ironically, his commitment to social reform, which was in part inspired by his observations as a reporter, would eventually cost him the position of editor of the *Globe*, a position he had once desired.

Kelso continued to advocate for social welfare reforms and battle governmental red-tape and scarce resources throughout his career. In 1893 the Ontario legislature day passed An Act for the Prevention of Cruelty to and Better Protection of Children, known as the Children's Charter, which established children's aid societies and child welfare regulation throughout the province. J.J. Kelso was appointed as the first provincial superintendent of neglected and dependent children, a position he held until his retirement in 1934. His initial annual salary was $1,000, and his annual budget of $4,000 offered few resources for his work. Nevertheless, by 1914 he had organized children's aid societies in all parts of Ontario and had helped organize them in Manitoba and British Columbia. In 1921 Kelso became administrator of Ontario's first Adoption Act and of the first Children of Unmarried Parents Act. Kelso also supported the immigration of boys and girls, having visited Barnardo Homes in Britain; he argued strenuously, however, for government regulation of agencies that handled immigration of juveniles, as they were called at that time. His proposals were adopted in 1897 in the first Ontario Act to Regulate Juvenile Immigration. Kelso and W.L. Scott also lobbied the federal government for a juvenile justice system, which was brought to be when Parliament passed the Juvenile Delinquents Act, 1908; this Act included many of the recommendations Kelso had made in Ontario in 1888. Kelso was a keen supporter of public playgrounds and helped form the Toronto Playgrounds Association (1906–1908). He maintained a lifelong association with the social gospel movement and served as an executive member of the Board of Moral and Social Reform of the Presbyterian Church (1908–10). He played an important role in the settlement movement (1908–17), having visited Hull House at the invitation of Julia Lathrop, who would later head the US Children's Bureau. At a lunch with Jane Addams, he met another Canadian, William Lyon McKenzie King, to whom he would later appeal to support the settlement house movement. As part of his advocacy for the establishment of a settlement house in downtown Toronto, Kelso appealed to the new president of the University of Toronto. In 1909 when the university established a settlement house, Kelso became a member of the first board of directors. He also pushed for the establishment of Central Neighbourhood House Settlement and was elected first chairman of the board in 1911, then vice-president until 1916, before he resigned from the board in 1917. He also approached President Falconer of the University of Toronto with the idea of a school for philanthropy, as early as 1908, because many students were going to New York and Chicago to study social work. In 1914 the first school of social work in Canada was established at the university, in part as a result of Kelso's advocacy. Kelso became much sought as an international speaker and was assistant secretary and vice-president of the National Conference of Charities and Correction; he participated in a White House conference on child welfare (1908) and an international prison congress (1910). In 1893 he called for state provision of mothers allowances (begun in 1920) and in 1905 for old age pensions (begun in 1927). He called for legislation to protect unwed mothers and their children sent to "baby farms." From 1905 to 1913, he travelled to other provinces to advocate for comprehensive child protection legislation. His influence in child welfare declined in the 1920s, as attitudes toward philanthropy began to change. Kelso then gave more time to his church activities as superintendent of the Sunday school at St. James Square Presbyterian church from 1919 to the church's closure in 1929. He was elected an elder of Bloor Street

United Church in 1931. He also focused attention on the Toronto Humane Society; as a founding member in 1887, he had continued on the board and became the treasurer in 1918, a position he held until 1935. He was required by government regulations on his seventieth birthday in 1934, but was informed by the government that he could continue to work; this extension was cancelled when a new government was elected. Kelso received many tributes at his retirement, including one from Charlotte Whitton, long-time director of the Canadian Welfare Council. One of his greatest honours was to be awarded the Silver Jubilee Medal in 1935 "in recognition of his services to child welfare and the humane treatment of animals" (Jones & Rutman 1981: 174).

In his latter years, Kelso's hearing and health began to fail, and he was diagnosed in 1930 with liver cancer; following an operation in 1932, his illness reoccurred in 1935 and he succumbed on September 30. In his obituary, the *Globe* stated that "all his actions, public and private were governed by kindness and consideration of others" (Jones & Rutman 1981: 178). On his death Kelso's contribution to child welfare and to the development of humane societies was recognized in international tributes and, most importantly, in those from his former wards. While he collected extensive memorabilia related to his career, Kelso never managed to write his memoirs. His personal papers were donated in 1974 by his son Martin to the National Archives in Ottawa. J.J. Kelso's vision created the child welfare and juvenile justice systems, large parts of the social safety net legislation, children's aid societies, settlement houses, and humane societies for the prevention of cruelty of animals now found throughout Canada. While the child welfare reform is arguable his greatest legacy, perhaps J.J. Kelso's most endearing legacy may be his Fresh Air Fund, which continues every spring with local newspapers' appeals to "send a child to camp."

[*Laura Taylor*]

RELATED ENTRIES

Child Abuse, An Act for the Prevention of Cruelty to and Better Protection of Children, Children's Aid Society, Child Welfare, Family & Youth Courts, Mothers Allowance, Services for Children, Services for Offenders, Social Welfare, Social Welfare History, Young Offenders Act, Youth Criminal Justice Act

REFERENCE

Jones, A., and L. Rutman. 1981. *In the Children's Aid: J.J. Kelso and Children Welfare in Ontario.* Toronto: University of Toronto Press.

Kingston Penitentiary

Kingston Penitentiary, which opened in 1835, is Canada's oldest penitentiary. Conceptualized from a state of near-revolt within the overcrowded local jails in Upper Canada in the nineteenth century, the first penitentiary was originally named the Provincial Penitentiary at Portsmouth. Kingston Penitentiary adopted its current name in 1867, when the government of the new confederation took over penitentiaries (Canada 1985). Throughout its history, with a mandate to protect the public through the incarceration of federally sentenced offenders, Kingston Penitentiary has served a dual purpose of confinement (secure custody) and reform. Reform in its earlier days meant "meditation, penitence, and reflection upon a life of crime" (Canada 1985: 6); a century later, however, the ideology of reform was geared to changing the behaviour and attitudes of those incarcerated, through the tools the social sciences brought to the reform movement of the 1970s. The role of the penitentiary has changed through time. After discontented inmates perpetrated a riot in 1971, Kingston Penitentiary became instead a regional reception centre where the placement of offenders into other penitentiaries in Ontario was decided. In 1981, prompted by inmate demographic changes to an increasingly diverse and vulnerable population, the mandate of Kingston Penitentiary was changed so that it then housed offenders with protective custody concerns at all levels of security. In 1996, in an effort to reduce the stigmatization of the "protective custody" label, Kingston Penitentiary reverted to a maximum-security prison, as it remains today.

Changes have also occurred within the penitentiary itself, in particular in response to offenders with symptoms of mental illness. Prior to the 1930s, when little was known about the causes and treatment of mental illness, such offenders sentenced to Kingston Penitentiary were locked away under the dining hall because of their inability to comply with prison rules, most prominently the "rule of silence." A history of the penitentiary reports that they were "beaten often enough, but they could not be silenced. They drove the prison routine to distraction and in retaliation the system mandated cruelties that drove them further into madness" (Canada 1985: 51). Many of these inmates found their way into a cell block newly constructed in the 1950s along the southeast wall known as the "prison of isolation"; after the riot in 1971, this cell block formally became the Regional Psychiatric Centre for Ontario. A clinical director oversaw the assessment and treatment of mentally disordered offenders, with direct reporting to the penitentiary warden. In the early 1980s the centre was renamed the Regional Treatment Centre for Ontario and the directorship was held by correctional manager, an associate warden, instead of a clinician; in some ways, these changes ensured that the primary mandate for the centre is as a federal correctional facility. Today, the centre is an active 144-bed accredited mental health facility that is foremost a federal penitentiary providing a full range of psychiatric assessment and treatment, in addition to a high-intensity program for sexual offenders. The centre now operates almost completely independently from Kingston Penitentiary; yet its location within the penitentiary retains the influence of its history and harsh environment.

The first social workers at Kingston Penitentiary were hired in the 1970s to work solely with the mentally disordered offenders at the Regional Psychiatric Centre. Social work disappeared when the centre's mandate switched to a more correctional focus in the early 1980s, until David Champagne was permitted to reintroduce its practice in 1993, initially as a pilot project and fully in 1995. Champagne had been employed with Correctional Services of Canada since 1983, initially as a case management officer, a non-clinical role in federal corrections; on completion of his master's degree in social work degree in 1992, Champagne advocated for the inclusion of social work at the centre. Through his dedication to social work ethics and standards of practice, Champagne has established a firm professional and comprehensive role for social work within the centre's multi-disciplinary teams. Champagne, a registered social worker, is the only current practitioner within federal corrections in the Ontario region. He provides a referral for consultation service to all offenders at the centre, with two major functions: comprehensive dis-

charge planning for high-need offenders, and assistance to address multi-faceted issues relating to families. Efforts are in place to expand the social work department from one to several. It is a rich environment for graduate students in social work to develop and finetune skills in working with a forensic population.

[*Arthur T. Bowers* and
Nancy Riedel Bowers]

RELATED ENTRIES

Clinical Social Work, Correctional Services, Criminal Justice, Forensic Practice, Probation, Services for Offenders

REFERENCE

Canada. 1985. *Kingston Penitentiary, the First Hundred and Fifty Years.* Kingston, ON: Correctional Services Canada.

knowledge base

The knowledge base for the study of social welfare is appropriately characterized as interdisciplinary. Social welfare is concerned with achieving concrete outcomes in the real world and so the most visible aspects of social welfare are statutory public programs and public assistance (i.e., old age security, protection of children and youth). Elsewhere in the public sector, such matters as taxation, fiscal policy, and trade policy impinge heavily on the welfare of Canadians and practitioners who wish to pursue advocacy for major change might wish to include them in their knowledge base. Social welfare cannot be defined solely as public welfare, as many public programs rely on the financial and/or administrative collaboration of private employers and non-profit organizations. Practitioners may work for any of the private organizations operating independent in-kind social welfare programs, such as shelter and meals for vulnerable populations. Practitioners may also practice within a broader sense of social welfare, anticipating and dealing with the harm done to people through the major processes in society (as in providing materially for the poor and those at risk, and supporting the socially alienated). As such, an understanding of harm done is a necessary step contributing to the development of institutional forms to prevent harm and promote welfare positively. The knowledge base for social welfare can be thought to include all relevant social science disciplines, but this implies the humanly impracticable task of mastering all of them.

The knowledge base may better be outlined from the inside: required factual data, the practices by which welfare is pursued, the theories by which the data may be understood and practices designed, and values at stake. The most fundamental data within the knowledge base concern demographics: numbers, age and gender distribution of people, migration, familial patterns, and changes therein. Certain economic data—income and wealth, employment, occupational structures—are also basic. Given state dominance in welfare, knowledge of the data of public finance is also necessary, both expenditure and revenue sources, and debt, as the overall budgetary pattern has more impact on general welfare than all welfare programs combined. Social welfare works in conjunction with major institutions of Canadian society (i.e., the family, the economy) whose evolution must be understood by practitioners. Knowledge of the history of welfare in Canada is essential, notably the expansion of the government role in the twentieth century and the continuing dynamics of responsibilities shared by the federal and provincial/territorial governments. Certain episodes in the histories of other countries can also be illuminating.

As social welfare is a practical matter, analysis of an issue is only a step toward doing something about it. Welfare programs operate in the world at large: while pursuing the core objectives of programs, practitioners may have to meet other demands, such as mobilizing resources. For public programs, political support must be sustained from multiple constituencies whose perceived interests vary; analogous constraints apply to private programs. Attention to history can enhance such practitioners' appreciation for the environment surrounding welfare programs. The administration of programs is complicated by the feedback effect: the program alters the behaviour of parties, sometimes unpredictably, perhaps altering the problem itself. The interrelated basic facts concerning a program are: the public statute or private charter under which it is administered; the eligible clientele and their contact with the administering body; the benefits provided; and the body responsible for administration.

Social welfare cannot address social issues effectively without a basis in theory: the consumption of substantial resources and interventions into people's lives need to be approached with a sound reason to expect success. Similarly, to be credible, critics must root their objections in a persuasive theory. Theory organizes data into coherent relationships. Different people may look at the same data and see different relationships. A theory ought to give way if in conflict with data; but this may be difficult both in principle, for theory guides the selection of data, and in practice, for few will readily give up a cherished theory, even when faced with incompatible data. One ought to understand not only one's own theoretical underpinnings, but also, at some level, other interpretations as well. Among relevant theoretical debates are those around the primacy, as unit of analysis, of the individual versus a collectivity (which collectivity is also debated), the range of freedom of action realistically open to people in society, and the level of objectivity attainable by an observer. Selecting one or more theories for practice should not reflect one's personal taste, but which explains society or a client's circumstances best. Error is inevitable if one's observations and analyses are determined by one's preferences.

The objectives of social welfare necessarily reflect values. Social values grow from many cultural and philosophical roots, and are shaped by personal and group experience. In a society as pluralist as Canada's, the goals that social welfare seeks to achieve may be contentious. Values are deeply ingrained, often working below the conscious level. Some theorists regard a person's value orientations—e.g., individualist, communitarian, authoritarian—as virtually beyond discussion; however, experience shows that values are subject to change. Many participants in welfare discourse accord nearly uncritical allegiance to programs that appear to express values with which they sympathize, and the reverse. But personal value systems are complex and people who share some values may be in conflict over others. Further, structures of values may be criticized for their internal consistency, and they must be tested for the consequences that ensue when they are exercised, despite the notorious propensity of believers to excuse harm done in the service of their ideologies. Values matter with regard to both means and ends. Lastly, advances in the natural sciences and in the emergent technologies exert vast effects in society. The knowledge base of social welfare must include enough awareness of the movement of science to enable practitioners to respond to its social implications.

[*Frank McGilly*]

RELATED ENTRIES

Aboriginal Issues, Demographics, Education in Social Work, Feminist Theory, Paraprofessionals, Practice Methods, Practicum Instruction, Progressive Social Work, Racism-Sensitive Social Work, Radical Social Work, Research, Social Welfare, Social Welfare Context, Social Welfare History, Social Work Profession, Theory & Practice

L

Lakehead University School of Social Work

In 1967 the Lakehead University Senate approved a program in social welfare toward a bachelor of arts degree. Based on recommendations in "Design for Development, Northwestern Ontario Region," the Ontario Ministry of Treasury and Economics recommended the development of a social work program at Lakehead University; at that time, northwestern Ontario was designated by the Ministry of Community and Social Services as an underserviced region, as only thirty-five to forty social workers working there had a professional degree. After a series of discussions with social workers there in 1971, a further feasibility study conducted in 1972 by Lakehead Dean of Arts, Dr. Tim Ryan, reinforced the need for a social work program in northwestern Ontario. In 1973, a joint bachelor of arts and bachelor of social work program was approved by the Senate at Lakehead University, to be administered by the dean of arts, Dr. Bill Melnyk, and a part-time chair, Jack Young; the division of social work admitted its first ninety-five students in 1973/74. By 1974 a full-time chair, Dr. James Chacko, the first full-time faculty members, and eleven sessionals had been appointed. With the approval of the Senate and the Faculty of Arts, the social work program became an honours bachelor of social work degree. In 1975/76 the program was admitted as a candidate for accredita-

tion by the Canadian Association of Schools of Social Work. The first accreditation was received in 1980; the school has been reaccredited in 1986, 1993 and 2000. A graduate master of social work program, approved by the Ontario Council on Graduate Studies in 1991, was first offered on a part-time basis in 1992/93; in 1995, permission was granted to admit students on a full-time basis and to offer graduate assistantships to full-time students. A review by the council in 1996 granted the master's program a classification as "good quality" and this program was accredited in 2003.

In 1975, the program was changed from a division to a department of social work and, in 2001, it became a school of social work. As a department, social work had been located in the Faculty of Arts and Science; in 2001, the school became part of the Faculty of Professional Schools. The Lakehead social work programs have consistently recognized the importance of professional social work education for northwestern Ontario. The school did address the drastic shortage of social workers serving the region, as revealed by the results of a 1989 alumni survey, which indicated that 293 of 417 graduates from 1974 to 1988 were working in northwestern Ontario. Moreover, more than fifty students have graduated from the honours bachelor program offered in Kenora, Geraldton, and Atikokan; the honours program is currently being offered through distance education for students in northwestern Ontario. In 1997 the masters of social work program was offered for study in Kenora. The school now offers a four-year honours bachelor of social work program, a one-year (i.e., twelve months) honours bachelor of social work program, and a masters of social work program. Within the context of a broad generalist social work education, these programs reflect multiple theoretical and conceptual bases of social work knowledge and practice; in particular, the programs emphasize relevance to the practice needs of this northern and rural region and regions farther north. The diversity of the population and communities within the region, particularly the prevalence of Aboriginal cultures, is specifically addressed within the curriculum. Issues drawn from northern and rural social work practice, and from community and context-based practice in general are addressed throughout the curriculum in policy, research, theory, and practice skills courses. The school maintains strong links through active involvement with communities throughout northwestern Ontario, provides continuing and professional development, and often collaborates with other agencies and the local branch of the professional social work association. Current information about social work studies at Lakehead can be found online at <www.lakeheadu.ca/~socwork/>.

[*Roger Delaney* and
Sharon Taylor]

RELATED ENTRIES

Canadian Association of Schools of Social Work, Education in Social Work, Faculties of Social Work, Ontario Association of Social Workers, Ontario College of Certified Social Workers and Social Service Workers

John Woodburn Langmuir (1834–1915)

Langmuir, John Woodburn, social welfare pioneer;
b. 1834, Scotland; d. 1915

J.W. Langmuir, who was to win a firm place in Canada's social welfare history, arrived in Canada from Scotland at age fifteen. He rapidly succeeded in business, served as an officer in repulsing the Fenian raids, became mayor of Picton at age twenty-four, and was appointed to a key position in the newly formed public service of Ontario at age thirty-four. His appointment as inspector of prisons, asylums, and charitable institutions in 1868 was opportune. The government of the new province of Ontario, rejoicing in its freedom from the constraints it endured before confederation, then had the constitutional and financial capacity to develop measures needed for the care, protection, and well-being of its citizens. J.W. Langmuir, creatively reporting to and working with provincial governments—notably that of the long time provincial premier, Oliver Mowat—brought into being a golden age of social welfare development. Year after year during his fourteen years as inspector, Langmuir presented superbly prepared proposals that won governmental acceptance for new or enhanced programs in corrections and mental health, new facilities for the deaf and blind, and support and direction for a wide range of voluntary social welfare and health services under the Charity Aid Act. In his administrative role, Langmuir drew selectively on contemporary expe-

rience in Britain and the United States, forming valuable links with American leaders in the developing field of social welfare. By the time of his departure in 1882—to found the Toronto General Trust—the province could boast of having one of the most complete systems of charities and corrections on the continent. Another of Langmuir's social welfare contributions was his chairmanship in 1890 of a provincial Royal Commission, a landmark endeavour in the history of social welfare. It received extensive testimony, made wideranging recommendations, and introduced a general philosophy of social responsibility for problems such as poverty and crime. It also made the case for an occupation requiring education, training, and skill—a calling that, within a few years, would be called social work.

[*Richard Splane*]

RELATED ENTRIES

Social Welfare History

League for Social Reconstruction*

League for Social Reconstruction (LSR), organization of left-wing intellectuals, founded 1931–32 in Montreal and Toronto, largely in response to the Great Depression. Although it had almost twenty branches elsewhere in Ontario and the West, the founding branches proved the longest lived and most active in political education. Led by historian Frank Underhill and law professor F.R. Scott, the LSR was critical of monopoly capitalism and demanded economic change by parliamentary means. Never formally linked with a political party, it made its sympathies clear with the annual reelection of J.S. Woodsworth as its honorary president. The Regina Manifesto (1933) of the Co-operative Commonwealth Federation (CCF) was largely written by LSR members. The league's ideas Found fullest expression in the books *Social Planning for Canadian* (1935) and *Democracy Needs Socialism* (1938), and in the *Canadian Forum*, acquired in 1936. Disillusionment with Socialism in the late 1930s weakened the LSR. World War II and the increased organizational demands of the CCF led to the LSR's quiet demise in 1942. Its influence on the CCF was great; its influence on Canada is still a matter for speculation.

[*Michiel Horn*]

*Used unedited by permission from *The Canadian Encyclopedia*. 2000. Toronto: McClelland and Stewart.

League for the Advancement of Coloured People

The Canadian League for the Advancement of Coloured People (est. 1924) formed with the two major objectives of attempting to unify the diverse peoples of African descent facing barriers throughout this land, and determining the nature and extent of these barriers. The struggle of peoples of African descent for freedom and equality in Canada is as old as the history of the country itself, a surprise to the many Canadians who believe it to be a new phenomenon. The league's efforts to counter the pervasive oppression endemic to the life experience of African Canadians and their descendants emerged as part of a continuous stream of collective protest against the uniquely inhumane conditions of slavery and its aftermath. The first African slave was brought to Canada on a Dutch ship in 1628, the start of a rich but unsavoury history before abolition of slavery in British territories in 1834. If Canadian historians acknowledge more than two hundred years of slavery in Canada, they tend to minimize its severity as compared to that in the American colonies, and emphasize somewhat romantic notions associated with the Underground Railroad as an escape from the southern experience of slavery after the 1850s. Yet slavery within Canada was sufficiently severe for escape attempts to be frequent (Winks 1971: 14), and for shiploads of people of African descent to plan organized protests (e.g., in 1792 and in 1800) in order to return to such point of origin as Sierra Leone. Moreover, Canada certainly did not always offer a safe haven; officials commonly recaptured escaped slaves or returned them for a bounty to their slave owners in the American colonies. By the late 1800s, people of African descent in Canada were already multi-ethnic, comprised of early settlers from slavery times and their descendents; Black Loyalist troops (both slaves and free persons) from the American colonies; Black Americans, lured by the promise of greater equality in Canada; and immigrants from what was then called the West Indies. Early attempts to form a collective front produced some divisions as, for example, West Indians were given certain rights as "British" by birth. Widespread anti-"Negro" sentiment grew sufficiently in Canada between 1909 and 1930 that African Canadians recognized the need for a unified struggle (Winks 1971: 284–85). In response, numerous self-help societies were initiated throughout the country, as were organized efforts to combat racism and its effects in Canada. The latter, although mostly based on US models, lacked direct affiliation with organized movements there. An early precursor to the league, the Niagara Movement (est. 1905) by a Black American, W.E.B. DuBois, was an exception. DuBois invited representatives from thirteen states and the District of Columbia to meet in Fort Erie, Ontario, having been unable to do so in Buffalo, New York, owing to discriminatory accommodation policies. No Canadians of African descent were invited to this meeting, which led to the emergence in 1909 as the National Association for the Advancement of Colored People, an organization that persists to this day in the United States.

The League for the Advancement of Coloured People was formally chartered in 1925 as the Canadian equivalent of the US association. The Canadian league differed from its US counterpart, in that it never achieved national status. It was operational only in Ontario, with affiliates in Dresden and, for a time, in Hamilton and Windsor. The league successfully sponsored a newspaper, *The Dawn of Tomorrow*, encouraged research into the history of Black people in Canada, sought to increase employment opportunities for Black people in London, Ontario, helped Black Canadians to continue their education, and worked with the London Juvenile Court (as youth court was then called). Unlike its US counterpart, the Canadian league did not press for fundamental change in the attitudes of the dominant culture, although it led one recorded protest against the depiction a Victory Loan poster in 1944 of Black Canadians as redcaps. Instead, the league became mainly a charitable organization distributing food baskets in mid-winter through funds donated to the segregated Beth Emanuel Congregation, one of the many Black churphes that took a leadership role in combating the deleterious effects of systemic racism. Nonetheless, during the couple of decades when it was operational, the league is said to have been more forward-looking than its equivalents in Nova Scotia and New Brunswick, where discrimination against Black people remained most persistent (Winks 1971: 419). While the severity of prejudice and discrimination against Black people in Canada has varied over time and from place to place, no part of Canada can be said to have been free—or to be free today—of race-based barriers similar to those in the United States and Britain. Until the 1960s, people of African descent faced overt prejudice and systemic discrimination in housing, education, employment, and the justice system, and in places of recreation and worship (Este & Bernard 2002). Constantly changing in its manifestation, the effects of slavery, fuelled by stereotypes and racial profiling, continue to be felt by Black people in Canada today (Christensen 2001: 198). Recent studies have indicated that the very issues that the League attempted to address remain today, largely fuelled by the continued denial of the existence, extent, and effects of anti-black racism in Canada (Kazemipur & Halli 2000). Issues of racialization and lack of full access to social services is but a reflection of the denial of racism, which is found in the wider society. The Canadian Race Relations Foundation, found online at <www.crrf .ca>, documents instances of racism and supports education to combat systemic discrimination in Canada.

[*Carole Pigler Christensen*]

RELATED ENTRIES

Diversity, Ethnocultural Communities' Services, Nongovernmental Organizations, Minorities, Race & Racism, Racism-Sensitive Social Work, Visible Minorities

REFERENCES

Christensen, C.P. 2001. Immigrant Minorities in Canada. In J.C. Turner and F. J. Turner (Eds.) *Canadian Social Welfare*. 180–209. 4th ed. Toronto: Pearson Education.

Este, D., and W.T. Bernard. 2002. Social Work Practice with African Canadians: An Examination of the African-Nova Scotian Community. In A. Al-Krenawi and J.R. Graham (Eds.), *Multicultural Social Work in Canada: Working with Diverse Ethno-racial Communities*. Chapter 13, 306–38. Toronto: Oxford University Press.

Kazemipur, A., and S.S. Halli. 2000. *The New Poverty in Canada: Ethnic Groups and Ghetto Neighbourhoods*. Toronto: Thompson Educational Publishing.

Winks, R.W. 1971. *The Blacks in Canada*. Montreal/ Kingston: McGill-Queen's University Press.

learning disabilities

Learning disabilities are defined as "a variety of disorders that affect the acquisition, retention, understanding, organization and/or use of verbal and non-verbal information" (LDAO 2001). While learning disabilities are considered to be the result of "genetic, other congenital and/or acquired neuro-biological factors" (LDAO 2001), development of the disorder impacts on an individual's emotional, family, and social functioning (Wiener, Harris, & Shirer 1990). The prevalence of learning disabilities in North America is reported as ranging from 4 to 10 percent (Interagency Committee on Learning Disabilities [US] 1987). Learning disability as a term was first used in 1963 (Dane 1990), marking the recentness of identification and study of this phenomenon. There is also a growing recognition of the impact of sociocultural factors on individuals' learning styles and problems, in turn affecting the understanding of learning disabilities, as well as assessment and intervention (Wiener & Siegel 1992). It is estimated that 50 percent of individuals with learning disabilities develop social, emotional, and behavioural problems (Kavale & Forness 1996), with a high prevalence of learning disabilities in clinical populations. Learning disabilities may interact with environmental, social, and emotional factors to disrupt personality development (Dane 1990). Children and adolescents with learning disabilities are inclined to suffer from depression, anxiety, and poor motivation (Heath 1992), and to have low self-esteem. Individuals with learning disabilities often exhibit inadequate interpersonal skills resulting in social rejection. Children in Ontario who do poorly in school have been found to be twice as likely to be identified as having a psychiatric disorder. This population is vulnerable to delinquent behaviour, both as victims and perpetrators. Studies report prevalence rates of learning disabilities in the youth crime population ranging from 30 to 50 percent (Brier 1989). Adolescents with learning disabilities are more than twice as likely to be arrested than are their peers without learning disabilities. Moreover, youth offenders with learning disabilities are more than twice as likely to be rearrested than are youth offenders without learning disabilities. As in other countries, bullying is pervasive in schools in Canada. Children and adolescents in special education are at particular risk for involvement in bullying, both as victims and bullies (Whitney, Smith, & Thompson 1994).

Learning disabilities may impede development across an individual's lifespan. Between 33 and 47 percent of students with learning disabilities drop out of school, a significantly higher rate than students without learning disabilities (Levin, Zigmond, & Birch 1986). Students with learning disabilities who drop out are at risk for continued disadvantage, both socially and economically. Many problems experienced by youth with learning disabilities continue into adulthood. The family of an individual with learning disabilities may represent either a risk or a protective factor, which may depend on the interaction of child and parent characteristics, socio-economic status, cultural variables, and availability of external support and resources (Dane 1990; Wiener & Siegel 1992). Other protective factors include self-esteem, self-awareness, and understanding of one's learning disabilities, appropriate academic support, attachment with teachers, peer relationships, and high school graduation.

Social work interventions aim to reduce risk factors and enhance protective factors. Social workers are advised to understand the interactions among the student, family, peers, institutions, and environment to recognize the significance of family, institutional and societal attitudes and behaviours toward the student, and to regard all aspects of the environment as potential targets for intervention. Social workers must maintain communication with such community resources with which children and adolescents are involved as therapeutic, recreational, academic, vocational, and religious resources. Intervention with the family may facilitate the family's ability to cope with the additional stresses as a result of learning disabilities, such as dealing with the stigma, advocating with the school, supporting siblings, and providing long-term economic and social support for the individual with learning disabilities. Social workers must recognize the

diversity of families and understand the meanings and impact of the learning disabilities for each individual and family. Individual treatment may be indicated, to offer the individual with learning disabilities a safe environment and relationship in which to deal with issues (Dane 1990). A key intervention consists of helping children and adolescents improve their ability to relate with peers. Group work enables individuals to recognize that they are not the only ones with learning disabilities, to interact with and receive feedback from peers, and to learn and practice social skills (Dane 1990; Mishna 1996). Social work's role and perspective in the field of learning disabilities has been under-represented as a result of an emphasis on academic aspects of the condition, along with a lack of focus on the psychosocial consequences and needs of the children, youth, and their families (Dane 1990).

[*Faye Mishra*]

RELATED ENTRIES

Bullying, Developmental Challenges, Developmental Challenges & Families, Minorities, Physical Challenges, School Social Workers, Services for People with Disabilities, Services for Youth, Wellness, Young Offenders Act, Youth Criminal Justice Act

REFERENCES

Brier, N. 1989. The Relationship between Learning Disability and Delinquency: A Review and Reappraisal. *Journal of Learning Disabilities* 22, 546–53.

Dane, E. 1990. *Painful Passages: Working with Children with Learning Disabilities*. Silver Spring, MD: National Association of Social Workers Press.

Heath, N.L. 1992. Learning Disabilities and Depression: Research, Theory and Practice. *Exceptionality Education in Canada* 2, 3, 59–74.

Interagency Committee on Learning Disabilities. 1987. Learning Disabilities—A Report to the US Congress. Washington, DC: US Department of Health and Human Services.

Kavale, K.A., and S.R. Forness. 1996. Social Skill Deficits and Learning Disabilities: A Meta-analysis. *Journal of Learning Disabilities* 29, 226–37.

LDAO. 2001. *Promoting Early Intervention for Learning Disabilities 1999–2002*. Toronto: Learning Disabilities Association of Ontario.

Levin, F., N. Zigmond, and J. Birch. 1986. A Follow-up Study of Fifty-two Learning Disabled Adolescents. *Journal of Learning Disabilities* 18, 2–7.

Mishna, F. 1996. In Their Own Words: Therapeutic Factors for Adolescents Who Have Learning Disabilities. *International Journal of Group Psychotherapy* 46, 265-73.

Whitney, I., P.K. Smith, and D. Thompson. 1994. Bullying and Children with Special Educational Needs. In P.K. Smith and S. Sharp (Eds.) *School Bullying: Insights and Perspectives.* 213-240. London: Routledge.

Wiener, J., P.J. Harris, and C. Shirer. 1990. Achievement and Social-Behavioural Correlates of Peer Status in Learning Disabled Children. *Learning Disabilities Quarterly* 13, 114-27.

Wiener, J., and L. Siegel. 1992. A Canadian Perspective on Learning Disabilities. *Journal of Learning Disabilities* 26, 340-50, 371.

legal issues

Law is a crystalline form of social policy in Canada that attempts to reflect the changing social context. Aspects of law provide the framework for governmental social services, client rights, and social worker powers. Understanding key aspects of law is essential for effective social work practice; otherwise the adversarial, hierarchical, and classist nature of law can disempower both clients and social workers. The discrepancy between the concepts of legal truth and ethical morality can be disconcerting. Major functions of the law to regulate, empower and obligate, resolve conflicts, and enforce adherence must be understood so that social workers know the parameters of their legal powers, and can assist clients and groups to become empowered when challenging powerful agencies to provide appropriate services. Legal processes and remedies, despite their reactive limitations, can be useful tools; for instance, increasingly social workers are supporting clients in taking legal action (civil and criminal) against perpetrators of abuse, or invoking the Canadian Charter of Rights and Freedoms to challenge repressive laws. Practitioners need to know equality rights in the Charter, anti-discrimination rights in federal and provincial or territorial human rights codes, and the rights of patients under provincial or territorial mental health acts. Distinctions need to be recognized between criminal process (in adult and youth courts) and civil process (in welfare, family, divorce, small claims courts, and quasi-judicial human rights tribunals). Practitioners working in schools need to be familiar with provincial/territorial education statutes, child welfare laws, and the federal Youth Criminal Justice Act, 2002.

Since many clients are dependent on services from governments and contracted agencies, social workers delivering services must understand notions of equity, the principles of due process and administrative fairness—often referred to as the rules of natural justice—which affect them as decision makers. In particular, practice must include familiarity with those principles, as court decisions are at best restorative, rather than transformative or redistributive, leaving to politicians the decisions for making changes that may be effective. Social work contributions to relevant commissions of law reform and inquiry are required. Court process can sometimes revictimize victims, humiliate complainants, and shelter some offenders from responsibility. Wherever possible, social workers need to assist clients to make informed choices about involvement in the legal system. Social workers might act as support persons for disempowered clients in giving instructions to lawyers, for witnesses in testifying and debriefing courtroom experiences, and for promoting alternatives such as diversion from court and restorative justice programs.

[*David Turner*]

RELATED ENTRIES

Accountability, Bioethical Issues, Codes of Ethics, Criminal Justice, Ethics, Forensic Practice, Family & Youth Courts, Interprofessional Issues, Kingston Penitentiary, Knowledge Base, Malpractice, Mediation Services, Practice Methods, Probation, Professional Liability, Services for Offenders, Services for Youth, Theory & Practice, Young Offenders Act, Youth Criminal Justice Act

Raoul Leger (1951–81)

Leger, Raoul, international social worker, social justice activist; b. Jan. 27, 1951, Bouctouche, NB; d. July 25, 1981, Guatemala

Raoul Leger was an Acadian social worker from New Brunswick whose work as a member of a multidisciplinary team on a pastoral mission in Guatemala led to the loss of his life through assassination. Leger graduated from Université de Moncton in 1974 with a bachelor's degree in social work, and in 1976 completed a master's degree in social work from the Maritime School of Social

Work in Halifax. He was employed with the New Brunswick Department of Community Social Services, working in the field of mental health as well. In January 1979 Leger left l'Acadie for Guatemala to be part of a social missionary project team sponsored by Société des missions-étrangères (Foreign Missions Society) of Montreal. In his dual roles as social worker and lay missionary, Leger's goal was to "help others to help themselves and one another" (Duguay 1999: 42). During the two and half years he spent working with people in Guatemala, he remained devoted to the causes of the poor, and fought against injustices through actions of solidarity with villagers and communities. His approach won him much respect and love from the people he served. Raoul Leger witnessed firsthand the terror and death threats experienced by the people alongside whom he worked, yet he chose to remain in the country striving toward the people's goal of freedom from oppression. In 1990 the New Brunswick Association of Social Workers awarded the first annual Raoul Leger award in his memory, to "remind us of the spirit that Raoul represents: Commitment and solidarity in the struggle for social justice and peace. Through his example, his simplicity and his sense of responsibility, he truly represents what a social worker is all about. By making this presentation each year, we are keeping this ideal alive." Raoul Leger has carved a significant place among the heroes and heroines who have emerged in Canada during the social work profession's historical development.

[*Linda M. Turner*]

RELATED ENTRIES

Church-Based Services, International Practice, Social Justice

REFERENCES

Duguay, Henri-Eugene. 1999. *Raoul: Un amour pas comme les autres*. Moncton, NB: McCurdy.

lesbian services

Sensitivity in social services for lesbians is a critical need, the recognition for which has long been understood within the gay and lesbian communities but is only coming to be understood within the profession. Until the last twenty-five years or so, professional services for lesbians were primarily aimed at punishing or attempting to cure such women of their "sexual deviance." Homosexuality was regarded as a criminal activity until 1969 and was classified as a mental illness in the third edition of the *Diagnostic and Statistical Manual of Mental Disorders* (DSM III) until 1973. Training schools, mental hospitals, and faith organizations participated in bizarre and often cruel programs to reform/cure women who exhibited lesbian behaviours or were considered unfeminine. At the same time, lesbians gathered to meet, socialize, and form informal networks of support, gradually become a community, until recently remaining underground, primarily in bars, coffee shops, and private homes. In the 1960s and 1970s the women's movement, feminism, and sexual liberation legitimized new expressions of gender and sexual identity which, in turn, enabled lesbians to become far more visible and to begin to organize around and advocate for their own needs. In fact, women's services, such as rape crisis centres, shelters, immigrant women's centres, and health clinics, often included a strong lesbian presence in both staffing and programming and led the way in the development of services that were at least inclusive of lesbians and their life experiences.

Currently, lesbian services exist within the three broad categories of unfunded grassroots groups, mainstream organization services, and lesbian-specific services. By far, the majority of services available to lesbians are offered through grassroots groups, which have generally grown from initiatives by a few individuals who recognized and became committed to the fulfilment of a specific need. These groups are informal and services are offered in private homes, community centres, universities, or locations in the community that relate to the identified need (i.e., parenting, coming out, social or recreational events, immigration, physical or intellectual disabilities). Grassroots groups may also organize around specific member characteristics, for example, nationality, ethnicity, culture, religion, age, or professional interests. Potential members usually find grassroots groups through word of mouth, the gay media, or the Internet. The existence of grassroots groups is vital for many lesbians, in that they provide a sense of connectedness and belonging within intentional communities; these services have some limitations, however. Since these groups are not long-term and have no paid staff, they come and go, depending on the interest and the energy of volunteers. As well, the availability and accessibility of grassroots groups vary greatly between urban and rural settings. In urban settings, accessing grassroots groups is fairly easy and anonymous through word of mouth, postings in the gay media, and bookstores; conversely, in rural settings, gay women may have to locate information through a network of people who are still mostly underground, often a difficult process that risks some degree of disclosure. Finally, urban or rural gay women who do not have access to a computer or gay media may have difficulty accessing information because it is not readily available in mainstream service providers. They may, as a result, experience isolation and a lack of sense of belonging. Mainstream organizations offer a paucity of lesbian services, despite the ongoing receptiveness to lesbian clients at least among services with a feminist orientation. Where mainstream services do include lesbian clients, they typically create space for lesbian clients within existing programs but rarely address heterosexist biases in the program or explore the different social contexts in which these women live. The experiences of lesbian women are often presented as a conspicuous addition, resulting in the fragmentation of lesbian lives through a limited acceptance and visibility within each context. Services offered generally address health and addiction/substance use, such as Alcoholics Anonymous or mental health counselling. Still, the availability of such services is spread through word of mouth, as lesbian clients experience some level of visibility. The largest percentage of the third category—lesbian-specific services—is provided by private practitioners, themselves often members of lesbian and gay communities who are aware of the needs and gaps that exist. These services include in their conceptual framework an understanding of the impact of oppression related to homophobia and lesbian invisibility. Private practitioners do offer a safe haven in that lesbian acceptance and visibility is implicit; however, most practitioners work on a fee-for-service basis, which presents a financial barrier and limited accessibility for many lesbians. Many lesbian and feminist private practitioners do offer fees on a sliding scale to address these obstacles. Within

the public realm, very few lesbian-specific services exist. A few groups and programs within community centres and counselling and health centres may offer services for coming out, substance use, partner abuse, and sexual health.

Gaps in lesbian services persist in relation to, among others, domestic violence, chronic mental illness, death and bereavement, and childhood physical and sexual abuse. Heterosexual and lesbian women share similar trauma from these experiences; however, the overall impact on lesbian lives will differ by virtue of their invisibility. Exclusionary practices in program funding, development, and implementation prohibit expansion of services for lesbians and contribute to the overwhelming oppression that lesbian women experience when their interactions with social services fail to recognize and address their unique needs. Current information on lesbian issues and services can be found online at < www.gaycanada.com>.

[*Andrea Daley* and
Anna Travers]

RELATED ENTRIES

Education in Social Work, Feminist Theory, Gay-Sensitive Services, Gender Issues, Natural Helping Networks, Mutual-Aid Societies, Parenting, Peer Counselling, Personal-Centred Theory, Self-Help Groups, Self Help & Mutual Aid, Sensitizing Concepts, Services for Women, Sexual Harassment, Sexual Minorities, Sexual Orientation, Sexual Problems & Services, Social Services, Social Work Profession, Theory & Practice, Women Abuse

life-model theory

The life-model theory of social work intervention emphasizes the exchanges between people and various aspects of their environment, and seeks to understand how various organisms, especially people, adapt to their environment. When exchanges between persons and their environment are positive, conditions supportive of adaptation emerge and, when they are negative, serious repercussions to persons occur. According to this theory, individual persons develop unique patterns of adjustment related to different historical times, patterns that are common to others growing up in similar times. Thus, people construct meanings within the historical and social times in which they develop. Throughout this development process, individuals meet stressors, which call into play patterns of responses that may be functional or dysfunctional. The life-model theory—principally developed by Dr. Carel Germain and Dr. Alex Gitterman in the 1970s—was the first social work theory to address the world of nature as an important aspect of a person's significant environment. The theory has continued to evolve in view of new developments in the theory itself and in practice.

The goal of life-model practice is to improve the fit between a person's perceived needs and capacities, and their support systems and resources. Under life-model theory, the way problems are defined by individuals affects what is to be done about them. Such stressors fall into three separate but inter-related types: different life transitions, pressures from the environment, and interpersonal difficulties. The skill of the practitioner drawing on this theory relates to deciding where and when to intervene in a client's stress-producing systems, necessitating the disciplined ability to make sensitive and responsive judgments about who the client is. To make such judgments, practitioners draw on expertise in gathering, organizing, and interpreting data, and assessing the changes occurring in a client's life. To organize and continually assess the client's reality, practitioners use schematic summaries of the presenting and changing reality. The social worker makes efforts to direct work with the client as well as with significant systems in the client's life. This approach to practice calls for a high integration between and among systems and methodologies from a perspective that builds on what is common and what is different in systems and methodologies. The life-model approach stresses, humanness, compassion, spontaneity, and individuality of practitioners, emphasizing the need to avoid a rote style of practice. This model has found considerable support among practitioners and instructors on practice methods in schools of social work. Life-model theory and practice reflects efforts at integrating methodologies and foci of intervention.

[*FJT*]

RELATED ENTRIES

Person-in-Environment Perspective, Theory & Practice

Dorothy Livesay (1909–96)

Livesay, Dorothy, poet, social worker, social activist; b. Oct. 12, 1909, Winnipeg, MB (of J.F.B. Livesay & Florence Randal); Governor General's Literary Award for Poetry, 1944, 1947; d. Dec. 27, 1996, Victoria, BC

Dorothy Livesay—poet, social worker, activist—studied modern languages at the University of Aix-Marseilles and graduated with a bachelor of arts from the University of Toronto in 1929. During postgraduate studies at the Sorbonne in Paris, where Livesay observed demonstrations against war, unemployment, and fascism, her already strong interest in social issues influenced her return to the University of Toronto in 1932 to study social work. As a social work student and already published poet, Livesay became involved with several progressive literary movements and joined the Communist Party as a way to help build a movement against war and fascism (Livesay 1991: 82). While working as a social work apprentice in Montreal, she encountered desperate families, who did not receive relief, and many unemployed people left powerless to fight evictions from their homes. This exposure prompted her involvement in demonstrations with the unemployed and against repressive political arrests by the Quebec government; however, during a sojourn as a social worker in a relief agency in New Jersey (1934–35) and appalled by overt racism experienced by Black Americans, Livesay first brought together her literary passions and her commitment to social justice. Livesay penned two of her most famous political poems, "The Outrider" and "Day and Night," the latter following Newfoundland poet E.J. Pratt's example in 1936; Desmond Pacey observed that, Pratt's poem "Day and Night," had caused a sensation: "Other poets ... in Canada had written social satire but this was the first poem by a Canadian unashamedly to preach social revolution" (Pacey 1957).

Livesay continued to practice social work professionally until 1937, when she married and was, therefore, compelled to quit her job at the Welfare Field Service in British Columbia, because of a policy that forbade married women to be employed in civil service jobs during the great depression of the 1930s. In the 1940s Livesay continued her career as an editor, journalist, poet, and educator. Foreshadowing second wave feminism,

Livesay's later poetry often focused on women's issues which, in her view, required a dual sense of interpersonal and social struggle rather than an individualistic focus (Moffatt 1995: 119). Livesay also understood the importance of international social involvement. In the early 1960s she worked as a teacher for UNESCO in Africa. In 1966 Livesay was awarded a master of education degree from the University of British Columbia and, in 1972, an honorary doctorate from the University of Waterloo. While most recognized for her work as a significant poet of her generation, Dorothy Livesay also left an important legacy for social workers. Her understanding of social change and social movements based on political struggle and work, personal engagement, lived experience, and personal relationships reveals a complex marrying of micro and macro intervention as a practice model (Moffatt 2000: 67). Her life and work reflect a rich and unique integration of personal responsibility and social change (Moffatt 1995: 1191). Livesay's concrete experience as a social worker and activist was an acknowledged source for her writing. In this light, her life is a reminder of the importance of the arts as a contributor to social justice.

[Suzanne Dudziak]

RELATED ENTRIES

Social Welfare Context, Social Welfare History

REFERENCES

Moffatt, Kenneth J. 1995 *Multiple Ways of Knowing: Social Work Knowledge and Ethics in the Technological Era.* Unpublished doctoral degree dissertation. Faculty of Social Work, University of Toronto.
———. 2000. *A Poetics of Social Work. Personal Agency and Social Transformation in Canada, 1920–1939.* Toronto: University of Toronto Press.
Pacey, Desmond. 1957. Introduction. *Selected Poems of Dorothy Livesay (1926–1956).* Toronto: Ryerson.

long-term care

Long-term care refers to a system of services and programs to address a broad range of health and housing for people of all ages. Core functions of long-term care programs include visiting professional health and personnel support services in a home or school to enable people with physical challenges to live as independently as possible, as well as facility-based care for people whose needs are best met in residential settings offering health and personal support round the clock. In general the provinces and territories are responsible for administration of long-term care services, most of which are mandated by the federal Canada Health Act. Certain aspects of residential long-term care, and some health aspects of home and ambulatory care are covered by extended-care services beyond the federal Act. For example, eligible clients can receive in-home services from a health-care professional, such as a nurse, social worker, or occupational therapist at no charge, while they may have to pay a per-diem rate for personal care services provided by community support workers. Similarly, persons living in a publicly funded care facility will not pay directly for costs of professional health services nor for medication, but will be expected to make per-diem payments toward "hospitality" expenses relating to accommodation, meals, and other optional but not medically essential services. (In British Columbia, for example, such per-diem charges range between $27 and $50). Significant in-home and residential long-term care is also provided by private, non-governmental operators, both for-profit and non-profit. Regardless of the basis for the service provision, operators must comply with regulations, standards, and licensing requirements set by provincial and territorial legislation. In private facilities, residents pay the full rate for services.

The presence and contribution of social work is evident across the continuum of long-term care. Practitioners work as members of multidisciplinary team employing a range of skills, knowledge, and expertise in government and private, in-home and congregate settings. At the direct service level, social workers frequently play a key role in assisting clients and families to adjust to the significant changes to daily living, to cope with chronic disease or condition management, and to make difficult decisions relating to terminal illness and palliative care. Long-term care lends itself well to social work practice that incorporates systems theory. As advocates and counsellors, social workers have the opportunity to engage with clients and their families on such practical matters as eligibility and application for funded services, determining and comparing costs, identifying entitlements, ascertaining private-pay options, and anticipating future care options. As administrators, social workers can exercise leadership at a macro scale to shape the development of service delivery, establish an environment in which colleagues, staff, clients, and families have chances to contribute to service delivery and future improvements, and to foster a supportive process for identifying and resolving concerns. Within long-term care, social workers also contribute to program planning and evaluation, and to policy development.

[*Wendy Carmichael*]

RELATED ENTRIES
Bereavement, Bioethical Issues, Caregiving, Clinical Social Work, Hospices, Managed Care, Palliative Care, Personal-Centred Theory, Practice Methods, Sensitizing Concepts, Social Welfare Context, Theory & Practice, Veterans Affairs Canada, Wellness

macro practice

Macro practice identifies social work that focuses on intervention within systems to bring about change perceived to be of benefit to society as a whole or to some targeted community within society. The scope of macro work is immense, ranging from work in small communities to meet an identified psychosocial need of particular citizens, to international issues that affect large numbers of people across geopolitical boundaries. Macro practice focuses on the formation, refinement, and changes of social policies at all levels of government. Competence in this kind of practice requires highly developed knowledge, understanding, and abilities to work effectively in political processes as well as in research (i.e., gathering, analyzing, and presenting data). Underlying these skills is the necessity for understanding the intricacies of intersystemic interaction. Canadian social workers over the decades have played major roles in macro practice, thereby influencing the development and refinement of the Canadian network of social security.

The term "macro practice" has come increasingly into use in the Canadian social work lexicon. Ongoing and sometimes acrimonious dialogue within the profession has attempted to promote the relative importance of practice at a macro scale compared to practice at a micro scale, and vice versa, rather than perceiving social work as a spectrum of practice, each facet of which has its intrinsic value. This debate is reflected in some curricula of faculties and schools of social work, where students are led or required to select one area of concentration over another. It is also reflected in the kinds of practica available for students and, often, in the kinds of positions available for graduates. Currently, the majority of persons seeking admissions to faculties and schools of social work tend to view social work from a micro perspective with the development of an interest in and commitment to macro practice emerging through the process of learning and direct experiences. One attempt to balance both macro and micro interests is a commitment to a generalist basis for the initial degree in social work, in keeping with the reality that much social work practice in Canada takes place in small communities (i.e., micro scale) and also needs competence in and commitment to systemic change (i.e., macro scale). Often knowledge and experience from micro practice provides insights for systemic issues need to be addressed within macro practice. Fortunately, the need for a comprehensive view of practice is reflected in a variety of social work legislation in all provinces and territories which to date have not identified separate competencies or separate bodies of knowledge for a specific concentration. Rather the legal emphasis is on the need to ensure for practitioners to be competent in the area in which he/she practices. Effective social workers recognize that micro and macro practice complement one another.

[*FJT*]

RELATED ENTRIES
Direct Practice, Generalist Practice, Indirect Practice, Mezzo Practice, Micro Practice, Theory & Practice

malpractice

From time to time, an individual social worker commits malpractice—that is, he/she acts in an unethical and harmful way in an intervention, either through lack of awareness or, much more rarely, malevolent intent. Only in very recent times have such unfortunate actions received much attention either within the profession or in society at large. Over the last century, social work has developed codes of ethics; the Canadian Association of Social Work has such a code, which is subject to periodic review, to which members are expected to follow. At the same time, however, the professions have developed little or no formal means to deal with allegations of violations of these codes (i.e., malpractice). Disciplinary action or release from employment for unethical conduct has generally been meted out by the agencies that employed the social workers who performed inappropriate behaviour. In very rare instances involving criminal activity, charges would be laid against the social worker. The conduct in such situations would have been assessed against agency or legal standards, rather than the profession's code of ethics. Further, practitioners operating consultancies either independently or in partnerships are not be subject to internal agency standards. In recent decades however, the profession's approach to accountability in the conduct of individual practitioners has changed, for several reasons. Social work has attained a higher profile within Canadian society, increasing contacts with the public and drawing on greater public expenditure and, thereby, attracting greater public scrutiny. The understanding of potential harm that inappropriate behaviour by social workers can do has increasingly become recognized. And the understanding of the rights of clients and social communities has grown to articulate concerns that previously remained inaudible, marginalized, or ignored. Further as each province has enacted legislation to control the practice of social work, complaint structures and review processes have emerged for publicizing and establishing procedures whereby complaints could be made and heard, and remedial or punitive action taken when malpractice has been found to have occurred. Contemporary society demands high levels of competence in the performance of human services and complementary accountability on the part of individual practitioners. The reality that social workers can be sued by clients on the basis of professional malfeasance or called before a professional or legislative tribunal is now more common. A concomitant reality is that many social workers now seek malpractice insurance.

While many allegations of malpractice on the part of social workers are found to be valid, many others are made without substance. To ensure protection of all parties concerned, the processes that have emerged to review and adjudicate allegations in provincial tribunals are complex and thorough, necessitating the use of lawyers and the incurring of significant administrative and legal costs. A particularly sensitive area with potential risks for abuse in social work practice relates to the nature of the relationship between social worker and client, particularly in micro work. Codes of conduct of various professional bodies are very explicit and detailed about appropriate and expected boundaries of professional conduct in this relationship. What constitutes appropriate competence in particular practice instances is a continuing area of study. As the profession assumes responsibility for more difficult psychosocial problems and as professional knowledge continues to expand rapidly, the challenge for each social worker to maintain an appropriate level of competence is daunting. The efforts must be fairly successful, however, as the record shows that—in spite of the greatly increased public interest in and response to malpractice by social workers in Canada—very few allegations of this type of unacceptable professional conduct have proven to be valid.

[FJT]

RELATED ENTRIES

Accountability, Bioethical Issues, Codes of Ethics, Ethics, Legal Issues, Professional Issues, Professional Liability, Recording

managed care

Managed care, as defined by the Canadian Managed Care Council (est. 1998), is "a process of quality integrated health, based on best evidence, which balances quality, access, and cost for the purpose of achieving optimum health for the individual" (Davis 1999: 22). In Canada the evolution of the concept of managed care has been subtler than it has in the United States, where it is a form of health care provision that is dependent on health maintenance organizations and preferred providers. Many people working in the delivery of health care services in Canada fear that their professions or legislators might move toward the US model of managed care. Because of its prevalence, the US model of health maintenance organizations has become synonymous with managed care; it has been subjected to a lot of undue criticism arising as a result of a few health care providers that place profit ahead of quality of service. A broader view of managed care, however, can embody a range of techniques and forms, including promotion of wellness, early disease identification, patient education, self-care, and financial incentives for providers. In a number ways, provincial and territorial health ministries have taken on many of the features of the US model of managed care, such as generic substitution and prior authorization, which have been used in Canada for several years to control costs associated with managed care. In the current dynamic environment, the private health insurance industry is beginning to use managed care techniques. In addition many of the major US providers of managed care are moving into Canada.

While the function of managed care may be slightly different in Canada, it is undoubtedly a model that is here to stay. A group of about twenty employers, insurers, academics, and pharmaceutical companies formed the Canadian Managed Care Council to monitor the evolution of managed care in Canada. Any time of change is a time of challenge, and some of the issues facing the social work profession as a result of the influence of managed care include:

- *the likelihood of competition for recognition by managed care providers*: The social work profession and various regulatory colleges will have to fight to retain their recognition within the managed care self-governance framework;
- *the promotion of managed care as a medical format*: with a primary focus on a medical model of healthcare delivery, physicians could play the role of gatekeepers, possibly reducing other professions to altered, secondary or tertiary status;
- *the potential for discrimination against small provider groups and sole practitioners*: economies of scale favour an increasing number of large providers to offer required services at lower cost and higher profit; and
- *the barriers statutory and regulatory prohibiting professional incorporation in some areas of the country and the limiting of cross-profession ownership of clinics*: Such prohibitions militate against the social work profession taking full

advantage of the transition to the managed care structure.

The transition to a managed care model of health care provision in Canada is inevitable. The social work profession must advocate for the interest of the profession while achieving governments' objectives in the public interest.

[*Peter Christian*]

RELATED ENTRIES

Canadian Association of Social Workers, Case Management, Integration of Services, Practice Methods, Theory & Practice, Wellness

REFERENCE

Davis, A. 1999. The Managed-care Solution. *Benefits Canada* October, 18–25.

Manitoba Association of Social Workers

The Manitoba Association of Social Workers is the voice of social workers in Manitoba, providing peer support to its members, links with social workers throughout the country, and a strong educative role for members as well as the public. Membership in the organization is open to persons holding a social work degree. It is also open to persons holding a welfare workers certificate from a Manitoba community college who have held a social service position for two years and provide relevant letters of recommendation. The association works closely with the Manitoba Institute of Registered Social Workers, with which it shares a common board of directors elected by the membership. This board sets policies, responds to social issues and carries out the work of the organization. Information about the Manitoba association and institute can be found online at < www.geocities.com/masw_mirsw>.

[*Dianne Cullen*]

RELATED ENTRIES

Canadian Association of Social Workers, Education in Social Work, International Federation of Social Workers, National Association of Social Workers (US), Provincial/Territorial Associations

Manitoba Institute of Registered Social Workers

The Manitoba Institute of Registered Social Workers is the regulatory arm of social work in

Manitoba responsible for certifying members and protecting the public through recognized ethical standards of practice. This body includes a disciplinary body to investigate complaints. Membership in the institute is open to persons practicing in social work and holding a social work degree from an accredited school of social work. Membership permits a member to practice as a Registered Social Worker / Travailleurs social enregistrés, and to use the designation "RSW" or "TSE" after their name. To maintain membership, registrants are required to maintain current knowledge through the completion of forty hours of continuing education. The organization works closely with the Manitoba Association of Social Workers, with which it shares a volunteer board of directors elected by the membership. The board sets policies and responds to social issues as well as conducting the business of the organization. With Manitoba Association of Social Workers, the institute is committed to the protection of the public in matters related to the practice of social work, to the support of members in relevant areas, and to social action. Information about the Manitoba institute and association can be found online at <www.geocities.com/masw_mirsw>.

[*Dianne Cullen*]

RELATED ENTRIES

Canadian Association of Social Workers, Education in Social Work, International Federation of Social Workers, National Association of Social Workers (US), Provincial/Territorial Associations

marital and family problems

Marriage breakdown occurs for many reasons, but a constant that has emerged from research is couples' inability to negotiate and solve ongoing problems without friction and negative feelings. Gottman and Silver say that some marriages work because the partners have "emotional intelligence and fondness and admiration for one another" that prevent the couple from being trounced by the four horsemen that spell doom for a marriage: "contempt, criticism, defensiveness and stonewalling" (1999: 65). The literature is clear that the odds of a marriage working and being rewarding for both parties depends on the maturity of one or both parties: not a new analysis, but some recent research is more specific. What determines the success or failure of a marriage depends on the balance of positive and negative interactions within the relationship. While in science a positive cancels out a negative, this is not so in marriages. Good working marriages function on the basis of positive emotional interactions and the ones that work best have at least five positive to one negative emotional incidents. Research demonstrates a phenomenon in marriage for how spouses think about the positive and negative actions in their partners. A partner in an unhappy marriage in some ways expects or anticipates negative behaviour from their spouse and when they get it, it reinforces their feelings and fears. Positive behaviour in unhappy marriages is treated with suspicion because the partner expects negative behaviour and thinks the positive behaviour is not going to last. In a happy marriage, a partner perceives negative behaviour as occasional and not lasting, while positive behaviour is seen as stable and internal to the partner. What the researchers conclude is that people who have a lot of emotional encumbrances from their past do not do well in marriages. Persons who as children experienced feelings of rejection from parents or parental figures without compensating feelings of caring and soothing, however, tend to feel unloved, rejected, and unsure of themselves. They may cope very well in temporary or superficial relationships but, when they become involved in an intimate, martial situation in a general sense their fears and needs are forced into the open and begin to have a deleterious effect on the relationship. People who have experienced rejection tend to look for faults and rejection in others as a protective measure, and suspect that things will go wrong for them. In some instances their expectation of being rejected is so strong that they unconsciously set people up to reject them. An insightful observer noted that the example of an anecdotal couple is "what's wrong 85 percent of the time in most marriages. If you consider yourself inadequate, you are always on the lookout for what is not there in yourself and your partner" (Gottman and Silver 1999: 264).

For couples who have children, marital problems usually become family problems. Family problems presented to family service agencies run the gamut of difficulties a family, couple, or individual faces at one time or another throughout his/her life. In a 1997 research project called "An

Assets Approach to Canadian Families," 75 percent of the clients presented one or more issues listed under the category of "family relationships and parenting." The most common problems presented were couple relationship, which made up 37 percent; health and disability affected 45 percent, and violence and abuse 39 percent. Other common issues included depression, parent/child problems, parenting, social relationships, divorce, and separation. "Poor" clients presented more issues than "non-poor" individuals (Michalski 1997). They are presented because the individual, couple, or family has not been able to resolve the situation satisfactorily themselves. Although family service agencies are only one segment of the many services to which a family might turn when confronted with a family crisis, they are representative throughout Canada of professional counsellors dedicated to assisting families, couples, and individuals for a wide range of family problems. Researchers have long studied what makes some families functional and some dysfunctional. Florence Hollis (1965) describes causes of interpersonal adjustment problems as:

> persisting infantile needs and drives may lead to exaggerated narcissistic needs, excessive dependence or hostility, fixations on early family figures, fear of separation and abnormalities in the expression of sexual and aggressive drives. [The breakdown in social adjustment may be caused by:] 1) infantile needs and drives left over from childhood which causes the individual to make inappropriate demands upon his adult world; 2) a current life situation which exerts excessive pressure upon him and 3) faulty ego and superego functioning.

Parad and Miller describe a family in individual crisis in terms of stress and threat: "1) the stress threatens important life goals such as health, securities or affectional ties, and 2) the threat posed by the stress appears impossible of immediate solution and overtaxes the immediate resources available to the ego" (1963: 146–47).

While family problems are as diverse as families, they usually have in common a degree of disruption in the family equilibrium, usually having to do with a conflict in interpersonal relations of members within the family or an outside influence which the family member(s) may not be able to deal with effectively. A publication of the Vanier

Institute on the Family states that "the family is universally recognized as the basic unit of society and continues to be the preferred structure for providing the emotional and material support that is essential to the development and well-being of its members" (Couchman & Ruffo 1994). Canadian families have undergone many changes in the past fifty years or so, the most significant being the increase of women in the work force, and of lone-parent families (Vanier Institute 1994: 3). The popularity of the common-law family in the early 1980s began to change the ways in which the family is structured and how it functions. The number of children born to married couples was still high in the early 1980s, but almost half of those couples had lived in common-law unions before marrying. About 13 percent of children of married couples who did not live together before marriage see their parents separate, while a startling 63 percent of children from unmarried common-law unions see their caregivers separate. The National Longitudinal Survey of children and youth indicates that for children in the six-to-eleven age range born to common-law parents in Ontario, the rate of family breakdown before the child is six years is 61 percent (Marcel Gratton 1999: 5–6). Each year more and more children are exposed to the break up of their parents at a younger age. Such statistics represent the immediate trauma and disruption of family members from abandonment, rejection, and lowering in standard of living. It should be said that the majority of children brought up in lone-parent homes grow up healthy; however, for those who exhibit poor developmental outcomes, the ingrained cumulative effects tend to show up when the adult becomes involved in an intimate "marital" relationship. There is also reasonably reliable evidence for the intergenerational transmission of divorce and, while it is not large, the trend does exist. It has been well-documented that parental breakup creates a variety of problems for the child, usually involving trust, attachment, and low self-image: "In terms of their health, behaviour, academic achievement and relationship, lone-parent children are distinguished by more negative scores than the general population" (Ross, Roberts, & Scott 1999: 15). Wallerstein and Blakesee indicate that even the most competent parent may experience "a diminished capacity to parent" (1989: 122). How families adjust to the various changes occurring in society is hard to say, but it is to be hoped that family social workers can help families to diminish the negative effects on children from family problems. Canadian families have encountered and handled with many challenges over the years and, no doubt, they will continue to change and adapt to the opportunities and demands of the future.

[*Frank MacDonald*]

RELATED ENTRIES

Aboriginal Issues, Abortion, Abuse, Addiction, Bullying, Crisis Intervention, Family Demographics, Family Research, Family Services Canada, Family Statistical Patterns, Family Therapy, Parenting, Peer Counselling, Poverty, School Social Work, Separation & Divorce, Services for Families, Sexual Problems & Services, Single Parents, Vanier Institute for the Family, Women Abuse, Wellness

REFERENCES

Couchman, R., and A. Ruffo. 1994. *Canadian Families.* Ottawa: The Vanier Institute of the Family.
Gottman, J. 1993. *What Predicts Divorce?* Mahwah, NJ: Lawrence Erlbaum Associates.
———. 1994. *The Family Therapy Networker.* May/June.
Gottman, J., and N. Silver. 1999. *The Seven Principles for Making Marriage Work.* New York: Three Rivers Press.
Hollis, F. 1965. *Casework, A Psychosocial Therapy.* New York: Random House.
Marcel Gratton, N. 1999. Growing Up with Mom and Dad? *Transitions.*[The Vanier Institute of the Family]. Spring.
Michalski, J. 1999. *Family Service Canada's Outcomes Project and Study of Family Strengths.* Ottawa: Canadian Policy Research Networks.
Parad, H., and R. Miller (Eds.) 1963. *Ego-Oriented Caseworks: Problems and Perspectives.* New York: Family Service Association of America.
Ross, D., P. Roberts, and C. Scott. 1999. Facts about Children of Lone Parents. *Transitions* [The Vanier Institute of the Family]. Spring.
Wallerstein, J., and S. Blakesee. 1989. *Second Chances: Men, Women, and Children a Decade after Divorce.* New York: Ticknor and Fields.
Vanier Institute for the Family. 1994. *What Matters for Canadian Families.* Ottawa: The Institute.

Leonard Marsh (1906–82)

Marsh, Leonard, social work occupations; b. Sept. 24, 1906, London, UK; d. May, 10, 1982, Vancouver, BC

Leonard Marsh was an empiricist with a strong pragmatic bent toward factual inquiry. During the great depression, Marsh was director of social research for the pioneering program, Research in the Social Sciences, at McGill University (1931–41) that focused on the crushing unemployment of the time. He suggested that unemployment should be treated by social welfare investigators as a subject for research rather than a subject for protest. Marsh had received his undergraduate education at the University of London in England, and attained a PhD in economics at McGill University in 1940. He published two books—*Health and Unemployment* (1938) and *Canadians In and Out of Work: A Survey of Economic Classes and Their Relation to the Labour Market* (1940)—that reflect the influence of England's William Beveridge, whose report ushered in the British welfare state. Marsh then became research adviser (1941–44) for the federal government's advisory committee on post-war reconstruction; there, he produced the document for which he is best known: his 1943 *Report on Social Security for Canada.* Marsh's report—which historian Michael Bliss calls "the most important single document in the history of the development of the welfare state in Canada" (1975: ix)—advocated a comprehensive social insurance program to be complemented by social assistance and children's allowances. For Marsh, the outcome of his detailed and comprehensive report would be "to lay the foundation of a social minimum" (1975: ix).

Leonard Marsh was very much a person of the enlightened modernity of his time; he believed that successful methods developed by the natural sciences could be refashioned for an assault on social problems. "The task of social engineering," he wrote in *Employment Research: An Introduction to the McGill Programme of Research in the Social Science* (1935), "demands the same scientific attitude and the same systematic appeal to facts." Social research needed to be encouraged in universities, including schools of social work, which he was optimistic could attract young people who would be trained to bring the approach and attitudes of the scientist "into alliance with their enthusiasm for social improvement and reform" (Marsh 1935: xi). Adopting a scientific approach to social problems did not, Marsh maintained, mean that one would be unsympathetic to the plight of those studied; in his view, a factual survey provided "the best foundation for the construction and the advocacy of improvements and reforms" (Marsh 1935: x). Many of his proposals were imbued with Keynesian thinking. He was also a great admirer of William Beveridge and had profited from reading Beveridge's seminal work, *Unemployment: A Problem of Industry* (1909, 1930), where the argument was made that "distress through want of employment is not a temporary but chronic evil." Anticipating in his own book, published in 1940, the recommendations he would make three years later, Marsh urged that a progressive and direct approach to the problem of inequitable distribution of income should be the establishment of a national system of social insurance. Legislation of this kind would, Marsh argued, begin to deal with the risks of unemployment, sickness, old age, and disability. From 1944 to 1946, Marsh worked for United Nations RRA, initially as an adviser on social welfare, then as a senior information officer. After his UN work, Marsh served as director of research at the University of British Columbia School of Social Work and, from 1966 until his retirement in 1972, he was a professor of educational sociology in the university's Faculty of Education. Throughout his life, Marsh maintained a firm belief that human beings were co-operative and he worried about the encroachment of "rampant individualism." He never lost his faith in the ability of, and need for, government to intervene in the social and economic life of society to blunt the sharp edges of unrestrained capitalism. Not long after Marsh's death one of his greatest admirers, York University historian Michiel Horn, wrote: "As a person Leonard earned affection and respect; as a social scientist and reformer he deserves our continued attention" (1986: 75).

[*Allan Irving*]

RELATED ENTRIES

W.H. Beveridge, Demographics, Income Security, Social Welfare Context, Social Welfare History

REFERENCES

Bliss, M. 1975. Preface to L. Marsh, *Report on Social Security.* University of Toronto. [Reissue of 1942 report.]

Horn, M. 1986. Leonard Marsh and His Ideas, 1967–1982: Some Personal Recollections. *Journal of Canadian Studies* 21,2.

Marsh, L. 1935. *Employment Research: An Introduction to the McGill Programme of Research in the Social Science.* Toronto: Oxford University Press.

Marsh Report

The 1943 *Report on Social Security for Canada* by Leonard Marsh was pivotal to planning for the post-war era, which began long before the Second World War ended. Indeed, an important part of the strategy for winning the war was the formulation and proclamation of plans for a far better world than people everywhere had experienced during the depression before the outbreak of war in 1939. Canada began the planning process with the establishment, early in 1941, of the Committee on Post-war Reconstruction, with Leonard Marsh as research director. Marsh had outstanding credentials and a precedent in Sir William Beveridge's 1942 report, *Social Insurance and Allied Services*, which represented post-war planning at its most creditable. Beveridge's report presented a social security plan for post-war Britain, outlining detailed plans for security "from the cradle to the grave" that captured worldwide attention. The Beveridge Report "created a sensation in Canada," in the words of Dennis Guest, and led to the decision to develop a Canadian equivalent and the assignment of this task to Leonard Marsh. The creation of the Marsh report was described by George Davidson in *Canadian Welfare* as "largely the product of a single man's mind." Marsh, himself, however, acknowledged the assistance of three outstanding social work leaders: Bessie Touzel, Stuart Jaffary, and George Davidson himself. The report made the case for the provision of at least a minimum subsistence budget for every Canadian family and a preference for a "desirable living" minimum budget. And, having outlined a defensible standard of living below which no Canadian family should be allowed to fall, the report offered proposals for meeting the principal contingencies that characterize industrial society. The most immediately significant proposal of the report was the case it made for a universal system of family allowances. Marsh described family allowances as "the key to consistency" in a comprehensive social security program. The Liberal government of Mackenzie King expressed its support for the report as a whole and seized on family allowances as the component it would adopt immediately. The promise of cash allowances—payments to every Canadian family with children—may well have won for the Liberal government the election of 1945. In proposing a universal program that required no test of means, need, or income, the Marsh report introduced the "demogrant model," that would be followed in later years in the old age security and youth allowance programs. The main proposals in the Marsh report, which formed an integral part of the proposals outlined in the comprehensive post-war reconstruction plans of 1945, lived on through the succeeding years when Canada attained the status of a welfare state.

[*Richard Splane*]

RELATED ENTRIES
W.H. Beveridge, Great Depression (1930s), Income Security, B. Touzel, Social Welfare Context, Social Welfare History

Paul Martin (1903–92)*

Martin, Paul Joseph James, politician, statesman; b. at Ottawa, June 23, 1903; d. at Windsor, Sept. 14, 1992

First elected to the House of Commons in 1935. Martin quickly took a prominent place in Liberal ranks because of his impressive educational background in philosophy, international relations and law. Prime Minister King appointed him parliamentary assistant to the Minister of Labour in 1943. He entered Cabinet in 1945 as secretary of state, and in 1946 became Minister of National Health and Welfare (now Health Canada). Faced with a government becoming increasingly conservative on social issues, Martin managed to introduce a system of health grants and, by threatening resignation, made Prime Minister St. Laurent accept national health insurance. He also undertook diplomatic assignments for the King and St. Laurent governments. In 1955 he negotiated an agreement that allowed the expansion of United Nations membership. Martin ran unsuccessfully for the Liberal leadership in 1948 and 1958. In 1963 Prime Minister Pearson appointed Martin secretary of state for external affairs, a portfolio he held until 1968, when he tried again for the leadership but lost to Pierre Trudeau. He was appointed government leader in the Senate (1968–74) and high commissioner to Britain

(1975–79). His memoirs, *A Very Public Life*, have been published in two volumes (1983, 1986).

[*John R. English*]

*Used unedited by permission from *The Canadian Encyclopedia*. 2000. Toronto: McClelland and Stewart.

RELATED ENTRIES
Health Canada

materialistic theory

The most familiar current-day materialist theory is historical materialism, the social-scientific method of Marxism. "The object is not only to understand the world, but to change it," said Karl Marx who, with Frederick Engels, worked out the analytical and practical methods of historical materialism. Human beings were seen as products of their environments, as well as of their human activities to take control of that environment. Owning or not owning the means to produce goods, relating to other people, and reacting to the elements create interests that divide people into social and economic classes; in Marxist terms, the struggle between and among those classes are explained as the means and goals human beings choose when they intervene in the material conditions of life. Historical materialism represents an advance along the path from determinism to human discretion to conscious human intervention in the physical and social world.

Materialist theory has a 2500-year history and trajectory beginning in India and Greece. The most direct influence in North America comes from Greek and German philosophical roots, where it was presented as a repudiation of idealism. Democritus, a deterministic materialist, is referred to as an "atomist" because he pointed out the fundamental material unit of life known in his time, the atom, and he saw the atom acting in mechanical ways. Human beings were viewed as subject to the same forces. Epicurus later put forth the view that, as atoms surrounded by other atoms respond to each other, they therefore have self-determination. Extrapolating from this idea, human beings engage in complex interactions, make decisions, and have relationships that are not predetermined but are open to differentiation, innovation, novelty, and discretion. This advance in a theoretical comprehension of the world laid the groundwork for a modern understanding of the human being in a complex universe. Materialist theory thus opens the way for a scientific knowledge of the environment, and explains how human beings have freedom to engage in quests for their own ends. Yet, this theory is not a description of a thing, as a given; rather it is a theory that explains how to deal with the never-ending process of birth, growth, building, dissolution, decay, and rebirth. Remaking the world anew is seen as the quality of human life. Materialist theory, like any other theory, is confronted with contending theories. Late twentieth-century alternatives to materialist theory have come from postmodernism—end-of-history, and chaos theories, among others—some of which mark a return to more deterministic or idealistic positions. Other theories lean toward ideas that knowing has limits, or that knowing is not possible in a scientific or practical sense: these are positions that materialism theorists continue to debate as they did in earlier era.

[*Ken Collier*]

RELATED ENTRIES
Theory & Practice

Nellie McClung (1873–1951)

McClung, Nellie Letitia née Mooney, social reformer, political activist, suffragist, MLA (AB); b. Oct.20, 1873, Chatsworth, Grey County, ON; m. Robert Wesley McClung, 1896; five children; d. Sept. 01, 1951, Victoria, AB

Nellie McClung was a leading activist and social reformer in the Canadian public domain during the first half of the twentieth century. She spent her early childhood in Grey County, Ontario, until her family moved to rural Manitoba. In school she developed a love of literature and independent thinking. Trained as a schoolteacher, she taught in rural and small town schools in Manitoba. In 1896 she married Wesley McClung and they had five children. A prominent suffragist and activist in the women's rights movement, McClung's feminist consciousness had bloomed early in her life as she recognized the arbitrary limits imposed on girls and women. Her deep spiritual beliefs also underpinned her lifelong work for social justice. Like many women of her time, she supported both maternal feminism and egalitarian feminism. She eloquently argued for women's rights in her six-

teen books, the best known of which is *In Times Like These*, a collection of suffrage and prohibition speeches published in 1915. This book and the major part of her writings were aimed at seeking changes for the status of women in the country as well as other needed social reforms in such areas as public health and prison reforms. As a writer, recitalist, and public speaker of national and international renown, McClung gave readings and public addresses that focused on improving rural living for women, children, and families, and educating others about her ideas for social reform. As a suffragist, both her pen and her political acumen helped secure the vote for women, first in Manitoba. She and other supporters of the Political Equality League, Manitoba's main women's suffrage organization, attended the Liberal convention; it was the first time in Canada that women addressed a political assembly and they played a key role in the Manitoba election campaign of 1914. Although not then a member of the Liberal party, McClung supported the Liberals for their position on suffrage and prohibition. She challenged the Conservative position that held women immigrants as ignorant and therefore undeserving of electoral franchise. The Conservatives under Roblin did win the 1914 election, but Roblin resigned soon afterward and another election was called for 1915. Although McClung was living in Alberta at that time, she returned to Manitoba to give election speeches. The Liberals won and, on January 28, 1916, the women of Manitoba became the first Canadian women to win the right to vote in provincial elections and hold provincial office. A pre-eminent suffragist, popular author, and orator with a social conscience, Nellie McClung was herself elected, becoming a Liberal member of the Alberta legislature (1921–26). In Edmonton, the Famous Five—McClung and Emily Murphy, Irene Parlby, Louise McKinney, and Henrietta Muir Edwards—launched the *Persons Case*; led by Emily Murphy, the five Alberta feminists petitioned the Supreme Court to clarify the term "persons" in section 24 of the British North America Act, 1867 (now Constitution Act, 1867) to determine whether women were eligible to sit in the Senate. The group appealed the decision to the Judicial Committee of the Privy Council in England and, in a landmark decision on October 18, 1929, the Privy Council defined the word "persons" as including both women and men, thereby enabling women to serve in the Canadian Senate. This decision had implications for the public position of women throughout the British empire. McClung was a Canadian delegate to the League of Nations in 1938, and became the first woman appointed to the board of governors of the Canadian Broadcasting Corporation (1936–42).

During her life, Nellie McClung advocated for old age pensions, compulsory education laws, regulations to improve housing for immigrants, laws to protect women's property rights, public health measures, and better working conditions in factories. McClung was also active in the Women's Christian Temperance Union, a prohibition society; as an expression of the religious and social ferment of the social gospel movement, the Women's Christian Temperance Union formed a central part of small town social and cultural life and supported general social reforms such as women's suffrage and mothers' allowances. She was concerned about the treatment of immigrants, the plight of Jewish refugees, and the denial of civic and other citizen rights to Japanese Canadians. McClung argued for collective approaches to such social issues as medical care for all regardless of ability to pay and location, and rural laundry and child care co-operatives. She believed that government had a fundamental role to play in ensuring the well-being of citizens and the equitable distribution of wealth.

[*Norma Jean Profitt*]

RELATED ENTRIES

Feminist Theory, Human Rights, E. Murphy, I. Parlby, Social Welfare History, Women's Christian Temperance Union

McGill University School of Social Work

The McGill University School of Social Work was born in 1918 from academic and community interests in developing scientific techniques to help improve poor social conditions in Montreal, which had been intensified by the First World War. The precedent had been set four years earlier by McGill's academic rival, the University of Toronto. Planning a federation of all city social welfare institutions, Anglophone leaders in Montreal looked to

McGill to provide training and research for its personnel. Most social workers in the city had come from the United States and, typically, returned after a few years' service. McGill's new Department of Social Work established was supported in part by the Department of Theology, whose students attended its courses during their professional training. The first director, John Howard Toynbee Falk, was an Englishman who had trained in the Oxford settlement house movement and the Fabian Society, whose ancestors had been social workers. Falk believed that a social work program should be composed of two elements: a theoretical basis of casework and practical fieldwork. Four students enrolled in that first year. In addition to their academic studies, they had conversations with the director in the mornings and spent the afternoons in fieldwork. As well as his educational responsibilities, Falk advocated on behalf of and, in 1920, was appointed director of the Montreal Council of Social Agencies. The new social work department at McGill had too few students, was running a deficit, and was under pressure from the theological college for more theoretical content, especially sociology. A university committee—of which Stephen Leacock was a member—recommended the establishment of a new department of sociology, whose director would also be responsible for the training of social workers. Falk resigned. In 1923 the McGill School of Social Work was founded with director Carl Dawson, recruited from the influential University of Chicago, who also maintained his appointment in sociology. In 1925 he became head of the first Department of Sociology at McGill (and in Canada); his work established sociology as a scientific discipline in Canada. Dawson emphasized empirical research, believing that solutions to social problems would emerge from scientific investigation. Social work students were encouraged to combine a master's degree in sociology with their professional training. A tension arose within the social work school between research-oriented sociologists and social workers who believed that the school should focus on the teaching of professional skills. For advice, Dawson turned to two alumni, who suggested the establishment of a graduate school offering a master's of social work degree following a bachelor of arts or science; instead, the board of governors decided to close the school at the end of the 1931/32 session. The Department of Sociology survived, owing in part to its participation in the interdisciplinary social science research project funded by a major grant from the Rockefeller Foundation; the project hired Leonard Marsh, an economist from the London School of Economics and a protégé of William Beveridge. The research generated under Marsh's guidance became an important foundation for social welfare programs in Canada after the Second World War.

Social work alumni of McGill's defunct department rallied to respond to its eviction from the university, keeping alive training programs for professional social workers in Montreal from 1933 until 1950. With nine students in 1933, they convinced McGill to give them rent-free premises and library access, and they persuaded members of the academic staff to teach; they financed the school through student fees, agency grants for contracted students, membership subscriptions, and donations. The list of trustees and subscribers in a progress report (1933–40) reads like a who's who of Anglophone Montreal, a testament to the effectiveness of alumni advocacy. A product of Anglophone and mostly Protestant Montreal, the school nevertheless began to attract francophone students, who had to obtain the diocesan bishop's consent to attend. Calling this program the Montreal School of Social Work, they offered a two-year professional course to graduates of approved universities. By 1940 fifty-three students had registered from ten Canadian universities; conditions were not ideal, however, as the school premises, which were shared with the nursing students, were neglected and so cold that students wore their outdoor clothing in class. The demand for qualified social workers continued to increase beyond the school's ability to fill it. Dorothy King, the director who guided the school through the difficult depression and war years, was a woman of dynamic spirit and dedication. Trained in England and the United States, King maintained high scholastic standards at the school and recruited high-calibre teachers from the university and community; Frank R. Scott, for instance, taught social legislation. In 1939 the school met the academic and budgetary conditions for admission into the American Association of Schools of Social Work (now, US Council on Social Work Educa-

tion). In 1945 with no change in curriculum, the university allowed the school to present its students for bachelor's and master's of social work degrees. Finally, in 1950, owing to efforts by King and other community leaders, negotiations with McGill principal, R. Cyril James, led to the school's readmission to McGill. The board of governors resumed responsibility for its operation, with a full-time staff of one and 150 students.

The next twenty-five years were an expansive period for the school, established in the Faculty of Graduate Studies and Research, under the direction of Dr. John J.O. Moore (1950–66). Faculty were recruited, community development programs were initiated, and anti-poverty groups organized; the school also expanded its commitment to international activities and development of knowledge appropriate to a fledgling profession. Dr. David Woodsworth, nephew of J.S. Woodsworth, oversaw the expansion into undergraduate programs during his directorship (1966–76). The school introduced a bachelor of social work program in 1969/70, one of the first in Canada, added a special bachelor of social work in 1975, and changed the two-year master's program to one year. An interdisciplinary program was arranged, an employment assistance program for industry was introduced and an inter-university research centre on social policy was established; the curriculum was reorganized to reflect these changes. These were turbulent years in Quebec, especially in Montreal, and the school struggled with its focus as an English program in a primarily French environment. Ideological differences that surfaced in the school during this period characterized debate for many years afterward. From the late 1970s, a period of retrenchment for all universities began, during which the directors of the school were confronted with severe budget cuts despite increasing enrolment: Myer Katz (1977–87), Peter Leonard (1987–91), Frank Gilly (1991–95), William Rowe (1995–2002), and Estelle Hopmeyer (acting, 2002–04). Nevertheless, staff continued to launch new initiatives for such social issues as multiculturalism, interpersonal violence, adoption, group work, disabilities, children at risk, and human rights advocacy training. A database on Canadian ethnic communities was created. A family violence clinic was founded. The curriculum was modified to include issues relating to changing social realities (e.g., loss and bereavement, ageing, HIV/AIDS, physical challenges, international social work, feminism, and anti-racism and anti-oppressive perspectives). Fieldwork training centres were diversified.

In 1987, the first chair in social work—named after Philip Fisher, a strong supporter of the school and social work education—was endowed with a $1.5-million grant from the Southam Foundation. A year later, two research centres were opened: one for applied family studies (through a grant from the Southam Foundation supplemented by a major bequest from an alumnus) and one for loss and bereavement. The McGill Couple and Family Clinic was established in 1995 and, in 1997, the first joint international initiative—the McGill Middle East Program in Civil Society and Peacebuilding—was developed in partnership with Israel, Jordan, and Palestine to provide graduate training in social work toward improvement of living conditions of the poor and disadvantaged in those countries. Project Interaction was established in 1998 as a service for gays, lesbians, and two-spirited persons. In 2002 six Indonesian students began graduate training in social work, under the auspices of the Indonesian Social Equity Project of the State Institute of Islamic Studies and the Canadian International Development Agency. The school is also an active participant in the new interdisciplinary master's program being established in Indonesia.

New degree programs have continued to evolve. Certificate programs were created to train northern and Aboriginal social workers. A joint master's of law and social work was designed for students with an interest in professional social work, family law, and human rights. Two doctoral programs were established: a bilingual joint program in conjunction with l'Université de Montréal in 1996, and an *ad personam* program in 1997. A continuing education program, developed from funds raised by alumni, was inaugurated for the school's seventy-fifth anniversary in 1993. Responding to 2002 legislation in Quebec that established professional credentials for marriage and family therapists, the school began discussions to develop a master's program to train such practitioners. The McGill School of Social Work has been and continues to be a major contributor to the field of social work in Canada, with its extensive research opportunities, an enrolment of more than 325 students in its various programs, field placement in diverse settings, and the awarding of more than 4,500 diploma throughout its history. It has been a vigorous journey since the first four students in social work met each morning with Mr. Falk. Current information on the McGill school can be found online at <www.mcgill.ca/socialwork/>.

[*Joan Keefler* and *William Rowe*]

RELATED ENTRIES

Aboriginal Services, W.H. Beveridge, Council on Social Work Education (US), Education in Social Work, Employee Assistance Programs, Faculties of Social Work, L. Marsh, Marsh Report, I. Munroe-Smith, F.R. Scott, J.S. Woodsworth

Agnes Macphail (1890–1954)

Macphail, Agnes Campbell, politician, teacher, social reformer; b. Mar. 24, 1890 at Proton Township, Grey County, ON; first woman elected to Canadian Parliament; d. Feb. 13, 1954 at Toronto, ON

Agnes Macphail was Canada's first woman to be elected to the House of Commons (1921–40), and Ontario's first female Member of the Legislature Assembly (1943–45, 1948–51). Following early training as a schoolteacher, Macphail entered federal politics in 1921 at the age of thirty-one as a representative of the United Farmers of Ontario. She spoke continually on the concerns and challenges faced by farmers and members of the working class. She was elected for three subsequent terms as an Independent candidate, until the 1940 election, when she was defeated, perhaps in part to a major snowstorm that prevented voter turnout. She then became the first woman to be elected to the Ontario legislature, where she sat twice as a Co-operative Commonwealth Federation party member. Recognized for her significant contributions to reforms in Canadian prisons, Macphail advocated for segregation, useful work and wages, trained guards, attendant psychiatrists, and a parole system, and demanded that a Royal commission be formed to look into conditions within which prisoners were living. She was instrumental in the creation of the Elizabeth Fry Society in Toronto, serving as honorary president. An avid supporter of and contributor to the co-operative movement in Canada, she sought equal opportunities for women in political parties and government. Macphail also spoke out strongly in favour of disarmament, reduced military spending, and international peace initiatives. In 1929 she was a Member of the Assembly of the League of Nations, where she was inspired by a speech made by President Jane Adams. Later, Macphail helped to establish equal pay for equal work for men and women in Ontario, and contributed to changes in the age at which people become eligible for old age pensions, as well as in the establishment of assistance for "war widows, and services to support citizens with disabilities. In a March 1993 pamphlet from the Agnes Macphail Recognition Committee, Charlotte Whitton called Macphail "The most important woman in public life that Canada has produced in the twentieth century."

[*Linda M. Turner*]

RELATED ENTRIES

Services for Offenders, Social Welfare History, United Farmers of Ontario

medication

Medication is increasingly becoming part of practice for social workers employed in mental health and psychiatric programs. Although always part of the working world of physicians, nurses, pharmacists, and other health care professionals, familiarity with medications has not traditionally been part of social work practice. This scenario is changing dramatically as social work practice in mental health programs becomes a key element in the multidisciplinary treatment of people with mental illnesses. Use of psychotropic drugs has long been a cornerstone in the treatment of psychiatric disorders and, sometimes, a variety of other mental health problems—but not without marked differences of professional opinion as to the efficacy of such treatments. Social workers are increasingly having to understand the use of psychotropic drugs as part of their client's overall treatment to ensure that the best possible options are available to the individuals in their care. A requirement of social work staff in most mental health programs, whether in-patient, outpatient, or community-based, is that they have a working knowledge of the main classifications of psychotropic drugs, including indications and contraindications for use, anticipated results, and

main side effects. This general working knowledge of pharmacology is important, as, by virtue of the frequency and intensity of the therapeutic relationship through a range of case management services, the social worker often monitors an individual's response to medication. It may also be the social worker, as part of their advocacy on behalf of clients, who asks a physician to consider the trial use of a medication or, conversely, to review the decision related to medication because of continuing problems with a client's response or noncompliance.

The treatment of people with mental illness underwent its most revolutionary change during the 1950s and early 1960s with the advent of psychotropic drugs to provide symptomatic treatment and improvement in the overall quality of life, beginning with antipsychotic drugs (i.e., chlorpromazine) and antidepressant drugs (i.e., amitriptyline). These discoveries led to the start of the exodus of people with mental illnesses from institutional settings and the accompanying development of community treatment models. Medications made it easier to treat individuals at home and in the community, which in turn, reinforced their connections with family and community as vital forces in their lives. When symptoms persist over time, do not seem to be responding to a person's own attempts to restore stability (e.g., proper nutrition, fitness, lifestyle, psychotherapy), and directly impede the person's overall level of functioning on cognitive, emotional, and behavioural levels, then the use of medication is an appropriate consideration. Considerable evidence indicates that the most effective treatment of clinical depression, for example, is a combination of antidepressant medication and psychotherapy—particularly cognitive-behavioural—to reduce the symptoms, then either medication or psychotherapy alone. The use of medication to treat psychiatric disorders continues to raise questions. As helpful as medication can be with initial and ongoing symptom relief, numerous mental health professionals continue to challenge the need for such interventions, arguing that this type of treatment is invasive, sometimes punitive, and prone to overuse and abuse. Many social workers may question the efficacy and even the ethics of administering drugs to change the way an individual thinks or feels, while many others advocate for the introduction of medication as part of a client's course of treatment. Social workers may find themselves on either side of medical arguments in terms of in relation to a particular client, or the use of psychotropic drugs.

Psychotropic drugs are generally classified into six primary categories: mild tranquillizers (e.g., Valium™, Ativan™, Xanex™, Buspar™); neuroleptics (formerly referred to as major tranquillizers or antipsychotic drugs (e.g., Risperdal®, Haldol®, Zyprexa®, Clozaril®); antidepressants (e.g., Prozac®, Paxil®, Rameron™, Effexor®); mood stabilizers (e.g., lithium carbonate, valproic acid, Epival®, Neurontin®); stimulants (e.g., Ritalin®, Dexadrine®); and antiparkinsonian agents for the treatment of side effects related to some of the preceding drugs (e.g., Cogentin®, Modicate®). As with any medication, these drugs may produce side effects, which usually arise a shortly after the first use, in much the same way that an allergic reaction might follow use of certain antibiotics. Side effects are usually grouped under such headings as anticholinergic effects (i.e., dry mouth, blurred vision, sweating), central nervous system effects (i.e., drowsiness, insomnia, excitement, confusion), extrapyramidal effects (i.e., fine tremor), cardiovascular effects (i.e., dizziness, arrhythmia), or such other more general effects as nausea, rash, weight gain, and sexual dysfunction. Additionally, long-term use of some neuroleptic medication may result in other conditions (e.g., tardive dyskinesia) characterized by involuntary movements of mouth, tongue, or hands. In general the most frequent reason for discontinuing the use of medication is a person's inability to tolerate side effects, which they perceive as problematic. Other reasons for discontinuing medication include, ironically, a favourable response with marked improvement in functioning to the point where clients decide they no longer require the drugs or, conversely, the perception that the medication is simply not helping. A problem associated with these scenarios is that, often, clients make the decision to stop using the medications without communicating this decision to their caregivers. The cost of medications may preclude compliance on the part of numerous people—not because they do not want or cannot benefit from the medication, but simply because they cannot afford them and do not have access to a drug plan which would cover these costs in whole or in part. A social worker may need to advocate on behalf of a client without the means to purchase medication that is an essential part of his/her overall treatment.

One reality of mental health treatment today is that it is becoming more difficult for individuals in need to have timely psychosocial or psychiatric assessment, particularly if their condition is not at the point of requiring hospitalization; as such, family or emergency physicians increasingly have the responsibility for making a provisional diagnosis and beginning treatment. It is often at this point that referrals are made for treatment to continue through a community mental health program, and that a social worker first picks up the case to complete an intake screening, comprehensive assessment, and development of appropriate treatment plans. Social workers can also help clients to obtain crucial and current information about the medication they are prescribed, to make an informed decision about using or continuing to use them. Most pharmaceutical firms now produce written and video information about an illness (e.g., depression, manic depression or bipolar disorder, anxiety, schizophrenia) and symptoms being treated by a particular medication as teaching aids for clients and family members; these are now generally factual, without a focus on a specific medication being promoted by the company that produced the information. In additional, pharmacists can be particularly helpful in supplying written information about the various medications clients use, listing symptoms for which use of the medication is appropriate, any side effects, and matters related to compliance. One situation with ethical dimensions that social workers see increasing is clients being overmedicated or inappropriately medicated on multiple combinations ("cocktails") of drugs, seemingly prescribed somewhat indiscriminately. Social workers can consider asking a physician to review the medication, or explain the use of multiple medications, perhaps commenting that the use of certain drugs seems problematic for the client This is not without some risk, particularly to interprofessional relations, if such questions or remarks are perceived as challenging a physician's authority, and beyond the social worker's frame of reference. However, should the circumstances seem appropriate without disrupting the smooth functioning of the multidisciplinary clinical team. Ideally, all information about treatment should be reviewed openly. Social workers may also encounter clients who abuse their medications by non-compliance with recommended dosages, or who ingest them in quantity as a means of self-injury or suicide; as one of the community treatment teams who is responsible for distributing the medication on any particular day, the social worker may be directly involved. The extent of the social worker's responsibility, however, is simply to take the professional precautions that are appropriate, not to ensure client compliance with medication nor to prevent an abuse of the medication. Where a practitioner has concern about client compliance or safety, in an effort to minimize risk, the social worker could negotiate with the client's physician to prescribe medication(s) one week at a time, and with local pharmacies to dispense medication(s) every few days or even daily.

The role of social work in mental health programs, particularly those that are community-based, continues to become more complex. One aspect of that complexity is the need to understand the use of psychotropic drugs in the overall spectrum of treatment services. With this increased understanding—and the increased comfort level that such understanding fosters—the social worker can become an even more pivotal player in multidisciplinary teams because of their well-defined role in client and systemic advocacy.

[*Brian R. Adams*]

RELATED ENTRIES

Addiction, Bioethical Issues, Clinical Social Work, Pharmacological Therapy, Psychotropic Medication, Substance Addiction, Therapy, Treatment

meditation

Meditation can be defined as, "any activity that keeps the attention pleasantly anchored in the present moment" (Meditation 2000), with the goal of help a person to come to know him/herself physically, emotionally, mentally and spiritually (Yoga and Meditation 2000). While meditation has been practised for centuries in many societies as a way to change and perfect the human being (Engel 1997), its early development was rooted in the spiritual traditions of Hinduism, Buddhism, Judaism, Christianity, and Islam (Meditation 2000). Forms of meditation that developed and moved through countries now known as India, Tibet, China, and Japan tend to be older and more varied in method (Engel 1997). Forms of meditation that arose in civilizations around the Mediterranean Sea—mainly Judaism, Christianity, and Islam—emphasized the handing down of experiences based on beliefs and looking into the soul to develop inner life (Engel 1997). Thus, meditation does not belong to any one culture or religion. Over time, meditative methods became transformed through encounters with existing cultures and the nature of religious traditions of adjoining societies, so that, for example, the Buddhist tradition was transformed into various local versions, including Taoist meditation and Zen Buddhism (Engel 1997). As a result, Zen, Buddhist, Taoist, and transcendental meditation—which all focus on quieting the busy mind and directing concentration to a single healing element (Meditation 2000)—are now practised. All forms of meditation can be classified into two groups: concentrative and mindfulness. Concentrative meditation focuses the attention on the breath, an image, or a sound (usually a mantra) to quieten the mind and allow for emergence of greater awareness and clarity (Meditation 2000); mindfulness meditation involves paying attention to continuous sensations, feelings, images, thoughts, and sounds without thinking about them or reacting to them in order to achieve a calm, clear, and non-reactive state of mind (Meditation 2000). Most forms of traditional meditation have several techniques in common. (Meditation 2000). First, the meditator must begin in a quiet place with a passive attitude, striving not to become distracted. Second, one must have comfortable or poised posture, usually with a straight spine; Hindus and Buddhists use yoga positions, while Christians usually use kneeling prayer, and Taoists use standing positions. Finally, an object is used to focus attention; in Hindu yoga, the attention focuses on sound (a mantra), while Buddhists focus attention on the meditator's own breathing. Some methods recommend looking at objects with open eyes, and others closed eyes in order to help induce relaxation.

As social work aspirations are grounded in certain religious and humanitarian views, practitioners aspire to respect and accept their clients and their aspirations (Harris 1990). In fact, the historical roots of the profession are tied to the spiritual dimension (Kilpatrick & Holland 1990). Meditation supports these aspirations by enhancing the spiritual lives of both social worker and client. Some available literature examines the physiological and psychological health benefits of meditation, as well as reasons for spirituality's importance to social work practice. It is a safe way to balance physical, emotional, and mental states, and its benefits include a decreased heart rate, decreased muscle tension, reduced blood pressure, and improved breathing (Meditation 2000); it is also known to lower levels of cortisol, a hormone released in response to stress. Thus, meditation has the potential as a method of stress reduction to address the spiritual lives of social workers and clients. However, literature concerning the use of meditation in social work, especially literature written from a Canadian perspective, has been lacking. Some research to determine how meditation can be used to alleviate the stress associated with social work is being conducted by professionals and graduate students but has yet to be published; as such, the profession is still exploring the use of meditation in Canadian social work practice. A social worker is "one who helps people who have social problems or who are under some heavy stress which they cannot cope with by themselves" (Harris 1990: xi–xii). Since many clients use spirituality as a means of coping, social workers can use meditation to help strengthen a client's ability to develop strategies to meet his/her basic needs and maintain mental health (Sermabeikian 1994). Social work strives for helping and healing and, by addressing the spiritual dimension and using such methods as meditation, both social worker and clients can achieve inner peace.

[*Joanne Zamparo*]

RELATED ENTRIES

Natural Health & Complementary Wellness, Practice Methods, Spirituality, Transpersonal Psychology, Treatment, Theory & Practice

REFERENCES

Engel, K. 1997. *Meditation*. Vol. 1, *History and Present Time*. Frankfurt: Peter Lang.

Harris, J.T. 1990. *Inner Peace: An Essential for Social Work Practice*. University of Waterloo, Renison College.

Kilpatrick, A.C., and T.P. Holland. 1990. Spiritual Dimensions of Practice. *The Clinical Supervisor* 8, 2, 125–40.

Meditation. 2000. Online at time of writing at <www.holisticonline.com/>.

Sermabeikian, P. 1994. Our Clients, Ourselves: The Spiritual Perspective and Social Work Practice. *Social Work* 39, 2, 178–83.

Yoga and Meditation. 2000. Online at time of writing at <www.crha-health.ab.ca/>.

Memorial University School of Social Work

Newfoundland's Memorial University College (est. 1925), became a degree-granting university in 1949 and, with a well-established arts and science program by the early 1960s, it was ready to move on to the development of professional programs. Prior to confederation in 1949, welfare and social services on the island were carried out by Canada's Department of Health and Welfare as well as by denominationally based agencies, staffed by people of varying educational backgrounds but rarely with professional training in social work. This changed after Second World War when numerous workers from Newfoundland with wide experience in the social services completed university social work programs at Dalhousie, McGill, and Toronto; on their return to work on the island, they provided leadership and encouragement to a growing number of aspiring social workers to undertake professional education, which at the time could only be done outside the province. Confederation and provincial status added further impetus and resources, with the shared federal/provincial goals of developing a well-educated and professional civil service. It was in this context that professional social work education at a basic level began in Newfoundland (now, the province of Newfoundland and Labrador). In 1964 the first social work courses were offered at Memorial University of Newfoundland as part of a two-year Diploma in Social Welfare. The following year, the Department of Social Welfare was established with a new four-year program, the bachelor of arts with a social welfare major. The department became the Department of Social Work in 1969 and, when approval was given in 1971 to offer a bachelor of social work, the original bachelor of arts program was phased out. In 1974 the department became the School of Social Work and an extensive curriculum review was undertaken, based on research on the long- and short-term needs for professional social workers in the province. The result was the introduction of a core of three new undergraduate programs. The first of these was a unique five-year generalist social work program for a bachelor's degree with an emphasis on a strong arts and science foundation of approximately twenty-five courses and a further twenty-five courses in social work, including two thirteen-week field placements. The aim of this program was to produce an annual cadre of young graduates to meet the expanding demands for qualified social work practitioners. The second new program was a one-year bachelor of social work for students with a bachelor of arts and experience working in a social service setting, and the third was a certificate program for employees in the provincial Department of Social Services, sponsored jointly with the university's extension service. The latter two programs were focused on providing opportunities, previously unavailable, for individuals with experience in and a commitment to social work to upgrade their professional qualifications and advance in a social work career. The primary objective in developing this curriculum was to graduate generalist practitioners with a broad range of skills who were able to work in widely varying settings and particularly in rural areas where there were limited financial and professional resources. This rapid evolution of programs reflected the support and commitment of the university, the provincial government, and the service community to the education of professional social workers in Newfoundland.

In the early 1970s, the school recognized the need for continuing education programs, particularly to support those social workers practising in areas distant from most services. To increase accessibility to potential students, the school began to offer evening and summer courses and was one of the first in the university to provide courses by distance education and educational television. It also became clear by the mid-1970s that many graduates from the school who filled supervisory, administrative, and research positions, were interested in more advanced and specialized educational opportunities then only available outside the province. In response to this need, in 1977, the school introduced a one-year master's program to a small group of mature and experienced workers. Two areas of specialization were offered, one in the analysis, design, and development of social services and the other in staff development in social service settings. In the same year the bachelor of social work was first accredited; it was re-accredited in 1982, 1989, and 1996. These programs, with ongoing revisions, became the core for social work education in Newfoundland through the 1980s. In 1996 the school, in collaboration with the Labrador Inuit Association, offered a diploma in social work program to a cohort of Inuit students; students with a completed diploma could choose to enter the regular bachelor of social work program. The growing need for advanced education beyond the master's program led the school to initiate in 1994 a small doctoral program, the first in the Atlantic region. The doctoral program is an intensive but flexible research-based program designed to be accessible to students who may complete part of the requirements for the degree off-campus. Students complete course work over five semesters and are required to write a comprehensive examination and a thesis, as the university calendar states that the "primary focus is social work practice within the socio-economic context of the Atlantic region and a secondary focus to provide an educational foundation to those who wish to pursue careers in social work education." Largely owing to its accessibility, this doctoral program now draws one of the largest student bodies in Canada, with students from the United States and other provinces of Canada; to date five students have graduated. In the nearly forty years since the beginning of social work education in Newfoundland, the school at Memorial has been continually challenged to meet the changing needs of its constituents and, in spite of resource limitations, has met these challenges handsomely. The coming years will doubtlessly provide a new set of challenges and the Memorial School of Social Work can be confidently expected to continue to respond well to them. Current information can be found about the school online at < www.mun .ca/socwrk/ >.

[*Jane Dempster*]

RELATED ENTRIES
A. Comanor, Education in Social Work, Faculties of
Social Work, Newfoundland and Labrador Associa-
tion of Social Workers

mezzo practice

Mezzo practice, a term of relatively recent origin in Canadian social work literature, refers to a
cluster of knowledge, skills, and commitment to
aspects of practice that are neither clearly macro
nor micro in nature but between the two. From
the earliest days, virtually all professional direct
service agencies were involved in community
work, education, political, and social action that
differed from direct work with clients—long called
casework—and from social action activities of
large community organization agencies. It has
long been recognized in practice that this non-
clinical component of practice—mezzo practice—
comprised techniques that differed from clinical
work and focused on systemic issues of a more
general nature than those dealt with as a part of
direct work with clients. Mezzo practice draws on
skills for work with community groups: gathering, analyzing, and presenting relevant data; political lobbying at a local level; work with media;
preparing and presenting briefs for public education; and inter-agency co-operation and planning.
Mezzo practice has served to minimize in part the
long-standing dichotomy in the field which has
at times sought to value either macro or micro
practice as ideologically superior. To date, no clear
body of literature focuses on this component of
the intervention spectrum, nor has it found a clear
place in the curricula of schools and faculties of
social work, where it is still common to have practice presented as a macro/micro dichotomy rather
than a continuum. Nevertheless, interest is growing and efforts by educators are increasing to
ensure that students understand and have some
readiness for this inter-systemic cluster of professional activities. Current interest in and commitment to a generalist bachelor's program in social
work stresses this concept of a continuum of practice and clearly recognizes this mid-range component of much social work practice; still, clear
identification and structuring of mezzo theory
and practice has not yet fully emerged. Further
discussion and analysis of practice profession-
wide is necessary to clarify whether in fact mezzo
practice is distinct from micro and macro practice, or whether it exists as a focused mid-point
on a continuum ranging between the profession's
macro and micro spheres of intervention, drawing
on knowledge, skills, and commitment from both.

[*FJT*]

RELATED ENTRIES
Direct Practice, Generalist Practice, Indirect Practice,
Macro Practice, Micro Practice, Theory & Practice

micro practice

Micro practice in the Canadian social work lexicon is sometimes viewed as co-terminous with
direct, or clinical, practice—or with the earlier
term, casework—wherein the individual client
is the area of direct concern. Micro practice
describes interventions by social workers directly
with individual clients, dyads, small groups, and
families, while not excluding work they do in the
significant systems in a client's life, such as the
family, that impinge on or function as resources
for the client. Micro practice as a concept seeks to
be theoretically and methodologically neutral, in
that it incorporates all approaches that may assist
intervention and stresses the interrelationship of
all aspects of practice. Within micro practice,
social workers need to practice responsibly and
ethically; paramount within the profession is the
need for ongoing research to identify the differential impact of various theories, methods, and techniques in responding to client needs and requests,
regardless of background or origin.

In its proper sense, micro practice identifies
one end of a continuum of social work, with macro
practice anchoring the other end and, perhaps,
mezzo practice occupying a mid-point between
them. Viewing the profession's fields of practice
as a continuum avoids dichotomies or ideological positions that seek to grant greater value to
either micro or macro practice. Practitioners
whose emphasis is on micro scale work also have
a responsibility to learn aspects of mezzo and
macro practice, as they often work with colleagues
whose emphasis is elsewhere along the profession's continuum. As well, with their focus on direct intervention with individuals, micro-focused
practitioners have the potential to influence their
mezzo- and macro-focused colleagues, and in turn

to be influenced by their work and approaches. As such, practice is advanced in a unitary manner rather than fragmented as different concepts of intervention become isolated from one another. This concept of a broad purview of the practice spectrum underscores the necessity of the professional in micro practice to draw differentially from the whole range of methods, approaches, and theories available to respond most sensitively to who the client is and how a practitioner can best respond. The concept of an ongoing responsibility to a diagnosis-based strategy, as an underpinning of micro practice, is essential.

[FJT]

RELATED ENTRIES

Direct Practice, Generalist Practice, Indirect Practice, Macro Practice, Mezzo Practice, Theory & Practice

military social work

Military social work developed from efforts to address the general welfare of members of the Canadian forces and their families. Attempts began to be made through the chain of command to ameliorate family problems to prevent them from having negative impacts on the military member, but until the middle part of the twentieth century, when individual rights and freedoms received greater recognition, the approach to general welfare was frequently paternalistic (e.g., until fairly recently, military members wishing to be married had to receive permission from their commanding officer). In 1939 social worker Stewart Sutton wrote to Prime Minister Mackenzie King to suggest that the Canadian army should consider developing a service to provide soldiers with confidential reports on problems at home and, where necessary, arrange for professionals to be available to assist their families. In 1942 when Sutton was director of the Kingston children's aid society, he was asked to join the Canadian army in Ottawa to establish a social work program. Sutton, who had received his professional training at the University of Toronto (1926–33), undertook basic officer qualification training and was appointed in 1942 to the welfare section of the directorate of special services, out of which grew the directorate of social science. These events are regarded as the birth of Canadian military social work. Sutton's first challenge was to educate his new employers concerning the role of social work and its potential to provide professional services to military members and their families. Active recruiting located candidates with a master of social work degree, and a job description was developed for a social welfare officer was developed. A network of social workers was set up in every military district to serve military families in Canada, and to provide direct service to members overseas. By January 1945 more than 5,500 requests for services had been received. At the close of the Second World War, the social workers that had been recruited for uniformed service were demobilized and returned to civilian life. Residual responsibilities that remained from their wartime role were delegated to the federal government's department of Veterans Affairs. Counsellors employed by the department were stationed around Canada and continued to conduct compassionate investigations, frequently calling on local children's aid societies or social services agencies for assistance, particularly in areas more distant from organized services.

In 1947 Professor Hendry of the University of Toronto School of Social Work was commissioned to complete a study on the social work and recreational needs of the armed forces (Canada 1974). Hendry's report observed that, until 1939, the handling of personnel problems in the armed forces had rested primarily with regimental or equivalent officers, and chaplains. By 1945 the army employed professional social workers at headquarters, districts, and certain large camps; the air force as well had such personnel at headquarters and in commands; and the navy had an officer stationed in Halifax with special responsibilities for personal problem situations. The role of each service's specialist was to act as consultant and advisor on social service matters, as a co-ordinator of referrals and as a liaison officer with community social service agencies. The ongoing need for such specialist services was accentuated because of the growth of a variety of personal problems affecting operational deployments. The use of counselling specialists was then seen as necessary to ensure the appropriate investigation of compassionate circumstances, liaison with community agencies to improve referrals, as well as the protection of confidentiality, and the promotion of client advocacy. The Hendry report accepted the historical premise that, from the perspective of the armed forces, welfare problems were initially the responsibility of regimental (or equivalent line) officers. A need for additional training of these individuals was identified, with greater emphasis on their responsibility in assisting service personnel under their command in solving personal and domestic problems. The experience of the Second World War shown that regimental (or line) officers needed assistance in handling social service problems. The Hendry report also supported the role of professionally trained consultants and advisors, which was seen to encompass: direct assistance to regimental officers, acceptance of referrals of more complex cases, liaison with civilian community agencies, and co-ordination and monitoring of referrals. The report also recognized that, while professional social workers employed in the Second World War had contributed in a positive way, they would have been even more successful had their particular skills been realized earlier, thereby avoiding their frequent inappropriate task assignment.

Action on the Hendry report was largely dormant until 1950–51 when it was resurrected by the air force. At the time, each service had a separate command structure, unified only at national defence headquarters. Group Captain Ernie McNab took the Hendry report recommendations to the personnel members committee, which was composed of senior personnel chiefs from each service. Encountering considerable difficulty achieving consensus, he elected to pursue, unilaterally, the introduction of social welfare and recreational branches to the air force and recruited Helen Margaret Sutherland, a social worker employed by the BC government, who agreed to join the air force for three years to set up a professional social work program. Sutherland was immediately met with some daunting challenges, the first of which was that she was operating in a male-dominated environment offering a service that had been done to that time by line officers. With support in some quarters, the social welfare branch began operating in 1952 serving the 32,600 members of the air force. One by one, social workers joined the service and were sent to newly established command positions throughout Canada. An advantage for one of the new social workers, Sub-lieutenant Clifford Roy Taylor, was that he retained his flying sta-

tus as a pilot and was therefore able to fly to the various locations in western Canada that he served and could more readily spread the word about the new service. In time, military social workers became accepted for their professionalism, and valued for their advice and recommendations. S. Lt. Taylor, who later succeeded Sutherland as the senior social welfare officer, was posted in 1957 to the air force station in Metz, France; from there, he was expected to serve Canadian forces in Paris, as well as England, Sardinia, and the Middle East. As social work officers began to move around, the need for standardization of service for quality assurance became apparent. As each officer took different emphases into his/her individual practice, units were often confused about what to expect from them. Further, new social workers came on board expressed concern about the possibility of making a career in this new enterprise, considering the small number of practitioners and the existing rank structure. During his tenure, S. Lt. Taylor was able to increase the number of squadron leader positions, but he was unsuccessful at increasing the rank of the senior position. In 1962 S. Lt. Taylor was asked to work toward unifying social work for the three armed services and, within weeks, his staff was expanded by an artillery officer, a female civilian, and an air force sergeant assigned for this project, as well as administrative and clerical support. Progress was slow as each service had particular ideas about how its social welfare services operated. In the next three years, the number of social work positions increased and, as S. Lt. Taylor was about to retire in 1965, approval was granted to increase the rank of the senior social worker. Taylor's successor, Lachlan Bruce MacQuarrie, became the first air force social worker to wear the rank of lieutenant colonel. One of the highlights of his career was during the Suez Canal crisis (1956–57), when he screened personnel for service in Egypt and Italy in support of the world's first peacekeeping force under the United Nations.

On unification in 1967–68, the Canadian forces social work service was formed and expanded to cover all three military services that comprised over 100,000 men and women. In 1971 the service was decentralized, with all social work officers outside of national defence headquarters being placed, on the establishment of commands, in regional support roles. Under Lt. Col. Doug Carter, who had become director in 1970, military credit unions and financial counselling began to be developed, and professionalism of military social work was advanced by enabling serving members to train for a master's of social work degree. In the 1970s the awareness and appreciation was growing for the clinical and mental health skills that professional social work could contribute to the services; consequently, as of January 1, 1979, the affiliation of military social work was changed to the forces' medical services cementing the long-standing relationship with medical personnel on bases and in units and locating social worker officers with medical units. While this restructuring was more consistent with a holistic health model, it challenged medical and social workers to work together effectively as multidisciplinary teams. Under Lt. Col. Hub Deveau, who became director in 1979, several goals of social work services were advanced, as he obtained video equipment for use by practitioners, developed standards of practice for social work reports and administration, and prepared an on-the-job training manual for the orientation of new members with considerable emphasis placed on professional development and capturing the collective practice wisdom of practitioners in the field. A professional journal, later called the *Society of Military Social Workers Newsletter*, was launched in his time, born from a desire to promote professionalism and bind military social workers separated by considerable geography and different command structures into a cohesive unit. Lt. Col. Deveau opened an international initiative to encourage co-operation with social work colleagues in other countries, and alternative employment opportunities, for example, teaching at Royal military colleges, promoting prevention education in drug and alcohol prevention programs, and as administrators and counsellors in alcohol rehabilitation programs. A specific initiative was taken with the land service toward defining a combat role for military social workers, particularly in treating psychological casualties. Social development services also continued, along with involvement in financial counselling and the administration of various benevolent funds through which serving and retired members could receive assistance; distress grants and loans were later expanded to loans for educational purposes, as further assistance to members and their families.

By 1983, when Lt. Col. John Hanson assumed directorship, the social welfare branch had grown to include one lieutenant colonel, twelve majors, and more than thirty captains, lieutenants, and civilian positions. And, by 1988, when his successor, Lt. Col. James Jamieson, took over, integration of military social work with medical services was well underway, one consequence of which was loss of its status as a directorate; instead, it became a section within a larger directorate and massive downsizing of national headquarters staff. The main impact of this change was to restrict the ability of the director—then, the chief social worker—to communicate with units and bases outside of national headquarters. During his term, Lt. Col. Jamieson was diligent in advocating for the interests of clients and their families, championing the cause of social work within the military, as well as creating expanded roles for social workers. He was instrumental in developing operational roles, particularly in stress management, including critical incident stress interventions. For the first time social worker officers were sent into operational theatres (i.e., Bosnia, Croatia, Rwanda, and Somalia). In 1994 he left direct military social work for the directorate of military family support, where he continues to the present as a civilian in the capacity of director. Trading jobs with him was Lt. Col. Richard McLellan, who then assumed the role of chief social worker. As director of military family support, McLellan had consolidated the fledging directorate and introduced new initiatives, such as a 1–800 telephone line for spouses and family members of service personnel serving with UN missions. As chief social worker, Lt. Col. McLellan led his section through the restructuring and downsizing of the forces' medical services. The review determined that mental health requirements in battle zones could better be addressed by psychiatrists and mental health nurses and, consequently, social work officers in uniform were no longer needed. By August 1996, a plan was in place to progressively reduce the numbers of social work officers to nothing. The service that gave birth to post-war uniformed military social work, the air force, came to the rescue, however, and insisted that uni-

formed practitioners be retained in their formations. The plan was modified so that the occupation military social worker was designated as
"military non-operational essential" and an establishment was approved, consisting of thirty-three
uniformed military social work officers (twenty-
seven at the rank of captain/lieutenant and six at
the rank of major), six full-time civilian social
workers, and a number of part-timers. Other
changes included the loss of the final lieutenant
colonel position, and the then-major who was
chief social worker was located within the directorate of medical policy headquarters in Ottawa.
In July 1998 Major Henry Matheson occupy the
senior major's position, when Lt. Col. McLellan
left the social work services to pursue some special
military projects. He developed services for injured and dying members and their families, an
initiative that led to formation of a quality of life
management office that now encompasses four
other areas of military life: compensation and benefits, accommodation, work expectations, and
family support. The legacy of uniformed military
social work continues into the new millennium.

[*James R. Arnett*]

RELATED ENTRIES

Practice Methods, Theory & Practice, Veterans Affairs
Canada

REFERENCES

Canada. 1945. *Social Services Personnel Newsletter.*
August.
Canada. 1974. *Social Work Twenty-First Anniversary.*
August.
Society of Military Social Workers. 1993. Newsletter:
42nd anniversary ed.

minorities

Traditionally, minorities have been defined as
communities or groups that differ from the dominant societies by their self-ascribed ethnicity, or
by the "race" attributed to them by others. More
recently, the notion that ethnicity is the sole determinant of minority status has been expanded to
include physically disabled people (Hopps 1982),
people living in non-traditional families, people
with different political, linguistic, or religious affiliations (Soydan & Williams 1998: 3), and women,
lesbian and gay people. As Hopps (1982: 3) has
pointed out, the number of minority groups
expands as new "offended" communities are identified or claim minority status. As a concept, it is
much contested in social work and social science
literature. Some authors do not define the term
but instead provide examples of "minority
groups." Views about acceptable terminology differ from region to region within Canada, and
change over time. Ideology influences terms used
within and between region. Consequently, Bissoondath (1994) who advocates integration for
ethnic minorities resists references to "hyphen-
ated-Canadians" (e.g., African-Canadians). Tulchinsky (1994), who applauds efforts to retain ethnic identity, emphasizes specific issues faced by
different ethnic communities as they have
attempted to do so. Some authors prefer alternatives, such as "otherness," to "minority." Many
scholars point to the inadequacy of defining
"minority" in numerical terms: Soydan and
Williams (1998) cite the example of the numerical
minority of Europeans in South Africa who successfully oppressed the far more populous "black"
and "coloured" peoples. Bolaria and Li (1988: 2–
23) note that in Canada "the historical experiences
of colonization and slavery are good examples of
racial domination in which Europeans were the
dominant group although numerically a minority
among the populations they colonized and en-
slaved." At a deeper level, some argue that a discourse about minority status detracts attention
from important dialogue about racism, discrimination, and oppression.

When the concept "minority" is used, it is often
contrasted with "majority," particularly in proposals that the culture and values of the social majority be transmitted through formal institutions,
such as schools, the media, and social agencies:
"The elite classes occupying the highest social,
economic, and political positions are drawn from
this (majority) group." In contrast, minorities
experience "unequal treatment and limited access
to the opportunity structure in the economic,
social and political spheres" (CASSW 1991: Appendix). Bolaria and Li (1988) consider that "the concept of majority and minority groups in race relations is defined by unequal power." Similarly Ng
(1993: 52) states that "European men, especially
those of British and French descent, are seen to be

superior to women, and to people from other racial and ethnic origins. Systems of ideas and practices have been developed over time to justify and support their notion of superiority. These ideas have become the premise on which societal norms and values are based and the practices become the 'normal way of doing things.'" Writing from a postmodern perspective, Williams (1998: 4) states that, as power is dynamic and cannot be permanently owned, the relation between minorities and majorities is constantly open to change. Consequences are well documented: people identified with minority communities are likely to receive inferior education, and health and social care (Bolaria & Li 1988: 25). Young (1988) writes about five different dimensions of oppression, emphasizing the exploitation, marginalization, and powerlessness of minorities, and the cultural imperialism and violence exerted by majority societies. Oppression may cause minorities to "reject their own heritage in pursuit of white culture and symbols that renders a higher social recognition. [Therefore] many minority cultures and institutions are dead before minority members abandon them because the majority group has defined their social insignificance" (Bolaria & Li 1988: 25).

Social work with minorities has many controversial aspects (de Anda 1997). Contemporary debates include those concerning the desirable balance between promoting assimilation or pluralism. Some suggest that culturally competent social work based on a knowledge and understanding of different minorities is needed, while others recommend that ethnocultural communities have their own practitioners and services. Still others advocate that social work focus on confronting racism and oppression in Canadian society. Despite these differences, social work scholars usually agree that it is important for social workers to develop the knowledge, skills, and commitment to challenge the systemic discrimination and oppression that affects minorities.

[*Rosemary A. Clews*]

RELATED ENTRIES

Aboriginal Issues, Culture, Deafness, Diversity, Gender Issues, Knowledge Base, Physical Challenges, Race & Racism, Racism-Sensitive Social Work, Sensitizing Concepts, Sexual Minorities, Visible Minorities, Visual Impairment

REFERENCES

Bissoondath, N. 1994. *Selling Illusions: The Cult of Multiculturalism in Canada.* Toronto: Penguin.

Bolaria, B., and P. Li. 1988. *Racial Oppression in Canada.* 2nd ed. Toronto: Garamond.

CASSW. 1991. *Social Work Education at the Crossroads: The Challenge of Diversity.* Ottawa: Canadian Association of Schools of Social Work.

de Anda, D. (Ed.). 1997. *Controversial Issues in Multiculturalism.* Needham Heights, MA: Allyn and Bacon.

Hopps, J.G. 1982. Oppression Based on Colour. *Social Work* 27, 3–6.

Ng, R. 1993. Racism, Sexism and Nation-building in Canada. In C. McCarthy and W. Crichlow (Eds.) *Race, Identity and Representation in Education.* New York: Routledge.

Soydan, H., and C. Williams. 1998. Exploring Concepts." In C. Williams, H. Soydan, and M. Johnson (Eds.), *Social Work and Minorities.* New York: Routledge.

Tulchinsky, G. (Ed.). 1994. *Immigration in Canada: Historical Perspectives.* Toronto: Copp Clark Longman.

Williams, L.F. 1988. Frameworks for Introducing Racial and Ethnic Minority Content into the Curriculum. In C. Jacobs and D.D. Bowles (Eds.) *Ethnicity and Race: Critical Concepts in Social Work.* 185–203. Silver Spring, MD: National Association of Social Workers.

Young, I.M. 1988. Five Faces of Oppression. *The Philosophical Forum* 9, 4, 270–89.

minority-sensitive practice

Minority-sensitive social work comes from the profession's commitment to work with marginalized, disenfranchised, and oppressed people. As Canada becomes increasingly multilingual, culturally pluralistic, and connected globally, it is vital that social workers understand the "complex interaction as well as the differences among race, class, and gender in social work practice" (Wilkinson 1997: 263). Indeed, after completing a national survey, the Canadian Association of Schools of Social Work (CASSW 1991) concluded that formal training in practice with multiethnic or ethnocultural communities should be included as a criterion of accreditation of social work programs. The assumption underlying this recommendation is that contemporary social workers need to be trained to communicate effectively with, understand, and work co-operatively with a variety of clientele. This philosophical and ideological commitment to fight oppression and work effectively with vulnerable people is the basis for minority-sensitive social work practice. Social work practice with culturally and ethnically diverse clients has been described as anti-oppressive, ethnic-sensitive, cultural-sensitive, cultural-relevant, cultural-competent, and transcultural practice. Minority-sensitive approaches to social work practice emphasize "diversity within the society with the focus on ethnic minority populations and, other population groups who have been marginalized or who have been denied access to power, goods, and opportunity because of their identification as a specific population (race, ethnicity, culture, class, gender, sexual orientation, religion, physical or mental disability, age, and national origin)" (de Anda 1977: xi). Competence in minority-sensitive practice can be defined as "an ability to provide services that are perceived as legitimate for problems experienced by culturally diverse persons" (Lum 1999: 278). In other words, social workers need the knowledge and skills to start to understand the client's circumstances.

Minority-sensitive practice approaches share five main characteristics: self-awareness, enlightened consciousness or attitude, knowledge, acquisition of skills, and cross-cultural experience or immersion. With regard to self-awareness, social workers need to be aware of and critically challenge their own values, biases, assumptions, stereotypes, and experiences of oppression. Increased self-awareness assists social workers to identify and change potentially harmful behaviours. Social workers also need to be cognizant of how they benefit from and act out positions of privilege and power. It is also useful to recognize that not every person identified with a minority conforms to commonly held characteristics of the community: many may want to change or be treated as having already changed. Enlightened consciousness or attitude: has been defined as the "fundamental process of reorienting one's primary worldview" (McPhatter 1997: 261–62). Enlightenment is gained through a process of self-awareness, experience, and critical reflection. Enlightened social workers demonstrate a willingness to learn about themselves and others, an ability to critique their own values and assump-

tions, a respect for difference, a non-judgmental attitude, and a commitment to social justice.

Social workers need to develop a knowledge base about their own, colleagues', and clients' cultures, encompassing individual and community history, diversity, rituals, beliefs, customs, values, and traditions. Central to this knowledge building, is the identification, acknowledgment, and celebration of difference between and among different ethnocultural communities. Knowledge should also include the history and biopsychosocial effects of oppression and inequality on client groups as well as an openness and respect for indigenous/local cultural knowledge. In order to truly hear and understand diverse clients' experiences, social workers need to develop and practice what Schulman calls "containment skills" including being able to tolerate silence, demonstrating good listening skills, refraining from interpreting the client's experience or problem from their own perspective, and having the patience to draw out those who have been traditionally silenced or ignored. McPhatter stresses the importance of engaging "a culturally diverse client's reality in an accepting, genuine, nonoffensive manner" (1997: 272). Skill acquisition is seen as cumulative, experiential, and self-reflective in nature. To assist in this skill development, social workers need regular feedback about using the above mentioned skills. This can be accomplished through peer review, self-evaluation, observation, and video/audiotaping. Lum (1999: 14) offers a useful survey, called the Social Work Cultural Competencies Self-Assessment Instrument, a Likert-type scale, which social workers can complete to measure their own level of cultural competence, including skills, attitudes, and knowledge.

Cross-cultural experience or immersion has been suggested as the most important way in which social workers can help clients from minorities through prolonged exposure to people of that group in a variety of settings. In other words, social workers need to develop opportunities to spend time with, learn from, and work with diverse clientele. This can mean working in locations where the clients live, being responsible to and for specific client populations, or teaming up with colleagues from different cultural backgrounds who can share access to, knowledge of, and social work experience.

Approaches to minority-sensitive practice have significant implications for social work agencies, particularly those that serve ethnically or culturally diverse clients. Ongoing evaluation of organizational processes and methods of providing client service can identify minority-sensitive or cultural competence of practitioners. Employers need to be aware of workers' assumptions, norms, biases, values, and interpersonal dynamics. How social workers treat one another in the workplace can be a significant indicator of minority-sensitive attitudes. Here are some questions related to adopting minority-sensitive practice in social work agencies:

- *Who should be hired to work with clients from diverse communities?* Should social workers work with clients across cultures, genders, or class? Is it unethical for social workers to work with clients out of their own cultural and ethnic identity? Under what circumstances, if any, is it appropriate for social workers to refuse to work with specific clients?
- *How should social workers be trained to meet the specialized needs of diverse communities?* Who decides what training is necessary and how much each worker should receive? What are the supports needed to assist social workers to acquire an adequate knowledge and skill base to work with diverse minorities and to cope with "cultural shock" should they experience it on working in unfamiliar social/cultural settings? Will agencies and/or government fund required cross-cultural training?
- *If indigenous knowledge is to be truly respected and valued, how much and what type of contribution can clients make toward social work policy, practice and research decision making?* What happens when local knowledge conflicts with agency and/or government legislation and policy?

Adopting a minority-sensitive approach to social work practice assists social workers to achieve increased understanding, communication, respect, and trust with clients and their communities. McPhatter (1997: 203) suggests that social workers might also become "not only culturally sensitive—which implies a reaction—but culturally enriched or transcultural." Such enrichment could have far-reaching benefits for social work

practice, education, and research. By seeking out, recognizing, and celebrating the knowledge derived from other cultures and societies, social workers could be better prepared to work collaboratively with all clients to ameliorate the biopsychosocial effects of inequity and to promote social change.

[*Susan Hillock*]

RELATED ENTRIES

Aboriginal Services, Diversity, Ethnic-Sensitive Practice, Ethnocultural Communities' Services, Knowledge Base, Minorities, Racism-Sensitive Practice, Sensitizing Concepts, Sexual Orientation, Theory & Practice, Visible Minorities

REFERENCES

CASSW. 1991. *Social Work Education at the Crossroads.* Ottawa: Canadian Association of Schools of Social Work.

de Anda, D. (Ed.) 1997. *Controversial Issues in Multiculturalism.* Boston, MA: Allyn and Bacon.

Lum, D. 1999. *Culturally Competent Practice.* Pacific Grove, CA: Brooks/Cole.

McPhatter, A.R. 1997. Cultural Competence in Child Welfare: What Is It? *Child Welfare* 76, 1 (January/February), 255–78.

Wilkinson, D. 1997. Re-Appraising the Race, Class, Gender Equation: A Critical Theoretical Perspective. *Smith College Studies in Social Work* 43, 3 (June), 217–41.

Simonne Monet-Chartrand (1919–93)

Monet-Chartrand, Simonne, pacifist, feminist, rights activist; b. Nov. 4, 1919, Montreal, QC; m. Michel Chartrand, 1942; d. Jan. 18, 1993, Richelieu, QC

Simonne Monet-Chartrand received her initial education from 1926 to 1935 at the boarding school Marie-Rose in Montreal, where she started her life-long passion of pacifism and social activism. In 1937 she became president of the school organization Jeunesse étudiante catholique féminine. In 1939 she travelled to Washington as a delegate to the seventeenth congress of the Pax Romana, an international organization of Catholic university students established in 1921 that was re-created in Rome in April 1947 as an international association of Catholic professionals and intellectuals. In 1942 Simonne Monet graduated from the University of Montreal, where she had studied French-Canadian literature and Canadian history. She further developed her humanism and social commitment with the increased militancy evident within the youth movements of the 1940s. Her marriage to Michel Chartrand, a Quebec socialist, nationalist, and trade unionist, boosted her public profile as a Quebec intellectual and lecturer; by the mid-1950s, she had became a media personality as the driving force, consultant, and panellist for public affairs broadcasts for the French-language Radio-Canada. In 1961 helped to found Voix des femmes / Voice of the Women of Quebec—a pacifist organization that drew on the movement of radical women opposed to violence—becoming a member of its national council. In 1966 she founded Fédération des femmes du Quebec. She became a writer, researcher, and freelance journalist in religious broadcasts for Radio-Canada during the late 1960s and early 1970s. Monet-Chartrand also distinguished herself through her writing, including remarkable literary reviews for *Châtelaine*, *La Vie en Rose*, and *Les Têtes de Pioche*. Understanding the importance of the written word, she wrote stirringly about women's issues in many regional and trade union newspapers. She worked for the trade union of Champlain teachers as director of information (1972–75). Her determination and conviction for justice and human rights led her to support social movements associated with promoting women rights, social justice, and peace. She was elected associate director of Ligue des droits de l'homme / League of Human Rights (1975–78), which she had joined in 1963, and became associate director of the League of Rights and Freedoms in 1977. Whether as a writer, public speaker, activist, panellist, or pacifist, she served as a role model for people of her own and future generations. Late in her life, Monet-Chartrand produced the four volumes of *Ma Vie Comme Rivière*, a compilation of excerpts from her materials written between 1981 and 1992 about Quebec politics, social justice, peace, and disarmament, and the rights of the individual. These volumes summarize fifty-five years of radical activism committed to Quebec's social movements. In 1991 Simonne Monet-Chartrand was recognized for her life-long support of Quebec artists with the title "Artiste pour la paix / Artiste for Peace."

[*Carlos J. Pereira*]

RELATED ENTRIES
Feminist Theory, Human Rights, Social Welfare History

mother's allowance

Mother's allowance was one of the first provincial experiments with formal income support programs in Canada. In 1916 Manitoba was the first province in Canada to pass legislation granting an allowance to poor widows and four years later, the western provinces and Ontario had similar legislation in place; by the 1950s, all provinces had some form of support for mothers raising children alone. These programs were not extended to the territories until later decades. At their onset, the programs were characterized by restricted categorical eligibility, stringent moral requirements, domestic supervision, and meagre financial support. Nevertheless they recognized the popularity of the idea for public support to poor mothers rearing their children alone. The programs inaugurated a role of the state as guarantor of well-being through direct intervention in the families of deserving widows and, in their many metamorphosed forms, they have persisted to the present. Many factors contributed to the widespread acceptance of supporting poor mothers. Early-twentieth-century women's movements advocated for paid motherhood as a way to prevent the dissolution of family ties and attending to the plight of dependent poor children. In addition by the First World War in Canada, the growth of slums, infant mortality, crime, and disease became increasingly associated with the instability of the family and support for motherhood received widespread sanction. Suffragists, such as Nellie McClung, argued for greater appreciation of women's maternal qualities and more humane values while Leacock, for example, emphasized female weakness, questioning women's ability to support themselves and their families on their own.

Mother's allowance legislation in Canadian provinces was also influenced by a series of events around the 1914–18 war. Widows and their children were popularized as prominent images of victims of misfortune in the discussion about the lack of adequate child care services and the need for the propagation of a physically and morally fit generation to inherit the nation. Examples of public interventions were provided by the implementation of the mothers aid programs in some of the American states and, as well, by support provided by the Canadian Patriotic Fund and local experiments by local councils of women. Grounded in their white middle-class origins, the women's organizations and social service leaders who came to dominate the mother's allowance campaign, insisted on a program with stringent eligibility criteria requiring moral evaluation and using their own values as standards. While supporting and encouraging poor mothers, women in these organizations also saw a role for themselves in the public world defined by a career in family management using professional tools for direction of the deviant and distressed families of the lower classes. The programs initially supported primarily poor widows with at least two dependent children but, gradually, eligibility criteria were enlarged to include wives of incapacitated men, deserted women, foster mothers, mothers with only one child, divorcees and officially separated mothers, wives of imprisoned criminals, and unmarried mothers, as well as previous residents of other provinces and immigrant mothers. By the 1960s most provinces did not place restrictions on the causes of single motherhood, but arguments around fathers' responsibility for their families still placed restrictions on certain mothers' eligibility through regulations around frequency of contact with men. Furthermore the type and amount of support varied. Financial support, reflecting a fear of discouraging industriousness, was contingent on assessments of need and contained by strict ceilings. In-kind and tagged benefits consisted of medical and dental assistance, support for fuel and winter clothing, and emergency funds in some cases. Supervision of mothers regarding their motherhood expertise, their household management, and their moral fitness have been central characteristics of the mother's allowance programs. The emphasis of the program also gradually shifted from the initial valuing of mother-work to integration of mothers into the workforce. By 1964 with the possibility of federal cost-shared funding introduced by the Canada Assistance Plan, provinces gradually passed new acts replacing the mother's allowance with other income support grants through new legislation.

Although characterized by meagre benefits and regulatory procedures, mother's allowance can be seen as an important point in the history of social welfare in Canada. This novel arrangement inaugurated support for mother-work and family life, as well as establishing the precedent for direct public intervention in certain types of motherhood: those outside of the family norm of support by a male parent. In doing so, the initiative separated this group of mothers from others and contributed to the development of a variety of mechanisms through which their lives were ruled and defined.

[*Iara Lessa*]

RELATED ENTRIES

E.H. Blois, Family Allowance Act, Income Security, Mother's Allowance Commission, Poverty, Services for Women

Mother's Allowance Commission (ON)

The Ontario Mother's Allowance Commission (est. 1920) administered the Mother's Allowance Act, which granted an allowance to certain poor mothers. It is an example of the ways in which provinces implemented this type of service. The commission was composed of five persons appointed by the lieutenant-governor, and two positions designated for women—an indication of the influence that women's groups had achieved on shaping the legislation. Members served without remuneration except for a per diem allowance for attendance at meetings, and paid expenses. The commission answered initially to the provincial labour department and, as of 1930, to the newly created public welfare department. It had autonomy, however, regarding the allocation and amount of each allowance within a budget defined by the provincial government and controlled all administrative aspects of the Act including the development of eligibility criteria. The Commission created ninety-six local boards in Ontario, each of which reproduced the central commission structure in being composed of five members, of whom at least two were women. The local board members served without any remuneration, and only their travelling expenses were reimbursed. Mayors of cities and separated towns, wardens of counties, and judges of judicial districts could nominate two board members, but appointment was ultimately a responsibility of the commission. Members tended to be citizens of good standing in the community, generally associated with the local political, social, and economic elite. Local boards received applications for Mother's Allowances, considered them in relation to the Act, and forwarded them with their recommendations to the commission. The boards reported quarterly to the commission, which supervised their work and granted their allowances based on their recommendations and the report of investigators. By the end of the 1920s, 110 boards were in operation, comprising more than 500 members.

This public structure of delivery, through its reliance on appointed rather then elected representatives, indicates a preference for handling the private matters of the family outside the public sphere of the state government: respected members of the public were considered better adjudicators of deservedness than civil servants, politicians or judges, as in the United States. The participation of white middle-class and usually Protestant citizens in these decisions was seen as representing the typical taxpayers' feelings and social commitments. Furthermore this extensive representation cultivated support among a wide range of labour, women, business, and charity constituencies who felt represented in the operation of the Act, leading in turn to relatively modest levels of opposition to the program. For the purpose of investigation and supervision, the commission divided the province into seventeen districts, each assigned an investigator including two who were bilingual in French and English. Investigators were all women which, in a historically male-dominated civil service, marked the formation of gender and professional relations: women were considered more akin to the nature and function of motherhood and were called on to serve professionally in the program. The investigators answered to the central commission, which passed to them the applications approved by the local boards for the regular home visits. These visits conditioned the allowance to intense, close, and direct supervision of beneficiaries based on specific class, ethnic, cultural, and moral values of investigators. This method of delivery contributed to the development of key observable indicators of good motherhood, which were ingrained in the evolving eligibility and decision-making structures associated with the support of motherhood.

In 1932–33, the Mother's Allowance Commission was compressed to three people and its composition changed to include one volunteer chair and two civil servants: the deputy minister of welfare and the chief investigator. Later, in 1944–45, the volunteer chair of the commission was replaced by another civil servant and, in 1948, the local boards were eliminated. In 1952 a new administrative structure was put in place: the commission was abolished and the director of the mother's allowance branch was made responsible for decision making and management of the program.

[*Iara Lessa*]

RELATED ENTRIES

Family Allowance Act, Income Security, Mother's Allowance, Poverty, Services for Women

multi-skilling

Multi-skilling, or the acquisition of multiple skills for practice, is primarily associated with health care practice and was much discussed among service professions in Canada in the 1990s. In the literature, which is limited, two forms are identified: intradisciplinary and interdisciplinary. In intradisciplinary multi-skilling, a person trains in two or more fields of practice within a single discipline (e.g., a generalist social work program and a certificate program in addictions); intradisciplinary multi-skilling is very similar to generalist social work practice. In interdisciplinary multi-skilling, a person trains—but is not professionally educated—in at least two tasks associated with two different disciplines (e.g., a social worker trains to perform occupational therapy functions) (Makely 1998). Social work was one of several professions that examined multi-skilling to determine its appropriateness for adoption. Interdisciplinary multi-skilling generates much debate within professions, as it is viewed by many as a development driven primarily by fiscal considerations—a measure to contain staffing costs (Makely 1998). The concept seems to have emerged from the need for affordable ways to provide a full range of services in areas or situations where it was not practical to supply services in a traditional manner. A small long-term care facility might, for example, hire a social worker to provide social work and recreation services where insufficient demand and funds could support two positions. As specialization and unionization increased, the resulting division of labour became too expensive for organizations, and they promoted multi-skilling as a way to obtain multiple skills from fewer people. Proponents of multi-skilling argue that this approach is a response to the demand for a more client-centred service and a method of ensuring that clients receive a full range of service despite the unavailability of specialized providers. Little research has been done to offer clear direction, particularly in relation to the impact of multi-skilling on clients. Potential benefits for clients are said to include less fragmented and more efficient service, a service that is client-centred rather than focused on role or territorial issues, and an improved quality of service that is more accessible to the client. It is thought that employers experience the following benefits: a more cost-effective service, less expense for traditionally expensive highly specialized tasks, reduced recruitment problems, and flexibility in staff assignment. Advantages perceived for staff include increased job satisfaction from more variety of duties, increased job security, and an increased sense of worth and value within the organization. Limitations identified in the literature reflect implications for staff and clients, the major ones being frequently cited as the quality of care/service declines from a focus on tasks and economics rather than professional judgment, uncertain staff competencies as a result of inadequate training; task-focused training, lack of licensing and accreditation systems, and unidentified liability issues. Deprofessionalization is a potential outcome of interprofessional multi-skilling; as well, diminished professional identity is likely to occur, and unions can easily become disempowered. An analysis offered by the Canadian Association of Social Workers in a 1999 position paper suggests that a major weakness of multi-skilling is that it fails to consider the complexity of people and the issues clients bring to professionals. The approach also does not address the large proliferation of knowledge that creates the need for specialized fields of practice (Rossides 1998). The multi-skilling approach has been debated and considered by service professions but has not received widespread acceptance. To date, research to confirm or refute identified benefits and concerns has been limited. Clearly, more consideration of the potential impacts of multi-skilling is needed, as the approach is more widely researched and implemented.

[*Ellen Oliver*]

RELATED ENTRIES

Case Management, Interprofessional Education, Interprofessional Issues, Knowledge Base, Theory & Practice

REFERENCES

Makeley, S. 1998. *Multiskilled Health Care Workers.* Indiana: Pine Ridge.

Rossides, D.W. 1998. *Profession and Disciplines Functional and Conflict Perspectives.* Englewood Cliffs, NJ: Prentice Hall.

Isabel Munroe-Smith (1914–94)

Munroe-Smith, Isabel (née Munroe), therapist, social worker, administrator, educator, social activist; b. July 10, 1914, Edmonton, AB; m. Norman Smith, 1981; d. Mar. 24, 1994

Isabel Munroe was educated in the Edmonton public and high schools and received a bachelor of arts in psychology from the University of Alberta in 1935. She took post-graduate studies in social work at the Montreal School of Social Work attached to McGill University (1935–37), where she received her bachelor of social work degree. Social work at that time had an eclectic base, borrowing heavily from sociology, psychology, psychiatry, and public health; professors in her program were almost entirely from the field, with two coming from the United States for sessional courses in casework and group work. On graduation, Munroe worked in foster care in Montreal for two years. She returned to Edmonton and, because of her interest in children, sought a position with child welfare. The provincial child welfare director, however, thought that social work was not needed in that department. Day care was similarly disinterested in social work at that time. Mental health clinics were looking for social workers but, because Munroe's father was a prominent physician in Edmonton, the Minister of Health was reluctant to hire her, as she "didn't need a job"; He was persuaded, however, that, if she were appointed to the Calgary clinic, his concerns about her relationship to her father would not arise. The Calgary Mental Health Clinic office was at city hall, where Munroe was receptionist, typist, psychologist, and social worker. Biweekly clinics were held at the well-baby clinic in the same building, when a psychiatrist and psychologist from the provincial psychiatric hospital at Ponoka, north of Calgary, would visit. Psychiatric diagnoses was made on the basis of a family and social history, and psychometric testing prepared by Isabel Munroe. The Calgary Mental Health Clinic served an area of 27,000 square kilometres, including the communities of Drumheller, in the northeast; High River, Clairsholm, and Lethbridge in the south; and Medicine Hat in the southeast. Clinics in these outlying areas were held two or three times a month.

With the coming of the Second World War three years later, Munroe's attitude was that "although war itself didn't bear thinking about... if there was a war it would be easier to live through it emotionally if you were in the midst of it" (1985 lecture). Volunteering to help the hard-pressed British social workers coping with evacuation programs, Munroe was sent by the Canadian Children's Service to Devonshire, England, to help move children from cities to rural communities. She was among twenty-five social workers, teachers, and nursery school workers assigned to corresponding program in England; Isabel Munroe was one of two mental health specialists. There, she had the opportunity to meet and work with Anna Freud. On returning to Canada in 1945, Munroe worked for the federal government in the early stages of the Family Allowance Program, "seeing a federal bureaucracy in action and maturing social work input as best one could (1985 lecture). Munroe returned to direct practice by taking a time limited appointment at a family service agency in St. Paul, Minnesota, then, three years later, travelled to Montreal to accept a teaching position at McGill University in the School of Social Work. After a brief tenure at McGill, she returned to Edmonton to work for ten years with the Family Service Association as a social worker and supervisor. At the time, only one professional organization existed for social work, the Canadian Association of Social Workers with branches in various cities. Munroe served on the executive of the local branches in both Montreal and Edmonton at a time when provincial organizations were forming. She was also part of a group lobbying for the establishment of a School of Social Work in

Alberta, which eventually emerged at the University of Calgary.

In 1968, Isabel Munroe became Dean of Women at the University of Alberta, a post she held until 1974. Student protests were gaining strength during her tenure and she was involved in the "mature women students project" to support a student push for daycare service at the university; Munroe concerned herself mostly with the needs of mature women coming into the university. After attending the International Social Welfare Conference in Nairobi, Kenya, she decided to stay in Africa for two years on a Young Women Christian Association world assignment, serving as a consultant in a girls' vocational school in Ghana. In 1981 she married Norman Smith, an Edmonton pharmacist and long-time friend. Munroe-Smith was much involved in charitable projects, among which were directorships in the United Way Centraide, YWCA, and planning for the daycare centre at the University of Alberta. At the First Presbyterian Church in Edmonton, she was an elder and involved in many projects there. In 1988 Isabel Munroe-Smith was awarded an honorary doctor of laws by the University of Alberta in recognition of her accomplishments.

[*Alex Munroe*]

RELATED ENTRIES

Canadian Association of Social Work, McGill University (School of Social Work,) University of Calgary (School of Social Work), YWCA

REFERENCES

Munroe-Smith, Isabel. (1985). Lecture presentation to Faculty of Social Work, University of Calgary, at Lethbridge.

Emily Murphy (1868–1933)

Murphy, Emily (née Ferguson), social activist, author; b. 1868, Cookstown, ON; m. Rev. Arthur Murphy, 1887; first woman magistrate in British Empire; d. 1933

Emily Murphy initiated the earliest women's movement for political and legal rights, including voting privileges and holding political office. She may be best known for her work as one of the "Famous Five" Alberta feminists who took the *Persons Case* to the Privy Council in England to seek recognition of women as "persons" under the law, which was achieved in 1929 (Wharf 1990). Murphy came from the political Ferguson family in Ontario, having an uncle who sat on the Supreme Court of Canada and three brothers who were lawyers (Cochrane 1977). Moving west with her husband, she has been described as "a kind of one-woman committee, forever on the lookout for injustices or irregularities, and she generally managed to be in the midst of some fight, great or small" (Savage 1979: 112–13). Much of her activism on behalf of rural women, particularly on property rights, was supported by her published writings. Following a trial in Edmonton where two women were asked to leave the courtroom during testimony deemed unfit for their ears, Murphy rallied her troops and campaigned for a court where women's issues could be heard (Cochrane 1977). In 1916 Emily Murphy was appointed the first magistrate of such a court, an honour which also made her the first female police magistrate in the British empire (Cochrane 1977: 45). She is said to have filled this position with compassion and competence, as, even without formal legal training, her natural authority and logical mind were suited perfectly to her work on the bench (Savage 1979). But the fact that women were not yet considered to be "persons" under section 24 of the British North American Act, 1867 (now, Constitution Act, 1867) led to a continual questioning of her authority (Cochrane 1977). She attempted to conquer that obstacle through her role as the first national president of the Federated Women's Institute of Canada, which forwarded a proposal to Ottawa asking for a woman to be appointed to Senate. In spite of numerous rejections, Murphy and the other four women persisted with their court case, which led eventually to the 1929 judgment by the Privy Council that women were legally entitled to the same political right to hold office as men (Wharf 1990; Cochrane 1977). Although Murphy herself was never granted an appointment to the Senate, she had set the stage for those who would do so in the future (Cochrane 1977: 48). Emily Murphy birthed in women a sense that there was more to life than that which was being handed to them. Social workers can proudly carry the torch of equality for women and pass on Murphy's vision of great things for women to future generations.

[*Anne MacGregor*]

RELATED ENTRIES

Nellie McClung, I. Parlby, Social Justice, Social Welfare History

REFERENCES

Cochrane, J. 1977. *Women in Canadian Politics.* Toronto: Fitzhenry and Whiteside.

Savage, C. 1979. *Our Nell.* Saskatoon, SK: Western Producer Prairie Books.

Wharf, B., (Ed.) 1990. *Social Work and Social Change in Canada.* Toronto: McClelland and Stewart.

music intervention

Among the many applications of music in social work practice, the use of specifically recorded songs in therapy with addicted clients is a strategy being currently studied by Gallant and Holosko of the University of Windsor. Their work is grounded in the principles of Alcoholic Anonymous (AA) and carried out at Brentwood Recovery Home. These researchers were originally challenged by the observation that many of their addictive clients were trapped in a learned helplessness mode, which allowed them to deny major issues in their lives and to avoid the spiritual discovery necessary for recovery. They observed that the use of specifically chosen music helped these clients to get in touch with their inner selves in a manner non-threatening, appealing, and readily embraced. In various research projects, such clients were offered expressions of prose, music, poetry, and songs composed by the researchers, and were guided to commit their own experiences to poetry and artistic expression. By combining this form of music and a group therapy modality with couples, one of which was an identified alcoholic, it was found that almost all clients benefitted from this form of intervention—especially those who reported that they enjoyed music. This study laid the groundwork for a more rigorous examination of the use of this type of spiritually oriented music for groups. In a later study, groups using this approach were compared with matched groups where music was not used. Differences between the groups favouring the use of music were found. An important theme of work with these groups includes a basis of spiritual values, which touches a need of these vulnerable people for forgiveness and reconciliation, and how music can dynamically evoke these central themes in therapy. From further interdisciplinary work with music therapists and composers, several collections of songs that facilitate this helping process have been published. As well, various projective instruments, which evaluate levels of grief and foreignness, have been developed. Ongoing research strongly supports the effectiveness of music with grieving clients; it has also found that clients are willing to integrate appropriately chosen music into their therapeutic journey.

[*Wilfred A. Gallant*]

RELATED ENTRIES

Practice Methods, Theory & Practice, Therapy, Treatment, Wellness

mutual-aid societies

"The sophisms of the brain cannot resist the mutual-aid feeling, because this feeling has been nurtured by thousands of years of human social life" (Kropotkin 1902: 277). As evidence of the veracity of Kropotkin's statement, in the twentieth-first century, mutual aid associations range from the highly organized credit unions and worker's mutual insurance societies to local chapters of the Heart Fund. More deeply rooted traditions for mutual-aid associations are the informal groups and societies that are so prevalent in rural communities and that are so helpful everywhere in economic hard times. Community social work practices are manifestations of these traditions, particularly the promulgation of organizational behaviours that can be successfully replicated when people request assistance in organizing for mutual aid. Scholarly social workers and educators in Canada have contributed very useful models for the construction of mutual-aid societies, often with an eye to group treatment (Shulman 1992; Wickham & Cowan 1986) or to community economic revitalization (Turner 2001: chap. 25). Sociological work on social networking is also instructive for building community-based mutual aid (Wellman 1979). Frequently, mutual aid association building, unlike other forms of community social work, is focused more in a social network or community of interest than in locality-based issues. Parents who are having a struggle with their teenage children, for example, may travel from all over a region to attend meetings of a semi-autonomous parent's group facilitated by a youth-serving agency. Not being alone with problems helps, as does sharing solutions. Friendship groups among vulnerable populations may be more locality based for a lack of transporta-

tion, and for both of these issues groups can be prepared for invigorating levels of autonomy.

In mutual aid groups generated through community social work, an initial process of group building helps associations to be autonomous in the long-term. Here, the typologies developed for treatment groups can be adapted for mutual aid group building. The groups are usually open, with group members selected by their involvement in the issue generating the need for mutual aid. Once they choose to join they can enter or leave at will. Size of the group varies with demand, with group members deciding. Assessment and pre-screening are usually limited to verifying that people are committed to the issue at hand. Worker awareness of fundamental stages of group process will facilitate a high level of group autonomy later on. A mutual aid group process typology looks something like this:

- *Initiation*: nervousness, holding back, or sometimes over-talking; sharing their story regarding the issue; and some reaching out or tentative contracting on group purpose;
- *Premature desire for structure*: several more experienced members may vie for power; different views on issue at hand expressed; more reticent members will defer, process information; worker support for more time for leadership to unfold; negotiate rules for group conduct; and initiate discussion of goals;
- *Networking*: making linkages; venturing forth with creative ideas for the group to consider; expression of fears, reservations; some assurances of mutual support;
- *Ownership*: comfort levels increase; members take on small rituals (e.g., coffee, recording); "safe" level for discussion of difference tested out; venture forth with idea for trial action re: issue; worker cedes some coordinating duties;
- *Transcendence*: confidence with group solidarity; eagerness for autonomy; wobbly leaving of the nest (i.e., agency); treating worker as welcome outsider.

Mutual-aid groups are like brewing good beer. If you give them good content, create a stable environment and as much time as they need, you'll get a superior outcome. Each of the above stages will take weeks, and they will overlap with each other as people come along at different times. A mutual aid group that is confident and mature can be semi-autonomous in one season. That is, do not expect to have them flying solo in less than three months. Even then the worker will have to judge how long a tether they will tolerate. All persons, as Peter Kropotkin said, have that mutual aid feeling... social work can expedites the process.

[*Ken Banks*]

RELATED ENTRIES

Citizen Participation, Natural Helping Networks, Non-governmental Organizations, Organizational Theory, Peer Counselling, Self-Help Groups, Self Help & Mutual Aid, Voluntarism

REFERENCES

Cossom, J. "Informal Helping and Mutual Aid," in J. Turner and F. Turner [eds.], *Canadian Social Welfare*, 4th Ed. Toronto: Allyn and Bacon. pp. 346–61.

Kropotkin, P. 1955. *Mutual Aid: A Factor of Evolution.* Boston: Extending Horizons Books.

Shulman, L. 1992. *The Skills of Helping: Individual, Families, and Groups*, 3rd ed. Itasca, IL: F.E. Peacock, 2001.

Wellman, B. 1979. "The Community Question: The Intimate Networks of East Yorkers." *American Journal of Sociology* 84, 5: 1201–31.

Wickham, E. and B. Cowan. *Group Treatment: An Integration of Theory and Practice.* Guelph, ON: University of Guelph, 1986.

My Neighbour

My Neighbour was a book written by J.S. Woodsworth in 1911 at the request of F.C. Stephenson for the Young People's Foreword Movement for Missions. In it, Woodsworth urged Canadians to begin rethinking traditions in relation to the responsibility to care for the needy in society. It served to establish Woodsworth as a leading personage in the social gospel movement with its strong commitment to social problems and their proposed solutions.

[*FJT*]

RELATED ENTRIES

Social Gospel Movement, Social Welfare History, J.E. Woodsworth

N

narrative theory

Narrative theory refers to the use of story as a metaphor for explaining how knowledge and experience are structured (Bruner 1990). Narrative theory, while not specifically associated with social work, spans a number of approaches to working with people as well as having a rich history and an independent research tradition (Manning & Cullum-Swan 1994). Two ideas are central to the narrative metaphor, the first bring that "reality"—or, what a person knows about the world and his/her experience of it—is constructed through personal proactive mental processes. The second central idea is that a person's understanding of the world is organized in the form of stories, which give meaning to experience, and shape relationships and behaviour. The constructionist position is often explained by distinguishing between the philosophical traditions of John Locke and Immanuel Kant. Lockean philosophy, associated with empiricism, assumes that people, their thoughts, and behaviour are a product of exposure and reaction to a single objective reality, which is an external environment; Lockean philosophers assume that, through a process of discovery, reality can gradually become known objectively. In contrast, Kantian philosophers assume that knowledge is wholly created by the organism/person and that what is regarded as reality is a product of a person's own active constructions; that is, all that a person can really know about the world is his/her own experience of it and the way in which he/she makes sense of it. Narrative theory assumes that story has a central role in forming the sense that a person makes of his/her experience, and in influencing a person's reactions and behaviour toward others. It is held that the sense a person makes is always an act of interpretation in which he/she arranges events in a sequence across time and in a way that provides a coherent description of him/herself and the surrounding world (White & Epston 1990). Stories are inseparable from language, which includes shared meanings and agreed-on descriptions that direct perceptions toward certain elements and omit others. Within social work, narrative theory is mostly associated with social constructionism, which recognizes that stories are embedded in the shared meanings of a social world. Meaning is not seen as fixed or invariant, but as multiple and changing and susceptible to the influences of culture, power, and historical contexts within which language and experience would be situated (Sands & Nuccio 1992). Accordingly, narrative theorists do not espouse "grand theory" or "universal truths" that imply a single correct version of reality.

Arguably, the process of living is so rich and complex that any single story can only reflect a fraction of that experience. In narrative theory, when one version of a story or event emerges as a generally accepted and preferred version of events, it is identified as the dominant narrative. Since many stories are possible about any single event, a great deal of lived experience falls outside dominant stories. A critical aspect of narrative theory for social work is making the effort to listen to stories that fall outside of the dominant narrative, as they are seldom heard and the voices, knowledge, and experiences associated with these non-dominant stories tend to be excluded. The effect is that some stories, and thereby experiences, become privileged while others are overlooked. Social work practice that is based on a narrative theory has emphasized the importance of examining a story that is given preference over others and of encouraging other stories about any particular issue or experience to surface. Narrative therapists seek to assist in the recovery of overlooked stories that may provide new and beneficial meanings for the client. They assume that new perceptions of a problem can promote new behaviours and alternative identities that challenge oppressed stories that people hold about themselves. Narrative social work, therefore, aims to support a client in locating facts about a problem that were previously overlooked and contradict prevailing accounts of their situation.

[*Keith Brownlee*]

RELATED ENTRIES

Hypnosis, Theory & Practice

REFERENCES

Bruner, J. 1990. *Acts of Meaning.* Cambridge, MA: Harvard University Press.

Manning, P.K., and B. Cullum-Swan. 1994. Narrative, Content and Semiotic Analysis. In N.K. Denzin and Y.S. Lincoln (Eds.) *Handbook of Qualitative Research.* Thousand Oaks, CA: Sage.

Sands, R.G., and K. Nuccio. 1992. Postmodern Feminist Theory and Social Work. *Social Work* 37, 6: 489–94.

White, M., and D. Epston. 1990. *Narrative Means to Therapeutic Ends.* New York: W.W. Norton.

National Action Committee on the Status of Women

The National Action Committee on the Status of Women—often informally called NAC—(est. 1972) is an umbrella organization for more than seven hundred women's groups and groups that support women's issues in Canada. NAC has a mandate to improve the status of all women in Canada by legislative, programmatic, and other legitimate avenues for social change. The express objective of the organization in its founding years was to "press for the implementation of the recommendations of the Royal Commission on the Status of Women at the federal level." The first focus was on social and economic issues including pay equity, pensions, child-care, poverty, education, and the inclusiveness of human rights codes. When abortion rights were debated publicly, NAC supported legitimizing abortion in the health care system. As an umbrella organization, the internal structure and politics are under continual challenges to maintain representativeness and to avoid constraints from the constitutions and commitments of member organizations. From the original thirty-one organizations, NAC has lost and gained members over the years according to the issues and the political climate. For example, women's organizations of the Catholic church left NAC when the legal right to abortion was contained in the list of NAC's key priorities; and the feminist organization, Federation des femmes de Quebec, left NAC in 1980 over constitutional issues emanating from the Charlottetown accord and during free trade debates. While a very broad range of cultural, political, economic and legal issues were debated, NAC also applied pressure to governments to improve the situation of women in the economy, in Canadian laws and in representation on boards and commission created by government. Until the constitution issues that arose in the 1980s, NAC worked to change legislation and programmes dealing with these issues and the rights of Aboriginal women in particular. The rise of women in the legal profession and the constitutional debates moved NAC's focus away from social and economic implications to rights under the Canadian Charter of Rights and Freedoms. NAC's prominence was eclipsed by the rise of the Women's Legal Education Action Fund (LEAF), whose approach was to fight issues in the courts instead of Parliament. NAC turned to issues related to violence against women, sexual orientation, and racism. This broader agenda resituated social and economic concerns on collective rather than individual rights, an approach not easily accommodated within the structure of liberal democratic law and institutions.

NAC emerged from a conference called Strategy for Change, held in Toronto on April 7–9, 1972, with more than five hundred women from throughout Canada. The conference had been organized by the National Ad Hoc Committee on the Status of Women. Many of the women involved in the conference organizing committee had begun meeting in 1966, when Laura Sabia, then president of the Canadian Federation of University Women, invited them to assemble to see what could be done to change the status of women in Canada. Leaders of thirty-two organizations formed a Committee for Equality of Women in Canada, which called on Prime Minister Pearson to establish a Royal Commission on the Status of Women; the commission chaired by Florence Bird was set up in February 1967 and reported in December 1970. Determined not to let the commission's recommendations languish, Laura Sabia in 1971 again called on the Committee for Equality of Women to take action. At that meeting, the National Ad Hoc Committee on the Status of Women was formed and planning began for the 1972 conference that was a turning point in Canadian women's history. The conference proved to be the first national confluence of long-standing women's organizations with newer feminist groups formed in the 1960s (e.g., rape crisis centres, New Feminists, Association for the Repeal of the Abortion Law, Ontario Committee on the Status of Women, Toronto Women's Liberation Movement), as well as individuals from most women's political, religious, and community organizations. From its founding meeting, NAC contained within it diametrically opposed views, and financial and organizational problems—but it also had a keen insight into the need to speak in a unified way on major issues of the day to a federal civil service that was dominated by male middle-class professionals of mostly European backgrounds. NAC's organizational focus and major issues were established in a series of meetings held over the next two years. Developing structure was difficult. Established women's organizations had formal constitutions, rules of order, and individual memberships—an apparatus that was rejected by the newer women's movement as reflective of patriarchal institutions. Throughout its history, the organization has struggled with such matters as well as regionalism and provincialism. As the first president (1972–74), Laura Sabia created a large and diverse executive of supportive volunteer women, a practice that has continued with each successive president. One account of NAC (Vickers, Rankin, & Appelle 1993) focuses on three periods: the founding era (1972–78), under presidents Sabia, Grace Hartman, Lorna Marsden (1975–77), and Kay Macpherson (1977–79); the transitional era (1979–82) under presidents Lynn McDonald (1979–81) and Jean Wood (1981–82); and an era of institutionalization (1983–88) under presidents Doris Anderson (1982–84), Chaviva Hosek (1984–86), and Louise Dulude (1986–88). The era that has followed these has been characterized by expanded issues that go well beyond the scope of ideas broached by the Royal Commission on the Status of Women. Under the presidencies of Dulude (1986–88), Lynn Kaye (1988–90), Judy Rebick (1990–93), Sunera Thobani (1993–96), and Joan Grant-Cummings (1996–2000), these issues included lesbianism, racism, refugee issues, global trade issues, and involvements with the UN agenda on women. While these expansions built on earlier concerns—NAC was active, for instance, in the 1975 UN women's conference—they redefined the founding purposes of the organization. In fact, constant vigorous debate over policy positions is a characteristic of annual meetings. NAC is typical of Canadian organizations that takes representation seriously, in that the costs of travel to meetings and its complex structure preclude broad participation; further, it has never been clear how many individuals in the member organizations that comprise NAC are aware of their affiliation with the umbrella organization or their ability to support its positions.

Working with senior public officials inside governments and with women in all sectors of the economy, NAC has lobbied successfully for changes in legislation, programs, and budgets of the federal government (e.g., pensions, part-time pay and benefits, divorce reforms, and rights of Aboriginal women). It has had a major impact on the appointment process of all subsequent prime ministers and some public inquiries (e.g., the Royal Commission on Equality in Employment (chaired by Rosalie Abella), the Royal Commission on New Reproductive Technologies (chaired by Patricia Baird), and the National Panel on Violence against Women). Often NAC works with other organizations, such as CABAL on abortion rights, unions on pay equity and trade, and national Aboriginal women's associations on their rights. The first Ottawa-based annual meeting, in 1976, also launched the annual lobby of federal politicians. Meetings with Cabinet ministers, opposition parties, and, often, the prime minister were a regular feature of this policy-making assembly. The success and influence of NAC has been so substantial that such counter-groups as REAL Women strove to lobby against many of NAC's positions—in particular, the rights of women in the paid labour force and the need for a national childcare program, and free and legal abortion rights met resistance from the homemaker's lobby. In the 1984 federal election, NAC chaired the first national debate of party leaders on women's issues, thereby raising the popular profile of the organization and putting women's issues on the election agenda. Since then NAC has commanded more sustained attention in the national media. Successful applications for grants from the federal government began in 1976, and individual donations and other private funding has supported NAC from the early 1980s. Cuts to government programs in the mid-1980s reduced NAC's budgets. Recent presidents have become full-time paid leaders and the organization has moved from its status as an inclusive volunteer social movement to an established organization of progressive women with a substantial budget and staff. This becalming is typical of social movements everywhere; NAC's thirty-year life span—a generation—follows a usual pattern in the institutionalization of a social movement. NAC's relative flexibility will likely accommodate the next generation, the so-called echo baby boom, which will come to prominence in the second decade of the twentieth-first century. Perhaps that generation can recreate the spirit of the original movement, seizing the power to determine women's rights in Canada for the twenty-first century. NAC has produced several different regular publications for its members and the public including *Status of Women News* (1973–85), *Feminist Action Feministe* (1985), and *Action Now* (1990). Information on NAC can be found in these publications and online at <www.nac-cca.ca>.

[Lorna Marsden]

RELATED ENTRIES

Feminist Theory, Non-governmental Organizations, Royal Commission on New Reproductive Technologies, Royal Commission on the Status of Women, Services for Women

REFERENCE

Vickers, J., P. Rankin, and C. Appelle. 1993. *Politics as if Women Mattered: A Political Analysis of the National Action Committee on the Status of Women.* Toronto: University of Toronto Press.

National Association of Social Workers (US)

The National Association of Social Workers (est. 1955) is the American equivalent of the Canadian Association of Social Work, albeit much larger and more complex in scope. With headquarters in Washington DC to facilitate its national social advocacy role, the organization reported its membership in 1996 as in excess of 150,000 with fifty-five chapters in fifty states. Its structural organization is comprised of a governing body, called the delegate assembly, which is made up more than three hundred delegates elected by the membership and which meets every three years. A twenty-five member board of directors is responsible for the allocation of resources and the implementation of policies set by the delegate assembly. This organization emerged from the work and commitment of five associations that represented different components of the profession such as the Association of Medical Social Workers and Group Workers, some of which had been in existence since 1918. The goal was to establish a body that could speak for the entire profession in the United

States. The association is engaged in a rich and broad spectrum of professional activities related to practice, standards, public policy, development, regulation, and international issues. Over its history, the association has published a broad range of professional materials in many formats, through the NASW Press. The journal *Social Work* is now in its forty-ninth year of publication; the press also produces the extremely useful *Encyclopedia of Social Work* and related materials that have influences much professional thinking and practice developments in Canada and elsewhere in the world. Canadian social work has benefitted greatly from the work of this organization. Information on the National Association of Social Workers can be found online at < www.naswdc .org >.

[*FJT*]

RELATED ENTRIES

Canadian Association of Social Workers, A. Comanor, International Federation of Social Workers, Provincial/Territorial Associations

National Congress of Italian-Canadians

The National Congress of Italian-Canadians (est. 1974) is a non-profit, apolitical umbrella organization representing Italian-Canadians in Canada. It was formed for the purpose of unifying Canadians of Italian descent so that they might have a sense of strength in their community and throughout Canada. With more than a dozen objectives, the congress provides assistance to members of the Italian-Canadian community in civic affairs, and in provincial and federal programs. In general it represents the community in projects of common interest and welfare with respect for economic and political issues affecting its membership. Fostering links to other organizations that were either formed by Canadians of Italian descent or have programs for them, the congress has affiliations with more than forty such organizations committed to rehabilitation, seniors, social services, and youth. Information about the congress can be found online at < www. canadese.org >.

[*Carlos J. Pereira*]

RELATED ENTRIES

Non-governmental Organizations, Social Services, Services for Elderly People, Services for Youth

National Council of Women of Canada

The National Council of Women of Canada (est. 1893) emerged during a time of widespread social reform and significant growth in women's voluntarism; it is Canada's longest existing women's organization. The council was founded five years after the founding convention of the International Council of Women in Washington, DC, with delegates from nine countries, which served as an umbrella organization for already established organizations. The founding objectives of the international council were to provide the opportunity for communication among women's organizations and a forum for women to discuss issues related to the welfare of women, families, and communities (Griffiths 1993). The first president of the international council, Lady Ishbel Aberdeen, played a significant role in the first years of the National Council of Women of Canada, helping to found the organization and serve as its first president during the years of her husband's appointment as Canada's governor general. Founding members included such pioneers as Dr. Augusta Stowe-Gullen, the first female medical doctor in Canada and a leader of the Canadian women's suffrage movement; and Henrietta Muir Edwards, who formed the Victorian Order of Nurses, wrote the first handbook on the legal status of women in Canada, and was one of the five women—with Nellie McClung, Emily Murphy, Irene Parlby, and Louise McKinney—to achieve a successful judgment in the *Persons Case*. The council's membership tended to include predominantly middle to upper class, well-educated women of European ancestry. This was a common profile for volunteers at the time, as these individuals had the time and financial support needed for such work. The Canadian council was structured to allow for membership through study groups, local councils, provincial councils, and nationally organized societies to enable engagement of municipal, provincial, and national governments. The National Action Committee on the Status of Women on its formation in 1972 used the structure of the National Council of Women in Canada as a model because of its effectiveness at lobbying (Vickers, Rankin, & Appelle 1993).

As a means to co-ordinate the social reform efforts of women in volunteer organizations, the council supplies women with information about public matters, offers a forum for debate and decision making, and organizes the presentation of members' concerns to the public and to official bodies—in particular, the Canadian government. As a member of the international council, the Canadian council also provides international links among women's organizations. Early reform efforts focused on improving conditions for female immigrants, factory workers, and prisoners. Members of the council have lobbied for women's suffrage, fought for the rights of mothers, and promoted women's appointments to boards, delegations, commissions, senior government positions, and senior positions in Canada's judicial system. The council has played a vital role in the formation of such institutions meant to enhance the welfare of individuals and families as the Victorian Order of Nurses, the Consumer's Association of Canada, and children's aid societies. In response to community and municipal concerns, council members have worked to promote adequate sewage systems, water purification plants, and controls to guarantee clean milk and bread (Griffiths 1993). Also at a community level, the council has fought for the promotion of the arts, such as development of local museums, art galleries, and music programs. The council brings issues of concern to the government in the form of policy statements and briefs, some recent submissions including Aboriginal peoples, social assistance standards, workplace child care, women as caregivers, and eradication of land mines. More conservative than some more recently developed women's reform movements such as the National Action Committee on the Status of Women, the council has been criticized for taking some stands seen as serving the existing social order (Strong-Boag 1976). Admittedly, the council's structure, with a commitment to consensus building, has influenced the council's focus and decisions; while this process has been challenged as slow and leading to the "lowest common denominator of opinion" among members (Strong-Boag 1976: 7), many of the council's initiatives have had egalitarian and humanitarian aims. The council has never been wed to one ideological view, but has been committed to finding common ground and common solutions among members across a broad spectrum of problem areas (Griffiths 1993). One of the council's

significant achievements has been its own survival with such a broad focus, particularly during times of waning mobilization. Not only is the council one of the first organizations to place women's politics on the public map in Canada, it has been successful for over a century in involving women collectively in Canadian politics. Information on the National Council of Women in Canada can be found online at <www.ncwc.ca>.

[*Sue McKenzie-Mohr*]

RELATED ENTRIES

N. McClung, E. Murphy, National Action Committee on the Status of Women, Non-governmental Organizations, I. Parlby, Services for Women, E. Stowe, Volunteers

REFERENCES

Griffiths, N.E.S. 1993. *The Splendid Vision: Centennial History of the National Council of Women of Canada, 1893–1993*. Ottawa: Carleton University Press.

Strong-Boag, V.J. 1976. *The Parliament of Women: The National Council of Women of Canada, 1839–1929*. Ottawa: National Museums of Canada.

Vickers, J., P. Rankin, and C. Appelle. 1993. *Politics as if Women Mattered: A Political Analysis of the National Action Committee on the Status of Women*. Toronto: University of Toronto Press.

natural health and complementary wellness

The field of complementary wellness has been growing in Canada, where people now have access to much literature on natural health and nutritional supplements are now sold in many drug and grocery stores. Consumers can also choose their own homeopathic remedies and herbal supplements at health food stores, as well as books on how to use them, and such complementary therapies as reflexology, reiki, and massage are among modalities gaining increased exposure. Many people are embracing the idea that individuals can assume a management role in their own wellness. According to a report on Canadian labour market trends (Canada 2000), the large ageing population wants lifestyle and wellness choices and is willing to pay for them. This mushrooming interest in and availability of complementary health care can make contributions to current social work practice, with which it has ready links. Social work has consistently sought to see the individual in context and, like complementary wellness, takes a holistic approach; whether the context is a societal inequity or the family, social work principles emphasize the need to consider the whole. Empowerment and equality are inherent objectives within social work toward the goal of wellness. Some of social works' most powerful medicines include the belief in the intrinsic worth of each individual, the right to self-determination, and the right to be truly heard free from judgment. Current curricula for universities offering social work programs have common threads beyond the basics, such as an emphasis on responding inequitable distributions of power, alleviating oppression, and learning cultural sensitivity, in particular, to Aboriginal peoples and immigrant communities; clearly, social work is not static, but is continually integrating changes to reflect the needs of the times. As such, the current practice of social work fits well beside the holistic model of personal wellness. This model has been influencing social work by offering such techniques and methods of stress relief for use by practitioners and/or clients, such as training in relaxational breathing exercises, in meditation, on eye movement desensitization and reprocessing, or on alternative nutrition. Beyond the understanding of wholeness at personal, familial, and societal levels—or rather, deeply inside it—is the micro-system of body, mind, and spirit. Complementing social work's view of the person as a whole are creative ways to involve all aspects of a person in treatment by drawing on natural health and complementary wellness. Social work can also apply other disciplines in the complementary and healing arts. Information is available, for instance, on the use of natural nutrition in addressing depression and anxiety. Energy psychology involves using accupressure points based on the meridian system of traditional Chinese medicine. Breathing exercises can open pathways for previously unexpressed emotional issues.

Foundational hallmarks of social work can be enhanced when practitioners engage the intellect, emotions, and spirit, as well as the body's physiology. The list of possible techniques is exciting, limited only by the extent of one's creativity. While it is too soon to tell how social work might benefit from other healing practices, it is quite likely that some social workers can derive personal benefit from relief of their work-related stress through some of these techniques. While some blending from prevailing influences is inevitable, maintaining the integrity of the profession is essential. A final consideration, however, is whether practices of natural health and complementary wellness can benefit clients by future research. Whether clients use them in addition to or instead of social work, widespread acceptance of natural health and complementary wellness has become part of the ways in which people heal and maintain their well-being.

[*Heather Harmony*]

RELATED ENTRIES

Culture, Diversity, Empowerment Theory, Ethnic-Sensitive Practice, Meditation, Natural Helping Networks, Wellness

REFERENCE

Canada. 2000. *Labour Market Trends and Opportunities.* LMI Unit. London: Human Resources Development Canada, Human Resources Centre of Canada.

natural helping networks

Natural helping networks are a wide range of resources that occur informally with or without the direct involvement of professional helpers and formal human services. The concept is of great interest to professional social workers because it acknowledges that most helping occurs, and indeed always has occurred, in natural or informal ways. Social workers may develop and employ particular skills and strategies to develop and support natural helping networks as a way of strengthening a family's or community's resources in conjunction with, or as an alternative to, social work services. The helping that takes place in natural helping networks tends to be defined in terms of its content, style, utility, and effectiveness by those who are engaged in the process whether in the role of giving/offering or receiving/rejecting help. Helping may convey significant cultural, religious, political, or ideological meanings, and may be quite different from the definitions of help that have their source in professional, scientific, or academic traditions. In natural networks, the helper may be a member of a family, a friend, a neighbour, a colleague, or a stranger who helps in a way that is not normally thought of as social work service (i.e., hairdresser, bartender, undertaker, postal worker, firefighter, or member of the clergy). The helper may be a peer sharing some important characteristic of the person being helped (i.e., age, gender, status, neighbourhood, ethnicity, role, problem, or issue). Some persons may become identified as natural helpers in the sense that they acquire a reputation for being particularly accessible, approachable, and useful. The helping itself may be emotional and/or instrumental, and occasioned by a crisis or by a more enduring need. It may be requested or unsolicited, and it may sometimes involve some expectation of reciprocity. Natural helping may also take place within a more formal structure, such as in self-help or mutual-help groups where expertise comes from participants' personal life experiences. These groups may be seen as alternatives to the formal services offered by professionals and are closely co-ordinated with them. Other types of natural helpers who might work with formal services include healers and spiritual advisers who are indigenous to an Aboriginal, religious, or other cultural community, and various "new age" and complementary wellness therapists and practitioners. Further, formal social services may emulate natural helping by offering roles and relationships designed to narrow the gap between helper and client, or to extend the reach of its resources, or to support, supplement, and complement what professionals do (e.g., surrogate parent/child relationships such as fostering and adoption, "befriending" programs, and direct services provided by indigenous workers, paraprofessionals, and volunteers). Within the context of professional group work, it is recognized that mutual aid processes among participants are central dynamics; in community development, a primary objective is collective empowerment for capacity building to meet local needs through internal and external action; and in organization practice, increasing attention is paid to the informal structures and dynamics within and between organizations, which play a significant role in task and maintenance processes. In many organizations, opportunities for informal communication and interaction are deliberately planned and encouraged as a means of fostering creativity, initiative, and teamwork.

Structures in which natural helping takes place, whether formal or informal, have frequently been characterized as systems and networks. For example, a support system for the caregiver of a chronically ill person may provide a structure for the provision of instrumental and emotional support from several informal and formal sources. In addition to the psychological and social processes— and, in particular, stress-relieving dynamics— involved in the provision of support, the use of terminology from systems theory entails such related concepts as boundary maintenance, equilibrium, organic development, feedback, and interdependence of parts and whole, all of which may be associated with natural qualities of the helping. In recent decades, the terminology of networks has also been used to characterize natural helping, including such related concepts as links or ties, density, centrality, multiplexity, connectedness and degrees of separation. This terminology suggests a focus on the routes that helping takes, without necessarily assuming dynamics of social solidarity and equilibrium, and without assuming physical proximity: a person's network may, for example, extend across space, with communication moving through electronic media. Network participants may transfer resources among one another without reference to a focal person. Weakly connected ties, because of their connections to other networks, may provide access to needed resources that other ties cannot. Concepts from both systems and networks emphasize the relational nature of helping within a larger social context and suggest that helping takes place in a social structure that is part of larger social structures. The social fabric of a society can therefore be seen to depend to some extent on the vitality of the helping interactions among its members and the degree to which social policies tend to strengthen and support these interactions. Historically, diverse intellectual and social roots can be identified for the concept of natural helping networks, these include Kropotkin's sociobiological ideas of mutual aid, the anti-intellectualism and anti-professionalism of the 1960s, nineteenth- and twentieth-century social movements that developed intentional communities, experiments in the use of paraprofessionals in poverty programs, the growth of the self-help movement, mental health approaches championed by Gerald Caplan, work on the idea of social support in the health disciplines, and the spread of alternative therapies in recent years. In Canada in addition to influences emanating from other parts of the world, important contributions were made by the co-operative movement with its roots in Saint Francis Xavier University in Antigonish; community development and adult education work in urban, rural, and isolated communities; the use of social animation in Quebec; the work of Todres in organizing a self-help clearinghouses, of Farquharson who applied related concepts in his work in remote areas of British Columbia, of Gottlieb who made a significant contribution in showing the connection between social support and helping networks, and Wellman and others who traced and conceptualized the patterns of helping networks from a mental health perspective in an urban community in Toronto. Wellman, a sociologist at the University of Toronto has been a leading theoretician in the development of approaches to social network analysis and in mobilizing networks of academics and others to develop new knowledge in this area.

In 1980, a symposium called Helping Networks and the Welfare State was held at the University of Toronto, bringing together researchers and practitioners from throughout Canada and beyond who represented a range of micro and macro applications. Since that time Canadian social workers have used these concepts as the basis for developing new forms of practice with young and elderly people, with families and communities, and in relation to a range of problems and issues. A persistent issue has been the tension between grassroots mobilization by ordinary citizens independent of government, and social policies designed to reduce the burden on the public purse by encouraging the development of natural helping networks. Another alternative involves designing social policies to ensure an interaction between the formal service system and natural helping networks that enhances the social welfare of all.

[*Ben Zion Shapiro*]

RELATED ENTRIES

Citizen Participation, Community Development, Empowerment Theory, Mutual Aid, Natural Health & Complementary Wellness, Networks, Organizational Theory, Paraprofessionals, Peer Counselling, Self-Help Groups, Self Help & Mutual Aid, Social Networks, Systems Theory, Theory & Practice, Wellness

networks

The word "network" has three usages current in the social work lexicon. Networks have emerged in recent decades as a concept of the competence and power of clusters of people in small and large systems to help individuals and groups attain desired psychosocial goals through their interaction. Although not originally, or even yet, a formal term in social systems theory literature, the concept of networks has developed from systems thinking as a useful and professionally popular term within social work. Even though social work has consistently stressed the importance of understanding the person-in-situation, the full richness and implications of this idea have only flowered in recent years. An underlying tangent of the term is that individuals, as social beings, attain the majority of their growth and development in interaction with other persons, groups, families, cultures, and political, religious, geographic, and historic systems. While persons are not directly connected to many of these societal subsystems, the more visible influences on a person's lives are the significant others with whom they interact. The awareness of the complexity of a person's intersecting systems of contact has considerable impact for social workers as they seek to understand the strengths and needs of each client, and where stresses and strains occur in the interactions with significant others and systems in a client's life. From a network perspective, work with and on behalf of a client may focus on areas in the client's life, where a practitioner can encourage potential change either to assist in a positive way or to reduce areas of stress; hence, a social worker needs to be aware of this spectrum of reality and seek to strengthen, alter, add to, or restrict it, or to limit its impact on a client's life. Although a relatively simple term, networking has had a strong impact of broadening the scope of social work interventions.

The word "network" is also used in a somewhat different and more administrative way in social work, to refer to the range of formal service resources that are available to a particular client; practitioners draw on this network to build from this range a structure that can maximize the impact on the client, minimize duplication and overlap, and establish strategies for the optimum effect on the client. Thus, networks are frequently associated with case management approaches to social service. As a concept, networking aims to maximize interaction or planned co-operation between/among services, or different components within a service, to avoid confusion and increase differential effects to help a client.

A third way in which the term "networks" is used is in reference to a country-wide structure of social, and health services, policies and programs—frequently identified as the social network. Again, the term reflects the concept of planned and unplanned linking of components of social services. This sense of network is viewed as an inter-influencing dynamic structure—a single entity that can produce a conceptual base for study to identify strengths, limitations, overlaps, and gaps in a manner that facilitates the planning of strategies for improvements. Network and networking do not comprise a theory of practice but, rather, a rich translation of systems theory concepts and operational strategies.

[FJT]

RELATED ENTRIES

Administrative Theory & Practice, Case Management, Integration of Services, Natural Helping Networks, Non-governmental Organizations, Organizational Theory, Peer Counselling, Social Networks, Systems Theory, Theory & Practice

neurolinguistic programming

Neurolinguistic programming, defined as a way to understand the structure of subjective experience (Adler 1996), is not actually a theory; rather, it is a model of change that is concerned with perception, language, attitudes, and beliefs within communication. The term "neurolinguistic programming" consists of three components, reflecting its nature: "neuro" referring to sensory perception (specifically visual, auditory, kinesthetic, olfactory, and gustatory); "linguistic" referring to language and non-verbal communication systems that order, code, and give meaning to perceptions; and "programming" referring to the ways in which individuals can learn about and modify thoughts, feelings, and communication patterns to change behaviour (Adler 1996). Neurolinguistic programming uses a series of techniques and tools to shift

an individual's subjective experience and, consequently, effect change in behaviour and foster problem resolution in a variety of relationships and contexts. Neurolinguistic programming is based on techniques pulled together from various disciplines, including psychology, linguistics, communication theory, and a belief in the unconscious (Lewis & Pucelik 1990). The originators of neurolinguistic programming, Richard Bandler and John Grinder (1975a and 1975b), examined the work of such master practitioners as Milton Erickson, Fritz Perls, and Virginia Satir to make these models of excellence explicit. The concepts and techniques of neurolinguistic programming have been applied to therapy, teaching, management, sales, and daily living. Neurolinguistic programming techniques foster communication change with an emphasis on aspects of communication that are outside of awareness, and draw on the belief advanced by Watzlawick, Beavin, and Jackson (1967) that all behaviour is communication, including observable patterns of interaction such as speech and body language, as well as less observable indicators of communication that reflect internal processes. The intent is to help individuals observe and use subtle sensory aspects of communication behaviours.

Neurolinguistic programming provides a method by which to analyze the structure of individuals' experiences and communication. According to its meta-model, analysis of spoken language (surface structure) can expose the speaker's mental map (deep structure); while the meta-model is based on language (Adler 1996), neurolinguistic programming is concerned with other forms of communication as well. Communication is comprised of representational systems, which refer to ways in which individuals represent and access experience, including the visual, kinesthetic, auditory, digital, or word symbols and rules, and olfactory systems (Lewis & Pucelik 1990). Specific questions are posed to elicit a person's views of reality and to facilitate change as appropriate. Along with the senses through which individuals process perceptual data, neurolinguistic programming posits that each representational system has specific qualities and characteristics, the details of which are important to identify and analyze: for example, for a person who is processing visually, it is necessary to determine the intensity of the colour, whether the picture has movement or is still, and so forth. According to neurolinguistic programming, certain categories of experience share similar structures for each individual: thus, happy experiences will have common structures, which may differ from the structures of unhappy experiences for that particular individual. The assumption is that a person who is helped to identify and change certain representational patterns can learn to change his/her emotional state and behaviour (O'Conner& McDermott 1996). People tend to favour one representational system over others, which is evident in the language the person uses as well as his/her posture and such body cues as breathing, tone, speed, and volume of the person's voice, and eye movements. One hypothesis is that the ability to identify and use the same representational system as the person with whom one is communicating will increase the effectiveness of the communication and strengthen the rapport that is established. For example, a person who represents his/her world visually may seek assurance that the listener "sees" what he or she is "portraying"; if a listener represents the world through an auditory mode, and responds that he/she "hears" what a speaker is "saying," the speaker may not feel understood. A listener who is "tuned in" to his/her own and to a speaker's representational system, however, may shift from his/her own preferred mode and assure the speaker that his/her does "see the picture," thereby fostering more effective communication. This technique of building rapport may be one that social workers find useful in forming therapeutic alliances with clients. Neurolinguistic programming also provides non-verbal rapport-building strategies, which require practitioners to use their own body movements, voice quality, and breathing rate; once mastered, these strategies enable practitioners to regulate the intensity of clients' affect states. For example, if communicating with an angry client who is speaking quickly and using large gestures, a practitioner could pace a client's gestures and speech on a smaller scale, and lead by gradually reducing his/her own rate of speech and body movements. using this technique, he client's anger is likely to become less intense (James 1989). Numerous techniques within neurolinguistic programming provide ways to identify and understand an individual's internal processes,

assumptions, and belief systems. A few of the major techniques include anchoring, reframing, and use of metaphor (Adler 1996; Lewis & Pucelik 1990).

According to the tenets of neurolinguistic programming, the meaning of communication is the response one gets, a principle that is compatible with social work principles (Angell 1996). The objectives for neurolinguistic programming practitioners are to learn how to assess another's/others' communication patterns; to become more aware of the effects of their own communication styles on another/others; and to modify communication patterns to fit each client. The tools of neurolinguistic programming will help the practitioner build the necessary rapport for the work. Another principle of neurolinguistic programming that is consistent with social work theory is the delineation of each individual's subjective experiences, rather than assuming a universal framework that can be applied to all. Finally, various empowerment principles are evident in neurolinguistic programming, for example, the belief that individuals already have requisite skills and resources within their repertoire (Bandler & Grinder 1979). Regardless of the social worker's theoretical approach, neurolinguistic programming techniques can be used to establish rapport with individuals, couples, groups, and within organizations and communities. Particular directive techniques can be integrated with such practice approaches as cognitive behavioural therapy. With a limited research base indicating mixed findings, neurolinguistic programming has yet to prove its applied effectiveness empirically (Angell 1996).

[*Debbie Levine*]

RELATED ENTRIES

Communication Theory, Information & Communications Technology, Theory & Practice

REFERENCES

Adler, H. 1996. *NLP for Managers: How to Achieve Excellence at Work.* London: Piatkus.

Angell, G.B. 1996. Neurolinguistic Programming Theory and Social Work Practice. In F.J. Turner (Ed.) *Social Work Treatment: Interlocking Theoretical Approaches.* 4th ed. New York: Free Press.

Bandler, R., and J. Grinder. 1975a. *Patterns of the Hypnotic Techniques of Milton Erickson, MD.* Cupertino, CA: Meta Publications.

———. 1975b. *The Structure of Magic I*. Palo Alto, CA: Science and Behaviour Books.

Bandler, R. and J. Grinder. 1979. *Frogs into Princes*. Moab, UT: Real People Press.

James, T. 1989. *NLP Practitioner Certification Manual*. Honolulu, HI: Advanced Neuro Dynamics.

Lewis, B., and F. Pucelik. 1990. *Magic of NLP Demystified*. Portland, OR: Metamorphous Press.

O' Conner, J., and I. McDermott. 1996. *Principles of NLP*. San Francisco, CA: Thorsons.

Watzlawick, P., J. Beavin, and D. Jackson. 1967. *Pragmatics of Human Communication*. New York: W.W. Norton.

New Brunswick Association of Social Workers / L'Association des travailleurs sociales du Nouveau-Brunswick

The New Brunswick Association of Social Workers/L'Association des travailleurs sociales du Nouveau-Brunswick (est. 1965) is the professional association and regulatory body for the profession of social work in that province. It was founded as a voluntary association by Carol Proctor, Marcel Arseneau, Joseph Laviolette, Norman Clavet, Stanley Matheson, Murray Manzer, and Constance Harrison. In 1988 it became a regulatory body assuming control of the practice of social work as well as the titles social worker and registered social worker under a private member's bill entitled An Act to Incorporate the New Brunswick Association of Social Workers, 1988. The objects of the association are to regulate the practice of social work and govern its members in order to serve and protect the public interest; establish, maintain, and develop standards of knowledge, skill, efficiency, and standards of qualification for the practice of social work, establish, maintain, develop, and enforce standards of professional ethics, promote public awareness of the role of the association and social work; provide means whereby its members may take action to pursue social justice and effect social change; and encourage studies in social work, and provide assistance and facilities for special studies and research. The association is governed by an elected board of directors composed of the five members of the executive, ten chapter directors, and one non social worker appointed by the government. The regulatory functions are carried out by three leg-islative committees: the committee of examiners, which approves all applications for membership and registration; the complaints committee, whose responsibility it is to investigate all complaints brought forth against a registered social worker; and the discipline committee that conducts disciplinary hearings and determines the consequences. There are also three standing committees for bylaws, education, and social action.

The minimum requirement for registration is a completed bachelor of social work. A person who does not have a degree may apply under the equivalency process if he/she has at least three years of experience in a social work position. If deemed to meet the criteria, a candidate can undergo a series of evaluations to assess level of knowledge, skills, and experience. All applicants must complete an application form; send a good character reference, an affidavit of diploma, provide two letters of reference; undergo a criminal reference check; and pay an administrative fee. Membership categories include regular, nonemployed, out of province, retired, and student. Annual re-registration occurs on or before April 1, and each member is required to complete a maximum of forty hours of continuing education credits in accordance with the association's continuing education policy, sign an agreement to abide by the code of ethics of the Canadian Association of Social Workers, and pay the appropriate dues. The head office of the association is located in Fredericton, New Brunswick. Current information about the New Brunswick Association of Social Workers/L'Association des travailleurs sociales du Nouveau-Brunswick can be found online at <www.nbasw-atsnb.ca>.

[*Suzanne McKenna*]

RELATED ENTRIES
Canadian Association of Social Workers, International Federation of Social Workers, National Association of Social Workers (US), Provincial/Territorial Associations

Newfoundland and Labrador Association of Social Workers

The Newfoundland and Labrador Association of Social Workers (est. 1993) is the professional association and regulatory body for social work in that province. The association was established with the proclamation of the Social Workers Association Act. This Act granted mandatory registration to the social work profession with control of the title social worker, as well as of the scope of practice of social work as defined by the Act. The mission—to ensure excellence in the social work profession—reflects both the regulatory mandate and the professional association functions of the organization. The present organization is the successor to the Newfoundland Association of Social Workers (est. 1952), formed by a small group of individuals committed to the growth and promotion of the profession of social work in the province. The earlier association had no regulatory mandate but persistent lobbying by members lobbied for regulation of social work practice was finally successful forty years later. The process initially involved the constitution of the Board of Registration for Social Workers in 1979 under the Act to Provide for the Registration of Qualified Social Workers. The purpose of that body was to provide for the voluntary registration of social workers and to implement regulations and standards to govern the practice of social work. The objectives of the present association by the statute are:

- to establish and maintain standards of professional conduct, knowledge and skill among its members and to ensure the general public the proficiency and competency of the practice of social work in the province and to serve and protect the public interest;
- to promote, increase and improve the knowledge skill, efficiency and proficiency of its members in all matters relating to the profession and practice of social work in the province;
- to regulate the practice of social work in the province and to govern the profession according to this Act and to protect the interest of members;
- to promote public awareness of the profession and practice of social work and to communicate and co-operate with other professional organizations for the advancement and best interest of the profession and practice of social work; and
- to encourage studies in social work.

The Newfoundland and Labrador Association of Social Workers provides such services to members as consulting on ethical concerns, continuing education, advocacy, social action, and promotional activities. In 2000 the association had a membership of about nine hundred individuals from all regions of the province who are registered to practice social work. The provincial office for the association is located in St. John's. Current information about the association can be found online at < www3.nf.sympatico.ca/nlasw >.

[*Lisa Crockwell*]

RELATED ENTRIES

Canadian Association of Social Workers, International Federation of Social Workers, National Association of Social Workers (US), Provincial/Territorial Associations

non-clinical practice

Non-clinical practice has a two-fold meaning in social work usage. It describes those aspects of practice that do not focus on direct work with individuals, dyads, small groups, or families but on efforts to bring about changes in the significant social systems or subsystems that differentially impact on society and its members. This meaning of the term encompasses those aspects of practice included under such methodologies as community work, social action, social policy, administration, and research. Non-clinical practice is also a designation also used in small systems, or direct work with clients, to describe those aspects of practice that do not take place through the process of interviewing. The understanding that frequently social work practice will not involve the client directly but with some aspect of his/her life that is affecting him/her is a long-term and critically important component of practice stemming from the profession's identification with the person-in-situation approach. Thereby, a practitioners will work directly with significant others in a client's life, or work to obtain needed resources for a client. Over the years, this essential non-clinical aspect of social work practice has also been referred to as indirect work and, unfortunately, through the complexities of the sociology of the profession, it has acquired an inferentially lower status than direct work, which is perceived as demanding more skill and knowledge. Non-clinical work is properly as, if not more, demanding of a practitioner, and it does not deserve to be relegated to practitioners with lesser qualifications. Like "therapy" and "treatment," "clinical" is a term that bears status for many practitioners, agencies, and clients and, consequently, is to be sought, while activities properly called non-clinical are often accorded a lower position in the list of "intra-familial" quality or status indicators.

[*FJT*]

RELATED ENTRIES

Clinical Social Work, Direct Practice, Indirect Practice, Knowledge Base, Research, Theory & Practice, Wellness

non-governmental organizations

Non-governmental organizations, commonly called NGOs, play a crucial role in social welfare throughout the world and are at the heart of the Canadian society's expression of democracy. Non-governmental agencies comprise the organizations that are generally not-for-profit and voluntary, as they are created to meet a purpose not being addressed by governmental or private, for-profit, agencies. This purpose or mission of social work NGOs is either to meet the needs of a particular group, such as immigrants and refugees, or address a specific issue, for instance, domestic violence. In contrast to government departments and agencies, NGOs are not empowered through legislation, and they differ from private organizations in that NGOs do not exist to make a profit for shareholders. A key feature that distinguishes social work NGOs from public agencies is that NGOs are self-governed; they should not be confused with such public organizations as health boards or school boards that are governed by boards of directors under legislation. Generally, an NGO's board of directors consists of volunteers, some of whom may be service users or have an intimate knowledge of the issue the organization aims to address. Being self-governed enables non-governmental agencies to be very flexible and to assume a strong role in public advocacy and social change. Often non-profit, such NGOs reinvest surplus moneys into the organization. This does not mean, however, that they are have charitable status for taxation benefits, as this status can only be granted to eligible organizations according to stringent criteria set by the Canada Customs and Revenue Agency. With respect to funding, NGOs can receive support from a number of possible sources, such as grants or service contracts with government, user fees, and grants from private philanthropic societies, where eligible.

Social welfare in Canada has been strongly influenced by non-governmental organizations. Canada's first attempts to care for the poor and marginalized, for instance, were carried out by religious-based NGOs, many of which persist to this day, along with many other sectarian and non-sectarian agencies. Non-governmental agencies have been advocates for marginalized and oppressed persons, taking stands on such fundamental social issues as child welfare, women's rights, immigration policy, and resource issues. They have also provided services when assistance has not been available elsewhere, for example, women's shelters, support services to persons with developmental challenges and their families, and hostels for the homeless. Beyond Canada, such organizations as the International Red Cross, OXFAM, and CARE, have been crucial in addressing human needs and social justice. The legislative advocacy and direct service provision roles assumed by NGOs still apply today. The Canadian Association of Social Workers and the International Federation of Social Workers are two examples of NGOs specific to the profession of social work, which exist to strengthen the social work profession through political advocacy and direct services to members, and to address social justice and development issues affecting clients and communities throughout the world.

[*Michael R. Woodford*]

RELATED ENTRIES

Assembly of First Nations, Associated Charities of Toronto, Barnardo Homes, B'Nai Brith, Caledon Institute for Social Policy, Canadian Labour Congress, Canadian Council on Child Welfare, Children's Aid Society, Chinese-Canadian National Council, Church-Based Services, Credit Counselling Canada, Fabian Society, Fred Victor Centre, Funding, Imperial Order of the Daughters of the Republic, Jewish Social Services, League for Social Reconstruction, League for the Advancement of Coloured People, National Action Committee on the Status of Women, National Committee of Women in Canada, National Congress of Italian-Canadians, Organizational Theory, Provincial/Territorial Associations, Salvation Army, Toronto Infants Home, United Way, Voluntarism, YMCA, YWCA

Nova Scotia Association of Social Workers

The Nova Scotia Association of Social Workers (est. 1963) was originally incorporated under a Nova Scotia statute, which provided for voluntary registration and protection of the title, registered social worker. Thirty years later, in 1993, legislation was enacted to regulate the titles registered social worker and social worker, and the practice of social work and to administer appropriate standards of social work practice. As a consequence of this change, all social workers practising in Nova Scotia are required to be registered with the association. With a current membership of about 1,400 members, the association maintains a register of members as well as a register of social workers engaged in practice, both of which are open to the public. The two main purposes of legal regulation of the profession are protection of the public from incompetence by preventing the practice of social work by persons without the requisite values, knowledge and skills required for competent social work practice, and development and promotion of the profession. The first of these two purposes is primarily performed by the board of examiners, which is part of the association but which operates at arm's length from other functions within it. The board is comprised of seven social work members appointed by the association and three non-social work members appointed by the Nova Scotia government. The board fulfils its mandate of ensuring competent social work practice by registering appropriately qualified social work candidates, and by investigating complaints against social workers who are alleged to be incompetent, accused of professional misconduct, or have breached the code of ethics. The board may also take appropriate action to discipline members in accordance with its mandate to protect the public interest. The second purpose, development and promotion of the profession, is fulfilled by the overall association. To ensure that members are competent and practice with high standards, the association provides educational opportunities to its membership, either by directly sponsoring educational seminars or by linking with other groups or educational bodies to do so. Each year, each member is required each year to engage in forty hours of professional development to update his/her skills. The association has adopted the code of ethics of the Canadian Association of Social Workers, as well as its own standards of practice to assist and guide practice by its members. As well, the association takes an active role in advocacy and social action by submitting briefs to commissions, task forces, and to the Nova Scotia and federal government departments on a wide range of social and health issues. The association believes that it has a responsibility to contribute to the development of social policy by drawing on members' firsthand knowledge and experience of ways in which the lives of individuals and families are affected by social factors.

The association strives to fulfil its mission and goals through the governance of an elected council, which meets regularly to conduct the business of the association. The council consists of the executive officers, chairs of standing committees, chair of the board of examiners, regional representatives, and special representatives. The membership as a whole meets at an annual general meeting, and at special membership meetings called occasionally for a specific purpose. Standing committees exist for social action, program, professional development, public relations, membership services, standards and ethics, private practice, and nominations. Current ad hoc committees established by council include social work in health care, and social work candidacy. Current information on the Nova Scotia Association of Social Workers can be found online at <www.nsasw.org>.

[*Harold Beals*]

RELATED ENTRIES

Canadian Association of Social Workers, International Federation of Social Workers, National Association of Social Workers (US), Provincial/Territorial Associations

Okanagan University College School of Social Work, Kelowna

In 1989, Okanagan University College in Kelowna, British Columbia, was given a mandate under provincial legislation to provide baccalaureate degree programs. In 1990 in a formal partnership with the University of Victoria, the university college developed a bachelor of social work program for study in the Okanagan region, with the University of Victoria giving the degrees. This program was accredited by the Canadian Association of Schools of Social Work in 1995 and, thereafter, the university college began in earnest to develop its own independent school of social work. Its 1996 mission statement, updated in 2000, reads:

> Based on a commitment to fundamental social work values and a vision of social justice, the BSW program prepares competent social workers for generalist practice. Graduates work at the individual, family, community and societal levels to promote social health and well-being in a diverse and changing society. The program fosters a pride in, and commitment to, the ideals of the profession through undergraduate and continuing education, contribution to the knowledge base of social work and partnership with the professional and larger community.

A comprehensive program review undertaken in 1998 with input from community professionals, students, alumni, and faculty resulted in the redesign of the integrated curriculum to reflect the mission statement. The university college conferred its first bachelor of social work degree in 2000. In recognition of the quality of the curriculum and overall development of the bachelor of social work program, in 2002, the national association awarded the Okanagan University College School of Social Work the full seven-year accreditation—a notable achievement for the first accreditation of a new school.

The current core faculty is comprised of nine faculty members (i.e., a director, a chair, and seven faculty) representing diverse ethnic backgrounds and sexual orientations. Five members of the faculty hold a doctorate and three others are working toward their doctorate. Community professionals also serve as sessional instructors, including designated First Nations and legal skills specialists. Approximately forty-five full-time students are admitted annually into the third year of the bachelor of social work program; the majority from the Okanagan region with increasing numbers from other parts of British Columbia and Alberta. Most baccalaureate graduates have remained in the region as professional practitioners and an increasing number have continued to pursue a

master of social work. The bachelor of social work at the university college is a four-year undergraduate degree. Students complete university arts courses in the first two years, followed by social work courses in the third and fourth years. The generalist social work curriculum is based on a solid core of required courses, in addition to a range of electives. A specialization in child welfare is also offered. Some highlights of the current program include collaboration between bachelor of social work and fine arts students in a creative "Art for Social Change" community project, an annual research conference to encourage faculty and community research activities, the creation of a First Nations student learning circle, and involvement in a First Nations healing conference.

Under the leadership of the director, the school has developed a four-year plan (2002–05) consistent with the university college's strategic directions. Several key initiatives are include in this strategic plan. The school is planning a master of social work program, owing to the increasing number of baccalaureate graduates in the region and the demand for practitioners with a master's degree. A social work research institute separate from the faculty will be formalized within the university college. Faculty members are engaged in community research within the region, province, and country; for example, a joint proposal by Okanagan University College and Laurentian University on homelessness has been submitted to the Community University Research Alliance for federal government funding. A new joint faculty appointment between social work and sociology can enable the development of an interdisciplinary gerontology program, considered to be vital given the ageing demographics of this region. In the current economic climate and pending retirement boom faced by many post-secondary educational institutions, the school is developing a plan to address the ongoing recruitment and retention of qualified students and faculty. Current information on the Okanagan University College can be found online at < www.ouc.bc.ca/ >.

[*Christine H. Lewis*]

RELATED ENTRIES

Board of Registration for Social Workers of BC, British Columbia Association of Social Workers, Education in Social Work, Faculties of Social Work

Ontario Association of Social Workers

The Ontario Association of Social Workers (est. 1964)—a bilingual membership association—is the professional association for social workers in that province, which in turn is a member of the Canadian Association of Social Workers. The association's fifteen branches share the mission of asserting the role of professional social workers, advancing their interests, and enhancing their contribution to social justice. Practising members are professional social workers with bachelor, master, or doctoral degrees. According to its strategic plan, which is reviewed annually, the association is committed to the pursuit of the goals of professional advocacy, social advocacy, and membership services. The association actively represents the interests and concerns of social workers by responding to the impact of government policies, programs, and legislation on professional practice, by advocating for recognition of the social work role and credentials, and by challenging misperceptions of the profession in the media, organizations, and communities. In 1982 the association established the Ontario College of Certified Social Workers as a voluntary self-regulatory body with a mandate to protect the public. Following a long-standing multi-pronged initiative in the 1980s and 1990s to vigorously seek social work legislation, in 1998, the Social Work and Social Service Work Act was passed and the college was replaced by the Ontario College of Social Workers and Social Service Workers. Another major professional advocacy initiative is association's active promotion of National Social Work Week. Every year, a poster and a wide variety of items promoting the profession are produced and distributed throughout Canada. The Ontario association embodies the social work profession's commitment to a civil and equitable society by engaging in social action related to marginalized populations and human rights violations, and promoting the profession's code of ethics. As the voice of social workers in Ontario, the association works though several standing policy committees (i.e., ageing issues, health, and school social work), as well as task forces or work groups on specific issues as they arise. The association addresses issues relating to, for example, women and children (including family violence), the elderly, persons with disabilities, health care, poverty, and social assistance. Social advocacy initiatives include making oral and written submissions to government and legislative committees; having representation on government ministerial committees; writing letters to the editors and opinion editorials for national, provincial, and local newspapers; and holding press conferences with media releases. In addition the association produces numerous professional practice publications—some of which have been the first of its kind in Ontario (e.g., Elder Abuse Handbook and the Social Work Statement on HIV/AIDS)—and serves as an important resource to social workers providing services to disadvantaged client communities. The range of professional and personal services provided to members includes, among others: discounted professional liability insurance; health, life, home, and automobile insurance; legal services; professional practice publications, guidelines, handbooks, and newsletters and journals addressing current policy and practice issues; continuing education workshops; job search materials and job bulletin; private practice orientation kit. Branch membership provides local and provincial opportunities to address the regional impact of government policies and programs, provide leadership through boards and committees on an array of professional and social issues, network with colleagues, access continuing education and local information, and enable social work students to learn more about the profession. Current information about the association can be found online at <www.oasw.org>.

[*Joan MacKenzie-Davies* and
Gillian McCloskey]

RELATED ENTRIES

Canadian Association of Social Workers, International Federation of Social Workers, National Association of Social Workers (US), Ontario College of Social Workers & Social Service Workers, Provincial/ Territorial Associations

Ontario College of Social Workers and Social Service Workers

The Ontario College of Social Workers and Social Service Workers (est. 1998) is the body charged to implement the 1998 Ontario Social Work and Social Service Worker Act. Under this Act, the Ontario Minister of Community and

Social Services, on the recommendation of the board of the college appoints the registrar. The board, which is responsible for the enforcement of the Act, comprises six people elected by member social workers, six social service workers, and six persons appointed by the minister for designated terms. Elections are structured so that all areas of the province are represented. The administrative functions of the college are carried out by the registrar and staff, and the policy making and disciplinary functions by the board.

[*FJT*]

RELATED ENTRIES

Canadian Association of Social Workers, International Federation of Social Workers, National Association of Social Workers (US), Ontario Association of Social Workers, Provincial / Territorial Associations

Ordre professionnel des travailleurs sociaux du Québec

The Corporation of Professional Social Workers of the Province of Quebec (est. 1960) is a voluntary association created by a private bill of the Quebec assembly. This initiative stemmed from the commitment of fifty social workers, the founders of the association, to the legal recognition of the profession in Quebec. Quebec's professional system was modified in 1974 with passage of new legislation for a provincial code to regulate all professional orders, including social work, the main objective of which was protection of the public. Under this legislation, the corporation was renamed Corporation professionnelle des travailleurs sociaux du Quebec. Social work was categorized as a profession of reserved title with the result that, while professional activities of a social worker may be exercised by non-members, the title "social worker" and the initials "sw" are reserved to members. With a view to ensuring the protection of the public, the Quebec association has put into place a regulatory framework, enshrined in government regulation, designed to shape the ethical and practical aspects of social work practice. All members are governed by a code of ethics and are subject to a disciplinary process co-ordinated by a social worker called a syndic. A disciplinary committee—chaired by a government-hired and -paid lawyer assisted by two social workers—hears cases involving infractions of the code of ethics and other regulations. Social workers are guided by regulations on record keeping, conciliation, and arbitration of professional fees, professional liability insurance, refresher training, professional inspection, and the cessation of practice. Other regulations govern admissions and administration of the association. It has also developed norms and standards for the practice of the profession in different settings and fields of practice and to fulfil its commitment to the continuing education of its members. As such, inspectors visit members in their offices to ensure their professional competence; and the association offers professional training to members throughout the year and holds an annual day of continuing education. The association also publishes a professional journal, *Intervention*, and a regular newsletter for its members. These initiatives are orchestrated by a number of committees bringing together lay leadership and the expertise of the personnel of the association. It is administered by a board of directors of nineteen social workers elected by regions, one marital and family therapist elected by all marital and family therapists, and four members of the public appointed by l'Office des professions, the provincial body with a mandate to oversee the application of the professional code. A five-member administrative committee is elected by the board: four social workers or marital and family therapists, and one public representative. Candidates for admission must hold a bachelor's or a master's degree in social work or a degree recognized as equivalent, and must inform the order of any criminal or disciplinary records in Quebec or elsewhere. Separate categories exist for regular, unemployed, nonpractising, retired, and out-of-province members. To attract young members, the association has established a preferential fee structure for new graduates. On November 30, 2001, the Quebec government conferred on the association the additional responsibility of regulating marital and family therapists. The head office is located in Montreal, Quebec. Current information on l'Ordre professionel des travailleurs sociaux du Quebec can be found online at < www.optsq .org/ >.

[*René Pagé*]

RELATED ENTRIES

Canadian Association of Social Workers, International Federation of Social Workers, National Association of Social Workers (US), Provincial/Territorial Associations

organizational theory

Organizational theory deals with organizations at a conceptual level, providing an abstract map of their goals, structure, functions, and environments. An expectation of a single clear and widely accepted definition of "organization" must remain unfulfilled, however, as many definitions exist, each with a specific epistemological or ideological foundation. In a survey, one hundred management scholars listed important organization theories, which were then reviewed to determine the twenty-eight most important organizational theories identified by more than ten of the surveyed scholars. Some scholars have even argued that there is no such thing as an organization (Wick 1976). With little consensus among organizational theorists, the variety of definitions that have been adopted confirms contradictory assumptions about the nature of organizations. In the social sciences, the concept of organization varies, depending on environment, culture, and language. Functionalists following Talcott Parsons, for example, define it as a social unit with particular purposes, primarily oriented to the attainment of a specific goal; although this functionalist paradigm dominated social sciences in the Euro-American world in the 1960s and 1970s, it has been challenged by proponents of other paradigms (Burrell & Morgan 1979). Corwin (1978), for example, defines an "organization" in one way as a unit consisting of individuals and patterns of interpersonal relationships among individuals, and more comprehensively as a co-ordinated collective that comprises autonomous units with adaptive structure, multiple normative systems, and permeable boundaries. Shafritz and Ott (1992) note that many theories attempt to explain and predict people's behaviour within diverse organizational structures, cultures, and circumstances. Just as with management theories, organizational theories can be described as a semantics jungle, which scholars have tried to manage by grouping together theories that focus, for instance, on time of creation, power, conflicting paradigms, as well as by descriptive or prescriptive nature. Among the numerous scholars in this field, the most creative is Morgan (1989; 1997), who uses different metaphors to illustrate why organizations exist and how they function. Burrell and Morgan (1979) provide the most useful guide to the organizational theory jungle, identifying ideology as a means of distinguishing theories from one another to provide a comprehensive view of their underlying assumptions:

- *Functionalist theorists* assume that society has a concrete existence and a systematic character oriented to producing a regulated state of affairs. This orientation is pragmatic and empirical.
- *Interpretive theorists* view the social world as a product of the subjective and inter-subjective experiences of individuals. Society is understood from the standpoint of an actor instead of an observer.
- *Radical humanist theorists* see reality as socially created and sustained. The analysis is pathologically conscious, as radical humanists are concerned with discovering how humans link thought and action as a way of transcending their alienation.
- *Radical structural theorists* view society as a potentially dominating force. With a material conception of the real world, these theorists assume reality to exist independently of the way it is perceived by people in their everyday activities.

As these four paradigms are founded on mutually exclusive views of the social world, each paradigm generates a theory that is fundamentally different from the others. An exploration of organizational theory as a whole reveals that this study has itself been guided by paradigm consisting of interrelated theoretical, methodological, and practical commitments. Since the end of 1960s, the study of organizational theories has proceeded "from orthodox consensus to pluralistic diversity" (Reed & Hughes 1992)—some even saying that it has become anarchistic—for numerous reasons. This movement toward diversity has emerged from the widespread increasingly pointed emphasis on cultural and symbolic processes through which organizations are socially constructed and on the way organizational analysis is academically structured. Further, macro power relations and the ideological systems that shaped organizational forms have become a focus of analysis; and finally, once organizational analysis was no longer restricted to the natural sciences, intellectual, and institutional space was created to allowed for approaches that focused on the complex interaction between theoretical innovation and social context. These developments, however, may lead to a crisis of incommensurability among organizational theories.

Professional social workers practise in organizational settings. Social workers who want to study organizations and communicate their findings can be guided by four focused considerations. First, to avoid differentiated findings and conclusions, it is most effective to study the same kind of organization. Second, to avoid miscommunications and endless debates over terminology, practitioner researchers need to speak the same academic or professional language. Third, each researcher needs to clarify his/her own position, theoretical or ideological position, and declared interests or commitments. Finally, each researcher needs to orient his/her work in time: for example, a modernist and postmodernist will have completely different paradigms for organizational theory. An understanding of the nature, boundaries, and functions of the organizations in which social workers practise is a crucial component of professional knowledge that continues to unfold.

[*Ming-Sum Tsui*]

RELATED ENTRIES

Accountability, Administrative, Boards, Non-governmental Organizations, Personnel, Social Policy Making, Supervision, Theory & Practice

REFERENCES

Burrell, G., and G. Morgan. 1979. *Sociological Paradigms and Organizational Analysis*. Portsmouth, NJ: Heinemann.
Corwin, R.G. 1987. *The Organization-society Nexus*. Westport, CT: Greenwood.
Morgan, G. 1989. *Creative Organization Theory: A Resource Book*. Newbury Park, CA: Sage.
———. 1997. *Images of Organization*. Thousand Oaks, CA: Sage.
Reed, M., and M. Hughes (Eds.) 1992. *Rethinking Organization: New Directions in Organization Theory and Analysis*. London: Sage.
Shafritz, J.M., and J.S. Ott (Eds.) 1992. *Classics of Organization Theory*. Pacific Grove, CA: Brooks/Cole.
Wick, K.E. 1976. Educational Organizations as Loosely Coupled Systems. *Administrative Science Quarterly* 21, 1–19.

palliative care

Palliative care can be defined as "a program of active compassionate care primarily directed towards improving the quality of life for the dying ... delivered by an interdisciplinary team that provides sensitive and skilled care to meet the physical, psychosocial and spiritual needs of both the patient and family" (Canada 1989: 1). Palliative care programs can include consultation, in-patient, outreach, and/or community-based services. In the community, individuals may receive care in their own home, a long-term care facility, or a hospice. Holistic palliative care draws on a complex interaction of physical and emotional factors. In providing family care, palliative care social workers provide important support throughout the continuum of care, whether in hospital or community settings. Primary reasons for referring patients to a palliative care program are pain and symptom management, and the need for psychosocial counselling. Toward pain reduction and symptom control, social workers may be considered secondary to physicians, nurses, and pharmacists; however, practitioners can offer specific techniques for relaxation, meditation, and imagery to assist individuals to feel that they have more control over and less anxiety about their situation. Social workers have a key role in providing psychosocial assessments to identify psychopathologies, risk factors, and other concerns for which intervention would be appropriate. Building on existing strengths and coping skills as well as support systems, social workers provide counselling to persons at the close of their lives and their families. Practitioners can help to alleviate anxiety and depression through the purposeful expression of conflicting feelings such as anger, helplessness, guilt, and sadness. Social workers can also help families to develop strategies and/or action plans that focus on current problem areas (i.e., finances, informing children, funeral arrangements, bereavement). Social workers can help individuals and families to negotiate the complex maze of health and social services at this stressful time. Responsibility for co-ordinating bereavement follow-up may also fall to social workers. In some situations—such as complex family dynamics or pathological grief reactions— palliative care social workers may continue to counsel family members following death. Other roles may include that of interdisciplinary team member, perhaps co-ordinator and/or facilitator of, team self-care. Social workers may consult on institutional policies and guidelines, participate in ethical deliberations and discernments, be active in program planning and development, and facilitate the provision of specific client information needs, or environmental enhancements; and practitioners are frequently educators to clients, team members, volunteers, community groups, and social work students.

Unlike Britain and the United States, where palliative care is rooted in the development of free-standing hospices, Canada's first palliative care programs were based in acute-care teaching hospitals. From their inception in the mid-1970s, palliative care programs have gradually incorporated a community focus. Most literature, however, notes that only about 5 percent of people dying in Canada receive palliative care, and the majority of these have a diagnosis of cancer. In 1988 a Canadian survey of palliative care programs found that only half of them employed social workers— a finding consistent with a 1985 US study in which only 48 percent of 463 hospices surveyed had social workers on their teams (Rodway & Blythe 1989). In June 1995 the Special Senate Committee on Euthanasia and Assisted Suicide recommended that within the restructuring of the health care system, palliative care programs should be made a top priority (Canada 1995). At present, with health care falling under provincial jurisdiction, there is no nation-wide standard for palliative care services or composition of the interdisciplinary teams who provide palliative care.

[*Janet Devreux*]

RELATED ENTRIES

Bereavement, Bioethical Issues, Caregiving, Clinical Social Work, Codes of Ethics, Ethics, Hospices, Long-Term Care, Personal-Centred Theory, Services for Elderly People, Veterans Affairs Canada, Wellness

REFERENCES

Canada. 1989. *Palliative Care Services.* Report of the Subcommittee on Institutional Guidelines—Guidelines for Establishing Standards. Ottawa: Health and Welfare Canada, Health Services and Promotion Branch.

Canada. 1985. *Of Life and Death.* Final Report of the Special Senate Committee on Euthanasia and Assisted Suicide. Chapter III. Palliative Care and Appendix M. Ottawa: The Committee.

Rodway, M.R., and J. Blythe. 1989. Social Work Practice in Palliative Care. In M.J. Holosko and P.A. Taylor (Eds.) *Social Work Practice in Health Care Settings.* 399–417. Toronto: Canadian Scholars Press.

paraprofessionals

Social work paraprofessionals are persons who have received specialized education beyond high school with recognized credentials in a field of social welfare activity. This term appears to have emerged simultaneously with and perhaps as a result of the rapid development of community college social service programs. Use of this term at its most positive seeks to grant a quasi-professional status to graduates of such programs. The emergence of social welfare paraprofessionals is part of a broader recognition that many tasks traditionally done by professionals could be carried out by other persons with adequate knowledge and training, thereby freeing professionals for more difficult tasks. In an informal way until the middle of the last century, this pattern had been underway in many fields where technicians or other persons with extensive experience had acquired a repertoire of skills that equipped them to carry out various tasks and responsibilities related to professional practices. This was certainly true of social work: over the last hundred years, professional practitioners have worked alongside many people carrying out diverse functions associated with social workers, people who identified themselves and have been identified as social workers but who had no formal social work education. Two factors bring some clarity to a clearer division of responsibilities and recognition in the general field of social welfare. The first was the development of community college curricula and recognized certification for formal status and recognition of a broad spectrum of occupations and activities; within social welfare, a cluster of paraprofessional designations such as social service, social welfare, child care, gerontological, and corrections worker gained recognition. The second factor was the rapid development of provincial legislation governing the practice of social work and the use of designated titles that clarify distinctions between social workers and paraprofessionals with other titles. This legal framework did not preclude the reality that, in some settings, persons with various titles and differing levels of training were carrying similar responsibilities. Implied in the differential use of the terms professional and paraprofessional are sociological status issues related to power, recognition, and legislative control of title and function. The dynamic in such boundary issues is also ongoing within broader fields of related human service such as social welfare, law, and health.

In social work in Canada, more recent developments impinge on the interrelationship between recognized professionals and paraprofessionals. The educational continuum from community college to university programs has undergone very rapid development. One change is in the increased recognition of community college coursework by universities, so that college graduates in social service and related fields can more readily complete university social work programs. Now, most Canadian faculties and schools of social work give some advanced standing to related coursework completed by college graduates. At the same time, greater definitional clarity is being achieved through legislative amendments to social work statutes throughout the country, whereby various jurisdictions award social work status to some community college graduates. The 1998 Social Work and Social Service Worker Act in Ontario, for instance, gives professional status to social service workers in Ontario, while maintaining a clear differentiation between their responsibilities and those of social workers. The term "paraprofessional" grants to a broad cadre of occupations and profession-related training formal recognition within society and within professions such as social work. The formal training for this recognized title prepares the paraprofessional for clearly recognized responsibilities that differ from those who have prepared for and become designated by a professional title. In social work, the continuum of knowledge and skills in training from a community college diploma through to a university doctoral degree has resulted in clearly defined and recognized paraprofessional and professional designations. Social work is among the first of the human service professions to do so.

[*FJT*]

parenting

Parenting refers to the raising of children to adulthood. Researchers and practitioners have concluded that parenting is a major determinant of child well being from infancy through adolescence, and that parents are the single most direct influence in their child's development (McCain & Mustard 1999). Research strongly suggests that the period from conception to age six is the most influential time in the life cycle for brain development and subsequent learning, behaviour, and health. Positive parenting throughout the preschool years prepares children for formal schooling with social competence, emotional confidence, and increased readiness to learn. Children who receive consistent nurturing and warmth, and appropriate stimulation throughout early childhood and into the school-age years do better in their cognitive, emotional, social, and physical development (McCain & Mustard 1999). But perhaps the most challenging parenting is during children's teenager years, when adolescents still require consistent parental controls but are striving for independence. Over the past forty years a wealth of parenting information has emerged on attachment research, child development, social learning theory, behavioural management, cognitive/behavioural therapy, family systems and ecological theories, psychodynamic theory, in addition to findings from a host of child and family studies. This knowledge base has identified important aspects of child development and family life as they relate to parenting and forms the foundation for numerous parenting intervention programs practised by social workers (Alaggia 2001). Family therapy practitioners provide parenting intervention, for example, when families experience difficult problems with their child's behaviour. Assisting parents through family therapy is common practice in children's mental health settings, child and adolescent units in hospitals, and medical and private practice offices. Approaches used are based on systems and ecological theories, which view change in one part of a system (i.e., the family) as creating change in the whole. Specifically, the child's problems are interpreted as symptomatic of larger issues in the family and interventions are aimed at the entire family, and related systems, with encouragement to refrain from scapegoating the child displaying problems and instead to identify and resolve the underlying family problems. Functional family therapy, structural family therapy, and the McMaster model of family therapy are frequently identified as ways to address parenting issues, especially establishing appropriate boundaries in the family, problem-solving skills, and behavioural controls (Cunningham 1988). Through parenting management training, social workers can instruct parents to deal more effectively with their children once problematic behaviours have surfaced, based on the premise that parents can act as critical change agents in the modification of child behaviour. To date, such programs are mostly used in clinical settings with children who have been identified as exhibiting socially inappropriate behaviours or who have been diagnosed with potentially serious behaviour disorders. As research has established developmental pathways for conduct problems and for aggressive and oppositional behaviour, identification and intervention with parents is possible to try to prevent future problems. Based on these findings, models of intervention for parent management training have been developed using social learning approaches, cognitive/behavioural therapy, and multi-systemic therapy. Parenting programs for abusive or neglectful parents are pertinent interventions for families identified by child welfare workers. Treatment for such parents is typically mandated by a court and, while interventions tend to be eclectic, a recently evolving model of multi-family group therapy has been developed for parents who have maltreated their children. The primary goals of this approach are to change behaviour in family members through alteration of intrafamilial interactional patterns, increase the responsiveness of family members to one another, and decrease isolation of families by working with other families. Owing to the serious nature of the problems and the risk level of children involved, the therapy is intensive.

Social workers also educate parents in preventive programs, the goals for which are to teach parents to deal effectively with normative child development. The most well-developed and tested parent education programs make use of videotaped parenting vignettes, role play, discussion, and written materials (Taylor et al. 1998). These programs tend to be implemented early in parenting from infancy to the pre-school years. Delivery of service is often community-based where parents meet in groups in places such as recreation centres, libraries, and child care centres. Social work intervention has benefitted from the wealth of child development and family research into parenting. Models have evolved to respond to parent needs for education, training, and therapy in raising healthy children. Practitioners can rely on well-established traditions of working with parents through interventions on inter-disciplinary teams in health and school settings, and in primary social work settings. In conducting family therapy, parent training, and/or education, interventions are aimed at strengthening parenting competence, discouraging negative parenting practices, and supporting positive approaches. As well as identifying and intervening on behalf of children displaying potentially serious problems, social workers are involved in prevention programs that promote parenting that limits future problems in children.

[*Ramona Alaggia*]

RELATED ENTRIES

Adoption, Child Abuse, Child Advocacy, Child Custody & Access, Child Welfare, Children's Aid Society, Family Allowance Act, Family Demographics, Family: Non-traditional, Family Planning, Family Research, Family Services Canada, Family Statistical Patterns, Family Therapy, Income Security, Mother's Allowance, Poverty, Pregnancy, Private Adoption, Services for Children, Services for Families, Services for Married People, Services for Women, Services for Youth, Sexual Abuse of Children, Single Parents, Toronto Infants Home, Vanier Institute for the Family, Wellness, Youth Criminal Justice Act

REFERENCES

Alaggia, R. 2001. *An Overview of Parenting Programs for Parents of Young Children: What Works?* Report prepared for The Parenting Alliance. Toronto: The Alliance.

Cunningham, C.E. 1988. A Family-systems-oriented Training Program for Parent of Language-delayed Children with Behaviour Problems. In J.M. Briesmeister and C.E. Schaefer (Eds.) *Handbook of Parent Training: Parents as Co-therapists for Children's Behavior Problems*. 133–75. Toronto: John Wiley and Sons.

McCain, M.N., and J.F. Mustard. 1999. *Early Years Study: Reversing the Real Brain Drain*. Toronto: Canadian Institute for Advanced Research.

Taylor, T.K., F. Schmidt, D. Pepler, and C. Hodgins. 1998. A Comparison of Eclectic Treatment with Webster-Stratton's Parents and Child Series in a Children's Mental Health Center: A Randomized Controlled Trial. *Behavior Therapy* 29, 221–40.

Irene Parlby (1868–1965)

Parlby, Irene (née Marryat), agrarian feminist, writer, politician; b. Jan. 09, 1868, London, UK; m. Walter Parlby, 1898; first female Cabinet minister (AB); d. July 12, 1965, Alix, AB

Irene Parlby was the first president of the United Farm Women of Alberta (1916). In 1921 she was elected to provincial legislature, and was later appointed to Cabinet as a minister without portfolio (1921–35). As such, she was the second woman to hold office in Canada and in the British empire. Throughout her terms of office, Parlby supported all programs that would benefit the welfare of women and children, including legislation to improve the quality of rural education, provide municipal hospitals and public health nurses in rural districts, enact a minimum wage for women, and require paternal child support. With Emily Murphy, Louise McKinney, Nellie McClung, and Henrietta Muir Edwards, Parlby was one of Alberta's "Famous Five" who petitioned the Privy Council in England in the *Persons Case*. Advocating for admission of women to the Senate, they challenged section 24 of the British North America Act, 1867 (now, Constitution Act, 1867), which stated that "women are persons in matters of pains and penalties, but are not persons in matters of rights and privileges." On October 18, 1929, the Privy Council reversed the Supreme Court of Canada's ruling on the case, declaring that women are persons in law "and eligible to be summoned and may become members of the Senate of Canada." In 1933, a memorial plaque was unveiled in lobby of the Canadian Senate honouring the "Famous Five." Every year since 1979—the fiftieth anniversary of the Privy Council ruling—five outstanding Canadian women are honoured with the Governor General's Award in commemoration of the *Persons Case*. In 1999 on the seventieth anniversary of this landmark ruling, a statue depicting the five Alberta feminists entitled "Women are Persons" was unveiled in the Olympic Plaza in Calgary, Alberta; further national recognition of these political pioneers occurred with the unveiling of an identical sculpture on Parliament Hill, in Ottawa on October 18, 2000. This was the first statue of female Canadian citizens on Parliament Hill. Irene Parlby was appointed as one of three Canadian delegates to the League of Nations in Geneva in 1930, and she became the first women to receive an honorary doctor of laws from the University of Alberta (1935).

[*Judy Barnes*]

RELATED ENTRIES

Feminist Theory, Human Rights, N. McClung, E. Murphy, Social Welfare History, Women's Christian Temperance Union

participatory research

Participatory research—studies carried out by one or more researchers alongside active participants, rather than as observers of passive subjects—has been part of Canadian social work for more than a quarter-century. Typically, in participatory social work research, representative working groups of community organizations and social movements define the study problem collectively, gather and analyze relevant data, and use their findings to take action to solve the defined problem. A wide range of methods may be used, such as theatre, art, role play, and other popular media; or community meetings, workshops, or focus groups. Computerized survey, mapping, and decision-support software may help to synthesize or analyze collected data. Academics and professionals may facilitate the research process, rather than direct it, as in more conventional research approaches. Before a study begins, all participants make a commitment for mutual learning and co-production, and decide how ownership of the knowledge generated through the research process is to be handled; some findings or recommendations may relate to confidential, controversial, or cultural knowledge that properly belongs to research participants and ought not to be shared in the public domain.

Influenced by and linked to similar approaches emerging under the leadership of such radical educators as Paolo Freire and Orlando Fals Borda, participatory research was given impetus and profile in Canada in the late 1970s by the Participatory Research Group of the International Council for Adult Education in Toronto. Other major centres of activity in participatory research, among others, include the schools of social work at Carleton and Dalhousie universities, the Native Studies Department at Trent University, University of Calgary's International Development Centre, and the International Development Research Centre and Participatory Development Forum, both based in Ottawa. In the 1990s, the research directors for the Royal Commission on Aboriginal Peoples encouraged use of participatory research principles in studies conducted for it, while many federal agencies (i.e., Justice Canada, Health Canada and the Canadian International Development Agency) have adopted the approach from time to time. Over the past twenty-five years, numerous Canadians have provided leadership in testing and refining participatory research applications in community work (Art Stinson, James Draper, David Smith, Elizabeth Whitmore, Rick Williams, Joan Kuyek, Gregory Conchelos), Aboriginal studies (Marlene Brant Castellano, Don McCaskill, Sandy Lockhart, Grace Hudson, Gerry McKay, Michael Robinson), feminist/ women's studies (Helga Jacobsen, Diana Ellis, Jan Barnsley, Anne Bernard, Lynne Dee Sproule), education (Bradley Cousins), rural planning (Harry Cummings, David Douglas), popular and labour education (Linda Yanz, Michel Blondin, Bev Burke, Rick Arnold, D'Arcy Martin, Barb Thomas, Carl James), the disability movement (Jack Pearpoint, Marsha Forrest, Judith Snow), popular art and media (Dian Marino, Deborah Barndt, Ross Kidd, Al Vigoda), and international development (Yusuf Kassam, Susan Smith, Tim Pyrch, Fiona Mackenzie, Françoise Coupal, Sheila Robinson, Terry Smutlyo).

Despite such widespread acceptance, participatory research has been the subject of debate and criticism. Beginning in the 1980s, and continuing today, feminist commentators have criticized participatory research for too often marginalizing or subordinating the voices of women, especially poor women, in processes that have been biased toward male leadership and middle-class perspectives. Also dissatisfied with past practices, anti-racist practitioners have sought new ways of integrating participatory research into the activism of Canadians who are not represented by views and assumptions of white, middle class, middle-aged citizens. In recent years, interest has grown among academics and practitioners alike in participatory evaluation. Contemporary applications in this area seek to reconcile the accountability requirements of funders for results and value-for-money in government and non-profit programs, with the needs, priorities, and perspectives of program users. Citizen-driven program evaluation—sometimes referred to as stakeholder or empowerment evaluation—is gaining prominence in public policy circles. Social work and other professions are continuing to explore the methods, contradictions, constraints, and opportunities associated with various forms of participatory evaluation and monitoring.

[*Edward T. Jackson* and
Budd L. Hall]

RELATED ENTRIES

Capacity Assessment, Citizen Participation, Community Development, Community Organization, Research

peer counselling

Peer counselling is simply people helping other people who are experiencing frustrations, worries, and other stressful life concerns. It can take place virtually anywhere, for children, teens, young adults, adults, and senior citizens. While elementary and secondary schools are probably the most popular sites for peer helping, some universities, colleges, hospitals, clinics, community centres, unions, businesses, and corporations have set up peer helping programs and services. Peer counselling is a generic description for such activities as peer tutoring, peer support, peer facilitation, peer mediation, peer conflict resolution, peer education, and peer ministry carried out by such facilitators as peer health workers, peer ambassadors, peer leaders, peer facilitators, peer mediators, natural helpers, peer support workers, peer helpers or peer learning assistants. While peer helping can include a variety of approaches, it differs from peer groups and from mutual help, self-help, and support groups. Typically, peer counselling can be distinguished by these characteristics:

- Peers are self-nominated or selected by members of their peer group(s).
- Peers are volunteers but may receive some type of compensation for their involvement.
- Peer volunteers receive from a qualified peer trainer needs-based, goal-directed, and experiential skill training.
- Peer volunteers are supervised on a regular basis.
- The more experience that peer volunteers have, the more they are involved in the selection, training, and supervision of other peers.

Peer counsellors fall under the general rubric of paraprofessionals (i.e., persons without extended professional training) who are selected from the group to be served, trained to perform some key function generally performed by a professional, and given ongoing supervision by a professional. Many benefits are cited from the use of peer counsellors. Services can be expanded and costs reduced, for example, because professionals are freed for other duties. Traditional counselling services can be enhanced by the unique abilities and skills of peer paraprofessionals, and opportunities arise to gain special insight into the needs and problems of the group being served, as peer counsellors bridge the gap between professionals and the diverse groups they serve. Peer counsellors benefit from the specialized human relations training, as well as the opportunity to help others and contribute to their own personal growth and development. The rapid expansion of peer programs throughout North America has been accompanied by a wide variety of roles for peers in helping one another. Peer programs are now widespread and associated with many community organizations, hospitals, telephone hot lines, and education, recreation, and seniors centres. Peer programs have been developed for diverse ethnic and cultural communities, specific health problems, health promotion, gifted children, children and adults with developmental or intellectual challenges, inmates, and many other special-needs populations.

[*Robin Wright*]

RELATED ENTRIES

Citizen Participation, Conflict Resolution, Coun-

selling, Mutual Aid Societies, Natural Helping Networks, paraprofessionals, Personal Social Services, Practice Methods, Self-Help Groups, Self Help & Mutual Aid, Theory & Practice, Therapy, Treatment, Wellness

person-centred theory

Person-centred theory—formerly referred to as client-centred theory—is an approach to psychosocial treatment that stresses a client's present experiences, with a focus on individual growth. It is a positive optimistic approach to intervention that strives to minimize aspects of authority in the helping relationship. This theory is principally identified with Carl Rogers (1980), who developed many of his early concepts through observing social work practitioners. Rogers was also influenced by the work of Jessie Taft, by functional thinking in general, and by the educational concepts of John Dewy. Rogers and those who followed him in the development of this theory were strongly committed to an empirical approach to knowledge building and the responsibility for self-evaluation of practice. The theory strongly emphasizes the critical aspect of individual experience and how phenomena are perceived: behaviour patterns developed by each individual are consistent with his/her view of him/herself; anxiety emerges when incongruity occurs between a person's sense of self and his/her experiences with others. Self-actualization is a basic human drive that takes place when a person perceives that he/she is loved and accepted. Effective practitioners must have a strong and genuine respect and value for the client, so that clients can find ways of achieving self-fulfilment. Client- or personal-centred theory, which stresses the critical import of a set of values from which the techniques of effective intervention emerge, is highly congruent with much of social work's value base and traditional style of interviewing. Despite its very close fit to contemporary social work practice, including the stress on evaluation, this theory does not have a high profile in Canadian social work practice; few schools of social work teach it as a discrete theory and, apart from a few Canadian authors (Rowe 1996), it is scarcely recognized in the lexicon of many practitioners. Nevertheless, the theory has made direct contributions to social work practice and persists indirectly to influence much of the values and practices of social workers.

[*FJT*]

RELATED ENTRIES

Abuse, Bereavement, Child Abuse, Counselling, Deafness, Developmental Challenges, Eating Disorders, Elder Abuse, Empowerment Theory, Environmental Issues, HIV/AIDS, Home Care, Individual Therapy, Hospices, Interprofessional Issues, Interviewing, Long-Term Care, Palliative Care, Play Therapy, Sensitizing Concepts, Sexual Abuse of Children, Suicide, Theory & Practice, Torture & Trauma Victims, Transactional Analysis, Visual Impairment, Vocational Rehabilitation

REFERENCES

Rowe, W. 1996. Client-Centered Theory, a Person-Centered Approach. In F. J. Turner (Ed.) *Social Work Treatment*, 69–93. 4th ed. New York: Free Press.

Rogers, C.R. 1980. *A Way of Being*. Boston, MA: Houghton Mifflin.

personal social services

Generally, personal social services are those professional, paraprofessional, and voluntary services that complement, supplement, or are in place of services and care rendered by families or friends on an individual basis to relations, friends, or other individuals. While today a wide range of services is available for persons who request them, these services have not always been sought or received on a voluntary basis: often, as in the case of child welfare services, compulsion has been involved. In the last thirty years in numerous countries, a cluster of social services has come to be perceived as having characteristics in common and significant where this was not previously the case. These services are now referred to as personal social services; often simply called "social services," they can usefully be distinguished as "personal," especially for purposes of international communication and comparison. In general social services are thought to comprise education, health, income maintenance, housing, and employment services. Personal social services can be thought of as the sixth or fifth social service, as the Fabian Society (1970) and others (i.e., Kamerman & Kahn 1976) have. The term itself came into more common usage after the report of the British Committee on Local Authority and Allied Personal Social Services was published (UK 1968). Personal social services regardless of nomenclature—whether called social services, general social services, personal care services, or social care services—can best be identified by their functions (Rodgers, Doro, & Jones 1975; Hepworth 1975–77). A comparison can be made with personal health services, since the mode of delivery of both sets of services is on a strictly to a person or individual. Whether as a consequence of industrialization or other factors, some personal needs are not met by the other social services. Over the last century, more and more measures of voluntary, public, and/or commercial provision have been made to respond to these unmet needs for specific groups or categories of people. Gradually, social workers and researchers recognized that these people come from all age groups and all social groups. In other words, while the incidence of social or unmet personal need may be higher for some groups than for others (i.e., lower income), in fact, everyone might potentially experience these needs at some time in their lives. In this context, then, it can be seen that child welfare services, housing for the aged, day care centres, homemaker services, transition homes, and rape crisis centres have characteristics in common—that is, in the words of Alvin Schorr (1974) that these "social services peculiarly demand personal delivery." Underlying these developments is an ongoing debate about the extent to which the state rightly or wrongly has taken over functions of the family. Suffice it to say that personal social services do relate to people in their private lives. Clearly many of the ills and circumstances that beset people are unsought: they do not voluntarily lose families and friends, or become old or disabled. Personal social services have been created to meet and mitigate some of these personal needs, needs that anyone might incur and that, in their private lives, they cannot always meet on their own.

When this type of service is considered holistically, it is far from comprehensive and far from meeting all recognized personal needs, let alone those current or future unmet needs that emerge as Canadian society changes. Even in the last thirty years, new personal social services have emerged such as transition homes for victims of family violence, independent living centres for persons with physical or developmental challenges, and brokerage services for persons with multiple problems. It is a social irony that personal social services emerged as a recognized sector of services in the period after 1973, and have continued to diversify even as economic prosperity itself has come under challenge in affluent countries for the first time since the end of the Second World War. Looked at broadly in historical perspective, personal social services have evolved from forms of state institutional care provided in the past for children, and for indigent, elderly, and disabled members of society as well as services less formally by religious organizations. Perhaps because institutions for children of the Poor Law-type were so unsatisfactory, a variety of special institutions were created for young people beyond or without the care and control of their families, or who were delinquent. But as such orphanages, industrial schools, and reformatories did not stem the tide of children and young people in need of some form of care, the state response was to create juvenile courts and child welfare services as the next response to the perceived needs of these children. Today, many publicly funded personal social services still provide a large measure of residential care, for example, foster care and group homes, which seek to provide a substitute family and supportive home environment. In some respects, child welfare services and the first measures of universal state financial supports (i.e., mother's allowances) given to families, especially widows with children, evolved alongside one another; in fact, financial support was introduced as a preventive measure to keep children from being brought into care, to keep families together. In this respect, some social services can be substituted for others or may be combined to produce better and more desirable results.

Personal social services have gained legitimacy and moved beyond the stigma that have been attached to use of them in the past, as people from throughout society now turn to them for assistance. On a conceptual and systemic level, it has become possible to identify a discrete personal social services sector that responds to a broad variety of human needs, which in the past may have been met by family and friends or, often, not at all. As Canadian society and economy become more complex—and new needs emerge—new types of personal social services are likely to emerge.

[*H. Philip Hepworth*]

RELATED ENTRIES

Fabian Society (UK), Peer Counselling, Personal-Centred Theory, Person-in-Environment Perspective, Poor Laws (UK), Poverty, Social Services, Social Welfare History, Voluntarism, Wellness

REFERENCES

Fabian Society. 1970. *The Fifth Social Service: A Critical Analysis of the Seebohm Proposals.* London: Fabian Society.

Rodgers, B., A. Doron, and M. Jones. 1975. *The Study of Social Policy: A Comparative Approach.* London: Allen and Unwin.

Schorr, A.L. 1974. *Social Services after Eden, or Who Promised Us a Rose Garden.* New York: New York University Press.

UK. 1968. Report of the Committee on Local Authority and Allied Personal Social Services. Cmnd. 3703. London: Her Majesty's Stationery Office. (Chair: Seebohm.)

person-in-environment perspective

The concept of person-in-environment captures the reciprocal interaction between an individual and the physical and social environments. It accounts for the dynamic interplay between the uniqueness of each individual and the contextual forces that have an impact on that person. An enduring and distinctive aspect of social work theory and practice, Greene (1999: 1) notes that "the person-in-environment perspective has been a central influence in the formation of the profession's knowledge base as well as its approach to practice." Viewed in this way, the human environment can be seen to be either supportive of an individual's growth and development, or potentially harmful; however, given the view that interaction between the individual and the environment is neither unidirectional nor static, and the complexity of such interaction accounts for variance of behaviour. In other words, individuals continually and concurrently shape, and are shaped, by their environment. Social workers can understand and contextualize human behaviour that is viewed from this holistic perspective, and understand that behaviour cannot be understood separate from the environment in which it occurs. Further, the person-in-environment perspective provides a broad mindset and a multi-system perspective, from which the practitioner may choose interventions. The construct of person-in-environment—which has also been referred to as person-in situation and person environment—is central to social work theory. In fact, the ecological perspective, the task-centred approach, the problem-solving model, ego psychology, and feminist theories all draw heavily on this perspective. Guided by this practice perspective, social workers must simultaneously attend to the person, the environment, and the transactions between them. In many instances, social workers are interested in improving both the client's immediate environment and the client's interaction with the environment. For example, an Aboriginal social worker assisting First Nation youths on a northern reserve would need to contextualize, for instance, the substance misuse by some teenagers and their parents, within the difficult social environment in which they live and the poor employment prospects they might look forward, as well as the rich cultural resources and natural environment available for learning coping and interpersonal skills. Maintaining a person-in-environment perspective guards against the tendency to attribute psychopathology to the individual while disregarding the conditions in which the behaviour arises and the individual's attempts to cope with the situation. Efforts to remove youths from the situation, attempts to treat them for addictions, and return them to an unaltered living situation will, in all likelihood, fail; at the same time, the person-in-environment perspective honours the uniqueness of the individual, "the person." The person-in-environment perspective reinforces social work's commitment to improving social functioning and the human environment.

Karls and Wandrei (1994) have initiated work to devise a person-in-environment, or PIE, classification for social functioning problems. This classification system is not diagnostic, as it does not attribute cause-and-effect relationships, but it is comprehensive in its assessment of a client's problems within this broad construct. The PIE system, which can provide social workers with a uniform language to describe the problems presented by clients, consists of four factors that capture various aspects of the overall client situation. The first factor—social functioning problems—captures an individual's performance in his/her family roles, other interpersonal roles, occupational roles, and special life-situation roles. The second factor—environmental problems—accounts for the social system in which the problem is identified, the type of problem, its severity, and duration. The third factor deals with mental health problems as outlined in the *Diagnostic and Statistical Manual of Mental Disorders* (DSM-IV), while the fourth factor accounts for physical health problems. Testing of the PIE system in a multidisciplinary rural mental health setting in Alberta found that the system was valuable for social work and non-social work members alike (Walsh & Ramsay 1994). While additional research is required in the development and application of this assessment tool, the person-in-environment perspective will undoubtedly continue to serve as a cornerstone in the theory and practice of social work.

[*Brian Rasmussen*]

RELATED ENTRIES

Biopsychosocial Theory, Ecological Theory, Environmental Issues, Individual Therapy, Life-Model Theory, Theory & Practice

REFERENCES

Karls, J., and K. Wandrei (Eds.) 1994. *Person-in-environment System: The PIE Classification System for Social Functioning Problems*. Washington, DC: NASW Press.

Walsh, K., and R. Ramsay. 1994. The PIE System: Canadian Field Test with a Multidisciplinary Mental Health Team. In J. Karls and K. Wandrei (Eds.) *Person-in-environment System: The PIE Classification for Social Functioning Problems*. Washington, DC: NASW Press.

personnel

The popular view that personnel in social services is principally comprised of social workers is in fact much more complex. Social workers are the predominant profession around which the social services are based; however, today's agencies are staffed by a broad diversity of professions and occupations to provide the range of services required. Even within the category of social worker, persons holding bachelor's, master's, and doctoral degrees with differing lengths of service/experience who are differentially responsible for the direct provision of psychosocial services offered.

As well, social workers carry responsibility for much of the supervision, training, administration of services, and, to an increasing extent, the conduct of research within the agency. Over the last several decades, a broad range of paraprofessionals and occupations from the rich spectrum of community college human services programs work alongside social workers. Staffing, depending on the agency and the services offered, will comprise persons who have been differentially trained in such areas as social service, child care, gerontological work, and family support. As agencies and services become more complex, members of other professions—such disciplines as psychology, nursing, education, play therapists, and financial counsellors—may work alongside social workers and paraprofessionals offering direct services or consultation. Other personnel are likely to be drawn from specialized financial and administrative spheres, particularly as funding and accountability become more complex. In the past when social services were in development, much direct service to clients was provided by volunteers; over time, these volunteers were replaced with professionally trained full-time staff. In recent years, the profile of the volunteer has once again assumed importance, where responsibilities carried out by volunteers might generally be covered by the concept of "friendly visitors" as well as a broad range of support tasks for clients, professionals, and the agency itself. As well as providing services, virtually all agencies, whether public or non-profit, have as part of its structure a board of directors that carries major responsibilities in planning, formulating strategies to achieve agency objectives, and fundraising; board directors, who are usually volunteers, also represent the agency in the community/communities in which it functions. Rather than representing only high profile groups in the communities, board directors to an increasing extent reflect social diversity and the community or populations served by the agency (i.e., single mothers, youth, seniors, physically challenged). The personnel of social service agencies, although still closely identified with professional social work, have become increasingly diverse as the needs served by the agency and state support served have become more complex. It is now common to find a range of staff positions that reflects the complexity of services, skills, and resources offered. Only in this way can the services respond to the complex psychosocial and systemic needs and wishes of the communities and the persons of which they are comprised.

[*FJT*]

RELATED ENTRIES
Administrative Theory & Practice, Boards, Education in Social Work, Organizational Theory, paraprofessionals, Supervision

pharmacological therapy

Pharmacological therapy is commonly prescribed for substance abusers, an extremely heterogeneous group. The use of a variety of intervention methods is necessary to assist in decreasing or stopping psychoactive drug use; treatment programs might include medical, psychiatric, harm reduction, and behavioural approaches. Addiction treatment, therefore, entails pharmacological interventions as well as traditional individual, family, and group psychosocial counselling. Further, the historic conceptualization of alcoholism and addiction as diseases, and associated involvement of the medical profession, have contributed to the use of a large number of pharmaceuticals as either an adjunct to or the primary method of treatment. Social workers need to be aware that such clients may have been prescribed a variety of different types of drugs, some of which may be psychoactive, to assist during their recovery from alcohol or other drug addiction. Four basic uses of pharmacological agents are used in addiction treatment: anti-alcohol drugs, antagonists, psychoactive drug substitutes, and drugs to treat concurrent disorders. Anti-alcohol drugs—referred to as antidispostropics—are prescribed with the intention of creating an adverse physical reaction when the individual consumes alcohol. The basic paradigm is that of conditioned avoidance/aversion: when taken before the consumption of any form of alcoholic beverage, these drugs produce a strong and unpleasant aversive reaction that is intended to deter further drinking. The most commonly employed drug for this is Anatabuse® (disulfiram). Treatment with alcohol-sensitizing drugs assumes that: an aversive reaction will occur after alcohol ingestion; the reaction will be sufficiently unpleasant to deter further drinking; and the ensuing reduction in alcohol use will result in overall improvement in the behavioural and medical problems that led to excessive drinking or resulted from it. Antagonists are drugs that block the effects of abused psychoactive drugs by occupying receptor sites in the brain where the drugs produce their effect. When used, antagonists extinguish the behavioural aspects of drug abuse; a drug user receives no positive reinforcement if the drug of choice is administered after the antagonist. Effective antagonists have been found for opioids with one, naltrexone, also used to treat alcoholics. As with the anti-alcohol drugs, the effectiveness of this method of intervention rests solely with the addicted person's willingness to take the drug.

Psychoactive drug substitution is simply the replacement of an abused drug with a "safer" alternative drug or an alternative form of the psychoactive substance. The alternative drug is theoretically used to slowly withdraw the addicted person until a time when he/she neither craves the original drug nor requires the substitute. Drug substitution is typically offered in conjunction with other treatment methods. The two most commonly used substitute drugs are methadone, used with opioids in a harm reduction approach, and benzodiazepines, used with both alcohol and other benzodiazepines. More recently, nicotine patches, using a transdermal method of administration, have emerged as a substitute for the nicotine obtained through smoking cigarettes along with the more traditional use of nicotine chewing gum. Drug dependence that involves heroin and other opioid agents is a chronic recidivist condition with a generally unfavourable prognosis; the outstanding characteristic elements include an overpowering drive or compulsion to continue to take the drug and to obtain it by any means for pleasure or to avoid the discomfort of withdrawal. The basic premise for opioid substitution therapy is that a suitable opioid agent administered daily by mouth is effective in the suppression of withdrawal symptoms and in the reduction of the use of illicit opioids. Of the many opioid agonist drugs that are available, methadone is currently the most widely used for maintenance treatment. No serious side effects have been reported with the therapeutic use of methadone. Nevertheless, methadone should only be provided to those who are able to curtail their excessive opioid use and

who are physically dependent. Drugs to treat concurrent disorders, such as alcoholism and other drug abuse, are frequently found in association with one or more mental health problems. For these persons, drug use may be a form of self-medication. Alcohol or drug abuse may also be a secondary to the primary problem of anxiety, depression, neurosis, or psychosis. (It was this belief that led to the unsuccessful trials with lysergic acid diethylamide (LSD) given to alcoholics in the 1960s; the rationale for use of LSD was that alcoholics would have a psychedelic experience or undergo an altered state of consciousness that would eliminate the need to misuse or abuse alcohol.) When psychopathology persists, particularly after initial sobriety has been achieved, a carefully selected medication may be necessary for treating concurrent mental health problems and to assist in maintaining sobriety. Most psychoactive drugs, however, produce a physical dependency after as little as four weeks of continuous use.

[*Rick Csiernik*]

RELATED ENTRIES

Addiction, Bioethical Issues, Clinical Social Work, Codes of Ethics, Ethics, Medication, Psychotropic Medication, Substance Addiction, Therapy, Treatment, Wellness

physical challenges

Language to describe people with physical challenges has varied widely. Prior to the 1970s, they were often referred to collectively as "the disabled" or "the handicapped"; then, "people with disabilities" was used to reflect the fact that a disability was only one characteristic of an individual and, in the 1990s, widespread use of the descriptor "disabled people" arose out of an intent to bring attention to issues of disability. Currently, "people with physical challenges" is accepted as an appropriate identifier. People with physical disabilities have suffered tremendously. Throughout the twentieth century, they have suffered humiliation and degradation—as a source of entertainment, for instance, in circus-like freak shows—social isolation, and even death (Linton 1998; Oliver 1990, 1996). Historically, sterilization was a frequently used intervention, performed in parts of North America under eugenics laws and bluntly orchestrated under Hitler's regime, during which nearly 250,000 persons with disabilities were executed (Chadwick & Dias 2000). Throughout North America and Europe, people with disabilities were hidden from society, kept in family attics or basements, or warehoused in state-run institutions (Linton 1998). Societies with little tolerance for difference, negated any realization or appreciation for the contribution that persons with physical challenges could make to a social order. Members of this community today may call themselves by such pejorative terms as "crip" or "gimp" to shock societal perceptions of normalcy and to empower themselves as a group (Linton 1998); similarly, members of this community have attempted to switch the political location of difference by referring to able-bodied persons as "temporarily able-bodied" or "tabs" (Bickenbach 1993). Language continues to play an essential role in the sociopolitical evolution of issues related to physical disabilities, as does the understanding of the concept of disability. Wendell (1996), for instance, defines disability as a social construction of biological differences between the disabled and the non-disabled, whereas Oliver identifies three components of disability: "the presence of an impairment, the experience of externally imposed restrictions and self-identification as a disabled person" (1996: 5).

Beginning in the early 1970s, the disability movement witnessed considerable "rights" action, initiated with the United Nations' commitment to the protection of rights and welfare of people with developmental as well as physical challenges. The UN defines disability as "a restriction or lack (resulting from an impairment) of ability to perform an activity in the manner or within the range considered normal for a human being" (UN 2000). In 1975 the general assembly passed a Declaration on the Rights of Disabled Persons, which encouraged international protection, and the International Year of Disabled Persons in 1981 facilitated "a global strategy to enhance disability prevention, rehabilitation, and equalization of opportunity, calling for full participation of persons with disabilities in social life and national development" (UN 2000). In recognition of this commitment and to provide a timeframe for governments to implement the recommendations, the UN. Decade of Disabled Persons (1983–92) was proclaimed. In 1993 the UN standardized rules on

equalization of opportunity for persons with disabilities and two years later the first international symposium on women with disabilities was held in Beijing, with more than two hundred women from twenty-five countries participating (UN 2000). The UN has been criticized, however, for its lack of implementation power, as people with disabilities continue to face insurmountable hardships throughout the world. Future initiatives for persons with disabilities need to focus on accessibility and inclusivity at the development stage of social planning for all nations. In this country, section 15.1 of the 1982 Canadian Charter of Rights and Freedoms recognized that "every individual is equal before and under the law ... without discrimination based on race, national or ethnic origin, colour, religion, sex, age, or mental or physical disability." A 1998 amendment by the Canadian Human Rights Commission required employers and service providers to accommodate special needs of persons with disabilities "short of undue hardship" and the definition of "undue hardship" continues to be specified by courts. While the disability community recognizes the significance of this addition, they call for more comprehensive legislation, similar to the US Disabilities Act 1990, prohibiting discrimination in all social interaction. In 1997 almost 30 percent of the complaints to the commission—where responsibility to bring a case forward is on the complainant—were discrimination toward persons with disabilities.

Social work practice has touched the parameters of disability on numerous fronts, such as within hospitals helping the newly diagnosed to cope with their disability; in rehabilitation services helping clients adapt their lifestyles; or in disability associations advocating for services and government legislation respectful of persons with disabilities. Social workers are not necessarily offering inclusive practice, however, when serving persons with disabilities, for example, failing to recognize the uniqueness of individuals, see clients' ability and potential, listen respectfully while focusing primarily on the disability (Gilson, Bricout, & Baskind 1998). The profession could pay increased attention to disability-sensitive practice. Given the historical struggles persons with physical challenges have faced in addition to living with their disability, social work is an appropriate profession to work alongside them, offering the profession's skills in self-determination, respect of diversity, and collectivization.

[*Judy MacDonald*]

RELATED ENTRIES

Canadian Charter of Rights and Freedoms, Developmental Challenges, Developmental Challenges & Families, Human Rights, Minorities, Minority-Sensitive Practice, Services for People with Disabilities, Wellness

REFERENCES

Bickenbach, J. 1993. *Physical Disability and Social Policy*. Toronto: University of Toronto Press.

Gilson, S.F., J.C. Bricout, and F.R. Baskind. 1998. Listening to the Voices of Individuals with Disabilities. *Families in Society* 79, 2 (March/April), 188–96.

Linton, S. 1998. *Claiming Disability: Knowledge and Identity*. New York: New York University Press.

Oliver, M. 1990. *The Politics of Disablement: A Sociological Approach*. New York: St. Martin's Press.

———. 1996. *Understanding Disability: From Theory to Practice*. London: Macmillan

UN. 2000. *The UN and Persons with Disabilities*. United Nations, Economic and Social Council, DESA, Division for Social Policy and Development. Online at time of writing at <www.un.org>.

Wendell, S. 1996. *The Rejected Body: Feminist Philosophical Reflections on Disability*. New York: Routledge.

play therapy

Play therapy has been described as "an interpersonal process wherein a trained therapist systematically applies the curative powers of play to help clients resolve their psychological difficulties" (Schaefer 1993: 3). The premise for play therapy as an effective treatment modality for children is the concept that plays is a natural form of self-expression that crosses cultures, religions, and genders. It offers children the opportunity to process and overcome experiences that are confusing, anxiety provoking, painful, or traumatic. Play provides a form of communication in which conscious or unconscious thoughts, feelings, perceptions, and desires can be symbolically expressed by children of any age and stage of social, emotional, and cognitive development. In a play therapy setting, the therapist can facilitate the re-experiencing of an unpleasant relationship or event with a more positive outcome (Schaefer

1993). Play becomes a symbolic language for children representing the conflict in a child's life while the toys are representative of the words used to describe the issues being played out. Child therapies can be described as non-directive or directive in nature: non-directive play therapy involves a child-centred approach whereby the therapist leaves the direction of the work to the child, whereas directive play therapy implies that the therapist directs and interprets the work. The difference between the two is related to the level of involvement on behalf of the therapist (Gil 1991). Theoretical models employed in therapeutic work with children emerged from adaptations to the application of the theoretical frameworks in adult therapy. Alderian play therapy purports that the therapist learn about the child's lifestyle and logic in order to facilitate a child's awareness of these areas and to alter self-defeating logic so as to move toward more positive logic, goals, behaviour, strategies for belonging, social interest, self-worth, use of creativity, and decision making (Kottman in O'Connor & Mages Braverman 1997). Child-centred play therapy focuses on the therapeutic relationship and the child as a whole being with the capacity for self-healing (Gil 1991). This model encourages a child to enhance his/her capabilities toward developing positive self-concept, self-responsibility, self-directedness, self-acceptance, self-reliance, and self-determination in decision making, while experiencing control, coping mechanisms, internal sources of evaluation, and self-trust (Landreth & Sweenie in O'Connor & Mages Braverman 1997).

Cognitive behavioural play therapy theoretically espouses an insight-oriented approach designed to change overt behaviours and controlling belief systems by incorporating cognitive and behavioural interventions into verbal and non-verbal play-oriented activities (Knell in O'Connor & Mages Braverman 1997). Emerging from object-relations and attachment theory is the developmental play therapy approach, whereby the therapist represents a mother figure who provides a solid sense of self through body contact and uses creative, playful touch to bring about therapeutic communication and relationship building (Brody in O'Connor & Mages Braverman 1997). Ecosystemic play therapy offers problem solving through alternative ways of understanding and experiencing life by employing structure, challenge, intruding, and nurturing techniques (Jernberg 1979) on behalf of the therapist to facilitate new understanding of an event (O'Connor in O'Connor & Mages Braverman 1997). Ericksonian play therapy focuses on the child's potential and resources to bring resolution to the present and the future. The therapist communicates with the child's conscious and unconscious mind through use of metaphors and storytelling with dolls and puppets (Marvasti in O'Connor & Mages Braverman 1997). Based on child-centred play therapy concepts, filial therapy—as developed by Bernard and Louise Guerney and associates in the 1960s and 1970s—encourages parents or caregivers as participants in the treatment process with the children as a means of reducing problematic behaviours and of enhancing the parent or caregiver-to-child relationship by assisting them in attaining the skills used by the play therapist (Guerney in O'Connor & Mages Braverman 1997). Gestalt play therapy assumes the principle of organismic self-regulation; through a process of reflecting and valuing their reality symbolically in play, the child constructs self-gestalts about his or her experience of self and significant others' responses to and reactions with them (Carroll & Oaklander in O'Connor & Mages Braverman 1997). Jungian play psychotherapy focuses on activating the individuation process, so that a child can develop a sense of identity and resolve traumatic experiences, while activating the child's self-healing potential, strengthening the ego-self, stimulating creativity, healing wounds, developing an interior life and sense of mastery, developing coping strategies, and understanding life's complexities with an openness for change (Allan in O'Connor & Mages Braverman 1997). From the psychoanalytic play therapy model—emerging from the work of Melanie Klein and Anna Freud in the 1930s—the therapist analyses the resistance and transference issues arising in the child's symbolic play and offers interpretations to the child to facilitate understanding and adaptive resolution on the child's behalf (Gil 1991; Lee in O'Connor & Mages Braverman 1997). Family play therapy includes theraplay, dynamic, and strategic techniques. Theraplay developed by Jernberg (1979) promotes positive interaction between parents or caregivers and children that contributes to building attach-

ment, esteem, trust, and adult/child interaction; and in this approach, learning from observation, the parents or caregivers become co-therapists (Koller & Booth in O'Connor & Mages Braverman 1997). Dynamic family play therapy promotes the resolution of relational challenges, including unresolved loss and separation, using techniques from movement, art, and drama to enhance spontaneous play and build trust, intimacy, and positive connections between family members (Harvey in O'Connor & Mages Braverman 1997). The premise of strategic family play therapy rests on the goals of dismantling dysfunction and stabilizing emotional and cognitive feedback mechanisms in family patterns of interaction. This is achieved through conjoint play as the medium for communication and change (Ariel in O'Connor & Mages Braverman 1997). The development of sand-tray therapy is attributed to the work of Dora Kalff (1980), based in Jungian theory; in it, the therapist interprets the child's symbolic representation of life through placement of objects in the sand tray and observes the child's healing process as he/she does so (Gil 1991).

[*Sheri Hardcastle*]

RELATED ENTRIES

Child Abuse, Child Welfare, Family Therapy, Narrative Theory, Personal-Centred Theory, Practice Methods, Services for Children, Services for Youth, Theory & Practice, Therapy, Treatment, Wellness

REFERENCES

Gil, E. 1991. *The Healing Power of Play: Working with Abused Children*. New York: Guilford.

Jernberg, A. 1979. *Theraplay*. San Francisco, CA: Jossey-Bass.

Kalff, D. 1980. *Sandplay*. Santa Monica, CA: Sigo.

O'Connor, K., and L. Mages Braverman (Eds.) 1997. *Play Therapy Theory and Practice: A Comparative Presentation*. J. Allan, Jungian Play Psychotherapy 100–30; S. Ariel, Strategic Family Play Therapy 368–95; V.A. Brody, Developmental Play Therapy 160–83; F. Carroll and V. Oaklander, Gestalt Play Therapy 184– 203; L. Guerney, Filial Therapy 131–59; S. Harvey, Dynamic Family Play Therapy: A Creative Arts Approach 341–67; S.M. Knell, Cognitive-behavioural Play Therapy 79–99; T.J. Koller, and P. Booth, Fostering Attachment through Family Theraplay 204–33; T. Kottman, Alderian Play Therapy 310–40; G.L. Landreth and D.S. Sweeney, Child-centered Play Therapy 17–45; A.C. Lee, Psychoanalytic Play Therapy 46–78; J.A. Marvasti, Ericksonian

Play Therapy 285–309; K. O'Connor, Ecosystemic Play Therapy 234–84. Toronto: John Wiley and Sons.

Schaefer, C.E. (Ed.) 1993. *The Therapeutic Powers of Play*. Lanham, MD: Jason Aronson.

Poor Laws (UK)

The Poor Laws, codified and reorganized in the Elizabethan era between 1597 and 1601, formed the foundation for social welfare in England and Wales until the passage of the Poor Law Amendment Act in 1834, which remained in effect until 1929 (Laybourn 1995). The English Poor Laws gave authority to the state to provide relief to the poor and indigent; at the time, by contrast, in other countries such as France, care for poor and disadvantaged people was a church and family responsibility. The Poor Laws strongly influenced the modern development of welfare states in Britain, Canada, and elsewhere, as the role of the state as provider for those in need became the foundation for welfare legislation. For instance, English-speaking Canada's first child welfare legislation, the 1879 Ontario Act to Provide For the Education and Support of Orphaned Children, gave the province authority over these matters. Not until the passing of the Quebec Public Charities Act in 1921 that state provision of services was extended to disadvantaged persons in French-speaking Canada (Yelaja 1985). Much of the ideology inherent in the English Poor Laws for state assumption of responsibility for social welfare persists still in Canada today.

[*Michael R. Woodford*]

RELATED ENTRIES

W.H. Beveridge, Church-Based Services, Fabian Society (UK), Income Security, Poverty, Sectarian Social Services, Social Welfare History

REFERENCES

Laybourn, K. 1995. The Poor Law, c.1780–1870s. In *The Evolution of British Social Policy and the Welfare State*. 15–36. Keele, UK: Keele University Press.

Yelaja, S.A. 1985. Introduction to the Profession of Social Work. *An Introduction to Social Work Practice in Canada*. 2–23. Toronto: Prentice-Hall Canada.

poverty

Poverty is an economic indicator of a person or family's lack of capacity to purchase basic needs (i.e., food, shelter, transportation, and clothing).

As such, people counted as poor in one country may not be in another country. Currently, the government of Canada is considering lowering the upper limit of this indicator (the poverty line), thereby reducing the number of Canadians counted by national statistics as living in poverty. According to the measure in place in 2000, nearly 18 percent of Canadians (one in five people) was living in poverty (NCW 2000). The majority of these people were women and children. By contrast, the top one-fifth of the population was earning about 44 percent of the total income per year, while the poorest one-fifth receives about 5 percent. During the 1990s, the disparity between affluent and poor Canadians was also growing, as taxes for the rich and for large corporations were dramatically cut, and the poor have grown poorer with increasing as globalization, the loss of jobs within economic restructuring and business downsizing, and drastic cuts to social assistance. At the same time, the number of middle class families has shrunk, further polarizing rich and poor (Ross, Scott, & Smith 2000).

Women and children face a high risk of poverty in Canada because of multiple structural factors and barriers. Roughly 40 percent of single women who are seniors are poor compared with 29 percent of elderly men. Families led by single mothers are four times more likely to be poor than single-father-led families. The unfortunate feminization of poverty results from multiple factors, including built-in labour market injustices, discrimination in pay, and inadequate funding and policies for child care, public assistance, and pensions (NCW 2000). Despite a declaration by the federal government in 1989 to eliminate child poverty by the year 2000, the number of children living in poverty increased in this period by 43 percent. Approximately 20 percent of children lived in poverty despite the fact that almost half lived in families who were working. Many parents and caregivers are employed in low-paying part-time jobs without benefits, while those receiving welfare live on very limited benefits. The National Council of Welfare determined that, in 2000, social assistance rates in Canada varied between 9 and 70 percent of Statistics Canada's poverty line, depending on location, household size, and type of benefit. As a result of improved public and private pensions, the poverty rate has dropped significantly among seniors, from 34 percent in 1980 to the present rate of 18 percent (NCW 2000). Nevertheless, there are still many poor seniors, especially women, stemming in part from inequities in the pension system and in part from the fact that many women had left the labour force for significant periods of time. The 45 percent of seniors who are disabled face further challenges, such as inaccessible housing and transportation and inadequate personal supports. Almost 60 percent of all Canadians with physical and developmental challenges are poor (Ross, Scott, & Smith 2000). Aboriginal peoples in Canada have been disadvantaged through the colonization, exploitation, and discrimination that has marked their interaction with non-Aboriginal society since contact. Unemployment exceeds 30 percent on reserves, where Aboriginal people generate incomes that are about 60 percent of what other Canadians earn (Ross, Scott, & Smith 2000); further, statistics have only recently been collected for the many Aboriginal peoples who live off reserve. As a result of multiple oppressions, Aboriginal peoples have much higher rates of suicide, school dropout, and incarceration than other Canadians (Morrisette, McKenzie, & Morrisette 1993). Approximately 36 percent of Canadians identified as members of visible minorities live below the poverty line (Ross, Scott, & Smith 2000). Many face discrimination and oppression in the delivery of social and economic programs. About 42 percent of immigrants coming to Canada are poor, especially those from so-called developing countries. Some distinctive characteristics mark poverty within different regions of Canada. On the east coast, for example, many people depend on natural resource exploitation (i.e., fishing, forestry, hunting) that is seasonal and low paying. Aboriginal peoples in the northern territories and provinces often rely on social assistance because they cannot earn a living from their traditional livelihoods, such as hunting and fishing, nor from local small-scale enterprise in their communities (Ross, Scott, & Smith 2000).

Theoretical explanations for causes of poverty in Canada and for potential solutions are diverse and affect ways in which social work practitioners view poverty and applicable interventions. Paralleling the rise in conservatism in politics, economics, and social policy making in Canada, right-

wing theoretical perspective on the causes of and solutions for poverty have been increasing. Conservative social functionalists hold that, to fill all the positions in society, different rewards must be provided (i.e., greater compensation is necessary to motivate people to strive for positions of higher status) and, therefore, a certain amount of poverty is inevitable to ensure the smooth operation of society. Closely connected is the economic trickle-down concept, adherents of which believe that, as an economy grows, benefits can be passed down to the poor. Solutions to poverty include the provision of private charity for the deserving poor and sanctions, such as the Ontario workfare program, to motivate others to work. A large segment of the Canadian population supports the theory of a poverty subculture, which sees poverty as a way of life and a value system passed from one generation to another; as the poor are seen as having, for instance, similar spending patterns, time orientations, and drinking habits, social welfare interventions from this perspective are devised to help change these values and patterns, and break the cycle of poverty. Ecological theory provides social workers with a more liberal view of how to intervene with an individual. This theory stresses that poor families often experience a chronic imbalance of stress over resources, which has the effect of disorganizing their natural networks and essential social systems. Human services that are fragmented and unco-ordinated often add to the problem. Proposed solutions from within ecological theory include dealing with people's survival needs before developmental needs, emphasizing services that promote family systems, using social supports including informal networks, and co-ordinating services to include multiple interventions and advocacy (Cameron et al. 1994).

Often human service programs stress a human capital theory. This classical economic theory considers poverty the result of a lack of such human capital as education, training, skills, and experience. Differences in levels of human capital result in differences in wages and income; little attention may be paid, however, to such systemic factors as discrimination. Instead programs such as training for welfare recipients focus on education and skills development. The dual labour-market theory emphasizes systemic factors that create inequities in wages and incomes; under this theory, the labour market is viewed as divided into a primary sector with stable employment, adequate wages, strong unions, and good career advancement, and a secondary sector characterized by unstable and often part-time jobs, poor wages and benefits, and few unions. Interventions thought appropriate for combatting poverty resulting from the disadvantages of being in the secondary sector include adequate minimum-wage protection, strong union legislation, pay equity, and affirmative action. Minority theory emphasizes the vulnerability or risk of certain people (i.e., seniors) to poverty; suitable interventions are thought to be development of such social policies as more extensive pension plans to bring more people out of poverty (Ross, Scott, & Smith 2000).

Postmodernism questions the concept of grand theories, faith in universal stable truths, and progress through science and rationality. Many human service institutions are considered to be oppressive. Social workers are urged to analyze and deconstruct existing programs critically, in order to understand how the poor in different segments of society are affected and to develop new interventions that respond to the diversity of human needs (Lessa 1998). Postmodern solutions include narrative therapy, which focuses on understanding the stories and experiences of individuals who are poor and marginalized. Feminist theories view poverty as caused by the unequal distribution of rights, wealth, and privileges that support patriarchal interests. Such theories—whether liberal, socialist, Marxist, or radical—stress the inequality of wealth and power between men and women. Solutions include understanding the impact of patriarchy and creating a more just society with more equitable relations: feminist therapists emphasize the empowerment of women through collaborative strategies, just therapy, and challenging social norms; community work by feminists focuses on organizing women to create social change; and feminist policies emphasize dealing with systemic issues and injustices that have produced the feminization of poverty. Radical economists maintain that capitalism promotes inequalities and creates class segregation, as a small economic elite controls the means of production and political decision making and policies. Control is effected by direct coer-cion, economic dependency, and the raising expectations through the provision of human services. Class conflict is inevitable and will bring about worker control over the means of production, either through violent revolution or concerted peaceful reforms. Social democrats in Canada, who also come from a class-based theory of poverty, feel that capitalism can be transformed through regulations and public policies. Closely connected is the anti-oppressive approach to social work practice that seeks to change a society based on exploitation, inequity, and oppression to one of emancipation and equality. Oppressions, which are seen as interlocking, include classism, sexism, colonization, racism, ableism, heterosexism, and ageism. Anti-oppressive practice interventions include promoting social justice, helping individuals redefine their problems, consciousness raising, empowerment, culturally sensitivity, collectivization, and creation of democratic institutions. Social policies from these perspectives aim to abolish excessive wealth, eliminate unemployment, emphasize human rights, and create a just and responsive society (Carniol 2000).

Postmodern theorists also point to economic grand theories that require deconstruction to alleviate poverty. The idea that poverty is increasing as a result of globalization has been increasing in many parts of the world. Canada has had stronger and more comprehensive social policies than the United States, and has produced fewer urban ghettos. The social safety net in Canada is rapidly being eroded, however, by pressures to harmonize human services between the two countries. Recent years have seen dramatic increases in Canada in the number of homeless people, reliance on food banks, and emerging private charities. Free-trade deals between Canada and the United States in 1990—and later with Mexico and South American nations—have resulted in massive job cuts as the economy in Canada became restructured, corporations amalgamated, and industries moved south to take advantage of lower taxes and wages. At the same time, the federal government has reduced corporate taxes and cut government expenditure for transfer payments, unemployment insurance, and human service programs. Wealth and power increasingly became concentrated in the hands of a few people. A much larger free-trade zone is being negotiated to include all of the Americas, except Cuba. Unlike the free-trade agreement throughout the European Union, the one in the Americas has not yet included significant environment or human rights protection.

Social workers in Canada have had to make some adjustments to practice as a result of changing social policies. Use of brief therapy is increasing, as government support for lengthy interventions is reduced. Protection, rather than prevention, is now emphasized in child welfare services. Many rely on the same clinical counselling interventions with poor people who face multiple oppressions that they do with other clients. Nevertheless, alternative ecological models of interventions (e.g., such as Better Beginnings / Better Futures) have been established; under this service model focuses on multiple risk factors of poor children, involves parents as lay helpers, stresses social supports, emphasizes community development, and provides comprehensive and flexible co-ordinated services at discrete stages of child development (Cameron et al. 1994). Independent living and resource centres more often apply a just therapy approach in responding to the needs of people with physical and developmental challenges; with this approach, clients comprise at least 50 percent of board members and provide such services as peer support, advocacy, referral, research, and service development. Such organizations stress client control, choice, and flexibility (Hutchison et al. 1996). Structural social work interventions with cultural sensitivity have been developed for immigrant and visible minority communities, and for Aboriginal peoples. Such programs may stress empowerment, holism, coping skills, and community development; Aboriginal social workers often draw on culture and the medicine wheel, encourage understanding the effects of colonization, involve elders as teachers, and assist in obtaining basic resources, advocacy, and community activism. This approach incorporates anti-oppressive social work interventions of replacing self-blame with a broader social analysis, empowerment techniques and collaborative social action (Morrisette, McKenzie, & Morrisette 1993).

Recent cutbacks in human services and the growing disparity between rich and poor are increasingly leading to structural interventions at the community level. Feminist groups are organizing about cuts that have greatly affected women and children, in support of more adequate day care, safe affordable housing and responsive services for women who have been abused. The withdrawal of the welfare state has led to more spontaneous grassroots initiatives, a focus on communities of interests and diversity, and emphasis on mutual aid, self-help, natural networks, and peer support. An increased interest has emerged in alternative economic development initiatives (e.g., community development corporations, local employment, co-operatives, local enterprise agencies, loan circles, and co-operative kitchens and gardens). Community action and organization are regaining importance, this time protesting against free trade, the lack of response to Aboriginal rights and land claims, growing racism, and the dismantling of the social safety net. Postmodern theories are increasingly being used to deconstruct government policies and bring together diverse interests in collective action. Structural theories have been utilized to create alternative federal and provincial budgets that propose job creation, strengthening social programs, investment in social housing, public transportation, and environmental programs, as well as raising taxes for corporations and the wealthy. As a result of efforts such as these, alternative visions based on liberation, equity, and local needs are emerging as social activists rally around poverty alleviation to bring about greater social justice and equality in Canada.

[*Peter A. Dunn*]

RELATED ENTRIES

Aboriginal Issues, Anti-oppressive Social Work, Canada Assistance Plan, Canada In & Out of Work, Family Allowance Act, Case Management, Food Banks, Great Depression (1930s), Healing Theory (Cree), Income Security, Mother's Allowance Act, Organization Theory, Personal Social Services, Poor Laws (UK), Single Parents, Social Assistance, Social Justice, Social Services, Social Welfare, Social Welfare Context, Social Welfare History, Social Policy & Practice, Social Work Profession, Theory, B. Touzel, Welfare State, Wellness, Workfare

REFERENCES

Cameron, G., J. Vanderwoerd, L. Peirson, and M. Cheung. 1994. *Promising Programs and Organizational Realities: Protecting Children and Support-*

ing Families. Waterloo, ON: Centre for Social Welfare Studies.

Carniol, B. 2000. *Case Critical: Challenging Social Services in Canada*. Toronto: Between the Lines.

Hutchison, P., P. Dunn, A. Pedlar, and J. Lord. 1996. *The Impact of Independent Living Resource Centres in Canada*. Ottawa: Canadian Association of Independent Living Centres.

Lessa, I. 1998. *Restaging the Welfare Diva: Case Studies on Single Motherhood and Social Policy*. PhD diss. Faculty of Social Work, Wilfrid Laurier University.

Morrisette, V., B. McKenzie, and L. Morrisette. 1993. Towards an Aboriginal Model of Social Work Practice. *Canadian Social Work Review* 10, 1, 91–109.

NCW [National Council of Welfare]. 2000. *Poverty Profile, 1998*. Ottawa: Minister of Supply and Services Canada.

Ross, D., K. Scott, and P. Smith. 2000. *The Canadian Fact Book on Poverty*. Ottawa: Canadian Council on Social Development.

practice methods

While social work practice in general has several distinct methods, sometimes referred to as modes, consensus within the profession has not been reached regarding their range and designation. There is general agreement in principle that, within the broad scope of professional social work activities, broad methods can be discerned to differ on the basis of client target, techniques and strategies, and requisite bodies of knowledge: individual, dyadic, group, family, and community practice methods; as well, some usage includes social policy practice, research, and teaching as distinct methods. The five foundational practice methods are the most enduring in social work. Practice with individuals—variously called casework, micro practice, individual therapy, one-to-one intervention, and counselling—involves a single social worker, dealing with an individual client from a broad range of theoretical perspectives. The strength of this method rests on the power of the helping relationship and, for many, it reflects the popular image of the contemporary social worker. Dyadic practice, which has only in recent years been identified as a distinct method of social work practice, has two clients as the direct focus of treatment; they are seen and worked with simultaneously. This method emerged from marriage counselling, later couple counselling; originally viewed as a subset of individual work or casework, this method has recently been as a separate and distinct methodology with implications of working with client dyads other than couples. Its particular challenge and potential stems from the complexities of triadic relationships and their application as therapeutic tools. Group practice methods—now also called group work, group counselling, group therapy, and group psychotherapy—was at one time also referred to as casework with groups. The power of this method draws on the potential of groups to build trust and mutually support one another in order to set and achieve individual and common goals. A method with a long history in social work, group practice has served as the basis for many social services. Family practice method—also called family work, family casework, family counselling, family therapy, family treatment, and family psychotherapy—focuses on the family as the critical social unit in a person's life as a complex social system with the ability to help or hinder the ongoing psychosocial development of members. Emerging from various theoretical approaches to family practice, a rich repertoire of techniques have been developed, which have in turn enriched other practice modalities. Even though social workers have long dealt with families, it was only in the 1950s when specific theories of family functioning emerged that this aspect of social work practice was identified as a distinct method. Community practice in Canadian is also known as community development, community organization, and at times social action. This method too has long historic roots in Canada, which recognizes the critical impact of community well-being on individuals and its potential to hinder or facilitate their psychosocial growth and development. This method builds on an understanding of the complexities of communities from small groups of neighbours to worldwide movements of people with common interests.

Earlier in the profession's history, social policy practice was often included as part of community work, but now is generally viewed as a separate practice method requiring separate but related knowledge and skills to those for community work. Social policy practice is a method that recognizes the power and influence of the body politic at all levels, as well as the differential impact that they have on the lives of citizens as a whole or in regard to people with special needs. As a social work method, it seeks to understand, critique, influence, and shape various social policies at all levels. Research became a separate method as a result of the great explosion of sophisticated quantitative and qualitative strategies and the massive potential of computers and related technology. Before that, social work had long acknowledged the ongoing responsibility to evaluate interventions and seek to expand and assess the profession's body of knowledge. As a separate methodology, research requires a high level of technical research knowledge; however, the expectation that all social workers need to have some competence in this area is reflected in the literature by the use of such terms as "scientific clinician," or the "clinical scientist" as a necessary description of all practitioners. Teaching has grown into a considerable practice method within social work, as the knowledge and skill bases, and the scope of theory and intervention techniques expand. Considerable literature relates to the many current aspects of social work education. As well, social workers occupy positions in influential national and international bodies, such as the Canadian Association of Schools of Social Work, and in most of the country's universities and colleges. Nevertheless, this field of practice is not ordinarily listed as a social work method; but teaching certainly has all the qualities of a separate and distinct methodology. The practicum is a particular component of the teaching method in social work that has shaped the form of education for the profession; field instructors for practica have contributed greatly to building an essential bridge between theory and practice and have become within the profession a cadre of front-line colleagues who function in both the academic world and that of direct practice.

Early in the profession's history, the widely held perception was that each individual practised in only a single method. Indeed, for several decades people identified themselves on the basis of a methodology, for example, as a caseworker or as a group worker. This identification has changed, as most practitioners today require competence in several different methods; thus, the perception of the contemporary social worker is one that of mul-

tiple methods, from which the generalist identity has emerged.

[*FJT*]

RELATED ENTRIES

Aboriginal Issues, Accountability, Assessment, Conflict Resolution, Counselling, Creativity, Crisis Intervention, Demography, Ethics, Diagnosis, Goal Setting, Healing Theory (Cree), Interviewing, Knowledge Base, Meditation, Peer Counselling, Practicum Instruction, Private Practice, Professional Issues, Program Evaluation, Quality Assurance, Recording, Research, Sensitizing Concepts, Social Work Practice, Spirituality, Technology, Theory & Practice, Therapy, Treatment, Youth Criminal Justice Act

practicum instruction

Practicum—also referred to as field practicum, field instruction, field education, field work—is a type of course or mode of study where students learn to practice social work through delivering social work services in agency settings. Educationally focused field instruction is provided so that students learn to integrate and apply theory to practice, to examine, critique, and test in action the knowledge, values, and principles studied in academic courses. In the practicum, students are exposed to a wide range of interventions and learn to use practice techniques, skilfully adapted to the dynamics of particular situations. They develop competence in performing social work functions through educationally focused feedback about their actual practice with a range of clients, groups, communities, or in administration, planning, or policy development activities. The practicum is a required and integral component of curricula in all undergraduate and many graduate programs in Canadian Schools of Social Work. Canadian social work educators and field instructors have developed a substantial knowledge base for the practicum, conducted federally funded studies, and organized national symposia on practicum (Rogers 1995). The practicum takes place within the context of two organizations, the university school or faculty of social work and the community social service agency or human service organization. Social work field education depends on the collaboration of service organizations, universities, and individual social workers (Bogo & Globerman 1995). Since many agencies do not reduce social workers' workloads for field instruction, field education depends on the commitment and voluntary participation of social workers and the organizations' support for their participation. In the health field, with the shift to programmatic hospital organizations and the lack of professional departments, social workers must also gain the support of the interdisciplinary team and program director before they can volunteer to become field instructors.

Many social work students and alumni consider the practicum as the core of their educational preparation for professional practice and personal development as a social worker (Kadushin 1991). They also regard field instructors, those social workers who guide students through the practicum, as central to their learning. Field instructors have primary responsibility for linking the student to the setting; teaching, co-ordinating, and evaluating the student's learning; ensuring that the agency's service standards are met; and liaising with the university. They have current practice experience and a commitment to social work education. Field instructors are employees of the service delivery organization, hold a social work degree, and have a minimum of two years of social work experience. Exceptions are made to these requirements when, for example, schools establish field units with a faculty field instructor, or appoint as field instructor persons who do not hold a professional social work degree and are working in innovative programs, under-serviced fields, or in locales where there are no social workers. The school provides liaison to ensure the incorporation of a social work focus. Studies repeatedly confirm the importance of the field instructor as pivotal in promoting student learning and satisfaction in field education. Recognizing that the competence of the field instructor is crucial for a quality practicum for students, schools of social work offer a range of training opportunities for both new and experienced field instructors (Rogers 1996). Schools appoint a faculty field liaison, a member of the university, to link class and field, monitor the practicum, evaluate student learning and field instruction, and consult and manage problems in learning. What constitutes the content for the practicum and what students should be able to do on completion is much debated. Fortune (1994) identified a core of common knowledge and skill that can be considered

the foundation field curriculum. The competencies include practice with individuals and families; professional commitment and development; practice in an organizational context; and practice that uses service delivery organizations and community resources. Each Canadian school develops practicum objectives or a competency model that reflects the mission and objectives of the specific educational program. Field instructors and students use this framework to develop individualized learning plans that reflect the student's learning needs and the agency's practice. Learning plans or contracts specify goals, guide the selection of learning assignments, focus the teaching and learning, and provide objectives for evaluating outcomes. The client, group, community, project, or policy assignment provide the focus for a range of teaching and learning methods including case discussion, written process, or summary reports, audio and videotape review, and practising with the field instructor.

[*Marion Bogo*]

RELATED ENTRIES

Education in Social Work, Professional Issues, Social Work Profession

REFERENCES

Bogo, M., and J. Globerman. 1995. Creating Effective University Field Partnerships: An Analysis of Two Inter-organization Models. *Journal of Teaching in Social Work* 11, 112, 177–92.

Fortune, A.E. 1994. Field Education. In F.J. Reamer (Ed.) *The Foundations of Social Work Knowledge*. 151–94. New York: Columbia University Press.

Kadushin, A.E. 1991. Introduction. In D. Schneck, B. Grossman, and U. Glassman (Eds.) *Field Education in Social Work: Contemporary Issues and Trends*. 1112. Dubuque, IA: Kendall/Hunt.

Rogers, G. (Ed.). 1995. *Social Workfield Education: Views and Visions*. Dubuque, IA: Kendall/Hunt.

pregnancy

Social workers encounter issues related to pregnancy in various community and regional services, and in collaboration with colleagues from other disciplines. Social workers develop, administer, and refer clients to programs and services that address the physical, social, emotional, and economic needs of individuals and families during and as a result of pregnancy. In the past pregnancy was viewed as a private matter within a family; when pregnancy issues were catapulted to the political forefront in the last century, it brought the social work profession in its slipstream. This movement effectively broadened the profession's current involvement in and focus on treatment with this client population. A Health Canada report (Canada 1999a) identified, as one of its initiatives, the need to improve and integrate preconception, prenatal, pregnancy, and postpartum programs to ensure essential assistance and support for mothers, fathers, and babies. Pregnancy services that compliment this objective include prenatal health and nutrition programs, individual casework, and parenting workshops; in recognition of pregnancy as a normal and healthy life event, they are offered in a range of interdisciplinary settings including family counselling agencies, pregnancy help centres, and hospitals. Pregnancy is a major life transition, yet, as a study by the Institute of Medicine (CCT 1995) indicates, about half of all pregnancies are unplanned; the degree of impact on the pregnant woman's life is determined by personal circumstances rather than the unintended nature of the event. For some, it is the forerunner to a personal crisis and is central to the need for clinical intervention, often by social workers employed in family counselling agencies or community health centres. The development of anxiety, depression, or relationship difficulties are typical problems for which pregnant women seek treatment. At times, issues of childhood physical and sexual abuse are brought to the fore. Pre-existing marital discord may reach intolerable levels with the impending arrival of a child and requests for marital counselling during this period may also occur. Research also indicates the prevalence of women abuse during pregnancy, one study indicating that more than half of reported cases of woman abuse were from women between the ages of eighteen to thirty-four the prime childbearing years (Rodgers 1994). Some clients who have experienced one or more losses through stillbirth or miscarriage may seek individual or group counselling as they begin another pregnancy.

Social patterns related to pregnancy have undergone many changes in the past twenty years. A major change is in the age of first-time mothers: whereas in 1987 about 19 percent of first births were to women aged thirty and over, by 1997, they had increased to 31 percent (Canada 1999b). Another issue is the pervasive concern about teenage pregnancies, despite the availability and social acceptance of contraception and birth control counselling in Canada: while statistics indicate that teenage pregnancies have steadily declined since 1994, more than 42,000 teenagers between the ages of fifteen and nineteen became pregnant in 1997 (Canada 2001b). Referrals for social work intervention for pregnant teens reflect the shared concern by professionals of the ongoing risks for this population, in particular, poverty and inadequate parenting. In 1993 the National Council of Welfare reported that 60 percent of single-parent families led by females were living in poverty; by 1998, almost one-fifth of children under the age of eighteen were living in poverty, a rate that places Canada as one of the worst of sixteen affluent countries (Canada 2001a). Support centres for young parents are community-based resources where social workers provide a range of services to teens, including pre-natal care, residential placement, and education in child development. In the case of adoption, social workers can be contracted to represent the expectant mother, while other practitioners are licensed to conduct the crucial home study of prospective adoptive parents. Research indicates that family support, attitudes, beliefs, and perceived consequences influence a teen's decisions regarding a pregnancy; social workers who strive "to develop better counselling strategies to ensure that choices are well thought out, realistic, reasonable, and consistent with the adolescent's overall future goals" can be crucial to this process (Cervera 1993). Social workers recognize inherent risks and hardships faced by pregnant teens, including problems such as delayed prenatal care, low birth weight, and pre-maturity. Work with this client population is rooted in the basic need to access services that can foster optimal care of both mother and child. Economic and social costs of teen pregnancy are well documented; for example, as between 50 and 70 percent of pregnant teens leave school (Miller in CCT 1995). Social workers can help teenage mothers to develop a plan to enhance their ability to continue their studies in an effort to avoid the poverty experienced by many teenaged mothers and their children. Social workers are one of the primary health professions advocating for the specialized needs of affected individual, organizations, and policies.

In health care settings, the current emphasis on the commitment to excellence in patient care is based on a family-centred approach; within this organizational structure, social workers play an invaluable part. The first professionals a pregnant teen is likely to contact are family physicians, obstetricians, and nurses, who often make referrals to community social workers when clients need more than medical intervention. Overall, despite the inception of program management, hospitals—particularly those affiliated with the Canadian Women's Health Network—continue to rely on social workers to undertake a range of essential tasks including prenatal counselling, crisis intervention, discharge planning, child protection screening, community referral, and post-delivery follow-up. Hospitals and community clinics are the primary sites where abortions take place: in 1971, there were 8.3 abortions for every one hundred live births, while by 1998, this rate had grown to 32.3 (Canada 2000). Considering the present rate of unintended pregnancies, the possibility of having an abortion is an option for some clients, including those whose personal value systems conflict with this choice; when this decision-making process is marked by ambivalence, the issue often becomes apparent in the office of a social worker who can afford a client the unconditional positive regard required to arrive at a decision. Social work intervention may also act as an avenue through which a client gains access to services to terminate a pregnancy. Workers in agencies where people are committed to pro-life positions, however, are mandated to respect the right to life of the unborn as well as the pregnant woman and other family members; as such, practitioners there are restricted in their ability to counsel women regarding abortion as an option. The social work profession has always worked closely with and advocated for client communities. Politically, the most notable pregnancy issue for many decades has been and remains abortion, with dissension between pro-life and pro-choice positions that sometimes involve social agencies; recently, for example, allegations arose that some pregnancy counselling centres were secretly encouraging women to carry their pregnancies to term and supporting their advice with moral and religious reasoning. Social workers may also face rights conflicts—those of the unborn child versus those of the mother—when they work with pregnant women who are abusing drugs or alcohol. Social workers, with their specialized training to assess the person-in-environment, is admirably prepared for the complexity of these and such other pregnancy issues as transracial adoption or the ethics of some reproductive technologies. Practitioners are thus an important voice in an interdisciplinary approach to treatment.

For some pregnant clients, social workers in a children's aid society may also intervene. The society's involvement is often the result of previous contact and subsequent concerns about the protection of the unborn child. Supervision orders may include requirements to attend counselling or substance abuse programs; some clients may be required to refrain from contact with an abusive partner, as the exposure of children to violence in the home, before and after birth, remains an ongoing concern. The implementation in Ontario of the 1997 risk assessment model for child protection identifies clear guidelines for determining degree of risk, including the occurrence of family violence. Greater vigilance by child protection workers is being shown to pregnant clients owing to the increased risk of abuse during this period. In one three-month study of children's aid societies referrals, 58 percent of the children suspected of being emotionally abused were in fact children exposed to violence in the home (Canada 2001a); the focus for children aid societies therefore remains the protection of the welfare of the child even before birth. Support, education, and advocacy are primary tasks undertaken on behalf of the pregnant woman and her social network regardless of the professional milieu in which this work takes place. Attending to the concrete needs of a pregnant client is critical to a successful treatment outcome. Social workers, however, reach beyond those tasks and also address mental health issues, which may pose a threat to the overall well-being of the client and the unborn child. The focus of intervention can therefore be as varied as the clients themselves: grassroots efforts to secure housing for a pregnant and homeless teen; traditional therapy for a once-childless couple awaiting the arrival of their newborn; monitoring a substance-abusing pregnant mother whose other children are already in care. The restructuring of health and social services and the growing emphasis on outcome measures has had direct impacts on service delivery by social workers in Canada. While at times fiscal and policy constraints diametrically oppose efforts by the profession, the psychosocial framework within which social workers operate is their unique and invaluable contribution to effective practice with this client population. Future directions for social workers with regards to pregnancy issues are likely to include continual critical appraisal of specific barriers faced by marginalized clients in accessing information and services about pregnancy, promoting responsible sexual behaviour, and taking leadership in advocating for research, programs, and policies designed to protect overall reproductive health.

[*Angela Townend*]

RELATED ENTRIES

Abortion, Adoption, Bioethical Issues, Ethics, Family: Non-traditional, Family Planning, Parenting, Private Adoption, Professional Issues, Royal Commission on New Reproductive Technologies, Separation & Divorce, Services for Children, Services for Families, Services for Married People, Services for Women, Single Parents, Toronto Infants Home, Wellness, Women Abuse

REFERENCES

Canada. 1999a. Births. *The Daily,* June 16. Ottawa: Statistics Canada.
———. 1999b. *Report from Consultations on a Framework for Sexual and Reproductive Health.* Ottawa, ON; Health Canada.
———. 2000. Responding to Abuse during Pregnancy. Part 2 (February). Ottawa: Health Canada.
———. 2001a. Population and Public Health Branch. The Canadian Incidence Study of Reported Child Abuse and Neglect. Ottawa: Health Canada.
———. 2001b. Sexual and Reproductive Health. Fact Sheet. Ottawa: Health Canada.
Cervera, N.J. 1993. Decision-Making for Pregnant Adolescents: Applying Reasoned Action Theory to Research and Treatment. Families in Society. *The Journal of Contemporary Human Services* 74, 6, 355–65.
CCT. 1995. *Contraceptive Use in Canada.* Toronto: Childbirth by Choice Trust.

private adoption

Adoption is the legal and binding transfer of parental rights from one family to another. In Canada adoptions are either public or private in nature and can occur domestically or internationally. In recent years, the Canadian adoption scene has witnessed a steady increase in private adoptions; in 1981, 22 percent of all infant adoptions were done privately and, by 1990, this number had risen to 59 percent (Daly & Sobol 1993). Private adoptions may assume three forms: licensee, independent, or identified (Wine 1995). Licensee adoptions involve a prospective parent(s) registering with an agency or individual that is regulated and licensed by a province or territory to oversee the legal and social work tasks central to the adoption; prospective parents are then placed on a waiting list with other couples or individuals until a suitable baby or child match is found. An identified private adoption is more self-directed, in that the individual or couple seeks out a birth mother placing her child for adoption, and a licensee and social worker are then hired to fulfil the necessary legal requirements. An independent private adoption is also self-directed but does not involve a third-party licensee; the birth parent and adoptive parents control much of the process and hire the necessary adoption professionals to satisfy provincial/territorial laws regarding their adoption. All Canadian provinces and territories allow various forms of private adoption to take place, but Quebec residents may not privately adopt children born in their own province; all other Canadian residents may privately adopt children born both within and outside of their respective province or territory. Most provinces and territories require as part of the screening process in adoption that a home study be completed, usually by a social worker; this report on the adoptive family, which must be completed before an adoption order is made, comprises an assessment by the social worker as well as a self-evaluation by the adoptive parents. Among the issues addressed in a home study are psychosocial functioning, medical history, employment and finances, personal values, marital relationship, parenting practices and beliefs, individual strengths, family of origin background information, and adoption expectations and concerns.

The social worker conducting the study meets individually and jointly with the prospective couple and, based on the information gathered in the meetings, provides a written report to the licensee or other professional overseeing the adoption. The report is then submitted with all other documentation (e.g., personal references) to the provincial/territorial adoption unit responsible for conducting a final assessment of the suitability of the prospective adoptive parents to adopt. The birth mother is also represented by a different social worker to guide her through the adoption process and assess, among other things, the sincerity of her desire to place her child for adoption. Prior to finalization of an adoption order, the social worker also makes post-placement visits to assess the overall adjustment of the child and the adoptive parents. Practitioners may also provide service during other periods including individual or family counselling related to post-adoption concerns, as well as pre-reunion counselling, which in some provinces or territories is mandated when the birth parent and the adoptive child have registered with the adoption disclosure register.

In open adoptions, both families share varying degrees of personal and identifying information, including decisions regarding ongoing contact. An increasing awareness of such adoptions has resulted in home studies being revised to address with adoptive parents their personal views regarding this often controversial issue. Consequently, open adoptions have also invited a critique of the laws regarding the confidentiality of adoption records; in Newfoundland and British Columbia, amendments to the legislation have already been made. In 2002 a private member's bill in Ontario amended adoption-disclosure legislation to make it possible for birth records to be accessed by adoptees. International adoptions are a more complex and costly form of private adoption, usually involving placement of children from poor and warring countries. Significant media coverage of children, usually orphans, whose living conditions are marked by poverty and oppression, has led to an increasing number of applications for intercountry adoptions. While public adoptions are facilitated and funded through the local children's aid societies or other units of local social services, the costs for private adoption are borne wholly by the prospective adoptive parents. Domestic adoptions presently incur costs between $4,000 and $6,000 and international ones up to $25,000 or more. While expensive, private adoptions are usually more expedient, with an average wait of twenty-one months, and most often involve healthy infants. Couples wishing to adopt through a public agencies may wait from seven to as long as twelve years; public adoptions are also often viewed as placing children who may pose challenges. For some, these differences have raised issues of equality and fairness: despite the expectation that both private and public adoption agencies will provide services that uphold the Canadian Charter of Rights and Freedoms, the adoption of a healthy infant by a lower-income couple or individual is becoming increasingly difficult. It has been estimated that, for every two domestic adoptions that occur in Canada, three international adoptions take place (Daly & Sobol 1993); this shift is a disconcerting one for some adoption workers in Canada who are committed to increasing public awareness about the plight of Canadian children awaiting adoption. The Adoption Council of Canada, a charitable organization based in Ottawa that recognizes the priority for placing Canadian-born children for adoption, noted in 2001, that more than 20,000 children in various forms of care were waiting for permanent placement with a family. Canada's Waiting Children is a program initiated by the council in 1997 to unite individuals and couples wishing to adopt such children; by the summer of 2001, this program had placed more than 120 children (Grove 2001).

[*Angela Townend*]

RELATED ENTRIES

Adoption, Family Planning, Marital & Family Problems, Parenting, Pregnancy, Services for Children, Services for Families, Services for Married People, Services for Women, Single Parents

REFERENCES

Daly, K.J., and M.P. Sobol. 1993. *Adoption in Canada: Report of the National Adoption Study*. Guelph, ON: University of Guelph.

Grove, J. 2001. Waiting for Parents: Canadian Kids Need Homes. *Transition Magazine* 31, 2 (Summer).

Wine, J. 1995. *A Family at Last. A Canadian Guide to Finding and Adopting Your Child*. Whitby, ON: McGraw-Hill Ryerson.

private practice

Private, or independent, practice is an autonomous form of social work self-employment, either wholly or in part, in which social work knowledge, skills, and values acquired through adequate education and experience are used to deliver professional services (Barker 1991: 181). Clinical and non-clinical practices, as well as those services provided under private contract, are included. Reimbursement for services may be negotiated directly with clients or determined by third-party organizations and funding bodies that determine the reimbursement rates. Standards for practice are set by the Canadian Association of Social Workers and provincial/territorial associations. In many provinces, private practice is limited to practitioners with a master's degree as minimum credentials. Over the past two decades private practice has been the focus of much controversy in social work literature, with critics of private practice arguing that it jeopardizes social work's historical mandate, creates professional value conflicts, and promotes a two-tiered system of services. Changes in the external environment beginning in the 1980s, however, have had a greater impact on the acceptance of private practice than has dialogue within the profession. While the discussion about it within the profession continues, private practice is now accepted as a legitimate form of social work, as attested to by growing number of social workers who identify themselves as private practitioners in either their primary or their secondary practice setting. Private communication with provincial/territorial associations indicates that there is a trend toward increasing participation in private practice; however, reliable Canadian statistics are not available, as the national association maintains statistics only on those social workers who have been approved as members of the National Registry of Social Workers in private practice. Factors that influence social workers to enter private practice include the promise of increased prestige and higher income, flexibility in scheduling, dissatisfaction with agency-based practice, the desire for more autonomy and control over working conditions, and opportunities to continue working directly with clients, with particular populations, or types of presenting problems. Historically, practitioners with ten or more years of experience entered private practice; current trends, however, note that less experienced social workers are now entering private practice. The 1990s witnessed a continuation of changing social mores, which have been marked by reductions in state responsibility for provision of services, restructuring of organizations, and downsizing. These changes have had a great impact on the working conditions of social workers in agencies, and opportunities for professional development and advancement within bureaucratic structures have been reduced. Cost-cutting measures have resulted in larger caseloads, and concerns have increased that the best interests of the clients are not being served. The increasing privatization of services within social services—resulting in community care access centres, employee assistance programs, and brief contracts—has provided more opportunities for social workers in the private sector.

Personality style may also influence a social worker's decision to enter private practice. Comparison of the personality characteristics of private practitioners with those in agency settings indicate that private practitioners tend to be more persevering, more tolerant of uncertainty and frustrations, more creative, and more resist to standard operating procedure (Seiz & Schwab 1992: 449). Studies also indicate that private practitioners report less psychological and somatic distress and higher levels of personal and professional satisfaction than agency practitioners (Jayaratne, Davis-Sacks, & Chess 1991). In the past private practitioners tended to use a predominately psychodynamic or systemic approach to serve a client population characterized by a middle class European background; current contracted services in employee assistance programs, community care access centres, and brief contracts have resulted in private practitioners now providing services to a client population previously under-served or not served at all in traditional settings. The changing marketplace has an impact on services provided by private practitioners, affecting both the client base and the services provided. The continuing thrust to privatization may necessitate an increasing focus on short-term interventions and psychoeducational programs. Private practice is not without stress, as for instance, social workers in private practice must balance clinical and administrative aspects of their business (e.g., advertising services, scheduling, contract negotiation, bookkeeping). Consideration must be given, for instance, to sliding fee scales, collection of fees, and utilization of collection agencies; in some instances, privatization has resulted in the undercutting of social work fees. Marketing requires considerable effort to maintain a private practice, and time is also needed for formal and informal case consultations and information sharing with professional colleagues and consultants. Maintaining confidentiality may pose challenges for private practitioners in addition to those for all social workers. Provision must be made for additional formal training, which may be required to stay current with emerging theoretical developments and practice models, and with updated technological equipment and software, which also requires training time.

As self-employed professionals, social workers in private practice are supported by their provincial/territorial associations through a variety of services to meet their needs. Directories of private practitioners are available through national and provincial/territorial associations. Malpractice and extended insurance are available for private practitioners registered with the national registry. Specific committees operating under provincial/territorial organizations focus on the political needs of private practitioners, including exemption from federal goods and services (GST) taxation and third-party reimbursements. The continuing development of private practice highlights the need to ensure that services provided continue to meet the ethical and practice standards of social work. Increasing interest by social work students in private practice necessitates that social work educators adjust curricula to meet these needs. Research on Canadian private practice realities, its prevalence and variations across the country would also prove insightful.

[*Sheila Faucher*]

RELATED ENTRIES

Creativity, Practice Methods, Practicum Instruction, Private-Sector Employment, Social Work Profession

REFERENCES

Barker, R.L. 1991. *The Social Work Dictionary*. 2nd ed. Silver Spring, MD: NASW Press.

Jayaratne, S., M.L. Davis-Sacks, and W.A. Chess. 1991.

Private Practice May Be Good for Your Health and Well-being. *Social Work*, 36, 3, 224–29.

Seiz, R.C., and A.J. Schwab, Jr. 1992. Entrepreneurial Personality Traits and Clinical Social Work Practitioners. *Families in Society: The Journal of Contemporary Human Services*, October, 495–502.

private-sector employment

Private-sector employment is the employment of social workers in the private for-profit sector of the economy. This form of work is non-traditional and relatively uncommon for social workers. Among trends affecting current social work employment are reduced employment and promotional opportunities in traditional settings as a result of governmental funding cutbacks and organizational restructuring, changes in the role and activities of social workers as a result of information technology, and globalization of the economy that is creating new challenges and opportunities in Canada for workers in all sectors. In response to these trends, social workers are seeking private-sector career opportunities within such existing and emerging opportunities as:

• *private practice* in various clinical and other specialties;

• *employee assistance programs* in large corporations;

• *management consulting*, conducted for public or private sector organizations, in such fields as strategic planning, program review, and facilitation services;

• *human resources*, such as employee recruitment, retention, and diversity awareness programs; and

• *organizational development*, including change management, work process redesign, and managing change.

Issues may arise in the acceptance of this new role by practitioners, social work educators, and certification or regulatory bodies. Some individuals and organizations challenge whether this type of employment is consistent with the history, values, and training of social workers. In addition social workers are required to adapt to the organizational culture generally found in the private sector, generally characterized by

• primary emphasis on revenue growth, cost savings, profitability and shareholder expectations;

- faster decisions, less consultation, generally longer or unpredictable hours of work;
- better technological tools and support, office facilities and learning opportunities; and
- compensation increases and promotions linked to individual performance and corporate financial results.

Employment in the private sector challenges social workers to deepen their knowledge and skills in such areas as business management, information technology, budgeting, financial management, operations, and human resources. Is work in the private sector a form of social work? Arguments for and against are current. Proponents claim that it is social work because practitioners help individuals and organizations to adapt and grow during times of difficult organizational and societal change. Critics are firm that it is not social work because practitioners are not addressing the needs of disadvantaged or other special needs individuals and communities. On balance, employment in the private sector is to be seen as social work, as the knowledge, skills, and values of social work are being provided to workers and organizations with special needs or difficult challenges. Private-sector employment expands the influence and relevance of the profession without lessening the core importance and dominance of more traditional social work practice.

[*Steven A. Raiken*]

RELATED ENTRIES

Employment, Globalization, Practice Methods, Private Practice, Privatization, Social Welfare History, Social Work Profession, Welfare State

privatization

In the narrowest sense, privatization refers to the transfer directly by government of the funding and delivery of services to the private sector, or the takeover by the private sector of services previously provided by government in a profit-making format, sometimes with government aid. Thus, an American company could, for example, provide in Canada some aspect of home care as a private enterprise, providing that it could show that the service can be done at least as well as did the government agency previously operating it. Privatization is generally related to the North America Free Trade Agreement, facilitated by the cross-

ing of borders by various forms of enterprise. The movement to privatization reflects a much larger world trend which holds that many services, deemed in recent decades to be best provided by government can be provided at least as effectively, if not more so by private companies. Historically, Canadian social work has followed the philosophical trend for state-run social programs as they emerged with the welfare state; current trends in the profession indicate that practitioners are adapting to such new career opportunities as private practice and jobs in private agencies. Indeed, ample evidence shows that that good quality social work services are being offered by private practitioners and practitioners in private agencies. Initially challenged as a contradiction in terms, private social work services have increasingly become part of social welfare. Many companies, for example, offer employees very comprehensive social work services on a private contractual basis. Rather than a question of principle or value, the desirability of privatization of some social services must be assessed on the basis of quality, confidentiality, accountability, effectiveness, and client satisfaction. In the related field of health care, the issue of privatization and its effect on service has given rise to fears that a two- or three-tiered system might reduce the quality of services available to clients in each tier. Already in Canada, some agencies that offer social service obtain their funding—and, therefore, some operational direction—from a variety of public, private, and client sources, which places them in a *quasi*-privatized situation. This mixed of financing is expected to increase within social welfare in the future.

[*FJT*]

RELATED ENTRIES

Employment, Globalization, Practice Methods, Private Practice, Privatization, Social Welfare History, Social Work Profession, Welfare State

probation

Probation is a court-ordered sanction where an adjudicated offender is placed under the control, supervision, and care of a probation officer in lieu of imprisonment, as long as the probationer fulfils certain standards of conduct. Probation, a common form of criminal sanctioning in Canada, affects the largest number of offenders who are conditionally supervised in the community. The practice of releasing offenders on their own recognizance rather than imposing a sentence gained legal authority in 1889 with the Act to Permit the Conditional Release of First Offenders in Certain Cases. By 1892 probation is mentioned in the Criminal Code and, in 1921, Code amendments required the offender to report to an officer of the court. The first probation service was in 1922, with the passage of the Ontario Probation Act, and this form of sanction saw major growth after the Second World War. Probation is a judicial function and a provincial/territorial responsibility, with all provinces and territories now having probation services. The maximum probation sentence is three years, which can be given in conjunction with a suspended sentence, fine, or term of imprisonment of less than two years. All probation sanctions include the conditions to keep the peace, be of good behaviour, and appear before the court as required by an agent of the court. Services provided by probation officers include pre-sentence reports to the courts and community assessment reports to parole boards as required. In recent decades, probation has been viewed by much of the public as a soft option for offenders. Probation services have worked to change this public perception by instituting risk assessment instruments, intensive supervision practices, and evidence-based programming (i.e., cognitive/behaviour treatment programs for substance abuse, domestic violence, and sexual offending). Multi-agency partnerships are also developing as a means to expanded services and supervision. Partnerships with police assist in the supervision of high-risk offenders. Treatment agencies often staffed by social workers are involved with offenders with special needs (e.g., substance abuse, mental health, or complex family issues). Probation participates in emergent drug courts. All of these new ventures are strengthening the role of probation within Canadian criminal justice. Probation today is based on careful assessment and differential supervision. The emerging style of supervision includes control through surveillance and assistance through treatment. By a careful melding of control and assistance, the objective for probation services to protect public safety is met. The benefits—lower costs, increased opportunities for rehabilitation, flexibility of programming, and reduction of the risks for re-offending— are likely to keep probation as a primary correctional policy.

[*Donald G. Evans*]

RELATED ENTRIES

Corrections Services, Criminal Justice, Family & Youth Courts, Services for Offenders, Youth Criminal Justice Act

problem-solving theory

Problem solving as a social work intervention has been defined as a "rational, goal directed process that includes actions to define the problem; to collect information on which to base decisions; to engage the client in goal setting and decision making; to produce change; and to evaluate progress" (Compton & Galaway 1999: 7). Problem solving theory is the foundation for many social work activities profession-wide. It is the basis for many interventions with individuals, families, groups, organizations, and communities, and provides a structure for social work in the fields of social planning and social policy. Problem solving is essentially the means by which humans move from experiencing an unmet need, want, or life problem to living in a more desirable state. Its basis is an innate human ability to reason, which emerges with the growing cognitive and interactive skills of a developing child. Ivey credits Benjamin Franklin with first outlining a logical system of decision making in these steps: define the problem or concern clearly; generate alternative possibilities for solution; weight the positives and negatives for each alternative in a simple balance sheet; select one alternative for action and see how it works (Ivey, Ivey, & Simek-Morgan 1993: 72–73). Ivey notes that all counselling and therapy models contain elements of this approach and, further, that the five-stage model of the interview incorporates it (Ivey, Ivey, & Simek-Morgan 1993: 76). Compton and Galaway base their social work method on later refinements of this process by John Dewey, in which he detailed the thought processes human beings go through when solving problems: termed "reflective thinking," Dewey "reduced effective problem solving to a set of procedural steps in a well-defined and orderly sequence" (Compton & Galaway 1999: 83). Helen Harris Perlman, who was the first theorist to interweave the theory into social work practice, described life as a continuous process of problem solving as people are challenged to make decisions, form judgments, and respond to the demands of their environment; she stated that this is "the work in which every human being engages from the moment of birth to that of death" (Perlman 1957: 53). Problem solving converges so well with the fundamental purposes of social work that it has been incorporated into the definition of social work generated by the International Federation of Social Workers: "The social work profession promotes social change, problem solving in human relationships and the empowerment and liberation of people to enhance well-being" (Hick 2002: 15). Problem solving has been referred to by some theorists as the foundation on which generalist practice is based (Compton & Galaway 1999: 9) and, with some modifications, as the basis for crisis intervention. Problem solving provides essential concepts for task-centred social work, planned short-term treatment, and the life model of practice. As an approach to helping people and modifying the social environment, problem solving is compatible with cultural- and gender-sensitive practice; while providing a framework for intervention, it also permits much flexibility in the actual change tactics employed, so that the unique situation, emotional state, goals, and resources of the client can be incorporated into the process to maximize the effectiveness of the response. Some critics object to the focus on "problem" as incompatible with social work's commitment to an empowerment approach, while proponents of an empowerment model note that it "draws its organizational framework from the problem-solving model [while redesigning the traditional approach through] language and concepts that emphasize strengths, empowerment, and working in partnership with clients at all system levels to promote competence" (Miley, O'Melia, & DuBois 1998: 105). Because problem solving involves a series of logical steps, both social worker and client have a cognitive road map to follow in moving toward resolution.

The expanded social work model developed by Compton and Galaway (1999: 93) outlines four phases of the problem solving approach as: engagement, assessment, intervention, and evaluation. Within these phases, they detail multiple actions and skills to be undertaken by both practitioner and client. In the engagement phase, they define the problem, determine the objectives the client wants to achieve, and negotiate a working contract. In the assessment phase, practitioner and client begin to collect data and develop a plan of action, segmenting the problem so that various aspects can be worked on with flexibility. In the intervention phase, the action plan is carried out by the client system, with the worker as needed, so that the client's goals, resources, and the changing psychosocial environment are paid full attention. In the evaluation phase, all participants assess the successes, partial success, or failure of the plan, and determine next steps, which may include the development of a new plan, the addressing of other difficulties, referral, or termination. In essence, problem solving is based on a natural process available to human beings, which has been identified as one used by effective thinkers. It is marked by clarity, logic, and power. As social work is a profession that exists for the purpose of solving personal, organizational, and societal problems, this approach is central to all its activities.

[*Rose Marie Jaco*]

RELATED ENTRIES

Brief Treatment, Task-Centred Theory, Theory & Practice

REFERENCES

Compton, B., and B. Galaway (Eds.) 1999. *Social Work Processes*. 6th ed. Pacific Grove, CA: Brooks/Cole.

Hick, S. 2002. *Social Work in Canada*. Toronto: Thompson Educational Publishing.

Ivey, A.E., M.B. Ivey, and L. Simek-Morgan. 1993. *Counseling and Psychotherapy: A Multicultural Perspective*. 3rd ed. Needham Heights, MA: Allyn and Bacon.

Miley, K.K., M. O'Melia, and B. DuBois. 1998. *Generalist Social Work Practice: An Empowering Approach*. Needham Heights MA: Allyn and Bacon.

Perlman, H.H. 1957. *Social Casework: A Problem-Solving Process*. Chicago: University of Chicago Press.

professional continuing education

Professional education that continues throughout a practitioner's career has always been expected of social workers; trends in current practice for an increasing emphasis on accountability have made this expectation more explicit. The challenge for social workers is to continue to provide high-quality competent social work services within ever-changing and uncertain times. Massive changes continue to occur in the workplace as a result of funding cutbacks, globalization, restructuring of systems and organizations, growing privatization of services, elimination of some programs, and deinstitutionalization. As a result, job security and predictable career paths are diminishing as current employment patterns challenge traditional service-delivery models and employment routes. For social workers, part-time and contract work with single or multiple projects is becoming more common with a subsequent movement into private or independent practice, and other non-traditional areas of practice. A second major impact—in particular from changes in tasks and programs—is that the source of and responsibility for professional development have shifted clearly from the employer to the employee. Related effects result from the demise of employer-supported educational experiences and the reduction or disappearance of supervision, compounded by the increasing change of accountability to functional service programs rather than to a social work manager. Several provincial/territorial professional social work associations require professional development or continuing education as part of membership, certification, or registration; as legislation of the professions is a provincial/territorial responsibility, there is variation throughout the country. The national guidelines of Canadian Association of Social Workers recommend forty hours of continuing education per year, which is also the minimum requirement for maintaining a listing in the National Registry of Social Workers in Private Practice.

Criteria for professional development or continuing education activities vary throughout the country and need to be relevant to the geographical and practice situations of social workers. Professional development opportunities abound, especially in large cities, while smaller towns, and rural and northern areas are less well served; the majority of programs are provided in English only. Even if events are offered close by, however, work pressures and agency demands may limit participation unless activities are scheduled to accommodate practitioners' workplace circumstances;

different responses developed to respond to these needs include lunch-time seminar series, and schedules that combine evening and weekends sessions. The proliferation in distance education through information technology may provide greater access and availability of learning opportunities; many faculties and schools of social work, and other training providers offer information about their continuing education—and foundation or graduate—programs online. For francophones, Le réseau d'enseignement francophone à distance du Canada can be used to access educational and training resources in French. And some Aboriginal social work programs are provided through distance education, for example, from Laurentian University in Ontario, and Arctic College in Nunavut and the Northwest Territories. The social work profession is charged with challenging its members to confront demands from the dynamic environment in which it is set, as an invitation to learn more and practice new skills, and to be imaginative, inventive, and resourceful for professional growth. Mandatory requirements have become instilled within the profession; now a culture of lifelong learning needs to be fostered as vital professional equipment.

[*Roberta Roberts*]

RELATED ENTRIES

Education in Social Work, Information Technology, Knowledge Base

professional issues

Social work faces this millennium as a well-established dynamic profession challenged by issues similar to those experienced by other human service professions. An age-old concern persists—at least in academe—as the profession continues to debate whether to expand its focus on systemic social change and minimize its direct service, or the reverse, or to seek a balance between the two; in practice, the profession seems to have moved toward the balance long sought for. Since regulation of the profession in Canada has moved firmly from advocacy to achievement, social workers are now grappling with the realization that such regulation places new demands for accountability on the profession; one response to these demands is the creation of new roles within professional associations to advocate on behalf of members. With increased recognition of the profession has come increased visibility and public scrutiny, at times through presentations at public inquiries or of policy recommendations and at others over high-profile tragedies, for instance, in child welfare or suicides; this reality has placed pressure on professional associations for increased public education about social work, and the concomitant need to understand and draw on the skills of public relations professionals.

Dramatic cuts in social welfare funding stemming from the ideology of welfare reform have resulted in the need for more aggressive social action from the profession to make the case for societal benefits of a strong social network. An important part of this challenge involves the ongoing need for well-designed research to support positive change with hard data persuasive analysis and to minimize the pejorative perception of social work as oversentimental with little substance. Within the profession interesting developments in educational requirements for admission to the profession have seen the dramatic increase in community college programs, and a trend in both community college graduates and experienced practitioners without formal education entering a range of university programs. In turn, graduates from community college programs have been demanding—and, in some provinces, receiving—social work status. At the other end of the educational spectrum, expansion in number and size of doctoral programs and in numbers of persons seeking admission to them marks an important Canadian development. Impacts from this development are likely to be felt in the quality of research, teaching, and policy formulation; as well, a significant number of social work doctors are practising outside academic settings, once thought to be the sole terminus for doctoral-trained personnel. The past overdependence on American literature and textbooks remains a challenge to the social work profession. Some indicators, however, suggest that a rapid growth in Canadian social work writing is responding to this issue and resulting in the emergence of a Canadian social work conceptual identity. One facet of literature publication with little progress is translation and sharing of theories and practice experiences between English- and French-speaking members of the profession, even though it has long been identified as an issue.

Recruitment to the profession remains strong with most schools and faculties receiving many more applications than they have places. Much progress has been made in the diversification of student bodies, especially in the recruitment of Aboriginal peoples. The gender imbalance within student bodies is persistently tipped, with about 80 percent of the students being female. As in other parts of the world, a growing sensitivity to, interest in, and willingness to become involved in international social issues is emerging within Canadian social work. This expanded purview of the profession's mission offers implementation challenges and opportunities to facilitate training and practice in this country in a way that enhances the impact the profession abroad. Overall, the social work profession projects the perception that is comfortable, mature, and able to use its growing influence and authority to address critical systemic and personal psychosocial issues facing the country as a whole, human services, and individual citizens.

[*FJT*]

RELATED ENTRIES

Accountability, Bioethical Issues, Clinical Social Work, Codes of Ethics, Diversity, Ethics, Ethnic-Sensitive Practice, Information Technology, Legal Issues, Knowledge Base, Minority-Sensitive Practice, Non-clinical Practice, Practice Methods, Practicum Instruction, Professional Liability, Racism-Sensitive Social Work, Recording, Sensitizing Concepts, Social Planning, Social Policy & Practice, Social Work Profession, Theory & Practice

professional liability

A social work practitioner's liability is his/her obligation to compensate a client harmed or put at risk through his/her improper or unethical professional conduct. Being a professional means attaining a specific degree of knowledge, skill, experience, autonomy, and judgment (Knoppers 1988). Society grants a practitioner professional status to denote his/her high attainment of skill, which reflects society's trust and expectation in that professional—in particular that he/she will place the client's needs and well-being above his/her own. These criteria do not wholly consider circumstantial detail in all cases. Social work is embedded in normative principles that define right and wrong, good and better, thereby providing the basis for professional judgment, intervention, and decision making (Yelaja 1982). Because what might help one person may not be good for another, each professional practitioner must exercise professional judgment, reasoning, and decision making based on his/her personal knowledge and experience. Being a professional means being accountable for that judgment, reasoning, and decision making. The notion of liability, which has existed in the law for centuries, is a relatively new social consideration, as society increasingly demands accountability from professionals. Liability is a legal obligation that social workers accept when they enter into practice. Among claims for liability that a social worker might incur are, for example, inaccurate documentation, breach of confidentiality, conflict of interest, and fraudulent misrepresentation. As with other human service professions, liability arises in any social setting and activity. Changing values, laws, knowledge, theories, concepts, standards, policies, intervention protocols—and the interpretation of them—have broadened the potential for and likelihood of lawsuits. All social work practice must therefore be based on and supported by all of these considerations. Most professional codes of ethics indicate that a professional should not use methods or techniques without the required or necessary training in intervention with clients. A practitioner can best protect him/herself by adhering to professional standards, thereby facilitating ethical practice. This is not to say that professional social workers cannot be held liable for honest mistakes: the notion of "acting in good faith" is not always an effective defence when a client alleges that harm has been inflicted. Liability can be incurred by doing nothing (i.e., an act of omission) or by doing the wrong thing (i.e., an act of commission). Practitioners are advised to maintain professional liability, or malpractice, insurance.

Current information technologies and media reporting allow the rapid and widespread publication of professional liability cases. While the most sensationally reported cases involving professional misconduct in social work are extreme violations—such as having a sexual relationship with a client—the reality is that many cases involving ethical and competent social workers who face lawsuits are rarely made as public (Besharov 1985).

Unfortunately, the competence and reputation of all professionals is often affected by high-profile cases. As with other accredited and legally accountable professions, social work has developed its own mechanism for holding members accountable, in order to protect the public. This accountability is formally established under prescribed standards and a code of ethics that define professional practice and responsibilities. These formal standards and codes have been developed—and are regularly reviewed for amendment—by the Canadian Association of Social Workers; many provincial/territorial associations of social workers have their own standards and codes as well. Adherence to these prescriptions dictates an expected conformity within the practice of social work. Registration of social workers is one form of public quality assurance, as regulatory bodies specify the criteria for a social worker to be identified as a professional. This is of particular importance, given increasing public scrutiny. Regulation of the profession also affords the public and the professional an opportunity for peer review. Complaints about practice are reviewed by a professional body with lay representation; peer review of a colleague's ethical practice offers an examination of professional expectation, as opposed to a public panel unfamiliar with professional standards (Yelaja 1982). As the profession of social work accepts its place among longer-established professions, it faces the idiosyncratic issues of public responsibility, accountability, and liability.

[*Patricia Erving*]

RELATED ENTRIES

Accountability, Bioethical Issues, Canadian Association of Social Workers, Codes of Ethics, Ethics, Information Technology, Knowledge Base, Legal Issues, Malpractice, Professional Issues, Program Evaluation, Provincial/Territorial Associations, Quality Assurance, Social Work Profession

REFERENCES

Besharov, D.J. 1985. *The Vulnerable Social Worker: Liability for Serving Children and Families*. Washington, DC: NASW Press

Knoppers, B.M. 1988. *Professional Liability in Canada: Canadian Institute for the Administration of Justice*. Cowansville, QC: Les Éditions Yvon Blais.

Yelaja, S.A. 1982. *Ethical Issues in Social Work*. Springfield, IL: Charles C. Thomas.

program evaluation

Program evaluation within social work practice has roots in the unparalleled expansion of the welfare state in Canada during the 1960s. Dramatic increases in spending on health and social services following passage of the Canada Assistance Plan, the Medical Care Act, and the Canada and Quebec pension plans gave rise to a call for greater accountability of public spending. In response, the federal government committed to the practice of program and policy evaluation, with the Treasury Board in 1977 approving its first formal policy requiring deputy heads to evaluate all programs within their jurisdiction; this policy was revised in 1991, reaffirming the practice of program evaluation as a mechanism for improved cost-effectiveness, and for decision making with respect to program changes including the decision to terminate (Canada 1991: 5). Program evaluation also became a part of practice within provinces and the non-profit sector. The role of an evaluator had been defined as that of a detached, value-free researcher, primarily concerned with assessing whether a program was meeting its objectives; over time, the role has become enhanced as more of a program consultant or developer. As such, an evaluator now is less detached, entering into detailed discussions with a program's service providers about how the program operates and what it is trying to accomplish; as well, the program consultant is expected to make recommendations about ways in which the program can be strengthened and perhaps to assist in implementing them. The appropriateness of the changed role of program evaluators is under debate. Program evaluation has four major research functions: outcome evaluation, evaluability assessment (program logic models), process evaluation, and needs assessment. Initially, the primary focus in evaluation practice initially was on program outcomes, that is, to find out whether a program was having the desired effect and within budgeted costs (Pancer & Westhues 1989: 71). Research designs traditionally associated with outcome evaluation are experimental and quasi-experimental. More recently, social worker researchers have argued for the utility of the single case design in assessing outcomes as well. Reflecting a move to a greater valuing of subjective as well as more objective data, the use of client satisfaction surveys has become widespread to assess the effects of participating in a social program. Social impact assessments, while not widely used, are a means of measuring the effects of programs that are intended to have a community-wide impact (e.g., a public education campaign on family violence). To determine whether a program is achieving its effects at a desired level of cost, evaluators borrowed cost-benefit and cost-effectiveness analyses from economists.

The second major function, evaluability assessment, developed from challenges evaluators often faced when undertaking outcome evaluations. A common difficulty was that program objectives were often not written down, or they had shifted from what was recorded when the program had begun in earlier years; sometimes the understanding of what program objectives were differed among service providers, managers and program participants. If an evaluator selected objectives for the program him/herself, or if he/she took as objectives what was stated in the original program description, those choices could well be at variance with the actual or current foci for program activities. As a consequence, the program would be evaluated against objectives that were no longer valid in the perception of service providers, service recipients, or perhaps funders. When this happened, or was perceived to have happened, the findings were not used (Patton 1978: 28–35). To address this problem, evaluators began to write about and document in literature pre-evaluation work, developing a program model, or evaluability assessment. An evaluability assessment examines the components of a program, the goals (or intended effects) of the program, the unintended effects of the overall program and each component, whether the program could realistically achieve the specified goals or produce the anticipated effects. The findings tell an evaluator whether to proceed with an outcome evaluation directly, or whether more program development needs to be done beforehand. Another common problem that became evident to evaluation researchers was that the programs they were asked to assess were often "black boxes"—that is, the service delivered was not clearly articulated, and little or no monitoring had been done to ensure that it was implemented as it was intended to be. This meant that, if an evaluator found that a program was meeting its objectives, he/she could not readily show how it could be replicated in another setting. Further, if the evaluator found that the program was not meeting its objectives, he/she could not state whether this failure was owing to theory or implementation. Evaluators responded to this realization by investing additional energies into developing evaluation research called process evaluation (also, monitoring or auditing). A process evaluation assesses program operations against program plans, specifically, whether the intended quantity and quality of service was being delivered. The final research function that has evolved since the 1960s is needs assessment. Needs assessments were designed initially to assess service or program requirements in a community. Now, they are also used to assess whether there is a continuing need for a program that has been operational for some period of time. Results of needs assessments are used to help community representatives argue their cases more effectively to justify funding for desired programs, and to help decision makers allocate resources in a way that is better aligned with social needs than a purely political process.

The effects of this evolution in the research practice of program evaluation on policy and program development has been fourfold. The greatest impact has been what might be called the democratization of the process. Where, once, policy development was the domain of politicians and a small number of senior bureaucrats, the contributions of service providers and service users can now be a major consideration in decision making. Second, policy makers are now provided with a perspective—the subjective experience of service users (often referred to as consumers or customers in current parlance)—that had not been heard or given much credence in the policy making process previously. Third, the link between policy and program has become so much clearer that it is possible to assess not only how well policy objectives are being realized but to identify the programs that are helpful in realizing them. This provides excellent guidance as to programs that ought to be continued or expanded, and those that might reasonably be discontinued. Fourth, the provision of a framework has provided a recognition of the uniqueness of each program and of each community's objectives within the context of

that program, while still seeing that program as part of a larger policy direction. This perspective permits a community to address its own particular needs with respect to its cultural or religious values, while still linking it with the broader policy initiatives of its province, territory, or country.

[*Anne Westhues*]

RELATED ENTRIES

Accountability, Agency-Based Research, Assessment, Canada Assistance Plan, Capacity Assessment, Case Management, Goal Setting, Information & Communication Technologies, Problem Solving, Quality Assurance, Recording, Theory & Practice

REFERENCES

Canada. 1991. Report of the Senate Standing Committee on National Finance: The Program Evaluation System in the Government of Canada. Ottawa: Senate of Canada.

Pancer, M. and A. Westhues. 1989. A Developmental Stage Approach to Program Planning and Evaluation. *Evaluation Review* 13, 71.

Patton, M.Q. 1978. *Utilization-focused Evaluation.* Beverly Hills, CA: Sage.

Rutman, I. 1980. *Planning Useful Evaluations.* Beverly Hills, CA: Sage.

Rush, B., and A. Ogborne. 1995. Program Logic Models. *Canadian Review of Program Evaluation* 6.

Suchman, E.A. 1967. Evaluative Research: Principles and Practice in Public Service and Social Action Program 1: New York: Russell Sage Foundation.

Weiss, C.H. 1972. Evaluation Research: Methods of Assessing Program Effectiveness. Englewood Cliffs, NJ: Prentice-Hall, 43–53.

progressive social work

Progressive social work is a general category covering a variety of practice frameworks or approaches—including, for example, anti-oppressive, anti-racist, feminist, narrative, and structural models—that are oriented toward the realization of social justice and empowerment and that are critical of more conventional approaches. This orientation to social work is informed by critical analyses from within such disciplines as sociology, psychology, political science, and anthropology that tend to focus on larger structural factors—such as income inequality and marginalized identity—that produce and reproduce oppressive social relationships, inhumane living conditions, and dysfunctional human behaviour. While social work has traditionally been seen as a profession that attempts to link social issues and personal problems, it has also been criticized for failing to consistently embrace issues of inequality and justice as central themes of practice (Carniol 2000; Mullaly 1997). On the other hand, contemporary progressive practice shares this concern and has its roots in movements that are specifically focused on social justice, such as civil rights, peace, and feminism (Ward & Mullander 1991). Drawing on criticisms that these and like movements have levelled at society, as well as on the perspective of liberation theorists, such as Paulo Freire, progressive social work educators and practitioners have argued that social work must reject the notion of a liberal apparently value-neutral practice based on technique. They see that approach as failing society and perpetuating oppressive and exploitative social relationships (Carniol 2000); rather, social work must become committed to issues of justice and social transformation. While the various models within progressive social work have differing foci, issues of class, race, gender, or sexual orientation may take precedent; at the same time, each model views all oppressions as ultimately intersecting and reinforcing, and holds to a more or less critical stance with reference to the existing political and social institutions and processes. Progressive practitioners hope to address social divisions and structural inequalities in the social work they undertaken, and to promote practice that is concerned with linking a client's personal issues of power, equality, social rights, and interdependence to broader societal issues. As a result, they tend to place a high value on self-reflection and the maintenance of a critical stance that challenges the status quo. Further, progressive practitioners argue that the linkage of private troubles with public issues must be seen as a crucial practice principle. Progressive models challenge more conventional social work approaches that view the worker/ client relationship as a key aspect of the work by asserting that power is at the core of any helping relationship—particularly so social work. The intention must be to develop relationships that are dialogical, that is, where issues of power are brought to the surface and mediated. The goal is to develop working relationships that are truly participatory rather then authoritarian, and where the authen-

tic voices of clients—their lived experiences and knowledge—are at the centre of intervention. Such practitioners argue that, rather than focusing intervention on individual change, they favour raising consciousness of the structural roots of problems to foster collective solutions that promote progressive change in the broader society.

[*Bill Lee*]

RELATED ENTRIES

Anti-oppressive Social Work, Citizen Participation, Ethnic-Sensitive Practice, Feminist Theory, Gender Issues, Minority-Sensitive Practice, Narrative Practice, Practice Methods, Racism-Sensitive Social Work, Radical Social Work, Social Welfare History, Theory & Practice

REFERENCES

Carniol, B. 2000. *Case Critical: Challenging Social Services in Canada*. 4th edition. Toronto: Between the Lines.

Mullaly, R. 1997. *Structural Social Work: Ideology, Theory and Practice*. 2nd ed. Toronto: McClelland and Stewart.

Ward, D., and A. Mullander. 1991. Empowerment and Oppression: An Indissoluble Pairing for Contemporary Social Work. *Critical Social Policy* 32, 21–30.

provincial / territorial associations

The first formal corporate and professional identity formed by Canadian social workers was through individual membership in the Canadian Association of Social Workers (est. 1926). Gradually, practitioners in large cities of various provinces established local branches of the national organization, which was located in Ottawa, to serve as a professional reference point as well as a forum and voice for local and provincial issues. In the 1970s, it became evident that separate structures based in each province were needed, in part because of the growing number of memberships in the local branches. Further, social workers were becoming interested in and committed to the need for legislative recognition and regulation of practice, which would have to be developed and passed by provincial legislatures, which are responsible for social welfare. Within a very short time, a professional social work association was established in each of the provinces, and one association was formed by social workers in the territories. As a result, the national organization ceased to an organization of individual members and became instead a federation of provincial/territorial associations. While each provincial association reflects particular characteristics and interests, the provincial/territorial associations collectively have much in common. Once established, each association advocated for some sort of legislative recognition by the province and territories. This long process is still underway, as the Ontario Social Work and Social Service Workers Act marks the last province to obtain some form of legislative recognition, which is still lacking in the territories. Each provincial association maintains at least minimum staff and an office, with the larger provinces having more elaborate structures. All have an elected board of directors, hold annual meetings, and contribute recommendations and issues of concern to the national association. The function of provincial/ territorial associations generally includes services to individual members (e.g., insurance, job searches, and professional advice), publish a newsletter and/or journal, work with the media to maintain a positive profile for the profession and educate the public on pertinent issues, and, most importantly, maintain lobbying on social welfare issues. Contact with other provincial/territorial associations is through membership in the national association, which holds an annual conference. An emerging joint issue on which provincial/territorial and the national associations are advocating together is portability between jurisdictions of credentials and qualifications to practice social work.

[*FJT*]

RELATED ENTRIES

Accountability, Advocacy, Alberta College of Social Workers, Association of Social Workers in Northern Canada, Board of Registration for Social Workers of BC, British Columbia Association of Social Workers, Canadian Association of Social Workers, Ethics, International Federation of Social Workers, Manitoba Association of Social Workers, Manitoba Institute for Registered Social Workers, National Association of Social Workers (US), New Brunswick Association of Social Workers, Newfoundland and Labrador Association of Social Workers, Nova Scotia Association of Social Workers, Ontario Association of Social Workers, Ontario College of Certified Social Workers and Social Service Workers, Order professionel des travailleurs sociaux du Quebec, Practice

Methods, Professional Issues, Professional Liability, Saskatchewan Association of Social Workers, Social Work Profession

psychoanalytic theory

Psychoanalysis—a combination of the Greek words *psyche* (soul or spirit) and *analusis* (set free)—is the study of the inner workings of the human psychological system. Psychoanalytic theory is the theoretical formulation derived from this spirit analysis, the recognized originator for which is Sigmund Freud. Working from the late 1800s to the 1930s, Freud and his associates developed both a theory of human psychological development—which they called metapsychology, a clinical theory, and a methodology for clinical practice. While the current status of metapsychology is questionable, many practitioners still use their clinical theory and methodology. His own writings indicate that, for Freud, this was a work in progress that stopped on his death. His work has been carried on by many others, beginning with his associates and continuing to the present. The main features of psychoanalytic theory that are relevant to social workers are the structural model, the drive model, and the stages of psychosexual development. The structural model is the one in which Freud introduced the id, ego, and superego as templates for the functioning of the psyche. The id represents the impulsive aspects of human nature (i.e., the child, in transactional analysis terminology), the ego the executive function (i.e., the adult), and the superego the moral and judgmental aspects of the personality (i.e., the parent). The ego's executive function involves finding compromises between the impulses of the id, the moral judgment of the superego, and the reality of the environment. The drives—generally referred to as libidinal and aggressive—were for Freud the energy sources for the psyche. The accepted scientific model in Freud's day was the mechanical model and he adapted his understanding of the human psyche to fit that model; just as a mechanical model needs a source of energy, so the psyche needs the drives. The drives are ignored by most, if not all, current psychoanalysts except the classical, or Freudian, analysts who attempt to remain true to all aspects of Freud's writings. The stages of psychosexual development—oral, anal, phallic, latency, and genital—trace the development of the ego as it develops the strengths and skills necessary to deal with the competing demands of the id, the super-ego, and the environment. In Freud's writing, these stages were defined by their libidinal aspects; later writers traced the development of the aggressive drive through these stages as well. The stages of psychosexual development are still relevant to understanding human development and are currently understood and interpreted independent of references to the drives. Psychoanalytically based theories, which have modified Freud's work while trying to remain true to his basic concepts include ego psychology and object relations theory. From the 1950s to the mid-1970s psychoanalytic theory, primarily in the form of ego psychology, was the dominant theory for clinical social work practice. Many social workers still base their theoretical understandings on psychoanalytic principles, while an increasing number is more oriented to ego psychology, self psychology, or one of the schools of object relations theory—loosely identified as British and North American schools—that have developed.

[*Robert Twigg*]

RELATED ENTRIES

Clinical Social Work, Counselling, Ego Psychology, Jungian Theory, Psychosocial Theory, Psychotropic Medication, Transactional Analysis Theory, Transpersonal Psychology, Theory & Practice, Wellness

psychosocial theory

Psychosocial theory has its roots in the origins of the casework movement but emerged as a distinct theory in the 1950s in the wake of psychoanalytic theory's initial impact on social work practice. Often viewed as having an overly psychoanalytical orientation, psychosocial theory has always kept a balance between person and situation to maintain its focus as a distinct theory. In its earlier period, it was known as the diagnostic school to distinguish itself from the functional school. The principal theorists are Florence Hollis and, in more recent years, Mary Woods. As a theory for practice, psychosocial theory has been open to new ideas and developments; its original concept of intervention focused principally on casework—dyadic as well as individual—and grad-

ually moved to work with groups and families to respond to client views and perceptions of practice. This built-in approach of ongoing evaluation and transformation of practice originated in the 1960s with Hollis's work on the content of social work interviews. The theory continued to develop by tapping the potential of other methods so that current treatment with a psychosocial theoretical foundation encompasses work with groups and families as well as with relevant systems in a client's life. An important component of this theory is its emphasis on understanding the client's value system and adjusting intervention to respond to ethnic and cultural factors. While still extant as a distinct theoretical body, the term "psychosocial" has become an integral part of the lexicon of all helping professions, thereby lessening its distinct identity.

[*FJT*]

RELATED ENTRIES

Biopsychosocial Theory, Psychoanalytic Theory, Theory & Practice

psychotropic medication

Psychotropic medication is a mood-altering prescription drug. Naturally occurring psychotropic drugs from specific plants and animal tissue have apparently been used for centuries. In 1949 Reserpine was used by medical doctors in India as a tranquillizer, a drug that stabilizes moods and calms patients; Reserpine is derived from the root of *Rauvolfia serpentina*, or Indian snakeroot, which was in use in Europe since the eighteenth century to treat nervous conditions and mental illness. Also in the late 1940s, Swiss chemist Albert Hofmann's discovery of the properties of lysergic acid diethylamide (LSD) is credited with beginning research into the relationship between the mind and drugs. The French physician Henri Lalorit was the first to identify the use of drugs to reduce anxiety and agitation.

Asking clients if they have been prescribed psychotropic medication, and whether they are taking it, are questions that social workers frequently overlook during initial assessments. While social workers lack full medical training, becoming familiar with addictive drugs and with their side affects and interaction with other medications is an important addition to practitioners'

FIGURE 1: Selected Psychotropic Medications

MINOR TRANQUILLIZERS (anti-anxiety drugs)

Generic name	Trade Name
Lorazepam	Avitant™
Oxazepam	Serax™
Triazolam	Halicon™
Diazepam	Valium™
Chloriazepxide	Librium™

MAJOR TRANQUILLIZERS (anti-psychotic drugs)

Generic name	Trade Name
Haloperiodol	Haldol™
Chlorpromazine	Largactil™
Loxapine	Loxapac™
Thiordazine	Mellaril™
Theothixene	Navane™

knowledge base. As well, they have a responsibility to educate clients about the risks of addictive drugs, the risks of voluntarily stopping medication prescribed for them, and the necessity of informing someone if they decide to stop taking them. Currently, psychotropic tranquillizers are divided into two groups: minor (anti-anxiety) and major (anti-psychotic), both of which are recognized as a major breakthrough for treating mental illness. Minor tranquillizers are usually prescribed for anxiety, stress, and tension, and major tranquillizers are sometimes prescribed for schizophrenia, the manic stage of manic depression (bipolar condition), and psychosis. Side effects were quickly identified as lack of co-ordination, drowsiness, light-headedness, and sedation; less common side effects include headaches, blurred vision, and dizziness. Documentation of addiction—commonly viewed as a compulsive need for a habit-forming substance, characterized by well-defined physiological symptoms of withdrawal—to these drugs began to appear in medical journals and books during the 1960s. They noted observations of a wide variety of such withdrawal symptoms as agitation, loss of appetite and weight, headaches, nausea, restlessness, anxiety, gastrointestinal disturbances, muscle spasms, and increased sensory perception. As abrupt withdrawal can cause severe symptoms, gradual tapering off

of psychotropic drugs is recommended and less likely to cause severe reactions. Dual addiction to psychotropic medication along with alcohol, some prescription drugs or addictive substances (i.e., street drugs), sleep-inducing medication, and painkillers is an additional danger. Blackouts and unconsciousness can occur if large amounts are consumed.

Psychotropic drugs are prescribed for twice as many adult females as adult men. Early theories of gender bias were attributed to pharmaceutical companies' advertisements depicting women as anxious and stressed; later theories identified Freud, society-wide culture, or physicians' paternalistic attitudes as possible originators of this gender bias. Regardless of the source, women continue to be overprescribed psychotropic drugs. Another population currently identified as experiencing high-risk prescribing is the elderly, as older people can experience more adverse reactions to psychotropic medication. In a 1996 study, 63,268 elderly Canadians were studied for the use of prescription drugs; one finding was that high-risk prescribing was most prevalent for psychotropic drugs and was higher among women than men. Researchers are currently studying the relationship between falls and fractures and the use of psychotropic medication. A widespread concern underlying issues relating to psychotropic medication is the powerful influence power of multinational pharmaceutical manufacturers which spend millions every year promoting use of these drugs. The federal government has responsibility to develop regulatory standards for drugs prescribed for Canadians. Regulation of psychotropic medication is under the Controlled Drug And Substance Act, 1997, replaced the former Narcotic Control Act, 1970, and parts III and IV of the Food and Drug Act. In August 1998, Health Canada began a review of the regulatory framework for benzodiazepines and certain psychotropic substances. Current information on therapeutic product programs at Health Canada can be found online at <www.hs sc.gc.ca>.

[*Dorothy McKnight*]

RELATED ENTRIES

Addiction, Bioethical Issues, Clinical Social Work, Medication, Pharmacological Therapy, Substance Addiction, Therapy, Treatment, Wellness

Q

qualitative research

Qualitative research is an umbrella method that covers various interpretative techniques used to understand a particular phenomenon under study. Attaching the term "quality" connotes the "nature of a situation which can be interpreted as an empirical, socially located phenomenon, defined by its own history" (Kirk & Miller 1986: 9). This method of research, which is being increasingly used, is best described through a clear definition, a historical perspective, and a review of the six major domains that encompass qualitative research traditions. Fundamentally, qualitative research within the social sciences involves the observation and analysis of people and other living creatures in their own environment; for human studies, the researcher has opportunities to interact with research participants in their own language and on their own terms. Identified with sociology, cultural anthropology, political science, psychology and social work, among other disciplines, qualitative research is often understood to be naturalistic, ethnographic, and participatory in nature (Kirk & Miller 1986: 9). The qualitative research method analyzes data originating in intuitive and often serendipitous situations that add to a richer description of participants under observation; analyses derived from these data form new explanations and theories grounded in the details. The goal of qualitative research is the development of grounded theory—a discovery process of theory based on data systematically obtained through social research. A variety of interpretative techniques are used by individual researchers to describe, decode, translate, and come to terms with the meaning—not the frequency or other quantitative characteristic—of certain more or less naturally occurring phenomena in the social world. In addition to the many interpretative techniques documented in literature, others may be devised by researchers as part of their research process: therein lies the flexibility of this method.

Qualitative research has seen a lengthy and varied historical growth in the human disciplines and has become an increasingly important mode of inquiry for the social sciences. Denzin and Lincoln (1994) have traced the origin of qualitative research in the twentieth century to the works of the classic Chicago school of the 1920s and 1930s, which established the importance of direct observation as a research method used for the study of collective human life; the work by Robert Park, who studied natural areas of Chicago and investigated the underlying patterns of development and change, and Everett Hughes, who developed vivid accounts of urban settings in Chicago, are recognized as pioneers in this school. The Chicago methodology established the down-to-earth approach that applies flexible and emerging techniques for qualitative research data gathering, analysis, and theory development (Glaser & Strauss 1969: vii). During the first half of the twentieth century, the fieldwork method of data gathering for research was developed within the discipline of anthropology, in particular, by Franz Boas, Margaret Mead, Ruth Benedict, Gregory Bateson, E.E. Evans-Pritchard, A.R. Radcliffe-Brown, and Bronislaw Malinowski; this style of inquiry sees a researcher travelling to a foreign setting to study the customs and habits of another society and culture. Contemporary fieldwork now includes research in the field and real-life research as major methods of data collection and analysis; fieldwork is now routinely conducted, for example, in communities of economically or socially marginalized segments of Canadian society. Qualitative research as an established method of inquiry and theory formulation has become a widely used tool by many disciplines, including social work, education, psychology, and nursing as well as by many national and international organizations. Academic institutions increasingly hire faculty with expertise in many research paradigms, and qualitative research is now represented in university and college settings within the United States and Canada.

To differentiate prominent methods of data collection in qualitative research, six major domains have been identified within qualitative research. Stemming from the discipline of education, these domains are applicable to the social sciences.

- *Human ethology* seeks to understand a range of behaviours in which people naturally engage. Data are gathered through observation and sometimes on videotape.
- *Ecological psychology* stresses the interactions of persons within their environment in shaping

behaviour. This method relies heavily on observational data.

- *Holistic ethnography* recognizes that human culture is a crucial concept and relies on participant observation.
- *Cognitive anthropology* assumes that participants' perspectives are organized into cognitive or semantic schemata (categories of meaning that are systematically related to one another). Data are gathered through long and detailed interviews.
- *Ethnography of communication* draws heavily on linguistics. Data gathered focus on verbal and non-verbal interactions, relying on participant observation and audio/videotapes of these interactions.
- *Symbolic interactionism* examines ways in which individuals take and make meaning in interactions with others.

Each of these six methods of data gathering and interpretation assumes that "the systematic inquiry must occur in a natural setting rather than an artificially constrained one such as an experiment" (Marshall & Rossman 1989: 10). The process of interviewing for research purposes can be structured or unstructured, employ cultural or topical interviews, oral histories, life histories, and evaluations. Among the strengths of observational methods of data collection are the researcher's ability to shift focus when new information becomes available and to combine insight with rigour. Having evolved during the nineteenth century, this flexible and emerging research paradigm will, no doubt, continue to grow and develop.

[*Nancy Riedel Bowers*]

RELATED ENTRIES

Capacity Assessment, Quality Assurance, Quantitative Research, Research, Theory & Practice

REFERENCES

Denzin, N., and Y. Lincoln (Eds.) 1994. *Handbook of Qualitative Research*. Thousand Oaks, CA: Sage.

Glaser, B., and A. Strauss. 1967. *The Discovery of Grounded Theory: Strategies for Qualitative Research*. New York: Aldine de Gruyter.

Kirk, J., and M. Miller. 1986. *Reliability and Validity in Qualitative Research*. Beverly Hills, CA: Sage.

Marshall, C., and G. Rossman. 1994. *Designing Qualitative Research*. Newbury Park, CA: Sage.

quality assurance

Quality assurance is a type of service evaluation program that assesses whether a service's intended outcomes are within accepted standards. Human service organizations, which often operate with insufficient resources and growing client needs and demands, face challenges in related to service quality. As a result, many agencies carry out service quality programs, such as quality assurance. With origins in the manufacturing sector, quality assurance processes, procedures and techniques have been adapted to human service organizations to assess services for appropriateness, consistency, and excellence and, where necessary, improve them to ensure that they meet client needs (Adams 2000). Such agencies may want to implement quality assurance to, for instance, increase organizational output, enhance their service/resource ratio, improve overall effectiveness and operations, or deal with specific criticisms or weaknesses (Adams 2000). Other motivating factors can range from a genuine concern that services are meeting client needs to resource containment goals. Consequently, quality assurance may be a one-time evaluation or a continuous process to improve agency outcomes. Service standards, usually called outcome indicators or measures—are at the core of quality assurance; they can be developed by an agency, ideally with the staff who are expected to meet them, or they can be derived from well-established programs or legislated standards. In mental health, health care, and child welfare, for example, national and international standards have been developed with accreditation systems; child welfare standards set by the Child Welfare League of America are commonly used in Canada. Standards alone, however, do not guarantee quality. Some confusion exists between the setting of standards and benchmarks; benchmarks emphasize best practices, whereas standards are minimum requirements. A crucial step in quality assurance is determining whether these standards are being met, for instance, through a combination of systematic data collection, file audits, or evaluation of workers' clinical activities (Weinbach 1998). When standards are not met, quality assurance assessments can recommend strategies for implementing improvements and for periodic monitoring to ensure that standards are met in the future.

As quality assurance focuses on outcome measures, a social service organization may give too much attention to reaching quantitative service objectives and too little attention to qualitative means for attaining them. A common criticism of purist approaches to quality assurance is that they often fail to consider sufficiently all aspects of an organization (Weinbach 1998); to respond to this criticism, most organizations now are committed to broader, more inclusive quality evaluation paradigms, such as total quality management. Galea-Curmi and Hawkins note that quality assurance is "less concerned with the promotion of optimal standards and client care," while total quality measurement is concerned with quality in terms of external and internal clients; they add that, within organizations applying total quality management, "the measure of quality is operationalized within processes designed to develop evolving standards of excellence, rather than adherence to externally imposed standards of conformity" (1996: 163–64). In practice, the many approaches to and variations of quality assurance have become blurred with other quality evaluation frameworks. Social work has generally accepted the value of evaluating the quality of services, critical issues about quality assurance, with its focus on service standards and outcomes, persist. Issues such as the purpose of quality assurance in an organization, the meaning of established standards, how standards are set and by whom, and the balance of outcome measures to related work processes, need to be addressed when considering quality assurance in today's human services environment. Other broad concerns likely to draw professional attention include the role of staff in service quality review and improvement, the commitment of organizations to address issues related to the fulfilment of standards and quality, and whether quality reviews are reflective of organizational activities as a whole.

[*Michael R. Woodford*]

RELATED ENTRIES

Qualitative Research, Quantitative Research, Program Evaluation, Research, Theory & Practice

REFERENCES

Adams, R. 2000. Quality Assurance in Social Work. In M. Davies (ed.), *Blackwell Encyclopaedia of Social Work*. 279–81. Oxford, UK: Blackwell.

Galea-Curmi, E., and F. Hawkins. 1996. Benchmarking. In J. Gunther and F. Hawkins (Eds.) *Total Quality Management in Human Services*. 163–81. New York: Springer.

Weinbach, R.W. 1998. *The Social Worker as Manager: A Practice Guide to Success*. Needham Heights, MA: Allyn and Bacon.

quantitative research

Quantitative research is one dimension along the knowledge-building spectrum. The logical structure of quantitative research flows from theory development, hypothesis testing, observations/data collection, data analysis, and findings. Typically, quantitative research is experimental or explanatory in nature. It may draw on inductive or deductive methods of formulating hypotheses—through a logical process based on general principles applied to a particular instance—to arrive at conclusions. Research designs in quantitative research range from classical experimental approaches with randomized control trials, through quasi-experimental designs without true randomization and single-case studies, to large-scale surveys. These methodologies involve the testing and validation of predictive, cause-effect hypotheses regarding social regularities. Quantitative methodologies are most useful to social workers with extensive prior knowledge and contact with professionals in the field, as this research emphasizes the measurement of variables and extensive statistical analysis of their relationships. The function of quantitative research is multifaceted. Quantitative research can provide a framework for social work practitioners to guide their work in practice effectiveness or examine outcome interventions. Quantitative research can also help generate and refine concepts and perspectives, clarify abstractions, produce methods of measurement, provide evidence for generalizations and theories, challenge accepted beliefs, and stimulate new hypotheses and knowledge building through the scientific method.

[*Rachel Birnbaum*]

RELATED ENTRIES

Program Evaluation, Qualitative Research, Quality Assurance, Research, Theory & Practice

R

race and racism

Race refers to major divisions within humankind alleged to be characterized by distinct physical features but factually vanquished by scientific discoveries about genetics since the 1960s. Views about the derivation and usage of the concept "race" differ. The 1991 Canadian Task Force on Multicultural and Multiracial Issues in Social Work Education defined race as "an arbitrary classification of populations conceived in Europe, using actual or assumed biologically determined traits (e.g., skin colour and other physical features) to place populations of the world into a hierarchical order, in terms of basic human qualities, with Europeans superior to all others" (CASSW 1991: Appendix A). Contemporary Canadian social workers hold different views about the use of this concept, including support for outright avoidance. The confusion generated by different usages of the term and the lack of empirical support for theories that there are genetic or clear physical differences between "races" has led some to conclude that the term is without utility and so avoid the term (Ujimoto 1990: 214). Collier (1993: 3) suggests that the term should not be used because it has justified the domination of one group by another and continuing usage carries with it the danger that it will continue to do so. Christensen (1995: 210), however, continues to use the term because "most people continue to refer to themselves and to other individuals and populations that are identifiable by skin colour as if these categories exist and have inherent meaning." Race-related concepts remain important for social work because historical perceptions about racial differences have been used to justify inequities and oppression of some persons and communities, from false notions about the inherent superiority of others. Systemic racism persists throughout Canadian society, often affecting the circumstances and life experiences of social work clients, despite Canada's multicultural laws.

There is less dispute about the existence of racism. Many manifestations of racism are narrated in autobiographical accounts of Canadians—confirmed by empirical studies—from diverse ethnocultural backgrounds, often part of communities marginalized from dominant societies. Porter's seminal study (1965) demonstrated that racist perceptions were an important determinant of economic and social status in Canada until the middle of the twentieth century; from data collected in 1931, 1951, and 1961, he showed that Caucasian people of British descent were at the top of the social pyramid, and Chinese and Aboriginal peoples were at the bottom. Since Porter's study, Lautard and Guppy have considered occupational differentials based on race, commenting that "the composition of the Canadian population has changed since Porter first wrote, but social cleavages based on ethnicity remain important" (1990: 189). Clear evidence exists that racism is experienced in personal interactions, as reflected and supported through cultural bias and ethnocentrism, and as evident in social structures and systems that afford continuing privilege to some people and obstacles to others. The challenge issued to social work educators to confront multiple and overlapping bases of oppression (CASSW 1999) and the values of social work reflected in codes of ethics both support racism-sensitive practice. In the 1990s an increased emphasis on the role of social workers in challenging oppression based on any features of diversity was reflected in changes to educational policy statements and accreditation standards for social work programs developed by the Canadian Association of Schools of Social Work. Humanitarian and egalitarian ideals of Canadian social work advocate practice that is sensitive to diverse cultures, ethnicities, and minorities in its broadest sense.

[*Rosemary A. Clews*]

RELATED ENTRIES

Aboriginal Issues, Diversity, J. Gandy, Chinese Immigration Act, W. Head, D.G. Hill, Immigrants & Immigration, Minorities, Racism-Sensitive Social Work, Refugees, Sensitizing Concepts, Visible Minorities

REFERENCES

CASSW. 1991. *Social Work Education at the Crossroads: The Challenge of Diversity.* Report of the CASSW Task Force on Multicultural and Multiracial Issues in Social Work Education. Ottawa: Canadian Association of Schools of Social Work.

———. 1999. Revised Accreditation Standards. Ottawa: Canadian Association of Schools of Social Work.

Christensen, C.P. 1995. Immigrant Minorities in Canada. In J.C. Turner and F.J. Turner (Eds.) *Canadian Social Welfare*. 3rd ed. 179–212. Toronto: Allyn and Bacon.

Collier, K. 1993. Anti-racism Approaches to CASSW Educational Policy. Unpublished Presentation to Committee on Educational Policy of CASSW. Ottawa: Carlton University Press.

Lautard, H., and N. Guppy. 1990. The Vertical Mosaic Revisited: Occupational Differentials among Canadian Ethnic Groups. In P.S. Li (Ed.) *Race and Ethnic Relations in Canada*. 189–208. Toronto: Oxford University Press.

Porter, J. 1965. *The Vertical Mosaic*. Toronto: University of Toronto Press.

Ujimoto, K.V. 1990. Studies of Ethnic Identity and Race Relations. In P.S. Li (Ed.) *Race and Ethnic Relations in Canada*. 209–30. Toronto: Oxford University Press.

racism-sensitive social work

Racism-sensitive social work is practice based on acknowledging that systemic racism exists in Canadian society, and that it has deleterious effects on all aspects of social work theory, policy, and practice (Christensen 2002). Recently, Canadian social work literature has focused on oppression within a framework of diversity in all of its human forms (i.e., children, seniors, sexual orientation, people with developmental or physical challenges), failing to highlight the unique role played by race, as it intersects with, and distorts, the effects of other forms of oppression. This parallels the trend in the United States and has led to a decline in emphasis—if not again minimizing—the effects of racism on children, seniors, gays and lesbians, physically or intellectually challenged people, and others who experience double jeopardy, making their experience to be unique within these specified categories. Race in this context continues to be a vital way in which most people "to refer to themselves and to other individuals and populations that are identifiable by skin colour as if these categories exist and have inherent meaning" (Christensen 1995: 210).

Attempts to address racism and its effects on social work began in the United States, as an outgrowth of the civil rights movement of the 1960s. Literature and research on this subject proliferated during the 1970s and 1980s there, with racial (or visible) minorities making major contributions. The governing bodies of the profession and the accreditation boards, the US Council on Social Work Education, produced numerous publications on this subject. The next region of the world to give serious attention to racism in social work was Britain, where the number of "Blacks" (i.e., anyone not of European ancestry) from former colonies, whether immigrants or British-born, became more vocal about the discrimination they were experiencing. Canada has always been multiethnic and -cultural: First Nations are diverse peoples, Africans of diverse ancestries have been arriving since the 1600s and 1700s, and diverse Asian peoples have been in Canada since the mid-1850s. While several authors (Christensen 1986) had made note of racial issues having an effect within social work practice, a review of Canadian social work literature prior to the late 1980s infers that Canada was racially homogeneous, but ethnically and culturally diverse, with only scant attention paid to Aboriginal peoples. Liberalization of Canada's racist immigration laws, which had placed limits on people of colour before the 1960s, led to an influx of people from Asia, the Caribbean, and South and Central America. Consequently, the literature of the 1980s addressed the need for cultural sensitivity training and the development of cross-cultural competence. Later, closely related to Canada's multiculturalism focus in the form of various federal and provincial laws and policies, multicultural practice models were proposed. These models often focused on the impact of the practitioner having to serve clients from many backgrounds in a given agency setting (Al-Krenawi & Graham 2002). Social workers in Canada have only recently begun to focus on the effects of racism—rather than cultural differences alone—as a factor to be considered in social work and social welfare. The 1991 report of the Canadian Association of Schools of Social Work Task Force on Multicultural and Multiracial Issues in Social Work Education recognized ethnicity, culture, and race—as the latter construct is commonly used—as potentially determining factors in the lives of students, faculty, and clients. Nevertheless, discussions about race and racism remain uncomfortable and controversial, as indicated by recent attempts to identify anti-racist course materials used in schools of social work nationwide. Currently, there are but few Canadian authors making race-based analyses central to frameworks examining issues in social work education and practice (Christensen 1996 & 2002; Herberg 1993; Razack 2002).

In the current literature, race-sensitive practice is most clearly linked to anti-racist social work, which differs from multicultural social work by its emphasis on the pervasiveness of racism in Canada, past and present, and on the need to actively seek to change social welfare policies and agency structures that consciously or unconsciously maintain oppression on the basis of race. Since the effects of racism manifest on both personal and societal levels, social work curricula must thoroughly examine macro and micro issues and incorporate this awareness during all practice methods, whether in communities, group work, or intervention with individuals, dyads, and families (Lie & Este 1999). Effects of racism must be addressed in students' fieldwork settings and not only in the classroom (Razack 2002). Race-sensitive social work recognizes that the social work curriculum is based on Eurocentric models; it also recognizes that most social work analyses are underpinned by the assumption that race-based privilege within social service institutions, as in the wider society, is acceptable. Among the major premises of racism-sensitive social work is that social work is inevitably political in nature; that personal problems may have structural causes, particularly for members of racialized and other marginalized communities; and that action must be taken to dismantle oppressive policies, institutions, and service systems. Efforts must go beyond multicultural understanding and improving cross-cultural competence. When racism is ignored, any analysis of social problems faced by clients, communities, and society is incomplete. As anticipated by Porter (1965), several recent studies suggest that anyone's place in the ethnoracial hierarchy in major Canadian cities is increasingly tied to employment opportunities, location of residence, educational experiences, contacts with the criminal justice system, levels of social mobility, well-being and health, and poverty (Kazemipur & Halli 2000). Racism-sensitive social work calls for transforming attitudes and belief systems that lead practitioners to ignore—or to support—differential treatment in social services and other societal systems based on misperceptions about race.

[*Carole Pigler Christensen*]

RELATED ENTRIES

Anti-oppressive Social Work, Diversity, Education in Social Work, Empowerment Theory, Ethnocultural Communities' Services, League for the Advancement of Coloured People, Minorities, Minority-Sensitive Practice, Professional Issues, Progressive Social Work, Race & Racism, Radical Social Work, Sensitizing Concepts, Social Work Profession, Theory & Practice, Visible Minorities

REFERENCES

Al-Krenawi, A., and J.R. Graham (Eds.) 2002. *Multicultural Social Work in Canada: Working with Diverse Ethno-racial Communities*. Toronto: Oxford University Press.

CASSW. 1991. *Social Work Education at the Crossroads: The Challenge of Diversity*. Report of the CASSW Task Force on Multicultural and Multiracial Issues in Social Work Education. Ottawa: Canadian Association of Schools of Social Work.

Christensen, C.P. 1986. Cross-cultural Social Work: Fallacies, Fears, and Failings. *Intervention* 74, 6–15.

———. 1995. Immigrant Minorities in Canada. In J.C. Turner and F.J. Turner (Eds.) *Canadian Social Welfare*. 3rd ed. 179–212. Toronto: Allyn and Bacon.

———. 1996. The Impact of Racism on the Education of Social Service Workers. In C. James (Ed.) *Perspectives on Racism and the Human Services Sector: A Case for Change*. 140–51. Toronto: University of Toronto Press.

———. 2002. Canadian Society: Social Policy and Ethno-racial Diversity. In A. Al-Krenawi and J.R. Graham (Eds.) *Multicultural Social Work in Canada, Working with Diverse Ethno-racial Communities*. Chapter 4, 70–97. Toronto: Oxford University Press.

Herberg, D.C. 1993. *Frameworks for Cultural and Racial Diversity: Teaching and Learning for Practitioners*. Toronto: Canadian Scholars Press.

Kazemipur, A., and S.S. Halli. 2000. *The New Poverty in Canada: Ethnic Groups and Ghetto Neighbourhoods*. Toronto: Thompson Education.

Lie, G.Y., and D. Este. 1999. *Professional Social Service Delivery in a Multicultural World*. Toronto: Canadian Scholars Press.

Porter, J. 1965. *The Vertical Mosaic*. Toronto: University of Toronto Press.

Razack, N. 2002. *Critical Antiracist and Anti-oppressive Perspectives for the Human Services Practicum*. Halifax, NS: Fernwood.

radical social work

Radical social work is concerned with the *radix* or root of social and personal problems and falls under the rubric of critical theory and conflict paradigms as originated by Karl Marx. Marx concluded that societies are organized through and by intersecting conflicting class interests, rather than ruled by consensus or order. What differentiates the conflict critical paradigms—including radical social work, from other paradigms is their focus on oppression, their criticism of traditional theory and philosophy, their exploration of social/theoretical alternatives, and their goal to act to create socio-economic and political change. Radical social work has been a part of the profession since the late 1800s, the days of the settlement house movement. Since then three key periods of social work radical activity have been identified:

- In the 1930s, such social workers as Bertha Capen Reynolds were involved in the rank-and-file labour movements of the depression, a period that has been called the golden age of social work activism. These social workers viewed personal poverty and unemployment as resulting directly from the socio-economic and political structures of the day. Unlike social worker Mary Richmond who accepted the concept of individual pathology, Reynolds and her colleagues espoused the fundamental analysis of social work problems, advocating instead for radical social action to transform social structures.
- In the 1960s, some social workers again moved toward analyses of social, political, and economic structural causes for personal problems in the context of the developing welfare state, the civil rights movements, and a re-emerging feminist movement. These radical thinkers also began to look critically at the practitioner's role as agent of the state and the profession's role in support of the status quo.
- The 1970s saw a re-emergence of interest in radical social work through the works of such key authors as Bailey and Brake (1975) and Galper (1975), who were following by Moreau (1979) and Leonard (1975). More recently, Wagner (1989) and Mullaly (1997) argue that neo-conservative trends and escalating human and environmental crises of the 1980s and 1990s have resulted in an increased interest in radical social work and fundamental analysis.

The term "structural social work" was first coined by Ward and Middleman (1974) to describe intervention into the social environment. Similar to radical social work, structural social work views social problems as arising from liberal, neo-conservatism capitalism (classism, racism, sexism) rather than the failings of individuals. Structural, or radical, social work also falls under the rubric of critical theory and radical social work as it is critical of traditional order and consensus-based social work theoretical models, has emancipatory intent, emphasizes action to transform society and social structures, and suggests alternative visions for how people might choose to live. It was first explored in Canada by Moreau (1979), later authors including Carniol (1992) and Mullaly (1997), further developed the theory, concepts, and key assumptions of radical/structural social work. Mullaly defines structural social work as "social work which analyzes how structural inequality in a capitalist society creates, influences, and perpetuates oppression and personal problems"; for him, the term "structural social work" is both descriptive, as it identifies problems caused by the social order, and prescriptive, as it suggests interventions directed at changing social structure (1997). Some of the key concepts involved in a radical/structural approach include:

- *oppression*: the unjust or cruel exercise of authority or power;
- *the feminist slogan of the "personal is political"*: how the socio-economic political context of a society is critical in shaping personality and personal situation (Mullaly 1997);
- *critical consciousness*: from Freire's concept of conscientization (1970), learning to perceive social, political, and economic contradictions, and to take action against the oppressive elements of reality;
- *collectivism*: co-operation rather than competition, an emphasis on duties rather than rights, on the good of the community rather than on the rights of individuals, on altruism rather than selfishness, which implies participatory decision-making (Mullaly 1997); and
- *transformation to change in composition or structure*: to change the outward form or appearance of; to change in character or condition.

Leonard (1975) proposes that the goals of self-determination and human dignity are fraudulent and impossible to achieve in a for-profit society, yet many social workers do hold these beliefs. He argues that social work practice has developed into highly individualistic, pathology-based medical models and social casework, with the attendant therapeutic goals of adjustment, rehabilitation, and resocialization. Similarly, he claims that social welfare was developed to ameliorate the harshest consequences of capitalism and ensure an effective, cheap labour force. Radical or structural theorists suggest that socialism offers a better foundation for egalitarianism and humanism and is more consistent with social work values (Mullaly 1997; Leonard 1975). They also assume that once oppressed people become politically aware, they will unite around common experiences of oppression and will work collectively to resolve it. Radical or structural social workers work to transform the oppressive conditions and social structures that cause negative effects on people. In other words, the goal is not just to critique existing structures but to develop alternatives—what Freire described as radical praxis—reflection on the world and action to transform it (Leonard 1975).

Given these assumptions, radical or structural social workers encourage clients and students to develop social praxis—the ability to critically reflect on their personal political situations and develop consequent personal and political plans of action (Moreau 1979). The primary targets for intervention are the oppressive practices of mediating institutions. Secondary targets include providing concrete help to achieve immediate tension-relief while developing increased awareness (critical consciousness). Indeed, the main justification for helping adaptation and coping of individuals, dyads, or groups is to further their critical consciousness and build power bases for fundamental social change. With this in mind, the radical/structural practitioner works with clients and colleagues to explore countersystems, unite service users, link with political, social, and union organizations, and support organizations (collectivization) and develop alternative power bases for social change. De Maria thinks that conventional education tutors how to live in capitalism and proposes that social work education has invariably created noncritical and nonactive, yet fully explored masters of compassion, who in turn are incapable or uninterested in challenging the sta-

tus quo or making fundamental social change. In response, he calls for the intentional radicalization of the social work student body, faculty, university, and classroom. De Maria (1992) advises social work educators to identify and confront relations among power, knowledge, and control, revise welfare history, listen to survivors, and hold conflict-based dialogues on utopian possibilities. Other radical skills that could be taught include alliance building, collectivism, whistle blowing, protesting, and activist interpersonal helping. In terms of research, both quantitative and qualitative methods are encouraged but with a view to link to *a priori* assumptions about oppression. Participation action research is often mentioned as an example of radical/structural research methodology. Under this model, the primary goal of research is not to seek truths but to assist oppressed groups of people to become empowered to make social change.

[*Susan Hillock*]

RELATED ENTRIES

Aboriginal Services, Anti-oppressive Social Work, Citizen Participation, Community Development, Community Organization, Diversity, Empowerment Theory, Healing Theory (Cree), Participatory Research, Practice Methods, Progressive Social Work, Racism-Sensitive Social Work, Sensitizing Concepts, Social Welfare History, Theory & Practice

REFERENCES

Bailey, R., and M. Brake (Eds.) 1975. *Radical Social Work*. New York: Pantheon.

Carniol, B. 1992. Structural Social Work: Maurice Moreau's Challenge to Social Work Practice. *Journal of Progressive Human Services* 3, 1, 1–20.

De Maria, W. 1992. Alive on the Street, Dead in the Classroom: The Return of Radical Social Work and the Manufacture of Activism. *Journal of Sociology and Social Welfare* 9, 13 (September), 137–58.

Freire, P. 1970. *Pedagogy of the Oppressed*. New York: Continuum.

Galper, J. 1975. *The Politics of Social Services*. Englewood Cliffs, NJ: Prentice-Hall.

Leonard, P. 1975. Towards a Paradigm of Radical Practice. R. Bailey and M. Brake (Eds.) *Radical Social Work* 3, 46–61.

Moreau, M.J. 1979. A Structural Approach to Social Work Practice. *The Canadian Journal of Social Work Education* 5, 1, 78–94.

Mullaly, Robert. 1997. *Structural Social Work*. Toronto: Oxford University Press.

Wagner, D. 1989. Radical Movements in the Social Services: A Theoretical Framework. *Social Service Review* June, 79–82.

Ward, G.G., and R.R. Middleman. 1974. *The Structural Approach to Direct Social Work Practice*. New York: Columbia University Press.

recording

A long-time component of social work practice has been the acceptance of the professional responsibility to maintain ongoing written reports of work with clients. Originally, recording such records was seen as necessary to assist in the processes of clarifying a diagnosis and treatment plan, and noting progress or change in a case. As well, records were often expected to include a report of the social worker's reactions to the client to serve as a basis for supervision. This latter type of recording, known as process recording, resulted in voluminous case records. Over the years, concerns began to be expressed over the amount of time, effort, and cost involved in process recording; in response to demands for greater efficiency in the use of resources and as a reaction to this style of supervision, many practitioners and agencies moved to a much more summarized type of recording. In contemporary practice, recording case notes continues to be surrounded by debate. Accurate records must be kept to meet societal expectations of social work accountability, as reflected in various legislative and accrediting processes. Such notes are needed to identify a client, to document ongoing judgments of the worker about the client and his/her/their presenting situation, to note client expectations, to record decisions about intervention, to keep track of regular progress reports, to document prognosis, and to provide a final summary and evaluation. Concerns about the data in such recording focus on confidentiality. For a long time, records were seen as confidential documents available not to clients but only to authorized personnel. In small agencies, authorized personnel would constitute only a small number of people; however, in major multi-faceted settings with large administrative staffs, many persons with differing professional and paraprofessional affiliations had access to records. In recent years, confidentiality and exclusive access to social work records has become less clear cut, as they can, for instance, become sub-ject to subpoena by a court. Further, there has been a strong movement in Canadian practice to make a client's records available to him/her; indeed, some practitioners make use of the record as a part of treatment and involve the client in their preparation and maintenance. Access to client records by various forms of outside scrutiny has made many social workers very cautious about what they document in client records. Motivation ranges from protection of clients to minimizing risks to themselves as potential evidence against them in allegations of professional misconduct. Thus, practitioners may feel caught in a conflict between meeting their ethical and mandated responsibility to record and potential risks to themselves and clients from record contents. The weakening of agencies' assurances to clients of absolute confidentiality of their records has resulted in the destruction of records as a matter of routine after a periods of time, usually several years, even though such destruction might be in violation of accreditation or legislative requirements to retain records. Researchers are also uncomfortable about records that have potential value for future studies and historical studies of practice being destroyed.

Other factors with considerable impact on recording are changes in technology and increased evaluation to meet demands for accountability. The availability of computers has resulted in client data collection and storage through coding, prescribed formats, and specific headings, as well as having practitioners enter their records through electronic processes. Moves to standardization of content and format have served to save practitioners time, and have also been of considerable assistance in gathering and analyzing data, service trends, outcome evaluations, and clearer understanding of time management. Improved evaluation methods have also resulted in agency conflicts as practitioners may view increased monitoring as administrative controls rather than adjuncts to treatment. A further challenge to contemporary recording stems from the diversity of theories driving practice, which may sit uneasily with efforts to standardize recording. Inherent within this diversity of theories and practice approaches diversity results are differing perceptions of the nature and scope of practice, frequently drawing on terminology and usage differences that do not mesh well with standardized data collection. Trends in recording and in data gathering and analysis have had a generally positive impact on practice for clients, practitioners, researchers, administrators and funders. The critical awareness of the potential for miscommunication and ethical concerns are signs of a healthy profession continually alert for risks to client and practitioner well-being.

[*FJT*]

RELATED ENTRIES

Accountability, Assessment, Capacity Assessment, Codes of Ethics, Communication Theory, Ethics, Information & Communication Technologies, Interviewing, Malpractice, Practice Methods, Professional Issues, Professional Liability, Research, Treatment, Theory & Practice

reflective practice

The term "reflective practice" was originally coined by Chris Argyris and Donald Schon (1974; Schon 1983) to describe the way professionals from various disciplines consciously apply knowledge and theory within practice. They argued that a technical epistemology of practice works well when a field of practice is narrow and routine, and when all that is required is the technical application of abstract, scientific knowledge to standardized problems; when the field of practice is diverse and ambiguous—as in social work—and when problems do not present themselves ready-made as textbook cases, knowledge of what to do is not readily available in an abstract format to be applied; rather, knowledge of what to do is acquired through the experience of practice, accumulating judgment by beginning to act in the situation, trying out alternative options, improvising and testing diverse ways of framing and organizing the relevant facets of the situation, and exploring the constraints and possibilities inherent in the situation itself. Reflective practice has generated interest among social workers who view the rational/technical epistemology of professional practice as an inadequate description of what social workers really do when they construct their knowledge-for-practice (Dean 1989; Papell & Skolnick 1992; Pilalis 1986). Knowledge accrued through reflective practice is concrete and local, rather than abstract and technical. It is knowledge of that situation in its uniqueness and particularity. Acquired by engaging the situation through conversation,

trying to influence it while listening for its backtalk, and continuously reflecting, the knowledge crafted inductively from the ground up fits the specific local context. For the reflective practitioner, the field of practice is not a static, passive recipient of expert knowledge. Because the situation itself "talks back," resists, and constrains the practitioner's every move, effective practice is not so much a matter of having the right expert knowledge, as of accommodating social work knowledge, judgment, and expertise to the demands of the context with great flexibility. This ability to reflect in the midst of action—rather than apart from action—combined with the unpredictable and improvisational unfolding of knowledge characterizes reflective practice.

Social workers who are excited by a reflective epistemology of practice espouse a concept of practice effectiveness that is based not so much on knowing the right solution(s), as on appropriately identifying the problem(s)—knowing in other words, how to construct practice worlds within which the practitioner's knowledge, values, and expertise are operational. This signature worldmaking component of reflective practice—through which countless unnamed details of a situation are identified and organized into a coherent problem—requires more than technical prowess. It requires a creative artistry that is learned not so much from textbooks as from apprenticeship to the values and discourses of the discipline. Schon and others have argued that professional education favours the learning of abstract theories, which, while embodying the central values of the profession, often fail to translate into practice behaviour. Instead, much of everyday practice tends to be governed by the tacit practice "wisdom" accrued from personal experience, some of which may not actually be wise (DeMartini & Whitbeck 1987). It is a kind of knowing-in-action that is learned by doing, and that is assimilated into a practice repertoire and embedded in automatic habits and skills, often without conscious critical deliberation. Like riding a bike or speaking with syntactical grammar: one learns what to do without necessarily being able to give a verbal description of the how one does it. Practitioners who are committed to surfacing and critically reflecting on the theories that govern their practice behaviour open themselves to truly transformative learning, learning that involves inquiry into the foundational assumptions and values of their practice worlds. When this kind of inquiry becomes fully reciprocal with others who are equally committed to critical reflection on their practice, they have the potential for a dynamic and mutually transformative dialogue and lifelong professional development.

[*Margaret Sellick*]

RELATED ENTRIES

Creativity, Interviewing, Theory & Practice

REFERENCES

Argyris, C., and D. Schon. 1974. *Theory in Practice: Increasing Personal Effectiveness*. San Francisco, CA: Jossey-Bass.

Dean, R. 1989. Ways of Knowing in Clinical Practice. *Clinical Social Work Journal* 17, 2, 116–27.

DeMartini, J., and L. Whitbeck. 1987. Sources of Knowledge for Practice. *The Journal of Applied Behavioural Science* 23, 2, 219–31.

Papell, C., and L. Skolnick. 1992. The Reflective Practitioner: A Contemporary Paradigm's Relevance for Social Work Education. *Journal of Social Work Education* 28, 1, 18–26.

Pilalis, J. 1986. The Integration of Theory and Practice: A Reexamination of a Paradoxical Expectation. *British Journal of Social Work* 16, 1, 79–96.

Schon, D. 1983. *The Reflective Practitioner: How Professionals Think in Action*. London: Temple Smith.

Regina Manifesto

The Regina Manifesto was the founding document adopted as party policy at a 1933 convention in Regina for the Co-operative Commonwealth Federation (CCF). The outgrowth of several small political movements ranging from social democratic through socialist and to communist, the CCF brought these parties' regional issues together, largely by pressures resulting from the great depression. The CCF became an alternative to the existing Liberal and Conservative parties, offering party policies and new hope for Canadians struggling to cope with the crushing social and economic effects of the depression. The major points of the Regina Manifesto, which was drafted in large part by members of the League for Social Reconstruction (such as F.R. Scott and J.S. Woodsworth), include:

- strong condemnation of the capitalist system for its "inherent injustice and inhumanity," "glar-

ing inequalities of wealth and opportunity," "chaotic waste and instability," and the "domination and exploitation of one class by another class";
- capitalism was to be replaced by a new social order, which would improve the life of all Canadian citizens and would be accomplished by a national planning commission, which would be responsible to the federal Cabinet and would lead to the socialization of a range of industries;
- acceptance of the family farm as the basis for agricultural production and increased purchasing power for the farm community by social control of the financial system;
- introduction of a welfare state, freedom of association, and collective bargaining for industrial workers, government regulation of wages;
- the end of sex discrimination;
- a uniform labour code;
- changes in the British North America Act (now Constitution Act, 1867) to give the federal government adequate power to "deal effectively with urgent economic problems which are essentially national in scope";
- immediate revision of the federal and provincial sources of revenue so as to produce "coordinated and equitable system of taxation throughout Canada";
- freedom of speech and assembly for all;
- humanization of the legal system; and
- an emergency program to cope with unemployment.

The manifesto ended with the words "No CCF government will rest content until it has eradicated capitalism and put into operation the full program of socialized planning which will lead to the establishment in Canada of the Co-operative Commonwealth." The CCF was eventually succeeded by the New Democratic Party (est. 1961).

[*Robert Twigg*]

RELATED ENTRIES

H. Cassidy, Co-operative Commonwealth Federation, League for Social Reconstruction, F.R. Scott, Social Welfare History, J.S. Woodsworth

religion

Social work has exceptionally strong religious roots, derived from generations of religious philanthropic persons and helping institutions preceding the twentieth-century secular social worker. Moreover, in a pre-secular society, social problems and their solutions had been widely understood and articulated through the prism of religion. Likewise, the compulsion to respond to human need has had religious dimensions, as it continues to have for many people, and particularly for practitioners of social work. In this context, religion entails the theological belief in a transcendent and/or immanent deity. It may also include the philosophical focus on one's relation to the cosmic order and human existence; the psychological states and behaviours associated with religious expression; and the anthro-sociological patterns, symbols, rituals, and stories around which communities relate to putative or supernatural powers (Canda & Furman 1999: 45). Interrelated with religion is spirituality, the latter term involving a person's "search for meaning and morally fulfilling relationships between oneself, other people, the encompassing universe, and the ontological ground of existence." Whereas religion tends to assume some deity/ies, spirituality may be understood "in terms that are theistic, atheistic, nontheistic, or any combination of these" (Canda & Furman 1999: 44).

The social concern and the development of the welfare state in Canada have been influenced by religious conviction. The Women's Christian Temperance Union and the Young Women's Christian Association, for example, were international Protestant organizations, founded in Canada in the latter half of the nineteenth century to assert women's rights. The social gospel movement, a loose coalition of Protestant clerics and laity emerged in the 1890s to apply social democratic Christian principles to prevailing public policy. B'Nai Brith Canada, formed in 1875 to extend well-established Jewish social services in the United States north, has itself expanded and created a network of related services. In Quebec, Semaines sociales was a forum in which Catholic clergy and laity likewise discussed social issues. The Social Services Council of Canada (est. 1907) was the creation of a number of diverse representatives from the trade union movement, Anglican, Methodist, Presbyterian, and Baptist churches, and others. Several Protestant clergy were important in the establishment and leadership of the Co-operative Commonwealth Federation (renamed the New

Democratic Party in 1961), including Methodist cleric and party founder J.S. Woodsworth (1874–1942) and Baptist minister Tommy Douglas (1904–86). Many of the country's oldest social service institutions have roots that are in some way associated with religious institutions or with personnel who were motivated by faith. Today a vital role in social development through local, national, and international structures is played by religions as diverse as Buddhism, Christianity, Hinduism, Islam, Judaism, traditional Aboriginal spirituality, and other traditions. A wide spectrum of religious coalitions also undertakes such work: the Canadian Council of Churches (est. 1944), the Inter-Church Committee on Human Rights in Latin America, Project Ploughshares, the Task Force on Churches and Corporate Responsibility, among others. Revelations in the 1980s and 1990s of abuse of children under the care of Catholic clergy, and of Aboriginal children at residential schools operated by the Catholic, Anglican, Presbyterian, and United churches has cast a dark shadow on the work of these institutions.

Mainstream social work scholarship has not devoted great attention to religion, with such rare exceptions as Charlotte Towle (1945) and theologian Reinhold Niebuhr (1932). Writings on existential/humanistic practice (Krill 1978) preceded other American scholarship authored mainly in the 1980s to the present time by Edward Canda, Alan Keith-Lucas, F.M. Loewenberg, Max Siproin, and others. Several social work journals explicitly focus on religious issues and communities, including *Christianity and Social Work*, published by the North America Association of Christians in Social Work, the *Journal of Jewish Communal Service, and Social Thought*. Other journals, such as *International Social Work*, have published numerous articles on issues related to diverse religious traditions. American scholars write about the importance of religion and spirituality to social workers, and as an issue that could be addressed in professional practice. Others consider the probability of still greater participation of religious institutions in social service delivery during the contemporary era of government cutback. Similar research could be undertaken in Canada, a country with lower levels of religiosity than the United States. Likewise, Canadians could consider the relevance to their country of recent US and UK scholarship calling for the inclusion of religion and spirituality as areas of diversity within mainstream social work education.

[*John R. Graham*]

RELATED ENTRIES

Bioethical Issues, B'Nai Brith, M. Bourgeoys, I. Bourget, Catholic Charities, Congrégation de Notre Dame, Church-Based Services, Cults, T.C. Douglas, Sister Mary Henry, Jewish Social Services, R. Leger, Meditation, Salvation Army, Sectarian Social Services, Social Gospel Movement, Spirituality, Women's Christian Temperance Union, J.S. Woodsworth, Women's Missionary Society, YMCA, YWCA

REFERENCES

Canda, E.R., and L.D. Furman. 1999. *Spiritual Diversity in Social Work Practice: The Heart of Helping.* New York: Free Press.

Krill, D.F. 1978. *Existential Social Work.* New York: Free Press.

Niebuhr, R. 1932. *The Contribution of Religion to Social Work.* New York: Columbia University Press.

Towle, C. 1945. *Common Human Needs.* New York: American Association of Social Workers.

remote practice

In Canada, remote practice refers to social work practice in small and scattered communities that are distant from human service organizations, where practitioners address local circumstances that often differ from those in the more populous urban-rural continuum in southern Canada. The label "northern practice" is also often used to reflect the geographic reality that much of Canada comprises predominantly rural landscapes with few built-up locations away from the urban and suburban areas where most Canadians live close to the American border. The term "remote" is more generic and encourages connections with similar practice settings elsewhere in Canada (e.g., on islands or outposts) and in the world that are not necessarily northern (e.g., Australian outback). For a long time social work in North America was satisfied with a simplistic distinction between urban and rural practice settings. By the mid-1980s, however, several Canadian authors were pointing out important differences between rural social work and the practice realities in remote communities in the northern provinces and territories. Collier (1984) connected the mission of remote social work with the state of underdevelopment

and exploitation experienced by most northern communities. Zapf (1985) argued that American rural social work theory was not sufficient to guide practice in northern Canada, where workers experiencing professional isolation encountered intense conflicts between the urban-based role for which they had been trained and the demands of northern communities. McKay (1987) called for the inclusion of a conflict perspective as a necessary adjunct to ecosystems theory for practice in northern Canada. A similar pattern was apparent internationally during the 1980s. Recognizing that isolated communities within predominantly rural regions differed in spatial issues and quality of life from rural areas close to major cities, the European Centre for Social Welfare Training and Research proposed a new category of "remote" or "isolated" practice setting. Reviewing patterns in the five Nordic countries, Lindholm (1988) found enough common traits to justify a separate identity and training for "Nordic practice." Rosenman (1980) reached a similar conclusion for the Australian outback.

The 1990s have witnessed a proliferation of Canadian literature on remote practice. *Northern Review* devoted an entire special issue to social work in northern Canada (Wharf 1992). A compilation of readings from northern Manitoba was published that same year (Tobin & Walmsley 1992). Grant MacEwan Community College published a collection of reflective essays on their experiences with Aboriginal social work outreach education in northern Alberta. Lakehead University's Centre for Northern Studies launched a Northern Social Work Series (Delaney & Brownlee 1995) with plans for additional books in the future. The knowledge base for Canadian social work practice overall has been expanded to include geographic factors that support the argument for recognition of remote practice (Zapf 1999). At this time, remote practice is not a fully developed model, but literature suggests an underlying worldview that emphasizes stewardship rather than exploitation and an approach focused on partnership and collaboration with the community through the constructive use of multiple-role relationships.

[*Michael Kim Zapf*]

RELATED ENTRIES

Aboriginal Issues, Aboriginal Services, Association of Social Workers in Northern Canada, Poverty,

Reflective Practice, Remote & Rural Practice, Sensitizing Concepts, Theory & Practice

REFERENCES

Collier, K. 1984. *Social Work with Rural People*. Vancouver, BC: New Star.

Delaney, R., and K. Brownlee (Eds.) 1995. *Northern Social Work Practice*. Thunder Bay, ON: Lakehead University Centre for Northern Studies.

Lindholm, K. 1988. In Search of an Identity—Social Work Training in the Nordic Countries. *Nordic Journal of Social Work* 8, 4–14. [Special English supplementary issue *Nordisk Sosialt Arbeid* on the occasion of IFSW's World Conference in Stockholm 1988.]

McKay, S. 1987. Social Work in Canada's North: Survival and Development Issues Affecting Aboriginal and Industry-based Economics. *International Social Work* 30, 259–78.

Rosenman, L.S. 1980. Social Work Education in Australia: The Impact of the American Model. *Journal of Education for Social Work* 16, 1, 112–18.

Tobin, M., and C. Walmsley (Eds.) 1992. *Northern Perspectives: Practice and Education in Social Work*. Winnipeg: Manitoba Association of Social Workers and University of Manitoba, Faculty of Social Work.

Wharf, B. (Ed.) 1992. *The Northern Review* 7. [Special issue on social work in northern Canada.]

Zapf, M.K. 1985. *Rural Social Work and Its Application to the Canadian North as a Practice Setting*. Working Papers on Social Welfare in Canada Publications Series 15. University of Toronto, Faculty of Social Work.

———. 1999. Geographic Factors. In F. J. Turner (Ed.) *Social Work Practice: A Canadian Perspective*. 344–58. Scarborough, ON: Prentice Hall / Allyn and Bacon Canada.

remote and rural practice methods

Social workers who undertake remote practice most often work with Aboriginal peoples, as they constitute most of the population in the northern provinces and the three territories. The circumstances of the north have required social work theory and practice to adapt to the distinct First Nations, Métis, Inuit, and Inuvialuit cultures there and to the psychological and social pressures produced by the encroachment of modern industrial development. Since the 1960s, major oil and gas, mining, and hydroelectric projects have had increasingly detrimental effects on Aboriginal pur-

suits, family roles, and values. Resulting pressures on Aboriginal societies are displayed through much higher levels of unemployment and social dysfunction than are found in the rest of Canadian society. Individual responses to stress range from high rates of alcohol and drug addiction, incarceration, and suicide. To deal with this social environment that differs dramatically from urban social realities in the much more populous and prosperous southern Canada, social work practitioners have had to adjust theoretical and practice approaches that are appropriate for southern Canada. Remote practice draws on the conventional multi-disciplinary model of treatment as well as Aboriginal concepts of healing and learning. Other factors that require adjustment of conventional practice approaches are the predominance of roles prescribed by the extended family and a focus on communal obligations, as opposed to the individual rights orientation of the dominant southern society. Practitioners are likely to build co-operative relationships with local leaders and staff, especially where an Aboriginal community has responsibility for social services and health care. Since most psycho-social services are absent from the north (i.e., for learning disabilities, mental illness, auditory/visual impairment), practitioners have to gain access to high-cost medical evacuation and travel on behalf of clients needing these specialized services; with health care cutbacks, access to both travel and services has decreased while needs increase. To address these needs, therefore, advancements in information technologies are increasingly being employed, such as video-conferencing to create virtual interdisciplinary conferences to co-ordinate a client's treatment plans. The development of and access to computerized databases of social service, employment, and educational opportunities are providing new tools for social workers to build integrated community-based treatment plans.

The challenges of remote practice are being met in part by the development of programs within existing schools and faculties of social work—such as those at Laurentian and Dalhousie—as well as Aboriginal schools of social work—such as the one at the First Nations University of Canada in Saskatchewan—to provide training for Aboriginal students to become social workers. The presumption is that Aboriginal social workers have the potential to provide more culturally appropriate social work practice. A continual problem in social work education, however, has been the retention of graduates in remote practice: the majority of practitioners are attracted to better paying positions in urban centres with increased opportunities for professional advancement. To counter this persistent brain drain, provincial and territorial governments are encouraging social work and other professionals to relocate to remote and predominantly rural areas by providing increased access to distance education for professional development in combination with compensation packages and improved working conditions, to be competitive with social service agencies in the urbanized south.

[*Mark Feldstein*]

RELATED ENTRIES

Aboriginal Issues, Aboriginal Services, Association of Social Workers in Northern Canada, Healing Theory (Cree), Poverty, Reflective Practice, Remote Practice, Sensitizing Concepts, Theory & Practice

research

The simplest definition of research is to "search again" (re-search) or to review and refine knowledge through repeated inquiry. Social work research can be broadly defined, as systematic procedures employed for the purpose of developing knowledge that can inform social work practice. Unlike so-called "pure" research, social work research has an applied component to it. It arises out of practice, policy, or social justice concerns and is designed ideally to inform social work practice, to find solutions to human problems or to promote human well-being. Currently, the are two dominant paradigms in social work research are quantitative and qualitative methodological approaches to inquiry. A paradigm is an orientation or underlying perspective held by a person, which organizes how one views the world, a problem or issue, or a research question. This way of thinking has been likened to conceptual lenses, which are shaped and tinted by our own values, experiences, assumptions, and beliefs. Where a researcher focuses attention is influenced by these lenses, and by where and how a researcher look for answers to research questions greatly influences what he/she finds.

Scholars have for years debated the relative merits of quantitative and qualitative approaches to research. More recently, it has been more widely acknowledged that each approach has an important role to play in social work inquiry, depending largely on the research question of interest. The primary difference between the two methodological approaches is that the data gathered in quantitative studies are numerical compared with non-numerical data for qualitative studies. Underlying the quantitative approach is the belief in the importance of careful empirical observation, a belief rooted in logical positivism, a philosophy of science that maintains that the scientific method is the appropriate tool for determining valid and factual knowledge. Quantitative methodological approaches to knowledge-building in social work inquire into predetermined questions or hypotheses and seek, through replicable and measurable means, to find facts that are generalizable. The analysis of data for this type of research requires the statistical manipulation of numbers or development of models. A researcher who wants to determine whether or not a cause produces an effect would select this method. To demonstrate that a social work intervention is effective in achieving a desired outcome, a quantitative method is normally used in social work research. Qualitative research approaches are most appropriate when a researcher seeks to understand the meaning of human experience. The approach to data collection is guided by more general research questions than those encountered in quantitative studies. In fact, the questions asked are not always clearly laid out at the onset of the study, but can emerge and evolve as the data are collected, analyzed and interpreted, often leading to new questions and further data gathering. The approach rests heavily on the creativity of the researcher and his/her ability to pursue rich sources of data and interpret them.

One of the key differences between the two paradigms is the system of logic they employ. Quantitative methods employ deductive logic, which, as described by Creswell (1994), begins when the researcher wants to test a theory using a hypothesis or research question that was derived from the theory. The researcher finds ways of measuring the concepts and variables, typically using scales or structured questions as indicators; finally, the hypotheses or questions are resolved through the statistical analysis of empirical data. Deductive logic begins with an abstract theoretical idea and moves toward hard empirical evidence or facts. The system of logic that underlies qualitative research is inductive reasoning, a way of reasoning that moves from the particular to the general. In this method, the researcher examines a large quantity of data obtained from a comparatively small number of individuals, cases, or events. The researcher meticulously examines and analyzes these data seeking to find relationships, patterns, similarities, and differences. Ideally, patterns that emerge point toward theory development (Creswell 1994). Thus, qualitative studies move from specific detailed observations toward more abstract generalizations and the development of theory.

[*J. Grant Macdonald*]

RELATED ENTRIES

Agency-Based Research, Assessment, Bioethical Issues, Caledon Institute for Social Policy, Canadian Capacity Assessment, Council on Social Development, Canadian Research Institute for Social Policy, Capacity Assessment, Demography, Doctorate, Ethics, Experimental Research Design, Family Demographics, Family Research, Intervention Research, Interprofessional Education, Interviewing, Knowledge Base, Participatory Research, Program Evaluation, Qualitative Research, Quantitative Research, Recording, Sensitizing Concepts, Survey Research, Theory & Practice, Vanier Institute for the Family

REFERENCE

Creswell, J.W. 1994. *Research Designs: Qualitative and Quantitative Approaches.* Thousand Oaks, CA: Sage.

role theory

Role theory is rarely taught as a discrete theory within Canadian social work theory and practice perspective, yet it has had much influence on the profession. Role theory encourages the understanding of roles projected by others and appropriate responses to them. The principal social work authors who have written about role theory are Herbert Strean (1971), Helen Perlman (1968), B. Biddle and Edwin Thomas (1966), and L.V. Davis (1966). Little social work research has supported role theory, which is viewed by many in the profession as currently being out of fashion. Developed within sociology, role theory concepts come from and have been used by several disciplines including the theatre, with its focus on how a person responds to the scripts of other. In seeking to understand and describe how individuals shape and are shaped by interactions with others, role theory has lent its rich vocabulary to social work and other fields, including social status, ascribed positions, role expectations, role set, role play, role reversal, role conflict, and role ambiguity. Each of these terms represent an effort to describe ways in which a person's functioning in his/her many societal behavioural expectations influences or is influenced by components of role behaviour. The theory strives to develop principles that promote understanding for what is happening to a person in his/her interactions with other people. Thus, the concept of role conflict offers insights for helping people to understand what happens to them in situations where role expectations (e.g., of a mother or employer) are incompatible. Role concepts have also been useful in developing social work diagnoses perspective, and in helping clients to understand how differing norms shape behaviour and result in stress or challenges for them. The theory also stresses the way role enactment can be used as a mask behind which one can hide one's identity. Of all the theories currently underlying social work practice, role theory is the most sociological and the least clinical; still, it has much potential for small and large systems practice, as it is highly congruent with social work's commitment to person-in-situation or -environment by seeking to understand how individual functioning is influenced by external realities. Social work literature discusses ways in which role concepts can be useful in working with individuals, groups, and families, usually by emphasizing applications for the concepts in assessing and diagnosing situations rather than in their direct use in treatment. While references to the concepts of role therapy appear occasionally, little has been done with it in an organized way. Authors who write about this theory from a social work perspective note that it helps to de-emphasize the inner life of a client and looks more to external influences of others.

[*FJT*]

RELATED ENTRIES

Theory & Practice

REFERENCES

Biddle, B., and E. Thomas (Eds.) 1966. *Role Theory: Concepts and Research*. New York: Wiley.

Davis, L.V. 1996. Role Theory and Social Work Treatment. In F.J. Turner (Ed.), *Social Work Treatment*. 581–600. 4th ed. New York: Free Press.

Perlman, H.H. 1968. *Persona: Social Role and Responsibility*. Chicago: University of Chicago Press.

Strean, H.S. 1971. "The Application of Role Theory to Social Casework." In H. Strean (Ed.) *Social Casework: Theories in Action*. Metuchen, NY: Scarecrow Press.

Albert Rose (1917–96)

Rose, Albert, professor, housing and social welfare policy authority; b. Oct. 18, 1917, Toronto, ON; Canadian Centennial Medal, 1967; d. Aug. 09, 1996, Toronto, ON

Albert Rose was a leading authority on public housing and the driving force behind the construction of Canada's first major low-rent rehousing project, Regent Park North in Toronto. Rose obtained a bachelor of arts in political science and economics at the University of Toronto (1939); at the University of Illinois, he achieved a master of arts in economics (1940) and doctorate in economics and statistics (1942). On leaving his wartime service with the Canadian Army Directorate of Military Intelligence in 1945, he became the research director of the Toronto Welfare Council in 1945. Three years later, Rose joined the faculty of the School of Social Work at the University of Toronto as an assistant professor and, in 1969, rose to the position of director. He was the first dean of the Faculty of Social Work (1972–76), after which he returned to full-time teaching; he was named professor emeritus in 1986 and continued teaching part-time until 1995. Rose's principal areas of scholarship and advocacy were housing policy, social welfare policy, urban affairs and metropolitan governance, social work education and practice, public administration, and gerontology. He was the author of six books—three of which are considered classics in their field, twenty book chapters, and over one hundred academic journal articles and research reports. He was known for his brilliant mind, his strong social conscience,

his meticulous research, his critical analysis of social welfare policies, his great sense of humour, and his personal concern and support for his students.

Albert Rose was a founding member of the Community Planning Association of Canada and an executive member of both the Toronto Citizen's Housing and Planning Association and the Toronto Civic Advisory Council. He wrote the council's 1951 report, "Proposals for the Metropolitan Area of Toronto," in which he recommended that Toronto become a federation of local governments rather than an amalgamation—a recommendation that was accepted by the provincial government and led to the formation of Metropolitan Toronto in 1954. As vice-chair of the Metro Toronto Housing Authority (1955–64), he was appointed as director to the first board of the Ontario Housing Corporation; later he became the first chair of the Metro Housing Authority when it was created in 1980. Rose served for many years on the boards of numerous community, provincial, and national social and professional organizations (i.e., Canadian Jewish Congress, B'Nai Brith, Ontario Council of Health, Institute for the Clinical Study of Addictions, Metro Toronto Home Care Program, Co-ordinated Services for the Jewish Elderly, and Jewish Vocational Services of Toronto). He was active on numerous committees and councils relating to the governance of the University of Toronto. And he was president of the Canadian Association of Social Workers (1971–73). Rose received many honours and awards, including the Bruels Gold Medal in Political Science and Economics at the University College, University of Toronto (1939); honorary life member of the Community Planning Association of Canada (1961); Senior Fellowship from Central Mortgage and Housing Corporation (1962–63); Visiting Research Fellow at the School of Social Welfare, University of California at Berkeley (1962–63); Long Service Award from the University of Toronto (1978); Outstanding Achievement Award from the Ontario Association of Professional Social Workers (1978); Award of Merit from the city of Toronto (1984); and the Voluntary Service Award from the Ontario Ministry of Citizenship and Culture (1986). In 1996 he was awarded an honorary Doctor of Laws by Ryerson University; at the convocation, Dr. Ellen Sue Mesbur described Rose as "a teacher who challenged our thinking, enriched our minds, and broadened our perspectives on the context of social work practice." Following his death later that year, Alan Barnes referred to Albert Rose in an obituary in the *Toronto Star* as "Ontario's father of public housing." His son, Jeff Rose, wrote of him: "Throughout his life of scholarship, teaching and social activism, he tamed his passionate intelligence to altruistic purposes, displaying the same personal qualities of moral engagement, service and decency that symbolized the kind of society he toiled to create."

[*Doris E. Guyatt*]

RELATED ENTRIES

Canadian Association of Social Workers, Social Welfare History, University of Toronto (Faculty of Social Work)

Rowell-Sirois Commission

The work of the 1937 Royal Commission on Dominion-Provincial Relations, chaired by Rowell and Sirois, stands among the most important inquiries in Canadian history. The appointment of the commission was one of several measures taken by Prime Minister Mackenzie King to provide a sound basis for reforming the structure and performance of Canadian governments. Dominion-provincial relations had been troubled since the confederation in 1867 and were becoming dangerously contentious during the years of the depression (1929–39). The commission held extensive hearings throughout Canada seeking the views not only from provincial and municipal governments but also from non-governmental organizations and individuals; it also commissioned studies by outstanding authorities on government and the state of the nation. Central to the broad range of the commission's recommendations were those relating to taxation; in simplified terms, it called for the provinces to withdraw from income taxes, corporation, and inheritance taxes. Instead, the commission proposed that the federal government compensate the provinces with financial transfers sufficient to equalize provincial revenues and to assure the basic needs of their citizens. The central government was also to assume the existing debts of the provinces and take responsibility for unemployment insurance and contributory pensions. Opposition from the provinces and the advent of the Second World War proved to be

obstacles to implementation of the commission's proposals; most were rejected or implemented piecemeal over many years. The federal government continued to employ the shared-cost approach for social programs that the commission had condemned. The Rowell-Sirois Commission did, however, set an enduring standard for the analysis of economic and social policy. Further, the commission's proposals relating to the sharing of resources to promote equalized living standards throughout the nation were enshrined in the Canadian constitution in 1982—thereby constituting its most notable contribution.

[*Richard Splane*]

Royal Commission on New Reproductive Technologies

In 1989, the Canadian government established the Royal Commission on New reproductive technologies to study the rapidly developing field of assisted reproduction. This inquiry was in response to more than a decade of debate about such technologies and their implications for Canadian society. The world's first human birth from in vitro fertilisation in 1978 enabled the separation of fertilization from sexual intercourse and pregnancy, permitting embryos to exist outside a woman's body as well as genetically screening for certain characteristics before being implanted. While raising the hopes of many infertile couples, however, these developing technologies also created profound social, ethical, economic, health, and legal concerns. They had the capacity for both benefit and harm, given the rapid changes these technologies were bringing to entrenched definitions of the roles and structure of families. The Royal Commission was chaired by Dr. Patricia Baird, a medical geneticist from the University of British Columbia, along with members from such fields as bioethics, medicine, science, theology, and law. The mandate of the commission was far reaching to assess the impact of reproductive technologies on society as a whole, as well as for specific groups (e.g., women, children, and physically challenged persons). The commission held public hearings throughout the country, established information meetings with national organizations, conducted surveys to explore attitudes and values of Canadians, and released fourteen research studies on related topics. From the contributions of more than 40,000 individuals and organizations, the commission was able to provide an analysis of infertility and reproductive technology practice in Canada that encompassed ethical, social, legal, medical, and scientific implications.

The final report set out some guiding ethical principles on which its recommendations were based, including: respect for human life and dignity, equality, autonomy, protection of the vulnerable, non-commercialization of reproduction, accountability, and balancing individual and collective interests. The commission recommended the outright prohibition of several practices such as human cloning; the commercialization of eggs, sperm, and embryos; sex selection; and commercial surrogacy. In addition the report called for the formation of a national governing body to oversee research into and treatment of infertility; this body could license clinics and practitioners; develop and monitor standards; evaluate new scientific developments in the field; study the long-term health of women undergoing procedures and of the children conceived from them; and establish a registry of births from such procedures as egg and sperm donation. Disagreement among commission members arose regarding the rights of children conceived from donor eggs or sperm to have access to identifying information about their donors. While the commission as a whole recommended that children should be informed about their birth origins, the mandatory disclosure of identifying information was not recommended. In a separate chapter to the report, one member (Scorsone in Canada 1993: 1062–63, 1113–21) advocated for the offspring of these technologies to have the same rights of access to identifying information as adoptees. Following the publication of the report, the federal government placed a moratorium on nine controversial issues, including sex selection, human cloning, and the buying and selling of eggs, sperm, and embryos. Despite this action, the widespread commercialism of sperm, egg, and embryo donation continued to flourish and commercial surrogacy increased. To a considerable extent, most infertility treatments became delisted from provincial government health insurance plans and were now accessible only to those who could afford to pay for them.

In 1996 the federal government introduced Bill c-47, the Human Reproductive Technologies Act. This bill aimed to prohibit many of the practices identified by the Royal Commission as being unsafe or unethical. It did not, however, allow for the establishment of the recommended regulatory body nor did it address practices that might be permitted under a licence. The draft was therefore criticized for being too punitive in nature, rather than setting a framework for properly regulated activities. As a federal election being called in 1997 before the draft bill had been fully considered by Parliament, the proposed Act did not become law. The subsequent Liberal government continued to work on revamping Bill c-47, but did not re-introduce the legislation before it called another election in 2000. At the beginning of this millennium, Canada remains without a regulatory framework. Scientific developments in reproductive and genetic technologies continue at a faster pace than society's ability to address their implications for future generations. As a profession, social work is ideally placed to evaluate the impact of reproductive technology from the perspectives of the individual family and broader social policy. The profession can contribute to developing services for infertile couples, and to advocate for the welfare of individuals conceived through assisted reproduction.

[*Jean M. Haase*]

RELATED ENTRIES

Bioethical Issues, Ethics, Family Planning, Federal Government, Pregnancy, Services for Women

REFERENCE

Canada. 1993. *Proceed with Care*. Final Report of the Royal Commission on New Reproductive Technologies. Ottawa: Royal Commission on New Reproductive Technologies (Chair: F. Baird).

Royal Commission on the Status of Women

The 1967 Prime Minister Lester Pearson established the Royal Commission on the Status of Women to examine the situation of women in Canada with a mandate to "inquire into and report upon the status of women in Canada and to recommend what steps might be taken by the Federal Government to ensure for women equal opportunities with men in all aspects of Canadian

Society." Florence E. Bird was appointed its chair, the first woman selected to head a public inquiry. In its work, the commission received briefs and letters from a large number of organizations and individuals representing all aspects of Canadian society. In addition to written submissions, some one thousand witnesses were heard in the many hearings throughout the country. The commission tabled its report in 1970, with 167 recommendations that went beyond the scope of its mandate. The recommendations ranged from changes to divorce legislation, visiting homemakers, family planning, a guaranteed annual income for single parents, and the need for shelters for homeless women and universal day care. The commission's work served as the basis for much of the activity of the feminist movement in the 1970s. It had and continues to have a strong impact on Canadian society resulting in a broad range of changes in policies, procedures, and attitudes, as well as formal legislation.

[FJT]

RELATED ENTRIES

Feminist Theory, National Action Committee on the Status of Women, Services for Women, Social Welfare History

Ryerson University School of Social Work

The Ryerson University social work program has evolved over the past thirty-eight years in a manner consistent with the evolution of the broader institution. Ryerson Institute of Technology (est. 1948) was the first institution in Ontario to provide education and training for technicians and technologists. In 1963 the Ontario legislature granted the institute autonomy under a board of governors responsible to the ministry of colleges and universities, and changed the name to Ryerson Polytechnical Institute. In 1971 Ryerson obtained the right to grant baccalaureate degrees in applied arts and technology, with the bachelor of business management added in 1977. In 1993 the Ontario government amended the institute's governance act to recognize Ryerson as a full-fledged polytechnical university, expanding the undergraduate education mandate to include scholarly, research, and creative activity and graduate programs. More recently, "Polytechnical" has been

dropped and the official name has been changed to Ryerson University. The special mission of Ryerson University is "the advancement of applied knowledge and research to address societal need, and the provision of programs of study that provide a balance between theory and application and that prepare students for careers in professional and quasi-professional fields."

Under the directorship of Professor Russell Jolliffe, the social work program commenced in 1964 with an enrolment of twenty-five students in a two-year certificate course. The bachelor of applied arts in social services degree program was established in 1971, with the first students graduating in 1973. In 1975 the program was revised to offer instead a three-year diploma, followed by a post-diploma academic year leading to the bachelor's degree; to enter the degree program, applicants were expected to complete one year of post-diploma social work experience. Work experience accumulated prior to coming to Ryerson or during their studies was also considered. With the implementation of the new program in 1976, the department became a provisional member of the Canadian Association of Schools of Social Work. A self-study for candidacy was submitted and accepted in 1978. The School of Social Work was the first school at Ryerson to receive a change in degree designation and, since 1991, has been awarding a bachelor of social work degree—which received its first accreditation in 1982 and has been re-accredited in 1989, 1996, and 2002.

The Ryerson School of Social Work has grown considerably, with more than six hundred full-time students and a hundred part-time students. Admission to the four-year direct-entry program is 160 students into each year, and a further 30 students are admitted with advanced standing into the third year of the program. The curriculum is based on a four-year integrated model that includes professional social work courses, professionally related courses chosen from sociology, psychology, politics, economics, philosophy, history, geography, justice studies, and a further set of liberal studies courses. Opportunities exist for students to compete a minor in sociology, psychology, or politics. Students complete a total of 910 field practicum hours over the course of their placements in the third and fourth year of the program. The school has benefitted from strong leadership, with only six directors: Russell Jolliffe (1964–79), Carol Baines (1979–85), Sheila Joel (1985–89), Ellen Sue Mesbur (1989–98), Susan Silver (1998–2003), and Akua Benjamin (2003–present). Currently, the school has fifteen full-time faculty, three support staff, and one field education co-ordinator. Given the priority of enhancing the diversity of the faculty, the school has begun to realize this goal through new appointments; the program now also includes faculty with such backgrounds as First Nation, Caribbean, Latin American, Asian, and South Asian. Sexual minorities are also represented, by both gay and lesbian faculty. The school will see further faculty transitions over the next years, as other faculty approach retirement.

In the fall of 1994 the school adopted a new mission, one that is significantly informed by an anti-oppressive perspective. This mission reflects the school's commitment to a set of core values and principles, including on-going attention to the rigour and relevance of the undergraduate degree program, which prepares graduates with the requisite knowledge, skills, and values to work with marginalized people and communities. The school continues to foster student-centred learning environments that engage and challenge students, which are responsive to life circumstances and societal forces that create barriers to the student experience. The school maintains this commitment to communities, expressed in its collaborative community-based research, community service, and educational relationships with field placement settings. Most defining is the ongoing struggle to stand with communities that experience oppression and marginalization as the commitment to social justice is pursued. Following the adoption of this new mission, the school embarked on an extensive process of curriculum review and restructuring. Structurally, a two-semester course on anti-oppression and human diversity was added, and the social work research course was expanded. The new curriculum was fully implemented in the 1998/99 academic year. Subsequently, four cohorts of students (561) have graduated from the new curriculum over the past four years. With the implementation of the new curriculum, a period of further intense self-reflection and evaluation within the school followed. As a community of educators with a deep commitment to the rigour and relevance of the program, the inclusive process of self-reflection will continue. In June 2000 Professor Russell Jolliffe, the founder and first director of the School of Social Work received an honorary doctorate from Ryerson. Current information about Ryerson University can be found online at <www.ryerson.ca>.

[*Susan Silver*]

RELATED ENTRIES

Education in Social Work, Faculties of Social Work, Ontario Association of Social Workers, Ontario College of Certified Social Workers and Social Service Workers

S

Salvation Army

The Salvation Army—founded in England by William Booth in the early nineteenth century—is a highly visible and much respected non-governmental organization providing social services firmly based in Methodist evangelism. This organization came to Canada in 1882 and quickly spread throughout the entire country. In addition to a program of street missions, the Salvation Army in Canada has established and maintained a broad range of institutions such as hospitals, men and women's shelters, and children's shelters, and has provided diverse services for prison inmates and former prisoners. They are particularly well known for their support to Canadian soldiers overseas in both world wars and for their active assistance in any social disaster. The army is strongly committed to offering social services and spiritual comfort to many needy people and groups in Canadian society. Although fully evangelical in its earliest years, the Salvation Army has introduced a professional component to its services so that, now, many of its officers have received social work training in Canadian schools and faculties of social work. Current information on the Salvation Army can be found online at <www.salvationarmy.ca>.

[*FJT*]

RELATED ENTRIES

Church-Based Services, Community Service, Non-governmental Organizations, Religion

Saskatchewan Association of Social Workers

The Saskatchewan Association of Social Workers (est. 1967) is both the professional association and regulatory body for social work in Saskatchewan. Established under The Social Workers Act, the association has been the voice for social workers in the province for more than thirty years. The association was founded by committed social workers who had been active in the development of the Canadian Association of Social Workers during a period when the decision was made to eliminate individual memberships in the national association and to develop provincial associations. Initially, social work was regulated only on a voluntary basis. An Act Respecting Social Workers (1993) proclaimed in 1995 restricts the titles of social worker and registered social worker to those who are qualified under the Act and are registered members with the association. Under the Act, the objectives of the association are:

- to establish, maintain and develop standards of knowledge, skill, and competence among its members for the purpose of serving and protecting the public interest;
- to establish, maintain, and develop standards of professional conduct among its members
- to promote, develop, and sponsor activities appropriate to the strengthening and unification of the social work profession;
- to provide a means by which the association through its members may take action on issues of social welfare;
- to edit and publish books, papers, journals, and other forms of literature respecting social work in order to disseminate information to members of the association as well as to members of the public at large; and
- to encourage specialized studies in social work among its members and to provide assistance and facilities for special studies and research.

An elected council of seven members executes the association's functions, with a government-appointed public representative to provide public accountability. The organizational affairs committee provides the executive function. Standing committees handle standards of practice, education, social policy, public relations, and professional conduct; the appointed discipline commit-tees are drawn from the discipline committee resource pool comprised of volunteers among the membership who are trained for discipline cases. In 1999 the association had about nine hundred members, which represents a relatively small proportion of potential members in the province. Eight branches around the province provide opportunities for members to support one another, and offer educational and social events for members. The association's office is housed in Regina in the Edna Osborne House, named for a former volunteer executive director and pioneer social worker in Saskatchewan. Information can be requested from < sasw@cableregina.com >.

[*Klaus Gruber*]

RELATED ENTRIES

Canadian Association of Social Workers, International Federation of Social Workers, National Association of Social Workers (us), Provincial/Territorial Associations

school social workers

Social work in schools has focused on biopsychosocial factors that have an impact on school performance and academic success, especially of children and youth. Balancing both child-centred and parent/family-centred interventions, school social workers have attempted to promote improved social functioning of families as well as parent/caregiver capacity. Some school social workers have also promoted literacy among adults and adult basic education. The development of social work has progressed to a significant degree in parallel with the development of public education. Today, professionals practising social work with children and youth and within school systems may be employed by a department of education or seconded to schools by another agency such as child welfare services, or they may act as a consultant to school personnel in the interest of children and families facing specific challenges. Interventions by school social workers may focus on individuals (e.g., newly arrived immigrants adjusting to the culture of school life), families (e.g., those facing the transition of a child with special needs beginning school), groups (e.g., a group to prevent pregnant teens from leaving school), formal organizations (e.g., developing partnerships among those concerned with social problems in high-risk families, and resource - centres for families and children), or communities (e.g., critical incident debriefing with parents/ caregivers, relatives, and children after a major accident, fire, or other incident). Themes of promotion and prevention have been dominant in school social work since its inception. School social workers may promote well-being in students and their families through such efforts as meal programs, youth development programs (to support effective biopsychosocial development) or parent/caregiver effectiveness programs (to encourage development of their capacity). Familial and student interventions that have dominated school social work focused on reducing academic failure, supporting attendance, and preventing early school leaving. As well, social workers have had a major role in prevention and early intervention with respect to the use and abuse of mood-altering substances. New initiatives may include risk control and harm reduction programs, such as those focused on children and youth who have been known to have been abused within their homes, or teens at risk for suicide. Other social work activities within the school system have focused on risk, protection, and safety, for which interventions may range from the seconding of a children's protection social worker to an inner-city school to investigate suspected child maltreatment, to the school social worker establishing group and street programs to combat bullying and teen gang violence. Social workers in schools may be called on to address such other protection issues as sexually intrusive children, sexual harassment, juvenile prostitution, protection of children with special needs (i.e., intellectually challenged or physically disabled), as well as early intervention into a broad range of anti-social activities that were once classified more generally as delinquency.

School social workers are often the first to hear disclosures of personal crises (e.g., teen pregnancy or suicidal ideation), familial crises (e.g., exposure to spousal violence), or peer crises (e.g., concern for other students who may have experienced date rape or continual bullying). Rare crises may arise from such collective experiences as sniper shootings, multiple deaths during a school trip, or the discovery of toxic materials. Some experiences often have post-traumatic stress and crisis states

associated with them, requiring the social worker to undertake crisis interventions, including critical incident debriefing. Through social work assessment and interpretation of psychological assessments, a broad range of counselling, and psychosocial education (i.e., aimed at reducing parent/child conflict), social workers help to promote student potential (i.e., building confidence in youths capable of going to university), address problems and needs associated with normal development (i.e., psychosexual development, use of contraception), or search for solutions to normal and anticipated problems in daily living (i.e., appropriate responses to peer pressure to engage in sexual intercourse). School social workers are also called on to address such complex problems as students with mental disorders or mental health risks, issues of identity and self-esteem, and conflict resolution. As few extended services are provided by a school system, a major responsibility is effective referral to health, education, employment and justice services, especially for disadvantaged families and for children and youth in marginalized social and economic communities.

The school is an ideal setting to encourage development of self-help and mutual-aid groups to support students or their families who may be facing such significant challenges as, for example, transgenerational clashes within immigrant families. Systemic interventions may require the social worker to mediate and advocate on behalf of children and youth within the school system— perhaps to sensitize school personnel to out-of-school factors contributing to a child's development, behaviour, and school performance. Such systemic intervention also necessitates a role in case management and case consultation. School social workers also advocate for systemic social change to promote acceptance of gay and lesbian students, diverse cultures, and teen parents, as well as raising community awareness on such issues as the link between academic performance and coming to school hungry. As society faces serious reduction in active public support for health, education, and social services, the challenge for school social workers continues to focus on finding creative solutions to erode the harmful effects of poverty on school performance, as well as to promote opportunities for students to rise above poverty. Schools, sometimes by default, are becoming social services. Within a more complex sociopolitical context, where risks continue to be denied or minimized, school social workers will continue to address more global social issues experienced at the level of individual schools, such as safe sex beginning at a young age, and violence in society encroaching on schools. Opportunities will arise to support respect for cultural diversity by continuing the current movement to provide education-related social support through family resource centres linked with a school.

[*M. Louise Osmond*]

RELATED ENTRIES

Bullying, Case Management, Child Abuse, Child Welfare, Diversity, Gangs, Group Practice, Immigrants & Immigration, Interprofessional Issues, Sensitizing Concepts, Services for Youth, Young Offender's Act, Youth Criminal Justice Act

Francis Reginald Scott (1899–1985)

Scott, Francis Reginald, poet, lawyers, educator, social activist; b. Aug. 01, 1899, Quebec City, QC; d. Jan. 31, 1985, Montreal, QC

Raised in a privileged household, F.R. Scott acquired a strong sense of social justice from his father, a canon in the Anglican Church. While studying history at Oxford on a Rhodes scholarship (1920–23), Scott read the fifth report of the Committee of the Anglican Archbishops in which the ethical relationship of Christianity to capitalism was questioned, which ignited his lifelong commitment to socialism. On returning to Canada, Scott began activities in response to what he perceived to be the manifest domination of the economy by a small number of men; he expressed his attitudes toward negative outcomes of capitalism—as reflected in his 1933 comment that it allowed "children to starve in order that dividends and interest may go on being paid to wealthy people" (Djwa 1987)—in his writing, notably in satiric poetry. Until the 1950s Scott worked in the political arena to rectify social and economic inequities wrought by capitalism. Toward the making of political change, which Scott stressed throughout his life as a constitutional lawyer and law professor, he co-founded the League of Social Reconstruction in 1932. The league was instrumental in founding activities of the Co-operative Common-

wealth Federation political party (CCF, renamed in 1961 as the New Democratic Party). In 1933 Scott and other league members helped to write the Regina Manifesto, the founding principles of the new socialist party. The Regina Manifesto articulated a belief in a strong centralized government that could provide universal health, education and housing services, as well as protecting the rights of all minorities within the country. These principles reflected the dire consequences of the depression. Between 1942 and 1950 Scott served as the party's national chair. Dedication to the law paralleled Scott's socialist beliefs; he insisted that positive change for all Canadians could only come through the legal and political framework and, ultimately, through constitutional amendment. The Canadian social reformer and fellow founder of the League for Social Reconstruction, J.S. Woodsworth, inspired Scott to work for a strong Canadian constitution with an entrenched bill of rights. From 1928, Scott taught constitutional law at McGill University, where he directly influenced at least one future lawmakers, Pierre Elliott Trudeau, who heard Scott lecture at l'Université de Montréal in 1943. Over the years, Scott and Trudeau shared a common admiration for and interest in each other's constitutional ideas for a just society and a strong federation; one observer has noted that: "with only slight exaggeration, it can be said that Canada acquired the Canadian Charter of Rights and Freedoms through an immaculate, personal transmission from Woodsworth to Scott to Trudeau" (Mills 1997: 45). For his *Essays on the Constitution: Aspects of Canadian Law and Politics*, Scott won the Governor General's award for non-fiction in 1977.

Championing the persecuted and the marginalized in court as well as in his teaching, Scott made history with several famous legal challenges. In 1959 he won against the government of then-Quebec premier Maurice Duplessis, to secure a Supreme Court of Canada judgment that reversed the Duplessis government's persecution of the Jehovah's Witnesses. In 1962 Scott successfully argued in the Supreme Court against censorship as represented by the proposed banning of the D.H. Lawrence novel, *Lady Chatterley's Lover.* Always the man—as his friend, writer Leon Edel, described him (in Winkler 1982)—to "speak fearlessly," Scott was one of the few to protest publicly the deportation of Japanese Canadians in 1946. Support for ethnic minorities, including his support for French Canada as a founding nation, did not in any way include the ethnic nationalism represented by Quebec separatism. Because he supported Trudeau's declaration of the War Measures Act during the October 1970 crisis, when the Front de libération du Quebec kidnapped two prominent government officials, Scott lost favour with some French-Canadian allies; in response, some wealthy anglophone Montrealers who controlled major newspapers in Quebec, as well as McGill University, blackballed Scott, the life-long socialist. Their actions prevented Scott from receiving timely credit for his hard work and dedication to Canada, Canadians, and the law for many years. Scott's eloquence and vision endure in his poetry, which in his own time received international and national accolades. In 1982 Scott's collected poems received the Governor General's award for poetry. One poem, "Creed" sums up the humanitarian belief that Scott held and which motivated him to work so tirelessly toward peace and justice through political process and the law:

> The world is my country
> The human race is my race
> The spirit of man is my God
> The future of man is my heaven.

[*Heather Haas Barclay*]

RELATED ENTRIES

Canadian Bill of Rights, Canadian Charter of Rights and Freedoms, Co-operative Commonwealth Federation, Human Rights, League for Social Reconstruction, Regina Manifesto, J.S. Woodsworth

REFERENCES

Djwa, S. 1987. *The Politics of the Imagination: A Life of F.R. Scott.* Toronto: McClelland and Stewart.

Mills, A. 1997. Of Charters and Justice: The Social Thought of F.R. Scott, 1930–1985. *Journal of Canadian Studies* 32, 1, 44–62.

Winkler, D. 1982. *F.R. Scott: Rhyme and Reason.* Montreal, QC: National Film Board.

sectarian social services

Sectarian social work, social work delivered by an organization whose members share a common faith/religious belief system, has been part of the Canadian social fabric since its historical beginning. Religious imagination, according to Cana-

dian literary critic Northrop Frye, has been the main influence shaping Canadian culture and its long-standing doctrinal and evangelical traits. Aboriginal societies provided for all their members' spiritual, physical, and psychosocial needs guided by shamen or medicine people. Such a holistic approach was possible when these societies pursued a nomadic lifestyle within vast ancestral territories. Sectarian social work provided by organized churches began with the arrival of the French in what became Lower Canada after Jacques Cartier's maiden voyage in 1534. The Catholic Church and various Catholic missionary orders in France brought to the French colony basic social services, supported by families, seigneurs, and herbalists. In addition to schools, they established primary charitable institutions such as l'Hôtel-Dieu, the general hospital, administered by religious orders and such workers as Jeanne Mance, Jean Brebeuf, and Bishop Laval. Marguerite Bourgeoys, often referred to as Canada's first social worker, arrived in Montreal in 1653 at the request of Maisonneuve to work among colonists and Aboriginal peoples; she founded a religious order to educate children and young women, and established La Providence, an institution to aid the indigent, as well as l'Hôpital général, an early rehabilitation centre where the sick and needy were taught trade skills (Turner & Turner 1986: 29–30). Sister Marguerite d'Youville (1701–71), another Quebec nun, was canonized (i.e., declared a saint by the Catholic church) on December 9, 1990, for her work taking the indigent and ill off the streets to a hospital staffed by her order of Grey Nuns, which she founded in 1737; this order sought assistance in the community to support patients ready to leave the nuns' hospitals—foreshadowing community development, an emphasis on a person's environment as a health determinant, and a holistic view of a person that are cardinal tenets of modern social work. A century later, in 1843, the Roman Catholic Bishop Monseigneur Ignace Bourget founded the Institut de la Providence to care for the aged and for infirm women; in the following quarter-century, his programs extended to the wave of new Irish immigrants, orphaned children, and the mentally ill. These and other Quebec church pioneers established a tradition whereby the needy were provided for by the church and/or the family. The Catholic Church in Lower Canada collaborated with the state to provide a complete social service system, which continued after the British takeover. This approach differed from the English tradition, which stemmed from the Elizabethan Poor Laws, whereby the state was recognized as the primary provider of relief for the indigent or disadvantaged members of society (Yelaja 1985: 6).

Elsewhere in Canada, the subsequent unfolding of social work in the Canadian Catholic sector closely resembled the development of the Church in the United States: the first priority after building churches and schools, was the foundation of hospitals, orphanages, correctional institutions, and homes for the aged, depending on the needs, funds, and availability of religious communities who staffed them (Villeneuve 1955: 23). The early history of colonization and development in the primarily Protestant maritime provinces witnessed a separation of church and state. In 1750 congregationalism broke up as a result of a religious revival started by Henry Alline, whose evangelical sect provided a new basis for fellowship and belief and led to the New Light movement, which fostered the idea of church separated from community. In Upper Canada, sectarian service development followed the same pattern. Methodists and Baptists began to arrive after the close of France's war on Aboriginal peoples in 1783. These evangelical sects were interested only in the salvation of individual souls. The Methodists set up schools and model villages with training in life skills and trades for Aboriginal peoples in parts of central Ontario. Catholic social services in Upper Canada were organized initially by Bishop Charbonnel (1850–60) of Toronto. Bishops could negotiate among their adherents and religious orders to obtain personnel and goods to meet the health, education, and welfare needs of their congregations. Early social work was provided by Sisters of St. Joseph (from France), Sisters of Loretto, Christian Brothers, and the Hibernian Benevolent Society. As well, Jewish social services were established and developed from the early 1800s.

By 1800, New Light and the Methodists were the dominant religious forces in Nova Scotia and New Brunswick. Social service needs were primarily served privately. With immigration to western Canada, other churches joined the sectarian delivery of social services and supported the development of social service delivery systems. From the early 1800s, Christian missions offered health care, education, and a range of social services to Aboriginal peoples throughout the subArctic and along the Pacific and Arctic coasts. In 1840 the English Wesleyan Society established a mission in Moosenee. In 1851 it deployed John Horden and his wife from England's the Exeter Church Missionary Society to serve "Englishmen, Eskimaux, and Natives" in Moose Factory. Horden, a Renaissance man—linguist, printer, and engineer—learned Inuktitut (the Inuit language), founded a day school, and introduced social service initiatives to the populace who came to revere him. Edmund James Peek followed Horden and his emphasis on serving both religious and earthly needs. The development of the Canadian west was not supported or aligned with one particular religious sect. The Anglicans, who assumed a leadership role in that part of the country until First World War, initially came to the west with a mission to Aboriginal peoples, whom the church supported financially, politically, morally and legally (i.e., in regard to land claims). With Catholics and Presbyterians, the Anglicans were an "influential minority" in the important development of institutional structure, education, and social services in the west, joined later by the Methodists. In 1924 this Bishopric of Rupert's Land, Northern Ontario, and Quebec was filled by an Aboriginal missionary, Fred Marks, who competently carried on serving the religious and social needs of this vast area.

The British North America Act, 1867 (now, Constitution Act, 1867) assigned state responsibility for social welfare provision to provincial governments. Sectarian non-governmental organizations, however, continued to be a strong presence in communities and the country at large. Toward the end of the nineteenth century the social gospel movement, "a combination of religious and social ferment" (Turner & Turner 1986) spearheaded by a combination of religious and social action organizations primarily in Protestant English Canada, targeted societal issues resulting from industrialism and urbanism. An example is the Metropolitan Methodist Church of Toronto, which in 1894 established the Fred Victor Mission (now, Centre) for transient and homeless men. J.S. Woodsworth, who was ordained as a Methodist minister in Winnipeg, was introduced to the slums and the life of the downtrodden at the Fred Victor Mission; in Winnipeg, Woodworth created the All People's Mission and many other community organizations to meet the social service needs of his community. Estrangement from the Methodist orthodoxy moved him on from the mission and community development to the area of social policy. In 1913 he organized the Social Welfare League, through which he became knowledgeable about rural and urban social problems, which eventually led to a twenty-one year career in the Canadian House of Commons. During these years, the Salvation Army was also active in a broad range of social services. In 1907 the Moral and Social Reform Council of Canada organized with Anglican, Methodist, Baptists and Presbyterians as well as the Trades and Labour Congress of Canada to declare Sunday a day free from labour. The churches became active in setting up departments of social services to run and co-ordinate expanding social welfare and social reform activities. They also spearheaded the more radical thrusts of the social gospel movement that developed between 1900–20. In 1913 the Moral and Reform Council of Canada changed its name to the Social Service Council of Canada. In March 1914 the council initiated the first National Congress on Social Problems, a gathering of social reformists motivated by religion. Delegates left the congress confident that it was possible to reconstruct Canadian society on Christian principles. The war shattered its dreams. The period between the world wars marked by the recession and depression meant adjustment to new circumstances for the churches as provincial governments developed responses to social needs. It was during this era that the profession of social work, emerging out of the liberal individualism of private charitable agency values and practices was an additional force with Protestant churches and other groups, which pushed for broad programs of social reform through social service councils. Also during this era, the churches' separation from professional social work which diminished and weakened the social reform element in Canadian life (Splane 1965: 69–70).

Sectarian social work continues to exist in the twentieth-first century in Canada in a modified form. Individual religious organizations and churches offer their own programs to communi-

ties they serve. An example of a modern successful church/state approach to local citizens' social service needs is the House of Friendship in Kitchener, Ontario. Begun fifty years ago, the house today has become a complex institution serving social service needs for a whole community. It was begun by Joseph Cramer, born in 1892 in Kiev to a wealthy Jewish family, which suffered during the revolution and fled to Canada, where he started a simple storefront mission where "the poor found food for body and soul." Today, offering many programs and services for individuals, families, groups, and the community—and supported by Mennonite churches, citizens, and government funds—the House of Friendship is a prototype of the development of sectarian social services working in tandem with government and community.

[*Anne Wilson*]

RELATED ENTRIES

Antigonish Movement, B'Nai Brith, M. Bourgeoys, I. Bourget, Catholic Charities, Church-Based Services, Citizen Participation, A. Comanor, Congrégation de Notre-Dame, Fred Victor Centre, Sister Mary Henry, Jewish Social Services, R. Leger, Non-governmental Organizations, Religion, Salvation Army, Social Gospel Movement, Social Welfare History, Voluntarism, Women's Christian Temperance Union, Women's Missionary Society, YMCA, YWCA

REFERENCES

Clark, S.D. 1962. *The Developing Canadian Community.* Toronto: University of Toronto Press.

Splane, R. 1965. *Social Welfare in Ontario, 1791–1893: A Study of the Public Welfare Administration.* Toronto: University of Toronto Press.

Turner, J.C., and F.J. Turner (Eds.) 1986. *Canadian Social Welfare.* 2nd ed. Chapters 4, 5, and 9. Toronto: Collier-McMillan.

Yelaja, S. 1985. *An Introduction to Social Work Practice in Canada.* Toronto: Prentice-Hall.

self-help groups

Within social work, self-help has been associated with self-help and mutual-aid or support groups. As such, self-help is typically thought of as non-professionals voluntarily coming together to assist each other with common problems and to provide mutual support and an exchange of information. Schopler and Galinsky (1993) distinguish self-help from mutual-aid or support groups with the view that the latter are usually linked with agency sponsorship and more formal leadership and intervention methods; self-help groups are mostly regarded more loosely as encompassing closed or open groups of varying duration, led by professional or lay facilitators or co-led by both. Central to a self-help group is the experience or phenomenon that participants have all experienced in common that comprises the reason for the group's existence, and that motivates mutuality, sharing, and reciprocity. These values accord self-help groups with the capacity for collaborative rather than hierarchical functioning and foster the empowerment of members rather than vest power in a professional leader; the commonality of purpose also facilitates a capacity for organization and advocacy. Self-help groups have been described as effective with a variety of problems and populations. Self-help groups are not without criticism (Toseland & Rivas 1998). The involvement of professionals has been questioned for its potential to undermine the essential quality—or at least compromising the autonomy—of such groups (Katz & Bender 1987). Professionals have been known to undermine the value or status of self-help groups on the grounds that they do not provide legitimate therapy (Kemp, Whittaker, & Tracy 1997). Self-help groups dominated by a charismatic leader have not been immune to negative influences from within, such as the fostering of dependence (Gartner & Reisman 1977).

A broader conception of self-help includes the vast array of available resources on the Internet, in books, audio and video tapes, and in herbal remedies used without medical supervision. Many clinical practitioners acknowledge that they incorporate such resources in their practice and describe them as helpful to their clients. Studies that have examined the effectiveness of self-help programs have concluded that they are helpful to participants and that the improvements achieved are superior to those in no-treatment control groups.

[*Keith Brownlee*]

RELATED ENTRIES

Citizen Participation, Group Practice, Natural Health & Complementary Wellness, Natural Helping Networks, Mutual-Aid Societies, Organizational Theory, Peer Counselling, Personal Social Services, Practice Methods, Self Help & Mutual Aid, Theory & Practice, Therapy, Treatment, Voluntarism, Wellness

REFERENCES

Gartner, A., and F. Reisman. 1977. *Self-Help in the Human Services*. San Francisco, CA: Jossey Bass.

Katz, A.H., and E.I. Bender. 1987. *The Strengths in Us: Self-Help Groups in the Modern World*. Oakland, CA: Third Party Associates.

Kemp, S.P., J.K. Whittaker, and E.M. Tracy. 1997. *Person-environment Practice: The Social Ecology of Interpersonal Helping*. New York: Aldine De Gruyter.

Schopler, J.H., and M.J. Galinsky. 1993. Support Groups as Open Systems: A Model for Practice and Research. *Health and Social Work* 18, 195–207.

Toseland, R.W., and R.F. Rivas. 1998. *An Introduction to Group Work Practice*. 3rd ed. Toronto: Allyn and Bacon.

self-help and mutual aid

In the self-help process, the service user is also the service producer. As an informal voluntary method of social support, self-help provides informational, affective appraisal and instrumental support. The self-help process relies on three major aspects of social learning: instruction, reinforcers, and models. Mutual aid is a related process wherein people who share common experiences, situations, or problems can offer each other a unique perspective that is not available from those who have not shared these incidents (Kurtz & Powell 1987; SHCT 2000). Groups offering self-help and mutual aid give their members an anchor, a reference point, companionship, and even a sense of belonging. Self-help is based on the principle of reciprocity, of mutual giving and taking. A central axiom of self-help is the helper/helpee principle, so that the more a person helps the more that person is helped and those who help most are helped most. Great value is placed on shared experience, with minimal social distance between helper and helpee. Social support is paramount, as help is not a privilege but a right to be shared with others. Characteristics commonly associated with self-help and mutual-aid or support groups include:

- free membership and participation
- the voluntary nature of all activities
- a not-for-profit approach with members controlling all resources
- the lack of financial support from external sources

- membership based on individual circumstances and situations
- structuring of meetings for mutual benefit of those participating
- constructive action toward shared goals
- an egalitarian philosophy, including a belief in participatory not just representative democracy, equality of status, and power within the group, and shared leadership and co-operation in decision making
- groups being member-led and -organized
- a lack of reliance on professional helpers
- each member making decisions for him/herself with the group as a whole being responsible for its decisions
- confidentiality of proceedings
- participants moving toward improving control over their own circumstances, giving themselves more command over their own lives
- a general avoidance of hierarchical and bureaucratic patterns of organization
- a lack of importance of outside societal status within group proceedings; instead status is conferred by personal involvement in the group (Adams 1990; Katz & Bender 1976; Pape 1990).

Self-help has become a recognized process for dealing with all types of problems in a setting where participants treat one another as equals, with openness, informality, friendliness, and active involvement. Self-help participants are not separated by education, class, or experience; typically, individuals join self-help groups to overcome feelings of rejection, isolation, and powerlessness or to break free from societal stereotypes; however, in many groups members must identify themselves as having a specific problem, many of which are compulsive. Professional service providers may participate in the self-help process at the request and sanction of the group but usually remain in an ancillary or consultative role. Self-help has no pre-appointed hours. Many groups operate so that, when no formal meeting is expected, participants can call a contact person or personal buddy or sponsor to discuss a difficulty or crisis when it arises.

One of the most significant characteristics of mutual aid groups is the fact that they are empowering and thus potentially de-alienating. Self-help arose out of societal needs that had changed dramatically and rapidly with the industrializa-

tion of the economy. The growth of self-help has occurred as a response to the pervasiveness of technology, unavailable and increasingly unresponsive human services, the complexity and size of institutions, and the increasing dehumanizing and depersonalizing aspects of the workplace. Hoehne (1988) attempted to explain the growth of self-help as the consequence of four critical factors:

- the fiscal crisis of the state leading to cutbacks in volume and quality of the services provided by governments at a time when demographic trends are leading to an increase of sectors of the population that are the most dependent upon government services (unemployed, working poor, homeless, single parent families);
- a rise in the proportion of chronic diseases due to increasing life spans;
- the erosion of the traditional extended family network; and,
- health care and social service systems that are still rooted in nineteenth-century models.

Hoehne claimed that increasing self-help use equates to deficiencies in existing health care and social service systems. Health problems are seen as individual problems and social problems are individual only in their consequences; yet the causes of both are collective. Within the dominant ideology, the state, still tends to equate social problems with the shortcomings of each individual. Social self-help groups pose a threat to the legitimation efforts of governments than do health self-help groups. By becoming organized, participants in social self-help groups take the first step in countering the blaming-the-victim paradigm of this ruling ideology.

[*Rick Csiernik*]

RELATED ENTRIES

Citizen Participation, Group Practice, Natural Helping Networks, Mutual-Aid Societies, Peer Counselling, Practice Methods, Self-Help Groups, Theory & Practice, Therapy, Treatment, Voluntarism, Wellness

REFERENCES

Adams, R. 1990. *Self-Help and Empowerment*. London: British Association of Social Workers.
Hoehne, D. 1988. *Self-Help and Social Change in Social Movements/Social Change.* Toronto: Between the Lines.

Katz, A., and E. Bender. 1976. *The Strength in Us*. New York: Basic Books.

Kurtz, L., and T. Powell. 1987. Three Approaches to Understanding Self-Help Groups. *Social Work with Groups* 10, 3, 69–80.

Pape, B. 1990. *Self-Help/Mutual Aid*. Toronto: Canadian Mental Health Association.

SHCT. 2000. *Directory of Self-Help/Mutual Aid Groups*. Toronto: Self-Help Clearinghouse of Toronto.

sensitizing concepts

Sensitizing concepts is one of the most venerable yet basic research tools in sociology and, increasingly, in social work. Originating with Herbert Blumer (1954: 7), a sensitizing concept uses the language and expression from the research participant's perspective and sensitizes the researcher to more fruitful lines of enquiry. The use of sensitizing concepts falls squarely in a theoretical tradition known as symbolic interactionism. In contrast to functionalism, symbolic interactionism assigns importance to the study of everyday social interaction, based on meanings people assign to the behaviours of others and themselves. Meanings also arise out of social interaction. Many ethnographies use symbolic interactionism and sensitizing concepts as a key in understanding the meanings of the things that people assign to what they say and do. The sensitizing concept of "being there" was one of Kathy Charmaz's *in vivo* codes taken from the everyday discourse of chronic illness (Charmaz 1991, 1995); being there is the support given at crucial times through concrete help but, even more significantly, staying with a person who is ill when he/she needs the comfort of the other's physical presence, concern, and touch. The way Charmaz used the term was embedded in a larger analysis for her 1991 book, *Good Days, Bad Days: The Self in Chronic Illness*. In another illustration, a speech therapist saw him/herself as doing "detective work" when trying to pinpoint speech problems in patients (van den Hoonaard 1997). A social researcher can take this ordinary everyday concept of the speech pathologist to explore other instances where professionals undertake detection; this concept is particularly effective when a social researcher thinks about ways that some patients (e.g., "hospital hobos") try to plant misleading clues for medical staff to uncover. As can be seen

from these illustrations, one of the chief strengths in using sensitizing concepts is their ability to serve as a kind of halfway house between data and theory—a moment of analysis where the perspective of research participants can play a powerful role in developing broader concepts and theory. Martyn Hammersley and Paul Atkinson (1983: 180) offer the advice that sensitizing concepts "are an important starting point … the germ of the emerging theory"; all such concepts take progressive distance from the data. Social researchers and practitioners—and all persons in everyday life—commonly use sensitizing concepts more than they realize. In daily life, people routinely cast the experiences and expressions of others—and of themselves—in some generalizing manner. In the normal course of experiencing society, people already work with abstract conceptualizations of others' actions or thoughts. People order their own experience and the experience of others into abstractions that involve a degree of taking distance from the social world. Architecture offers a useful analogy. The Finnish architect Reima Pietila constructed homes where logs retain their original size and length: a practical illustration of how one has mastered original data (here, logs) to construct something (homes) beyond the data. The use of sensitizing concepts seems to fit nicely into current thinking. Current human and social sciences are defined by, on the one hand, the morass of postmodern relativism and the study of lived experiences and by, on the other, the persistence of nineteenth-century positivism. The latter is an especial blinder masking current social patterns. By use of sensitizing concepts, practitioners can circumvent the problem of institutional definition of client problems and more readily come to understand and rely on the ways in which clients define their world—and their own problems.

Recent Developments

Interest in the use of sensitizing concepts has reawakened since publication of *Working with Sensitizing Concepts* and several articles in *Kwalon*, the Dutch sociology journal on qualitative research. Canadian, Dutch, and Swedish scholars have taken an active interest in sensitizing concepts; for example, Robert A. Stebbins in Canada connects the use of sensitizing concepts to the process of exploration in science (2000). In social work, the strength of sensitizing concepts became evident in the work of Rosemary Clews (1999: 11) as a key to understanding the world view of another person. Use of sensitizing concepts make good sense, because it keeps researchers' feet in the data-gathering and analytical stages, which in theory and in practice should not in any event be separated.

[*Will C. van den Hoonaard*]

RELATED ENTRIES

Aboriginal Issues, Abuse, Anti-oppressive Social Work, Bereavement, Deafness, Developmental Challenges, Disaster Practice, Diversity, Ethnic-Sensitive Practice, Gay-Sensitive Practice, Immigrants & Immigration, Lesbian Services, Long-Term Care, Minorities, Minority-Sensitive Practice, Palliative Care, Person-in-Environment Perspective, Physical Challenges, Poverty, Progressive Social Work, Racism-Sensitive Practice, Research, Social Work Profession, Suicide, Theory & Practice, Torture & Trauma Victims, Vicarious Traumatization, Visual Impairment, Vocational rehabilitation

REFERENCES

Blumer, H.G. 1954. What Is Wrong with Social Theory? *American Sociological Review* 19, 3–10.
Charmaz, K. 1995. Personal communication with author, October 3.
Clews, R. 1999. *Doing Qualitative Research for a PhD: A Case Study of Resolving Challenges.* Presentation at Sixteenth Qualitative Analysis Conference in May at Fredericton, NB.
Hammersley, M., and P. Atkinson. 1983. *Ethnography: Principles in Practice.* London: Tavistock.
Stebbins, R.A. 2000. Exploration: Its Place in Qualitative Research. [Work in progress.]
van den Hoonaard, W.C. 1997. *Working with Sensitizing Concepts.* Thousand Oaks, CA: Sage.

services for children

Children's services consist of a system of services to dependent and or neglected children provided by federal and provincial/territorial governments often in partnership with private organizations such as children's aid societies. Services are designed to supplement or substitute parental care as well as address problems of delinquency, mental health, and education. Child welfare service assists abandoned and neglected children through the provision of foster family care, residential care, and adoption. Legal services are available for children and youth as well as special youth court services, probation, and secure facilities when needed. Each province has children's mental health services consisting of treatment and counselling through both outpatient and inpatient care facilities. Children in the territories are usually sent to facilities in the nearest province. A range of educational services is available for children with special needs and abilities through legislation supporting inclusiveness of children into regular classrooms. Children's development and best interests are the primary concern in service principles. The model for social services that stressed limited public responsibility for social problems to deserving persons, including children, originated with, in England, the Elizabethan Poor Laws (1597–98) and, in France, the Catholic church's various charitable institutions. Both influences came to Canada as colonial administrators and churches established social structures here. Charitable organizations relied primarily on private contributions and volunteer assistance for the services they delivered to children with the belief that social problems involving children resulted from the personal moral failings of the parents as the ideological basis for saving child. As an influx of immigrants to Canada during the 1820s taxed the limits of the volunteer model of service delivery, a system of public and private charities evolved to care for abandoned and neglected children. Legal responsibility over local and private matters, such as social programs, was assigned to the provincial governments under the British North America Act, 1867 (now, Constitution Act, 1867); it was not until the latter part of the 1800s, however, that governments responded to the plight of children. with the enactment of child protection legislation. Government children's services evolved and grew. In 1891 the first children's aid society was established in Toronto by J.J. Kelso as a charitable enterprise and, largely through his advocacy, the first Child's Protection Act was passed in 1893 by the province. This Act addressed the problem of sending children to indentured work programs for room and board in rural communities, as well as the growing numbers of destitute and homeless children in urban communities. The focus for child and family services continued to be changing the morals and behaviour of delinquent children and of parents assumed to be neglecting them. The legislation gave the provincial government the authority and responsibility to intervene in cases of child cruelty or neglect and the removal of children from a home. Soon similar legislation was enacted elsewhere in the country.

The federal government played an increased financial role as the need and demand for social programs increased following the Second World War, with the rapid expansion and professionalization of children's services. Federal/provincial cost sharing and universal entitlements became the standard for social service funding until very recently, when universal social welfare services, including children's services, began to be eroded. Universal health care, income security to children's parent(s) based on need, and free access to educational opportunities to the completion of high school are provided now through targeted cost-shared federal-provincial programs; for example, the federal government has terminated the universal family allowance, a guaranteed income benefit paid to mothers for each child, and replaced it with a tax-credit system. About 20 percent of all Canadian children are now living below the poverty line. Statistics Canada indicated an increase of 58 percent in the number of poor children in Canada between 1989 and 1995. Factors cited for the increase in child poverty included decreases in family income, parental unemployment, and increases in the number of single-parent families.

Currently, the provision of child welfare services to support and supplement parental responsibilities are the subject of intense debate. Fiscal cuts and growing support for reform of children's services legislation have been present over the past decade. The structure of the delivery system throughout the provinces and territories has been under review and in some cases modified. Some provinces, such as Ontario, mandate child welfare services through a system of children's aid societies, while the majority (i.e., British Columbia and Saskatchewan) provide the same programs through centrally controlled government delivered services. Others, such as Alberta have shifted from a government delivered service system to a privatized community-based system built on participation by interested organizations and local community governance of service delivery. Each

province and territory tends to honour the major principles of least intrusive intervention, family support for protection, nurturance, and safety of children, permanency planning, and wherever possible, non-adversarial approaches through family preservation ideology. Services are expected to contribute supports and resources promoting family autonomy and independence. Services are offered to children in their own homes and are designed to improve parental/caregiver ability to care for their children. The changing approach to the delivery of children's services to more decentralized models allows for greater local control of service delivery and a greater mix of public, voluntary, and private involvement in addressing children's problems. Approximately 50,000 children reside in permanent out-of-home care services in Canada. The population of older youth in care (30% are aged 15 or older) is rising; they often have complex problems requiring such long-term services as child welfare, special education, mental health, youth criminal justice, and vocational. Challenges to the system of children's services include the issues of stability and quality of family care. Aboriginal, Black, and Asian children are overrepresented in the out-of-home care population, in some provinces and territories representing 50 percent or more of this child population. In many instances, First Nations, Inuit, Inuvialuit, and Métis have developed community-based child welfare services, special youth justice programs, education, and to a lesser degree mental health services in their communities to provide more adequate services to their children. In the past decade a comprehensive and distinct system of youth criminal (formerly, juvenile or young offender) justice was developed with its own legislative framework under the Young Offenders Act, 1980, and its later amendments. Facilities developed under this system operated separately from the child protection and mental health systems. Principles guiding services to young offenders are intent on protecting society from children and youth who engage in criminal behaviour, protecting the legal rights of youth (age twelve to eighteen), and recognizing the special status and needs of young persons with respect to due process. Many young offenders have been or are currently involved with both child protection services and mental health services. Intervention programs such as alternative measures, dispositional options, and custodial facilities vary from jurisdiction to jurisdiction. Adjustments to this system are being implemented in accordance with the Youth Criminal Justice Act, 2002, which came into effect on April 1, 2003.

Among Canadian children and youth, a high prevalence (between 5 and 30%) of children's mental disorders and mental health problems, such as suicide, substance abuse, emotional, and behavioural problems, has been documented. The dual lack of a comprehensive service strategy and of acute specialized services to meet the mental health needs of children throughout the country is apparent. Some hospitals provide a few in-patient beds, but community-based services are minimal in most urban communities and exceptionally rare in rural communities. Preventive initiatives are also sparse and the fragmentation of mental health services makes it difficult to assess needs and service requirements. Brief therapy is the most common intervention, with some children receiving long-term services in treatment facilities under the child protection system. A comprehensive vision of child, youth, and family services that includes the integration and co-ordination of children's services is integral to service delivery.

[*Barbara Thomlison*]

RELATED ENTRIES

Adoption, Bereavement, Bullying, Child Abuse, Child Advocacy, Child Custody & Access, Child Welfare, Children's Aid Society, Crisis Intervention, Family Research, Family Services Canada, Family Therapy, Parenting, Peer Counselling, Pregnancy, Private Adoption, Services for Youth, Sexual Abuse of Children, Single Parents, School Social Workers, Services for Elderly People, Services for Families, Services for Married People, Services for Offenders, Services for People with Disabilities, Services for Refugees, Services for Women, Services for Youth, Social Services, Theory & Practice, Toronto Infants Home, Vanier Institute for the Family, Young Offenders Act, Youth Criminal Justice Act, YMCA, YWCA

services for elderly people

The ageing of human populations, especially in affluent industrialized societies, results from the combination of increased longevity and declining fertility, both of which are associated with the rapid social and economic development characterizing much of the twentieth century. Although Canada's population is still relatively young by international standards, it will age more rapidly as the populous baby boom generation (i.e., those born during the twenty years following the Second World War) reaches its senior years. The proportion of Canada's population aged sixty-five years and over is projected to reach 16 percent by 2016 and 23 percent by 2041. This latter percentage represents about 10 million people, 1.2 million of whom will be age eight-five and older. Based on present estimates of life expectancy, in 2041, 56 percent of the population age sixty-five and over will be women and 44 percent will be men (Canada, 1997; Denton & Feaver 1998). Given the fact that, in general, problems of health and mobility increase with age, clearly the need for services to support this growing segment of the population will increase significantly in coming decades, particularly for those in the oldest age groups. Canada's publicly administered, high-quality health care system continues to serve as a fundamental source of security for persons of all ages; escalating costs of health care and the anticipated pressures of an ageing society, however, have led to a sometimes strident debate over the sustainability of publicly funded health care services and the potential role for private for-profit alternatives. A central issue is the division of costs and responsibilities among federal and provincial/territorial governments in the context of increasing provincial and territorial autonomy. At the level of service delivery, the reorganization and consolidation of hospitals, health personnel shortages, wait times for non-elective procedures, and availability of technologically advanced diagnostic equipment have attracted widespread political and media attention. While public resources continue to be concentrated on acute hospital-based care, the health care needs of an ageing population call for a shift in emphasis. An expansion of institutional and long-term care in communities is becoming increasingly urgent, as is the need for coherent policies on home care and support for family caregivers. Health promotion and accident prevention strategies, including access to information and specialized services on chronic conditions ranging from arthritis and diabetes to dementia; public safety awareness campaigns to reduce accidents and falls; improved access to primary care providers, particularly family physicians; and improved systems to monitor prescription drugs will help to maintain health and contain costs.

The majority of older Canadians live independently in private housing, and most prefer to continue there for as long as they are able. Historically, housing services for elderly persons unable to afford market rents were provided by the federal Central Mortgage and Housing Corporation; during the 1980s, the national housing policy shifted away from a uniform approach and toward a philosophy of ageing in place, which suggested the need for a range of options to meet changing housing and care needs over time. In the 1990s, the federal government devolved responsibility for all types of assisted housing to the provinces and territories. The current emphasis of the federal government, by funding research and providing information on housing alternatives, is to encourage private developers and not-for-profit organizations to develop housing options for older people. Rent subsidies are also available for low-income elderly people and low-cost loans or grants for residential repair are available to qualified owners and landlords. The withdrawal of direct federal responsibility for affordable housing has had a number of consequences for the elderly; for example, in the mid-1990s, Ontario declared a moratorium on the construction of new subsidized housing for the elderly, removed rent controls, and devolved responsibility for assisted housing to municipalities. Private markets have failed to provide a sufficient supply of affordable rental housing, placing elderly people with low incomes at risk of poor or no housing. Regardless of auspices, housing for the elderly must be integrated with a range of health and social services to facilitate successful ageing in place. A challenge for the future will be to develop and expand a range of appropriate housing alternatives for the elderly, including home sharing, congregate living and continuous care residences.

Canada's retirement income system—consisting of public transfers, a publicly administered contributory pension, and tax-assisted private savings and pension plans—has succeeded in all but eliminating severe poverty among elderly people, with the exceptions of unattached women and some ethnocultural minorities (Myles 2000). The maturation of this system enabled the majority of workers to leave the workforce at or before the age of sixty-five. However, the gradual erosion of public benefits and the rapidly changing nature and uncertain future of employment raise questions about the future income security of elderly Canadians. Present policies place a strong value on individual and corporate responsibility for retirement income security and make a number of questionable assumptions about people's ability to make sufficient provision for their own income security in old age.

[*Malcolm Stewart*]

RELATED ENTRIES

Abuse, Bereavement, Bioethical Issues, Elder Abuse, Family Demographics, Marital & Family Problems, Family Research, Family Services Canada/Services à la famille—Canada, Family Therapy, Home care, Hospices, Long-Term Care, Palliative Care, Poverty, Services for Families, Services for Married People, Services for Women, Social Services, Theory & Practice, Vanier Institute for the Family, Veterans Affairs Canada

REFERENCES

Canada. 1997. *A Portrait of Seniors in Canada*. Ottawa: Statistics Canada.

Denton, F.T., and C.H. Feaver. 1998. The Future Population of Canada: Its Age Distribution and Dependency Relations. *Canadian Journal on Aging* 17, 1, 83–109.

Myles, J. 2000. The Maturation of Canada's Retirement Income System: Income Levels, Income Inequality and Low Income among the Elderly. *Canadian Journal on Aging* 19, 3, 287–316.

services for families

Family services in Canada trace their origins to the Charity Organization Society (est. 1877) in the United States. The society's network was primarily concerned with the needs of the disadvantaged and believed that their plight could be ameliorated through the abolition of public relief, the co-ordination of private philanthropy, and by a rational system of charitable administration; accordingly, the society promulgated seven major principles: interagency co-operation, community education, individualization, adequacy of relief, repression of begging, preventive philanthropy, and personal service. Gradually, the society moved away from its focus on financial security for families and began to examine the importance of the relationship between the individual and the family. Following the great depression of the 1930s, the society began to reorganize and, in 1946, many of its local organizations became private family service agencies. Subsequently, they became affiliate members of the Family Service Association of America, now called the Alliance for Children and Families. Family Services Canada/Services à la famille—Canada is the equivalent membership organization in this country. Family services are duly organized not-for-profit corporations with the primary purpose of providing social services for families. As voluntary agencies, they have a board of directors, which is representative of the communities they serve, responsible for establishing governance policies, and accountable to its membership, as well as an executive director or chief executive officer to carry the responsibility to oversee the total range of programs and services. While family services were once almost entirely funded by charitable donations, client fees, and other non-government sources, many have become more dependent on contracts from governments to survive in an increasingly competitive environment.

Family services agencies are primarily staffed by social workers who provide a broad array of therapeutic services, including individual, couple or dyad, family, and group therapy. These specialized services recognize individual and family values and goals, accommodate variations in lifestyles and emphasize growth, development, and situational change. Many family service agencies focus on preventing problems from surfacing in families through the provision of family life education; such services focus on a learning and sharing process designed to help families progress, understand, and deal adequately with those patterns of community, individual, and family living that are situational and stress producing. Numerous family service agencies also provide services that are planned, proactive, comprehensive, and based on a systematic procedure for identifying areas in which the agency will advocate on behalf of families. It is important to note that many family service agencies still offer the traditional support services of the Charity Organization Society; for example, community support services promote autonomy, quality of life, and overall well-being of individuals, including those with special needs, through direct services to clients, as well as support to the client's families and friends. These services may include day care for the elderly, friendly visiting and security checks, homemaking/home care, information and referral, transportation and accompaniment services, family support services, and support services for disabled seniors, adults, and/or youth. Particularly in Ontario, credit/debt counselling services are affiliated with family service agencies; these services focus on promoting money wise money management for consumers through the provision of budget counselling; debt management; and community education. Finally, family service agencies have become a major provider of employee assistance services. Employee assistance programs are designed to promote employee health and well-being and provide help to employees who are experiencing difficulties because of a personal, family, emotional psychological, or substance abuse problem.

[*David Rivard*]

RELATED ENTRIES

Bereavement, Bioethical Issues, Credit Counselling Canada, Employee Assistance Programs, Family: Non-traditional, Family Planning, Family Research, Family Services Canada/Services à la famille—Canada, Family Therapy, Parenting, Peer Counselling, School Social Workers, Services for Children, Services for Married People, Services for Refugees, Services for Women, Social Services, Theory & Practice, Vanier Institute for the Family

services for married people

Throughout Canada, the spectrum of services that focuses specifically on marriage from any perspective is provided by practitioners in many disciplines, including social workers. Indeed, the preponderance of these services may be provided by physicians, clergy, psychologists, and marriage and family therapists. Even those services provided by social workers are occasionally provided by non-professional persons under the direction of and quality control by professional practitioners. While services for marriages carries the common inference that they are for troubled marriages, many of them are for the preparation and enhancement or enrichment of marriages that would be perceived by most as healthy, or to address crises in families. Family serving agencies of many kinds and religious organizations are quite extensively involved in the latter, usually through group work. Mandates and funding for social work services for married people vary significantly in nature and amount from jurisdiction to jurisdiction, and from community to community. They can be broadly characterized in nature as public, voluntary, or private. Significantly, marriage does not seem to be even a low policy priority for the usual sources of mandates and funding for human services—in spite of the readily apparent relationship between the quality of marriage and the well-being of the associated family, individuals, and community. Pernicious consequences of broken marriages for families, their individual members, and community are well known but have yet to be effectively substantiated by a body of credible research findings. This lack of research contributes in part to the problem of eliciting a higher policy priority for enhanced social work services for married people. Social work needs to focus research efforts toward these relationships. Almost equally as paradoxical, Canadian faculties and schools of social work have generally not prepared graduates for either remedial or preventive work with married people. They do not appear to be addressing effectively the knowledge, skill, personality attributes, and commitment required for professional specialization to work with couples and families in marriages. Consequently, those who have chosen to practise in this specialty have had to pursue independent study to acquire the essential knowledge and skill through post-graduate on-the-job supervision, reading, workshops, and seminars.

Generally speaking, the public sector in the respective jurisdictions of all levels of government throughout Canada seems to be the least likely to encourage and sponsor social work services that focus in meaningful ways on the well-being of marriages. The primary focus and priorities in the public sector tend to be adverse conditions that may have been consequences of dysfunctional marriages (e.g., child welfare, children's mental health, youth criminal justice, adult mental health, substance abuse, domestic violence). Associated mandates and funding required for quality pro-

fessional services for those marriages are uncommon; however, physicians might argue that public sector support is provided but to their remedial services for troubled marriages, for which they see themselves as well qualified. Indeed, they deliver many services at considerable cost to the taxpayer. In a small number of situations, medical professionals engage other professionals, such as social workers and psychologists, who are expected to specialize in providing complementary services; in effect, they facilitate access to the necessary public sector mandate and funding. They also make appropriate referrals to those other disciplines located elsewhere in their communities. Many public sector services (i.e., those for developmentally challenged, mentally ill, and indigent persons) do make appropriate referrals for their clients to such community resources as family service agencies that offer social work services related to marriage. When managed well, these agencies are exceedingly important and valuable for those clients. Rarely do these referring agencies provide dollars to pay for those complementary services. Within the Canadian military, a small number of professional social workers is mandated to provide services for marriage as required without cost to the user. Within the voluntary sector, most of the services for married people are provided by clergy, many of whom have professional degrees in social work. As such, they can offer effective services for marriage as required by their parishioners, including clinical casework, or marriage preparation, and marriage enrichment. Professional services for marriage from other social work practitioners within the voluntary sector are limited; relative to need, that sector does not generate a significant amount of funding for this purpose and, as the cost is substantial, it likely could not realistically include these services. Further, partnering with public and private sectors to this end has not materialized. Family service agencies seem to be the principal recipients of voluntary sector funding for marriage.

Throughout Canada, the private sector provides a venue for many professional social workers who specialize in services for marriage. Mostly located in urban centres, these practitioners offer services for fees and function as autonomous professionals without the kind of deleterious restraint that may be associated with employment within a public or voluntary organization. The private sector is also a source of mandates and funding for professional services (social work and others) for marriages that come through the medium of employee assistance programs. Many private and public employers provide such services for the purpose of helping employees with marriage-related problems to maintain a high standard of job performance; they purchase these services from social workers in private practice, for-profit companies that specialize in the delivery of such programs, and from not-for-profit agencies, notably family service agencies. The focus may be remedial and/or enrichment in nature. The type and amount of service may be left to professional judgment and discretion, or it may be so prescribed by an employer as to constrain their capacity to be helpful in a meaningful way. The prognosis for improved funding for services for married people in any of the three principal mandating/funding sectors seems exceedingly poor. This regrettable situation stems from decision makers not being made aware of the potential positive return on an investment there, the expense of the services, and the fact that service providers have only begun to demonstrate positive outcomes in scientifically credible ways.

[*Jack Spence*]

RELATED ENTRIES

Education in Social Work, Employee Assistance Programs, Family Demographics, Family: Non-traditional, Family Planning, Family Research, Family Services Canada/Services à la famille—Canada, Family Therapy, Group Practice, Military Social Work, Parenting, Separation & Divorce, Services for Children, Services for Elderly People, Services for Families, Services for Women, Sexual Problems & Services, Social Services, Social Work Profession, Theory & Practice, Women Abuse

services for offenders

Services to offenders are offered within two broad categories, one in the community and one in institutions. Services provided in the community may be instead of, preceding, or following a sentence of incarceration. Services instead of or preceding incarceration may be bail programs, in which accused people are provided with supervision, assistance finding housing and jobs, and other support services as an alternative to spending time in pre-trial custody. Court worker programs provides services to First Nations and other Aboriginal peoples who need help to mediate the court process or other services. People charged with crimes may also be diverted from the court process and given the opportunity to participate in programs that address the problem that brought them before the courts, for example, support groups for people charged with shoplifting. Other services provided in the community may be as a condition of probation either instead of incarceration or following a provincial/territorial sentence, or as part of a parole plan. Support may be provided to the offender by the probation or parole officer but the majority of services offenders receive in the community are provided by such voluntary agencies as the Elizabeth Fry Society (for women) or the John Howard Society (for men); part of the mandate of these societies, beyond the provision of direct services, is to advocate for humane treatment of offenders and to engage in research and public education. The Salvation Army and other faith-based organizations are also active in the provision of support services to offenders. Probation and parole services contract with such organizations as these and with other for-profit, not-for-profit, and private practitioners to provide individual and group services to offenders in their care. As well, services that are generally available to community residents are also available to offenders (i.e., family service associations, substance abuse services, psychiatric out- or in-patient services); many offenders, however, find that they are not positively viewed by many mainstream community agencies.

Services to offenders within institutions vary considerably from jurisdiction to jurisdiction, and from institution to institution. Basic programs usually found in most institutions are educational, focused on both academic and training skills, and provided by qualified teachers. The other most frequently occurring programs are support groups, such as Alcoholics Anonymous and Narcotics Anonymous, provided by volunteers. Some institutions may also have Aboriginal programs that are culturally based, such as Native Sons and Native Daughters programs, provided by local Aboriginal agencies. Faith-based services and programs are also usually offered, depending on the interest and commitment of churches in the local community where the institution is located. Many institutions also have staff social workers and/or psychologists who provide individual and group counselling for offenders. The range of services offered by professional helpers is quite variable; many group programs focus on behaviourally specific issues, such as anger management, stress management, and life skills. In the federal correctional system, some institutions specialize in working with certain groups of inmates: for example, Okimaw Ohci Healing Lodge in Maple Creek, Saskatchewan, works with female Aboriginal offenders serving a federal sentence. Other specialized institutions include the Regional Psychiatric Centre in Saskatoon, Saskatchewan, and the Regional Treatment Centre in Kingston, Ontario. Some provinces and territories have specialized institutions in which treatment programs are offered to identified offender groups but these are rare.

Canadian scholars and practitioners have made significant contributions in criminal justice literature on the effectiveness of correctional programs. The general thrust is that services for offenders must be designed to address the complexity of multiple problems backgrounds of offenders; that implementation strategies should include consideration of organizational, program, and practitioner variables; and that the services should be based on current research into what works.

[*Margaret M. Wright*]

RELATED ENTRIES

Correctional Services, Criminal Justice, Forensic Practice, Mutual-Aid Societies, Peer Counselling, Salvation Army, Self-Help Groups, Self Help & Mutual Aid, Services for Children, Services for Elderly People, Services for Families, Services for Married People, Services for Offenders, Services for People with Disabilities, Services for Refugees, Services for Women, Services for Youth, Social Services, Theory & Practice, Young Offenders Act, Youth Criminal Justice Act

services for people with disabilities

As late as the turn of the twentieth century people with disabilities—such as developmental and physical challenges—were generally invisible in public life (Driedger 1992). Within Canada, fledgling constituency-based consumer movements

united in 1976 to form the Coalition of Provincial Organizations of the Handicapped, now known as the Council of Canadians with Disabilities. The coalition was instrumental in lobbying for persons with disabilities to be included in the Canadian Charter of Rights and Freedoms, achieved in 1983. Consumers have also voiced a perspective regarding service delivery, focusing on independent living and highlighting the importance of consumer control and choice. More than 16 percent of Canadians, and 30 percent of Aboriginal Canadians, have some type of disability (Canada 1991a, 1991b). As biomedical advances continue and the proportions of older people in our population increase, persons with developmental or physical challenges become important clientele for social workers. No unifying piece of legislation comparable to the US Disabilities Act 1990 has been passed in Canada to define disability and to outline the rights of disabled persons and the legal obligations of society toward them. The 1980 definition of the World Health Organization—that disability represents a change in ability to carry out daily activities related to an impairment of body functioning, resulting in a handicap or social barrier—still forms an important reference point for professionals. The current definition of the International Classification of Functioning, Disability, and Health introduces a strengths-based orientation; however, its complex matrix of body functioning, activities, and participation, and its contextual factors, each evaluated for positive and negative influences, is more difficult to apply.

The range of personal support needs for people with developmental or physical challenges can be great: among others, assistive devices for greater independence in self-care, communication aids, sign-language interpreters, guide dogs for the hearing and visually impaired, accessible transportation, attendant care to support self-care, and accessible housing. These personal support needs are met through a plethora of public and private service providers in both the health and social service systems (Roeher Institute 1993). Significantly, many such services levy user fees. Health care services in Canada are administered by the provinces and territories, and are governed by national standards under the Canada Health Act, 1984. Many important community-based services are available for persons with disabilities, such as home care, physiotherapy, occupational therapy, and social work, all funded under extended services in the Canada Health Act. Extended services, however, are not subject to the five principles of the Act (i.e., comprehensiveness, universality, reasonable access, portability, public administration), which apply only to insured services (i.e., hospitalization costs and physicians fees) (Bolaria & Dickinson 1994). Thus, in- and out-patient acute and rehabilitation services are free, but longer-term community services are delivered by public and private service providers with varying user fees. The result is a patchwork of essential services to support health, wellness, and independence for which access is complicated and often not affordable (Roeher Institute 1993). While financial compensation for health-related expenses is available through the federal disability and medical expenses tax credits, neither adequately compensates for actual costs.

While the Canadian Human Rights Act was amended in 1998 to require employers to accommodate the needs of persons with disabilities, "short of undue hardship," the Canadian Human Rights Commission reported in 2002 that employment equity remains problematic. Persons with disabilities on social assistance are disproportionately represented. For those whose disability prevents them from "substantially gainful occupation" and whose disability is "long-lasting or indefinite," the Canada pension plan provides a disability pension (Romaniuk 1995: 1777). Provinces may provide their own forms of disability support, for example, BC's disability benefits program (2001), which provides both income support and access to enhanced health benefits. Those whose physical disability resulted from a workplace accident can apply under a workers' compensation plan, available throughout the country as administered by appointed board. Others may qualify for long-term disability insurance (CCSD 1996). As well, the federal employment insurance program has sickness benefits.

Services for persons with physical and developmental challenges in Canada are provided through a complex matrix of health, social services, and income security initiatives under the auspices of federal, provincial/territorial, municipal programs delivered by both public and private providers. Considerable variance exists throughout the country and the complexity of service delivery is a significant barrier for many people. Social workers often provide not only counselling services but important skills in navigating and educating people to use these complex systems.

[*Beverley Antle*]

RELATED ENTRIES

Canada Health Act, Deafness, Developmental Challenges, Developmental Challenges & Families, Diversity, Peer Counselling, Personal-Centred Theory, Physical Challenges, Sensitizing Concepts, Services for Children, Services for Elderly People, Services for Families, Services for Married People, Services for Offenders, Services for Refugees, Services for Women, Services for Youth, Social Services, Theory & Practice, Visual Impairment, Wellness

REFERENCES

Bolaria, B.S., and H.D. Dickinson. 1994. *Health, Illness and Health Care in Canada.* Toronto: Harcourt Brace.

Canada. 1991a. *Aboriginal Peoples Survey.* Ottawa: Statistics Canada.

———. 1991b. *Health and Activities Limitation Survey.* Ottawa: Statistics Canada.

CCSD. 1996. *Maintaining a Social Safety Net: Recommendations on the Canada Health and Social Transfer: A Position Paper.* Ottawa: Canadian Council on Social Development.

Roeher Institute. 1993. *Nothing Personal: The Need for Personal Supports in Canada.* North York, ON: The Institute.

WHO. 2001. ICF Introduction. Geneva: World Health Organization.

services for refugees

Refugees are a special category of newcomers to Canada, invoking different policies from those applied to immigrants. Refugees have different settlement needs from other immigrants and can avail themselves of different services, owing in large part to their experiences in their countries of origin. While immigrants choose to migrate to reunite with family members living in Canada or to contribute to Canada's economy, refugees seek protection in this country. As a signatory to the 1951 Geneva Convention relating to the Status of Refugees, Canada has adopted within its Immigration Act the classification of Convention refugees, persons with a well-founded fear of persecution based on race, religion, nationality, political opinion, or membership in a particular social group. Such refugees are outside their country of nationality and are unable—or by reason of that fear unwilling—to be protected by that country, or, not having a country of nationality, are outside the country of their former habitual residence and are unable or—by reason of that fear—unwilling to return to that country. In practice, refugees in Canada are considered to belong to one of two basic classifications: government-assisted refugees and refugee claimants. Government-assisted refugees are individuals who are granted Convention refugee status or are recognized as members of humanitarian-designated classes (i.e., people in refugee-like situations) before arriving in Canada; on arrival in Canada, they become landed immigrants. Within this classification is a special category for women at risk. Government-assisted refugees are eligible for assistance from the federal government in terms of transportation loans and income support during their first year; they also qualify for federally funded settlement services, such as language training, assistance with housing and accessing community services, interpretation services, orientation services, employment counselling, and paraprofessional counselling. Citizenship and Immigration Canada does not support professional counselling within settlement agencies, even though many social workers and other professionals provide such counselling services in these organizations throughout the country. Refugee claimants are persons who arrive in Canada and then apply to be recognized as Convention refugees; they are sometimes referred to as in-land asylum seekers. Refugee claimants go through the refugee-determination process, in which they have to establish that they are either persecuted or fearful of persecution; while going through this process, refugee claimants are not eligible for federally funded settlement services, such as language training, but rely on provincial / territorial, municipal, and community services. Income support for refugee claimants is a provincial/territorial service for which they must apply. In some communities, established settlement agencies provide services to refugee claimants on behalf of the respective provincial / territorial or municipal government. Elsewhere, concerned citizens, religious, or ethnocultural bodies—usually volunteers—provide services and significant support to refugee claimants.

While the needs of Convention refugees and refugee claimants may be very similar, the settlement services available to each classification within Canada differ. All have pragmatic needs ranging from housing to language training that are similar to the needs of other immigrants. Such assistance should be provided in a culturally sensitive and appropriate manner. Refugees and refugee claimants often require considerable support as they begin to settle and negotiate the new environment, particularly those who are escaping a war zone or persecution. In addition to the challenges of migration and settling into a new community, refugees who have experienced trauma or torture may seek intervention for such mental health problems as post-traumatic stress. The Centre for Victims of Torture, located in Toronto, is an excellent resource. For some refugees, settlement is a transitional crisis in which their sense of identity is continually challenged; short-term crisis intervention may assist some, while others may need some form of longer-term support. Many refugee claimants experience delays in the settlement process, and may feel considerable instability while their refugee-determination status is under examination; the prospect of being deported or returned to a place from which they were escaping causes many to feel great anxiety. In addition to the needs experienced by other refugees, refugee claimants require information about the determination process and need assistance in preparing and presenting their claim; as they may not be eligible for legal aid in some provinces or territories, the determination process can be very stressful. Refugee claimants often appreciate emotional as much as financial and other support throughout the process. In addition to their counselling and support roles, social workers also advocate for policy changes to ensure equitable social policies that meet the needs of refugees and refugee claimants. Given the vulnerability of these newcomers, this advocacy is of fundamental importance and has acquired renewed intensity in the current context of economic rationalism, neo-conservatism, and racial profiling.

[*Michael R. Woodford*]

services for women

The status of women has always been influenced by factors related to entrenched societal philosophies, traditions, and convention: they have been "burdened with the weight of inherited customs, attitudes and laws" (Wade Labarge 1971: i). While settlers to this country brought these influences with them, they quickly found that men and women had to work together—much as women in Aboriginal societies shared in the tasks needed for life to continue, while maintaining their nurturing role. Sharing the difficult tasks for survival accorded some women a position of economic importance in the community (Wade Labarge 1971). Education gradually brought new employment and/or financial opportunities for some, but by the nineteenth century women's contributions to settlement were still not reflected in the legal and political framework (MacLellan 1971). In accordance with English common law, unmarried women over the age of twenty-one in Canada had many of the same personal and property rights as men but, when a woman's marriage was terminated, she lost her independent existence; she could not vote or own property and had no legal rights to her children (MacLellan 1971). Changes in legal rights and services for women came as a result of the industrial revolution, women's economic contributions during two world wars, the women's suffrage movement, the granting of the federal vote to most women in 1918, and the entitlement as a result of the *Persons Case* of women to enter the senate in 1929 (Wade Labarge 1971). Women were granted protective labour, property, and citizenship rights and finally began to receive recognition as mothers; in every case, however, Aboriginal women received these rights and services years after their non-Aboriginal counterparts. Laws such as the Deserted Wives and Children's Act and the Mother's Allowance

Act were passed in the early twentieth century to provide for women and their children if a father was unwilling or unable to support them (MacLellan 1971). Married women also gained equal guardianship of their children in all provinces by 1923. By the 1970s, women's rights and benefits continued to accrue—with, for instance, $800,000 worth of family planning research—but adequate resources focused on women's needs was still lacking. In 1972 the federal government raised tax exemptions, increased unemployment insurance benefits, and proposed a family income security program in an attempt to place larger sums of money in the hands of low-income mothers. In this time period, 8.6 percent of all families in Canada were led by women, some of whom were single parents, with 28.7 percent living in poverty and/or on welfare (CCSD 1976). The federal government also indicated its willingness to address the need for daycare, but required the co-operation of provincial governments, as it fell to their jurisdiction; further, many Canadians viewed the idea of working mothers placing children in daycare as controversial. Regardless of these federal initiatives, women in need still lacked adequate gynaecological, psychiatric, and family planning clinics, as well as affordable housing options. In 1969 there were 62 family planning clinics in all of Canada and, as of 1973, only 25 percent of all hospitals provided abortion services (CCSD 1976). Many women could not afford decent housing or were discriminated against by landlords/ladies who feared they would not pay their rent; although public housing was available, by the end of 1973, only 111,000 units were available in all of Canada—far less than required (CCSD 1976).

The United Nations declared 1975 to be International Women's Year with the intent to "focus attention on improving the status of women, to promote awareness of the changing role of women in today's society" (IWYS 1975: 1, 1). Plans to accomplish these goals in Canada included an educational and promotional media campaign, regional and national conferences, the removal of barriers to equality in legislation and regulations, and the provision of funds for various projects. For their part, the federal government promised to consider the concerns of women when developing future policies and programs. In order to demonstrate this commitment and change attitudes about women, they sponsored a "Why Not?" campaign in 1975. Unfortunately, the campaign ignored those women who struggle to support themselves and their children in low-paid work; it could have focused instead on reasonable incomes, access to education, and adequate daycare (CCSD 1976). Since 1975 services for women in Canada, especially those designed to meet their social and health needs, have dramatically increased. The provision of such services by the public sector (federal, provincial/territorial, and municipal agencies), as well as the establishment of women's organizations and research initiatives, now focus public attention on issues that face single, married, lesbian, and elderly women: low incomes, sexual assault, spousal abuse, disability rights, spousal benefits, breast cancer, and reproductive rights. Many government agencies have increased funding for single mothers and women's health research and have established a variety of daycare, education, and housing programs. More organizations now focus on women's issues, including the Centres of Excellence for Women's Health, the Canadian Research Institute for the Advancement of Women, the Canadian Women's Health Network, the National Action Committee on the Status of Women, and the Canadian Association of Sexual Assault Centres. International Women's Day on March 8, 2000, highlighted the role such organizations play in improving a woman's standard of living. Some of the first shelters and women's centres formed around 1975, but it was not until the 1980s that issues of violence against women began to be widely addressed. As of April 1988 throughout Canada, 470 shelters had been set up, offering women and their children counselling and advocacy services, parenting skills, and housing referrals (Canada 1999). As well, more family planning clinics now exist to support women's reproductive rights.

Although the recognition is now widespread that such services are essential, serious inadequacies still exist. Government funding for programs and research is dwindling and, currently, less than 4 percent of foundation donations are specifically designated for women's issues. More shelters are needed and attitudes toward sexual assault need to be improved, especially for rural and Aboriginal women. Available programs and services for rural and Aboriginal women are still

lacking and some of the services that are offered may not be culture- or racism-sensitive (Torjman 1988). Problems persist in the welfare and childcare systems, as benefits continue to fall below the poverty line (Torjman 1988). Poverty for widows and single elderly women is still persistent. The recognition of women's needs has certainly increased throughout the twentieth century—but much more still needs to be done.

[*Joanne Zamparo*]

RELATED ENTRIES

Aboriginal Issues, Abortion, M. Bourgeoys, Crisis Intervention, Family Planning, Feminist Theory, Gender Issues, Sister Mary Henry, Lesbian Services, L. Holland, D. Livesay, N. McClung, A. Macphail, Mother's Allowance, I. Munroe-Smith, E. Murphy, National Action Committee on the Status of Women, National Council of Women in Canada, I. Parlby, Pregnancy, Royal Commission on New Reproductive Technologies, Royal Commission on the Status of Women, Separation & Divorce, Sexual Harassment, Sexual Minorities, Sexual Orientation, Sexual Problems & Services, Single Parents, Social Services, K. Stovold, E. Stowe, Theory & Practice, Toronto Infants Home, B. Touzel, Women Abuse, Women's Christian Temperance Union, Women's Missionary Society

REFERENCES

Canada. 1999. Status of Women Canada. *The Daily* (June). Ottawa: Statistics Canada. Online at time of writing at <www.swc-cfc.ac.ca>.

CCSD. 1976. *Women in Need: A Sourcebook*. Ottawa: Council on Social Development.

IWYS [International Women's Year Secretariat]. 1975. *International Women's Year Newsletter Bulletins* 1, 1; 2, 9.

MacLellan, M.E. 1971. History of Women's Rights in Canada. In *Cultural Tradition and Political History of Women in Canada*. Studies of the Royal Commission on the Status of Women 8. Ottawa: The Royal Commission on the Status of Women in Canada (Chair: F. Bird).

Torjman, S. 1988. *The Reality Gap: Closing the Gap between Women's Needs and Available Programs and Services*. Background Paper. Ottawa: Canadian Advisory Council on the Status of Women.

Wade Labarge, M. 1971. The Cultural Tradition of Canadian Women: The Historical Background. In *Cultural Tradition and Political History of Women in Canada*. Studies of the Royal Commission on the Status of Women 8. Ottawa: The Royal Commission on the Status of Women in Canada. (Chair: F. Bird.)

services for youth

A wide range of social welfare programs has been developed for young people between the ages of twelve to eighteen over the past century in Canada. These services are distinct from those focused primarily on children or on adults. They emerged initially in the late nineteenth century out of the awareness that youth had special needs and challenges which, if not met, could lead to serious anti-social behaviour that could well continue into adult life. At the time, cities were expanding along with industrialization and the resultant social problems. Services designed for young people then were, for the most part, of a social and educational nature with a strong moralistic tone, often sponsored by churches; notable was the Young Man's Christian Association (YMCA). Initially, these services were educative, skill learning, and citizenship activities for after-business hours or after-school; the activities were geared at enhancing social behaviours along with a strong element of community service and voluntarism (e.g., the Boy Scouts and Guide Guides organizations). As times, a subdued military flavour can be detected, as in the range of cadet organizations and today's Rangers. Some services—for example, the YMCA and later YWCA—recognized the need for residential resources for unattached youth; these were combined with responsive neighbourhood centres for recreation and education. Although begun from an educative and social framework, over time, services for youth began to take on counselling and therapeutic functions, principally in structures for what used to be called juvenile delinquency and in the field of mental health. The emergence of juvenile court structures under the Juvenile Delinquents Act, 1908, stemming from the recognition that a more therapeutic rather than a punitive response to redressing difficulties experienced by youth was more effective and with longer-term benefits for society and youth. Probation services for youth were developed and continue to develop, provided sometimes through such autonomous organizations as the John Howard (for males) and Elizabeth Fry (for females) societies or in conjunction with other community services, such as family agencies. Community services will expand as the Youth Criminal Justice Act, 2002, is implemented. The other major area of youth services where therapeutic components have emerged is in the mental health field. The growing awareness that many of the problems of youth stemmed not only from societal and systemic circumstances, but as well from complex family and interpersonal issues, including childhood abuse, sexual abuse, and neglect.

Canadian society continues its commitment to services for youth, both for general welfare—the education, recreation and sports, and therapeutic services already well established—and many more specific approaches to respond to such issues as substance abuse, suicide, HIV/AIDS, homelessness, and identity (i.e., culture, ethnicity, diversity, sexual orientation), and systemic discrimination of all forms. Youth crisis hot-lines are now available nationwide. As well as seeking services, young people are participating and volunteering with enthusiasm to community activities that reflect their social commitment, often through such long-established organizations as YMCA, YWCA, Boy Scouts, Girl Guides, religious or faith-based groups, and environmental associations. In recent years, many agencies and services are moving to include youth in as many aspects of their activities and initiatives as possible; hospitals, services for seniors, family agencies, and various group homes have developed highly effective ways of encouraging young people to commit time toward their services. Many young people have found their way into community service positions, or to consider becoming a human service professional as a vocation to extend their community volunteer work.

[FJT]

RELATED ENTRIES

E.H. Blois, Criminal Justice, Crisis Intervention, Gender Issues, HIV/AIDS Peer Counselling, Probation, School Social Workers, Services for Children, Services for Families, Sexual Orientation, Social Services, Theory & Practice, Volunteers, YMCA, YWCA, Young Offenders Act, Youth Criminal Justice Act

separation and divorce

Separation in this context refers to the circumstance when a married or cohabiting couple stops living together, either by one person's decision, by mutual agreement, or by a judicial order (also called a decree of judicial separation, more common in Quebec than elsewhere). Divorce is the legal term that specifies the termination of a marriage contract. A separation contract could be arranged through a mediator, while a divorce has to be proceeded by a provincial/territorial court. Both separation and divorce have emotional, social, and legal implications. The emotional implications of divorce are associated with increases in depression as people experience the loss of a partner, lifestyle, hopes, some belongings, and income (O'Connell Corcoran 1997). Men may confront greater emotional adjustment problems than women as a result of the loss of intimacy, social connection, financial struggles, and/or interruption of a parental role; this may be more true for a father who leaves the marital home than for a custodial father who may feel supported by extended family and community. For women, the socio-economic challenges may be even greater than for men, as they may become the main emotional and financial custodian for the family. They may have to confront more social stigma than men and receive less support, in some cases. Regardless of the gender, the person who starts the separation has an easier adjustment process by comparison to the person who did not. A very common way to identify the stages of divorce has been to draw a parallel with the stages of crisis and grief: denial, anger, bargaining, depression, and acceptance or resolution. A person may move back and forth through these stages several times until he/she can accept the separation and move on with life. Several other models for looking at the stages of separation come from a clinical perspective. One model, gathered by Everett and Volgy (1991), look at three stages that identify the components of a systematic process. First, the family moves through a period of dysfunction where members and their roles disengage. Then, family members establish or renew their relationships with friends and extended family, perhaps after moving to a new house, school, or community (i.e., network coupling stage). Finally, the parent/child subsystem redefines itself and goes through an adjustment process (i.e., structural recoupling stage). Everett and Volgy (1991), and O'Connell Corcoran (1997) talk about several steps in the divorce process, which can be a guide for clinical intervention:

- *heightened ambivalence or disillusionment of one party* (early warning signs, problems are real but not acknowledged);
- *distancing or expressing dissatisfaction*: couple may look for counselling, give a last chance to save the marriage, usually relieved that problems are vented;
- *pre-separation*: fantasies and actions, pseudo-reconciliation, and pre-divorce fantasies; physical separation: deciding to divorce and acting on the decision;
- *recurring ambivalence*: usually reflects issues of uncertainty and the legal reality and costs;
- *potential disputes*: could happen through mediation or be very adversarial;
- *adjustments*: regaining sense of control, making plans for the future; and
- *post-divorce co-parenting*: remarriage, blended family issues, and dual family functioning.

Regarding the emotional effects of divorce on children, a therapist has to look at such factors as the age of the children, the level of conflict between parents during and after separation, the amount and quality of involvement of the non-resident parent, parenting skills and agreement on child rearing, openness to discuss the divorce, financial stressors, other causes of stress (i.e., moving, structural changes, either parent's romantic links to other people). Much of the children's adjustment will be related to the quality of the parent/child relationship before the separation, and to the parents' ability to separate the divorce from the children and attend to the children's needs. Even in the best of cases—where parents separate by mutual agreement and avoid involving the children in their conflicts—children present certain reactions; some of the most typical behaviours in children are denial (especially in young children), fear of abandonment, a need for detailed information, depression, either immaturity or parentalization, fantasies of parent reconciliation, feelings of blame or guilt and acting out, and anger toward peers, siblings, and/or parents. The family may also have to move to a less safe environment, which may expose children to unfortunate behaviours and activities. Generally, children of divorce may receive less attention and supervision, as parent may have to work longer hours to sustain the family financially. Children who are unsupervised or spend long periods alone or with their peers often engage in premature sexual behaviour and minor criminal activity (Ross, Scott, & Kelly 1995). Divorce has a direct connection to poverty, afflicting a large proportion of women and children and bringing even more stress to both.

[*Rita Ortiz de Waschmann*]

RELATED ENTRIES

Bereavement, Family Therapy, Services for Children, Services for Families, Services for Married People, Services for Women, Services for Youth, Social Services, Wellness

REFERENCES

Everett, C., and S. Volgy. 1991. Treating Divorce in Family-Therapy Practice. In A. Gurman and D. Kniskern (Eds.). *Handbook of Family Therapy*. Vol. 11, chap. 16. New York: Brunner/Mazel.

O'Connell Corcoran, K. 1998. *Psychological and Emotional Aspects of Divorce*. Online at time of writing at <www.mediate.com>.

Ross, D.P., T. Scott, and M. Kelly. 1995. Child Poverty: What Are the Consequences? In H. Wintersberger (Ed.) *Children On the Way from Marginality towards Citizenship. Childhood Policies: Conceptual and Practical Issues*. 67–100. Vienna: European Centre Vienna.

settlement house movement

The settlement house movement was started in Victorian England, initiated by some university-educated middle-class Christians who saw increasing class inequality and deteriorating living conditions of the poor as a crisis of conscience (Reinders 1982: 40); they decided to serve the poor by integrating them into middle-class neighbourhoods. In 1884 Samuel Barnetts established the first settlement house, Toynbee Hall, in the east end of London, which was seen as a deterrent to revolution by the poor that would cause instability. With the success of Toynbee Hall, the movement spread to North America during the late nineteenth and early twentieth centuries. Hull House in Chicago, one of the earliest settlement houses in North America, was established in 1889 by Jane Addams, a significant figure in the social work profession. Influence by Hull House, Mary Lawson Bell and Sara Libby Carson in 1902 opened the first settlement house in Canada, the Evangelia Settlement, in Toronto (Irving, Parsons, &

Bellamy 1995). As with the settlement house movement England and the United States, universities also played a crucial role in Canadian. J.J. Kelso, a social work education pioneer, who admired the idea of bridging the gap between educated young university men and women and the poor, was a keen proponent of settlement houses for the University of Toronto: two university-sponsored secular settlement houses were established, University Settlement and Central Neighbourhood House. Most settlement houses share philosophical ground similar to that laid down by Jane Addams in her famous article "The subjective necessity for social settlements [is] the solidarity of the human race" (Addams 1999). This philosophical ground defines the three motives behind the settlement house movement: to extend the domain of democracy from political aspect to other social dimensions in the local community, to foster a full progression of the human race, and to actualize the humanitarianism of Christianity (Addams 1999: 95). To achieve these philosophical objectives, settlement houses adopted a generic service model (Hillman 1960; Irving, Parsons, & Bellamy 1995), which can be further divided into four major categories: social, educational, humanitarian, and civic. This generic model is reflected in the three characteristics of settlement house services. First, settlement houses take a holistic perspective of human needs, often offering a full range of basic services to all members—rich and poor, young and old, men and women—of the community. Second, settlement houses rely on volunteers in all levels of operation. Participation by volunteers reflects the civic development functions of settlement houses and manifests the movement's ideal of local democracy. Civil functions of settlement houses are also related to the movement's concerns about poor social conditions, from poverty and bad housing to undesirable public health and unemployment; in collaborations with universities, settlement houses have conducted social research and surveys to expose the problems in the community and to encourage collective resolution (Irving, Parsons, & Bellamy 1995). Third, the services of the settlement houses are flexible, timely, and local. Because the focus of settlement houses is always local, their response to service needs is always expeditious; in turn, settlement houses have developed many creative services. Daycare is one of the creative endeavours initiated by early settlement houses. Where settlement houses are located in multiethnic immigrant areas, they have become the major service networks helping immigrants to settle and integrate into their new society.

Settlement houses are also known as community or neighbourhood centres (Ramey 1992). Nowadays, most settlement houses no longer serve a small neighbourhood. Instead, as reflected by the mandates of its national umbrella organization, the Canadian Association of Neighbourhood Services, settlement houses have evolved into community-based, multi-service agencies throughout Canada. Recently, these agencies have had to struggle with such new challenges as urban renewal, which upsets the stability of the community. A high level of social mobility in the community is detrimental to the sense of belonging that settlement houses need and rely on. Professionalization of the movement has also distanced the houses from community members. Financial dependence on government and United Way funding has led to fragmentation of the integrative functions and minimizes the social reform capacity of most settlement houses. Finally, the social control image of the settlement houses is under attack from many radical social activists. Despite all these difficulties, settlement houses are still the major social service backbone in urban Canada as community-based multi-service agencies serving thousands of people in their own community.

[*Miu Chung Yan*]

RELATED ENTRIES

Anti-oppressive Social Work, Citizen Participation, Natural Helping Networks, Radical Social Work, Social Justice, Social Welfare History, Theory & Practice, United Way, Wellness

REFERENCES

Addams, J. 1999. *Twenty Years at Hull House*. Boston, MA: Bedford / St. Martin's.

Hillman, A. 1960. *Neighbourhood Centers Today: Action Program for a Rapidly Changing World*. New York: National Federation of Settlements and Neighbourhood Centers.

Irving, A., H. Parsons, and D. Bellamy. (Eds.) 1995. *Neighbours: Three Social Settlements in Downtown Toronto*. Toronto: Canadian Scholars Press.

Ramey, J.H. 1992. Group Work Practice in Neighbourhood Centers Today. *Social Work with Groups* 15, 2/3, 193–206.

Reinders, R.C. 1982. Toynbee Hall and the American Settlement Movement. *Social Service Review* 56, 1, 39–54.

sexual abuse of children

The specific acts to be considered child sexual abuse have been the subject of much debate. Legal definitions based on the Criminal Code are relatively clear, but definitions used in research and clinical practice vary, reflecting a lack of societal consensus. Two major issues for debate include the age limit separating children—and perhaps youth—from adults, and whether a significant age difference must exist between a child and an offender before an act is considered child sexual abuse. Almost all definitions of acts involving a child require that the perpetrator's intent is a sexual purpose or stimulation; most definitions also include what has been called contact sexual abuse: "the touching of the sexual portions of the child's body (genitals or anus) or touching the breasts of pubescent females, or the child's touching the sexual portion's of the partner's body" (Finkelhor 1994: 33). Some definitions include such non-contact sexual activities as exhibitionism, voyeurism, the involvement of the child in the making of pornography, and verbal sexual propositions or harassment. The lack of consensus for defining child sexual abuse is accompanied by the virtual impossibility for keeping accurate statistics of incidence and prevalence because of the hidden nature of offences. For incidence statistics, researchers must rely on cases reported to child protection agencies and criminal justice officers; research has shown that many experiences of child sexual abuse are never reported. Prevalence statistics are generated from retrospective surveys of adults, which are limited by the possibility that some adults may fail to disclose abusive experiences, or that some—researchers say relatively few—may fabricate or exaggerate their experiences. Findings from a 1984 Canadian national survey and other surveys indicate that the majority of perpetrators are known to the victims (i.e., a neighbour or family friend), but a minority is a family member (Leventhal 1998). In an analysis of the 1984 survey a decade later, a Canadian social work researcher pointed out that customary sampling techniques in community surveys usually fail to include deviant populations; as victims of severe and long-standing child sexual abuse are likely to enter such populations, "a general population survey is likely to underestimate the amount of serious, long term abuse" (Bagley 1995: 34). Victims of abuse by close family members are more often seen in clinical situations, apparently because such abuse is associated with greater distress than that evoked when abuse is perpetrated by others. According to practitioners, girls are more likely than boys to be abused by family members and, for boys, the abuse is more likely to be associated with force and threats. The large majority of offenders against both girls and boys are male, but some females do engage in the sexual abuse of children. Victims are found in all classes and ethnocultural communities; among cases reported to professionals, lower income families are overrepresented but to a lesser degree than for other types of child maltreatment (Finkelhor 1994). Children with physical or intellectual disabilities are at increased risk (Sobsey & Varnhagen 1991). Some studies have shown that girls living with stepfathers are at an increased risk compared with girls living with biological fathers (Bagley 1995). Factors associated with parental inadequacy, unavailability, conflict, and a poor parent/child relationship also seem to put children at increased risk for child sexual abuse—but all these markers are relatively weak for reliable prediction of child sexual abuse (Finkelhor 1994). Children vary in their response to sexual abuse. It is also difficult to separate the effects of sexual abuse from other aspects of family structure, which may have negative effects on children (Bagley & Ramsay 1986). Children experience some decrease in their distress when they are believed and have family support. The most common problems seen in children within two years after abuse is identified are fear, anxiety, depression, anger, aggression, and sexually inappropriate behaviour. These difficulties persist, as the most frequent problems seen in adults who have been sexually abused as children are depression, self-destructive behaviour, anxiety, feelings of isolation and stigma, poor self-esteem, difficulty in trusting others, a tendency toward revictimiza-

tion, substance abuse, and sexual maladjustment. More severe long-term effects tend to be associated with the use or threat of force and many incidents of sexual abuse over a long period.

In 1980, growing concern about the increase in reported incidence of child sexual abuse led to the federal government establishing the Committee on Sexual Offences against Children and Youth, which reported in 1984. The Badgely Report found, as a result of the committee's national survey, that 22 percent of females and 10 percent of males had experienced serious and unwanted sexual abuse before the age of eighteen, involving at least the touching or fondling of the genital area, and including forcible sexual assault and intercourse (Canada 1984: 175–93). In 1988, in response to recommendations by the 1984 report, changes were made to the Criminal Code and the Canada Evidence Act to enhance successful prosecution of child sexual abuse cases, provide better protection and improve the experience of child victim/witness, and bring sentencing in line with the severity of the offence. A special advisor on child sexual abuse was appointed in 1987 to the minister of National Health and Welfare, who reported in 1990 with seventy-four recommendations. In the years following, the federal government committed substantial resources to prevention, protection, treatment of victims and offenders, professional education, and evaluation of innovative programs.

[*Carol A. Stalker*]

RELATED ENTRIES

Abuse, An Act for the Prevention of Cruelty to and Better Protection of Children, Bereavement, Child Abuse, Adoption, Child Advocacy, Child Custody & Access, Child Welfare, Children's Aid Society, Clinical Social Work, Parenting, Poverty, Sensitizing Concepts, Services for Children, Sexual Problems & Services, Single Parents, Social Services, Social Welfare, Therapy, Treatment, Torture & Trauma Victims, Vicarious Traumatization, Welfare, Wellness

REFERENCES

Bagley, C. 1995. *Child Sexual Abuse and Mental Health in Adolescents and Adults: British and Canadian Perspectives.* Aldershot, UK: Avebury.

Bagley, C., and R. Ramsay. 1986. Sexual Abuse in Childhood: Psychosocial Outcomes and Implications for Social Work Practice. *Journal of Social Work and Human Sexuality* 4, 33–47.

Canada. 1984. *Sexual Offences against Children*. Committee on Sexual Offences against Children and Youth. Ottawa: The Committee (Chair: R. Badgely).

Finkelhor, D. 1994. Current Information on the Scope and Nature of Child Sexual Abuse. *Future of Children* 4, 31–53.

Leventhal, J.M. 1998. Epidemiology of Sexual Abuse of Children: Old Problems, New Directions. *Child Abuse and Neglect* 22, 481–91.

Sobsey, D., and C. Varnhagen. 1991. Sexual Abuse and Exploitation of Disabled Individuals. In C. Bagley and R.J. Thomlinson (Eds.) *Child Sexual Abuse: Critical Perspectives on Prevention, Intervention and Treatment*. 203–16. Toronto: Wall and Emerson.

sexual harassment

Sexual harassment is generally regarded as any unwanted sexual behaviour—verbal or physical—directed toward an individual or group by a person(s) of the same or opposite sex who is aware, or ought reasonably to be aware, that the attention is unwanted and offensive. Sexual harassment includes any promise of reward or threat of reprisal related to compliance with unwanted sexual behaviour or attention, and the creation of a hostile environment when unwanted sexual behaviours or pornographic materials are displayed. The harassment may comprise a single or repeated episodes. The many forms of sexual harassment include suggestive comments, insistence on sexual contact, unnecessary touching, offensive gestures, or demands for sexual contact. Usually an attempt by a person to assert power and control over others, sexual harassment is unrelated to sexual desire and can escalate toward sexual assault or aggravated sexual assault. Sexual harassment often occurs in the workplace or at schools and universities but is prevalent in other public places and in almost any social situation. It may be directed at a person's sexual orientation, ethnocultural background, disability, or any other personal characteristic. Women—in particular young single women—are more often sexually harassed than men. The perpetrators of sexual harassment are usually men with no particular profile. In a national poll, one-third of women working outside the home reported being sexually harassed at work. Student surveys at Canadian universities found that half the female respondents experienced some form of sexual harassment on campus. Sexual harassment has existed for as long as individuals have walked in public. Until recent decades, it was not named as such and was generally accepted as a matter between two people rather than a social or legal concern.

The term "sexual harassment" was coined in the late 1970s in the United States by a women's activist group. In Canada the women's movement identified sexual harassment and public awareness of it was raised by the National Action Committee on the Status of Women, which now advises the federal government and the public on matters related to sexual harassment. Locally, individuals now find information and services from sexual assault and crises centres. Research on sexual harassment indicates that women and men conceptualize it differently, as women are more likely than men to define less explicit behaviour as sexual harassment. Behaviour constituting sexual harassment has been found to be dependent on the specific context of the situation, the specific setting, the participants' understanding of the situation, their past interactions with each other, the nature of their relationship (e.g., supervisor/subordinate or colleague, instructor/student, coach/athlete). The most widely cited theories on the causes of sexual harassment are outlined in three models (Tangri, Burt, & Johnson 1982). In the natural/biological model, men are viewed as naturally sexually aggressive and behaviour that women find offensive is viewed as the normal courtship behaviour of men. In the organizational model, harassment is a function of organizational hierarchies where those with more power can extort sexual gratification from subordinates. In the sociocultural model, a person's sex, rather than their organizational position, is more of an indicator of the likelihood to harass, as men are viewed as privileged members of society asserting power over others through sexual harassment. Alternative theories acknowledge a relationship between sexual harassment and power, sex and violence in society. A prominent view of sexual harassment based on feminist theory is that it has multiple dimensions related to power and control of women by men, the sexualization and objectification of women, the attempts of men to subordinate and economically exploit women, and men's socialization and subsequent feelings of superiority.

Sexual harassment is illegal. Within the work place, sexual harassment is prohibited by specific laws contained in the Quebec Charter of Rights and Freedoms, the Canadian Charter of Rights and Freedoms, and the Canada Labour Code. Other laws that can be invoked in situations arising from sexual harassment are contained in the Act Respecting Industrial Accidents and Occupational Hazards, the Act Respecting Labour Standards, and the Employment Insurance Act. The Canadian Human Rights Act also prohibits sexual harassment and provides recourse and protection for workers employed by federal business or corporations. Employers and educators are required by law to ensure that employees and students are not subjected to sexual harassment; among other steps, they must establish, issue, and make available a policy to outline procedures to be followed if an individual(s) is harassed. Individuals also have the right, through the Canadian Human Rights Act, to make a complaint and seek recourse through federal and provincial/territorial human rights commissions. In additional, individuals may wish to seek reparation through the courts. Consequences from sexual harassment involve disruption of work or school performance, absenteeism, loss of income or lower grades, and impairment of interpersonal relationships. Psychological and emotional effects include depression, anger, low self-esteem, post-traumatic stress disorder symptoms, and feelings of helplessness; physical or health-related effects may include weight loss, sleep disturbances, disordered eating, and gastrointestinal disorders (Koss et al. 1994). The consequences extending to employers, educators, and agencies include staff turnover, medical claims, reduced productivity, litigation, and even out-of-court settlements (Kaplan 1991 in Gould 2000). The social work role in addressing sexual harassment is to empower those who have experienced harassment while working to end sexual oppression. Social workers will need to have a working knowledge of the judicial system and procedures for taking legal action. Clinical interventions may involve individual, family, dyadic, and/or group therapies with the goal of validating those who have been sexually harassed and encouraging them to empower themselves. Sup-

portive therapy, psycho-education, and advocacy are also essential components of clinical social work. Policy and organizational interventions exemplify the values and skills of social work toward strategies to defeat sexual harassment within organizations and communities.

[*Marilyn Parsons*]

RELATED ENTRIES

Counselling, Gay-Sensitive Services, Gender Issues, Lesbian Services, National Action Committee on Status of Women, Sensitizing Concepts, Services for Women, Sexual Minorities, Sexual Orientation, Sexual Problems & Services, Sensitizing Concepts, Theory & Practice, Treatment, Wellness, Women Abuse

REFERENCES

Gould, K.H. 2000. Beyond Jones v. Clinton: Sexual Harassment Law and Social Work. *Social Work* 45, 3, 237–48.

Koss, M.P. et al. 1994. *No Safe Haven: Male Violence against Women at Home, at Work and in the Community.* Washington, DC: American Psychological Association.

Tangri, S.S., M.R. Burt, and L.B. Johnson. 1982. Sexual Harassment: Three Explanatory Models. *Journal of Social Issues* 38:33–54.

sexual minorities

Sexual minorities are, generally, people who possess sexual desires that fall outside of the sexual behaviours of the majority, such as lesbian, gay, bisexual, and transgendered orientations and identities. Intense activism among people with a sexual orientation that is not heterosexual has gradually raised public awareness and achieved legal and other formal recognition; social and health care services for gay men and lesbians, however, continue to be poor or insensitive. Within sexual minorities, bisexual and transgendered people fare even worse. Transgendered individuals are those who live in a gender other than their biological gender at birth (i.e., individuals born female live as men). Bisexuals are people who are sexually attracted to both men and women; because the concept is misunderstood by many people, bisexual individuals are not often accepted into heterosexual, lesbian, or gay social circles (CLGRO 1997). Stereotypes abound, so that bisexuals find themselves labelled as not fully out lesbians or gays, untrustworthy, incapable of monogamy, and promiscuous. Over the past ten years, many lesbian and gay groups have expanded their mandates to include bisexuals; some bisexual-specific groups have formed throughout the country, but they have not, as yet, coalesced as a movement with a powerful voice. Thus, public education on bisexual issues has been limited. What underscores all social issues faced by bisexuals is their need to be understood and accepted. As bisexuality is considered a sexual orientation, it is protected in most human rights legislation throughout Canada. Despite this protection, a lack of widespread social acceptance persists and bisexuals face issues of self-acceptance and disclosure to others related to coming out, similar to those faced by lesbians and gays; difficulties with self-esteem, relationships (familial, intimate, friendships), career, or absence of role models (CLGRO 1997; Mulé 1999) are further complicated by factors of socio-economic status and multiculturalism. Facing these challenges is difficult, in and of themselves, and add to the pressures of having a sexual orientation that generally elicits insensitivity.

Transgendered people are in an even more oppressed state than bisexuals because they have a very low public profile and no legal protection. Because the number of self-accepting transgendered people is very low, by comparison to gays, lesbians, and bisexuals who have come out, organizing and activism have been minimal. Only a few groups have formed in Canada around the issues of transgendered people. With no legislative protection in human rights policies for these people and little public awareness, transgendered people suffer social rejection and discrimination. Most experience so much intolerance that they are unable to find employment in the mainstream workforce; many turn to the sex trade to survive (CLGRO 1997). Transgendered people often take hormones or undergo genital surgery to change their physical appearance. Transvestites, known as cross-dressers, wear clothing and attire associated with the opposite sex so that they can choose when or where they will present themselves as one gender or another (CLGRO 1997). Availing themselves of these opportunities can comes at a considerable economic and equitable health care costs for transgendered people. Those in the process of or having completed the transition to their chosen gender face challenges accessing such services as housing and counselling where they are gender-specific (i.e., women's shelters, detox centres). As a population, transgendered people require understanding, sensitivity and respect for their pursuit to live their lives in the gender of their choice (CLGRO 1997).

The social work profession has been slow to recognize and respond to the needs of gay men and lesbians but even slower to integrate the existence and experiences of bisexuals and, to an even lesser extent, transgendered people. Issues related to bisexuality and transgenderism are unfortunately being coattailed onto gay and lesbian issues. Formal academic training and professional development in social work rarely mention the smallest sexual minorities and, when they do, usually assume that bisexual and transgender issues are similar to those of gay and lesbian people (Mulé 1999; van Wormer, Wells, & Boes 2000). Bisexual clients and bisexual social work practitioners are starting to raise awareness in the profession in Canada. Transgenderists are only beginning a similar education process. Understanding, sensitivity, and service development for sexual minorities are areas for potential growth in the social work profession. Further, the profession can work alongside activists from sexual minorities to redress the lack of funds and absence of social policy on their issues and needs.

[*Nick Mulé*]

RELATED ENTRIES

K. Belanger, Gay-Sensitive Services, Gender Issues, Lesbian Services, Minorities, Sensitizing Concepts, Sexual Minorities, Sexual Orientation, Sexual Problems & Services

REFERENCES

Castle, S. 1997. *Guidelines: A Manual for Transsexuals and Their Caregivers.* Vancouver, BC: Zenith Foundation.

CLGRO. 1997. *Systems Failure: A Report on the Experiences of Sexual Minorities in Ontario's Health-Care and Social-Services Systems.* Toronto: Coalition for Lesbian and Gay Rights in Ontario.

Mulé, N. 1999. Social Work and the Provision of Health Care and Social Services to Sexual Minority Populations. *Canadian Social Work* 1, 1, 39–55.

van Wormer, K., J. Wells, and M. Boes. 2000. *Social Work with Lesbians, Gays and Bisexuals: A Strengths Perspective.* 22–24. Boston, MA: Allyn and Bacon.

sexual orientation

Sexual orientation is an "enduring emotional, romantic, sexual or affectionate attraction to individuals of a particular gender." Sexual orientation defines who one is emotionally and intellectually drawn to in an intimate way, but differs "from sexual behaviour because it refers to feelings and self-concept [and it] emerges for most people in early adolescence without any prior sexual experience" (APA 2002). Research indicates that sexual orientation is established early in life, and that complex genetic, biological, and social factors contribute to its development. Sexual orientation is generally classified as heterosexual, bisexual, or homosexual, with the range often viewed as a continuum. Dr. Alfred Kinsey (1948) pioneered this concept of a continuum, "where some individuals are exclusively attracted to members of the [opposite] sex, a similar percentage experience exclusively same sex attraction, and the rest of the population is attracted to members of both sexes to a greater or lesser degree." These variations in sexual orientation seem to have always existed across history and cultures, thereby reflecting an essential aspect of the human experience (Bohan 1996). For this reason, it is vital to define each of the three main categories of sexual orientation, heterosexuality, bisexuality, and homosexuality. Heterosexuality is defined as the sexual desire or preference for people of the opposite sex. Bisexuality is sexual or romantic attraction or behaviour toward some members of more than one sex, and people may be more attracted to one sex than the other, to both sexes equally, or may find people's sex unimportant. Lastly, homosexuality is defined by "feelings of love, emotional attachment, or sexual attraction to persons of one's own gender" (Campbell 1996: 327). Female homosexuals are commonly referred to as lesbians, "pertaining to the sexual preference or desire of one woman for another" (Mosby 1998: 928). Statistically, great variance exists in the prevalence for each of these categories of sexual orientation, but the majority of Canadians identify themselves as heterosexual. With respect to homosexuality, the most-quoted statistic, which was initially reported by Kinsey, "says that one in ten people identifies her or himself as exclusively gay or lesbian." This statistic is believed to be roughly the same all over the world, in all times, cultures (and) climates. No widely accepted statistic for the prevalence of bisexuality exists and no Canadian studies are available. In 1948 Kinsey and his colleagues did find "that almost 37 percent of white American men fell somewhere between the two extremes of the scale (exclusively heterosexual and exclusively homosexual,) and that rarely did anyone fall exactly in the middle" (Zinik 1985). Part of the difficulty in estimating the prevalence of bisexuality is that many such persons commonly identify themselves as either heterosexual or homosexual, even though they have experiences and/or fantasies beyond either orientation: "The most that can be said, then, is that judging from the various studies, approximately 15 percent of American men and 10 percent of American women ... show some degree of homosexual behaviour in their sexual history" (Zinik 1985: 302).

[*Susan Hanna*]

RELATED ENTRIES

K. Belanger, Gay-Sensitive Services, Gender Issues, Lesbian Services, Minorities, Sensitizing Concepts, Sexual Minorities, Sexual Problems & Services

REFERENCES

APA. 2002. Public Information on Sexual Orientation. American Psychiatric Association. Online at time of writing at <www.apa.org>.

Bohan, J.S. 1996. *Psychology and Sexual Orientation: Coming to Terms.* New York: Routledge.

Kinsey, A.C., W.B. Pomeroy, and C.E. Martin. 1948. *Sexual Behavior in the Human Male.* Philadelphia, PA: W.B. Saunders

Zinik, G. 1985. Identity Conflict or Adaptive Flexibility? Bisexuality Reconsidered. In *Bisexualities: Theory and Research, Journal of Homosexuality* 11,1/2: 7–21.

sexual problems and services

Since psychosocial interventions by individuals and communities converged in the late 1800s to create what became social work, the profession has expressed a concern for problems, issues, and the promotion of well-being associated with psychosexual development, sexual intimacy, and sexual expression. Social work focus has ranged from human development and potential (i.e., counselling and psychosocial education to promote of the sexual well-being of marriages) to issues of social justice (i.e., rights for sexual minorities). Professionals committed to scientifically based social work and evidence-based practice have contributed to knowledge and skills for helping client systems, ranging from teens at risk for pregnancy to the sexual needs of such marginalized people as those with developmental delays. To promote psychosocial change, social workers might select to work with individuals (e.g., sex offenders or persons experiencing sexual dysfunction), families (e.g., parents of a sibling incest offender), dyads (e.g., couples experiencing difficulty with sexual intimacy), groups (e.g., survivors of sexual assault suffering from impaired sexual functioning), formal organizations (e.g., social action for HIV/AIDS prevention), communities (e.g., trauma debriefing for a community in which religious staff has been responsible for sexual abuse of children in their care), or societies (e.g., efforts by international organizations to ensure that women have access to safe contraception and/or abortions, or to challenge such oppressive cultural practices as female genital mutilation). One of the assumptions underpinning social work intervention and service development is that sexual intimacy and sexual expression represent a normal and basic biopsychosocial need that transcends the reproduction of the species. Community awareness activities, psychosocial education, and counselling may promote healthy and humane sexual attitudes, activities, and relationships, as well as sexual satisfaction. Social work intervention may also enable the affirmation of diverse normal sexual orientations (e.g., bisexuality), gender identity (e.g., transsexuality), or sexual identity (e.g., cross-dressing).

The driving forces for many interventions and services, however, have often helped client systems assess and ameliorate problems, risks, harmful impacts, and needs derived from non-normative variations in sexual interest or behaviour (sometimes characterized as sexual deviance), sexual dysfunctional, or otherwise inappropriate aspects of sexual intimacy and sexual expression. As well, social workers may help clients adjust to problems with sexual development, such as those associated with Klinefelter's syndrome. Such assessments have resulted in social policy and program initiatives—both historical (e.g., policies and programs to prevent juvenile prostitution) and current (e.g., to prevent sexual exploitation of children by pedophiles). Some programs and

interventions have focused on prevention, as with unwanted teen pregnancies, while others have goals of harm reduction, such as through free condom distribution and needle exchange among people with a high risk of HIV infection. Yet others have enabled early detection of: problems directly related to sexual expression (e.g., sexualized children), unintended consequences (e.g., unwanted pregnancy), or concomitant risks (e.g., fetal alcohol syndrome). Social workers have had to focus on ensuring protection and safety; they have been among world leaders in sex abuse investigation, early detection, and the assessment and treatment of children who have experienced incest or sex abuse. As case plans progress, some interventions may support safe and healing family reunification, after parent/child incest. Other protection foci include sexual harassment, the protection of the disabled, the elderly, and animals from sex exploitation or abuse. Some children and adults suffer post-traumatic stress and crisis as a result of undergoing such experiences as sexual harassment, date rape, partner/marital rape, aggravated sexual assault, sexual exploitation (e.g., unwilling participation in pornographic production), or the contracting of a sexually transmitted disease. While impacts vary from one individual or situation to another, many clients seek crisis intervention support and stabilization in order to resume a more normal life; these are sometimes provided through specialized rape crisis or mental health trauma services. Crisis and trauma interventions often address impacts on sexual identity, sexual functioning, and intimacy in pair bonds, including trauma bonds. Through assessment, psychosocial education, counselling, and therapy, social workers help address problems with intimacy and sexual expression that may have as their biopsychosocial genesis: biochemical developmental barriers (e.g., Klinefelter's syndrome), biomedical and biophysical barriers (e.g., a mastectomy), negative body image (e.g., associated with sexual humiliation), past experiences that have impacted psychosexual development (e.g., having been beaten for sexual self-stimulation), sex anxiety (e.g., fear of sexual performance failure), sex guilt or shame (e.g., associated with what a person misperceives as an abnormal fantasy), lack of sex knowledge (e.g., not understanding partner sexual responses), sexual behaviour patterns that inhibit sexual relations (e.g., lack of sufficient foreplay), relational issues associated with sharing intimacy or a sexual moment (e.g., permitting vulnerability, trusting), negative sexual self-image (e.g., a self-perception of not being sexually attractive), sexual identity barriers (e.g., a self-perception of having to be a passive recipient of sexual attention), or identity confusion (e.g., a lesbian trying to think, feel, and relate to others as if heterosexual). In addition the use and abuse of chemicals, or mental health problems, such as depression or mania (bipolar disorder), may have an impact on sexual attraction, interest, desire, arousal, and performance.

While everyone can benefit from some variety in intimacy and sexual expression, individuals or couples may experience much distress should disorders of sexual expression be developed or maintained. Among the problems in sexual functioning that clinical social workers may help address are severe hypoactive sexual desire or aversion, hyperactive sexual desire or sex addiction, erectile disorders, premature ejaculation, male/female orgasmic disorder, female arousal disorder, sexual pain disorders, and vaginismus. As well, social workers within mental health, correctional and family services may help address assessment, treatment, and control of sexual deviation (e.g., pedophilia, exhibitionism, voyeurism, frotteurism, sexual sadism, sexual masochism, zoophilia and bestiality, telephone scatophilia, and triolism). While these are variations in sexual expression, they have harmed or may cause risk or harm to the individual or others. Practitioners are trained to recognize that, whether defined as disordered or perverted, persons experiencing these expressions often present themselves as tortured souls— as do their victims, no matter how resilient.

Beyond direct clinical responsibility, social workers often enable development of self-help and mutual-aid opportunities to support persons facing significant challenges such as couple/marital infertility, the risk of sexual re-offending, coping with the harm of sexual abuse as a survivor of ritual abuse. Social workers also advocate for systemic social change (e.g., raising public awareness about female sex offending) and joining with others in collective social action (e.g., promoting the decriminalization of prostitution and other sex trade work for better regulation and protect

of workers, as is being attempted in Holland). Future social work policy, research, and intervention may focus on such less well understood concerns such as sibling incest, Internet pornography addiction, sexualized and sexually intrusive children, and sexual oppression and exploitation. The profession may also join growing global concerns about the sexual exploitation of children, youth, and animals.

[*M. Dennis Kimberley*]

RELATED ENTRIES

Child Sex Abuse, Clinical Social Work, Counselling, Direct Practice, Gay-Sensitive Services, Gender Issues, HIV/AIDS, Lesbian Services, Mutual-Aid Societies, Peer Counselling, Self-Help Groups, Self Help & Mutual Aid, Sensitizing Concepts, Services for Married People, Sexual Minorities, Theory & Practice, Therapy, Treatment, Torture & Trauma Victims, Vicarious Traumatization, Wellness, Women Abuse

single parents

A single parent is a person who is bringing up a child or children without a partner. The term gained currency in the 1960s unifying a variety of family situations which until then had been understood as different—for example, the death of one parent, the abandonment of the family by one partner, a birth out of wedlock, a divorce or separation. The proportion of single parent families has remained almost constant in Canada: in 1931, they represented 14 percent of all families and, in 1996, 15 percent; in the late 1950s widowhood was the status of the majority of single parents (60+%), while in 1996 only 20 percent of single parents were widowed. As of the 1970s, a majority of single parents were divorced or separated, a figure that reached 60 percent in 1996. Most commonly in Canada, single-parent families are composed of a mother and her children: in 1996, the proportion of female- to male-headed single-parent families was four to one; and one in every five Canadian children lived with a single parent. In 1996 about 16 percent of all Canadian children lived with their single mothers, in comparison to 3 percent with their single father (Canada 1996, 1984). Single-mother families invoke a complex set of social structures, values, and judgments fuelled by professional and scientific discourses. The predominant social perception of a family in affluent industrialized societies is still that it is headed by a male breadwinner financially responsible for his wife and their children; families that deviate from this conception are considered incomplete and problematic. This structure is conceived as the most effective unit for resource expenditure and results for society, and contemporary consumption requirements most often can only be fulfilled if a family has two incomes. Structural barriers to stable well paying jobs prevent most single-mother families from rising above poverty; most also experience housing difficulties. More than half of single-mother families report an annual household income of less than $20,000; as well as posing a burden on social spending, single mothers' poverty also significantly affects their children's academic, behavioural, and emotional situations as well as placing the health and adjustment of teens at risk.

Research evidence shows that as many as 40 percent of all Canadian women may experience single motherhood at some time in their lives (Desroisiers, le Bourdais, et Lehrhaupt 1994). Despite this fact, single motherhood is seen as a problem and, by some, as a moral issue. Teenage unwed mothers and young divorcees are pathologized, often being portrayed in the media as deviants. As well, single mothers, in certain arguments, pose a problem to the family as an institution, threatening this basic unit of society with breakdown and disorganization. Further, single motherhood has been used as one of the reasons to attack sex education, divorce laws, abortion, obscenity, homosexuality, and contraceptives. The search for a solution to single motherhood by those who perceive it as a problem in affluent societies has irrevocably linked women raising children alone to the system of welfare: women raising children alone should be supported to carry out their social reproduction functions adequately; but single motherhood should be socially discouraged through hardship to contain the numbers of those entering it and to limit the costs to the system. Over the last century, much attention has been focused on employability and training of single mothers; a mother who is the sole breadwinner, however, continues to have bleak prospects. In a weak position in the marketplace, single mothers find that both salaries and the number of high-level entry jobs are declining, as are the chances for improvement through train-

ing, individual mobility, or collective bargaining (Baker 1994). Despite the decreasing likelihood that a single mother can maintain her family through the marketplace, the rationalities for public support are increasingly being questioned. Although diverse, single mothers remain in the majority a disadvantaged group whose relative position has not improved significantly despite repeated social policy efforts to do so.

[Iara Lessa]

RELATED ENTRIES

Adoption, Bioethical Issues, Child Custody & Access, Family Demographics, Family: Non-traditional, Family Planning, Income Security, Parenting, Peer Counselling, Poverty, Pregnancy, Private Adoption, Separation & Divorce, Services for Women, Services for Youth, Toronto Infants Home, Wellness

REFERENCES

Baker, M. 1994. Family Poverty and Work/Family Conflicts: Inconsistencies of Social Policies. *Canadian Review of Social Policy* 33, 45–61.

Canada. 1984. Census. Ottawa: Statistics Canada.

———. 1996. Census. Ottawa: Statistics Canada.

Desroisiers, le Bourdais, et Lehrhaupt. 1994. *Vivre en famille mono Parentale et en famille recomposée: Portrait des Canadiennes d'hier et d'aujourd'hui.* Montreal, QC: Institut National de la Recherche Scientifique.

David Smith (1906–2000)

Smith, David, community development theorist and practitioner, adult educator; b. 1906, Hamilton, ON; d. 2000, Barrie, ON

David Smith was one of Canada's most accomplished practitioners, theorists, and exponents of the study-group method of community development. The role of the community practitioner, Smith believed, is to facilitate the learning process of small groups of citizens by releasing their potential for critical thinking and shared analysis of common problems and for taking action together to solve those problems. He believed that study-and-action groups could promote citizen-driven issues and hold all institutions—public, private, and non-profit alike—accountable for their policies and services. In fact, Smith saw this micro collective learning process as the key tool for protecting, enabling, and renewing democracy itself. David Smith's professional and intellectual output spanned five decades, beginning in the 1930s when Canada was an agrarian nation, and continuing to the global information age of the 1990s. His efforts helped to strengthen the organizational capacity of farmers, teachers, trade unionists, policy makers, social workers, librarians, aid officials, environmentalists, peace activists, community health advocates, and regional planners, among many others. In 1995 his collected writings were published as *First Person Plural: A Community Development Approach to Social Change*. Smith earned bachelor's and master's degrees in philosophy at the University of Toronto. After teaching at Regina College, Smith returned to Ontario in 1936, where he was appointed director of the Community Life Training Institute in Barrie. An experimental rural extension service sponsored by the University of Toronto and the Canadian Association for Adult Education, the institute worked with local leaders in Simcoe County to create hundreds of new rural organizations for marketing, production, social services, culture, and education—all generated through study-and-action groups. In 1946 Ontario elected a government that was hostile to the institute and Smith left; he was invited to become the first director of adult education in Saskatchewan's new Co-operative Commonwealth Federation government, which embarked on an activist agenda of social reform. In his new role, Smith mounted adult education programs in the schools and established a number of new institutions for residential adult education, human relations, acts, and public affairs, including, among many others, the Saskatchewan Arts Board. Smith served as adult education expert with UNESCO in Thailand (1953–58), where he advised on community development and teacher education programs, promoting a role for expatriate professionals as learners and facilitators, and the use of study groups in program evaluation. Returning to Barrie in 1959, he began working as an independent consultant on conferences, education, and training. During the 1960s and 1970s, he organized national conferences on a wide range of issues, including natural resources, pollution, ageing, problems in metropolitan centres, housing, and community health clinics. Smith's clients included the federal and provincial governments, the United Nations, and such non-

profit groups as the Quakers, who engaged him to run training institutes on non-violence; Smith employed the study-and-action group method in all of his consulting assignments. In the 1980s, as he phased out his professional work, he continued his interests in community health and, as a volunteer, in peace. With his partner, Mary Stevenson, Smith was instrumental in organizing a community health centre for seniors in Barrie, which opened in 1990. A prodigious correspondent with friends and colleagues, Smith frequently contributed critical letters to such publications of the political left as *Canadian Dimension, Canadian Forum*, and *Next-Year Country*. David Smith died in 2000 in Barrie, Ontario, the site of his earliest—and most recent—successful applications of the study-group method of community development.

[*Edward T. Jackson*]

RELATED ENTRIES

Community Development, Participatory Research

Goldwin Smith (1823–1910)

Smith, Goldwin, social work occupations; b. Aug. 13, 1823, Reading, Berks., UK; d. June 07, 1910, Toronto, ON

When Goldwin Smith arrived in Toronto in 1871, where he would live for the last forty years of his life, he was renowned as a classical scholar, historian, Victorian liberal, significant journalist, versatile author, and notable controversialist. During illustrious years in his Britain and at Cornell University in the United States, he wrote and lectured on the foremost issues of the time: colonial emancipation, extension of the franchise, socialism, religion and evolution, slavery, and the American Civil War. In Canada, writing as "The Bystander" in various media, including his own periodical, he engaged vigorously in Canadian affairs in community, provincial, and national spheres. While he raised the general level of public discourse, his attacks on the narrow partisanship of party politics and on the colonial mentality of some community leaders often made him a centre of controversy. Smith made his major contributions to social welfare locally in Toronto, where he made people aware that rapid industrial development and urban growth had brought social problems that required new preventive and remedial measures. He became a leader in a range of endeavours that included the National Conference of Charities and Corrections, the development of the Newsboys Home, the Industrial School for Boys, libraries, hospital boards, athletic clubs, the Toronto Women's Christian Association, and the Associated Charities of Toronto, of which he was a founder. Smith also made low-interest loans to persons buying their first home. Of notable importance was his advocacy of public welfare administration to meet the needs of the growing numbers of unemployed and homeless. When, in response to his strong advocacy, Toronto's city council finally appointed a welfare officer in 1893, Goldwin Smith paid the salary for the position for two years. His associated plea for the appointment of trained "visitors" for specific welfare duties was an early harbinger of professional social work. Goldwin Smith and his wife bequeathed their extensive grounds to the city of Toronto as a public park, and their home, the Grange, which had been an ideal base for their many contributions to community life, to the Toronto Public Library. Through many adaptations, the Grange carries the legacy of Goldwin Smith into the twenty-first century at the heart of the Art Gallery of Ontario and the Ontario College of Art and Design.

[*Richard Splane*]

RELATED ENTRIES

Associated Charities of Toronto, Church-Based Services, Non-governmental Organizations, Sectarian Social Services, Social Welfare History

social assistance

An important component of Canada's social security system, social assistance is a network of public programs intended to ensure a minimal level of income for all citizens. In contrast to universal programs (e.g., old age security) and insurance programs (e.g., employment insurance), social assistance is available only to those in financial need. It is considered to be the program of last resort, as applicants must have attempted to secure income from market and all other legitimate sources prior to applying. The first half of the twentieth century gave rise to many of Canada's major social programs. After many citizens served their country in the First World War, government pensions were demanded for mothers raising children on their own and for elderly peo-

ple. During the great depression of the 1930s, relief was demanded for the multitude of unemployed workers. A fundamental change had occurred in the dominant perspective regarding poverty causation: fault was then seen to be located in the economy rather than in the individual. Economists favoured solutions based on the ideas of John Maynard Keynes that advocated government intervention to correct the flaws of the unfettered market. The period between the Second World War and the 1970s was the golden age in the development of Canada's social security system. Universal programs were instituted, such as old age security and family allowance as well as such insurance programs as unemployment (now, employment) insurance and the Canada pension plan. Social assistance programs varied widely throughout the country until they were consolidated with the establishment of the Canada Assistance Plan, which provided the provinces with cost-shared funding and instituted nationwide standards for the provision of social assistance. In the early 1970s, retrenchment and cutbacks to social programs began amidst economic recession and heightened concern with government deficits and continued through the late twentieth century. Keynesian economic theories gave way to neo-liberal economic strategies, which favour a free market and minimal government intervention. In April 1996 the federal government replaced the Canada Assistance Plan with the Canada Health and Social Transfer to provide block funding to the provinces and territories without conditions or standards—other than a guarantee of Canadian's mobility rights—in social assistance provision. Evident in these historical developments is the transition from residual to institutional perspectives regarding social assistance. Dominant until the late nineteenth century, the residual perspective held that people should seek sustenance for survival through the family and the market and, only after these resources were exhausted, should they turn to the church, community, and charities. In contrast, the institutional perspective became increasingly preeminent through the twentieth century to 1970, espousing government acceptance of collective responsibility for adequate incomes for all citizens; it was the perspective underlying Leonard Marsh's recommendations for a comprehensive network of programs in his 1943 *Report on Social Security for Canada*. In the late twentieth century, the further transition characterized by erosion of the earlier programs to what has been identified as a post-institutional phase (Graham, Delaney, & Swift 2000: 21).

Jurisdictional arrangements for social assistance are grounded in Canadian constitutional arrangements, whereby the provinces have authority over social programs. This constitutional jurisdiction poses challenges should the federal government wish to develop nationwide programs and policies, as illustrated by the foiled first attempts to establish a federal unemployment insurance program, the resolution of which required an amendment to the Constitution Act, 1867. Responsibility for social assistance, however, has stayed with the provinces and has been extended to the territories, with levels of federal funding and delivery standards varying over time. Ontario, Manitoba, and the Northwest Territories, in turn, have delegated responsibility to municipalities for the delivery of short-term emergency assistance while retaining the legislative authority for eligibility criteria and decision-making power for benefit rates. Responsibility for social programs in Aboriginal communities differs as well. Eligibility criteria and levels of provision are central to current social assistance in Canada. Eligibility considerations include reasons for being in need and applicants' level of financial need. Reasons for being in need are stated as categories, such as lack of employment, family breakdown, and inability to work, and eligibility requirements or conditions are tied to these categories; for example, proof for someone applying in the reason category "employable, but unemployed" might include employment termination papers, and the eligibility requirement might include actively seeking employment. Similarly, a person with physical or intellectual challenges would have to provide a medical certificate that he/she is unable to work, and a single parent would usually be required to pursue child support. Level of financial need is assessed through a needs test that compares applicants' resources to allowable assets and income. Allowable assets vary with the applicants' category and province or territory; for example, employable persons in Nova Scotia and Manitoba are not allowed any liquid assets, while

disabled persons in five provinces are permitted $3,000 in assets. Allowable income is any amount that is less than the benefit level for the family unit and the calculation of income generally exempts tax credits and a portion of earnings, the latter in recognition of employment costs as well as being an employment incentive; in Ontario in 1998, for example, single individuals were allowed a basic exemption of $143 plus 25 percent of any additional earnings, and single parents were allowed a basic exemption of $275 plus 25 percent of additional earnings. Eligibility requirements include proof of assets and income as well as ongoing reporting of income (NCW 2000). Provisions under social assistance legislation include basic assistance and special assistance. Basic assistance is intended to meet regular expenses (e.g., shelter, utilities, food, clothing, and personal needs) and special assistance is available for some extraordinary needs (e.g., prescription drugs and dental care). Amounts for basic assistance vary from jurisdiction to jurisdiction as well as by such variables as family size, age of children, and applicant employability. As examples, the range and median annual incomes throughout Canada in 1998 are provided (NCW 2000) for the two most common categories of social assistance recipients: single employable people (56% of all cases) and single parents (29%) (CCSD 1998). These incomes include basic assistance plus other "income-tested" benefits provided through the tax system such as the federal child tax benefit, the goods and services tax credit, and provincial/ territorial tax credits. For a single employable person, the lowest rate of $1,323 was in Newfoundland, the highest rate of $8,101 was in the Yukon; and the median of $5,533 was midpoint between the rates in Prince Edward Island and Manitoba. For a single parent with a two-year-old child, the lowest rate of $11,088 was in Alberta, the highest rate of $18,967 was in the Northwest Territories, and the median of $12,588 was midpoint between the rates in Nova Scotia and Prince Edward Island. The high cost of living, owing to heating costs, resulted in the higher rates in the Yukon and the Northwest Territories (then including the land area that is now Nunavut). Lower rates cannot be explained by lower costs, however; the low rates in Newfoundland reflect severe cuts in 1996 to benefit levels for single employable persons, and the low rates in Alberta reflect the steady decline in benefit levels under the conservative provincial government. In 1996 approximately 10 percent of Canadians were receiving social assistance, which represented an annual expenditure of $13.7 billion (Clark 1998). However, the number of recipients has been declining in response to tightened eligibility requirements from 2.93 million in March 1996 to 2.27 million in March 1999, for example (NCW 2000).

The current reality of less generous social assistance provision in Canada is reflective of the global ascendance of neo-conservative philosophies and the accompanying pressures for neo-liberal economic policies. Ideologies emphasizing individual blame, rather than collective responsibility, foster more restrictive social programs. Restrictions to Canadian social assistance programs began in 1990 with a federal cap to limit expenditures under the Canada Assistance Plan, closely followed by provincial/territorial cutbacks through tighter eligibility criteria, lower benefit levels, and more stringent conditions. A prime example of tighter eligibility criteria is the change in several provinces so that single parents are no longer eligible for social assistance for the lack of a principle provider but, depending on the age of their children, are now considered to be employable. Another example relates to changes in allowable assets so that an owned residence is no longer an exempted asset and liens may be placed on recipient's homes. Scaling back of benefits for employable recipients occurred in all provinces and territories in the 1990s; most dramatically, Ontario in 1995 cut benefits by 21.6 percent to all recipients except elderly and disabled people. Reductions throughout the country deepened the poverty experienced by people living on social assistance. Single parents receiving social assistance in Alberta in 1998 had incomes that came within only 50 percent of Statistics Canada's low income cut-off poverty line and single employable people in Newfoundland received incomes that represented only 9 percent of these poverty lines (NCW 2000). More stringent conditions are evident in welfare-to-work programs (reviewed by Gorlick & Brethour 1998), where employment programs for social assistance recipients now emphasize the shortest route to employment and fewer long-term educational or supportive oppor-

tunities are available than in previous years. In many provinces, requirements mandating unpaid community participation for employable social assistance recipients, including single parents, have been introduced under workfare programs. In the absence of national standards, however, wide variance in specific rules is permissible and evident throughout the country; the single-parent exemption from seeking employment because of child-care responsibilities is dependent on the age of the youngest child—ranging from six months in Alberta to seven years in British Columbia. Overall, a punitive tone has become entrenched in social assistance programs. The national child tax benefit introduced in 1998 clawed back payments from social assistance recipients by all jurisdictions but Newfoundland and New Brunswick. Welfare snitch lines are now commonplace. International comparisons indicate that, despite global restructuring, many European countries have maintained more generous social programs than Canada; in relation to requirements, the Netherlands and Australia allow single mothers to care for their children at home. Canada spends more on social programs—of which social assistance is only a small portion—than the United States. However, at 12 percent of Gross Domestic Product excluding health expenditures in 1995, Canada falls well below the average of 16 percent for member countries of the Organisation of Economic Cooperation and Development (OECD 1999).

[*Linda Snyder*]

RELATED ENTRIES

Canada Assistance Plan, Church-Based Services, Great Depression (1930s), Employment Insurance, Employment Insurance Act, Family Allowance Act, Great Depression (1930s), Income Security, Marsh Report, Mother's Allowance, Mother's Allowance Commission, Poor Laws (UK), Poverty, Social Insurance Number, Social Policy, Social Planning, Social Security, Social Welfare, Social Welfare Context, Social Welfare History, Unemployment Assistance Program, Unemployment Insurance Act, Welfare, Welfare State, Workfare

REFERENCES

CCSD. 1998. *Estimates of Distribution of Social Assistance Cases and Recipients by Family Type*. Fact Sheet (March). Ottawa: Canadian Council on Social Development. Online at time of writing at <www.ccsd.ca>.

Clark, C. 1998. *Canada's Income Security Programs.* Ottawa: Canadian Council on Social Development.

Gorlick, C., and G. Brethour. 1998. *Welfare-to-Work Programs in Canada: An Overview.* Ottawa: Canadian Council on Social Development.

Graham, J., R. Delaney, and K. Swift. 2000. *Canadian Social Policy: An Introduction.* Toronto: Prentice Hall / Allyn and Bacon.

NCW. 1999. *Welfare Incomes 1997 and 1998.* Ottawa: National Council of Welfare. Online at time of writing at <www.ncwcnbes.net>.

OECD. 1999. The Battle against Exclusion. *Social Assistance in Canada and Switzerland.* Vol. 3. Paris: Organisation for Economic Cooperation and Development.

social development

Social development can be defined as "a process of planned social change designed to promote the well-being of the population as a whole in conjunction with a dynamic process of economic development" (Midgley 1995: 2). Several conceptual features are embodied in this definition. Social development is viewed as interdisciplinary; as progressive and interventionist in nature; as invoking a sense of process where growth and change are explicit; as inextricably linked to economic development; and as inclusive of various strategies for achieving its goals (Midgley 1995: 26–28). The 1995 World Summit on Social Development declared that: "Social development is inseparable from the cultural, ecological, economic, political and spiritual environment ... and is clearly linked to peace, freedom, stability and security both nationally and internationally" (Wilson & Whitmore 2000: 16). While not a dominant approach to social welfare in Canada, social development has become part of a growing debate in social work about approaches to social well-being since the demise of the welfare state. Unlike residual approaches to social welfare, the goals of social development focus on improving people's material conditions and building human capacities to achieve greater individual and collective self-reliance. In contrast to institutional approaches to social welfare, social development encourages grassroots and popular participation as major means for people to empower themselves and press for social policies and programs that meet their needs and promote their

rights. Social development as an approach to welfare gained currency among newly independent nations in Africa and Asia and, to a lesser extent in Latin America, following the Second World War. State intervention was favoured as a way to move so-called underdeveloped countries incrementally into modem industrial economies; many of these modernization schemes, as development theorists have pointed out, resulted in widespread dependency rather than national self-reliance. While some dependency-creating approaches were replaced by community development projects, the implementation tended to remain top-down and reliant on state intervention: "In response to criticisms that local communities were left out of the process of development, the United Nations, among others, returned to a 'community or popular participation' model, giving priority to community-based programs and citizen participation" (Wilson & Whitmore (2000: 132). In this context, social development is closely associated with community development, which can be viewed conceptually as the major approach for accomplishing social development goals. Popular participation that is organized by or with a community and directed toward macro change to meet the social needs of the population as a whole can be said to be engaged in social development.

[Suzanne Dudziak]

RELATED ENTRIES

Canadian Council on Social Development, Capacity Assessment, Citizen Participation, Community Development, Participatory Research, Social Policy & Practice, Social Welfare History, Theory & Practice, Wellness

REFERENCES

Midgley, J. 1995. *Social Development: The Developmental Perspective in Social Welfare.* Thousand Oaks, CA: Sage.

Wilson, M.G., and E. Whitmore. 2000. *Seeds of Fire: Social Development in an Era of Globalism,* Halifax, NS: Fernwood.

social gospel movement

The social gospel movement in Canada was part of a larger movement within the Protestant churches in Europe, England, and North America between the 1880s and the 1920s. Methodists spearheaded the Canadian movement, accompanied by Presbyterians, Anglicans, and other Protestant denominations. The social gospel movement was more a social than a theological or evangelical movement. Rather than a single coherent movement, it encompassed a diversity of active individuals and groups united by an emphasis on social justice. According to Canadian historian, Ramsay Cook (1985), social work in Canada was developed as a secular replacement for the social gospel movement. The Canadian social gospel movement took a distinct and sometimes more radical form than in the United States, particularly in the prairies, attributable to the rapid social change occurring in Canada at the turn of the century. The development of the prairies, characterized by the rise of industrialization, extensive immigration from Europe, and rapid urban growth, resulted in important changes in Canada's social as well as economic structures. Major social problems, related in particular related to labour, capital, immigration, and urbanization, included terrible working conditions, widespread unemployment, and housing and health problems. In response, the churches sought ways to help young ministers who were ill equipped to support parishioners experiencing these problems. Realizing that the wretched conditions of the urban poor were not caused by individual failings but, rather, by structural factors, activist church leaders collectively reinterpreted Christian teachings provide a framework for faith-based responses. Social gospel theology was characterized by sin and redemption in social rather than individualistic terms. The leading US theologian, Walter Rauschenbush, for instance, emphasized the notion of the kingdom of God on earth being called on to redeem society from social ills. This theology provided the underpinnings for the movement's social vision, which was based on a critique of capitalism and a focus on the problems of labourers. More radical social gospellers believed a complete restructuring of society was needed, especially a rejection of capitalism in favour of a kind of Christian socialism. As they continued to struggle with how to live out their faith in the social realm, social gospellers' strategies for change became more secularized and the main goals of the movement became political, economic, and social change. For a time, however, the movement remained strongly rooted in a faith-based motivation for many of its leaders and members.

Increasing secularization is partly demonstrated in the development of national councils to work for social change: in 1907, for example, the Moral and Social Reform Council was founded by Protestant churches to work collaboratively on social change goals. In 1914 this council changed its name to the Social Service Council of Canada to reflect an increasing shift to a more scientific base for change; it remained, however, firmly rooted in Christian principles with the churches remaining as key players. In 1918 the council launched the journal *Social Welfare*, and in 1925, the council was replaced by the Canadian Association of Social Workers. Community practice and the more radical forms of social work in Canada can trace important aspects of their heritage to the social gospel movement. Social gospellers founded many settlement houses, where community practice and group work often originated; settlement houses also influenced some of the early schools of social work. Further, the social gospel movement influenced early Canadian feminism and the Canadian political scene. The Co-operative Commonwealth Federation (est. 1932) was co-founded by prominent former social gospeller J.S. Woodsworth, and Tommy Douglas and David Lewis, early leaders of the party's replacement, the New Democratic Party, also had strong ties to the social gospel movement.

[*Silvia M. Straka*]

RELATED ENTRIES

Anti-oppressive Social Work, Canadian Association of Social Workers, Co-operative Commonwealth Federation, Church-Based Services, Great Depression (1930s), T.C. Douglas, Feminist Theory, League for Social Reconstruction, N. McClung, *My Neighbour,* Sectarian Social Services, Settlement House Movement, J.S. Woodsworth

REFERENCE

Cook, R. 1985. *The Regenerators: Social Criticism in Late Victorian English Canada.* Toronto: University of Toronto Press.

social insurance number

Created in 1964, the social insurance number (SIN) acts as a client account number for the administration of federal programs, such as, initially, the Canada pension plan, employment insurance, Canada student loans, and garnishment regulations under the Family Orders and Agreements Enforcement Assistance Act. Starting in 1967, the SIN was used for tax reporting purposes. The authority to collect, or request, and use the SIN is tied to specific legislation. For instance, for income-tax purposes, an employer can collect an employee's SIN to provide him/her with a record of employment and other information, as can provincial/territorial or municipal agencies that report financial assistance payments, and institutions (i.e., banks, credit unions, or caisses populaires) that pay interest. Many other types of organizations use the SIN as a client number; legislation does not exist restricting them from asking for it, but a person need not comply. To work in or receive government benefits in Canada, one must possess a social insurance number. To obtain one, a person must provide an original or true certified copy of a primary document that proves his/her identity and status in Canada. A temporary number is available for an individual permitted to work in Canada temporarily. As access to a social insurance number also provides access to a great deal of personal information stored within many federal computer systems, citizens are advised to keep their number private. More information about the social insurance number can be found online at <www.hrdc.gc.ca>.

[*Michael R. Woodford*]

RELATED ENTRIES
Personal Social Services, Social Assistance

social justice

The 1991 edition of the *Social Work Dictionary* defines social justice as "an ideal condition in which all members of a society have the same basic rights, protections, opportunities, obligations, and social benefits." Advocates for social justice in essence view social problems, exploitation, oppression, and violence as products of systemic inequities; these inequities create social arrangements and conditions that promote the potential development of one group of people at the expense of others, that elevate the human potential of one group of people over others, and/ or that deny the human potential of one or more groups of people (Delaney 1995). Achieving a social

climate that can support the ideals of social justice requires a major shift from social values and ideologies that espouse political, social, and economic inequity, domination, possessive individualism, selfishness, competition, separation, hierarchy, private property, disregard for community and environment, and power-over thinking to social values and ideologies that reflect equality, co-operation, community, connection, individuality, mutuality, commonality and power-with thinking (Delaney 1995). The Canadian Association of Social Workers code of ethics clearly states that social workers are to promote social justice, and advocate for equal distribution of resources and for equal access of all persons to resources, services, and opportunities. For social workers and social justice advocates, supporting equality recognizes the shared journey of all humans to fulfil their potential to become more fully human and that human potential cannot be fulfilled if its fulfilment restricts or denies any other human being's opportunity for fulfilment (Delaney 1995).

In Canada, efforts to achieve social justice have focused on issues of equality and rights. Powerful coalitions formed by social justice advocates managed to achieve agreement on a society governed by equality of general rules (i.e., laws apply to all citizens equally), equality of civil rights (i.e., guarantees of individual liberty and equality before the law), and equality of political rights (i.e., right to vote and seek political office). Guided by the foundation work of the Montpetit Commission in the 1930s and the Rowell-Sirois Commission, Marsh's *Report on Social Security*, and the United Nations Universal Declaration of Human Rights in the 1940s, Canada's federal, provincial, and territorial governments began enacting progressive social legislation reflecting a growing commitment to social justice. Issues associated with equality of outcome are essentially concerned with distributive justice, that is, with the allocation of such resources as wealth, housing, and health care (Reamer 1993). Equality of opportunity, however, has had a greater impact on Canadian social policy than equality of outcome; for example, former prime minister Pierre Trudeau viewed equality of opportunity as the cornerstone for a just society rather than "the procrustean kind of equality where everyone is raised or lowered to a kind of middle ground" (1990: 358). For Trudeau, a just society had to ensure equality of French with English, and equality of economic opportunity regardless of where one lived. Not surprisingly, Trudeau's vision is reflected in the 1982 Canadian Charter of Rights and Freedoms, to which he was committed; while granting all Canadians protections against unfair discrimination, the Charter does not include economic or social rights (Mishra 1995), such as the right to a decent-paying job, the right to adequate housing, or the right to social assistance. Further, Canada's commitment to distributive justice has slowly become eroded since the 1980s. In 1995–96 the federal government departed from the goals of economic opportunity and income redistribution when it replaced the 1967 Canada Assistance Plan with the Canada Health and Social Transfer. In 1999 the Centre for Social Justice reported that, between 1973 and 1996, middle-income Canadians dropped from comprising 60 percent of the population to 40 percent, and the richest 10 percent of families increased their income from 9 times to 229 times that of the poorest 10 percent. Child poverty rates have been increasing, unemployment and underemployment rates remain high, cuts to social assistance programs are increasing, and employment insurance usage is decreasing (88% of unemployed workers in 1990 to 43% in 1997 [NCW 1997]). Canada has slowly been losing its standing as a compassionate country and has received criticism from the United Nations to that effect in 1998 and 1999. Social work's values promote the notion that, when social justice prevails, both society and its citizens benefit from the participation of citizens in the social order (DuBois & Miley 1996). This commitment to social justice places social workers in conflict with the goals of corporatism that advocate for a social and economic world dominated by corporations and their needs, thereby reducing people "to the status of a subject at the foot of the throne of the marketplace" (Saul 1995: 80). Social work's commitment to social justice as the basis for a social transformation that can restore hope and possibility in an age of cynicism and despair reflects social work's role in a real world as well as its moral responsibility to influence that world based on the principles and knowledge that inform the profession.

[Roger Delaney]

RELATED ENTRIES

Anti-oppressive Social Work, K. Belanger, E.H. Blois, Citizen Participation, T.C. Douglas, J. Gandy, J.T. Harris, W. Head, D.G. Hill, J.J. Kelso, Knowledge Base, League for Social Reconstruction, R. Leger, Marsh Report, N. McClung, A. Macphail, E. Murphy, Nongovernmental Organizations, Rowell-Sirois Commission, Social Gospel Movement, Social Planning, Social Welfare History, Social Work Profession, B. Touzel

REFERENCES

Delaney, R. 1995. The Philosophical Base. In J.C. Turner and F.J. Turner (Eds.) *Canadian Social Welfare*, 12–27. 3rd ed. Toronto: Allyn and Bacon.

DuBois, B., and K. Miley. 1996. *Social Work: An Empowering Profession*. 2nd ed. Toronto: Allyn and Bacon.

Mishra, R. 1995. The Political Bases of Canadian Social Welfare. In J.C. Turner and F.J. Turner (Eds.) *Canadian Social Welfare*. 59–74. 3rd ed. Toronto: Allyn and Bacon.

NCW 1997. *Another Look at Welfare Reform*. Ottawa: National Council on Welfare.

Reamer, F. 1993. *The Philosophical Foundations of Social Welfare*. New York: Columbia University Press.

Saul, J.R. 1995. *The Unconscious Society*. Concord, ON: Anansi.

Trudeau, P.E. 1990. The Values of a Just Society. In T. Axworthy and P.E. Trudeau (Eds.) *Towards a Just Society*. 357–85. Markham, ON: Viking.

social network

In Canadian social work usage, the term "social network" has to a great extent replaced the term "welfare state," used over the past several decades to denote countries or political systems with highly developed and comprehensive social welfare structures. Social network has emerged as a more politically neutral term stemming from the observation that all countries, regardless of their political system, have some structures for providing some welfare services and benefits to some of its citizens, even countries that sought to deny that such services existed on grounds that they are capitalist democratic structures. All societies recognize the need for some type of social network to respond to citizens' needs. Services vary among and within countries, depending on the priority accorded such needs, given the inherent history, cultural and political values, and traditions. In Canada where much of the health and social service structure is deemed to be the responsibility of provinces and territories, considerable variance in social networks is noted among jurisdictions. As social work has become more aware of the variations between and within countries, researchers and advocates have expressed considerable interest and study aimed at ascertaining the differential effectiveness of differing approaches to the provision of social welfare services, the variables that influence and create such differences, and factors of comprehensiveness and economy.

[FJT]

RELATED ENTRIES

Capacity Assessment, Citizen Participation, Community Development, Community Organization, Integration of Services, Natural Helping Networks, Networks, Peer Counselling, Personal Social Services, Self-Help Groups, Self Help & Mutual Aid, Social Development, Social Policy & Practice, Social Welfare State, Systems Theory, Theory & Practice, Wellness

social planning

Social planning emerged as a field of practice in social work in the early twentieth century from the need to co-ordinate services, set standards, and improve working relationships among the plethora of agencies responding to human service needs that arose during and following the First World War and the great depression of 1930s. The activities of social planning are inextricably linked with the auspices under which it takes place. In its earliest days, social planning was largely concerned with information sharing, service co-ordination, and attempts to address new areas of social problems. Social workers have, from time to time, played key roles in senior government circles and championed the recommendations of social workers and social planning councils at grassroots levels. The enactment of the Canada Assistance Plan in the 1960s is but one example of this dynamic. The aspirations of social planners have often been much higher than the level of resources available to them to pursue their efforts; a consequence is that, often, they have prepared plans, proposals, and models that remained unexecuted.

Some of the best efforts in social planning have depended on moral suasion to be effective, since the authority and funding to carry out recommendations have not accompanied them. The lack of ongoing funding and mandate have been perennial concerns, especially for some of the smaller social planning organizations. The scope of social planning has greatly broadened over the years. One widely recognized model was developed in Ontario during the 1990s by a local social planning council and later endorsed by a provincial network of social planning councils (Halton Social Planning Council & Volunteer Centre 2000). This model sees social planning's purpose as two-fold: fostering social development for community well-being and living conditions, and encouraging social change. The values of social planning councils encompass community, voluntarism, diversity, equity, and social justice. Operating principles are independent from the public sector and funders, community accountability through volunteer elected boards of directors, action-based research and experience, citizen participation, inclusiveness and promotion of diversity, empowerment (in particular, community leadership building), and integrated comprehensive perspective. This model's list of strategies, roles, and functions shows how far social planning has come since the rudimentary efforts of the early twentieth century. The list contains research on trends, needs and issues; policy analysis and development; convening people and facilitating discussion of issues; building partnerships and collaboration among disparate community groups; building community awareness of social issues; developing needed services, fostering community development and undertaking advocacy and social action to promote specific changes, especially in government policy.

The mechanism under which social planning is carried on has traditionally been the social planning council. In the earliest days, these organizations were often known as welfare councils. In the latter part of the twentieth century, the word "welfare" has been replaced by the words "social development" as officials sought to put a more positive face on their work and depart from old remedial notions. Social planning councils began as associations of social agencies operating on a voluntary basis without mandate. Their role was to study human need and suggest appropriate responses. Their research findings were often useful to funding bodies, such as governments or United Ways, which needed data on which to base funding decisions. This function remains an important one. Over the years social planning councils have grown in sophistication, both in term of the activities they undertake and the people they involve in their work. Board members of social planning councils now include individuals from all walks of life from the corporate sector and local government to social assistance recipients and agency professionals. The most successful social planning councils are usually located in larger communities and receive funding from local donations, fees paid by individuals or agencies, United Ways, and governments at one or more levels to cover basic costs. In addition many are recipients of special project funding to carry out commissioned research. In smaller communities, social planning councils have struggled to maintain themselves as funding sources have become more stringent. Some Canadian cities have their own social planning departments, which focus on planning for municipal services. Some provinces have provincial social planning councils. The Ontario Social Development Council, for example, was founded in 1909. It focuses on issues at the provincial level and offers local social planning bodies a forum for sharing their work and contributing to the provincial perspective. At the national level, the Canadian Council on Social Development (est. 1971; originally the Canadian Welfare Council) undertakes a wide variety of research projects and issues regular publications containing information on a wide range of social issues.

[*Gary D. Davies*]

RELATED ENTRIES

W.H. Beveridge, J. Gandy, Capacity Assessment, Community Development, Community Organization, L. Marsh, Social Policy Making, Social Policy & Practice, Theory & Practice

REFERENCES

Halton Social Planning Council and Volunteer Centre. 2000. *Independent Community-Based Social Planning in the Voluntary Sector*. Online at time of writing at <www.worldchat.com>.

Social Planning for Canada

Social Planning for Canada was a volume published in 1935 by the League for Social Reconstruction (est. 1932). The league gave voice to intellectuals who were critical of capitalism and sympathetic to fundamental social reforms that could alleviate the worst effects of the great depression of the 1930s (Bellamy & Irving 1986: 44). This book laid out a plan of reform to deal with the broad range of societal problems produced by the depression. It led to further publications, which in turn strongly influenced the emergence of an unemployment relief program for Canada.

[*FJT*]

RELATED ENTRIES

Great Depression (1930s), League for Social Reconstruction, Social Welfare Context, Social Welfare History, Unemployment Assistance Program, Unemployment Insurance Act

REFERENCE

Bellamy, D., and H. Irving. 1986. Canadian Social Welfare. In J.C. Turner and Francis J. Turner (Eds.) *Canadian Social Welfare* 2nd ed. Toronto: Collier-McMillan

social policy

The foundation for a strong and distinctive Canadian social policy is in the 1940 report of the Rowell-Sirois Commission on dominion-provincial relations. From Confederation in 1867 to the 1930s, Canada had developed social services similar to those that existed in Britain and in the United States but this royal commission made the existence of these services and equity of access to them a Canadian imperative (Canada 1940: 2, 128). This initiative launched Canada on a path along which social policy has served to define major differences in social security, health, and cultural policy between Canada and the United States, and on which Canadian social policy is widely seen as essential to national unity and identity. Social policy in Canada is a broad term; included within its boundaries are social welfare policy measures including income security and child welfare, health policy and programs, educational policy and programs, ethnic and cultural identity policies, and marriage, divorce, sexual orientation, and other personal relationship policies. Social policy is also influenced by—and influences decisions in—such other major policy fields as economic policy, tax policy, labour policy, housing policy, foreign affairs, and criminal law. Social policy refers principally to the actions of federal, provincial/territorial, and municipal governments, as established through social policy objectives. Some of these objectives are reactive: the field of income security measures (i.e., social assistance, employment insurance, workers compensation, pensions), for instance, is a reaction to the income inequalities and instabilities that are inherent capitalist economies. Other forms of social policy are proactive: municipal social planning provides one example, while another and different example is Aboriginal assimilation policies attempted through the Indian Act. The formal activities of Canadian governments are not the only source of social policy; sometimes social policy has been implicit in the assumptions that are made about people's interrelationships, and explicit only when those assumptions are challenged; an example would be the mid-century assumption that men would be the principal wage earners in each family household and that a bias in social policy toward ensuring male head of household employment was normal. Whether a social policy is right or wrong is a matter for judgment. Frequently, social policy perspectives change over time and in different contexts: during the twentieth century, Canadians have seen major changes in social policy toward women, Aboriginal peoples, gays and lesbians, visible minorities, and persons with physical and developmental disabilities. From these examples, it is only reasonable to conclude that social policy is constantly changing and is a reflection of contemporary community values and public awareness. It is also reasonable to conclude that present policies will seem as outdated by the end of the twentieth-first century as the policies of the early twentieth century appear in today's contexts.

Changes to formal social policy is a function of the Canadian state, which includes all internal levels of government, the courts, human rights commissions and similar bodies, and the administrative organizations and agencies through which Canadians receive social benefits and human services. Sometimes these administrative organizations take the form of government ministries and agencies but just as often they take the form of non-profit and co-operative organizations, which operate with the sanction and often financial support of the state. Change takes place through highly visible formal processes. as when governments pass legislation or courts and tribunals make rulings, as well as through largely invisible measures of accommodation and change, as when administrative polices are modified and new non-profit agencies are formed to meet unanticipated social conditions. While most Canadian social policy is produced within the Canadian state, increasing concerns have been raised that international agreements, such as the North American Free Trade Agreement, could lead to restrictions on the ability of the Canadian state to have independent and distinctive social policies (Courchene 1994: 4). This concern is linked to the concern that social policy is becoming subservient to economic and trade policy, a change that some see as a necessity (Courchene 1994: 317*ff.*), while others reject it as a surrender of fundamental Canadian interests (Clarke 1996: 71*ff.*). The concept of "Canadian social policy" suggests a single unified entity that Canadians experience in a similar way. The truth is much more complex, as the distinct differences exist from the historical experiences of, for example, Aboriginal peoples, French and English colonists, immigrants from Europe and elsewhere, and refugees. There are also major differences in experience owing to geography, gender, cultural and ethnic origins, and sexual orientation. A major challenge for Canadian social policy is how to recognize, respect, and support these differences rather than to submerge them within common and dominating policies and institutions (Armitage 22–24, 124–29). As social policy affects all aspects of collective life, social workers are immersed in social policy every day of their working lives. Sometimes social workers are the enforcers of social policy, as when they establish benefit entitlements or investigate allegations of abuse; sometimes they challenge existing forms of policy and develop new ones, as when workers advocate for clients and develop new agencies or programs. Quite often, social workers will be found doing all these things at the same time. Although social work can claim no special power in making social policy, it has a proud history of being a weather vane indicating where policy was needed. Social work has also been an important source of ideas that have been incorporated into formal social policy.

[*Andrew Armitage*]

RELATED ENTRIES

Caledon Institute on Social Policy, Research, Rowell-Sirois Commission, Social Planning, Social Policy Making, Social Policy & Practice, Social Welfare Context, Social Welfare History, Social Work Profession, Wellness

REFERENCES

Armitage, A. 1996. *Social Welfare in Canada Revisited: Facing Up to the Future.* Toronto: Oxford University Press.

Canada. 1940. *The Report of the Royal Commission on Dominion-Provincial Relationships.* [Rowell-Sirois Commission] Toronto: Ryerson.

Clarke, T. 1997. *Silent Coup.* Ottawa: Canadian Centre for Policy Alternatives; Toronto: James Lorimer.

Courchene, T. 1994. *Social Canada in the Millennium.* Toronto: C.D. Howe Institute.

social policy making

Social work exists within a context of diverse social policies, and most public and private human services—e.g., health care, family services, economic programs, and education—operate within this social policy framework. These services may be seen as "purposeful social units; that is, they are deliberately constructed to achieve certain goals or to perform tasks and conduct programs that might not be as effectively or efficiently performed by individuals or informal groups" (Lauffer 1984: 14). Public and private agencies have policies about services to be provided, eligibility for services, and fees to be charged (Gambrill 1997: 26); in turn, public and private service programs and procedures are influenced by federal, provincial/territorial, and municipal policies. The nature of social policies and the impetus for services within affluent welfare states can be classified into functionalist, conflict, and class conflict views of society (George & Wilding 1985: 1–18). The functionalist view of society considers social services as a societal subsystem whose function is to assist the orderly operation of the entire society; from this perspective, the main task of social services is to promote social integration and acceptance of society's basic values either through prevention or treatment, and social policy is thereby seen as

non-political and non-ideological. The conflict view of society considers social services as the results of compromises in the resolution of conflicts between different segments of society with differing interests (i.e., classes, special interest groups, and political parties). These compromises result in unstable situations, continually open to change and dependent on unequal power distribution among these different societal interests; from this perspective, social policy—whether brought about by policy activism, by pressure from special interest groups, or by the election of a political party to introduce particular policies—will reflect the results of societal conflict. The class conflict view of society, which also considers that social services results from conflict in society, sees the main conflict as between the owning class and the working class; from this perspective, social services help to maintain the relative stability of society through coercion, economic dependence of workers on paid employment, and legitimization of values that are claimed as society-wide but in fact reflect and serve the owning class. Examples of these values include a work ethic toward paid employment, support for the market system, primacy of the nuclear family, and approval for military nationalism. As such, social policy is seen as designed to serve the needs of the dominant class in society, which requires a politically stable, healthy and educated work force. To be effective, social workers in the policy field need to be sensitive to the differing values evident within segments of society that hold varying perceptions of policies.

[*Garson Hunter*]

RELATED ENTRIES

Organizational Theory, Social Policy, Social Policy & Practice, Theory & Practice

REFERENCES

Gambrill, E. 1997. *Social Work Practice: A Critical Thinker's Guide.* New York: Oxford University Press.

George, V., and P. Wilding. 1985. *Ideology and Social Welfare.* London: Routledge.

Lauffer, A. 1984. *Understanding Your Social Agency.* Beverly Hills, CA: Sage.

social policy and practice

Social policy and social practice are intrinsically interconnected, and social workers are involved everywhere along the continuum that encompasses both. Social policies range in level and scope, which includes grand and ordinary issues: "The grand issues include the distribution of income and wealth, the distribution of political power and corporate prerogatives" (Lindblom 1979: 523). Grand issues at one end of the continuum are the concern of international organizations, national governments, and, in recent years, multinational corporations and the World Trade Organization. Ordinary social policy issues are those that affect people in their day-to-day lives, including health and social service programs and planning for the orderly development of communities. Ordinary issues, and the making of social policies by provincial governments and social agencies, are the primary concern of most social workers. As such, the optimum style of policy making includes practitioners, users of services, and other citizens. Social policies in Canada exist at the national, provincial/territorial, region and community, and agency levels. The federal government sets policies in matters such as employment, taxation, and income security and national standards for health care and environmental regulation. Provincial/territorial governments have responsibility for administering health care and child welfare, among other social services. Regional or county councils may manage responsibilities within their area and help to co-ordinate social policy making and implementation in communities; social policies in predominantly rural areas, for instance, may differ from those for a large city surrounded by suburbs. Social agencies, even at the neighbourhood level, also make policies, and practitioners are likely to be most involved in policy making at this level.

Policies are expressed in the form of legislation and of statements or directives by social agencies. Whereas policy is concerned about what is to be done in general, practice in social work refers to the specific work carried out with individuals, groups, dyads, or communities. Social policy making can be viewed as the choosing of courses of action in situations where many options or approaches could be selected, and where the final choice is heavily influenced by the values of those who make policy; thus, policy makers holding conservative values may be convinced that social welfare programs create dependency and should be provided only in situations of dire need and

for short periods of time, whereas, policy makers of a social democratic persuasion may view social programs as basic necessities that are required by many people when roles and circumstances change. Regardless of the level or scope of the policy, the policy-making process is typically characterized by clashes in values. The present approach to policy making means that, typically, elected individuals and senior managers at the apex of organizations, including governments, make the final choices and the approaches to implementation. Depending on the organization, the experience and knowledge of direct service practitioners and people who use services is rarely considered; therefore, policies are frequently developed in the absence of this very important information. Yet once enacted, the translation of policy to practice places responsibility on practitioners who implement social policies. Implementation may be relatively smooth when practitioners welcome the introduction of new policies that are helpful to their practice and provide new benefits to clients. Policies may be ignored or sabotaged, however, should practitioners see them as unnecessary, limiting worker discretion to make professional judgments, imposing increased work demands, or ignoring some client communities.

A more positive style of policy making on both philosophical and practical grounds would be inclusive. The philosophical rationale for inclusive social policy making is based on the principle of affected interests—that is, that citizens have a right to participate in matters that affect them. This rationale is supported by the work of such scholars as Marshall (1997), Drover (2000), and Kingwell (2000) who argue that citizens are entitled to benefits from the society in which they live and to play a role in shaping policies. An active and participatory role for citizens has been achieved in a very incomplete fashion in Canada, where citizen participation in social policy making is largely restricted to the "well off, the well spoken, and the well educated" (Wharf Higgins 1999: 293). People who receive services from health and social service agencies are conspicuous by their absence from policy making. The pragmatic argument for an inclusive style insists that the absence of service users and direct service practitioners is a major reason for many of the problems apparent in much social policy, in particular the failure to address adequately the needs of service users and the concerns of practitioners. An inclusive approach to policy making could begin to address these shortcomings in at least these three ways:

- Policy action groups could be established in provincial/territorial ministries and social welfare organizations. These groups might consist of representatives from throughout the organization, including service users, and could be assigned the responsibility for reviewing existing policies and suggesting revisions or new policies.
- Policy communities could be created to bring together individuals from the public and private sectors to comment on existing policies and suggest new directions. At the federal level, for example, representatives from Human Resources and Development Canada, the Canadian Labour Congress, the Canadian Council on Social Development, and the Caledon Institute on Social Policy might meet on a regular basis to consider issues relating to employment, taxation, and income security. Similarly, at the provincial/territorial level, policies in child welfare, day care, and other personal service programs could be improved by establishing policy communities that include the voices of social workers and service users.
- A complementary strategy would be to reorganize large and complex social welfare organizations such as provincial/territorial departments, into smaller community-based agencies, funded by the state. Organizations with a low level of bureaucratization can help promote an exchange of ideas and information between policy makers, practitioners, and users of service.

The right of service users to self-determination has been a cardinal social work value since the early days of the profession. Given this value, it would seem to be incumbent on social workers to advocate for inclusive approaches to social policy making within their own agencies and in broader policy-making arena.

[*Brad McKenzie* and *Brian Wharf*]

RELATED ENTRIES

Case Management, Citizen Participation, Community Development, Community Organization, Interprofessional Issues, Professional Issues, Social Planning, Social Policy, Social Policy Making, Social Work Profession, Theory & Practice

REFERENCES

Drover, G. 2000. Redefining Citizenship in a Global Era. *Social Work and Globalization*. Special Issue 29–49.

Kingwell, M. 2000. *The World We Want: Virtue, Vice and the Good Citizen*. Toronto: Viking.

Lindblom, C. 1979. Still Muddling, Not Yet Through. *Public Administration Review* 39, 6, 517–26.

Marshall, T.H. 1977. *Class, Citizenship and Social Development*. Chicago: University of Chicago Press.

Wharf Higgins, J. 1999. Citizenship and Empowerment: A Remedy for Citizen Participation in Health Reform. *Community Development Journal* 34, 4, 287–307.

social security

Social security is a term whose definition varies from one author and one country to another. American definitions, in contrast, harken from 1930s New Deal legislation and tend to be restricted to particular forms of income security or more narrowly, social insurance. William Beveridge, a principal architect of the UK welfare state that emerged after the Second World War referred to a Ministry of Social Security that could be responsible for all national and local systems of social insurance and national and voluntary assistance (Beveridge 1943: 72). Andrew Armitage claims a broader Canadian usage, defining social security as "income programs plus social services" (1996: 193). Social services as an expansive term covers the provision of such non-income services as day care, adoption, protection, or probation; income programs provide entitlement—usually as cash—to protect against such risks of life as poor health, unemployment, dependency, disability, old age, or death or injury of a wage earner. Canadian income security programs comprise three types: income- or means-test, social insurance, and universal (Ross, Scott and Smith 2001: 128). Income- or means-test programs are provided to individuals or families whose incomes fall below a set threshold—that is, they meet an eligibility requirement; examples include social assistance, guaranteed income supplements, spouse's allowances, and child tax credit benefits. Social insurance programs are based on contributions from workplace earnings, with benefits and premiums rising with a worker's earnings up to a defined income ceiling; examples include the employment insurance program and Canada and Quebec pension plans. Universal programs are payments made to all people within a specific category, such as being over or under a certain age (i.e., children, senior citizens); examples are the family allowance (1944–42) and old age security (1951–). Dramatic changes started to be made to universal programs in the 1990s. A selective child tax credit benefit replaced the family allowance in 1992. In 1989 the tax system started to claw back old age security so that a growing number of higher- and middle-income earners received partial or no benefits, calling into question whether the program could any longer be described as universal. Social security programs came to the fore in Canada in the twentieth century as part of the broader emergence of a welfare state. Their roots extend from European contact. In New France, the Catholic Church had the responsibility for caring for the elderly, sick, and orphaned; in Nova Scotia and New Brunswick, an English Poor Law assigned care of the poor to local jurisdictions, while in other provinces with no Poor Law, such as Ontario, voluntary charities became especially important. Social assistance—called unemployment relief up to and including the great depression of 1930s—has important municipal and local roots. Under the Canadian constitution, social welfare is a provincial responsibility. In times of dire economic circumstances in the first half of the twentieth century, major income security programs were developed by both federal and provincial governments, including workers' compensation (1914 first in Ontario), mother's allowances (1916 first in Manitoba), old age security (1927 as federal/provincial cost-shared and selective), unemployment insurance (1940, federal program, now called employment insurance), family allowance (1944, federal), and old age security as a universal program (1951, federal).

Various programs grew further in the period of welfare state expansion, such as the Canada and Quebec pension plans (est. 1966), guaranteed income supplements for pension plan recipients (1967), and old age security spouse's allowance (1975). In 1971 unemployment insurance was extended to previously excluded workers, such as those in the fishing industry, and to include sick-

ness and maternity leave. Most importantly, the Canada Assistance Plan (1966–96) was developed to provide a stable source of federal transfer payments to the provinces to cost-share provincial delivery of health, education, and social services; gradually reduced in scope beginning in the mid-1970s, the plan was replaced in 1996 by the less robust Canada Health and Social Transfer in an era in which federal government standards were being eroded. Significantly, the tax system has also become increasingly a modest instrument for income redistribution through various credits and benefits. From the mid-1970s, and with accelerated impact in the late 1980s and 1990s, income security programs were radically transformed. Social program budgets were reduced relative to inflation and population growth and, in many instances, in absolute terms. Federal government transfers to the provinces and territories did not keep up with inflation. Severe cutbacks occurred in employment insurance, social assistance, and workers' compensation, among other programs, occasioning reduced levels of entitlement, restricted access, and restricted program arrangements. Family allowances were eliminated. Universality is now all but dead, as a liberal ideology and the political economy of globalization have become exceptionally influential. In the 1980s, food banks started to appear and were abundant by the 1990s. Child poverty is now especially pronounced. Privatized social service, community care, and the marketplace are being trumpeted as increasingly important to social policy. The ability of social security programs to respond effectively to social problems appears, to many observers, to be commensurately imperiled.

[*John R. Graham*]

RELATED ENTRIES

W.H. Beveridge, Church-Based Services, Family Allowance Act, Income Security, Mother's Allowance, Mother's Allowance Commission, Personal Social Services, Poor Laws (UK), Poverty, Sectarian Social Assistance, Social Planning, Social Policy, Social Services, Social Welfare History, Unemployment Assistance Program, Unemployment Insurance Act, Welfare State, Workfare

REFERENCES

Armitage, A. 1996. *Social Welfare in Canada Revisited: Facing Up to the Future*. Toronto: Oxford University Press.

Ross, D.P., K.J. Scott, and P.J. Smith. 2001. *The Canadian Fact Book on Poverty, 2000*. Ottawa: Canadian Council on Social Development.

social services

Social services in Canada refers to the network of voluntary and publicly sponsored agencies, institutions, programs, and services that exist for the purpose of providing a broad range of psychosocial assistance to individuals, families, and groups. Social welfare in Canada has a complex structure, offering within it a broad spectrum of services. The means by which social services are structured and financed are just as complex and diverse: for instance, funding through foundations, churches, benevolent organizations, private enterprises, and complex arrangements of government support (e.g., direct grants, transfers of public funds, and direct provision of services). Included in the concept of social services are social security and social assistance. While there is a tendency to include as social services only those that provide some type of concrete assistance—either through direct payments or payments in kind, such as clothing, food or housing—social services also encompasses many non-financial services such as counselling and various forms of psychosocial therapy. In recent decades, with increasing fiscal pressures, many social service agencies have debated the possibilities of charging clients fees or of having certain services provided through insurance plans—neither of which appeal to social services agencies that adhere to the conventional approach of helping people freely, as an extension of charitable works. Their overall goal for offering services is to enhance the psychosocial well-being of clients in the best possible way; and the provision of social work treatment through a fee-for-service system is not technically outside the purview of social services. Another area where distinctions are unclear relates to social services linked to health issues. The line between some forms of rehabilitation services, counselling services, various aspects of after care or personal and family adjustment to physical conditions clearly fall into a grey area between social services and health care. The formal distinction between such services rests for the most part with the funding and sponsorship of the service in a particular location; thus, a service in one situation might be designated as a social service where a similar service elsewhere could be designated as health care. This distinction is most imprecise in regard to services for persons with mental illnesses who are discharged from health care facilities: many follow-up services are provided by the social service network but are funded by health care funding sources. The distinction between health care and social services becomes further blurred in government structures; until recently, the federal government ministry for these areas was the Department of Health and Welfare. As the movement to more holistic approaches to health, growth, and strength from a biopsychosocial perspective increases in importance, the division between health care and social services may disappear.

[*FJT*]

RELATED ENTRIES

Aboriginal Services, Biopsychosocial Theory, Church-Based Services, Clinical Social Work, Community Service, Crisis Intervention, Ethnocultural Communities' Services, Gay-Sensitive Services, Integration of Services, Jewish Social Services, Health Canada, Lesbian Services, Non-clinical Practice, Non-governmental Organizations, Personal Social Services, Psychosocial Theory, Sectarian Social Services, Sexual Problems & Services, Services for Children, Services for Elderly People, Services for Families, Services for Married People, Services for Offenders, Services for Physically Challenged People, Services for Refugees, Services for Women, Services for Youth, Social Policy Making, Therapy, Theory & Practice, Wellness, Workfare

social services workers

Social services workers are usually graduates of two-year diploma programs in social services work offered by community colleges; they may also hold an undergraduate university degree in a related discipline. In some cases, previous experience working in a human services environment in a volunteer capacity may replace the formal necessity of a diploma or degree. The social service worker designation has been formalized in some provinces through the establishment of professional colleges (e.g., the Ontario College of Social Workers and Social Services Workers). To use an ssw designation after their names, social services workers in these provinces must be registered with their respective colleges. In 1998 Human Resources Development Canada, noted that 75,000 people were employed as community and social services workers, an increase of 76.7 percent from 1988. These are professions where 81 percent of workers are women. Government spending restraints in health and social services have affected these workers negatively in the last few years. In 2000, Human Resources Development Canada noted that 95 percent of social services workers are aged fifteen to fifty-four, with only 5 percent falling among people aged fifty-five and over; 33 percent are aged fifteen to twenty-nine; and 31 percent are aged thirty to thirty-nine, and forty to fifty-four. Job prospects are currently rated as fair by the department, and this trend is expected to improve over the next decade as the Canadian population overall increases in age.

Social services workers receive practical skills and some theoretical education in social work practices, and many are educated in issues related to social work codes of ethics. All have completed practica in social service agencies. Different colleges place higher or lower levels of emphasis on theoretical constructs as well as practical training. Social services workers are employed in entry-level positions in government agencies, private services, and non-profit non-governmental organizations. These span a broad spectrum of human services including children's services, agencies serving older adults, mental health services, child welfare, developmental services, addictions services, Aboriginal outreach programs, rehabilitation services, family services, drop-in centres, welfare and other social assistance programs, agencies serving victims of domestic violence, immigrant and newcomer services, correctional programs, and many others. Social services workers wishing to move into positions of more responsibility generally seek higher education.

[*Patricia Spindel*]

RELATED ENTRIES

Clinical Social Work, Community Colleges, Multi-skilling, Non-clinical Practice, Personal Social Services, Practice Methods, Professional Issues, Social Services

social welfare

Social welfare refers to the broad network of policies, services, and resources that assist people to obtain basic needs from sources beyond the economic system to attain optimum biopsychosocial functioning. In Canada the structure of social welfare is complex, stemming from the historic development of sectarian and state social services, volunteer activities, private philanthropy, and special interest groups. Social welfare sparks divergent views. Most Canadian recognize that people need help when they are confronted by accidents and natural disasters, disease and economic crises, or—to a lesser extent—systemic inequities over which they have no control or influence. That Canadians in need have a right to assistance come from perceptions about citizenship and the rights of citizens to a sufficient share of goods and services to live fulfilling lives. Negative associations about social welfare are widespread, as a result of often misguided beliefs that many recipients are undeserving; this insensitivity is interesting, given that most Canadians are recipients of some kind of social welfare at some time in their lives. An accompanying belief within Canada, sometimes fostered by politicians and media, is that many recipients are abusing or exploiting social welfare, with a resultant clamp down on all recipients, widespread drastic reductions in benefits, and punitive elements introduced into some programs. This wish to reduce benefits is further complicated by fiscal struggles between municipalities, provinces/territories, and the federal government as to who should pay for what and whether user-pay systems should be developed. Social workers in this context face difficulties in advancing the case that the vast majority of persons need social welfare financial assistance and other types of services because of inadequacies and unevenness in the economic system, rather than from personal inadequacy or bad intentions. Even the most extreme critics of current social welfare acknowledge the need for at least some forms of public assistance; differences derive from variance over responsibility and what services are to be provided. A further challenge to the concept of social welfare is whether Canadians ought to assist people in need in other parts of the world: should globalization of social welfare needs parallel globalization of the world's economies? In fact, Canada has done well in responding to international assistance, especially in response to environmental disasters or war. Canadians have far less consensus about appropriate responses to structural challenges in this country that result in such problems as poverty and homelessness. The perception in the past that social welfare is an identifying characteristic of a particular form of government is now discredited, as it is now recognized that even the most totalitarian governments have a system of social welfare. The diversity of social welfare programs worldwide provides Canadians with an opportunity to study and learn as well as teach from other systems, as this country continues making changes to the systems of social welfare through ongoing evaluation.

[*FJT*]

RELATED ENTRIES

Canada Assistance Plan, Income Assistance, Income Security, Poverty, Program Evaluation, Sectarian Social Services, Social Assistance, Social Planning, Social Policy, Social Security, Social Services, Social Welfare Context, Social Welfare History, Welfare, Wellness, Workfare

social welfare context

Social welfare in Canada has been shaped by the enormous physical, economic, and social diversity of this country. Tradition, the Canadian Charter of Rights and Freedoms, multi-party parliamentary democracy, and demography have contributed to a balancing of individual rights and the common good that has produced a program of social welfare that is expected to provide a social safety net. Federal equalization payments to the provinces and territories are used to ensure the provision of comparable programs throughout the country, despite disparate regional economic resources. The relationship between the federal and the provincial governments, including responsibilities for social welfare responsibilities of each government is outlined in the British North America Act, 1867 (now, Constitution Act, 1867). The 1867 constitutional statute also made Canada officially bilingual, thereby requiring that government services, including social welfare, be provided in both English and French in many communities, as implemented through the Official Languages Act, 1985. Under the constitution, the federal government is also responsible for matters related to:

- *economic unity and for programs ensuring income maintenance* (as implemented through Canada Assistance Plan Act, 1985; Employment Insurance Act, 1996; Canada Pension Plan Act, 1985; Old Age Security Act, 1985; and Pension Benefits Standards Act, 1985, which were consolidated as Canada Pension Plan, Old Age Security and Pension Benefits Standards Act, 1998);
- *health care* (as implemented through Canada Health Act, 1985);
- *immigration* (as implemented through Immigrant and Refugee Protection Act, 2001);
- *First Nations* (as implemented through, for instance, Indian Act, 1985); and
- *northern development* (as implemented through the Department of Indian Affairs and Northern development Act, 1966).

Provinces with major jurisdiction in relation to property and civil rights are responsible for the delivery of public services including health, education, and welfare. Compliance with federal standards is achieved through funding mechanisms that require services delivered by provinces and territories to meet federal standards and guidelines (e.g., Canada Health Act and Canada Mortgage and Housing Act, 1985). Moving from an agrarian and natural resource–based economy with a population comprised mostly of Europeans, the population of Canada has grown to 28.5 million people—now mostly urban residents—comprised of a multiplicity of origins and cultures, as result of highly controlled, economically driven immigration. Immigration has continued to support a private agrarian and industrial economy moving by the end of the last century to a major international technology sector with significant government subsidies and political support. While many Aboriginal people have sought urban life and opportunities, a significant segment of the Aboriginal population has remained on reserves or in communities with a predominantly Aboriginal population; currently, land rights, self-government, and program and service provision are being renegotiated with First Nations and Inuit and, in some provinces and territories, with Métis.

To meet needs throughout Canadian society, social policies have been developed on the assumption that full employment is the foundation for meeting basic needs. Governments and business have been seen to have, in varying degrees, a social contract concerning the welfare of the workforce. The popular sense has been that governments are held responsible for the provision of basic services, such as education and health care of quality and with universal access. Entitlement programs in these areas—including support of a separate Catholic system, family tax credits, old age security and benefits, and minimum income supplements—are fundamental to Canadian social welfare. The voluntary sector, which receives both federal and provincial tax relief, supplements entitlement services and includes a diversity of services such as food banks, co-operative housing, and personal counselling. The availability of, access to, and range of services provided is highly variable from community to community. Private social service provision is rare in Canada; where it exists, it is usually funded from individual and corporate philanthropic trust funds that target specific health or social problems, often supplementing voluntary or government-sector initiatives. At the outset of the twenty-first century, Canada has emerged as a multicultural, bilingual, prosperous nation with a high standard of living. Nonetheless, unemployment rates have fluctuated by season and region, averaging 6.8 percent in 1999; consequently, many people remain in poverty. They have inadequate food, clothing, shelter, and lack access to timely and appropriate medical care. Poverty in absolute and relative terms is on the rise and many communities are facing the loss of their farming, fishing, and manufacturing bases. Immigration quota remain the primary way of supporting and replacing an ageing workforce. As in many industrial nations, the political climate in the last decade has become conservative and, as a result, social welfare programs have been reduced in scope. Increasing numbers of children are found on welfare roles; decreasing eligibility for only the most minimal welfare benefits has served to increase the gap between the wealthy and the poor in Canadian society. In many provinces, support for social welfare has been privatized, such as for youth correction and treatment facilities, and an increasing proportion of health services, especially for long-term care. Canada is moving away from its social contract roots and toward the centrality of an internationalized market economy. If the future of Canadian social welfare is premised on a conviction that the marketplace is the most appropriate major provider for social needs, it is likely to become quite different.

[*Susan Watt*]

RELATED ENTRIES

Aboriginal Issues, Canada Health Act, Canadian Charter of Rights and Freedoms, Citizenship and Immigration Canada, Counselling, Diversity, Employment, Employment Insurance Act, Family & Youth Courts, Food Banks, Human Rights, Indian & Affairs Northern Canada, Long-Term Care, Poverty, Rowell-Sirois Commission, Social Welfare, Social Welfare History, Unemployment Insurance Act, Voluntarism, Welfare State

social welfare history

Social welfare history, in the context of Canadian social work, encompasses the evolution of social policies, the profession of social work, and those institutions that are associated with them. Canadian social welfare emerged in seven stages. The first, pre-European contact, represented a complex system of community social concern among diverse Aboriginal peoples. The next stage, early European contact, saw the establishment of Catholic eleemosynary, medical, and educational institutions in colonial New France. During a third stage, British colonialism created Poor Law institutions in Nova Scotia and New Brunswick but not in Upper Canada (renamed Ontario). Throughout British North America, local charities and an emergent municipal system of poor relief reinforced a local basis of social welfare. A fourth stage, from confederation in 1867 to the Second World War, saw the British North America Act, 1867 (now, Constitution Act, 1867), assign responsibility for social welfare to, and made municipalities creatures of, the provinces; to the federal government came responsibility for Aboriginal peoples and lands, banking, currency, and external relations; and jurisdiction in agriculture, immigration, and taxes were to be shared by the provinces and the federal government.. The country's first school of social work at the University of Toronto opened in 1914, and the Canadian Association of Social Workers was created in 1928. Emergent social policy legislation included workers' compensation (1914, first in Ontario), mother's allowances (1916, first in Manitoba), and old age security (1927, as federal/provincial cost-shared and selective). Research into social conditions, which had trickled in the late nineteenth century, became more abundant and complex in the first half of the twentieth century. The Second World War ushered in a fifth stage, a comprehensive welfare state strongly oriented to Keynesian economics and universality; included were a national system of unemployment insurance (1940, now called employment insurance), universal family allowance (1944), and a blueprint for the welfare state (the Marsh Report, 1943). The 1950s and 1960s expanded further on these principles with the creation of a universal federal old age security system (1951), the Canada Assistance Plan (1966) as a cost-sharing agreement between the federal government and the provinces, the Canada pension plan (1966), a national system of health care, and the subsequent expansion of these programs. A sixth stage, a welfare state crisis, began in the mid-1970s with marked decreases in federal transfers to the provinces, and culminated in the 1980s, 1990s, and 2000s, with significant reductions in many of the welfare state's core programs. The less robust Canada Health and Social Transfer replaced the Canada Assistance Plan in 1996. Federal standards of service delivery became more difficult to enforce. Family allowances were eliminated in 1992, old age security ceased to be universal in 1989, and most income security programs were cut drastically. The 1982 Canadian Charter of Rights and Freedoms, and growing human rights legislation, have recognized the rights of the historically disempowered: Aboriginal peoples, members of ethnocultural and religious minority communities, women, gays and lesbians, and people with disabilities, among others. This sixth stage of crisis is giving way to a seventh, in which principles of universality appear moribund. Neo-liberalism and globalization are pre-eminent, and new relationships between civil society and the state, and new conceptions of community and individual rights, are developing (Rice & Prince 2000).

In Canada, the study of social welfare remained a relatively marginal area of mainstream historical inquiry until the 1970s. Before then, the Canadian historical profession had been preoccupied with economic, then political, and finally political biographical analysis—in which there could be some—in practice, little—overlap with the concerns of social welfare. Some of Canada's earliest social welfare histories were written as theses for master of social work programs. The country's first major monograph (Splane 1965)—the product of a doctoral dissertation in social work—remains a significant contribution to the field; studies published prior to Splane tended to be relatively uncritical of social welfare institutions. The emergence of social history rendered social welfare a more popular topic and, in the 1970s and 1980s, a second flash of social welfare historical writing was lit by issues related to socio-economic class, then issues related to women. A third conflagration of writing, from the 1980s to the present, reflects the now explosive growth in social history in Canada, fed by multitudinous historiographic influences from other countries and from the social sciences; the number of topics and the variety of approaches have increased commensurately. Research has become more sophisticated, with the introduction of discourse analysis, the perspectives of the socially excluded, and the critical rethinking of previous assumptions. A more subtle and nuanced conception of power relations is now evident. Greater consideration is given to diverse forces influencing social work and social policies, such as secularism and religiosity, the ambiguous role given to class relations, or women's empowerment, among other topics (Graham 1996). Guest's 1997 history of Canadian social policy remains the best in a single volume; at time of writing, a comparable single-volume study on the national evolution of social work had not yet been published.

[*John R. Graham*]

RELATED ENTRIES

Aboriginal Issues, Associated Charities of Toronto, R.B. Bennett, W.H. Beveridge, E.H. Blois, Canadian Council on Child Welfare, Canadian Council on Social Development, Canadians In & Out of Work, H. Cassidy, Church-Based Services, Citizen Participation, Co-operative Commonwealth Federation, Co-operative Movement, Dawn of Ampler Life, "Democracy Needs Socialism," Great Depression (1930s), T.C. Douglas, Education in Social Work, Fabian Society (UK), Ginger Group, Income Security, J.J. Kelso, J.W. Langmuir, League for Social Reconstruction, D. Livesay, L. Marsh, Marsh Report, N. McClung, A. Macphail, S. Monet-Chartrand, E. Murphy, My Neighbour, I. Parlby, Personal Social Services, Poverty, Progressive Social Work, Radical Social Work, Regina Manifesto, A. Rose, Sectarian Social Services, Settlement House Movement, G. Smith, Social Gospel Movement, Social Planning, Social Welfare, Social Welfare Context, E. Stowe, Strangers Within our Gates, Toronto Infants Home, B. Touzel, J.S. Woodsworth, Workfare

REFERENCES

Graham, J.R. An Analysis of Canadian Social Welfare Historical Writing. *Social Review Service* 70, 1, 140–58.

Guest, D. 1997. *The Emergence of Social Security in Canada.* Vancouver: University of British Columbia Press.

Rice, J.J., and M.J. Prince. 2000. *Changing Politics of Canadian Social Policy.* Toronto: University of Toronto Press.

Splane, R.B. 1965. *Social Welfare in Ontario, 1791–1893.* Toronto: University of Toronto Press.

social work profession

Although it has changed greatly in its century-long history, social work in Canada stands as a well recognized and respected senior profession within human services. From a legislative viewpoint, the profession is regulated in each of the ten provinces by registration or by licensing with varying degrees of control of title. In the academic world, faculties and schools of social work exist on most campuses in the major Canadian universities. Education and training for social work is offered for bachelor, masters, and doctoral degrees. At this time, the bachelor of social work is recognized in existing legislation as the entry-level degree into the profession. Doctorates are far less common, even though the numbers conferred have increased rapidly in the last decade. Standardization of content of university programs is maintained through the accreditation process of the Canadian Association of Schools of Social Work. Professional organization is now administered through a national as well as provincial and territorial associations. The national body, the Canadian Association of Social Workers is now more than seventy-five years old and stood, for a long time, as the sole voice of the profession in

the setting and maintaining of professional standards. With the profession moving to legislative recognition, which rests with provincial and territorial governments, individual members of the national association moved to establish provincial/territorial organizations, which themselves became the members of the national association. Individual practitioners thus hold membership in the Canadian Association of Social Work by virtue of their being members of the various provincial organizations. An estimated 15,000 social workers hold professional status in Canada, practising across a broad spectrum of private and public services, agencies and clinics, at all levels of government and in senior academic roles. Further, in recent decades, practitioners have moved into various forms of autonomous private practice at micro and macro levels, as well as into new areas of practice such as industry. Some of these developments have caused concern within the profession as to whether these entrepreneurial developments manifest a movement away from the profession's basic concerns for social issues and social justice. The knowledge and practice base of the profession are dynamic, in a continual process of development evident in the research arm of academe, the range of research sponsored and carried out by government, and the increasing amount of and commitment to program evaluation in response to societal demands for accountability. Practice developments and research outcomes are promulgated through a steadily expanding amount of publication in textbook and in journals ranging from scholarly journals to professional association newsletters. International practice is another expanding area for Canadian social work as Canada becomes more involved in global projects, frequently in response to disasters and in conjunction with issues related to Canadian immigration policies. Social work continues to be a highly attractive profession to large numbers of young students and as a second career to mature students. Admission to faculties and schools of social work remain highly competitive with increasingly more stringent requirements being set. Throughout the profession, a commitment to social justice for everyone in society and high levels of social action from micro to macro remains strong and consistent.

[*FJT*]

social work theory

One of the distinguishing marks of Canadian social work is the diversity of its theoretical base. At this time in the profession's development in North America, some thirty different bodies of theory-driving practice are being utilized. Formerly, the profession was strongly influenced by psychodynamic theoretical orientations that stressed individual pathology. As with practice in other countries, Canadian social work has moved to a more holistically oriented understanding of the complex interface of persons and systemic issues. Practitioners here have welcomed this theoretical diversity, in contrast to the more acrimonious struggles that have taken place in other countries for supremacy by particular theories. Differences in theoretical emphases and preferences do remain among faculties and schools of social work and within agencies, but they are tolerated rather than contested. One of the ways that accommodation has been made to the extant spectrum of theoretical diversity is the commitment to the generalist approach in curricular requirements of the accreditation process. This approach tends to stress problem-solving theories while providing an conceptual overview of the spectrum of theories underlying social work practice.

In the early 1960s, the profession became concerned with some of its own internal struggles around methodologies, as was occurring in other countries as well. Some feared that the proponents in the group work/casework dichotomy might split the profession, these concerns becoming heightened by similar divisions over theoretical differences. At the same time, promoters of

Canadian social work advancing the notion that a mature profession should have its own theoretical base, rather than borrowing theoretical concepts from other disciplines, were searching for a single theory to mark the profession. Dr. Gordon, a Canadian practising in the United States, became highly attracted to systems theory as a body of knowledge that could unite social work and provide a basis for a social work theory. Others realized, however, that diversity is also a sign of maturity in a profession, knowledge belongs to all disciplines, and that, once a theory is adopted or integrated into a profession's theoretical spectrum, that profession needs to take responsibility for it. From these broad discussions emerged the concept that social work theories—with an emphasis on the plural—were necessary as a base for practice in a discipline as complex as social work; each theory adds to the richness of practitioners' understanding of the professional vocation and mission. Thus, Canadian social work is driven by a cluster of theories incorporated, refined, and applied in practice. Some theories—such as psychodynamic and psychosocial—have been adopted and adapted from other disciplines, and others—such as task and problem solving—have been developed uniquely to social work and have, in turn, been and are being incorporated by other professions' theoretical bases. Crisis, client-centred, and systems theories have been developed in conjunction with other professions' theories, and still others—such as existentialism, meditation, and hypnosis—are emerging from very distinct thought systems in which some components are useful to social work practice. As social workers moves to make more effective use of the current theoretical spectrum, the profession's scholars and researchers are exploring emergent theories such as chaos and postmodern. The Canadian social work profession now has a complex and highly diverse theoretical base, with theories absorbed from without as well as developed from within. The challenge of this diversity is reflected in discussion, debate, and dialogue about what faculties and schools of social work are to teach and how to teach it to ensure that all students acquire an adequate theoretical foundation without moving to overly prescriptive accreditation and regulatory requirements. Ideally, the profession needs to ensure balance in its practice structure and style so that clients continue to benefit from the richness that flows from a diverse theoretical orientation to practice.

[*FJT*]

RELATED ENTRIES
Education in Social Work, Knowledge Base, Racism-Sensitive Practice, Social Work Profession, Theory & Practice

spirituality

A longing for spirituality has emerged in the rapidly changing societal context in which contemporary social work practises. This emergence is redefining the meaning of holistic social work practice, as practitioners now commonly include spirituality and the growing global search for spirituality is having an impact on every aspect of social work practice. Clients are requesting that their clinicians be knowledgeable of and able to respond to spiritual issues in their lives. In social work education, students are increasingly demanding the same from social work educators. In workplace settings, staff are asking for spiritual sensitivity from their leaders, as they struggle to address their spiritual needs in the context of their work lives. Reasons for this emergence of spirituality are many. Faced with contemporary unpredictability, people are searching for anchors that can secure their lives in these turbulent times. Traditional life anchors such as church, family, and work have become increasingly less reliable. The overemphasis on individualism and materialism in affluent industrialized societies has led to a fragmentation of communities, which is resulting in a longing among citizens for more profound and meaningful connections to one another, to themselves, and to something greater than themselves. Demographic factors are also contributing to the current interest in spirituality, as the baby boom generation enter mid-life with its associated questions about bigger purposes in life, what is really important to be done or to become in the second half of life, and how to leave a mark on the world. People are also beginning to question whether a disproportionate emphasis on work is appropriate within spiritual destiny because it dissipates physical, social, psychological, and spiritual energies.

Evidence is growing that social work is responding, albeit more slowly in Canada than in the United States where the importance of spirituality in the lives of clients has been acknowledged in the curriculum policy statement of the Council on Social Work Education and in the American Psychiatric Association's *Diagnostic and Statistical Manual of Mental Disorders*. More than eighteen American social work programs already offer specialized courses on spirituality and that number is rapidly increasing. In Canada only a handful of courses on spirituality in social work practice are being offered, even though interest does seem to be increasing, as evident in more frequent inclusion of spiritual themes at social work conferences, seminars, and workshops. Spirituality in social work practice remains controversial. While its inclusion is gaining support, spirituality's role in social work practice and education continues to be debated; many in the profession object or, at least, are cautious about the integration of spirituality in social work. Listening to and considering opposing views can inform proponents of potential difficulties and encourage the need for further study, research, and debate. Clearly, however, the growing literature, research, and broad spiritual renaissance within society are affecting social work and the profession needs to keep responding to spirituality at least as a prevalent social phenomenon. Social work will continue to be challenged to remain open to the expanding spiritual developments in the world. Some of these new developments can usefully build knowledge that can potentially enrich the lives of the members of the profession and those of the people it serves. Spirituality has the potential to transform social service organizations into more nurturing, respectful, and healing places of work for social workers. Social workers in such organizations could give more to their clients as they themselves are nurtured spiritually in their work. The integration of spirituality into social work practice presents an unprecedented opportunity for the profession to deepen its impact on society.

[*Hugh Drouin*]

RELATED ENTRIES
Aboriginal Services, Church-Based Services, Ethnocultural Communities' Services, Jewish Social Services, Meditation, Religion, Sectarian Social Services, Theory & Practice, Therapy, Transpersonal Psychology, Treatment, Wellness

St. Thomas University Department of Social Work

The bachelor of social work program at St. Thomas University in Fredericton, New Brunswick, has been in operation since September 1980, emerging from several years of co-operative effort with the Maritime School of Social Work at Dalhousie University, the social work department at l'Université de Moncton, the New Brunswick Department of Social Services, and the New Brunswick Association of Social Work. The Department of Social Work at St. Thomas University is situated in a small Catholic liberal arts university that has a tradition of concern for the dignity and worth of the individual, a history of responding to social issues, and a commitment to education that is humanistic rather than technical. After relocating from Chatham to Fredericton in 1964, the university began to expand its course offerings in psychosocial fields, and many of its graduates went into the helping professions. The move to establishing a social work education program at St. Thomas was logical and congruent with the university's heritage. The roots of formal social work education at St. Thomas go back to 1972 when the first social work course (theory and method of social intervention) was approved; since no social work department existed at the time, the course was entitled Psychology 491 and was offered as an extension course in Saint John in 1974. In subsequent years, the course was offered on the Miramichi and in Moncton. In the early 1970s, more than 80 percent of social service workers had no social work education and the Department of Social Services of New Brunswick had begun to assess the training needs of its workers. The department approached St. Thomas and, as a result, in 1975 the certificate in social work was instituted; modelled after an already existing certificate at l'Université de Moncton, the certificate program was designed for the educational and training needs of the government department's social work staff. The certificate program continued to be offered until 1989 with passage of the Act to Incorporate the New Brunswick Association of Social Workers, when the bachelor of social work became the minimum requirement to practice social work in New Brunswick and the certificate program became obsolete.

In 1976, St. Thomas took an interim step toward establishment of a bachelor of social work program by developing a major in applied social sciences, which included a core of social work courses and a practicum. To accomplish this goal, the Department of Social Work was formed and the first faculty were hired. A further step toward the bachelor of social work was accomplished in 1979, when discussions with Dalhousie's school of social work and with l'Université de Moncton resulted in an agreement that St. Thomas would provide the first year (five social work courses) of Dalhousie's decentralized bachelor of social work program to English-speaking students of New Brunswick. With the support of the New Brunswick Association of Social Workers, the New Brunswick Department of Social Services, l'Université de Moncton, and the University of New Brunswick (St. Thomas's sister university), an application was made to the Maritime Higher Education Commission for a bachelor of social work program. This application was approved on June 28, 1980 and, in September 1980, the first students were admitted into the bachelor of social work at St. Thomas. In 1982 in response to requests from the Union of New Brunswick Indians, the provincial Department of Social Work developed two initiatives with funding from the federal Department of Indian affairs. The department instituted a certificate in social work in drug and alcohol studies to meet training needs for Aboriginal drug and alcohol counsellors; as well, a bachelor of social work degree was offered on a part-time and extension basis, in response to the need for trained social workers in Native Child and Family Service agencies. In 1990 approximately thirty Aboriginal students graduated with a bachelor of social work degree. These programs were funded only on a one-time basis but the need for Aboriginal social workers was ongoing; in 1997, therefore, St. Thomas's social work department introduced an Aboriginal initiative as part of its long- term commitment to introduce specialized content in the curriculum, to increase access for Aboriginal students to the program, and to enhance the learning environment for Aboriginal students.

The department of social work's most recent initiative occurred in 1999 with the introduction of a post-degree program for graduates from an undergraduate social work program. This development was the outgrowth of a lengthy debate within the university regarding the small number of students entering directly from high school who were accepted into the professional years of the social work program. The St. Thomas University Department of Social Work, which has received three accreditations (1986, 1993 and 2001) from the Canadian Association of Schools of Social Work, continues to offer a vibrant and dynamic program. The department recently developed a mission statement based on the values of openness, respect, collegiality, mutuality, accountability, and reconciliation—and is developing a reputation as a structural school that responds from these values. To this end, the curriculum reflects the belief that much of the suffering and inequity in society is rooted in the social order. As a result of an extensive curriculum review process, the department anticipates that it will establish a master of social work degree in the near future. Current information can be found online at <www.stu.ca/>.

[*Brian Ouellette*]

RELATED ENTRIES
Aboriginal Services, Dalhousie University Maritime School of Social Work, Education in Social Work, Faculties of Social Work, New Brunswick Association of Social Workers

Kathleen Stovold (1911–2001)

Stovold, Kathleen, social activist; b. May 11, 1911, Tunbridge Wells, Kent, UK (of S.W. Stovold & Elizabeth Quinn); m. George Young (d. 1943), Leonard Stovold; son: Charles Young; d. Apr. 07, 2001, Vancouver, BC

Kathleen (Kay) Stovold emigrated to Canada during the Second World War as a widowed British war bride with a young son. She subsequently married Len Stovold, a marriage of fifty-four years' duration. She initially became aware of problems experienced by seniors through her work as a volunteer seniors counsellor at a local neighbourhood house. A personal experience in hospital reinforced her conviction that health care needed certain kinds of improvements. These joint experiences led to Stovold's commitment for more than thirty years to make the world a better place for seniors and people with disabilities. Although she was not a trained social worker, Stovold was often referred to as an advocate, a policy advisor,

and a skilled communicator. She became known throughout British Columbia for her three years' work on a seniors' advisory committee to the provincial government. She founded the West End Seniors Network in Vancouver and long served as its president. In November 1999, the Vancouver mayor and council honoured her at city hall with "Kay Stovold Day" and, in 2000, Volunteer Vancouver presented her with the Community Service Award. She was considered as the informal information and referral source for current and emerging resources for all aspects of services for elderly and disabled people. Kay Stovold's concern for seniors drew her into numerous boards, work groups, and conferences, among which were the St. Paul's Hospital Advisory Committee, the City Council Special Seniors Advisory Committee, New Horizons, and Health Department Committees, the BC Seniors Medication Awareness Project, the Association of Advocates for Care Reform, housing committees, and palliative care consultation. Kay Stovold's memorial service on April 19, 2001 was attended by many august persons. It was said that she "could walk with kings nor lose the common touch."

[*Mary A. Hill*]

RELATED ENTRIES
Services to Elderly People, Services to People with Physical Disabilities

Emily Stowe (1831–1903)

Stowe, Emily Howard (née Jennings), instructor, physician; b. May 01, 1831, Norwich, ON; m. John Stowe, 1856; three children (the eldest, Dr. Augusta Stowe Gullen); first female physician in Canada; d. Apr 30, 1903, Toronto, ON

Emily Stowe was strongly guided by her family's deep-rooted Quaker beliefs in her passion for education for all people and for women's equality with men stemmed from those beliefs. In 1854 Stowe attended a Normal school and received her first-class teacher's certificate; from teaching in a one-room school she proceeded to become the first principal. A short time after her marriage to John Stowe, her husband contracted tuberculosis and she returned to work to support her family and pay the medical bills. Having decided to become a physician, she applied in 1865 to the University of Toronto, which rejected her application as women were not accepted at university at that time. She decided to study in the United States, where Elizabeth Blackwell had become the first American female physician and had opened a women's medical school. In 1867 when Dr. Stowe returned to Toronto to practise medicine, she became Canada's first female physician. Not long afterward, an Act of Parliament was passed to state that medical doctors who had trained in the United States would be required to take a matriculation examination to obtain a licence to practise medicine in Canada. Dr. Stowe applied but was not accepted until 1870; she and her only female colleague, Dr. Jennie Trout, were harassed by professors and fellow students in an effort to dissuade women from entering the profession. In spite of being sued, being threatened with prison, and constantly being scrutinized by the Ontario College of Physicians and Surgeons, Dr. Stowe continued to practise illegally until the 1880s, when the college finally granted her a licence.

As Dr. Stowe travelled throughout Ontario providing medical care for women, she began to educate women about their rights and encouraged debate on the need for the education of girls as well as boys. She organized the first suffrage organization in Canada, called the Toronto Women's Literary Club (est. 1877), which was changed in 1883 to the Toronto Women's Suffrage Association; members discussed such topics as better education and working conditions for women in factories. In 1881 she sent a deputation to the Ontario government requesting women's voting rights, a process that would take much time to achieve. In 1882 she petitioned the legislature to allow women into the University of Toronto, which led to the admission of women in 1886/87. Another of Dr. Stowe's accomplishments was to be selected president of the Dominion Women's Enfranchisement Association, which fought continually against injustices toward women. In 1896 she participated in a mock parliament organized by the association where the featured debate was whether to permit men the right to vote.

Dr. Emily Stowe passed away on April 30, 1903. Throughout her life, she remained a gentle and compassionate woman who nevertheless advocated against discrimination and prejudice to blaze a trail for other women. Her daughter, Dr. Augusta Stowe Gullen followed her directly,

also as a physician. Her actions had a direct impact on women's right to vote, the education of women, and medical services for and by women.

[*Adele Eamer*]

RELATED ENTRIES
Services for Women, Social Welfare History

Strangers within Our Gates

A book authored by J.S. Woodsworth, *Strangers within Our Gates*, was published in 1908 for the Young People's Foreword Movement for Missions. It reflected the philosophy and ideology of the Social Gospel Movement. The principle focus of the book was a critique of the overall question of immigration in Canada and in particular promoted policies of non-European immigration.

[*FJT*]

RELATED ENTRIES
Immigrants & Immigration, Social Gospel Movement, Social Welfare History, J.S. Woodsworth

substance addiction

Addiction—derived from the Greek word *addicto* (bound or devoted, or bondage to a practice)—used to refer to behaviour engaged in by compulsive drug users in search of their substance(s) of choice but is now more expansively applied to describe any type of compulsive behaviour. Historically, people were considered to be addicted if they exhibited a physical and/or psychological dependence on a chemical agent or activity; implicit in this idea is an inability to resist using a substance or engaging in a behaviour to the point where the dosage and/or frequency becomes compulsive. At the turn of the twentieth century, addiction had a behavioural meaning: it referred to compulsive drug seeking and the losing of personal control to drugs that also involved a breakdown in lifestyle (i.e., family, work, leisure activities). In the 1950s and 1960s, addiction became more closely associated with the unpleasant physical reactions that occurred with termination of drug administration; those who were addicted continued to take a drug to avoid the negative physical reactions that occurred during withdrawal of the drug from bodily systems. In 1964 The World Health Organization moved away from use of the term to refer to the abuse of psychoactive drugs and began to use the more precise and narrower concept of addiction as dependence; dependence was further divided into the two distinct components of physical and psychological. The concept of addiction expanded beyond drug taking to other behaviours, such as eating, sex, shopping, and gambling. A further factor added to the idea of addiction is the socioenvironmental context, so that addiction now includes a social experience that in and of itself can bring about dependency to a substance or behaviour in a person who is otherwise well. Individuals become dependent to a particular state of body/mind. In this way, addiction can also be considered for the disorganizing effect that it has on an individual's life and how it can create crises. Addiction occurs along a continuum, and even those with extreme addictiveness show a capacity to act in a way other than addicted under certain circumstances. Veterans of the Vietnam War provide a dramatic example, where 75 percent who tested drug-positive after their tour of duty claimed that they had become addicted in Vietnam. One third continued using drugs, but less than 10 percent of veterans showed signs of what could be classified as dependency.

Within dependency to a psychoactive drug are two distinct types: physical and psychological. Physical dependence is a physiological state of cellular adaptation that occurs when a body becomes so accustomed to a drug that it can only function normally when the drug is present. Without the drug, the user will experience physical disturbances or illnesses, known as withdrawal; withdrawal symptoms can be prevented or promptly relieved by the administration of a sufficient quantity of the original drug or often by one with similar pharmacological properties. When different drugs are used interchangeably to prevent withdrawal symptoms, patients can experience cross-dependence. The development of physical dependence can be important in the maintenance of drug-taking, not only because of its negative reinforcement but also because administration—either to alleviate or to prevent withdrawal—can theoretically lead to additional positive reinforcement. Instead of returning a body to the neutral state of homeostasis, an overshooting effect can result in further positive reinforcement. Physical dependence is usually pre-ceded by serious personal psychological, social, and even physiological complications. Physical dependence can occur with chronic use of most depressants, opioids, and stimulants. Among the hallucinogens, physical dependence has not yet been demonstrated except with long-term use of cannabis products. Psychological dependence—also referred to as behavioural or emotional dependence—occurs when a drug becomes so important to a person's thoughts or activities that he/she believes that he/she cannot manage without it. Psychological dependence may range from a mild wish to a compelling emotional need for a periodic or continuous use of a drug and may include feelings of loss or desperation if the drug is unavailable. In the case of psychological dependence, a person begins to feel and eventually believe that he/she needs the drug effects—feeling relaxed or aroused—because he/she cannot cope with diverse life situations without these effects. In many instances in maintaining chronic drug use, psychological aspects are considerably more important than physical dependence. A major problem in dependency and addiction is not the physical aspect, as withdrawal can usually be successfully achieved within several days, but the far greater likelihood that the individual will return to chronic use for psychological reasons. Subtle yet persistent psychological and social factors are more than adequate to maintain the behaviour of drug consumption even after a successful detoxication process.

[*Rick Csiernik*]

RELATED ENTRIES

Addiction, Bioethical Issues, Crisis Intervention, Employee Assistance Programs, Industrial Social Work, Medication, Pharmacological Therapy, Psychotropic Medication, Therapy, Treatment, Women's Christian Temperance Union, Wellness

suicide

Suicide is a frequent cause of death in Canada, with about 4,000 incidents recorded each year. While suicide and suicide-related issues are ordinarily viewed as matters for physicians and the police, social workers are frequently involved. Many persons who turn to social workers for assistance often feel overwhelmed by their circumstances to the point where they consider suicide a possible course of action. Practitioners who sense a client's ambivalence about such a final act can with great sensitivity help to move him/her toward less dramatic and final alternatives. Because suicide is not a topic for open or public discussion, clients tend to conceal their thoughts about it, which means that their ambivalence may be obscured. Practitioners need to be alert to its possibility in clients under extreme distress or depression. Even when persons do not move to actively attempt suicide, or are unsuccessful in repeated attempts, they may feel considerable guilt and fear for having considered or attempted it; therapeutic assistance may be required. A practitioner who remains unaware that a client is contemplating suicide may be ineffective in intervention attempts with that client, who persists to be stressed as he/she struggles with despair alone; as well as the client, other significant people in the client's life may also seek professional help around a suicide incident or knowledge that the client is feeling suicidal. Such help is usually focused on resolving feelings of guilt, anger, confusion, and loss. Much suicidal behaviour follows patterns, so that significantly higher rates of suicide among particular persons or groups or locations may influence others. While the majority of suicides tend to be acts of desperation, the question of assisted suicide—in which a person actively seeks help to end his/her life—is becoming a more common occurrence, especially for workers in chronic and palliative care practices. Clearly, such requests involve complex ethical and legal issues in the helping professions. Social workers, with their commitment to understanding and modifying the interaction of persons within systems, are well placed to be alert to such patterns and their causes. Enhanced understanding can lead to whatever social action or social policy goals are deemed to be appropriate in each situation. Suicide is a topic that is usually avoided in therapeutic situations by clients and social workers alike, when in fact it is a critical component of many presenting situations; it is also a topic about which all social workers need to be more knowledgeable and comfortable.

[*FJT*]

RELATED ENTRIES

Bereavement, Bioethical Issues, Clinical Social Work, Crisis Intervention, Ethics, Long-Term Care, Palliative Care, Personal-Centred Theory, Sensitizing Concepts, Wellness

supervision

Supervision is a relationship used as a tool in the helping process. In a clinical social work context is "an interactional process in which a supervisor has been assigned or designated to assist in and direct the practice of supervisees in the areas of teaching, administration and helping" (Munson 1993: 10). Human situations are varied and complex, requiring the use of professional judgment in how to use helping skills most appropriately for each client. Because judgment and emotions are involved, supervision is used to provide a way for the social worker to step back from the process and gain perspective. Supervision can be formal or informal case discussion, but "the profession demands that the professional judgments and actions of a social worker be supervised by another professional social worker" (Kimberley 2000: 451). Supervision examines the most appropriate use of agency resources and how best to address the needs of clients. The transforming process of social work intervention occurs within a context where society often has harsh and negative attitudes toward the poor, the ill, and the deviant. In addition supervision provides a link between the agency and the profession, and to the values and ethics that govern the profession. In social work training, supervision is first encountered in field experience: "Field instruction, though derived from the school curriculum and from an older model of apprenticeship, is a unique approach to professional education which demands thoughtful preparation by the school and the agency" (Bogo & Vayda 1998: ix). Social work students require both a knowledge base and a skills base as well as a set of professional values to aid their judgment. Practice skills are learned in the field experience, which also provides opportunities to encounter ethical issues and ways to balance client need with agency mandate—and, often, agency resources. Practice skills and applied ethics are integrated with knowledge acquired in the classroom. To have the most benefit, supervision needs to occur in a climate that is conducive to learning uncomplicated by authority issues: "the nature and extent of the supervisor's authority is vague, unstructured, and limited in sanction. Even with student practitioners, authority is vague because the supervisor is often a remote representative of the social work faculty ... and because trainees are encouraged to prepare to be autonomous practitioners" (Munson 1993: 36). Social work practice now draws on multiple models of helping, and supervision in the field experience must take this into account: "Individual approaches to learning, affected by a whole range of human diversity variables, must be honoured and respected while maintaining the integrity of expectations and course objectives. The field instructor must be a knowledge provider, a demonstrator, a model and a critic, but, of equal importance, the field instructor must also be a learning partner, learning facilitator and a critical inquirer of his/her own practice" (Rogers 1995: 530).

Post-degree social work supervision has administrative, educational and supportive components that can be difficult to balance "In many agencies, the educational and supportive aspects of supervision have been devalued in favour of the administrative aspect" (Elliott 1990: 2). Elliott interprets this defence mechanism as emanating from anxiety that operates in many agencies, becoming heightened during fiscal restraint and increasing pressure on social workers to do more with less. A hardening of attitude toward those in need can occur: "The social work profession has become increasingly identified with bureaucratic systems and technocracy [and many] work in situations where legislation, regulations, policy, procedures, and standards govern their activities" (Schmidt et al. 2001: 89). The administrative component for supervision covers accountability of social workers, ensuring program guidelines are adhered to, seeing that agency procedures are kept, so that the agency can function effectively according to its guidelines. Appropriate use of scarce resources, liability, and funding accountability are all part of the agency's commitment to its staff and to ensuring that staff meet agency needs and standards: "the role of social workers has shifted to one of social control, reflecting more punitive social policies that have been put into place" (Schmidt et al. 2001: 89). In clinical supervision, more attention is paid to the educational and supportive components of the work, as social workers use more of themselves as a treatment tool. Creating a positive learning climate is necessary, as social workers' tasks are public and observable; their humanity is under scrutiny. A successful supervisory relationship can be seen to have three main components: shared meaning (i.e., having a common approach to therapy, what it is, what the role of the therapist is and how people change; what is expected of supervision), trust (i.e., creating a safe and respectful space, transparency and honesty), and how issues related to power and authority are addressed (Kaiser 1992: 55–60). The supervisory role evolves from instructing at the beginning of the process, to guiding, then consulting as a colleague as social workers' skill, competence, confidence, and independence grow. Training in supervision skills lags behind training in other areas of social work, as evident by the first fieldwork symposium for faculties of social work not being held until 1987. Within agencies, becoming a supervisor is based more on experience than on having acquired professional development in supervision skills and theories of adult learning: "Supervision is not a mechanical process; it requires a positive working relationship with staff" (Shulman 1982: 14). This area of the social work profession is gaining needed attention.

[*Alex Munroe*]

RELATED ENTRIES

Administrative Theory & Practice, Boards, Clinical Social Work, Education in Social Work, Organizational Theory, Paraprofessionals, Peer Counselling, Person-in-Environment Perspective, Personnel, Practicum Instruction, Social Work Profession

REFERENCES

Bogo, M., and E. Vayda. 1998. *The Practice of Field Instruction in Social Work: Theory and Process.* 2nd ed. Toronto: University of Toronto Press.

Elliott, N. 1990. *Practice Teaching and the Art of Social Work.* Norwich, UK: Social Work Monographs.

Kaiser, T.L. 1992. *The Supervisory Relationship: A Study of the Relationship between Supervisor and Supervisee in the Clinical Supervision of Marriage and Family Therapists.* Doctoral diss. from UMI Dissertation Services Ann Arbor, MI.

Kimberley, D. 2000. The Profession of Social Work: An Integrative Perspective. In J.C. Turner and F.J. Turner (Eds.) *Canadian Social Welfare.* 4th ed. Toronto: Allyn and Bacon.

Munson, C.E. 1993. *Clinical Social Work Supervision.* New York: Haworth Press.

Rogers, G. 1995. Field Education: A Pedagogy of Its Own. In G. Rogers (Ed.) *Social Work Field Education: Views and Visions*. Dubuque, IA: Kendall / Hunt.

Schmidt, G., A. Westhues, J. Lafrance, and A. Knowles. 2001. "Social Work In Canada: Results from the National Sector Study. *Canadian Social Work* 3, 2.

Shulman, L. 1982. *Skills of Supervision and Staff Management*. Itasca, IL: Peacock.

survey research

Survey research refers to the application of systematic measurements to a sample of people, groups, organizations, or communities to obtain comprehensive data patterns. As a frequently used mode of observation in the social sciences, survey research has become well recognized as a research method in social work. Major applications of survey research are for gathering data on health conditions, unemployment rates, incomes, crime rates, services and expenditures and various psychosocial problems. Survey data are only meaningful and informative about larger populations when the same variables are measured in carefully selected samples. The process of testing hypotheses is indirect and characterized by making "causal inferences" based on population variance and comparison. The origins of survey research are traceable from the rulers of Ancient Egypt who had censuses conducted to help administer their lands. In Europe, surveys carried out in the nineteenth and twentieth centuries served to inform governments about social interventions and, later, in detecting patterns of social changes as the welfare state became established. In his 1915 publication *The Measurement of Social Phenomena by British*, survey researcher Bowley emphasized the need for standardized definitions and practical sampling. In Canada survey research has informed the government, particularly through the work of Statistics Canada, for many years. The National Council on Welfare, a citizens' advisory body to the federal government, analyzes and interprets data from survey research, which are made available to the public. Survey research involves the careful sampling of a population, the collection of data through the design and administration of questionnaires, and analysis of survey data for the formulation of findings and, perhaps, recommendations. With respect to sampling, a researcher considers the sample size, the generalizability of the sample to a larger population, and the strategy to be used for selecting respondents. Questionnaire design is also critical, in that decisions need to be made regarding the extent to which a researcher draws on, for instance, previous literature, to devise questions likely to produce reliable and valid results. As well, a researcher may consider using consultants who are expert in questionnaire design, and whether to pre-test or pilot questionnaires (Fowler 1988). Methods of data collection in survey research can range from structured or unstructured personal interviews or telephone interviews to mailed questionnaires, which can be self-administered or agency recorded. Once data have been collected, they must be prepared for analysis. This phase of the research involves organizing the data, designing a code for computer processing, coding or "turning responses into standard categories," data entry into computer software, and checking the data for accuracy. Information obtained in survey research is generally cross-sectional, in that it is gathered at one point in time but not about past events. Surveys with data being collected at multiple points in time are longitudinal in design. Two other types of survey research interviews cohorts of a defined group at specific intervals (i.e., every five years), or interviews and follows the same individuals over time (Kirk 1999).

The advantages of survey research probably account for its popularity. It is economical and efficient, as large populations can be studied through surveys of small samples and information can be collected quickly. Survey research is also particularly useful in describing, explaining, and exploring attitudes and orientations, and determining probable causality. The main disadvantage of survey research is the problem of nonresponse to questionnaires: representivity and validity of a sample can be greatly reduced if the response rate is only 20 percent. A second concern is that survey research is not as strong as research that uses a control group to establish causal relationships. Survey research is the most common type of research found in the social work literature. As a structure of inquiry, it seeks to provide objective and unbiased observations of the human condition while using systemic data collection procedures. During recent years, secondary analysis—the analysis of survey data collected by another researcher, often for purposes other than those of the original researcher—has become an important aspect of survey research. It is especially useful for social work students or researchers who may have minimal research funds. Observations and correlation of survey data is valuable because of its potential to inform social work practice. Social workers must be concerned about whether data obtained are generalizable and to what extent those surveyed are representative of the larger population. It is predicted that survey research will continue to be "the most common structure of inquiry in social work" (Kirk 1999).

[*Marilyn Parsons*]

RELATED ENTRIES

Assessment, Capacity Assessment, Demographics, Interviewing, L. Marsh, Recording, Research

REFERENCES

Fowler, F.J., Jr. 1988. *Survey Research Methods.* Vol. 1, 9–12. Newbury Park, CA: Sage.

Kirk, S.A. 1999. *Social Work Research Methods: Building Knowledge for Practice.* 191–92. Washington, DC: National Association of Social Workers Press.

systems theory

Systems theory—or, social systems theory—is an application of general systems theory to four human systems: the individual, the family/small group, the organization, and the community. Many graduate and post-graduate professional schools in Canada and the United States have a social systems curriculum framework, historically offering specializations in casework, family therapy and group work, administration, and community development (including social planning and social policy advocacy). The father of general systems theory was Ludwig von Bertalanffy (1901–72). Born and educated in Austria, he was multi-disciplinary in competence (biology, physics, psychology) and in later years was a professor at McGill University in Montreal. Scholars have commented of Bertalanffy that "he became dissatisfied with the ability of linear-based, cause-and-effect theories to explain the growth and change he saw in living organisms. It occurred to von Bertalanffy that an explanation of this growth and change might lie in the relationships and interactions between those parts comprising the organism rather than in the parts.... It was an idea that revolutionized science" (Chess & Norlin 1988). While still in Europe von Bertalanffy had sketched aspects of his new body of theory by 1928, but his views were not widely known elsewhere until the publication of his works in English (1950, 1968). As early as 1969, the Council on Social Work Education in New York City published a small volume in which two of the six contributors, Schulman and Lathrope, called attention to the distinction between purely academic discussions of systems theory and emerging practice that focused on an applied use of the theory (Hearn 1969). Schulman distinguishes between "social system" and "institutional system" and Lathrope between a "master model for practice" and a "working model of concrete cases" (Sanders 1958; Rahn 1981). More recently, Warren, Franklin, and Streeter (1998) have provided a stimulating update of systems theory as formulated by its originator, Ludwig von Bertalanffy; those authors presented an informed and optimistic perspective on non-linear dynamic extension of systems theory to social work practice and applied theory research. Of particular interest are fresh insights as to why social systems theory does not supplant other theoretical contributions to social work but may indeed provide the basis for converting the present somewhat bewildering diversity of theories and conceptual approaches into a new and coherent interdependency. Warren, Franklin, and Streeter review an emerging focus on stages of self-change—which they characterize as pre-contemplation, contemplation, planning, action, and maintenance—and their implications for a more autonomous client context for assessment, diagnosis, and social work intervention. Clearly implied is the client's use of dynamic developmental and cultural categories of meaning, feeling, thought, and understanding to solve problems and achieve self-directed change. Positive uses of internal disequilibrium are emphasized, along with an implied reaffirmation that the person is not the problem—but the problem is the problem (Warren, Franklin, & Streeter 1998).

In departing from a linear causality model, von Bertalanffy introduced systems theory by drawing on the concept of living organisms developing and surviving based on feedback of information from internal subsystems and the external environment. This information is routed to one dominant subsystem at each of the four social system levels, a subsystem that carries responsibility and authority for final decision making around choices that have an impact on the organism. Applying this theory, one can recognize than an organism's central nervous system and cortical stem can represent an individual in society; the organism's mother (matrilineal), father (patriarchal), or the marital pair consensually (post-patriarchal) can represent the family; the organisms within a location can represent the board of directors in an organization; and larger numbers of organisms can represent communities or part of a community (i.e., elected council, provincial legislature, or federal parliament in post-feudal societies). Thanks to a unique capacity for vocabulary building, language development, and cultural evolution, each person within a social system is able to use information feedback to self-steer not only for survival but for other goals as well as build knowledge, work toward self-actualization, care for neighbours and others in society, develop third-party dispute settlement procedures, promote economic development, and educate the young in a moving equilibrium of safety and satisfactions conserved by an evolving culture. Social systems theory, described at a pure theory level of discourse, has been and continues to be a great gift from academia to practitioners. Without such contributions, there would be little for professional schools and practitioners to apply to real-life situations—as true for social work as for such engineered products as satellites, computer applications, or automated manufacturing equipment within inanimate systems. Graduate and post-graduate professional schools of social work, clinical psychology, medicine, and psychiatry have taken special responsibility to pioneer the applications of such theories to animate systems. In the context of the individual, medicine has long identified a roster of biological subsystems and their interdependency; medical diagnosis has long recognized the importance of first identifying in which specific subsystem a problem is focused: cardiovascular, respiratory, gastrointestinal, muscular-skeletal, central nervous subsystem, among others. Psychology subsequently greatly enlarged the knowledge base for the central nervous system. Developmentally based theory, cognitively

based theory, crisis-oriented theory, and task theory have added richly to an understanding of the interactions between biological maturation, evolving family structure, and the products of an evolving culture that are stored, retrieved, and dynamically active in human functioning (Turner 1999). In the context of the family or small group, a subsystem nomenclature, which includes the marital pair, parent/child roles, and sibling relationships has proven useful. In the context of organizations, identifiable subsystems with distinct and differentiated functions can include the policy board, the management and supervisory unit, staff units serving the organization, and line units serving clientele. Ambiguity and conflict around role expectations between/among members of these distinct structural units is well documented as a major source of organizational dysfunction and distress. In the context of the community, a different set of institutionalized subsystems can be identified, historically evolved, and very much available as possible trouble spots, and a locus of disequilibrium and intervention for the community development and policy advocate practitioner. Clearly, the political subsystem is dominant, with identifiable educational, economic, religious, professional, ethnic, transportation, and communications subsystems (i.e., boards of education, business corporations, church and synagogue bodies, professional associations, along with the organization of government itself: parliament, prime minister, and ministry departments at the federal level). While recognizing the organic interdependency of subsystems within each of the four social systems levels, the component relationship transience between them is also noteworthy: individuals composing the family or small group, small groups composing the organization, and organizations composing the community/society.

The literature of social systems theory struggles a bit in finding ways to distinguish between the system and subsystem of a living organism, and the information content flowing through them. The problem is somewhat similar to distinguishing anatomy from physiology, which J.G. Miller (1965) discerned as one between "maintenance energies" and "signal energies"; in some respects, the distinction between pure theory and applied theory is also analogous here. In the context of the individual, clearly, information and knowledge content—which at any time is stored and retrievable in the brain stem—can vary widely from person to person with no differences in structure or function. In the context of the community, the substantive content of legislation and approved programs—including related civil society constituency action—can vary from century to century and from state to state. Structure occasionally has changed too, as with the post-feudal transfer of the power of the purse and authority from monarch to parliament and the emergence of the democratic state. In the 1950s and 1960s in North America, the structural/functional debate created a great stir in academe focused implicitly on the necessity for yet further structural change in the political subsystem. Marxist students, in response to Talcott Parson's *The Social System*, argued that only a change in the structure of the democratic and capitalist state could bring hope for the future, while non-Marxist scholars insisted that changes in the content of legislation within democratic state structure could best do the job. A somewhat similar debate in more recent decades has emerged between radical and socialist feminists, on the one hand, and liberal feminists and their scholarly allies, on the other, as to the marital subsystem of the family: should the structure of the marital pair subsystem be displaced, or should the substantive content of role expectations between husband and wife change. Pure theory, including general systems theory, apparently can remain fairly free from controversy until the applied dimensions of the theory are articulated. Yet for the prevention or treatment of human distress, the content rather than the structural dimension supplies crucial change to history and to real-life situations.

[*Sheldon L. Rahn*]

RELATED ENTRIES

Community Organization, Ecological Theory, Mutual Aid, Natural Helping Networks, Networks, Self-Help Groups, Self Help & Mutual Aid, Social Policy & Practice, Social Work Profession, Social Work Theory, Theory & Practice

REFERENCES

Chess, W.A., and J.M. Norlin. 1988. *Human Behavior and Social Environment: A Social Systems Model*. Toronto: Allyn and Bacon.

Hearn, G. (Ed.) 1969. *General Systems Theory: Contributions toward a Holistic Conception of Social Work*. New York: Council on Social Work Education.

Miller, J.G. 1965. Living Systems: Basic Concepts. *Behavioral Science* 10, 193–237, 380–411.

Rahn, S.L. 1981. *General Systems Theory Applications to Community Development Practice*. Presentation at a conference on Community Development in the 1980s sponsored by the Faculty of Social Work, University of Michigan and the School of Social Work, University of Louisville, February 18–19.

Sanders, I.T. 1958. *The Community: An Introduction to a Social System*. New York: Ronald Press.

Turner, F.J. (Ed.) 1999. *Social Work Practice: A Canadian Perspective*. Chapter I. Toronto: Allyn and Bacon.

von Bertalanffy, L. 1950. The Theory of Open Systems in Physics and Biology. *Science* 3, 23–29.

——. 1968. *General Systems Theory: Foundations, Development, Applications*. New York: George Braziller.

Warren, K., C. Franklin, and C.L. Streeter. 1998. New Directions in Systems Theory: Chaos and Complexity. *Social Work* 43, 4, 357–72.

task-centred theory

Task-centred theory—developed by and specifically for social work—views intervention as a brief structured process with a clearly defined profile of activities. Problems are defined by the client and not by the social worker, and the relationship with the client is central, as it is the medium in which problem solving occurs. The focus of the process is to help clients plan and carry out a series of tasks as a strategy of problem solving leading to a positive outcome; therapy involves formal contracting over the steps to be taken by either party—practitioner or client—toward a solution. The relationship is supportive with a high degree of expectancy that something is going to happen and change. Although originally developed as a model for one-to-one intervention, research has demonstrated that it is effective in work with families, dyads, and groups as well as a useful underpinning for case management. An optimistic approach to practice, task-centred theory embraces the values that people want to change, want to participate actively in the process of change, and are willing to take responsibility for the tasks they agree to undertake in their contract. As task-centred theory stresses the need to build practice on an empirical base, it has a strong research base. The principal authors of task-centred theory were Dr. William Reid and Dr. Laura Epstein. The theory evolved in the late 1960s when considerable interest was focused on the possibility for using much briefer intervention than models that had emerged from psychodynamic traditions. Research had indicated that many clients appeared to benefit considerably from brief contacts with a social worker, and from active involvement in resolving a problem(s) they brought to a practitioner. The original conceptualization of this theory focused on the concepts of problem as developed by Helen Harris Perlman and those of task as formulated by E. Studt. This therapeutic approach is very popular in Canadian social work and is frequently taught in schools and faculties of social work.

[FJT]

RELATED ENTRIES

Brief Treatment, Goal Setting, Theory & Practice

technology

Any description of social work in Canada at the beginning of the twentieth-first century has to acknowledge the role of information technology in practice. Information technology refers to computer hardware and software and such related equipment as telephones, faxes, cellular telephones, and scanners that people use to create, manage, use, and transmit information. Canada is one of the most wired countries in the world; penetration rates within the country of telephone, cable, and video recorder are among the highest in the world, and a recent research survey identified Canadians as the world leader in time spent per user on the Internet. Computer competency has become a new expertise required of social workers. In a major sector survey of social work employers in Canada, the need for enhanced skills in computer technology was identified as the Achilles heel, or largest gap, of the three background skills (Stephensen et al. 2000). An earlier Canadian study found that social work staff were favourably inclined toward computers, even though they identified such specific problems as inaccurate data, failure of computers to increase productivity, and an increase in paperwork linked to computerization (Gandy & Tepperman 1990). Almost all Canadian social workers now employ technology in some form on a daily basis. One of the first tasks new social workers face when beginning employment is becoming competent with the agency information system used to track client information, services, and, in some cases, outcomes. Increasingly, social workers find themselves spending more time in front of a computer and less in direct contact with clients; this trend is becoming a major concern especially in fields such as child protection where documentation is a significant part of the role. Computers are used for such functions as word processing, appointment scheduling, record keeping, communication (i.e., email), accessing information internal to the organization (i.e., from an agency intranet), or externally (i.e., from the Internet), financial and human resource management, statistical analysis, and professional presentations. Clinically, computers are being used by some social workers for assessment, intervention, and evaluation (MacFadden 1999).

The graphical component of the Internet continues to provide substantial resources for social workers and their clients. Social agencies are increasingly positioning themselves on the Internet through websites that offer such features as information about their services, maps, links to other important information and resources, volunteer recruitment, job vacancies, donation opportunities, and areas where committee work can be conducted online. Agencies are making websites available that can be searched for the availability of particular services and features to aid in matching client needs with these specialized resources (e.g., < www.oarty.net >). Social work therapy is being offered online in various forms— such as e-therapy and therapy email (Murphy & Mitchell 1998)—and e-support groups are increasing in numbers. Internet-based training and education are becoming more available to social workers; Dalhousie University's Maritime School of Social Work began offering the first Internet-based master's of social work Program in Canada in September 2001 (< is.dal.ca/~schsw/distance/ >). Schools of social work are enhancing their websites from merely providing information to encouraging direct student use in course selection and registering, accessing, and maintaining their own student records. Specialized websites exist that contain links to hundreds of social work resources (e.g., <www.nyu.edu/socialwork/www rsw>). Some sites contain important information on various cultures and customs. (e.g., <cwr.uto ronto.ca/cultural>). As information technology continues to transform social work, ethical concerns persist on such issues as confidentiality, privacy, depersonalization, and the lack of equal access of Canadians to this technology, resulting in a digital divide of technological haves and have nots. The challenge remains for social workers to become familiar with and competent in ethical and effective use of technology, and to keep themselves current as technology and software change rapidly.

[*Robert J. MacFadden*]

RELATED ENTRIES

Communication Theory, Ethics, Information & Communication Technologies, Social Work Profession, Theory & Practice

REFERENCES

Gandy, J., and L. Tepperman. 1990. *False Alarm: The Computerization of Eight Social Welfare Organizations.* Waterloo, ON: Wilfrid Laurier University Press.

MacFadden, R.J. 1999. Information Technology in Social Work Practice: Challenges and Opportunities. In F.J. Turner (Ed.) *Canadian Social Work Practice* 448–76. Boston, MA: Allyn and Bacon.

Murphy, L., and Mitchell, D. 1998. When Writing Helps to Heal: E-mail as Therapy. *British Journal of Guidance and Counselling* 26, 21–31.

Stephensen, M., G. Rondeau, J. Michaud, and S. Fiddler. 2000. *In Critical Demand: Social Work in Canada.* Ottawa: Human Resources Development Canada.

theory and practice

The activities of social workers practitioners— as for any professionals—are presumed to be based on a recognized and sanctioned theoretical base for which the profession and the individual practitioner are to be held accountable. To what extent this commitment is fulfilled in contemporary Canadian social work practice has yet to be fully demonstrated. In their training and in the post-graduation process of continuing education, all social workers are now exposed formally or informally to some components from a rich theoretical spectrum. While social work in North America initially suffered from a deficit of theory, the contemporary challenge is how to teach and how to determine among some thirty bodies of theory which is/are most appropriate as conceptual bases for practice. What remains to be demonstrated are matches of approaches to practice in particular situations with a single theory or a combination of theories. The relating of theory and practice is of particular importance in the current climate of accountability and pressures to demonstrate the effectiveness and efficiency of practice. In the sociopolitical sphere of the profession, the most common response to selection among the theoretical diversity is to train social workers in a generalist emphasis, which postulates a multi-theory approach to practice; the principal drawback of a generalist emphasis is that it stresses problem solving, which is a more limited goal of intervention. In some ways, a social worker cannot but act from some conceptual framework; the difficulty for assessment may be identifying which theory or from which part of the spectrum of theoretical bases a particular practitioner is acting. Some practitioners view theory almost as a pejorative concept that inhibits practice by making it overly cerebral; they may argue that effective practice stems from an ability to respond quickly and sensitively to an individual client in an empathic way that avoids direct application of theory. Long-time practitioners are sometimes said to have acquired practice wisdom; although not specifically defined, practice wisdom appears to describe the knowledge and skill developed by experienced practitioners, usually thought to be based on practice alone. Implicit in this concept is an attitude that perceives theory as somehow antithetical to practice; it is also likely that theory has become absorbed into the practice techniques of experienced practitioners that they are no longer acutely conscious of it. Since theory is developed and refined from such accumulations of practice skill, an essential ongoing challenge for the profession is finding effective ways to remind experienced practitioners of the theory/ies underlying their practice and to have them articulate and explicate to researchers ways in which they may be adjusting this theoretical base. This process can permit the profession to continue to enrich practice by a more focused and direct application of theory, and to further expand theory by drawing on practitioners' experience to better understanding the basis of effective intervention.

[*FJT*]

RELATED ENTRIES

Education in Social Work, Practice Methods, Research, Social Work Profession, Social Work Theory; (*Theories:*) Administrative Theory & Practice, Anti-oppressive Social Work, Behaviour Theory, Biopsychosocial Theory, Cognitive Theory, Communication Theory, Constructivism, Ecological Theory, Ego Psychology, Empowerment Theory, Functional Theory, Generalist Practice, Gestalt Theory, Healing Theory (Cree), Jungian Theory, Knowledge Base, Life-Model Theory, Materialist Theory, Narrative Theory, Neurolinguistic Programming Theory, Organizational Theory, Personal-Centred Theory, Person-in-Environment Perspective, Problem-Solving Theory, Psychoanalytic Theory, Role Theory, Social Planning, Social Work Theory, Systems Theory, Task-Centred Theory, Transactional Analysis Theory, Transpersonal Psychology; (*Practice:*) Aboriginal Issues, Administrative Theory & Practice, Advocacy, Anti-oppressive Social Work, Brief Treatment, Caregiving, Case Management, Citizen Participation, Conflict Resolution, Counselling, Creativity, Credit Counselling, Crisis Intervention, Demography, Direct Practice, Disaster Practice, Education in Social Work, Environmental Issues, Ethnic-Sensitive Practice, Ethno-cultural Practice, Forensic Practice, Generalist Practice, Goal Setting, Group Practice, Home Care, Indirect Practice, International Practice, Interviewing, Knowledge Base, Legal Issues, Long-Term Care, Macro Practice, Managed Care, Mediation, Mezzo Practice, Micro Practice, Military Social Work, Minority-Sensitive Practice, Multi-skilling, Music Intervention, Natural Helping Networks, Networks, Non-clinical Practice, Peer Counselling, Practice Methods, Private Practice, Private-Sector Employment, Professional Issues, Professional Liability, Program Evaluation, Quality Assurance, Radical Social Work, Racism-Sensitive Social Work, Recording, Reflective Practice, Remote Practice, Remote & Rural Practice Methods, School Social Workers, Self Help & Mutual Aid, Sensitizing Concepts, Social Policy & Practice, Social Work Profession, Spirituality, Technology, Therapy, Treatment

therapy

Therapy refers to the functions of a social worker in the process of addressing intra/interpersonal problems of clients from an identified theoretical perspective. As such, it is of importance to practitioners of micro social work. Implicit in the process of therapy is the goal of building on a client's inherent strengths and available systemic resources to bring about some change in life of the client or the client's significant systems, usually involving a better understanding of him/herself and others, and the way in which he/she functions in particular situations and with particular people. Often, the change is effected by helping the client identify and come to understand some aspect of their personality that they hitherto have unaware of. The importance of such enhanced self-awareness varies with different theories but, overall, practitioners are committed to the importance of the therapeutic relationship as one of the critical and powerful media of change. Inherent in the concept of therapy is the need for high competence in skill, knowledge, and training as well as access to supervision and consultation by therapists; as such, therapy has come to be viewed by many in the profession as having a higher status than counselling. Some consider that therapy is a more precise term for intervention. Others perceive use of the term as inappropriate in Canadian social work, as "therapy" is said to presume pathology on the part of a client and control over the client by the social worker—rather than basing practice on client strengths and a collaborative client/practitioner relationship. Aside from discussions within the profession on appropriate terminology, there are three advantages to identifying therapy as a form of social work practice. First, some clients and potential clients identify their problems as ones that require therapy, and view social workers as the right profession for this service. Second, some insurance companies and vendors will cover clients' costs for therapy but not those for counselling or casework. Third, some provincial legislation identifies social work among professions that are recognized as competent to provide therapy and psychotherapy and, thereby, giving access to health insurance benefits for such services. In those provinces, social workers who use the term "therapy" can increase the resources available to clients.

[*FJT*]

RELATED ENTRIES

Abuse, Addiction, Bereavement, Bioethical Issues, Child Abuse, Clinical Social Work, Codes of Ethics, Counselling, Deafness, Developmental Challenges, Eating Disorders, Elder Abuse, Ethics, Empowerment Theory, Environmental Issues, Family Therapy, HIV/ AIDS, Individual Therapy, Long-Term Care, Medication, Palliative Care, Pharmacological Therapy, Play Therapy, Psychoanalytic Theory, Psychotropic Medication, Sexual Abuse of Children, Substance Addiction, Suicide, Torture & Trauma Victims, Transactional Analysis, Treatment, Visual Impairment, Vocational Rehabilitation Wellness

Thompson Rivers University School of Social Work and Human Service

In September 1990 the University College of the Cariboo in Kamloops (renamed Thompson Rivers University in 2005) began offering the bachelor of social work degree in partnership with the University of Victoria. This initiative was developed in response to the growing need for undergraduate degree education in interior and northern areas of British Columbia and specifically as part of the university-college concept, Until 1997 the Cariboo social work students graduated with University of Victoria degrees and met all entrance, curriculum, and graduation requirements of the University of Victoria. In 1996 the university-college attained independent degree-granting status from the BC government and accreditation with the Association of Universities and Colleges in Canada. While development of an independent mission statement, curriculum, and academic policies had been underway for several years, the university-college received candidacy status with the Canadian Association of Schools of Social Work in 1997, when it admitted its first Cariboo-only bachelor of social work students. Kamloops, located in south-central British Columbia, is in an area with a somewhat diverse rural population and many First Nation communities. The School of Social Work has been committed to principles of social justice, equity, and respect for diversity since its inception. In 1996 this was the first BC school of

social work to develop and publicize an equity admission policy, which reserved 25 percent of admission seats for minority applicants; the goal was implemented with some public controversy, but the school furthered its goals of educating the public about structural barriers for disadvantaged students and increasing the diversity of its students. With other BC schools of social work, Thompson Rivers has been part of a number of major provincial social work initiatives. In response to the Gove Inquiry into Child Protection in BC, the school offered a twelve-month concentrated bachelor of social work program to staff in the BC Ministry for Children and Families who held degrees in other disciplines. This successful initiative led to the development of a child welfare specialization within the bachelor's degree program, which was offered for the first time in 2000. In response to the growing educational needs of the community, the school has entered into two recent educational partnerships. To further the commitment to Aboriginal peoples, the school began offering the full bachelor's program to First Nation students at the Nicola Valley Institute of Technology in Merritt in 1998. And, in response to the growing demand for graduate social work education, the university has collaborated with the University of British Columbia to offer its master's of social work program in the Kamloops region. From its beginning as a small community college offering one-year certificate programs in human service work (which it still offers), the University College of the Cariboo (Thompson Rivers University) has already developed a rich history as a unique school of social work striving to be responsive to the diverse and changing needs of the community. Current information about the social work programs can be found online at < www.cariboo.bc.ca/social work/ >.

[*Grant D. Larson*]

RELATED ENTRIES

Board of Registration for Social Workers of BC, British Columbia Association of Social Workers, Education in Social Work, Faculties of Social Work

Toronto Infants' Home

The Toronto Infants' Home (est. 1875) was instrumental in providing early child welfare services in Toronto and advocating for many of the policies and procedures that formed the foundation of the child welfare system in Toronto and Ontario. The Infants' Home for destitute mothers and their babies was opened through the advocacy and fundraising efforts by Dr. Fenton Cameron and Ann Cameron; they had worked for more than twenty years in the face of Victorian disdain for these women and infants. The home focused on preparing mothers to breast-feed their babies and to train as a domestic servant, while encouraging mothers to place their children for adoption in a boarding group home or with relatives. The Infants' Home began in a six-room home, originally operating as a small nursery in conjunction with the Burnside Lying-In Hospital, where unwed mothers delivered their babies. Within twenty-five years, it had developed into a 150-bed facility that also accepted babies who had been abandoned or rescued from "baby farms." The home was responsible for all adoption services until 1891 and advocated for the licensing of children's boarding homes, which occurred in Toronto in 1887 and throughout Ontario in 1898. In 1877 the name was changed to the Infants' Home and Infirmary to reflect the many child residents who were under the age of two and received medical care there, as, at that time, the Hospital for Sick Children did not accept children under two years of age. Initially, the home focused on medical issues, in response to the high child mortality rate of the time, but evolved over time to provide combined medical and social services. Gradually, the home again changed its focus to foster care provision, rather than institutional care, for children and infants, as a means to increase health and reduce mortality. In 1919 the long-time executive secretary of the home, Vera Moberly (1919–45), was a nurse and social worker; Moberly was instrumental in developing nursing foster homes in Toronto where babies and their unmarried mothers could live together. In 1926 the Infants' Home closed as a shelter and became a child placement agency, which worked in co-operation with the Toronto Children's Aid Society, whose focus was mainly child protection. The home changed its name in 1942 to the Infants' Home of Toronto; in 1947, the home built a new facility, the Infants' Home Receiving Centre. In 1951 the Infants' Home of Toronto and the Toronto Children's Aid Society merged to provide comprehensive child protection and child placement services in tandem.

[*Susan Preston*]

RELATED ENTRIES

Adoption, Child Advocacy, Child Welfare, Children's Aid Society (Toronto), Non-governmental Organizations, Parenting, Pregnancy, Services for Children, Services for Women, Single Parents, Social Welfare History, Wellness

torture and trauma victims

Victims of torture and trauma experience a disconnection from the foundational belief in human life as hopeful and meaningful. The nature and extent of the precipitating event, the resilience and resources of the individual, and the accessibility and timeliness of reconnecting interventions determine the existential outcome for victims of torture and trauma. An all-out assault on psychological defences protecting an individual's sense of identity and trust, trauma can derive from accidental or deliberate causes. Trauma can result from natural disasters (e.g., floods, tornadoes, earthquakes) and from accidents (e.g., airplane crashes, fires, widespread food poisoning), where trauma is not related to a misuse of social power, as it is when trauma is caused deliberately. In childhood physical abuse, rape, murder, war, and torture, among others, trauma occurs as much as a result of the terror of the experience as of the recognition of the perpetrator's deliberate attempt to gain and preserve power over the victim. Nowhere is this truer than in the act of torture, the "long-term strategic destruction of physical, mental and spiritual capacity" (Suedfeld 1990). All trauma, be it accidental or deliberate, results in the victim's sense of disempowerment, but trauma engendered by torture has overwhelming implications of disempowerment not only for the individual but, by basic design and objective, for an entire community. Unlike other types of trauma, torture can become state-sanctioned: that is, the very structure set up to protect the security and safety of individuals and communities deliberately sets out to destroy not individual persons, but the individual's contextual supports—family, community, and culture—as well. Endemic trauma and torture has occurred recently in countries such as Rwanda, Kosovo, and Iraq. Colonial

powers in many powers have tortured or traumatized indigenous peoples; Canada, for example,
is on record for forcibly apprehending Aboriginal
children to educate them apart from their parents, language, and culture. Today, many Aboriginal individuals and communities continue to suffer the effects of trauma brought about by their
residential school experiences. Just as events of
trauma and torture can be categorized over a wide
range, effects from trauma and torture in victims
also vary. The fourth edition of the *Diagnostic and
Statistical Manual of Mental Disorders* describes
the most commonly understood effects as symptoms of post-traumatic stress disorder, including
depression, nightmares, flashbacks, and somatic
disorders resulting from a disturbance of the auto-
nomic nervous system. Psychodynamically, effects
of deliberate trauma and particularly of torture
include a profound combination of shame, guilt,
mental disorganization, pessimism, lack of trust,
and social isolation. People do not have to
undergo torture directly to experience symptoms
or effects, such is the insidious nature of this form
of brutality when it is aimed at domination
broader than that of the direct victim. Relatives
of victims who disappear or who return broken,
community observers who experience the betrayal
of neighbours, at times, even the torturers themselves may experience symptoms and effects. One
of the most articulate exponents of the traumatic
effects of indirect experience is former UN peace-
keeper General Romeo Dallaire, who publicly
detailed the agonizing pain and mental collapse
he experienced on returning to Canada from the
1994 Rwandan genocidal war.

Estimates suggest that as much as 30 percent of
the world's refugee population experience torture
as well as the trauma of war and loss. Of these refugees, many are women and children. Their access to home, country, and employment resources
are very limited; further, effects of trauma and torture will persist, depending on the duration of
their trauma; for example, some refugees are given
the opportunity to escape through such govern-
ment-sanctioned programs such as the airlift of
some Kosovars to Canada in 1999. Others may be
incarcerated in camps or may be transients in
countries refusing them any residency status.
Some victims of trauma and torture have solid
social supports as a stabilizing resource, for exam-

ple, family overseas who provide refugee sponsorship. As more of a victim's immediate family
and community are directly and deliberately traumatized, the less the victim can call on his/her
own resilience. In victims of torture and trauma,
resilience does not have measurable properties.
Often only after a person has been resettled or
his/her life conditions have been reorganized does
the full impact of the trauma hit. Time can increasingly unsettle some victims (van der Veer 1992),
as evident from the number who commit suicide
years after the event.

A key resource to all victims of torture and
trauma is the timeliness of appropriate intervention. The lives of victims of deliberate torture
and trauma must be rebuilt, requiring short- and
long-term interventions; however, psychosocial
effects of torture and other examples of deliberately perpetrated trauma are such that shame,
guilt, and lack of trust may constrain a victim from
seeking help. While many victims of torture live
in Canada—12,000 living in Calgary alone (Canadian Red Cross 1995), the ongoing agony they
experience is largely unknown to, and/or unrecognized, by the Canadian public (Hossie 1991).
Therefore, outreach to victims of torture must
include a raising of the awareness of the need,
which includes acceptance of their plight as well
as the provision of a various connecting services
that can offer medical and psychosocial interventions. Again, an impediment relating to trauma
treatment, which even in the most glancing of
interventions requires acknowledgment by the
victim, is the victim's own suppression of memory;
so horrible, so agonizing are these memories that
most victims prefer to suppress such pain (Herman 1992). Because of an overall low level of
awareness in Canada of the enormity of torture
combined with most victims' overt preference to
avoid reliving their torture and trauma, an option
might be to treat only symptoms of torture and
trauma in a non-contextual way. Most experts on
torture and trauma agree, however, that medication or somatic intervention, albeit of significant
value, will not address the deep-rooted issues of
disconnectedness from self and from community.
Ideally, programs to intervene with victims of torture and trauma, such as the Canadian Centre for
Victims of Torture in Toronto, use medical, psychosocial, and volunteer befriending components

to rebuild people's lives. In every intervention, experts stress the importance of openness to, and non-judgment of the victim to fully understand the experience and to reintroduce trust. In turn, as victims become stronger, their experience can provide empathic support to other victims and the voices to educate around the needs of victims in what the director of the Canadian Centre for Victims of Torture, Mulugeta Abai, himself a victim of torture, calls circles of healing. Throughout Canada, social workers engage more and more in helping victims of torture and trauma and in the process realize the importance of operating within micro, mezzo, and macro spheres: that is, intervening instrumentally and psychodynamically with individuals and their families, raising awareness and advocating within their communities for more services to victims of torture and trauma, and seeking greater justice within a world, which continues to sanction the use of torture.

[*Heather Haas Barclay*]

RELATED ENTRIES

Abuse, Bereavement, Child Abuse, Clinical Social Work, Crisis Intervention, *Diagnostic and Statistical Manual of Mental Disorders*, Disaster Practice, Elder Abuse, Personal-Centred Theory, Sensitizing Concepts, Sexual Abuse of Children, Suicide, Vicarious Traumatization, Wellness, Women Abuse

REFERENCES

Canadian Red Cross. 1995. *Survivors of Torture Volunteer Support Program.* Calgary, AB: The Society.

Herman, J.L. 1992. *Trauma and Recovery.* New York: Basic Books.

Hossie, L. 1991. Hiding Our Eyes from Horrible Truths. The *Globe & Mail.* 10 September.

Suedfeld, P. (Ed.) 1990. *Psychology and Torture.* New York: Hemisphere.

van der Veer, G. 1992. *Counselling and Therapy with Refugees.* Chichester, UK: John Wiley.

Bessie Touzel (1904–97)

Touzel, Bessie, social justice activist, Canadian and international social worker; b. Sept. 03, 1904, Killaloe, ON; Jubilee Medal (1935), Coronation Medal (1953), Confederation Medal (1967); d. Apr. 24, 1997, Ottawa, ON

Bessie Touzel began her social work career, after receiving her Diploma in Social Work in 1928, with the Neighbourhood Workers Association settlement services in the east end of Toronto. She witnessed profound human suffering during the great depression of the 1930s; attracted to Marxism, she became motivated for radical action to improve people's lives, particularly those of women. Serving as director of public welfare services in Ottawa (1933–36), she developed one of the best relief programs in the province. When the forty women case workers she had hired were arbitrarily fired by Ottawa's council to be replaced by eleven male detectives to investigate welfare fraud, Touzel resigned her position. From 1937 to 1947, she was executive director of the Toronto Welfare Council and, in the 1940s, also served as advisor to the Marsh Committee on Social Security, which led to the development of the Family Allowance Program. As director of the welfare council, Touzel helped to develop the first research-based minimum standard for social living (i.e., a poverty line). Her report, entitled "The Cost of Living: a Study of the Cost of a Standard of Living in Toronto," was published by the council in 1939. It was the first attempt to quantify welfare standards based on research, as Touzel had had 116 low-income families keep detailed journals of what they spent on basic necessities for one year. The report identified a gap of 32 percent between the basic needs of these families and their actual expenditures. A further research report in 1941 established that food allowances were 40 percent below the minimum required for health. The provincial government cut subsidies to Toronto by 50 percent but, under Touzel's leadership, the city implemented a higher food allowance without provincial support. The province was forced to develop more adequate standards for welfare payments. Touzel also led a struggle by social agencies and women's groups to establish a public welfare committee to oversee the city's welfare department. In 1947 Touzel resigned her position as director of the Toronto Welfare Council when the board decided not to continue issuing new editions of her cost of living report. In the late 1940s, she was commissioned to conduct a major review of welfare services in New Brunswick; when the Saint John River flooded, she was called on to use her enormous skills to organize relief. Touzel continued her crusade for social justice as director of the Ontario Welfare Council until she retired in 1964. She then served for two years on a United Nations assignment as advisor to the government of Tanzania. There, she advocated for women, families, and children; for example, she was a founding member of the Voice of Women, which worked with other women's groups to improve the status of Tanzanian women.

In addition to international and national honours, Touzel received the City of Toronto Award of Merit (1959); the Outstanding Contribution To Social Work Award, Eastern Ontario Branch, Ontario Association of Professional Social Workers (1985); and the Order of Ontario (1987). In 1994 she was awarded an honorary doctor of laws from the University of Toronto, as well as the Most Distinguished Graduate Award from the university's Faculty of Social Work. On September 15, 1998, the Social Work Alumni Association and the University of Toronto Faculty of Social Work sponsored a tribute to Bessie Touzel; during it, her nephew, John Patton, said of her that: "Above all, the passion and righteous indignation of her lifelong struggle for social justice was tempered by her boundless generosity of spirit and never-failing sense of humour" (FSW 1998: 3–7). On the same occasion, Margaret Hancock, a founding member of the Network for Social Justice and current Warden of Hart House, University of Toronto, said that Touzel was "someone who acted on her principles throughout her life to create systems for a socially just society, someone who made a difference and who continues to make a difference through each of us" (FSW 1998: 22–33). The press release for the tribute stated that Touzel had "provided leadership as a practitioner, administrator, advocate, for the poor and analyst/critic of social policy. She demonstrated that it is possible to influence decision makers using research coupled with commitment to the values based on social justice and equity."

[*Doris E. Guyatt*]

RELATED ENTRIES

Canadian Welfare Council, Family Allowance Act, Marsh Report on Social Security, Poverty, Social Justice, Social Welfare History

REFERENCE

FSW. 1998. Proceedings of the Bessie Touzel Tribute (September 15). 3–40. Faculty of Social Work, University of Toronto.

Trades and Labour Congress of Canada*

Trades and Labour Congress of Canada, the second Canadian central labour organization, was founded in 1883 on the initiative of the Toronto Trades and Labor Council. A successor to the Canadian Labor Union (1873–77), it first met in Toronto as the Canadian Labor Congress but changed its name to TLC at its second convention in 1886. Largely controlled by the Knights of Labor, the TLC initially brought together trade unionists from Ontario, but by 1900 the organization had become national in character. In 1902 at the Berlin (Kitchener), Ontario, convention, however, its expulsion of all unions, which were also American Federation of Labor chartered bodies ended its near hegemony of the Canadian labour movement. Thereafter the movement was splintered by national unions, by overly socialist and syndicated bodies, and by the rise of Industrial Unionism.

In 1919 political tension within the TLC reached crisis level, and socialist and industrial unionists bolted to form the One Big Union. After the defeats suffered by industrial unionists during the massive 1919 strike wave, the TLC re-emerged as the major central body. Its next challenge came with the renewed drive for industrial unionism led by the Workers Unity League and later by the Committee for Industrial Organization (funded 1935; became Congress of Industrial Organizations (CIO) in 1938). Again splits in the USA between AFL and CIO supporters led to a reluctant 1939 expulsion of Canadian industrial unionists from the TLC. The renegades founded the Canadian Congress of Labour (CCL) in 1940. Rapid growth of industrial unionism during and immediately after WW II left the CCL as the major labour power.

After a hysterical witch-hunt against communists in both labour centrals in the late 1940s and early 1950s and the merger of the AFL and the CIO in the USA in 1955, the CCL, and the TLC united in 1956 to create the Canadian Labour Congress.

[*Gregory S. Kealey*]

*Used unedited by permission from *The Canadian Encyclopedia*. 2000. Toronto: McClelland and Stewart.

RELATED ENTRIES

Employment, Non-Governmental Organizations

transactional analysis theory

The transactional analysis theory of treatment was developed by Canadian-born psychiatrist Eric Berne (né Bernstein, 1910–70), who was greatly influenced by the work of Charles Darwin and Erik Erickson (1902–94). The theory is built on three basic assumptions: that people are born healthy, that people are capable of solving problems in their lives, and that people are essentially good and capable of leading healthy satisfying lives. Transactional analysis stresses the importance of understanding interpersonal interaction or transactions; while it acknowledges the existence of the unconscious, it puts more importance on what is actual happening in people's lives. It is a highly flexible approach to practice that has demonstrated positive effects in social work with dyads, groups, and families as well as individuals. Thomas Harris presented various life positions that people adopt in relation to others, characterizing this theory as "I'm okay; you're okay." As an approach to treatment, transactional analysis is applicable to all ages and stages, as well as a wide range of populations. Because its value base is congruent with that of social work, it has become very attractive to social workers. One of the identifying components of this theory that made it very popular is the unique vocabulary it developed; such terms as strokes, games, rackets, and scripts that are used to describe various ways in which people relate to others come from transactional analysis. It is a theory with a reasonably strong research base and is very open in its responsibility to assess its differential effectiveness. This theory views its strength as lying in its positive optimistic approach to treatment, one that minimizes a more classical psychodynamic interpretative form of therapy. Even though it is consistent with social work values, mission, and tradition, transactional analysis is not a theory that is frequently addressed as a discrete entity in the curricula of Canadian schools and faculties of social work.

[FJT]

RELATED ENTRIES

Clinical Social Work, Ego Psychology, Personal-Centred Theory, Psychoanalytic Theory, Theory & Practice, Transpersonal Psychology

transpersonal psychology

Transpersonal psychology is part of a growing wave in the literature of professional social work that recognizes the spiritual dimension of human nature. Often referred to as the fourth force in psychology following Freudian, behavioural, and humanistic forces, transpersonal psychology draws on the other three forces and goes beyond traditional approaches to see humans as institutive, mystical, psychic, and spiritual. With the growing interest in spirituality and its place in social work practice, a renewed interest has been expressed in transpersonal psychology. For the transpersonal therapist, spirituality refers to "the experience of wholeness and integration, irrespective of religious beliefs or affiliation" (Cowley 1993). Seen as the bridge between science and the spiritual traditions, transpersonal psychology is a theory that focuses on spiritual growth, spiritual emergencies, and the transformation of consciousness. The word transpersonal refers to "that which is through the persona, beyond the persona, correcting the personas" (Hendricks & Weinhold 1982). As the word *persona* (Latin root of the word person) means "mask," transpersonal means through the mask, beyond the mask, or connecting the masks. A key concept in transpersonal psychology is self-transcendence, involving the development of a sense of self that is deeper, broader, and beyond the boundaries of the ordinary. Self-transcendence is often achieved through life experiences that have been labelled spiritual, mystical, religious, occult, magical, or paranormal. Early stirrings of transpersonal psychology can be found in the writings of Carl Jung, an early follower of Freud who later rejected the tendency in Freudian thought to pathologize human nature; instead, he postulated that all mental illness after age thirty-five was spiritual in nature. Jung also introduced the concept of the collective unconscious whereby the deepest part of the human psyche was transpersonal, or common, to all humanity; he believed that all humans had the potential to access an inexhaustible data bank of the unconscious or spiritual realm. Through the use of active imagination, the analysis of dreams, and archetypes, the human psyche is able to connect with this collective unconsciousness and ultimately the infinite. His writings became the basis for the human potential movement that led such theorists as Abraham Maslow, Rollo May, and Carl Rogers to develop a more expansive, positive and holistic understanding of what it means to be fully human. Abraham Maslow is often identified as the founder of transpersonal psychology. Maslow's hierarchy of needs, which culminates in self-actualization, is introduced to students in most social work programs; prior to his death, however, Maslow added a further level to his hierarchy, which he labelled transcendence, or the surrender of the self into a higher sense, as the need that grows out of self-actualization. Individuals who attain this level of growth have strong contact with the spiritual dimension, are capable of going beyond the limitations of personal identity, and have a deep sense of eternity and the sacred.

Social work literature on transpersonal approaches is limited and the theory is not taught widely in Canadian social work programs. The inclusive and holistic nature of this theory seems to be congruent with current social work approaches, but adhering to transpersonal psychology may require a paradigm shift from traditional and reductionistic approaches that value goals and problem solving to more expansive and qualitative approaches that values ways of knowing and expanding levels of consciousness. A positive advantage of exposure to transpersonal thought is the opportunity to explore such topics such as diverse spiritual experiences, mystical states of consciousness, mindfulness and meditative practices, shamanic states, the use of ritual, the relationship between spiritual experience and disturbed states, and the transpersonal dimensions of encounters with the natural world. As social work explores ways to incorporate spirituality into social work practice, and to identify a social work response to ecological crises, the various approaches to transpersonal psychology may provide a theoretical model that introduces an expanded view of human nature as well as intervention that go beyond the traditional view of helping (Cowley 1999).

[*Brian Ouellette*]

RELATED ENTRIES

Meditation, Psychoanalytic Theory, Spirituality, Transactional Analysis Theory

REFERENCES

Cowley, A.S. 1993. Transpersonal Social Work: A Theory for the 1990s. *Social Work* 38, 5 (September), 527–34.

———. 1999. Transpersonal Social Work Practice with Couples and Families. *Journal of Family Social Work* 3, 2, 5–21.

Hendricks, G., and Weinhold, B. 1982. *Transpersonal Approaches to Counselling and Psychotherapy*. Denver, CO: Love.

treatment

Broadly speaking, social work treatment is an approach to intervention that utilizes practice theories to restore, maintain, and enhance biopsychosocial functioning. While the role of treatment in social work practice has been debated historically and currently (Haynes 1998), it continues to be a mainstay. An explicit definition for social work treatment is not straightforward, for a diversity of theoretical and practice reasons (Turner & Turner 1999). Social work treatment may be used with an individual, couple, family, or group, or with larger systems of an organization or community. In some cases, social work treatment incorporates multiple levels of practice. Similarly, no single social work practice theory dominates the treatment landscape. In fact, social work treatment may be characterized by a plethora of theoretical constructs and approaches to intervention. Rather than listing all the established social work treatment approaches, it may be more meaningful to identify common practice principles that characterize treatment. First, irrespective of theoretical diversity, all forms of social work treatment embrace a person-in-environment perspective. This perspective is a broad construct that views human behaviour within the context of the social environment. The person-in-environment perspective captures the reciprocal influence of the individual and their immediate surroundings; that is, the way individuals shape, and are shaped, by their environment. It contextualizes behaviour within a broader perspective and provides social workers with a framework to intervene at various levels. In the absence of the person-in-environment perspective, client problems are viewed as emanating primarily from within the individual. The person-in-environment perspective guides all phases of the assessment and intervention process. Social work treatment seeks to identify and actively utilizes client strengths. The identification of and respect for the client's capacity is a significant part of the helping process. In the absence of a strengths perspective, the worker may unduly focus on a client's weaknesses, deficits, or shortcomings. At the same time, social work treatment does not ignore the client's current limitations, which may constitute the very nature of the request for help and/or the desire for personal growth.

In conjunction with a focus on the client's strengths, social work treatment attempts to empower the client. From this perspective, treatment aids a client or client group in the attempt to gain, or regain, control over their lives and to enhance their own personal or external resources. The empowerment of clients, while important in all treatments, is most valuable when working with clients who are members of oppressed and marginalized communities. An empowerment perspective thwarts a paternalistic tendency on the part of a practitioner to determine what is good for the client. Social work treatment recognizes the centrality of the helping relationship as a cornerstone of the treatment process. A social worker's warmth, genuine concern, and empathy are thought to contribute significantly to the change process (Coady 1999). Efforts to establish empirically the efficacy of one approach over another are confounded by the ubiquitous influence of the helping relationship. In many cases, the absence of a positive interpersonal connection spells failure for the helping process; further, treatment is a collaborative venture. Therefore, treatment is not something that is done to people in need, but rather is a joint effort to achieve a client's goals. The nature of this collaboration has been referred to as a therapeutic alliance in which the worker and client share a positive bond and work toward a shared vision of tasks and goals. A strong therapeutic alliance has been associated with positive outcomes. Collaboratively, the dyad works toward the development of a shared understanding of problem(s) presented. More recently, the subjectivity of a social worker's experience in the helping relationship has been granted more influence; consequently, the worker's self-reflective capacity and purposeful use of self are considered

important variables in the treatment relationship (Hanna 1993).

Social work is driven by an organizing principle of social justice, which has increasingly become a central force in social work treatment. Recognition of this aspect of social work treatment aids the worker in attending to oppressive forces that are having a negative impact on a client's life. Social work treatment incorporates an understanding of the diversity that influences all aspects of people's lives. For instance, a person or group's ethnic, cultural, or religious influences, sexual orientation, and unique individual characteristics are just some of the diverse qualities that need to be taken into consideration in the treatment process. In addition to characterization by these principles, social work treatment can be broadly described as a nonlinear process that includes assessment, diagnosis, contracting, intervention, evaluation, and termination.

[*Brian Rasmussen*]

RELATED ENTRIES

Addiction, Attention Deficit Hyperactive Disorder, Assessment, Bioethical Issues, Brief Treatment, Clinical Social Work, Conflict Resolution, Counselling, Crisis Intervention, Deinstitutionalization Movement, Developmental Challenges, *Diagnostic and Statistical Manual of Mental Disorders*, Diversity, Developmental Challenges & Families, Ethics, Family Therapy, Hypnosis, Individual Therapy, Interviewing, Managed Care, Mediation, Medication, Meditation, Music Intervention, Peer Counselling, Personal Social Services, Person-in-Environment Perspective, Pharmacological Therapy, Play Therapy, Psychotropic Medication, Recording, Self-Help Groups, Self Help & Mutual Aid, Sensitizing Concepts, Social Work Profession, Social Work Theory, Substance Addiction, Task-Centred Theory, Therapy, Wellness

REFERENCES

Coady, N. 1999. The Helping Relationship. In F.J. Turner (Ed.) *Social Work Practice: A Canadian Perspective*. 5, 8–72. Toronto: Prentice Hall / Allyn and Bacon.

Hanna, E. 1993. The Implications of Shifting Perspectives in Countertransference on the Therapeutic Action of Clinical Social Work. Part ii: The Recent Totalist and Intersubjective Position. *The Journal of Analytic Social Work* 1, 3, 53–79.

Haynes, K. 1998. The One Hundred-Year Debate: Social Reform versus Individual Treatment. *Social Work* 43, 6, 501–09.

Turner, J.C., and Turner, F.J. (Eds.) 1999. *Social Work Practice: A Canadian Perspective.* Toronto: Prentice Hall / Allyn and Bacon.

Unemployment Assistance Program (1956–66)

Unemployment in varying degrees was a fact of life in Canada from earliest times. It became a matter of increasing public concern as the economy was transformed from farming and other forms of primary production mostly in rural areas to industrial and, especially in recent decades, urban production. The importance and magnitude of unemployment had not been envisaged or provided for in the Canadian constitution of 1867. Initially, the federal government took the position that meeting the needs of the unemployed was a responsibility of the provinces and their municipalities. This continued to be its view during the severe unemployment following the First World War and throughout the depression of the 1930s. All the senior government agreed to do was to provide relief money to the provinces on a year-to-year basis and, in the mid-1930s, to set up work camps for unemployed men. Pressed for action, the federal government in 1935 appointed a Royal Commission on unemployment; this commission recommended that the federal government assume the major responsibility for unemployment. Two other principal recommendations were for unemployment insurance to provide benefits to unemployed persons who had built up entitlement while employed, and unemployment assistance for unemployed able-bodied persons with less than full entitlement for insurance but capable of and available for employment.

After securing an amendment to the constitution, the federal government established an unemployment insurance program that went into effect in 1940. The commission's recommendation on unemployment assistance proposed federally funded and administered offices associated with the insurance offices but paying less generous benefits than those eligible for unemployment insurance. Unemployment did not surface immediately after the Second World War but became a

major problem in the mid-1950s. A sustained outcry forced the federal government to act but on a different basis than had been proposed earlier. With the agreement of the provinces, the federal government established in 1956 a federal/provincial shared-cost program which, when amended in 1957, provided federal sharing in assistance to all unemployed persons not receiving unemployment insurance benefits. The unemployment assistance program differed in important respects from existing shared-cost programs for aged, blind, and disabled Canadians. It left to the provinces the terms, conditions, and amounts of assistance granted to persons who were unemployed and in need. The coverage, moreover, was not limited to single individuals; the amount granted by a province to meet the needs of the applicant and his/her dependents was shareable. In addition coverage was extended to persons in homes for special care (e.g., nursing homes, hostels for indigent transients, homes for the aged, poor houses, and alms houses). All provinces joined the program and, as unemployment continued into the 1960s, it became the largest public assistance programs, extending aid by 1965 to some seven hundred thousand recipients with combined federal/provincial payments exceeding twenty million dollars. Flaws in the unemployment assistance legislation and the desirability of enacting a broader program that would permit the inclusion of recipients in other assistance measures led to the enactment in 1966 of the Canada Assistance Plan, a broader measure designed to assist the provinces in more fully meeting the social assistance needs of their people. Thus, in addition to providing assistance to thousands of persons in need, the unemployment assistance program provided an essential stepping stone for the Canada Assistance Plan, Canada's basic social safety net from 1966 to 1995.

[*Richard Splane*]

RELATED ENTRIES

Employment, Great Depression (1930s)

Unemployment Insurance Act

In November 1990, Parliament passed An Act to Amend the Unemployment Insurance Act and the Employment and Immigration Department and Commission Act. By this Act the federal government ended its contribution to the unemployment fund after a fifty-year history of participation. This Act was aimed at deficiencies in the original legislation especially around alleged disincentives to work. In general this Act resulted in more restrictive eligibility regulations and higher premiums, which were then to be paid solely by employers and employees.

[*FJT*]

RELATED ENTRIES
Employment, Social Welfare Context

United Farmers of Ontario *

United Farmers of Ontario (UFO), a farmers' educational social and political organization formed March 1914 in Toronto. The UFO united several small Ontario co-operatives, the Grange and the Farmers' Association. Immediately after the founding of the UFO, the same farmers organized a "twin" company, the United Farmers' Co-operative, to buy supplies and sell produce for Ontario farmers. The UFO grew slowly until late WW I, when labour shortages, inflated costs and a general dissatisfaction with existing political parties led to a rapid growth in membership. Auxiliary organizations, the United Farm Women and the United Farm Young People, helped to mobilize rural areas.

In 1919, with over 50,000 members, the UFO entered politics and won a plurality in the provincial election, E.C. Drury, a Barrie farmer and long-time rural leader, was chosen premier. The UFO-labour coalition formed an honest and efficient, if unimaginative, administration that significantly improved rural education, transportation and hydroelectric services. After its defeat in 1923 the UFO declined steadily. Maintaining the enthusiasms of the early period proved difficulty; many effective farmers were drawn to work with the United Farmers' Co-operative, and the destruction of the federal Progressive Party was disheartening. During the 1930s, under the idealistic leadership of Agnes Macphail, H.H. Hannam and Leonard Harman, the UFO organized folk schools and supported the Farmer's Sun and the Rural Co-operator, and promoted orderly marketing. It briefly supported the Co-operative Commonwealth Federation. In 1944 the UFO joined with other farm groups to form the Ontario Federation of Agriculture. In 1948 the United Farmers' Co-

operative became the United Co-operatives of Ontario, today is one of the largest farmer-owned companies in Canada.

[*Ian MacPherson*]

*Used unedited by permission from *The Canadian Encyclopedia.* 2000. Toronto: McClelland and Stewart.

RELATED ENTRIES
A. Macphail, Co-operative Commonwealth Federation, Co-operative Movement

United Way

The United Way is a movement through which voluntary donations are raised and distributed to local projects and agencies, many of them for social welfare. This movement had its roots in the United States in the latter part of the nineteenth century and in Canada in the early part of the twentieth century. Over the years, the name that described this community or federated campaign (e.g., Community Fund, Community Chest, United Appeal, and Red Feather) until 1973, when the name United Way was adopted. In 1998, 125 local United Way organizations throughout Canada raised $284 million, to fund more than 4,300 agencies/programs and directed grants to more than ten thousand organizations. Local United Way organizations are autonomous, governed by a local board of directors, and represented by a national organization, United Way Canada, with offices in Ottawa, which provides leadership and services to its members by consultation, development, education and training, and marketing and communication. The mission statement of the United Way is "To promote the organized capacity of people to care for one another," describes the vision of the movement. The basic tenet of the United Way can be stated as volunteer driven both in its campaign function and its allocation process of community review. The emphasis is on the development of voluntarism in all areas of the community. The basic structure of a local United Way follows a uniform pattern: campaign and fundraising, planning and assessment, and allocation of funds. The campaign is characterized by the establishment of an annual goal based on the needs of the community in the health and social service field as evinced by member agencies and other indicators in the community. The planning and assessment requirements of each United Way organization are either provided in-house or obtained from relevant community agencies. In recent years, a divergence among United Ways has developed over philosophy and, consequently, operations. More traditional views hold that agency membership in the United Way is its raison d'être; the ability of a United Way, without undue intrusion, to monitor agency programs and budgets is the essential ingredient in the concept of accountability to donors and the credibility of the campaign appeal rests on accountability. According to proponents of this view, a grant program and project funding to non-members can still be included, as can accepting and transferring designated donations to non-members. The other more recent view—prompted by the proliferation of local causes, agencies, and campaigns—holds that the United Way must become a large umbrella, which can provide a distribution centre for all or most of the charitable giving in a community. To some extent, this position does not address the implicit guarantee that donations to United Way will fund efficient agencies and effective programs.

An issue that arose over the years and caused some difficulties to United Ways and their donors was the question of designation or donor choice—that is, a donation would go to a specific agency. The origin of this matter is found in the likes and dislikes of donors for individual agencies. The United Way provided a solution by allowing positive and negative designations. This solution provoked the two issues as to whether designations should be promoted, and whether designations would be in addition to agreed allocation to agencies. In the past many health agencies have been reluctant to seek membership or affiliation with a local United Way. This position has been based on each health agency having a specific constituency and believing that the agency had its particular and sometimes emotional appeal to donors. On the other hand, the United Way has contended that its campaign has provided an opportunity for agencies, particularly of the counselling variety, to compete for funding on a level playing field. The stance of United Way as a non-ideological umbrella organization enables it to attract business, labour, community leaders, and governments. From time to time, government relations have been difficult, as some governments had a penchant for contributing toward projects

and presuming—without actually asking—that United Way would be continue to fund operations on termination of federal funding. This pattern was an obvious irritant to United Way and other donors. In addition some governments have unilaterally downloaded programs to communities with the expectation that they be funded wholly by churches, United Way, and other local sources. To its credit, United Way has refrained from criticizing government in order to maintain its total constituency. Its unequivocal position, however, is that basic human needs are the joint responsibility of governments. Assessing the impact of the United Way movement on the profession of social work is difficult. An inescapable fact, however, is that the United Way movement has been a catalyst for the development of voluntary agencies in the private sector; for many years, this has meant the staffing of these organizations by social workers to a far greater extent than the staffing of government programs. Current information about United Way Canada can be found online at <www.unitedway.ca>.

[*Gerry Gaughan*]

RELATED ENTRIES
Non-governmental Organizations, Voluntarism

Université de Moncton, École de travail social

La création de l'École de travail social de l'Université de Moncton coïncide avec les grands bouleversements des années 1960. Ces derniers furent marqués au Nouveau-Brunswick par le programme de "Chances égales pour tous," lancé par le premier ministre de l'époque, Louis J. Robichaud. Cette réforme transforma les systèmes d'éducation, de santé, de justice, et des services sociaux, ainsi que le système local de taxation, à l'échelle de toute la province. À cette époque, l'Association canadienne des travailleurs sociaux approuve le baccalauréat en service social comme exigence minimale pour la pratique de la profession. C'est donc en 1968 que le département de service social fut institué à l'Université de Moncton et deviendra en 1985 l'école de service social rattachée à ses débuts à la Faculté des sciences sociales. Aujourd'hui elle fait partie de la Faculté des arts et des sciences sociales. La question d'éducation post-secondaire représente un acquis fondamental dans l'histoire acadienne, et le travail social est à l'avant-garde de ce phénomène. Les débuts de la formation en service social ont été initiés par le professeur Normand Doucet. Les enseignants et enseignantes de l'époque étaient essentiellement formés pour la pratique. Plus tard, vers la fin des années 1970, les dimensions du programme s'élargirent pour tenir compte de la complexité et de la pluralité sociale. Pour relever un tel défi, le département recruta des enseignants détenteurs d'un doctorat. Actuellement, l'école compte parmi ses nouvelles professeures certaines de ses propres diplômées qui ont complété un doctorat en travail social.

Les programmes actuellement offerts à l'école de travail social comprennent un programme de baccalauréat de cinq ans ainsi qu'un programme de maîtrise. Le programme de premier cycle accorde une grande importance à la formation générale, à la recherche-action, aux politiques sociales ainsi qu'à l'expérience terrain est exigée une formation à la supervision pour les superviseurs et superviseures de stage. Le programme permet au moins une occasion d'enseignement en petit groupe au cours de chaque année du baccalauréat. Il existe trois portes d'entrée: une pour les adultes avec baccalauréat connexe, une deuxième pour les adultes avec expérience et dans ces deux cas, la durée des études est de deux ans. La troisième porte d'entrée, et la plus générale, est réservée aux étudiantes et étudiants provenant du secondaire. Cette voie exige une formation préparatoire au travail social de deux ans avant l'admission au programme du baccalauréat proprement dit de trois ans. Nos diplômées et diplômés bilingues du baccalauréat sont sollicités par des employeurs provenant des provinces de l'Île du Prince-Édouard, du Québec, de l'Ontario et de la Colombie-britannique, ainsi que certains États de la Nouvelle-Angleterre. L'école a admis des étudiants et étudiantes à son programme de maîtrise pour la première fois en 1987. Ce programme, axé sur les composantes de recherche-action, de politique sociale et de mémoire action, s'adresse à des étudiants et étudiantes à plein temps mais aussi à des professionnels qui sont admis à temps partiel. L'école a déposé son premier bilan en vue de l'agrément du programme de maîtrise en avril 2003.

L'école est membre de l'Association canadienne des écoles de service social et bénéficie d'un plein agrément pour son programme de baccalauréat. Sur le plan international l'école a développé des accords avec l'Institut de travail social et de recherches sociales de Montrouge en France, et avec l'Institut national du travail et des études sociales de Tunis en 1987. Depuis 1999, elle est partenaire avec le groupe Communauté européenne–Canada, SANGHA. Chacune de ces ententes a permis l'échange de personnel et d'étudiantes. En plus, l'école a une longue histoire de stages à l'extérieur de l'Acadie. On enregistre des placements dans au moins six provinces canadiennes ainsi que huit pays répartis sur trois continents. L'école a récemment développé un partenariat avec le ministère des services familiaux et communautaires. Les dates suivantes correspondent à des événements importants dans la vie de l'école: mention en service social, Baccalauréat ès arts (1966), département de service social (1968: premiers diplômés en 1970), introduction d'un certificat en service social (1969), création d'un Baccalauréat déconcentré, en conjonction avec l'Université Dalhousie (1976), création d'un certificat en alcoologie et toxicologie (1977), obtention du statut d'école (1985), mise sur pied d'un comité consultatif de l'école (1985), et introduction de la maîtrise en travail social (1987). La mission de l'école s'énonce comme suit: "offrir des programmes de formation qui reflètent les réalités et les aspirations de la population acadienne." Cette orientation a pris depuis les origines un enracinement de plus en plus solide à travers les réalités dynamiques en Acadie et au-delà des frontières de cette dernière. On peut découvrir information courant à <www.umoncton.ca>.

[*Louis J. Richard* and
Katherine Marcoccio]

RELATED ENTRIES
Education in Social Work, Faculties of Social Work, New Brunswick Association of Social Workers

Université de Montréal, École de service social

La première école de service social au Québec fut celle de l'Université McGill, desservant la population de langue anglaise. Dans le Québec francophone, il faudra attendre les suites de la crise économique de 1929 pour voir apparaître les premiers signes d'une professionnalisation du travail social. Jusqu'à cette époque, les indigents et nécessiteux étaient pris en charge par l'Église catholique par l'entremise de ses communautés religieuses et de ses institutions. Les bouleversements socio-économiques de l'époque font toutefois prendre conscience de l'importance des besoins et de la nécessité de développer une main d'oeuvre professionnelle qualifiée dans ce secteur d'activités. En 1939, les premiers enseignements en service social destinés aux francophones sont dispensés dans les locaux de l'Institut des Soeurs de Notre-Dame-du-Bon-Conseil. Ces "cours de service social" étaient le résultat d'une initiative conjuguée de Soeur Marie Gérin-Lajoie, directrice et fondatrice de l'institut et de Monseigneur Gauthier, Archevêque de Montréal. Cette première école vécut une année. Elle fut remplacée par "l'École catholique de service social" créée en 1940 et dont les locaux étaient situés à l'École des Hautes Études Commerciales rue St-Denis. Assez rapidement son appellation fut modifiée et devint "l'École de service social de Montréal." Contrairement à la première école, qui offrait un enseignement générique sur les oeuvres et l'action sociale, la seconde école proposait un enseignement bilingue sur l'intervention en service social à partir du modèle professionnel de cours en casework, group work et organisation communautaire. Quelques années plus tard, le nouveau département des relations industrielles de l'Université de Montréal, sous la gouverne du Père Bouvier, entreprit d'offrir une formation en travail social. Le programme d'études favorisait un service social paroissial et industriel. Le développement parallèle de ces deux programmes et écoles aux orientations bien distinctes, illustre les difficultés rencontrées à l'époque pour préciser et définir la notion de service social. Le conflit fut résolu en 1948 par la fusion du segment travail social du département de relations industrielles et de "l'École de service social de Montréal" en une nouvelle section de service social intégrée à la Faculté des sciences sociales, économique, et politique de l'Université de Montréal (Groulx 1993).

Jusqu'en 1967, l'École de service social de l'Université de Montréal était partie intégrante d'une université francophone catholique et ses directeurs étaient des prêtres ou des religieux. Ainsi le Père André-Marie Guillemette o.p. et l'abbé Shaun Govenlock furent ses directeurs dans les années cinquante et soixante. En septembre 1967, l'Université de Montréal devenait une institution publique et non confessionnelle. Une femme, madame Marguerite Mathieu, fut alors nommée à la tête de l'École de service social en tant que première directrice laïque. Depuis ses premières années d'existence l'école offrait un seul programme, la Maîtrise ès arts (M.A. service social), lequel avait reçu l'agrément du Council on Social Work Education des États-Unis. Avec la réforme de l'éducation au Québec, l'école ajouta le baccalauréat spécialisé en service social (1968) puis modifia sa maîtrise pour en faire une maîtrise ès sciences (M.Sc. service social). Par la suite, elle développa successivement une maîtrise, programme de qualification professionnelle, à l'intention des personne provenant d'autres disciplines que le travail social (1977), un certificat en action communautaire (1982), et accepta la responsabilité de deux diplômes d'études supérieures spécialisées soit le diplôme en administration sociale (1987) et le diplôme interventions en toxicomanie (2001). Au niveau, doctoral l'école est impliquée, depuis sa création en 1988, dans le programme de doctorat multidisciplinaire en sciences humaines appliquées. C'est toutefois en 1996, qu'elle reçoit l'autorisation du ministère de l'éducation supérieure du Québec d'offrir un programme de doctorat en service social. Offert conjointement avec l'Université McGill, ce programme de troisième cycle bilingue présente des caractéristiques uniques, Son but est de répondre aux besoins pressants de formation pour des professeurs, des analystes en politique sociale, ainsi que des chercheurs au Canada et au Québec.

L'école de service social dessert actuellement plus de 500 étudiants à travers ses huit programmes, soit environ 325 au premier cycle, 150 au second cycle, et 25 au doctorat. Elle compte maintenant vingt professeurs réguliers et est orientée de façon intensive vers la recherche. Elle joue un rôle de premier plan dans la formation et la recherche en service social au Québec, au Canada et de plus en plus à travers le monde. On peut découvrir information courrant à <www .esersoc.umontreal.ca>.

[*Gilles Rondeau*]

RELATED ENTRIES
Doctorate in Social Work, Education in Social Work, Faculties of Social Work, Order professionel des travailleurs sociaux du Québec

Université de Sherbrooke, Département de service social

Le Département de service social de l'Université de Sherbrooke a été fondé en 1964. Fait assez inusité, la formation qui y a d'abord été offerte, a été celle d'un programme d'études post-maîtrise à temps partiel conduisant au Diplôme d'Études Supérieures en Service Social. Après huit ans d'existence, le département offrait quatre programmes: le diplôme, né en 1964 et qui sera fermé en 1974; le programme de baccalauréat à temps plein créé en 1967 et dont la formule de formation pratique de l'époque, soit le régime coopératif, le distinguait de tous les autres programmes de formation en service social de même niveau; le programme de maîtrise offert dès 1970; et le programme de certificat créé en 1972 qui visait essentiellement le perfectionnement des techniciennes et techniciens en assistance sociale. Mais cette évolution très rapide n'a pas été sans problème. En 1970, la contestation étudiante se manifeste sous la forme d'un département parallèle qui, s'exprimant durant quelques mois, oblige une révision des rapports département-étudiants et permet l'introduction d'un modèle de gestion pédagogique renouvelé. Ainsi, deux déterminants majeurs imposent une révision fondamentale du programme de baccalauréat en 1974. D'abord le ministère des affaires sociales faisait connaître la politique de non-rémunération des stages coopératifs: une refonte donc du système de formation pratique devenait nécessaire. Même chose pour les activités pédagogiques qui devaient se redéfinir en fonction des profondes modifications apportées aux services sociaux par la loi 65.

À partir de 1975, après un an de suspension des admissions pour fins de révision, le programme de baccalauréat accueille aussi bien des étudiantes et étudiants à temps plein qu'à temps partiel. Il s'offre alors selon deux cheminements: un cheminement de formation initiale qui s'adresse aux étudiantes et étudiants détenant un DEC après leur formation générale au CÉGEP et un cheminement de formation en cours d'emploi pour les techniciennes et techniciens en assistance sociale sur le marché du travail. En plus d'être offert à Sherbrooke, ce programme est dispensé en région (Saguenay Lac Saint-Jean, Alma, et région du bas du Fleuve). Si ces années furent fertiles en modifications de toutes sortes au sein de la pratique du service social, encore-là le développement du département et de ses programmes ne se fera pas sans heurts. Menacé de fermeture en 1974, il doit suspendre ses admissions durant un an pour revoir en profondeur ses programmes de formation en même temps qu'il fait face à des confrontations importantes au sein des membres du corps professoral. D'ailleurs, les services d'un médiateur sont retenus en 1987. Malgré ces difficultés, le département continue d'accueillir des étudiantes et des étudiants en grand nombre. Il offre un programme de maîtrise en service social aux détenteurs d'un baccalauréat en service social qu'il dispense à temps partiel. Également, il propose, en sus des programmes longs, un programme de certificat en service social de trente crédits qui s'adresse aux détentrices et aux détenteurs d'un DEC ayant de l'expérience sur le marché du travail. Trois transformations majeures concomitantes introduisent des changements significatifs dans les services sociaux institutionnalisés et viennent influencer les programmes de formation. D'abord, la loi 24 portant sur la protection de la jeunesse, implantée en janvier 1979, a déjà entraîné une véritable réorientation des pratiques. Ajoutons qu'encore à cette étape de son développement, le Département de service social connaît des tensions au niveau de sa gestion interne et des rapports de travail entre les membres du corps professoral. Si bien, qu'en 1989, l'Université de Sherbrooke met sur pied un comité spécial externe d'évaluation des programmes et des enseignements du Département de service social. Deux transformations fondamentales auront des conséquences majeures pour le Département de service social au cours des années 1990–95. La première se situe à l'interne et touche l'ajout d'une masse critique de nouveaux professeurs. La deuxième, extrinsèque au département, concerne l'ensemble de la réorganisation de la santé et des services sociaux au Québec qu'occasionne l'entrée en vigueur de la loi 120. Cette dernière reconfigure l'ensemble des services sociaux et de la santé et ses effets sont majeurs pour la profession du travail social. La disparition des Centres de services sociaux, instances essentiellement constituées de travailleurs sociaux en est un bel exemple. Cette loi repense aussi le type de recherches sociales subventionnées par le Conseil québécois de la recherche sociale, qui devra maintenant mettre l'accent sur la recherche en partenariat avec les milieux de pratique.

Le Département de service social procédera en 1990 à une révision mineure de son programme de baccalauréat et pourra offrir, dès septembre 1991, un programme ajusté dans son contenu et dans sa cohérence. De plus, cette démarche de révision se prolongera au programme de maîtrise qui verra le jour en septembre de l'année suivante et sera reconnue par l'Ordre professionnel des travailleuses et travailleurs sociaux du Québec l'année suivante soit l'année 1993. Nous assistons à l'engagement de six nouveaux membres du corps professoral dont un à la direction du département. Spécifiquement, les activités de recherche connaissent un essor sans précédent dans l'histoire du département. Encore une fois, le Département de service social a connu au cours des années 1996–2003 deux grandes transformations qui sont de toute évidence interreliées. Elles sont marquées par la nouvelle gouvernance des finances publiques au Québec dont la manifestation la plus notable consiste à l'atteinte du déficit zéro. Bien que le département n'ait pas actuellement de troisième cycle, six professeures et professeurs participent activement à celui en gérontologie dont l'ouverture est prévu en septembre 2003. La période est aussi marquée par la consolidation des activités d'enseignement. Ainsi, le programme de baccalauréat en service social obtient l'agrément en 1996 de l'Association canadienne des écoles de service social. Cette accréditation confirme la qualité des enseignements. Par contre, compte tenu de la nouvelle politique de l'Ordre professionnel des travailleuses et travailleurs sociaux du Québec, qui imposera prochainement le diplôme de maîtrise pour l'obtention du titre de travailleur social, nous nous préparons à repenser de manière significative l'articulation des programmes de baccalauréat et de maîtrise. On peut découvrir information courrant à <www.usherb.ca>.

[*Benoit van Collen*]

RELATED ENTRIES
Education in Social Work, Faculties of Social Work, Order professionel des travailleurs sociaux du Québec

Université du Québec à Montréal, École de travail social

L'école de travail social de l'Université du Québec à Montréal (ét. 1969) est formée de près de 700 étudiants, dix-sept professeurs réguliers, environ une vingtsime de chargés de cours, une chargée de formation pratique et trois personnes de soutien administratif. Elles s'inscrivent dans le contexte de la création de l'Université du Québec et dans une conjoncture de remise en question de l'enseignement universitaire et des services sociaux et de santé traditionnels au Québec. L'Université du Québec visait à démocratiser l'éducation universitaire, décloisonner les champs disciplinaires et donner accès à une formation de premier cycle plus générale et fondamentale. Cet objectif se traduisit au niveau du fonctionnement administratif par la mise en place d'une structure différente des autres universités: la double structure. D'un côté, des modules, composés d'étudiant-e-s et de professeur-e-s, assument la gestion des programs et la responsabilité pédagogique des étudiant-e-s. Ils commandent leurs cours à plusieurs départements dont un principal vis-à-vis disciplinaire. De l'autre côté, les départements composés de professeur-e-s regroupés autour d'un champ disciplinaire, sont responsables de la prestation des enseignements commandés par les modules et du développement de la recherche. Ces instances sont autonomes l'une par rapport à l'autre tout en étant aussi interdépendantes pour la réalisation d'un programme d'étude. C'est dans ce contexte qu'en 1970, est créé un module de travail social, après avoir été une sorte de pré-module à l'automne 1969. Il offre un programme de baccalauréat en travail social avec deux options, l'une clinique et l'autre collective. De 1970 à 1976, l'enseignement et la gestion du programme sont assurés par des professeur-e-s affecté-e-s au programme de travail social mais rattaché-e-s à plusieurs départements dont ceux de sociologie, psychologie, science politique et histoire. De même, les deux options relèvent de deux départements différents et fonctionnent comme deux sous-programmes nettement distincts. La non départementalisation du travail social reposait sur un choix consciemment fait par les premiers artisans du travail social à l'Université du Québec à Montréal qui avaient misé sur la multidisciplinarité pour le développement d'une approche du travail social ouverte, alimentée par les apports complémentaires de divers départements. Donc un refus de former des travailleurs sociaux repliés sur eux-mêmes, une volonté de se démarquer d'une formation corporatiste et professionnaliste. Ce choix n'était pas sans générer quelques difficultés: impossibilité pour les professeurs à constituer une équipe ayant un minimum de cohérence, difficulté de développer un cadre intégrateur pour une formation spécifique au travail social, net clivage entre les options individuelle et collective, tensions idéologiques persistantes. Suite à une situation de crise, un rassemblement de professeurs en travail social est créé en 1977. Dès lors suit une étape de structuration de 1978 à 1980 autour des deux instances du module et du rassemblement de travail social. Du côté du module, professeur-e-s et étudiant-e-s opèrent une refonte fondamentale du programme en vue de l'adoption d'un nouveau en 1979. Du côté du rassemblement, les professeurs se dotent d'une définition du champ d'étude spécifique au travail social et engage un processus de départementalisation qui sera actualisé en 1981. Après avoir fonctionné pendant quinze ans selon la structure traditionnelle uqamienne composée d'un département et d'un module, un comité conjoint rasssemblant les deux instances est constitué en 1995 pour mettre en œuvre la création d'une École de travail social. L'objectif est de mettre en place structure unifiée, intégrant les ressources et programmes de formation dans un espace commun visiblement identifié au champ professionnel du travail social tant à l'intérieur de l'Université du Québec à Montréal que dans la communauté. En 1999, l'école de travail social est créée comme une nouvelle structure à part entière à l'Université du Québec à Montréal.

La mission de l'école de travail social est de former des travailleuses sociales et des travailleurs sociaux critiques et compétents, capables d'intervenir avec autonomie et créativité dans une perspective de changement social. L'école favorise une approche intégrée axée sur l'interaction fondamentale entre l'individu et le contexte social, le changement individuel et le changement social. Elle met de l'avant une prise en compte des dimensions suivantes: la transformation des rapports sociaux de sexes, de classes, d'âges et d'ethnies, l'appauvrissement des populations, l'exclusion et la précarité sociale, la diversité culturelle, les droits socio-économiques et humains, les nouvelles pratiques sociales. Cette mission s'articule autour de trois champs d'activités: l'enseignement, la recherche et les services à la communauté. L'école chapeaute seule ou conjointement avec d'autres départements, un ensemble de programmes de premier et de deuxième cycle. Le programme de baccalauréat en travail social constitue le plus important de ceux-ci. Il s'agit d'un programme de trois ans contingenté à 135 étudiants par année, dûment accrédité par l'Association canadienne des écoles de service social pour la première fois en 1990. Il s'articule autour de trois axes: l'axe de formation théorique (corpus théorique de base du travail social et de ses problématiques), l'axe de formation méthodologique (corpus des méthodes d'intervention) et l'axe de formation pratique (stages en milieu de pratique). Depuis ses origines, le programme comportait un tronc commun et deux options complémentaires: l'intervention sociale auprès des individus et des petits groupes et l'intervention sociale auprès des communautés. En mars 2002, cette division a fait place à une formation intégrée des méthodes et approches d'intervention, rendant obligatoires à toutes et tous les étudiants les cours des deux options traditionnelles. Les deux premières années visent à procurer à l'étudiant-e les connaissances théoriques et méthodologiques de base d'une intervention sociale intégrée. La troisième année est consacrée aux stages répartis sur les deux trimestres et réalisés en concomitance avec deux séminaires d'intégration à l'université. L'école assure également la gestion d'un certificat de premier cycle en gérontologie sociale, fournit des cours à d'autres programmes en sciences humaines et participe au programme de formation continue de l'Université du Québec à Montréal en lien avec les milieux de pratique. Au deuxième cycle, l'école assume la direction de la maîtrise en intervention sociale, programme conjoint avec le département de sociologie, Il s'agit d'une maîtrise de type recherche visant à former des intervenant-e-s capables d'allier recherche et pratiques sociales. Le programme s'articule autour de la problématique du renouvellement des pratiques sociales et offre, entre autres, un ensemble de concentrations et programmes courts en économie sociale, études sur la mort, toxicomanie et gérontologie sociale. Il s'offre des concentrations en trois domaines : études sur la mort et mourir, toxicomanies et économie sociale. A l'automne 2003, s'ajoutera également une concentration de type professionnel.

Exerçant une fonction de soutien à la formation et au développement social et pédagogique, les activités de recherche revêtent divers axes: compréhension des réalités et problématiques sociales, développement des connaissances relatives aux pratiques d'intervention, examen des politiques sociales et de l'organisation des services sociaux et de santé, analyse du développement professionnel en travail social. Ces activités sont menées soit sur une base individuelle ou d'équipes de recherche, soit autour de laboratoires, soit en partenariat avec différents organismes et groupes de recherche locaux, nationaux et internationaux. L'école assume la direction de la revue nouvelles pratiques sociales et du laboratoire de recherche sur les pratiques et les politiques socials. Ce volet occupe une place centrale à l'école de travail social. Elles regroupent les multiples réponses aux demandes venant de la communauté interne et externe de l'université et inclut divers projets et activités de recherche, de formation, de consultation et d'intervention impliquant un partenariat avec des acteurs de la communauté. Créer une plus grande synergie entre les trois niveaux d'activités de l'école, adapter les programmes aux nouvelles réalités et pratiques sociales, renforcer le partenariat avec les milieux de pratique, consolider les partenariats en coopération internationale, tels sont entre autres quelques axes de développement que s'est donnée l'école de travail social de l'Université du Québec à Montréal pour les années à venir. On veut trouver l'information courrant aux programs à l'université à <www.uqam.ca>.

[*Michèle Bourgon* and
Pierre Maheu]

RELATED ENTRIES
Education in Social Work, Faculties of Social Work, Order professionel des travailleurs sociaux du Québec

Université du Québec en Outaouais, Programme de travail social

Sise sur les rives de la rivière Outaouais, dans la nouvelle ville de Gatineau, l'Université du Québec en Outaouais (uQO), anciennement l'Université du Québec à Hull (uQAH), est une des universités en région faisant partie du réseau de l'Université du Québec (uQ). Ce réseau structure ses programmes de formation selon deux régies : le *module*, qui encadre les étudiants selon les programmes de formation identifiés, et le *département*, qui encadre les ressources professorales, professeurs et chargés de cours. L'uQO oeuvre sur un territoire de 33,000 km^2, constitué principalement par la région administrative de l'Outaouais; celle-ci présente une densité démographique plus élevée que celle de la moyenne des régions du Québec. L'uQO offre, dans la région métropolitaine de l'Outaouais (Geatineau) et dans d'autres localités périphériques, ses activités dans diverses disciplines : sciences de la santé, sciences de l'éducation, sciences socials, travail social, psychologie, psychoéducation, sciences de l'administration, sciences comptables, relations industrielles, informatique, génie informatique, arts, design et bande dessinée, traduction et rédaction. Au total, l'uQO offer plus d'une quarantaine de programmes de premier cycle (certificat et baccalauréat), des programmes de deuxième cycle en éducation et andragogie, administration et finance, informatique, psychoéducation, relations industrielles, sciences comptables, sciences infirmières, développement régional, traduction et rédaction, et en travail social, et un programme de doctorat en éducation.

Les premières études en travail social offertes dans la région de l'Outaouais (1974) le furent grâce à la mise sur pied d'un certificat en travail social. Ce programme visait à répondre à des besoins spécifiques du milieu. Comme les organisms, les intervenants et les usagers des services sociaux avaient besoin d'un programme unversitaire plus poussé pour stimuler la réflexion et les services sociaux au plan regional, le programme de baccalauréat spécialisé en travail social (BTS), sous la responsabilité du Module du travail social, fut implanté à l'automne 1977. Depuis, plusieurs versions du programme ont eu cours suite à des évaluations statutaires, internes à l'Université, et à des évaluations pour l'agrément par l'Association canadienne des écoles de service social (ACESS) (1986; 1993; 2000). Le programme offre une compétence professionnelle de base en travail social et vise la formation de travailleurs sociaux capables de concevoir, d'offrir des services ou des programmes d'intervention destinés aux individus, aux familles, aux groupes et aux communautés, dans une perspective de changement personnel et de changement social. Le programme est reconnu officiellement par l'Ordre professionnel des travailleurs sociaux du Québec (OPTSQ).

D'une durée de trois ans et structuré autour de 90 crédits universitaires d'activités de cours formels, de laboratoires et de stages, le programme est contingenté à 50 étudiants à temps complet. Les étudiantes à temps partiel sont également acceptés. Les étudiants sont admis au programme à la suite de leur formation collégiale (Cégep) générale ou spécialisée en technique de travail social ou l'équivalent, ou sur la base d'une experiénce jugée adéquate. La majorité des étudiants et étudiantes inscrits au programme proviennent de la region immédiate, l'Outaouais et l'est francophone de l'Ontario; plusieurs étudiants du reste du Québec et de l'étranger s'ajoutent.

Le programme jouit d'une précieuse et constante collaboration de la part des organisme du milieu, tant du réseau de la santé et des services sociaux que du réseau des organismes communautaires. Ainsi, ces organisations permettent aux étudiantes d'y faire des stages de formation et d'y trouver, à la fin des études, des sources d'emplois intéressants et stimulants. Le haut taux de placement des diplômés témoigne de la qualité de la formation offerte à l'UQO. Certains étudiants poursuivent des études de deuxième cycle en travail social à l'UQO. Depuis 1995, un programme de maîtrise en travail social orienté sur le renouvellement des pratiques d'intervention sociale leur est offert (deux ans à temps partiel). Les professeurs sont présentement à élaborer un volet professionnel à cette maîtrise, et certains travaillent à l'élaboration d'un programme-réseau de doctorat en travail social, programme projeté en collaboration avec plusieurs universitiés de l'UQ.

[*Jean-Marc Meunier*]

University College of the Fraser Valley Department of Social Work and Human Services

The University College of the Fraser Valley offers a unique program of studies leading to a bachelor of social work degree that can prepare students for generalist social work practice in a multicultural environment. Graduates of the program are prepared to assist individuals, groups, and communities in enhancing personal, family, and community life and to promote social change. Based on egalitarian ideals, social work is dedicated to the promotion of individual, family, and community development, and seeks to ensure that people have access to the economic, political, and social resources necessary to enhance personal well-being and self-determination. To achieve these aims, social workers also advocate for social change and social justice in the belief that the basic and continuing improvement of social conditions are fundamental to individual, family, and community growth and development. In 1991 Fraser Valley College became the University College of the Fraser Valley with the capacity for granting university degrees, along with similar institutions at Malaspina, Cariboo, and Okanagan, as an attempt to solve issues of access to education in areas other than the lower mainland. Until the appropriate legislation was tabled, the degree had to be granted in co-operation with an existing BC university. During the early 1990s, faculty at the university college consulted extensively with other schools of social work throughout Canada about bachelor of social work programs. After exploring a range of partnerships with BC universities, the university-college's bachelor of social work program advisory committee conducted consultations that led to the signing of an agreement in October 1992 between the university-college and the Open Learning Agency (i.e., open university) to offer a bachelor of social work in partnership between the two institutions. With funding for the program approved in May 1994 by the BC Ministry of Education, the program was developed by university-college faculty in conjunction with a planning committee composed of faculty and administration from both institutions, as well as input from faculty at Ryerson, British Columbia, Victoria, and McMaster universities. The first class—of third-year students—started the program in 1994 and the first graduates were in 1996. In 1995 University College of Fraser Valley had become a candidate for accreditation by the Canadian Association of Schools of Social Work and, in 1997, the university college was recognized by the Association of Universities and Colleges of Canada as a degree-granting institute. The partnership with the open university was dissolved.

The program is geared primarily toward meeting entry-level practitioner needs in communities of the Fraser Valley; students are drawn, however, from both the Fraser Valley and the lower mainland. A focus of the program has been, and continues to be, on the preparation of generalist social work practitioners to work in a multicultural society. A child welfare specialization, or concentration, in conjunction with the other BC schools of social work was begun in 2000 with additional funding provided by the BC Ministry of Children and Family Development. Each year, both full- and part-time students are admitted to the program at the third-year level and approximately thirty full-time equivalent students are admitted. Students enter the program from either a liberal arts background or a social service background; many are mature students with a good deal of work experience. A consistent feature of the program has been the use of prior learning assessment to recognize the often significant theoretical and practical social work learning that students bring. With a total of nine full-time faculty, plus sessionals, the program maintains strong ties with the BC Association of Social Workers and the Board of Registration for Social Work. Faculty teach, do community service, and engage in research projects in the community. Current information about the University College of the Fraser Valley Department of Social Work and Human Services can be found online at <www .ucvf.bc.ca/swhs/>.

[*Gloria Krupnick Wolfson*]

RELATED ENTRIES

Board of Registration for Social Workers of BC, British Columbia Association of Social Workers, Education in Social Work, Faculties of Social Work

University of British Columbia School of Social Work and Family Studies

In response to economic, social and health problems following the First World War as well as concerns about families and children in care, the University of British Columbia School of Social Work—the third oldest in Canada—began in 1929 as a diploma program called Courses in Social Service. Impetus for the program came from two professors—one from economics and one from sociology—with senior workers in voluntary agencies and public health and welfare programs, who were also its instructors. Lacking faculty, trained supervisors, financial resources, and regular office and classroom facilities, the program survived because of the conviction, energy, and determination of its originators. Three women graduated in 1930. The curriculum was general, emphasizing casework method and public welfare through the initial stage (1929–43). Because faculty and alumni aimed to develop a university program with professional standards, they made connections to the American Association of Schools of Social Work (as the Canadian association had not yet been formed). In 1940 the program's title was renamed social work and a bachelor of arts became a prerequisite; these moves propelled the program closer to becoming a separate educational entity with full-time faculty. In 1942 a provincial grant enabled the appointment of the first full-time faculty member and two years later the first director was recruited. In 1945 the program became the Department of Social Work in the faculty of arts and science, gaining provisional membership in the American Association of Schools of Social Work. The program increased its emphasis on professional education and the development of professionals. A group work specialization began in 1945, and a research requirement in 1948. In 1946 when the university recognized a distinctive curriculum, the diploma was replaced with a bachelor of social work degree to be awarded after one year of post-baccalaureate studies, with a master of social work degree awarded after a second year. The first accreditation by the American Association of Schools of Social Work was awarded in 1947. Academic and administrative changes culminated in 1950, when the University of British Columbia board of governors redesignated the department as a professional school within the faculty of arts. This amazing expansion derived in part from federal government plans, aimed initially to make university education available to war veterans, so that, in 1943, the funding of social programs and professional education was increased. The established curriculum and program remained relatively stable until the early 1960s.

The 1960s saw the beginning of continuous curriculum evaluation, review, and revision in response to changes in Canadian social services and social work education, to faculty concerns, and to student and community demands for education that was more relevant to immediate field issues. In 1965 the bachelor of social work was terminated and a two-year post-graduate master of social work began; a master of social work community organization specialization had been introduced in 1963. Then, all graduate students were required to take casework, group work, and community organization methods and to choose one method as their fieldwork specialization. Growth occurred in the number of faculty, students, field placements, and in continuing education non-credit courses. Also coming from the debates over relevancy and evaluation was the establishment of a Canadian educational accrediting body, the Canadian Association of Schools of Social Work—faculty from the University of British Columbia being among its founders; the School of Social Work became a charter member. One of the association's early decisions was to recognize the bachelor of social work as the first professional degree in social work. In 1974 an undergraduate bachelor of social work program was reintroduced, requiring two years of liberal arts and two years of social work. The three traditional methods were now team-taught with the objective of graduating generalist practitioners with the range of approaches to method. Two years later a one-year concentrated bachelor of social work program was introduced for persons holding a bachelor of arts degree and social work experience. In 1976 a one-year master of social work program was recognized as a graduate program within the faculty of graduate studies. This master of social work program was focused on the analysis of social welfare problems and the processes appropriate to addressing such problems. Three major areas of educational concentration were offered: family needs, health needs, and socio-economic needs. Students had significant influence on course content and indeed, from the late 1960s on, have participated actively in the school's governance. The fiftieth anniversary of the school was marked in

1980 and the social work alumni division was activated. The 1980s, however, brought an end to sixteen years of stability and relative prosperity: numerous faculty retired, including the director, and his replacement took over just as provincial government support diminished drastically to result in the loss of three faculty positions and the termination of the off-campus program begun in 1980 in Prince George. Cutbacks in faculty continued, dropping from twenty-two full-time positions and three joint appointments in 1985, to nineteen and a half in 1989, before settling at sixteen in 1992, despite maintaining stable student enrolment.

From 1985 to 1993, efforts to consolidate decreasing faculty resources continued, along with efforts to revise the programs to meet the demands of the expanding knowledge base and changing needs of multicultural students and clients. Working to fulfil the university's mission to enhance graduate programs and to reflect the interests and abilities of new faculty, the school emphasized research-based course content and student research activity; an interdisciplinary doctoral program was also introduced. Despite the loss of faculty, including field faculty, curriculum review and development continued and, in 1988, the master of social work focus moved from a problem-centred to a practice- and research-centred approach, with two practice perspectives: interpersonal development and social development. The continuing education program—an integral part of the school from its beginning—was severely cut back, however. In 1991 the concentrated bachelor of social work was discontinued; a generic bachelor of social work began, with a focus on gender, race, class, and cultural issues. For the first time, study of the problem preceded study of method. A unified master of social work introduced, in 1994, offered a program in which students and their faculty advisors structured their own study pattern, and in which specialization could be initiated in child, family, and community well-being; social development; and practice with diverse populations. Up to fifteen of the thirty-three credits required for graduation could be taken outside the school, in recognition of the connections between social work and other disciplines. In spite of continuing unforeseen changes, in 1992, a First Nations faculty position was designated and, in 1997, the position of field co-ordinator became a full-time faculty position. While the faculty has been drastically downsized, its collective qualifications, teaching reviews, research, and community involvement have never been higher. As well, the number of graduate students has continued to increase and, in September 1999, a master of social work distance delivery program was inaugurated in conjunction with the University College of the Cariboo and the Okanagan University College. As part of the university's April 1999 restructuring, negotiations over a three-year period resulted in a new School of Social Work and Family Studies—resulting from the union with the school of nutrition and family science; its purpose is to "enhance the educational, research and community service goals of both divisions. Each unit will retain fundamental integrity of degree structures and accreditation standards" (Faculty of Arts minutes October 13, 1998). Review and development continues in all programs including distance education and interprofessional education, joint undertakings with the other five BC schools, faculty research capacity, and the evolving structure and relationships within the new school. Current information about the University of British Columbia's School of Social Work and Family Studies can be found online at <www.swfs.ubc.ca/>.

[*G. Elaine Stolar*]

RELATED ENTRIES

Board of Registration for Social Workers of BC, British Columbia Association of Social Workers, Education in Social Work, Faculties of Social Work, L. Holland

University of Calgary Faculty of Social Work

The case for establishing a school of social welfare—as it was first called—in Alberta was made between 1962 and 1964 through an initiative of the Alberta Association of Social Workers and substantial grant support from the Junior League of Calgary, culminating in the presentation of a research report and brief to the provincial Cabinet. Today, we take for granted that the University of Calgary is home to social work; however, at the time, considerable and vigorous debate occurred. With the decision to have the school of social welfare at the University of Calgary came a provincial mandate to recognize the responsibility to provide social work program opportunities to the province con-

sistent with resources and priorities. With a start-up budget of $55,965, the school began in 1966, under the leadership of Dr. Tim Tyler, offering a master of social work degree based on a bachelor of arts degree. In September 1967 the first cohort of sixteen students registered and graduated in 1969. One early faculty member has observed that: "we were all attracted to the idea of building a creative master of social work which could include but would go beyond direct services to individuals; which would call attention to and challenge students to address the root cultural, political, and societal dimensions of life … to fashion an master of social work program that would help students to challenge stale, status quo thinking. I recall the excitement. It was pioneering work." In March 1970 an accreditation report was submitted to the US Council on Social Work Education—the accreditation body for all graduate schools of social work in North America at the time—and accreditation was granted in February 1971. By that time, planning for an undergraduate program was well advanced and the bachelor of social work program in Calgary admitted students to the program in September 1971, convocating its first graduates in November 1973. The following year, the bachelor of social work program received accreditation through the Canadian Association of Schools of Social Work. To fulfil its mandate, the school was extremely sensitive to the needs of practitioners and offered courses whenever possible on a demand basis throughout the province. When there is sufficient interest, regular credit and non-credit courses can be offered on packaged learning, tutorial, or reading terms. Staff are available to meet with agencies, professional associations, and other groups to develop specific practitioner and agency training programs tailored to the needs of the community, group, or organization. To this end, a bachelor of social work cohort program was offered with Blue Quills Native Education Council in 1978. In these current initiatives to deliver the program in ways that facilitate access to the program for those who reside outside of major centres, as well as to those wishing to maintain jobs, the school echoes the past. To be responsive to the Edmonton region, the University of Calgary's division of continuing education and the social welfare school shared responsibility to co-ordinate degree-credit courses leading to a bachelor of social work. The cost

($11,500) was contributed by the division of continuing education with the school providing visiting lecturers for part-time classes. In a co-operative spirit, the Edmonton program was located on the main campus of the University of Alberta in Assiniboia Hall. Within the context of the provincial mandate, undergraduate courses have also been offered in Lethbridge since the mid-1970s. By 1981 the needs in Lethbridge had grown so significantly that a proposal to offer the bachelor of social work degree was approved housed on the University of Lethbridge campus by in 1982.

In 1975 the school had been granted faculty status and, in 1989, the name was changed from social welfare to the Faculty of Social Work. The faculty has seen four deans: Tim Tyler (1966–78), Len Richards (1978–83), Ray Thomlison (1983–98), and Gayla Rogers (1999–2004). From a complement of twelve full-time academics, six support staff, and approximately twenty students in 1969/70, the faculty now numbers thirty academics, fourteen support staff, and more than five hundred students. In 1993 the faculty moved into a state-of-the-art facility in the Professional Faculties Building. In 1994 the doctoral program began and, in that same year, an international concentration was developed—unique in Canada—within the community organization management and social policy specializations of the master of social work program. That year, a transfer agreement was signed between the faculty and six Alberta social work diploma providers to ensure allocation of 20 percent of the undergraduate seats to diploma holders who had completed the requisite additional arts courses. In 1998 a part-time master of social work program began in Edmonton on the basis of an outside tuition policy and, in 1999, the faculty received five-year funding from the provincial government to provide the bachelor of social work program to rural, remote, and Aboriginal communities in Alberta. For the faculty, the millennium is a benchmark. For the first time, the faculty has a female dean and a faculty that operates administratively on the principle of collegial governance. What began as a shift to participatory and transparent decision making in 1996 has now become the modus operandi based on principles of accountability, participation, equity, and transparency. The faculty is undertaking curriculum redesign in all programs, seeking student and community input, and developing more rigorous evaluation tools. The faculty took a stance to set priorities for continuous learning and professional development by hiring a part-time director in 1999 to coordinate offerings in this area, mainly partnering with social service agencies in the province. Building alumni relationships is also a focal area. In 1998 the faculty celebrated twenty-five years of bachelor of social work convocants and, in 1999, thirty years of master of social work convocants. The University of Calgary Faculty of Social Work has graduated 4,614 students in its thirty-three-year history. Current information about the university's social work programs can be found online at < www.fsw.ucalgary.ca/ >.

[*Gayla Rogers* and
Elsie Johnson]

RELATED ENTRIES
Alberta College of Social Workers, A. Comanor, Education in Social Work, Faculties of Social Work, I. Munroe-Smith

University of Manitoba Faculty of Social Work

The Faculty of Social Work at the University of Manitoba celebrated its sixtieth year of operation in the 2003/04 academic year. It had its distinguished beginnings anchored in the early work of J.S. Woodsworth and the Canadian Welfare League, which resulted in the establishment in 1914 of one of the first training programs for social workers in Canada. The First World War and the great depression constrained further development until 1943 that the School of Social Work had its formal beginnings within the faculty of arts and science. Under the leadership of Dr. C.E. Smith (1943–53), the school moved from offering a one-year diploma to a two-year graduate program leading to a master of social work degree. It was the first university-based social work program between Toronto and British Columbia and, for many years, was the only school serving the three prairie provinces. Professor Helen Mann and other staff at the school made an important contribution to the development of social work education in North America in the period 1953–68; they provided strong leadership in laying the groundwork for the development of an undergraduate degree program in most North American schools. These efforts led to the development of the faculty's bachelor of social work program, which admitted its first class for the 1968/69 academic year. Between 1968 and 1974, the school was faced with the need to reconceptualize its master of social work program necessitated by a new first degree program. The outcome was a twelve-month master of social work degree modelled on the British tutorial system of focused self-study. The program accepted its first group of students for the 1972/73 term. Since its inception, the school has had a strong commitment to affirmative action and extending the accessibility of its programs to non-traditional student populations and underrepresented minorities. From 1979 to 1984 three major decentralized programs were established to strengthen ties between the school and these marginalized constituencies. In September 1981 students were admitted to a four-year bachelor of social work program at the Winnipeg Education Centre, which focused on the preparation of social workers for inner-city social work practice; by the fall of 1984, about fifty students entered the program, of which about half were Aboriginal students. In January 1983 the first class was taught for a two-year certificate in child and family services offered to the staff of three First Nation child and family service agencies. Finally, in 1984, the faculty officially opened its northern program in Thompson to offer accessibility to the bachelor of social work degree to northern, predominantly Aboriginal, people; this program focuses on preparing social workers for practice in rural and remote northern communities. In the mid-1980s the emphasis in Manitoba on developments in the area of child and family services in Aboriginal and non-Aboriginal communities led to the development of the Child and Family Services Research Group within the school; initially funded by the federal Department of Health and Welfare, this group is now established as a source of collaborative research between the professional community and the faculty.

During the years 1984–89, the school also applied to the University of Manitoba Senate for faculty status, which was received in recognition of its academic standards and stature within the university and in the community. In 1994 as part of its commitment to extend access and inclusion, the Faculty of Social Work implemented a bold innovative approach to the delivery of its bachelor of social work program by distance education and off-campus means to the province. This strategy was extended in 1999 to the delivery of its master of social work program off campus. After twenty years of consultation and planning, the faculty implemented its doctorate program and admitted its first doctoral students in the fall of 2000; the intent of this program is for graduate students to become social work educators and researchers. The program includes a unique special emphases on social work practice and Aboriginal peoples, and feminist approaches to social work practice. In the later 1990s the faculty refined its mission statement and extended its mandate to add a focus on international social development. The faculty has advanced its international social development initiatives in the Ukraine, Russia, Mexico, and China. Its efforts in these international projects have been focused on promoting international social development through inclusive social work education and participatory research in all partner countries. The faculty is the only professional social work program in Manitoba; as such, it provides the only professional social work degree preparation at the bachelor, master, and doctoral levels in the province. It relies heavily on collaborative partnerships with community, voluntary and government, health and social service agencies for the bachelor and master programs. Field placements, and faculty and student research opportunities. Current information about the University of Manitoba's social work programs can be found online at <www.umanitoba/faculties/social_work/>.

[*Donald M. Fuchs*]

RELATED ENTRIES
Education in Social Work, G.D. Erickson, Faculties of Social Work, Manitoba Association of Social Workers, Manitoba Institute for Registered Social Workers

University of Northern British Columbia Social Work Program

The University of Northern British Columbia social work program opened its doors in the fall of 1994 with the introduction of the master of social work degree, followed one year later with the admission of undergraduate students to a bachelor of social work program. The origin of the two-degree programs lay in extensive community demand spearheaded by social workers and the northern branch of the British Columbia Association of Social Workers for the establishment of the two-degree programs. The development of a two-degree program also resulted from broad consultations with community agencies and the BC Ministry of Social Services. The mission statement emphasizes critical social thinking and social justice: "Social work education at the UNBC is committed to a program of studies that is informed by a central concern for human rights, personal empowerment, community change and social justice. It has as its foundation an analysis of power in relation to class, race, ethnicity, gender, sexual orientation, age and abilities. Incorporating critical social thinking including structural, feminist and anti-racist analyses, the Program focuses on social work in northern and remote areas, Aboriginal and cross cultural issues, women and human services and community practice and research. It continues to develop in collaboration with regional, national and global communities. The Social Work Program seeks to provide its graduates with intellectual, practical and professional skills and knowledge rooted in progressive values that promote beneficial change. By acknowledging the holistic, interdisciplinary and activist nature of social work and its commitment to social justice, the curriculum and governance of social work education at UNBC will strive to provide a self-reflective balance between theory and practice; research, teaching and community service; and critical self-awareness and respect for the ideas of others." The bachelor of social work degree is designed to prepare students for beginning level, generalist social work practice with individuals, families, groups, and communities. As well as the main campus in Prince George, three regional campuses—at Terrace, Quesnel/Williams Lake, and Dawson Creek/Fort St. John—offer bachelor of social work education. The child welfare specialization in the bachelor of social work program, introduced in 2000, prepares students for child protection responsibilities and other positions in government and non-profit child welfare services. The master of social work program is available on a full- or part-time basis for practitioners with a bachelor of social work and can be completed through a thesis or practicum route. The aim of the master of social work is to provide students with advanced social work research, policy, and practice skills.

The master of social work offers students an integrated research, policy, and practice concentration in one of the key thematic areas: social work in northern and remote areas, Aboriginal peoples, women and the human services, and community practice, and research. Some initiatives were taken to increase access to graduate social work education in our province. In 1998 a two-year master of social work degree was introduced for practitioners without a bachelor of social work degree. In April 2000 the university and Yukon College signed an agreement that put into motion the combined master of social work and master of science in community health. The master of social work curriculum, which is identical to that in Prince George campus, is specially designed for working social work practitioners in the Yukon. The bachelor of social work degree was fully accredited in 2000 by the Canadian Association of Schools of Social Work. Two years later, the accreditation board approved a further five years for the accreditation of the bachelor of social work program. The master of social work degree was granted candidacy for accreditation status in 1998. Application for the full accreditation of the master of social work program was submitted to the Canadian Association of Schools of Social Work in October 2002. The university's social work program is the leading provider of professional social work education in northern British Columbia. As the newest school of social work in this province, strong partnership link major health and social welfare agencies and ministries. Undergraduate and graduate students benefit directly from this well-established dialogue and from exchanges with professional, government, and community-based services. Current information about the university's social work programs can be found online at < www.unbc.ca /socialwork/ >.

[*Kwong-Leung Tang*]

RELATED ENTRIES

Board of Registration for Social Workers of BC, British Columbia Association of Social Workers, Education in Social Work, Faculties of Social Work

University of Regina Faculty of Social Work

Canadian social work education and practice has been shaped by ideas emerging from the prairies, especially those of the social gospel movement and the women's suffrage movement, which were particularly active in western Canada during the early years of the past century. Reforms championed by the Co-operative Commonwealth Federation (later, the New Democratic Party) in Saskatchewan have greatly influenced the development of social welfare in Canada. This history is integral to the development of social work education at the University of Regina, as is the special relationship with the school of Indian social work at the First Nations University of Canada. The faculty's programs of teaching and research, and many other activities are enriched by this relationship, which have been part of the history of the university's history and of the school of Indian social work. In recent years, the programs have benefitted significantly by contractual agreements for delivery of social work education through Yukon College (in Whitehorse, Yukon) and Aurora College (in Fort Smith, Northwest Territories). Briefly, the University of Regina grants three accredited social work degrees (master and bachelor of social work and bachelor of Indian social work) and two certificates (one in social work and one in Indian social work). The master of social work is located on the Regina campus, while the bachelor of social work is delivered in three locations in Saskatchewan (Regina, Saskatoon, and Prince Albert) and in the Yukon (Whitehorse at Yukon College). The bachelor of social work is also delivered across Saskatchewan through a system of regional colleges. The certificate in social work is delivered only through Aurora College in the Northwest Territories. The bachelor of and certificate in Indian social work are offered through the First Nations University of Canada. Program development and delivery is guided by the faculty mission statement:

> The social work program of education, research and community service is designed to prepare students for critical generalist social work practice with diverse peoples. Informed by the principles of social justice, the social work program encourages students to identify the needs of the disadvantaged, marginalized and oppressed; to develop the commitment, knowledge, values, attitudes, and skills required to confront structural inequalities; to address personal issues; and to empower individuals, families, and communities to realize their full potential.

The Faculty of Social Work programs are delivered to approximately six hundred undergraduate students and eighty graduate students. The faculty is proud of its accomplishments over the years, many of these reflected in publications disseminated through the Social Policy Research Unit (est. 1972), the research arm of the Faculty of Social Work. The unit's main goal is to conduct critical analytic research to promote social justice and enhance individual, family, and community development. The unit receives funding from the university and through various research contracts and grants. Current information about the University of Regina's social work programs can be found online at < www.uregina.ca/socwork/ >.

[*Sharon McKay*]

RELATED ENTRIES

Education in Social Work, Faculties of Social Work, Saskatchewan Association of Social Workers

University of Toronto Faculty of Social Work

The Faculty of Social Work at the University of Toronto (est. 1914) is the oldest school of social work in Canada and one of the oldest in North America. At the time of its founding, social work was an emerging profession. Social problems were widespread and the charity organization movement was growing at an unprecedented rate; while well intended, these relief practices were poorly organized, inefficient, and lacked central administration. Advancement in social work training was clearly needed. Shortly after the University of Toronto established the first school of social work, later renamed the Faculty of Social Work. In the early 1950s the School of Social Work at the University of Toronto responded to the critical need for advanced graduate education by inaugurating a doctoral program in social work. Until the 1980s the University of Toronto was the only Canadian school producing social work doctoral graduates and, consequently, junior faculty members for the new social work departments that began to proliferate throughout the country during a remarkable thirty-year period of growth in this field following the Second World War. In these post-war years, the faculty was instrumental in raising the profile of social work, by comparison with other disciplines such as medicine and law. Faculty members strove to impress on their non–social work colleagues the importance of social work research and scholarship in the field of social sciences. Change was most keenly felt in the 1960s, when widespread student activism rocked campuses in North America. The Faculty of Social Work was, like others, challenged with respect to its perceived conservative, parochial, and authoritarian conventions. During this period of transformation, entire faculty meetings were devoted to the subject of faculty/student relationships, and student became involved in curriculum development, faculty governance, and policy development. By the end of the 1960s about 10 percent of the master of social work student population had received undergraduate degrees in countries other than Canada, and throughout the 1970s and 1980s, the movement to embrace cultural pluralism gradually became society-wide. At the Faculty of Social Work, teaching and research began to reflect populations and subjects that had traditionally been excluded, such as visible minority communities, women, persons with disabilities, single-parent households, working mothers, and mature students. New partnerships were forged with agencies and practitioners in the field to enhance field education opportunities and open up joint research undertakings, as well as provide the faculty with valuable input on programs. These critical years in curriculum development at the faculty reflected major developments in social work education, both domestically and abroad. Notably, at a time when bachelor of social works were first being introduced in Canada, the faculty made the decision to remain focused on the master and doctoral programs, while offering an entry route for bachelor of social work graduates; this latter development was a major factor in attracting students from throughout Canada and beyond. Indeed, the faculty experienced a major spurt of growth in the student body during this time.

The year 1989 marked the beginning of a period of significant growth for the University of Toronto Faculty of Social Work. The faculty flourished as the university injected new resources into its programs; during the second half of the 1990s, however, post-secondary education became a primary target of government cutbacks. In 1995 the University of Toronto embarked on a campus-wide planning process to assist academic divisions to

work through these challenging times. The Faculty of Social Work identified these top priorities during this planning phase:

- increased support for high-quality scholarship and research of faculty and students;
- expansion of the doctoral program and refinement of the master's program;
- further advancement of anti-racism, multiculturalism, and Aboriginal issues initiatives;
- enhancement of teaching and learning effectiveness;
- further promotion of links between scholarship, research, and teaching;
- fostering of interdisciplinary partnerships; and
- expansion of fundraising activities.

Since 1995 the faculty has demonstrated significant progress in achieving these goals. A comprehensive self-study, including an external review, was undertaken in 1999 and highlighted the faculty's accomplishments. As part of this review process, a survey was conducted to obtain comparative data from the top ten US schools of social work as identified by the *US News and Work Report* (1998); overall, this comparative analysis provided clear evidence that the University of Toronto's performance ranks very well with that of the top-ranked US schools. The success of this earlier planning phase has provided a solid foundation for the next cycle of university-wide strategic planning. The faculty's new comprehensive academic plan has strengthening the core as its integrative theme and responding to diversity to achieve excellence as its primary focus. Throughout these decades of change, the Faculty of Social Work has been transformed in many new and exciting ways while maintaining its singular commitment to the pursuit of excellence in social work education. The faculty is extremely proud of its staff and graduates who have played important roles in forging a strong Canadian social work identity, through their important contributions to social work research, scholarship, and professional practice. Current information about the university's social work programs can be found online at <www.utoronto.ca /facsocwk/>.

[*Wes Shera*]

RELATED ENTRIES

H. Cassidy, Education in Social Work, G.D. Erickson, Faculties of Social Work, Ontario Association of Social

Workers, Ontario College of Certified Social Workers and Social Service Workers, A. Rose, J.W. Willard

University of Victoria School of Social Work

The University of Victoria School of Social Work is committed to being a leader in critical social work thought, First Nations social work education, child welfare policy and practice, and distance education delivery. The school's view of the profession of social work stresses social justice, anti-racist and anti-oppressive social work practices, and critical enquiry that respects the diversity of knowing and being. The School of Social Work admitted its first students to the bachelor of social work degree program in 1976 and its the first distance education courses were offered in 1978. In 1988 the bachelor of social work program has been re-accredited. In 1986 a program was established for a cohort of social workers in a Vancouver Island First Nation; a similar arrangement was established with the North West Band Social Worker's Association in Terrace in 1990 and with the Nicola Valley Institute of Technology in Merritt in 1991; at the request of the North West Band Social Worker's Association, the school developed an off-campus master of social work program in Terrace in 1995 for First Nation students in the north. By 1993, the distance education program was made available throughout British Columbia and, in 1997, to Alberta, the Yukon, and the Northwest Territories. In 1990 the school began collaborations whereby students in the Okanagan University College and the University College of the Cariboo could pursue the bachelor of social work degree under the University of Victoria's school program regulations; this mentoring and transitional relationship continued until 1997/98, when the university-college programs were ready to grant degrees directly from their institutions. In 1991 the school was a founding partner—with the school of child and youth care, and the school of nursing—in the establishment of multi-disciplinary graduate education; in 2000, the school took sole administrative responsibility for the master of social work program, while maintaining the interdisciplinarity of the curriculum. In 1996 the Gove Inquiry on Child Protection in BC recommended changes in social work education to strengthen child welfare and

child protection content. Development work to respond to these recommendations was done collaboratively between the BC schools of social work and the ministries of advanced education, and children and families. Revised bachelor of social work degree regulations were approved in 1999 to enable students to follow a specialized track within the bachelor program that provides a critical focus on child welfare policy and practice issues and related skills. Two other specializations were subsequently developed: one in First Nations, and one in First Nation child welfare to help Aboriginal students pursue their interests.

The school's graduate students and master of social work graduates fill many critical roles in social work education, in provincial government, and its agencies, in Aboriginal child welfare agencies, and in social work consulting practice. The external reputation of the master of social work program is very strong with qualified applications exceeding available spaces by three to one. As of 2002 five of the forty graduates of the master of social work degree program have continued their graduate education at the doctoral level. The school has from its beginning had a commitment to contributing through research and scholarship to the development of social work practice and social justice. The earliest form of this commitment was the Sedgewick Society, through which faculty contribute their time and scholarship to publications serving social work clients and the social work community; in 1986 this commitment took a new form in the development of the community-based Child, Family, and Community Research Program; in 2001 this program was subsumed under the newly formed Research Initiatives for Social Change Unit, which broadened the scope of research involved and reflected the current mission of the school. In 2002 the school was successfully re-accredited. The school continues to experience a strong demand for its bachelor and master of social work degrees. Over the last few years, faculty renewal has been a continuous process. Financial and personnel resources have been, and continue to be, strengthened; a committed community of faculty, staff, practicum agencies, and students continue to challenge themselves and one another to pursue the vision set out in the school's mission statement. Current information about the University of Victoria's social work programs can be found online at <www.uvic/socw/>.

[*Wendy Seager*]

RELATED ENTRIES

Board of Registration for Social Workers of BC, British Columbia Association of Social Workers, Education in Social Work, Faculties of Social Work

University of Waterloo, Renison College

In the year 2001, Renison College received full accreditation from the Canadian Association of Schools of Social Work for its bachelor of social work program. This program, the newest social work program in the country, was established in 1996 by the Senate of the University of Waterloo, of which Renison is an associated college. The program is comprised of three terms over twelve months and applicants are required to hold an undergraduate bachelor's degree and to have completed ten prerequisite courses. Although a new program, the bachelor of social work was build on a long tradition of undergraduate teaching in social work and social welfare courses, which offered students the opportunity to complete a diploma in social work. During these years, in addition to its cadre of full-time social work professors, Renison College drew on expertise in the region, including a long-standing co-operative arrangement with its neighbour Wilfrid Laurier University. At this point in its development the bachelor of social work is giving special attention to developing close relationships with First Nations in the area. As well, it has developed an exchange program with the University of Arizona. Current information about the university's social work programs can be found online at <www.reni son.uwaterloo.ca/>.

[*Francis J. Turner* and
Joanne C. Turner]

RELATED ENTRIES

Education in Social Work, Faculties of Social Work, Ontario Association of Social Workers, Ontario College of Certified Social Workers and Social Service Workers

University of Western Ontario School of Social Work

A department of social welfare (est. 1969) was founded at London, Ontario, at King's College, a denominational Catholic affiliate of the University of Western Ontario; now known as a school of social work, it was originally mandated to offer only an undergraduate program in social welfare. Conflict over its social work or social welfare focus and the college's apparent inability to support the program financially without government funding resulted in considerable disharmony within the department and the College over the next few years. In 1972 under a new director, curriculum revisions reoriented the program to focus more strongly on preparation for the practice of social work. These issues were partially resolved in late 1973, when the Ontario government announced full funding for denominational colleges and it was discovered that grants to the college for social work students would be at one-and-a-half times the standard undergraduate rate. As internal and environmental relations became more harmonious, the department increased its autonomy and self-regulation, defined its priorities, refined its policies, and developed a curriculum that became increasingly more oriented to preparing students for professional social work practice. The Department of Social Welfare became the Department of Social Work in 1974; implications from that change for professionally focused education were more solidly accepted by the college and the university. The department successfully completed requirements for program accreditation with the Canadian Association of Schools of Social Work in 1978. The associated mission statement declared that the "Bachelor of Social Work Program at King's College provides a learning environment directed toward developing and fostering competence and excellence at the first professional level of Social Work education and practice." This emphasis on teaching aimed at practice competence was further consolidated during a major curriculum review accomplished between 1980 and 1983. The new curriculum was implemented incrementally over the academic years 1982/83, 1983/84, and 1984/85, and was at the forefront of a successful re-accreditation review in 1986. The underlying principle was integration between courses in each of the three program years, between the program years, and between classroom and practicum components of the program.

The Ontario College of Certified Social Workers was established in 1982 at a meeting of the Ontario Association of Professional Social Workers held at King's College. This event solidified further the school's connection with the community of social work practitioners in Ontario. It also fortified the strong collegial relationship maintained between the school and the western branch of the Ontario Association of Social Workers. A new program structure was adopted in 1990–91, a program for part-time students began in 1991–92, and the honours bachelor of social work program was reaccredited in 1994. Previously, the overall structure required that students complete the equivalent of one university year, including an introductory social welfare and social work course, before applying for entry to the professional program in year two; under the new structure, students enter the program in year three, after completing the equivalent of two years of university-level preparation. Preparatory studies include courses providing an introduction to social welfare and social work, an introduction to social work practice, and introductory research methodology and statistics in social work. These changes were designed to ensure the admission of students with a strong academic foundation, and to facilitate access for mature students or graduates from other disciplines. More than half the students admitted each year now possess at least one completed university degree. The department officially changed its name to become a school of social work in 1994.

The school has always enjoyed strong support from organizations providing human services in London, Ontario, and its environs. Many students are drawn from that geographic area, while others have come from around the world. Graduates are often employed by local service agencies and many go on to post-graduate studies in social work. The fieldwork component of the program has always been well supported by local service agencies and an Association of Field Practice Educators serves as one major link between the service community and the school. Various efforts to establish a post-graduate master of social work program at the school have been thwarted by a lack of resources. A renewed venture in that direction envisions this long-term goal being achieved early in this millennium. Current information

about King's College's social work programs can be found online at < www.uwo.ca/king's/ >.

[*Kenneth H. Gordon*]

RELATED ENTRIES
Education in Social Work, Faculties of Social Work, Ontario Association of Social Workers, Ontario College of Certified Social Workers and Social Service Workers

University of Windsor School of Social Work

The University of Windsor has played an important role in the development of social work education in Canada. With the launch of the first bachelor of social work program in the country in the autumn of 1966 and the establishment of a master of social work program in 1968 the university and the school has demonstrated its ongoing commitment to meeting the needs of the community and its citizens, and to advancing the cause of social justice. Uniquely situated on the banks of the Detroit River at the foot of the Ambassador Bridge to the United States, the University of Windsor's school affords students the opportunity to study in one of the most culturally diverse regions of Canada. Accredited by the Canadian Association of Schools of Social Work, the school continues to offer baccalaureate and graduate education to individuals seeking professional preparation. Drawing on the knowledge and experience of a dedicated faculty, the school's programs combine classroom learning with field education in more than a hundred social service settings spanning both sides of the border. In addition the school has become the co-sponsor of a combined undergraduate honours degree program in social work and women's studies and is one of many interdisciplinary collaborations envisioned for the future. Current information about University of Windsor's social work programs can be found online at < www .uwindsor.ca/socialwork/ >.

[*G. Brent Angell*]

RELATED ENTRIES
G.D. Erickson, Education in Social Work, Faculties of Social Work, Practicum Instructor, Ontario Association of Social Workers, Ontario College of Certified Social Workers and Social Service Workers

V

Vanier Institute of the Family

The Vanier Institute of the Family (est. 1965) was formed by Governor General Georges Vanier and his wife Pauline. Founded as an organization committed to the promotion of the well being of families in Canada, the Vanier Institute bases its activities in Ottawa on the premise that strong families are the essential element in the healthy development of children. It states its mission as: "to create awareness of, and to provide leadership on, the importance and strengths of families in Canada and the challenges families face in all their diverse structures." The institute operationalizes this mission through a broad spectrum of activities encompassing the dissemination of information, supporting and carrying out research, and advising governments, corporations, and faith-based organizations on issues related to family policy. Throughout its work, the institute stresses the importance of helping families tap their inherent skills and powers to assist themselves. More information about the Vanier Institute for the Family can be found online at <www.vifamily.ca>.

[FJT]

RELATED ENTRIES

Family Allowance Act, Family Demographics, Family: Non-traditional, Family Planning, Family Research, Family Services Canada, Family Therapy, E.D.O. Hill, Parenting, Research, Services for Children, Services for Elderly People, Services for Families, Services to Married People

Veterans Affairs Canada

Veterans Affairs Canada is the federal department that repays the nation's debt of gratitude to those whose courage has contributed to the freedom of Canadians during wartime, and to global peace and security as an ally and peacekeeping partner. The department meets its responsibilities through programs for disability pensions, income support, pension advocacy, health care, and commemoration. The department seeks to provide these services in a caring manner consistent with its mission statement, which is "to provide exemplary, client-centred services and benefits that respond to the needs of veterans, and

other clients and their families, in recognition of their services to Canada; and to keep the memory of their achievements and sacrifices alive for all Canadians." Program and service delivery are based on a philosophy of care that emphasizes a broad concept of health that encompasses the determinants of health, veterans' autonomy and self-sufficiency, veterans' choices and quality of life, and promotion of health and self-care. Veterans Affairs Canada provides services to a highly diverse clientele including armed forces and merchant navy veterans, former—and in some cases current—members of the Canadian forces, certain civilians, former—and in some cases serving—members of the Royal Canadian Mounted Police (RCMP), and survivors and dependants of the aforementioned groups. In 2000–01 an estimated 204,903 veterans, eligible Canadian forces members, qualified civilians, and their families received benefits and services. The department's portfolio expended $2.1 billion, employing 3,317 full-time staff in a national network of headquarters, regional, and district offices throughout Canada. Wartime veterans with service in the First and Second World Wars and the Korean conflict are the largest group served by the department. At age seventy-nine, veterans in this group receive a services delivered through a client-centred continuing care model that focuses on later life and end-of-life care interventions; continuing care is provided in a veteran's community and in long-term care beds, as needed. The second largest population served is regular members of the Canadian Forces who have served Canada in peacetime, many on peacekeeping missions around the world; their average age is fifty-nine. Veterans Affairs, with its partners, such as the Department of National Defence, are developing a model of service delivery to address common problems facing this population, including stress, repetitive strain injuries, chronic pain, and issues related to rehabilitation and reintegration into civilian life.

Of especial interest to social workers are the Veterans Affairs Canada health services programs: the Veterans Independence Program and the Treatment Program. The Veterans Independence Program provides home support and institutional care nationally, to help veterans remain healthy and independent in their own homes or communities to the extent that health needs cannot be met through existing provincial/territorial or community programs. The federal program offers a wide array of services including home care, ambulatory health care, transportation, home adaptations, and health promotion. With an emphasis on prevention, service interventions often begin early in the process of functional decline and continue for longer duration than related provincial/territorial programs. The program is also veteran-centred so that veterans can receive moneys in advance, subject to cost ceilings, to choose a service provider. Beds in community care facilities are available when veterans are no longer able to function at home. Veterans may also be eligible for payment of a wide range of treatment benefits including aids to daily living, oxygen therapy, prescription drugs, prosthetics, special equipment, vision care and audio, dental, hospital, medical, and nursing services. The Veterans Independence Program is functionally administered through the Veterans Affairs district offices throughout Canada. Service needs are determined by a multi-dimensional functional assessment administered by an area counsellor, who often has social work or nursing qualifications. A multidisciplinary team—including nurses, occupational therapists, and physicians—may be called on in planning appropriate care. A screening tool is used by client service agents in ongoing reviews to identify changes in health needs that may trigger reassessment or modification to care plans.

Over the years, Veterans Affairs Canada has made important contributions to the development of social welfare programs and policies, among them the pioneering of public disability pensions after the First World War, the passing of the Veterans Charter after the Second World War, and a comprehensive legislative package for veterans on a national scale previously unknown in the areas of health care, rehabilitation, education, housing, and income support. In the 1980s and 1990s the department has provided leadership in community-based geriatric care with the introduction of the Veterans Independence Program, a national continuing care program. Currently, the department is piloting models of care in the treatment of stress-related and other injuries in addressing the needs regular Canadian Forces members, many who have served in at least one of the more the fifty special duty and peacekeeping missions since the Second World War. Information about Veterans Affairs Canada can be found online at < www.vac-acc.gc.ca >.

[*David Pedlar*]

RELATED ENTRIES

Crisis Intervention, Home Care, Hospices, Long-Term Care, Military Social Work, Palliative Care, Wellness

vicarious traumatization

Vicarious traumatization refers to the effects on workers who respond to victims of trauma, which authors began to describe as early as 1974. With a particular focus on emergency service personnel, these experiences were commonly explored as an aspect of burnout or countertransference. Researchers in the 1980s noting stress reactions among therapists working with traumatized individuals also referred to the phenomenon as an element of countertransference. Not until 1990 did reference to the constructs burnout and countertransference in describing this phenomenon come under scrutiny; in response, vicarious traumatization was proposed (McCann & Pearlman 1990) as a better way to encapsulate the enduring and pervasive schema alterations, and resulting behaviour changes related to the cumulative effects of working with those who have experienced trauma. The terms compassion fatigue and secondary traumatic stress disorder were also suggested (Figley 1995); others have described helpers' experiences without using particular terms, or have used these terms interchangeably to describe the same phenomenon (Stamm 1997), and still others continue to describe this experience as an element of countertransference. The parameters of this concept remain unclear; it has been described broadly as "helper-encounters with another's traumatic material" (Stamm 1997: 2) and "the transformation of a helper's inner experience resulting from empathic engagement with clients' trauma material" (Saakvitne & Pearlman 1996: 40). For example, while vicarious or secondary trauma has been used to describe the effects of indirect exposure to highly stressful experiences through the role of helper, differentiating direct and indirect exposure can be challenging. In particular, emergency service personnel may work in environments in which their safety is directly at risk. One must distinguish whether effects of such an experience are from indirect exposure of assisting traumatized individuals, the direct exposure of the unsafe environment, or some combination of the two. As well, discussion continues whether this phenomenon is a natural and inevitable reaction to engaging empathically with a traumatized individual and their material (Pearlman & MacIan 1995), and/or a disorder under the rubric of post-traumatic stress disorder (Figley 1995; Stamm 1997). No consensus has emerged for a uniform term or a clear taxonomy as yet; much of the development of this concept has been theoretical, with a recent shift to empirical study of the construct. Much of the literature exploring this concept has been field-specific. While work in the 1980s was dominated by a focus on emergency service workers, the experiences of health care providers (i.e., physicians, nurses, emergency room personnel) and social service providers (i.e., social workers, psychologists, therapists, child protection workers) have received greater attention in the 1990s. A few authors have explored vicarious traumatization in other professional areas, for example, those participating in research and teaching that involves traumatic material who may feel particularly helpless when facing this material without the opportunity to intervene or assist (McCammon 1995). This phenomenon has also been studied in jurors, clergy, corrections workers, drivers of vehicles who witness suicides or accidents, media personnel who witnessed executions, and Holocaust Memorial Museum staff.

Vicarious traumatization has been described as a cumulative process that may involve only a short-term reaction or may produce long-term changes in beliefs, values, and behaviour (McCann & Pearlman 1990). Symptoms may parallel those common to post-traumatic stress (e.g., avoidance, flooding, and hypervigilance)—although at less severe levels than those directly exposed; such impacts can have detrimental influences on functioning in both one's personal and professional life. For example, numbing and other avoidance strategies may lead a helper to experience personal isolation, and may also lead that helper to limit clients' disclosure of painful material or avoid empathic engagement with clients. McCann and Pearlman (1990) provide a theoretical framework for understanding the psychological impact of working with those who have experienced trauma; based on their constructivist self-development theory, they stress that a helper's unique responses to traumatic material are a result of interactions between salient characteristics of the traumatic situation (e.g., nature of the clientele, organizational contextual factors, sociocultural context) and unique therapy characteristics (e.g., psychological needs, cognitive schema, personal trauma history, and level of professional development). Those new to trauma work, those working with a greater number of clients dealing with trauma, and those with a personal history of trauma have described particularly negative effects from their work (Pearlman & MacIan 1995). Very recently, there has been a call to broaden the understanding of the effects of trauma work on the helper, recognizing both positive as well as negative effects from this work. In particular, Stamm has coined the term "compassion satisfaction" to describe potential positive effects of helping. Strategies to cope with and transform the challenges of trauma work have been recommended, such as increased supervision and support for newer and survivor trauma therapists, and limiting trauma work in therapists' caseloads (Pearlman & MacIan 1995). Further suggestions incorporate such individual and workplace strategies as professional development, debriefing with colleagues, self-care and nurturing activities, creating meaning, challenging negative beliefs and assumptions, participating in community-building activities, and maintaining awareness of one's needs, balancing life activities, and connection with others (Saakvitne & Pearlman 1996).

[*Sue McKenzie-Mohr*]

RELATED ENTRIES

Abuse, Bereavement, Child Abuse, Clinical Social Work, Crisis Intervention, Disasters, Elder Abuse, Sensitizing Concepts, Sexual Abuse of Children, Torture & Trauma Victims, Wellness, Women Abuse

REFERENCES

Figley, C.R. (Ed.) 1995. *Compassion Fatigue: Coping with Secondary Traumatic Stress Disorder in Those Who Treat the Traumatized*. New York: Brunner/ Mazel.

Haley, S.A. 1974. When the Patient Reports Atrocities: Specific Treatment Considerations of the Vietnam Veteran. *Archives of General Psychiatry* 30, 191–96.

McCammon, S.L. 1995. Painful Pedagogy: Teaching about Trauma in Academic and Training Settings. In B.H. Stamm (Ed.) *Secondary Traumatic Stress: Self-care Issues for Clinicians, Researchers, and Educators.* 105-20. Lutherville, MD: Sidran Press.

McCann, I.L., and L.A. Pearlman. 1990. Vicarious Traumatization: A Framework for Understanding the Psychological Effects of Working with Victims. *Journal of Traumatic Stress* 3, 1, 131-49.

Pearlman, L.A., and P.S. MacIan. 1995. Vicarious Traumatization: An Empirical Study of the Effects of Trauma Work on Trauma Therapists. *Professional Psychology: Research and Practice* 26, 558-65.

Saakvitne, K.W., and L.A. Pearlman. 1996. *Transforming the Pain: A Workbook on Vicarious Traumatization.* New York: W.W. Norton.

Stamm, B.H. 1997. Work-related Secondary Traumatic stress. PTSD *Research Quarterly* 8, 2 (Spring), 1-7.

visible minorities

Visible minorities is often used in the context of understanding culture and ethnicity, usually to refer to small social communities with observable ethnic or cultural traits, such as skin colour or religion, that are different from those of the majority population. On the surface, the term refers mainly to the observable characteristics and small numbers. For some people, however, use of the word "minority" to refer to culturally diverse ethnic communities is objectionable, as it carries a connotation of inferiority or insignificance; therefore, some people prefer use of "people of colour" to refer directly to the persons whose skin colour is not white. Others may use the term "racialized population" to reflect the challenges and stereotypes facing people because of their ethnicity. In recent decades, increases in immigration rates to Canada and changes in patterns are resulting in less European and more immigration from non-European countries; consequently, the size of the overall ethnocultural population and the diversity of visible minorities in Canada has been on the rise. In Canada an official definition stated in the Employment Equity Act, 1986, specifies that visible minorities are persons who are non-Caucasian in race or non-white in colour; notably, this definition excludes Aboriginal peoples (Canada 1998). The federal government keeps separate statistical records of Aboriginal populations. In 1996, 11.2 percent of the Canadian population was classified as from visible minorities; this percentage represented an almost 20 percent increase from 1991. People of Chinese, South Asian, Black, and Arab or West Asian societies are the four largest visible minority communities in Canada, accounting for almost three-quarters (73.4%) of the 3.2 million visible minorities in the country (Canada 1998).

Social workers in Canada are likely to encounter a more culturally diverse clientele, given this increase in visible minority immigration. Practising with sensitivity to ethnicity, culture, and racism is essential. It is also important for social workers to understand the social implications of being a member of a visible minorities—including Aboriginal persons—in this country. Visible minorities may be disadvantaged in many ways; their vulnerability is most often reflected through the discriminatory and inequitable treatments they receive. While many visible minorities have been contributing to Canadian society and have many outstanding achievements, research findings indicate that visible minorities frequently face racial and systemic discrimination in such aspects of their lives such as education, employment, interaction with police, public media, access to services, health care system, judicial system, among others (CRRF 2000; Gardner-Hofatt, Hoffart, & Pruegger 2001; Henry & Tator 2000). Relatively small population size could mean that individual members may feel isolated and lack a sense of belonging if they live and work in places without other people from their community. While many visible minorities are immigrants from other countries who continue to maintain their own cultural heritage, many others are Canadian born and may or may not share the same cultural values, beliefs, and customs of their ancestors or more recent arrivals. Social workers must be aware that such diversity of experience exists within visible minority communities, and avoid assumptions about homogeneity. Issues and challenges faced by visible minority immigrants who are new to this country are wholly different from those of visible minorities who were born here. Should population trends continue to grow, some visible minority communities may no longer be small in numbers; social workers need to understand that an increase in population size may not automatically bring an increase in equity. As long as the power to control and discriminate continues to rest with the privileged in society, and as long as inequities prevail, the disadvantaged status of visible minorities is likely to continue. Social workers committed to building a just and equitable society can welcome colleagues and clients alike from within disadvantaged communities, and remain committed to social changes to remove maltreatments and barriers that prevent many members of visible minorities from living well every day.

[*Daniel W.L. Lai*]

RELATED ENTRIES

Aboriginal Issues, Culture, Deafness, Diversity, Ethnocultural Communities' Services, Minorities, Minority-Sensitive Practice, Race & Racism, Racism-Sensitive Social Work, Sensitizing Concepts, Sexual Minorities

REFERENCES

Canada. 1998. Census (1996): *Ethnic Origin and Visible Minority Population.* Nation Series 6 [CD-ROM]. Ottawa: Statistics Canada.

CRRF. 2000. *Unequal Access: A Canadian Profile of Racial Differences in Education, Employment and Income.* Toronto ON: Canadian Race Relations Foundation.

Gardner-Hofatt, D., B. Hoffart, and V. Pruegger. 2001. *The Calgary Cultural and Racial Diversity Task Force.* Background Paper. Calgary, AB. Online at time of writing at <www.gov.calgary.ab.ca>.

Henry, F., and C. Tator. 2000. *Racist Discourse in Canada's English Print Media.* Toronto: Canadian Race Relations Foundation.

visual impairment

Vision impairment refers to the extent to which a person has lost the ability to see. Although total blindness is a condition much noted throughout history, it is relatively rare and, as a result, little literature has been devoted to it. That blind persons live in absolute darkness is a common misperception; in fact, the majority of persons considered to be legally blind generally retain some perception of light and shapes. Blindness by law is determined by his/her measurement of acuity (ability to perceive detail) on the basis of distance and visual field: at its simplest, a person who retains vision of 10 percent or less is legally blind. The origin, onset, and extent of vision loss is tremendously varied (Tuttle 1996) and, therefore,

services to ameliorate the impact of blindness and visual impairment are necessarily multi-dimensional. The primary social agency that offers assistance to the visually impaired in Canada, the Canadian National Institute for the Blind (est. 1918) was formed with a charter from the federal government. Its primary concern at the time was to address the immediate needs of veterans blinded during the First World War. The focus of the institute and similar other agencies has shifted from sheltered workshops and residential schools toward goals for full integration and enfranchisement. The majority of visually impaired persons in Canada have lost their sight as a result of age-related conditions, the most common of which are macular degeneration, diabetic retinopathy, glaucoma, and cataracts; the terminology used to refer to vision loss after years of sight is "adventitious" blindness. The impact of the onset of low vision may be compounded by other restrictions associated with later life, such as failing health or mobility, and social isolation (Orr 1991). A fundamental task in the provision of services to older visually impaired persons is to ensure that rehabilitation efforts are not compromised by ageist notions of debilitation and dependence as allegedly normal conditions of old age. For younger visually impaired adults, employment opportunities have significantly advanced over the past fifty years as a result of improved access to education and adaptive technology. Voice-activated and Braille-compatible computer software, talking calculators, and many other high- and low-tech communication tools have helped blind persons to enter the modern workplace. In those provinces or territories where assistive devices are not subsidized by government programs, the high cost of adaptive technology remains a barrier to employment. Children who are congenitally blind can obtain support to ensure access to schools and classrooms; rehabilitation for enhanced mobility and orientation are a particular challenge for a visually impaired child who has difficulty understanding spatial and perspective relationships. Important factors to help children to access information include Braille literacy and keyboarding ability; a recent development is the use of tactile maps. The development of fine-motor skills at an early age is crucial for such children. Visually impaired persons my seek social work assistance with advocacy and education to other service provision in addition to biopsychosocial counselling; for example, when working with a blind client who is also a victim of spousal assault, or aged and in need of opportunities for socialization, the social worker may be called on to ensure access to community services and facilities available to sighted persons. In such cases, the condition of blindness or visual impairment is secondary to the problem presented.

A recent project of the Canadian National Institute for the Blind outlines the importance of developing partnerships with communities, of respecting the tradition of oral culture in the transference of information, and of understanding the importance of inclusive and culturally respective interventions when offering or providing services; the Northern Vision Project in consultation with Aboriginal communities throughout Canada endeavoured to identify specific needs of Aboriginal adults—rate of vision impairment is more than 2.5 times greater than that for other Canadian adults—in accessing and using information and resources related to vision care. Social work counselling has been identified as a vital precursor to rehabilitation and a predictor of its success. The community development model of social work has also played a role in responding to the needs of visually impaired persons, particularly those in developing countries. The World Health Organization has promoted community-based rehabilitation in an effort to provide timely and accessible intervention in rural communities (Yeadon 1991).

In the 1950s Dr. Louis Cholden, a psychiatrist and leading expert on the psychological impact of vision loss, was among the first to emphasize the importance of counselling and psychosocial well-being in the rehabilitation process. Dr. Cholden (1958) described adjustment to blindness as progressing within three distinct areas: physical restoration, education, and psychological rehabilitation. Physical restoration begins with a medical consultation that can ensure optimum physical status as well as information about corrective intervention to maximize remaining vision. Educative efforts can involve teaching/learning specific skills related to living with vision loss, such as using Braille, a white cane, or a guide dog.

Dr. Cholden described psychological rehabilitation by emphasizing that "any of our efforts in the first two classes of rehabilitation will be wasted unless we know where we stand in relation to the third class … the differences between amazing stories of rehabilitative success and clients who have been unable to do anything independently lie in the psychological sphere, in the attitudes of these people toward their handicaps" (Cholden 1958: 63). Some have suggested that the psychological adjustment to blindness can be considered an extension of normal human capacity to deal with any of life's challenges, such as the stages of bereavement. Rehabilitation for the blind engages the most ephemeral of materials, such as attitudes, ideas, concepts of self, aspirations, ambitions as wispy and formless as cobwebs yet the things that determine the meaning and the direction of living (Cholden 1958: 115). The complexity of issues related to adjustment to blindness and vision impairment calls for the expertise and theoretical insight of a range of professions. The discourse of social work, guided by the foundational principles of client determination, empowerment, and holistic assessment, may serve to address the less measurable and more indeterminate objectives of adjustment: self-esteem, well-being, and fulfilment. Current information about visual impairment services provided by the Canadian National Institute for the Blind can be found online at <www.cnib.org>.

[*Gail Wideman*]

RELATED ENTRIES

Bereavement, Deafness, Developmental Challenges, Developmental Challenges & Families, Minorities, Personal-Centred Theory, Physical Challenges, Wellness

REFERENCES

Cholden, L. 1958. *A Psychiatrist Works with Blindness.* New York: William Byrd.

Orr, A. 1991. The Psychosocial Aspects of Aging and Vision Loss. *Journal of Gerontological Social Work* 17, 3/4, 1–14.

Tuttle, D. 1996. *Self-esteem and Adjusting with Blindness: The Process of Responding to Life's Demands.* Springfield, IL: Charles C. Thomas.

Yeadon, A. 1991. Far Too Little, Far Too Slow: Toward a New and Immediate Strategy of Rehabilitation for the Elderly Visually Handicapped. *Journal of Gerontological Social Work* 17, 3/4, 181–96.

vocational rehabilitation

Vocational rehabilitation is a service provided to individuals who have experienced illness, injury, or disability to help them reach their ultimate level of functioning and develop their employability. Rehabilitation may involve assisting clients to return to their pre-disability occupation, or determining alternate occupations based on their functional and vocational capabilities. Services are usually implemented through a team comprised of the client, his/her family, vocational rehabilitation co-ordinator, medical professionals (including physicians and physical therapists), and employers. Vocational rehabilitation begins with a comprehensive assessment with the client's medical status, current functional abilities, psychosocial condition, and economic status, as well as details of vocational background (e.g., education and training, employment history, transferable skills, and interests). Barriers that may influence the client's return to work—including workplace issues (e.g., unsupportive management or workplace conflict), demographic issues (e.g., age, education level), or health issues (e.g., addictions, chronic symptomatology, or ongoing therapies)—are also identified. Discussions with the client's employer and medical professionals are often a part of these assessments, which, on completion, establish the foundation for the client's goals and appropriate directions for vocational rehabilitation. The vocational rehabilitation co-ordinator or case manager assists the client to plan rehabilitation based on the assessment by establishing vocational goals and providing support for the client throughout the development and implementation of the plan. The co-ordinator ensures that plans are jointly managed with clients, their employers, therapists, and health care providers. The co-ordinator also provides leadership with return-to-work programs and promotes positive attitudes regarding persons with physical disabilities. A successful rehabilitation process is characterized by ownership remaining with the client, honesty, transparency, and open communication with all people involved to avoid misunderstandings.

Social workers are well suited to the role of vocational rehabilitation co-ordinator, as their training in assessment and case management is beneficial to the vocational rehabilitation process. Employers of such co-ordinators include auto insurance companies, long-term disability insurance companies, the Canadian Paraplegic Association, and provincial/territorial worker compensation boards. They require competence in written and oral communications, assessment, negotiation, facilitation, and team building. Social workers offer a unique contribution to the process of vocational rehabilitation, given the profession's commitment to helping clients work toward their goals. Social workers' foundation in client advocacy work is also beneficial since vocational rehabilitation can require advocating for entitlements from the workplace, unions, and/or insurance companies.

[*Debbie I. Curtis*]

RELATED ENTRIES

Employee Assistance Programs, Employment, Health & Unemployment, Industrial Social Work, Personal-Centred Theory, Person-in-Environment Perspective, Physical Challenges, Sensitizing Concepts, Services for People with Disabilities, Social Work Profession, Wellness, Workers Compensation

voluntarism

Voluntarism or volunteerism refers both to individuals freely offering their time and talents in support of a community or society's well-being, and to the involvement of voluntary organizations in social welfare. Sparse documentation exists about the entire nature and extent of voluntarism in Canada, yet these activities clearly constitute a fundamental feature of Canadian society and a central expression of its values. Formal volunteer activities cover a gamut from direct service to consumers, to board and committee participation, fund raising, advocacy, education, and administrative support. In addition to formal volunteer roles in organizations, many people provide untold service to others on an informal basis, offering free care and support to relatives, neighbours, and friends. The National Survey of Giving, Volunteering and Participating reported that, in an average year in the 1990s, about 7.5 million Canadians (i.e., 31% of the population aged fifteen and over) indicated that they volunteered to help non-profit organizations (Hall et al. 1998: 10). More than 40 percent of the population in each of Manitoba, Saskatchewan, and Alberta volunteered, compared with the national rate of 31 percent. One-third of all volunteers accounted for 81 percent of total volunteer hours; in most age groups, the rate of doing volunteer work was stable or increased slightly during the last decade, with the exception of a significant increase— almost double—in volunteering among young people (Hall et al. 1998).

Voluntarism is a subject of major importance to social work practitioners who often work alongside volunteers in all practice milieu. An enduring hallmark of Canadian society is the enormous number and wide range of voluntary organizations and associations that contribute to the well-being of citizens, and the great numbers of individuals who undertake volunteer service and fundraising within them. The history of many voluntary agencies demonstrates the indispensable role that individual volunteers played in their establishment. The majority of voluntary organizations continue to use volunteers in various aspects of their work, even though professional staff now occupy primary roles in most. Volunteers work in many areas, among them social services, health, education, arts and culture, sport and recreation, and faith-based organizations. A recent survey (McFarlane & Roach 1999: 5) of 72 Canadian non-profit agencies in crisis services for women and services for children and youth from Ontario to British Columbia demonstrated that 91 percent of agencies surveyed have volunteers in addition to volunteer board members; these agencies used volunteers regardless of the amount of government funding received. On average, the agencies had 60 volunteers, contributing 6,673 hours of service annually, or 3.3 hours/person/week—the equivalent of 3.5 full-time staff, on average, for each agency. With prolonged and severe funding cutbacks in all human service areas, agencies have come to rely on volunteer assistance more of late, making voluntarism even more important. And, while recognizing that volunteers in Canada make an astounding contribution, agencies do express some concerns about rising voluntarism. Volunteers are not paid a salary, but do cost agencies for their recruitment, training, co-ordination, supervision, retention, and related insurance expenses. The supply of volunteers in a community is finite—particularly when difficult

economic times compel most family members to work; so competition for volunteers in any community may be demanding. Significant implications for Voluntarism are arising from the ageing of Canada's population. Adult children may now find themselves with elderly, ailing parents to care for and support; such shifts are likely to produce considerable strain between public service provision and resource allocation, and the volunteer resources and voluntary, non-profit organizations in Canadian communities. Volunteers, like professionals, can suffer burnout in demanding care and support roles, especially in the absence of support and relief for themselves. Governments usually determine grants or contracts with agencies on the assumption that formal and informal volunteers can fill any gaps; similarly, governments have been reducing public funding of human services on the assumption that the voluntary sector can fill gaps created by this diminished public responsibility. Yet government policy and legislation have given little attention to buttressing volunteers and the organizations that rely on them; for example, the emphasis on community care for previously institutionalized populations places much higher expectations on informal caring and volunteer help, without providing adequate resources and supports for such demanding work.

[*John Cossam*]

RELATED ENTRIES

Capacity Assessment, Caregiving, Church-Based Services, Citizen Participation, Community Development, Community Organization, Community Service, Foundations, Fundraising, Mutual-Aid Societies, Natural Helping Networks, Participatory Research, Peer Counselling, Self-Help Groups, Self Help & Mutual Aid, Social Welfare Context, United Way

REFERENCES

Hall, M., T. Knighton, P. Reed, P. Bussiere, D. McRae, and P. Bowen. 1998. *Caring Canadians, Involved Canadians: Highlights from the National Survey of Giving, Volunteering and Participating.* Ottawa: Statistics Canada.

McFarlane, S., and R. Roach. 1999. *Making a Difference: Volunteers and Non-profits.* Calgary, AB: Canada West Foundation.

W

welfare state

The welfare state, a term that emerged in many countries following the Second World War, identifies political systems that attempted to provide comprehensive state-supported health and social services to all citizens. Welfare states, such as Canada, Britain, Australia, Sweden, and New Zealand, among others, instituted a system that respected the range of people's biopsychosocial needs encountered throughout a lifetime—from cradle to grave. In its original conception, it was viewed in a non-political sense, so that welfare state could be a descriptor of a country with highly developed health and social services; the term soon became implicitly associated with socialistic, as opposed to capitalist, ideologies for what constituted an optimum political system. For some observers, this ideological association turned welfare state into a pejorative term, as implementation was considered to be detrimental to the optimum development of a country; from this perspective, a welfare state would place an overly heavy demand on a country's economic resources and, therefore, would limit that country's ongoing development. As a result, welfare state gradually came to be identified only with programs that offered financial assistance to people in need; those who took a pejorative view of such programs alleged that too many of those benefitting were abusing the system or were, in the centuries-old claim, the "undeserving" poor. The global movement to politically conservative governance has sought to weaken efforts to build welfare states. On balance, a thorough understanding of the requisites for any modern society includes some kind of social welfare system, regardless of political persuasion. The reality is not either/or but, rather, a continuum of human services, as countries vary in the nature, extent, effectiveness, and structure of their social and health care programs. In this context, all countries are welfare states to a greater or lesser extent, along a broad range of types, varieties, attitudes, commitments, and methods for supporting their human service systems. Being viewed as a concept lacking precision and overly identified with political ideologies, the term "welfare state" is now less commonly used in contemporary social work literature. The more commonly used concept is that of a social network, which can be applied to all countries and all parts of the human services continuum.

[*FJT*]

RELATED ENTRIES

R.B. Bennett, W.H. Beveridge, Canada Assistance Plan, Great Depression (1930s), Income Security, Marsh Report, Poverty, Social Welfare, Social Welfare Context, Social Welfare History, Unemployment Assistance Plan, Wellness

wellness

Wellness is a concept of increasing importance in Canadian social work, as it seeks to move social work and its goals from a focus on pathology, treatment, and problem solving to a more holistic approach that fosters health and growth in persons, families, and systems. For several decades, theories that underscored attempts of helping or curing clients strongly influenced intervention through some form of personal or systemic structural change, or through the seeking of solutions for identified problems; social work theory and practice was driven more by a restore-and-repair thrust than by the development of human potential and the seeking of optimum functioning. This latter, more positive thinking, was greatly influenced by theories drawing on existentialism and feminism. The seeking of wellness in working with clients stems not from a naive denial of the existence of pathology nor of personal and physical limitations, but from an understanding that, when they do occur, they need to be addressed and assisted. A wellness approach is emphatic about the potential for people, even under the most repressive and constrained circumstances, to build on their ability to identify their needs, to grow, and to achieve the improvements they desire. In this framework, the role of the social worker is to help clients to empower themselves, so that clients can identify the extent and sources of their potential and become aware of their inherent capability and belief in themselves; professionals can draw on strategies and resources to assist clients to seek and achieve their own highest possible well-being. Wellness does not negate problems and pathological behaviours but, rather, stresses the need for detailed knowledge of them and other factors that limit clients; practitioners can apply relevant theories, skills, techniques, and resources to help clients educate themselves and address their concerns. As well, a wellness approach stresses the need for a rich knowledge and appreciation of human potential and its capacity to set and seek goals of attainment, to achieve satisfaction within the scope of a person's potentials, and, when necessary, to seek support and aid from enriching, sustaining, and fostering environments and systems. Important positive impacts of this holistic and optimistic approach to social work practice can be seen in the tremendous advantages gained by people who were formerly institutionalized, such as elderly people and people with developmental or intellectual challenges, physical challenges, and mental illness.

[*FJT*]

RELATED ENTRIES

Abuse, Addiction, Assessment, Attention Deficit Hyperactive Disorder, Bereavement, Bioethical Issues, Canada Health Act, Clinical Social Work, Deafness, Deinstitutionalization Movement, Developmental Challenges, *Diagnostic and Statistical Manual of Mental Disorders*, Disasters, Eating Disorders, Environmental Issues, Ethics, Healing Theory (Cree), Health & Unemployment, Health Canada, Health Determinants, HIV/AIDS, Home Care, Learning Disabilities, Long-Term Care, Managed Care, Natural Health & Complementary Wellness, Person-in-Environment perspective, Physical Challenges, Practice Methods, Self Help & Mutual Aid, Services for, Settlement House Movement, Social Systems Theory, Social Work Theory, Suicide, Substance Addiction, Theory & Practice, Therapy, Toronto Infants Home, Treatment, Visual Impairment, Youth Criminal Justice Act

Wilfrid Laurier University Faculty of Social Work

The first school of social work at Wilfrid Laurier University was the Graduate School of Social Work (est. 1966) at what was then Waterloo Lutheran University. The school—the ninth social work program in a Canadian university and the first since 1954—offered a master of social work. The program began with a class of twenty-one students in its first year and fifty-nine in its second. The first dean, Dr. Sheldon Rahn, was appointed in January 1966. He and a group of five senior faculty members seconded from the University of

Toronto developed the first curriculum, acted as the admissions committee, and consulted on the hiring of faculty members in the new school. Dr. Rahn also consulted extensively with leading social work educators in the United States. The school was first accredited by the US Council on Social Work Education in 1968. The newly formed Canadian Association of Schools of Social Work awarded full accreditation to the school in 1974, and the program has been accredited by the Canadian association ever since; it and ceased its affiliation with the American accrediting body in 1982. Dr. Francis J. Turner was the first faculty member appointed in 1966 and, in 1969, he succeeded Sheldon Rahn as dean, serving in this position until 1980, when he became Academic Vice-President at Laurentian University. During these years the program achieved a national reputation for the excellence of its graduates. Within the newly named Wilfrid Laurier University, the Graduate School of Social Work became the Faculty of Social Work in 1974. Dr. Sherman Merle was dean from 1980 to 1983, when Dr. Shankar Yelaja was named acting dean; after a search, he was named dean in 1984 and served until his sudden death in 1992. Jannah Mather served as dean from 1994 to 1999, and after serving a year as acting dean, Luke Fusco was appointed in 2000 to a five-year term as dean.

The Faculty of Social Work at Wilfrid Laurier has always had a strong commitment to educating advanced practitioners at the MSW level. It is also committed to research and scholarship providing an environment within which faculty and students can pursue scholarly activities. In 1987 Dr. Yelaja welcomed the first class of doctoral students of social work; the degree designation was changed to Ph.D. in 2000. Throughout most of its history the Faculty of Social Work has offered two major concentrations—Work with Individuals, Families, and Groups and Community Development and Social Planning—and since September 2003 it has offered students concentrations in Work with Individuals, Families, and Groups or the newly designed Community Practice, Policy, and Organizations, as well as the option of integrating concentrations. The Faculty of Social Work has always been committed to international social work education. For more than thirty years practicum students have been placed in a variety of countries on all continents. The Faculty of Social Work has also collaborated with other disciplines in the university: since 1968, there has been a joint master of social work and master of divinity or master of theological studies. More recently students in a master of music therapy program take some of their required courses in the Faculty of Social Work. While it has shared a building with the Seminary, the School of Business and Economics, and with the Faculty of Music, the faculty will move to its own accommodations September 2006. Current information about Wilfrid Laurier's social work programs can be found online at <www .wlu.ca /fsw/ >.

[*Luke Fusco*]

RELATED ENTRIES
Council on Social Work Education (US), Doctorate in Social Work, Education in Social Work, Faculties of Social Work, Ontario Association of Social Workers, Ontario College of Certified Social Workers and Social Service Workers

Joseph William Willard (1917-?)

Willard, Joseph William: public servant; b. Sept. 24, 1917, Hamilton, ON (of Archibald Willard & Janet Warren); m. Geraldine Margaret née, Sept. 17, 1942; children: John William, Kathy Jean; d. unknown

Joseph William Willard attended the University Toronto, where he received a bachelor of arts in political science and economics (1940) and a master's degree in political science (1944). From Harvard University, he received distinctions including Littauer Fellow (1945–46, 1946–47), and achieved a master of public administration (1946), a master's degree in economics (1947), and a doctorate in economics (1954). In his early years he was involved with the YMCA Ontario Boys' Work Board, but his employment commitment was to public service, first in the federal departments of National Defence and Labour. While with the Department of Labour, he worked on the Unemployment Insurance Commission and was assistant editor of the *Labour Gazette*. Dr. Willard was director of research and statistics (1947–60,) within the federal Department of National Health and Welfare (now Health Canada), but he is probably better known for his position as deputy minister of that department (1960–73). While in this position, Dr. Willard represented Canada in UNICEF, holding the positions of chairman of the program committee and

chairman of the board. In the 1950s and 1960s, Dr. Willard's interest in national and international health and welfare were exemplified by his attendance at many international conferences, among others, the International Labour Conference, American Regional Conferences of International Labour Organization, International Conference on Mental Health, International Conference on Social Work, and First International Conference of Ministers of Social Welfare. He was the keynote speaker at the International Conference on Social Welfare. Dr. Willard was also rapporteur and chair on the United Nations Social Commission and was a member of the World Health Organization's Expert Committee of Public Heath Administration. He was a member of the International Labour Organisation's committee of Experts on Social Security, becoming the chair in 1966. As well, Dr. Willard was a consultant for countries studying their health care systems, and for the World Health Organization survey of public health services. Nationally, Dr. Willard was research advisor for the Joint Commission of the House of Commons and Senate on Old Age Security.

Dr. Willard belonged to such organizations as the Canadian Association of Social Workers, Canadian Welfare Council (now Canadian Council on Social Development), Canadian Public Health Association, Canadian Political Science and Economic Association, American Economic Association, American Public Welfare Association, American Public Health Association, and National Association of Social Workers (US). In 1972 he was awarded an honorary doctor of laws degree from McMaster University. After leaving his post as deputy minister of national health and welfare in 1973, Dr. Willard became vice-chair of the Canada Labour Relations Board. Dr. Willard's many awards testify to his commitment to helping others: the Gold Medal from the Professional Institute of Public Service Canada, the Award of Honour from Baron de Hirsch Institute (Montreal), the Community Service Award from the City of Winnipeg, and the Trans-Canada Alliance Award for special efforts toward German-Canadians in Canada.

[*Michelle Wolfe*]

RELATED ENTRIES
Health Canada, YMCA

women abuse

Women abuse refers to the physical and psychological abuse of women by their intimate partners or ex-partners, whether male or female. Core issues that distinguish marital conflict from abuse are control and jealousy. The most frequent abuse of women is psychological or emotional, consisting of degrading comments or slurs, often sexually demeaning in nature; financial abuse—the withholding of sufficient funds to cover basic needs such as food, shelter and clothing—is common even when the woman is employed. Men who abuse their wives have also been known to threaten or abuse family pets or farm animals as a strategy to control their partner's behaviour and to frighten her and any children in their care. Threatening to kill a woman if she were to leave the relationship and/or take children with her is also a relatively common strategy; a partner's threat to take his own life is not unknown and may indicate an increased risk to women and their children (Tutty & Goard 2002). Physical violence occurs in many abusive relationships: it is often present throughout the relationship and severity may increase over the years. Psychological abuse is always a factor when women are physically abused: the threat of repeated violence may control a vulnerable woman's actions even if she is rarely hit. The force of the violence generally outweighs the import of the precipitating issue, as women are not simply pushed, shoved, or slapped; they are beaten or injured, especially where they are most vulnerable. Women often identify their first pregnancy as the onset of physical violence; their partner may direct his physical aggression at the baby in her belly or other female parts such as her breasts or genitals. Men also sexually abuse women and are considerably more likely to stalk women after they leave a relationship (Tutty & Goard 2002).

The 1999 General Social Survey on Victimization concluded that "7 percent of people who were married or living in a common-law relationship experienced some type of violence by a partner during the previous 5 years. The 5-year rate of violence was similar for women (8%) and men (7%). This amounts to approximately 690,000 women and 549,000 men who had a current or former partner in the past 5 years and reported experiencing at least one incident of violence" (Canada 2000: 5). The extent to which men also report being victimized by women partners has raised questions about why services and resources for men have not also been widely developed. The consequences of abuse against women by male partners are generally more serious and recurrence is reported to be frequent: "Sixty-five percent of women compared to 54 percent of men were assaulted on more than one occasion, 26 percent of women as compared to 13 percent of men were victimized more than 10 times. The abuse more often results in women being injured: 40 percent of women compared to 13 percent of men reporting violence in the past five years were injured" (Canada 2000: 5). Men are more likely to murder wives than the opposite: Fitzgerald (1999: 35) noted that spouses were the victims in 18 percent of all solved Canadian homicides and 48 percent of family-related incidents; he also reported that: "over the two decades, three times more wives than husbands were killed by their spouse (1,485 women and 442 men)." Women are at more risk after they have separated from their abusive partner and children are much more likely to be murder victims when men are the perpetrators of family violence. To assist women in leaving abusive relationships, Canada has a network of more than five hundred shelters for abused women funded by provinces and territories. In the year ending March 31, 2000, Statistics Canada (1999–2000) noted that 96,359 women and dependent children were admitted to 467 shelters. While a minority simply needed housing, more than 80 percent were leaving abusive homes: over half were women with dependent children, 73 percent of whom were under ten years of age. Children who are exposed to domestic violence may, themselves, be abused by their parent or may become traumatized by witnessing the violence and are prone to be abusive when they become adults. Other services for abused women offered by shelters and community agencies include support groups, counselling for children, prevention programs, and assistance with access to housing and social assistance.

[*Leslie M. Tutty*]

RELATED ENTRIES

Abuse, Bereavement, Clinical Social Work, Crisis Intervention, Marital & Family Problems, Pregnancy,

Separation & Divorce, Sensitivity Concepts, Services for Women, Therapy, Torture & Trauma, Treatment, Wellness

REFERENCES

Canada. 2000. *Family Violence in Canada: A Statistical Profile*. Ottawa: Statistics Canada.

————. 1999–2000. *Transition Home Survey*. Ottawa: Statistics Canada.

Fitzgerald, R. 1999. *Family Violence: A Statistical Profile 1999*. Ottawa: Statistics Canada.

Tutty, L., and C. Goard. 2002. Woman Abuse in Canada: An Overview. In L. Tutty and C. Goard (Eds.) *Reclaiming Self: Issues and Resources for Women Abused by Intimate Partners*. Halifax, NS: Fernwood.

Women's Christian Temperance Union

The Women's Christian Temperance Union (est. 1874) was of many women's organizations that emerged in Canada in the early to mid-nineteenth century to work for and lobby for a wide range of needed social reform as well as providing direct services to many needy groups in society. The union, founded in Owen Sound, Ontario, held that abuse of alcohol was the root cause of many social problems and, on this premise, the members lobbied for total prohibition of all alcohol in Canada. The organization quickly spread throughout the country and worked on other projects such as suffrage and mother's allowances. Nellie McClung was a prominent member of the Women's Christian Temperance Union in Alberta. Their lobbying was successful, in that prohibition legislation was enacted by the provincial and federal governments during the First World War. The repeal of this legislation greatly weakened the Women's Christian Temperance Union, which gradually ceased to have an influence on Canadian social issues.

[*FJT*]

RELATED ENTRIES

Addiction, Church-Based Services, N. McClung, Non-Governmental Organizations, Religion, Sectarian Social Services, Services for Women, Social Welfare History, Substance, Women's Missionary Society

Women's Missionary Society

The Women's Missionary Society (est. 1914) was closely linked to the Presbyterian Church, which has for more than a hundred years provided a broad range of social services to many disadvantaged people throughout Canada through local groups of volunteers. The Women's Missionary Society is significant in the history of Canadian social welfare and social services because of its longevity and ability to respond to changing needs. Its roots derive from a group of women in Montreal known as the Ladies Auxiliary Association organized in 1864 to assist the Church of Scotland in its work among the French. From this organization emerged the present-day Woman's Missionary Society, which has local bodies functioning in all parts of Canada. Over the years, this organization has been and continues to be involved in a wide range of projects aimed at meeting diverse needs of citizens, especially in such remote areas as the Klondike in the early 1900s, where the society set up hospitals. The society publishes a journal entitled *Glad Tidings*, which focuses on current issues facing society and the church. Current information on the Woman's Missionary Society can be found online at < www.presbycan.ca >.

[*FJT*]

RELATED ENTRIES

Church-Based Services, Non-Governmental Organizations, Religion, Sectarian Social Services, Services for Women, Women's Christian Temperance Union

James Shaver Woodsworth (1874–1942)

Woodsworth, James Shaver, minister, social activist, politician: b. July 29, 1874, Etobicoke, ON; d. Mar. 21, 1942, Vancouver, BC

J.S. Woodsworth, the son of a Methodist minister, also studied to become a minister. As a young theology student and minister he worked in the slums, first in Toronto in an association with the Fred Victor Mission (now, Centre) and later in Winnipeg, where he was instrumental in founding the "All Mission" and several other social services to attempt to meet needs of the desperately poor people he encountered. From this work emerged Woodsworth's understanding of the extent of social injustice existing in Canadian society as its economy was industrializing. In addition to his direct work with the poor, he developed views and proposed solutions in writing, among which are his two best known, *Strangers within Our Gates*

(1909) and *My Neighbour* (1911). Woodsworth's work and publications led to his appointment in 1913 to the position of Secretary of the Canadian Welfare League for the western provinces. He was a strong critic of the government's position in the First World War, especially on the issue of conscription; his views rendered him very unpopular in some circles. Later in his career, Woodsworth worked in Vancouver for several years as a longshoreman, while continuing his activities as a speaker and advocate for the poor through his identification with the social gospel movement. This role led his to involvement in the Winnipeg General Strike of 1919 a role that increased his reputation as a highly visible and influential spokesperson for the needs of people in the workforce. This in turn led Woodsworth to a formal role in the political arena: from 1921 until his death in 1942, he held the federal seat of Winnipeg North Centre continuously. As a member of Parliament, he continued to advocate for legislation that might lead the country's economy to be more co-operative and humane. Among his many accomplishments, he played an essential role in the passage of the first old age pension legislation in 1927, as well as an instrumental role in the development of the Co-operative Commonwealth Federation, the predecessor of the present New Democratic Party. Woodsworth probably would not have identified himself as a social worker, but what he stood for and what he accomplished greatly reflect the goals and values of the social work profession. He taught Canadians much about the commitment to social justice, and the art and science of bringing about social change. His life inspired many to join in his causes and has led many into the social work profession—including one of Woodsworth's own grandsons.

[*FJT*]

RELATED ENTRIES

Co-operative Commonwealth Federation, Fred Victor Centre, *My Neighbour*, F.R. Scott, Social Gospel Movement, Social Welfare History, *Strangers within Our Gates*

workers compensation

Workers compensation refers to a government-administered program that funds people who become hurt or disabled in their workplace. Prior to 1915 workers injured on the job could only recover damages by suing their employer. In defending suits brought against them, employers could rely on such factors as whether the worker's actions contributed to the accident, whether the accident was caused by a co-worker, whether the worker was aware of the risks of the industry and had, therefore, voluntarily assumed the risk by accepting the job. While some workers' claims were successful, barriers made pursuit of claims difficult for most workers to proceed; successful claims could financially ruin small employers and eliminate the job opportunities they provided. In 1912 in recognition of these concerns, the Ontario government commissioned Sir William Meredith to study ways to deal fairly and effectively with the impact of accidents and deaths at work; in his 1914 report, Meredith proposed that a workers compensation system be set up in Ontario, based on five principles:

- *security of payment*: The worker is guaranteed compensation for as long as the disability exists.
- no-fault system: It is not necessary to prove negligence in order to receive benefits;
- *no right to sue*: Injured workers compensated through this system in general would be barred from suing their employer; a few instances were suggested as exceptions;
- *collective liability*: To protect small firms from the high costs of serious accidents, all employers in a given business contribute to an accident fund according to the nature of their business;
- *independent administration*: The administration, the Workers Compensation Board, is to be an agency independent of government with no right to appeal its decisions to the courts.

The principles enunciated by Meredith form the cornerstone of the current compensation system in Ontario and elsewhere in Canada; a legislative package brought the first workers compensation board into existence, often considered as a historic compromise. Since the inception of the legislation, numerous changes have been made, the most extensive occurring in 1985 in benefits and administration. The major change in benefits was from 75 percent of gross wages to 90 percent of net wages; the top end of wages covered was increased substantially and the method used for determining average wages was changed. Improvements were made to the benefits paid for those whose spouse or supporting parent had been killed on the job. As well, employers were then required to pay a workers' wages for the day of the accident. In terms of administration, a major change was made to workers compensation procedures. Several new agencies were created. The Workers Compensation Appeals Tribunal was created to function as a final level of appeal from decisions of the board; the tribunal has a panel of medical assessors available to provide independent medical evidence. Two agencies were created whose mandate was to provide information, advice, and representation to employers (the Office of the Employer Adviser) or injured workers (the Office of the Worker Adviser), respectively. The Industrial Disease Standards Panel was also established with responsibility for making recommendations on compensation criteria for occupational diseases.

Automatic cost-of-living increases began in January 1, 1986, a wage-loss system came into effect on January 2, 1990. These represented very significant changes to the benefits paid to workers. A limited obligation was placed on employers to re-employ workers, and a dual-award system was introduced compromised of a benefit for the physical injury by way of a non-economic loss award and a benefit for the replacement of lost wages associated with the injury, that is, the future economic loss award. The non-economic loss was calculated by taking into consideration the results of the report of a medical assessor in conjunction with the use of the American Medical Associations Guidelines for the rating of disabilities, along with a worker's age at the time of injury, and a ceiling on benefits. The future economic loss was based on either the actual earnings of the worker in modified work or what the board deemed the worker capable of earning in suitable employment, whether the worker actually had such employment. As of January 1, 1995, and April 3, 1995, other changes brought mandatory mediation with respect to some disputes, additional payments to workers whose injuries occurred before 1990, and partially de-indexed benefits; as well, the governance of the workers compensation board was changed. Effective on January 1, 1998, even more significant changes occurred, as for the first time since the original legislation, mandatory time limits were set for the reporting of an injury by a worker and for bringing an appeal. The emphasis of the amending legislation was on safety and co-operation between workplace parties to resolve disputes. The basis for benefits was reduced from 90 percent of net earnings to 85 percent, and the basis for calculating the effect of inflation was reduced. Amendments bound the decisions of the Workplace Safety and Insurance Appeals Tribunal to board policy and limited the mandate of the offices of worker and employer advisers. The Industrial Disease Standards Panel was eliminated. The most recent changes enacted are well reflected in the name of the legislation, The Workplace Safety and Insurance Act. The workers compensation board in Ontario is now known as the Workplace Safety and Insurance Board.

[*Shirley Clement*]

RELATED ENTRIES

Employment, Industrial Social Work, Vocational Rehabilitation

workfare

Workfare refers to a wide range of programs that require recipients of public welfare to engage in various forms of labour in return for benefits. Workfare became widespread in the 1990s; although the term was new, the idea was not. In its most recent revival, it emerged from a continent-wide popularly supported political platform that one of the major causes of deficits in public financing was payments to unemployed persons. This platform draws on highly publicized misperception that serious abuse of welfare benefits was widespread. To provide incentives, workfare designates work assignments for eligible applicants who, should they refuse an assignment, are refused further payments. Through workfare, governments were able to reduce significantly the number of persons receiving public assistance; these data have been used to support the success of the program.

Over the decades, social workers committed to helping unemployed persons have found that some persons receiving public assistance could attain necessary skills and experience, perhaps through training or retraining to re-enter the labour force. Some factors that can contribute to the success of workfare are that it be voluntary and non-coercive in nature, and that designated work experiences be meaningful rather than make-work projects. Programs that have helped people learn or update skills required to hold regular employment have a strong educative component with backup counselling services. Social workers also recognize, however, that many persons receiving public assistance for unemployability are unlikely to find regular employment for a number of personal and systemic reasons (e.g., single parent with several young children, trauma recovery, illiteracy, substance abuse, mental illness). Clearly, most persons who are unemployed but capable of employment and who are on public assistance would prefer to be employed, and would be employed if positions existed to match their capabilities. In fact, abusers of the welfare system comprise only a small percentage of all recipients (research suggests about 5%). Punitive workfare programs deny the reality that all persons have a right to resources to live, just as individuals have a right to other societal services such as health care and education, which are free from such punitive attitudes.

[*FJT*]

RELATED ENTRIES

Employment, Income Security, Vocational Rehabilitation

Shankar Yelaja (1936–92)

Yaleja, Shankar, social work educator: b. Aug. 11, 1936, India; d. Sept. 14, 1992, Waterloo, ON

Dr. Shankar Yelaja received a master of social work degree in Bombay, India, and a doctorate in social work focusing on social policy from the University of Pennsylvania in Philadelphia. After teaching in social work at the University of Western Virginia, Dr. Yelaja joined the newly established graduate school (now, faculty) of social work at Waterloo Lutheran University in Waterloo, Ontario, in 1967. That university is now Wilfrid Laurier University. While at Wilfrid Laurier, Dr. Yelaja contributed much to the development of the social work program. He taught courses in social policy and social work ethics. As well as publishing numerous articles for professional journals and contributing chapters to books, he published three books:

Canadian Social Policy, Authority and Social Work, and *An Introduction to Social Work Practice in Canada.* Dr. Yelaja also acted as consultant to several social service organizations. Dr. Yelaja was appointed acting dean in 1983 and dean in 1984. As dean, Dr. Yelaja was instrumental in establishing in 1987 a doctoral program in social work. As well, the Centre for Social Welfare Studies was instituted in 1986 with support from Wilfrid Laurier University and the Ontario government. Throughout his term as dean, which he held until his death in September 1992, Dr. Yelaja maintained the high standards in all aspects of the social work program.

[*Rose Blackmore*]

RELATED ENTRIES

Functional Theory

Young Offenders Act

The Young Offenders Act, 1982, came into effect on April 2, 1984 to replace the Juvenile Delinquents Act originally enacted in 1908 and amended several times. As new legislation to deal with young persons who break the law in Canada, the Young Offenders Act changed the minimum age of liability from seven to twelve, and the legal upper age limit for an adolescent from sixteen to eighteen throughout Canada. The objective of the new Act was to provide a law to deal with young people that balanced the protection and interests of society with the rights and needs of young persons. The Young Offenders Act tended to place more emphasis on the protection of society than did the preceding legislation but maintained the concept of youth courts having a distinctive identity that held onto the ideal of rehabilitation of young persons brought before the courts. Rather than charging youth with the all-encompassing charge of delinquency, as under the Juvenile Delinquents Act, the Young Offenders Act legislated the charging of the young person with an offence under the Criminal Code or another statute. Youth court judges acted as impartial arbiters between the Crown and the accused, allowing judges to consider the special needs of young persons on a case-by-case basis. Judges were not only expected to rule on guilt but also to decide what was to be done with the accused once a guilty verdict was established. Judges could then request more information to help with their disposition of the young person, which may have included a predisposition report (under s.14) prepared by a probation officer, a mental health assessment (under s.13), or both in certain cases. The Young Offenders Act introduced tighter restrictions to the length of such dispositions as custody, probation, and community service as opposed to the option under the Juvenile Delinquents Act of open-ended dispositions. In keeping with the principle of least intrusive measures, as set out in the Young Offenders Act, one measure allowed for either alternative or no measures—usually reserved for cases involving first or less serious offences. Initially, the maximum custody sentence a young person could receive was three years; however, later amendments to the Act extended custody terms in cases that involved homicide and extreme violence. Further, in cases involving serious violence, the initial Young Offenders Act allowed for a Crown attorney to request that a young person be transferred to an adult court; later amendments shifted the onus onto the defence attorney to argue that his/her client's case ought to be heard in youth court. Under the Young Offenders Act, as under the previous legislation, youth court judges were still unable to order a young person into treatment; however, as part of a probation order, a young person could be requested to attend or be amenable to treatment recommended by a probation officer. In addition a judge was able to order an accused to reside at a specific place as a condition of his/her probation order. Public commentary on the Young Offenders Act, which was characterized by extreme opinions in support and against, frequently pointed to the challenges faced by youth court judges in their attempts to balance social accountability for criminal charge(s) committed, and each young person's rehabilitation needs. While many citizens expressed concerns that the protection of society was not being upheld by the Young Offenders Act, others who worked with the youth complained about the limited emphasis on and resources available for meaningful rehabilitation. The Young Offenders Act was replaced in April 2003 by the Youth Criminal Justice Act.

[*Jeff Packer*]

RELATED ENTRIES

Community Service, Criminal Justice, Family & Youth Courts, Probation, Offenders, Services for Offenders, Services for Youth, Youth Criminal Justice Act

Young Men's Christian Association*

Young Men's Christian Association (YMCA) worldwide charitable organization that offers a wide range of opportunities for the development of persons in spirit, mind and body and service to the human community. Founded in London, England, in 1844 by George Williams, it spread rapidly to other cities where groups of young men wished to protect themselves against the temptations of modern urban life. The first North American association appeared in Montreal in 1851 and a Canadian National Council was organized in 1912. The YMCA's original goal was the spiritual improvement of young men and for many years it was closely tied to the Protestant evangelical churches. Today, it serves people of both sexes and all ages, walks of life, races and religions. The Canadian YMCA is among the largest providers of programs in fitness, recreation, child care and employment training, and has promoted camping, adult education and international development projects. In 1998, 280,000 Canadians held memberships in the YMCA, while over a million people used its available services.

[*Diana Pedersen*]

* Used unedited by permission from *The Canadian Encyclopedia*. 2000. Toronto: McClelland and Stewart.

RELATED ENTRIES

B'Nai Brith, Church-Based Services, Cults, C.E. Hendry, Industrial Social Work, Jewish Social Services, Meditation, Religion, Sectarian Social Services, Services for Youth, Social Gospel Movement, Spirituality, J.W. Willard, Women's Christian Temperance Union, YWCA

Young Women's Christian Association*

Young Women's Christian Association (YWCA) cooperates closely with the Young Men's Christian Association (YMCA) in many Canadian Communities but has retained its distinct identity. Two organizations providing religious fellowships and boarding house accommodation to young women were crated in England in 1855, and amalgamated in 1877. The rapid growth of the YWCA as an international movement was linked to the increasing concentration in cities of large numbers of young unmarried women seeking employment, especially in factories. The first Canadian branch was organized in Saint John, NB, in 1870, and a national body was created in 1895. Sharing the Protestant evangelical orientation of the YMCA, early YWCA programs combined attempts to increase employment and educational opportunities available to young women, with a concern for their physical and moral welfare. The Canadian YWCA today is actively working to improve the social legal and economic position of all Canadian women. Some half million Canadian annually make use of YWCA facilities in one way or another.

[*Diana Pedersen*]

* Used unedited by permission from *The Canadian Encyclopedia*. 2000. Toronto: McClelland and Stewart.

RELATED ENTRIES
B'Nai Brith, Church-Based Services, Cults, Jewish Social Services, Meditation, I. Munroe-Smith, Religion, Sectarian Social Services, Social Gospel Movement, Spirituality, Women's Christian Temperance Union, YMCA

Youth Criminal Justice Act

The federal Youth Criminal Justice Act, 2002, received royal assent on February 19, 2003, and came into effect in April 2003, as an attempt to respond to the concerns of Canadians about the effectiveness of the previous legislation, the Young Offenders Act, 1982, which the Youth Criminal Justice Act replaced. Following country-wide consultation, the Act stands as the government's commitment to renewal of youth justice. As before, accused young people between the ages of twelve and eighteen are subject to the provisions of this new Act. They are dealt with in courts separate from adults and, if convicted, are subject to different penalties and usually held in separate custodial facilities. Sentences for youth, similarly to adults, can range from absolute discharge to a period in custody. Custodial sentences can be in open or secure facilities and can be imposed for up to ten years in the most serious of crimes, first-degree murder. Young offenders can be transferred to the adult court system and receive adult penalties if a judge in a hearing is convinced that such a move would be in the interests of justice. Youth are not entitled to parole but can have their sentences reviewed by a judge, perhaps gaining access to a less restrictive custodial sentence.

The new legislation has four principal features.

First, within a framework that ensures consistency throughout the country, the Act recognizes the different needs within provinces and territories. Second, the Act treats violent and non-violent crimes differently and, in the case of less serious crimes, underlines the importance of accountability and the effectiveness of responses that involve the offender's community, victims, and family. Third, the Act stresses an integrated approach that focuses on all aspects of youth crime, including prevention, education, and employment. Fourth, underlying the legislation is a strong emphasis on the priority of children and youth for the country, to protect their rights and to ensure opportunities to develop their full potential. In the application of the Act, the courts are permitted considerable variation in decisions, particularly regarding the seriousness of the crime and if/when a youth can be dealt with in an adult manner including publication of his/her name. Throughout, taking responsibility for one's actions is stressed. In addition to formal court proceedings, emphasis is placed on community structures that can offer a range of options for dealing with youth offenders; instead of court proceedings, these options might include such things as diversion programs, community service, or repair of harm done (i.e., restitution). Roles of social workers within these community structures and options are likely to be enhanced. Funding has also been allotted to support federal youth justice strategies. A period of five years has been set as an implementation phase to ensure optimum effectiveness of this new regime, especially in families, schools, and communities.

[*FJT*]

RELATED ENTRIES
E.H. Blois, Bullying, Correctional Services, Criminal Justice, Forensic Practice, Family & Youth Courts, Gangs, J.J. Kelso, Legal Issues, Parenting, Practice Methods, Probation, Services for Offenders, Services for Youth, School Social Workers, Wellness, Young Offenders Act

Selected Resource Materials

APA. 1994. *Diagnostic and Statistical Manual of Mental Disorders.* 4th ed. Washington, DC: American Psychiatric Association.

Barker, R.L. 2003. *The Social Work Dictionary.* 5th ed. Washington, DC: National Association of Social Workers Press.

Brilliant, E.L. (Ed.) 1995. *Encyclopedia of Social Work.* 19th ed. Washington, DC: NASW Press.

CASW. 1983. Code of Ethics. Ottawa: Canadian Association of Social Workers.

Canadian Who's Who. [var. yrs.] Toronto: University of Toronto Press.

Shore, M. 1987. *The Science of Social Redemption; McGill, the Chicago School, and the Origins of Social Research in Canada.* Toronto: University of Toronto Press.

Turner, F.J. (Ed.) 1996. F.J. Turner (Ed.) *Social Work Treatment.* 4th ed. New York: Free Press.

——. 1999. *Adult Psychopathology: A Social Work Perspective.* 2nd ed. New York: Free Press.

——. 2002. *Social Work Practice: A Canadian Perspective.* 2nd ed. Toronto: Pearson Education.

Turner, J.C., & F.J. Turner (Eds.) 2005. *Canadian Social Welfare.* 5th ed. Toronto: Pearson Education.

WHO. 1992. *International Classification of Diseases and Related Health Problems.* 10th ed. Geneva: World Health Organization.

Who's Who in Canada. [var. yrs.] Toronto: International Press.